C# 13 and .NET 9

Guide to C# 13, .NET 9,
data management, and deployment strategies

Jefferson S. Motta

bpb

www.bpbonline.com

To View Complete
BPB Publications Catalogue
Scan the QR Code:

www.bpbonline.com

Dedicated to

To the sisters: M. A. A.

Prof. Cássio Saldanha, *My Mentor*

Natali Fonseca

About the Author

Jefferson S. Motta is currently working as a consultant with over 25 years of experience in desktop, web, and cloud development. His professional journey began in 1994 as a programming intern at Janssen Consultoria, where he helped develop an MRP II System for the Olvebra Group.

In 1996, he founded Menphis - Intelligent Systems, focusing on IT solutions for Olvebra and new clients. His most notable achievement was the development of Advocati.NET, a management system for law firms that has earned a respectable place in Brazilian legal technology. The system has undergone continuous improvement for over 20 years and is built using C# 13, ASP.NET Web Forms, and WinForms .NET 9.0, incorporating elements of artificial intelligence and big data.

Jefferson has been a pioneer in technological innovation, developing applications with artificial intelligence as early as 2012, followed by implementing bigdata solutions and automated control systems for physical equipment. In 2005, he created a management system for Medical Clinics.

He has made significant contributions to the tech community as an editor at C# Corner, a respected platform for technical articles. As a four-time MVP, his articles in English have garnered over 850,000 views, elevating him to approximately the 90th position in the global ranking.

He is also a graduate with a software engineering degree and has a diverse educational background, including digital marketing analysis (SENAC), digital security (Sisnema), and various technical courses.

About the Reviewer

Rositsa is an experienced engineering manager with 20 years of experience in the software industry, with a significant portion of that time leading teams that developed Telerik UI components for .NET MAUI, and Telerik UI for WPF and WinForms.

Her focus is on building high-performing teams that enjoy crafting software that they are proud of. She has also been a Microsoft MVP for .NET for the last 5 years (2020-2025).

Acknowledgement

Hey there! We want to thank everyone from the bottom of our hearts who helped make this book happen!

First, a big hug to our family and friends who stuck by us throughout this journey. Your love kept us going when things got tough, you know?

We owe a big debt of gratitude to the team at BPB Publications, who gave us expert publishing support. You guys were amazing in helping us navigate this crazy world of book publishing!

We can't forget the reviewers, technical experts, and editors who gave us that honest feedback to improve our manuscript. Your suggestions made all the difference!

Last but not least, a special thanks to you, the reader of our book. Your support means everything to us!

Thanks to everyone who pitched in to make this book a reality. You rock!

Preface

If you are new to programming or an experienced professional looking to enhance your skills, these pages will provide you with the information and tips you need to succeed in the .NET ecosystem, which is constantly evolving.

From Chapter 1's Introducing to C# 13 and .NET 9 to Chapter 16's Packaging and Deployment, each chapter is carefully organized to build on what you already know while presenting new ideas at a pace that you can easily handle.

In this book, you will discover the remarkable flexibility of the C# language and the .NET system. It will guide you through object-oriented programming, working with data using Entity Framework Core, utilizing LINQ to modify data in a concise and elegant manner, and leveraging ASP.NET Core and Blazor for modern web development.

I hope that this book not only helps you learn how to code but also inspires you to do so, providing you with the tools to solve complex problems in innovative ways and adding your own unique perspective and will to the world of software development.

Chapter 1: Introducing to C# 13 and .NET 9 - This chapter guid you through the key stages of configuring your development environment and acquiring fundamental knowledge of C# programming. This first chapter establishes a solid foundation for your coding journey.

Here, you will find the step-by-step installation procedure for the .NET **software development kit (SDK)**—an essential tool for any developer—as well as guidance on how to select an appropriate **integrated development environment (IDE)**.

Chapter 2: C# Fundamentals - Originally part of the .NET framework, C# has proven to be a top option in software development for Microsoft because of its scalability, dependability, and simple syntax. The first part looks at the basic structural guidelines and conventions needed to write C# programs. From here, the trip delves into an in-depth study of data types, revealing the nuances of integers, floats, strings, and Booleans—the fundamental building blocks of data storage and processing.

Chapter 3: Harnessing the Code - In this chapter, we will use iterative techniques to explore iteration and learn how to effectively navigate data. We will clarify type conversion and type casting as we proceed, thereby equipping you with the tools to properly manage data. Furthermore, we will cover the principles of robust error management and exception handling, enabling you to produce consistent and reliable code.

Chapter 4: Functions In-depth - In this chapter, we will find ways to improve your code's modularity and adaptability. Techniques for exception handling are discussed to ensure robustness and to safeguard your code from unexpected errors. The need for unit testing in C# is also addressed since it helps to preserve code quality and dependability.

Chapter 5: Building Apps with OOPs- In this chapter, thorough investigations of key ideas such as encapsulation and abstraction will help to create strong and safe programs. Moving into advanced subjects, we explore inheritance and polymorphism, which enable dynamic behavior and code reuse. Along with static and instance members, you will investigate constructors, acquiring a clear knowledge of how objects are initialized and controlled.

Chapter 6: Mastering Interfaces and Inheriting Classes- This chapter explores polymorphism, which enables objects to take on multiple forms; examines inheritance as a foundational concept in object-oriented programming, facilitating code reuse; and discusses the value of interfaces as contracts for class behavior. Mastering these basic concepts will help you build a solid foundation to enhance your programming skills.

Chapter 7: .NET Toolbox - Forming one of the basic data types within the .NET framework, strings are crucial in many applications. They provide many features for text manipulation. Focusing on the string class and its closely related types—such as DateTime, TimeSpan, encoding, and regex—this chapter guides you on an in-depth exploration of the System namespace. We will demonstrate their practical applications in various situations and reveal the architectural ideas and design choices that underpin these classes

Chapter 8: Data in Motion- This chapter covers the fundamentals of file operations in .NET, including reading and writing text files, handling file and directory exceptions, and guaranteeing safe file operations. We also examine the key role of .NET streams in supporting data reading and writing across various sources, including files, networks, and memory. You will also learn about .NET serialization, a strong tool for transforming data structures or objects into digital forms for storage or transport.

Chapter 9: Data Handling with EF Core - This chapter explores **Entity Framework Core (EF Core)**, a sophisticated **Object-Relational Mapping (ORM)** framework designed for .NET applications. EF Core simplifies processes and increases output by utilizing .NET objects instead of SQL queries, thereby enabling efficient data management.

Chapter 10: LINQ Unleashed- This chapter delves into the intricacies of **Language Integrated Query (LINQ)**, a powerful C# feature that enables programmers to query and manipulate data seamlessly across multiple data sources. You will learn to use LINQ with various data types—including collections, databases, XML, and JSON—by means of a coherent and expressive syntax. You will also investigate leveraging LINQ operators, lambda expressions, and deferred execution to create efficient designs and adaptable queries.

Chapter 11: ASP.NET Core the Future of Web Development- This chapter introduces a modern and flexible framework meant for creating web apps and services, ASP.NET Core. Among its cross-platform support, great performance, modular architecture, and strong security, the fundamental features and benefits of ASP.NET Core will be revealed. Through hands-on activities, you will acquire knowledge of building a simple web application, investigating its architecture, adding features, running tests, refining features, and efficiently deploying it.

Chapter 12: Building Powerful Websites with Razor- This chapter covers Razor Pages, a key feature of ASP.NET Core that utilizes a page-oriented approach to transform web development. Emphasizing obvious separation of concerns and effective data management, Razor Pages simplifies the process by combining C# and HTML into a single file. Using Razor syntax, Tag Helpers, layouts, and partials, you will learn how to create and control Razor Pages using the .NET Core framework to build dynamic and responsive online applications. Form management, user input processing, data validation, and fundamental **Create, Read, Update, Delete (CRUD)** activities using Razor Pages are all covered in the chapter.

Chapter 13: Website Development Using MVC Pattern- This chapter explores the **Model-View-Controller (MVC)** architecture within the ASP.NET Core framework, a powerful tool for creating modern web applications. You will learn to create views and controllers, set up MVC routing, use Entity Framework Core to handle data, apply strong form validation, and use ViewModels to simplify your development process.

Chapter 14: Mastering Web Services- This chapter provides a comprehensive overview of the various web service domains within the .NET environment, including an analysis of their potential as well as their challenges. Emphasizing strong security policies against current cyber threats, it unpacks the complexity of building and using web services from basic ideas like RESTful APIs in ASP.NET Core to advanced technologies like gRPC and GraphQL.

Chapter 15: Blazor for UI Development- This chapter explores Blazor, a state-of-the-art UI framework using C# for both client-side and server-side programming. Key subjects are thoroughly investigated in it, including Blazor component development, project organization, form handling and validation, JavaScript interoperability, CRUD operations with Blazor and Entity Framework Core, differences between Server and WebAssembly models, routing, and application testing.

Chapter 16: Packaging and Deployment- This chapter explores the complexities of packaging and distributing .NET applications, including a thorough guide to components and libraries, NuGet's important role, and the process of publishing code for deployment. It highlights the importance of .NET Standard and .NET Core libraries, assembly versioning, the **Global Assembly Cache (GAC)**, and strongly named assemblies.

Code Bundle and Coloured Images

Please follow the link to download the
Code Bundle and the *Coloured Images* of the book:

https://rebrand.ly/i244egu

The code bundle for the book is also hosted on GitHub at
https://github.com/bpbpublications/C-Sharp-13-and-.NET-9.
In case there's an update to the code, it will be updated on the existing GitHub repository.

We have code bundles from our rich catalogue of books and videos available at
https://github.com/bpbpublications. Check them out!

Errata

We take immense pride in our work at BPB Publications and follow best practices to ensure the accuracy of our content to provide with an indulging reading experience to our subscribers. Our readers are our mirrors, and we use their inputs to reflect and improve upon human errors, if any, that may have occurred during the publishing processes involved. To let us maintain the quality and help us reach out to any readers who might be having difficulties due to any unforeseen errors, please write to us at :

errata@bpbonline.com

Your support, suggestions and feedbacks are highly appreciated by the BPB Publications' Family.

Did you know that BPB offers eBook versions of every book published, with PDF and ePub files available? You can upgrade to the eBook version at www.bpbonline.com and as a print book customer, you are entitled to a discount on the eBook copy. Get in touch with us at :

business@bpbonline.com for more details.

At **www.bpbonline.com**, you can also read a collection of free technical articles, sign up for a range of free newsletters, and receive exclusive discounts and offers on BPB books and eBooks.

Piracy

If you come across any illegal copies of our works in any form on the internet, we would be grateful if you would provide us with the location address or website name. Please contact us at **business@bpbonline.com** with a link to the material.

If you are interested in becoming an author

If there is a topic that you have expertise in, and you are interested in either writing or contributing to a book, please visit **www.bpbonline.com**. We have worked with thousands of developers and tech professionals, just like you, to help them share their insights with the global tech community. You can make a general application, apply for a specific hot topic that we are recruiting an author for, or submit your own idea.

Reviews

Please leave a review. Once you have read and used this book, why not leave a review on the site that you purchased it from? Potential readers can then see and use your unbiased opinion to make purchase decisions. We at BPB can understand what you think about our products, and our authors can see your feedback on their book. Thank you!

For more information about BPB, please visit **www.bpbonline.com**.

Join our book's Discord space

Join the book's Discord Workspace for Latest updates, Offers, Tech happenings around the world, New Release and Sessions with the Authors:

https://discord.bpbonline.com

Table of Contents

CHAPTER 1
Introduction to C# 13 and .NET 9

Introduction

Welcome to our journey into the world of C# (pronounced C-Sharp) and .NET (pronounced dot-Net) programming. This opening chapter aims to set the stage for our coding study, helping you navigate the initial, crucial steps of setting up our development environment and knowledge of C# programming. We start exploring the process of selecting an appropriate **integrated development environment** (**IDE**) and guide you through installing the .NET **software development kit** (**SDK**), an essential tool in our C# toolkit.

We will also understand the fundamental understanding of the .NET platform, a versatile framework central to C# programming. Moreover, we will delve into the diverse types of applications that can be crafted using C#, showcasing the extensive adaptability of this programming language.

Structure

This chapter covers the following topics:

- Introduction to C# and .NET
- Choosing the right tools for C# programming
- Understanding application types in C#
- Deploying cross-platform applications

- Role of integrated development environments
- .NET Framework vs. .NET Core
- Overview of C# and .NET ecosystem
- Installing and configuring Visual Studio
- Exploring Visual Studio Code for C# development

Objectives

In this chapter, we aim to provide you with a comprehensive understanding of C# and .NET programming. Throughout this section, you will gain familiarity with the C# language and the .NET platform, learning about their functionalities, advantages, and their place in the broader programming landscape. We will guide you through setting up your development environment, including the installation and configuration of essential tools like Visual Studio, empowering you to select the right tools for various C# programming tasks, thereby enhancing your productivity and efficiency. Additionally, you will explore the diverse range of applications that can be developed using C#, from desktop and web applications to mobile and cloud-based solutions. Another crucial aspect will be to understand the intricacies involved in deploying cross-platform applications, along with platform-specific configurations and deployment techniques. By comprehending the role and utility of IDEs in streamlining the software development process, you will be better equipped to make informed decisions.

Furthermore, you will gain insights into the key differences between the .NET Framework and .NET Core, aiding you in choosing the appropriate platform for your specific development needs. We will also provide an overview of the C# and .NET ecosystem, acquainting you with related frameworks, tools, and libraries such as **.NET Multi-platform App UI (.NET MAUI)**, Unity, and ASP.NET. Finally, you will receive hands-on guidance for installing and configuring Visual Studio, preparing you to embark on your development journey. By the end of this chapter, you will have established a solid foundation in C# and .NET programming, empowering you to create and deploy your own applications confidently.

Introduction to C# and .NET

C# is a modern, in constant evolution, open-sourced, object-oriented programming language developed by *Microsoft*, envisioned as a part of their **.NET initiative**. The language was designed to offer a mix of the best features from languages like Java™ and C++ while incorporating unique elements that deliver power and development flexibility.

Much like Java™, C# is a statically typed, object-oriented language, emphasizing safety and simplicity in its syntax. Both languages share similarities like garbage collection, exceptions, and the extensive use of libraries for different functionalities. They also provide capabilities for threading and synchronization, which are vital for modern, multi-threaded software.

However, there are differences, too. One significant distinction is that while Java™ was built with a *write once, run anywhere* philosophy and is thus platform-independent, C# was primarily designed for Windows development. But with the introduction of .NET Core and its evolution into .NET 5 and beyond, the latter has become increasingly cross-platform, supporting Android, Linux, iOS, and macOS.

The .NET, or Microsoft .NET initiative, is a comprehensive software development framework introduced by Microsoft in the late 1990s and officially launched in 2002. It represented a strategic initiative to provide developers with a unified, cohesive environment for developing applications that could run on Windows platforms and beyond.

At the core of the .NET initiative was the idea of language interoperability, which would allow different high-level languages to communicate seamlessly with one another. Using the **Common Language Runtime (CLR)** and the .NET **Framework Class Library (FCL)**, developers could write applications in various .NET compatible languages, such as C#, Visual Basic .NET, and F#.

Tip: Interoperability refers to the ability of different systems, devices, or applications to connect and communicate in a coordinated way without any effort from the end user.

Another significant aspect of the .NET initiative was the concept of managed code. Managed code is executed by the .NET CLR, which offers services like garbage collection, exception handling, and security, simplifying application development by automating routine or complex tasks.

The .NET Framework also introduced the idea of **software as a service (SaaS)**, highlighting the web services aspect of development. It is a model where the software is provided as a service over the Internet, which can be used by other software applications, irrespective of platform or language.

The .NET Framework, from 1.0 to 4.8, is closely tied to the Windows operating system, forming the backbone of many applications from Microsoft and other enterprises. Microsoft continues to maintain .NET Framework 4.8 despite the arrival of its new brother, .NET Core.

Hence, the .NET initiative represented a significant shift in the approach to software development by Microsoft, emphasizing interoperability, service-oriented architecture, and managed code, making application development more streamlined and efficient.

C# programming and the .NET platform form a potent combination. They have continued to evolve from their beginnings to the present day with a new **long-term support (LTS)** version every two years, offering programmers a robust, versatile, and efficient environment for creating powerful, modern applications. The LTS means it gets updated and receives security fixes for three years after the official launch. A non-LTS version is released every two years, with one year of support. So, we have one new version of .NET every year. Despite sharing roots and similarities with Java™, the pair has charted its unique path in the programming world. With their recent cross-platform capabilities, they are showing no signs of slowing down.

What is new in C# 13

In this chapter, we will see the innovative elements that C# 13 introduces.

Let us briefly describe how it has grown since its first release. Generics were introduced with C# 2.0, allowing us to design classes, interfaces, and functions with placeholders for the data type they store or use. It enabled more type-safe collections and increased performance by eliminating boxing and unboxing requirements. Iterators and partial types were also implemented, improving how we wrote code and organized our projects. C# 3.0 introduced many new improvements, the most notable of which was **Language-Integrated Query** (**LINQ**), which provided an SQL-like syntax for querying data sets directly from C#.

C# 4.0 improved interoperability with other languages and systems, making it more dynamic and versatile. Key features include the dynamic type, which allows operations to avoid compile-time type verification and defer binding until runtime. It made coding with COM objects, dynamic programming languages, and reflection easier and less error-prone.

C# 5.0 added the `async` and `await` keywords, significantly simplifying asynchronous programming. These keywords enabled developers to construct asynchronous code that is easy to read and maintain while approximating synchronous code in structure. C# 6.0 and 7.0 included syntactic sugar and new capabilities such as expression-bodied members, pattern matching, and tuples, reducing code complexity and boosting readability and conciseness. C# 8.0 included nullable reference types and more powerful pattern-matching capabilities, which improved the language's type safety and control flow. C# 9.0 and 10.0 were designed to make the language more concise and expressive by introducing records for immutable data structures, init-only properties, and pattern-matching improvements. C# 11, which builds on these advancements and becomes the language to the language of the year 2023.

C# 13 introduces several new features and changes to improve the programming experience, streamline syntax, and give additional functionality.

The primary constructors' feature, which has been expanded to be usable in any class and struct, is a significant addition. Unlike prior versions, which restricted primary constructors to record types, developers can now use this feature more liberally, allowing for more straightforward and concise class and struct definitions.

Collection expressions are another novel feature in C# 13. This feature reveals a more concise syntax that facilitates the generation of common collection values, encouraging code brevity and enhancing readability. This improved syntax is intended to give developers a more efficient way of working with collections.

C# 13 improves lambda expressions with default lambda parameters. This enables developers to assign default values to lambda expression parameters. This enhancement offers flexibility and simplicity to the definition and use of lambda expressions in diverse circumstances.

Furthermore, an alias of any type is a new feature introduced with Visual Studio 17.6 Preview 3. This feature increases the language's adaptability by enabling more robust and flexible type aliasing.

Inline arrays were also implemented to the C# 13 runtime as part of the previous .NET 9 preview. This enhancement enhances the language's array handling features, resulting in a more integrated and fluid array utilization experience.

Finally, interceptors are introduced as an experimental feature, providing new code generation and modification opportunities. Interceptors allow generators to reroute code, allowing for context-specific optimization and improving generated code functionality and efficiency. This broadens the scope of code modification and optimization options in C# programming.

The primary constructors extend to all classes and structs, letting us add parameters directly to class declarations for property initialization and method/property accessor usage.

Lambda expressions now support default parameter values, streamlining methods, and local function argument handling. The using alias directive no longer limits to named types. Creating semantic aliases for tuples, arrays, pointers, and other types is now possible.

Choosing the right tools for C# programming

Choosing the right tools can drastically impact our efficiency, code quality, and work. Each tool serves a specific purpose and choosing which tool to use can mean the difference between a smooth workflow and a choppy one. Let us have a detailed look at the essential pillars of C# programming tools.

Integrated development environment

The IDE is the platform where we write our code. Microsoft's Visual Studio is an excellent IDE for C# programming. It is a fully featured tool that offers an integrated debugger, a code editor with IntelliSense (an auto-completion tool to increase speed and accuracy), support for various project configurations, and much more. However, it is possible to use a lighter solution using Visual Studio Code. It is a more streamlined editor that still supports a wide range of languages and has robust community support for extensions.

Compiler

This tool translates our high-level C# code into low-level machine code that our computer can understand. The .NET Compiler Platform, or Roslyn, is an open-source set of compilers for C# and Visual Basic. Roslyn goes beyond simple compilation, providing APIs that enable a deep understanding of our code. It enables better code analysis and refactoring, leading to cleaner, more efficient code. It comes automatically with the Visual Studio installation setup.

Libraries and frameworks

Libraries are sets of precompiled routines that our program can use, while frameworks define a universal, reusable software environment that provides functionality as part of a larger software platform. The .NET Framework is a fundamental tool for C# programming, providing an extensive library that allows us to build various types of applications, from desktop to web-based. ASP.NET is an excellent choice for web development, offering a robust **Model-View-Controller** (**MVC**) framework.

Source control

Managing the various versions of our code, especially in a team setup, can be complex. For this work, we have global market tools like Mercurial, GNU Bazaar, and Git. Most developers use Git, which lets you easily track changes, revert code to previous versions, and create branches to work on new features saving the main codebase from break. To work safely with Git, we have cloud repositories like **Amazon Web Services** (**AWS**) CodeCommit, Bitbucket, Azure DevOps Repos, and GitHub. GitHub was acquired by Microsoft in 2018, and they use it as a repository for Microsoft Windows source code.

Unit testing

Ensuring our code works as expected is crucial. NUnit, xUnit, and MSTest are popular frameworks for unit testing in C#. They allow you to create small, isolated tests for individual units of our code, helping to catch bugs early in the development process and contributing to overall code integrity. We are going to use MSTest in this book.

Understanding application types in C#

C# is versatile, and we can use it to develop various types of applications. From console to web, mobile, and desktop applications, each serves unique needs.

In software development, requirements are the defined needs that a particular software should fulfill. They are guidelines that describe what the system should do and include functional (tasks the system must perform), non-functional (system performance), and user requirements.

Understanding these requirements is essential in developing effective software, ensuring it meets users' needs and adheres to specifications for optimal performance and functionality.

Differences between types of applications

Console applications run in a console or terminal, usually a black screen that mostly untechnical people think is a hacker thing. They are text-based and ideal for simple tasks or automation scripts running with scheduling or firing manually from the command prompt. They can run locally or in the cloud environment.

Web applications run in browsers and are accessible universally via the Internet. They are built using web technologies and served from a remote server. This server can be on-premises (local server) or cloud computing from various suppliers like AWS or Microsoft Azure.

Mobile applications are designed for handheld devices, optimized for touch interfaces, and often use device-specific features. It mainly uses a remote server to complete its tasks and save data. The applications can vary from an image editor to a bank account.

Desktop applications run directly on a computer, offer high performance, and can fully utilize system resources, suitable for more complex tasks. These applications can be client-server accessing and processing data from a remote server.

A complete solution can consist of several applications, each to attend to one need from the requirements.

This knowledge is the key to becoming a versatile developer, enabling you to design targeted solutions for various software requirements.

Console applications

A console application is a computer program that is created using a text-only computer interface. These programs are mostly used for work automation and as a steppingstone to learning the C# programming language. They are text-based and executed on a terminal window, like a command prompt, rather than a **graphical user interface (GUI)**.

Windows Forms applications

Windows Forms (WinForms) is a GUI class library in Microsoft .NET. It provides a platform for developing rich, interactive user interfaces for Windows desktop applications. With C#, we can create WinForms applications that include buttons, text boxes, drop-down menus, and other standard UI components. This type of application is event-driven, responding to user interactions via the GUI.

Windows Presentation Foundation applications

Windows Presentation Foundation (WPF) is another UI framework for building Windows desktop applications. It offers more advanced features than Windows Forms, such as vector graphics, animations, and media support. WPF uses **Extensible Application Markup Language** (**XAML**) for declarative layout, which allows for a clear separation of design and logic. WPF also uses hardware acceleration to render graphics, making it a powerful choice for graphically intensive applications.

ASP.NET applications

ASP.NET is framework-specific for building web applications. Using C# with ASP.NET, we can create dynamic websites, web services, and web APIs. ASP.NET supports multiple programming models, including Web Forms, MVC, and Razor Pages. With the recent introduction of ASP.NET Core, we can now build cross-platform web applications running on Windows, Linux, and MacOS.

Blazor applications

Blazor is an ASP.NET technology that allows you to create interactive web UIs in C# rather than JavaScript. WebAssembly is a real .NET operating in the browser. You can build full-stack web apps using the power of .NET and C# without writing a single line of JavaScript.

Blazor enables you to host components in any online browser using WebAssembly, on the server using ASP.NET Core, or in native client apps. It provides a simple, composable, declarative, and efficient component model that is versatile and reusable. Blazor components can be used on the web as well as in hybrid native apps for mobile and desktop.

Mobile applications with .NET MAUI

.NET MAUI is a platform that allows us to develop mobile applications using C# and .NET. It provides tools to build Android, iOS, and Windows apps, with a large portion of code sharing across platforms. It can reduce the time and resources needed for developing and maintaining an app on multiple operating systems.

Game development with Unity

Unity is a popular game engine for developing 2D and 3D video games. It uses C# as one of its primary scripting languages, enabling developers to control their games' physics, gameplay, and artificial intelligence. Unity's powerful features and the ability to export games to multiple platforms have made it a top choice for game developers.

Universal Windows Platform applications

Universal Windows Platform (**UWP**) allows developers to create applications running on many Windows devices, including PCs, tablets, phones, and even Xbox. A UWP app uses a single, unified API layer, ensuring that the application behaves consistently across all devices.

.NET Multi-platform App UI

The .NET MAUI is not entirely a type of application. However, it is a framework for building native device applications that span mobile, tablet, and desktop platforms. It is essentially an evolution of .NET MAUI.Forms, simplifying the options for .NET developers and unifying the .NET platform across different types of applications.

Subtypes of .NET MAUI

Within the realm of .NET MAUI, we can create different subtypes of applications, each catering to specific requirements and use cases. Let us explore these subtypes in detail:

- **Cross-platform development**: With .NET MAUI, we can write an application once in C# and run it on multiple platforms, including Android, iOS, macOS, and Windows. This unified approach leads to a significant reduction in both development time and resources.

- **Single project structure**: .NET MAUI introduces a new single project structure, which simplifies the process of building cross-platform applications. It consolidates common resources like images and app icons into one place, making them easily accessible across different platforms.

- **Native features access**: Even though .NET MAUI allows for cross-platform development, it does not sacrifice access to native features. We can tap into native APIs to utilize platform-specific capabilities or customize a specific platform's look and feel.

Model-View-ViewModel and Model-View-Update architectures

.NET MAUI supports the traditional **Model-View-ViewModel** (**MVVM**) pattern many developers are accustomed to from .NET MAUI.Forms and the new **Model-View-Update** (**MVU**) pattern for state management are similar to how **user interfaces** (**UIs**) are built in popular web libraries like React and Angular.

C# is flexible, and for each task in the global solution, a correct type of application can be done with excellence.

Choosing between a web-based or desktop application can be significant because web-based applications can run both on desktop and mobile with some adjustments. Primarily, it would help if you thought about your end-users. They are from the global Internet, or they will be accessed from a local network or **virtual private network** (**VPN**).

If your customers use only Windows operating system for desktop solutions, you can develop a Desktop application using WinForms or WPF. But, if you have a mixed client OS, like macOS and Windows OS, you should consider developing a .NET MAUI application according to your specific equipment resources needs, like a camera, USB port, or sign certificate.

Deploying cross-platform applications

Creating applications that run on multiple platforms is an invaluable asset in software development. Leveraging the power of C# and the .NET Framework, we can devise a strategy to help navigate the complexities of cross-platform deployment.

Choosing the right framework

With C# and .NET, we have a range of options, including .NET MAUI, .NET Core, and Blazor, a framework for building interactive web UIs using C# instead of JavaScript. The choice depends on the nature of the application, the target platforms, and the project's specific requirements.

Requirements

The requirements vary from project to project according to the application requirements.

Let us see the main requirements according to the platform:

- **Windows desktop applications**: If we need to build a traditional Windows desktop application, you can use WPF or WinForms. Both frameworks provide rich UI capabilities and access to the full range of Windows APIs.

- **Web applications**: There are multiple options for web applications based on your preferences and requirements.

    o **ASP.NET WebForms**: This mature framework for building web applications provides a visual drag-and-drop design experience. It is based on server-side controls and event-driven programming.

    o **ASP.NET Core**: This is the latest version of ASP.NET and provides a cross-platform, high-performance framework for building modern web applications. It is recommended for new projects and supports the latest web development technologies and supports MVC pattern.

- **Cross-platform mobile applications**: .NET MAUI allows us to build native mobile applications for iOS, Android, and Windows using C# and .NET. It provides a shared codebase across platforms, enabling code reuse and rapid development.

- **.NET MAUI**: .NET MAUI is the next evolution of .NET MAUI.Forms, which simplifies the development of cross-platform apps. It supports building applications for iOS, Android, macOS, and Windows.

- **Progressive Web Applications (PWA)**: Blazor is a web framework that allows us to build interactive web applications using C# instead of JavaScript. It enables you to write client-side and server-side code in C#, allowing for rich interactivity and performance.

Pros and cons of choosing WFP and WinForms

This section discusses the advantages and disadvantages of WPF.

The pros of WPF are as follows:

- **XAML and a rich user interface**: WPF enables the development of rich user interfaces with modern UI elements and styles, utilizing XAML for declarative UI design.
- **Data binding**: It has powerful data binding capabilities that make it easy to connect UI elements to data sources.
- **Hardware acceleration**: WPF leverages hardware acceleration to render UI elements, enabling better and more performant graphics and animations.
- **Custom controls**: It allows for greater flexibility in building custom controls, and the UI can be substantially customized to meet specific demands.
- **Scalability**: Since WPF programs are naturally scalable, they may be adapted to multiple screen sizes and resolutions.
- **Integration with .NET**: Because it is part of the .NET ecosystem, it can be easily integrated with various .NET technologies and frameworks.

The cons of WPF are as follows:

- **Learning curve**: For those accustomed to WinForms, grasping WPF requires a learning curve.
- **Limited in-box controls**: WPF's in-box control suite may appear limited compared to WinForms.
- **System requirements**: WPF apps have more significant system requirements for smooth operation due to enhanced graphics capabilities.
- **Backward compatibility**: WPF programs may not operate on older Windows versions, such as Windows 2000 or earlier.

This section discusses the advantages and disadvantages of WinForms.

The pros of WinForms are as follows:

- **Wider adoption**: Since WinForms has been around longer and is more extensively used, more community and third-party assistance is available.
- **Documentation and examples**: A wealth of documentation and examples accessible online to assist in resolving common problems and guiding development.
- **Support for Visual Studio**: The design experience in Visual Studio for WinForms is mature and user-friendly, making the development process more manageable.

- **Third-party controls**: To enhance the functionality and appearance of WinForms applications, a range of third-party controls are available.

The cons are as follows:

- **Antiquated UI**: Compared to newer UI frameworks such as WPF, the appearance and feel of WinForms applications may appear antiquated.
- **Limited customization**: Creating highly customized and dynamic user interfaces in WinForms might be more complex and require more manual code.
- Investing in third-party controls to improve the UI/UX may involve significant costs.
- **No hardware acceleration**: Unlike WPF, WinForms does not use hardware acceleration to render UI elements.

The decision between WPF and WinForms is heavily influenced by the project's specific requirements, such as the level of UI customization and richness required, system compatibility, and the development team's skills. WPF may be more suited for applications that require a contemporary, scalable, and highly flexible user interface. In contrast, WinForms may be better suited for more traditional applications that require rapid development and broad compatibility.

Designing for cross-platform compatibility

Successful cross-platform development relies heavily on ensuring that application design is compatible across platforms. For this reason, we develop our programs with platform neutrality in mind. This guarantees that the code will run correctly on any system.

Our C# code should be developed primarily to maximize code reuse across platforms. It improves the code's maintainability by cutting down on redundancy. Using techniques like dependency injection and abstraction, code reuse and modularity may be improved by separating platform-specific code and dependencies.

Despite our best efforts, we may sometimes need to resolve platform-specific functionality. Thus, we must be prepared to do so. Different platforms may call for different features or implementations due to variations in user interface traditions, hardware availability, or protection schemes. Therefore, to deliver a natural and intuitive user experience, a piece of our code may need to adapt explicitly to these platform-dependent capabilities.

In addition, .NET provides tools like .NET MAUI that make it easier to construct cross-platform compatible apps by abstracting platform-specific APIs and providing a single API surface for creating cross-platform code.

We can accomplish a high degree of cross-platform compatibility without sacrificing the quality of the user experience on any platform by striking a balance between shared code and platform-specific implementations.

Utilizing .NET's cross-platform tools

The .NET Framework provides a powerful and complete collection of tools designed to make programming more accessible and more streamlined across many platforms. The .NET **command line interface** (**CLI**) is a good example; it is a cross-platform tool that lets programmers build and run projects, add dependencies to existing ones, and create new ones from the command line.

MS Build, the Microsoft and Visual Studio build platform, is another vital tool from .NET for cross-platform programming. In contexts where Visual Studio is unavailable, MS Build may still be used to develop projects and solutions and coordinate and build products. Building dependency diagrams, conditional builds, and multi-targeted builds are all part of this process.

Assuring reliable performance and functionality across a wide range of OSs and environments is a significant goal of cross-platform development, and these tools help developers effectively manage and handle these challenges. Therefore, the flexibility and efficiency of the development process are greatly improved by .NET's cross-platform capabilities.

Deploying with platform-specific configurations

Implementing extensive and comprehensive testing is critical in the software development lifecycle to ensure our program runs smoothly across all targeted platforms. This detailed evaluation of the application's functionality can be accomplished with unit testing frameworks such as NUnit or xUnit.net. These testing frameworks allow us to develop and run tests that validate the functioning of specific components of our application, guaranteeing that each unit of code performs as intended.

In addition, built-in testing tools provide a selection of other testing approaches, including integration testing, system testing, and user interface testing. The application's functionality, component connections, and user interface are analyzed using these instruments.

Using these thorough testing approaches, we can ensure that our application behaves consistently and as expected, regardless of the platform it is running on. It, in turn, boosts the robustness and reliability of our program, giving us confidence in the quality of the product we give to end customers.

Ensuring thorough testing

Thorough testing is essential in the software development lifecycle to ensure that our program runs smoothly across all targeted platforms. Unit testing frameworks such as NUnit or xUnit.net can be used to perform this comprehensive evaluation of the application's functionality. These testing frameworks give us the tools we need to develop and run tests that validate the functioning of specific components of our application, guaranteeing that each unit of code works as it should.

Furthermore, built-in testing tools provide a variety of other testing methodologies, including integration testing, system testing, and user interface testing. These tools evaluate the application's general functioning, component interactions, and user interface.

Using these thorough testing approaches, we can ensure that our application behaves consistently and as expected, regardless of the platform on which it is run. This boosts the resilience and reliability of our program, providing us confidence in the product we give to end customers.

Implementing a CI/CD pipeline

Using a **continuous integration and continuous deployment (CI/CD)** pipeline is a fundamental practice in modern software development that improves efficiency and consistency. The CI/CD methodology automates the integration of code changes from all contributing developers into a single repository or mainline. This continuous integration aids in the early detection and resolution of conflicts or errors, improving code quality and minimizing the time required to resolve issues.

The code is automatically submitted to various tests following integration in the continuous testing phase. These tests may include unit tests, integration tests, and system tests, among others, to assure the application's stability and dependability, reducing the chance of introducing defects into the production environment. The continuous deployment phase automatically releases the tested modifications into the production environment after successful testing. This method ensures that new features and upgrades are delivered to end users promptly and dependably. The CI/CD pipeline accelerates the software development process and dramatically improves its robustness, dependability, and efficiency by automating key processes in the development lifecycle.

Windows applications deployment

Deploying C# apps on Windows entails utilizing the capabilities of specific Visual Studio deployment techniques, namely ClickOnce and MSI deployment. ClickOnce is a robust deployment tool that allows us to publish Windows-centric apps to various platforms, including a website, network file sharing, and even physical media such as a CD-ROM. This technique stands out because of its automated updating feature, security provisions, and user-friendly interface, which ensures a seamless user experience.

The MSI deployment method, on the other hand, encapsulates our application into a Windows Installer package, marked by the `.msi` file extension. This strategy allows developers to have more control over the installation process. It has many customization options, including modifying the user interface to specific requirements and tastes. It also allows you to change system settings during installation, giving you a dynamic and adaptable approach to Windows application distribution. As a result, these approaches, which Visual Studio supports, provide a smooth and efficient deployment process that caters to a wide range of deployment circumstances.

WebForms applications deployment

The tools provided by Visual Studio, which provide developers with a complete range of web publishing strategies, considerably simplify the process of distributing web applications, mainly when created in C#. The publish wizard, an intuitive guide that guides developers throughout the distribution of their apps to various sites, is a crucial utility. These can range from a web server to a **File Transfer Protocol** (**FTP**) server to cloud-based platforms.

The deployment procedure essentially collects all of our application's necessary files into a single `.zip` file, ensuring all components are bundled together for ease of transfer. Following that, the package is delivered to the developer's designated location. Throughout this process, Visual Studio's integrated features help you streamline deployment, check dependencies, configure the environment, and ensure the application runs smoothly on the destination server. This comprehensive deployment method increases efficiency and reduces potential errors, ensuring that your web applications are well-positioned for success.

Console applications deployment

When publishing console applications, we choose the right framework-dependent or self-contained deployment strategy depending on our application needs. As the name suggests, framework-dependent deployment relies on a shared system-wide version of .NET. This results in smaller deployment packages.

However, if we need to distribute the application to an environment where .NET may not be installed, we opt for self-contained deployment. This bundles .NET with our application, ensuring it can run independently of its deployed platform.

Mobile applications deployment

Deploying mobile applications, particularly when using C# and Visual Studio, necessitates the construction of app packages that are tailored to the specific requirements of each app store. Developers must generate either **Android Package Kit** (**APK**) or **Android App Bundle** (**AAB**) files when deploying to the Google Play Store for Android devices. For the Apple App Store on iOS devices, **iOS App Store Package** (**IPA**) files are created with the .NET MAUI. iOS toolset. Each platform has its own set of configuration settings and criteria that must be followed, including but not limited to versioning, package name, and security permissions.

Visual Studio and App Center collaborate to make app deployment easier. Here is how to use the App Center with Visual Studio to deploy:

- **Creating an application binary package**: To begin, you must package your program as a binary file for distribution. You can make this file by hand or with App Center Build. Build can be configured to distribute automatically in a branch's build settings.

○ You must create a signed software bundle or APK file for Android. Choose Build | Generate Signed Bundle/APK in Android Studio and follow the wizard instructions to build the app bundle or APK.

○ For iOS, you must create an IPA package for your software. To archive your app, navigate to Product | Archive in Xcode. Use the appropriate provisioning profile to export the archive.

○ You must create an app bundle for macOS. To archive your app, navigate to Product | Archive in Xcode. Use the appropriate provisioning profile to export the archive.

○ App Center for Windows allows you to distribute Windows app packages such as `.appx`, `.appxbundle`, `.appxupload`, `.msi`, `.msix`, `.msixbundle`, `.msixupload`, or `.zip`.

- **Distributing the package**: To distribute a package using App Center, go to App Center, then to your app, then to Distribute | Groups, and finally to New Release. Follow the wizard's instructions. Choose the Release area in the first step to look for the file you wish to upload or drag and drop the file onto the area.

Visual Studio App Center combines a variety of standard services into a DevOps cloud solution. We can use App Center to create, test, and distribute applications. Once the app is deployed, developers can use the analytics and diagnostics services to monitor its status and usage.

You can also use the Deploy with App Center Task to deploy your apps from Azure DevOps to App Center. This makes managing your deployments easier.

Visual Studio has a user-friendly interface that allows you to specify and maintain these settings, streamlining the process.

Android deployment generating APK and AAB Files

We generate an APK or an AAB file for Android. The APK serves as the keystone for installing our app on an Android device, as it is a compressed file package containing all the vital resources and code necessary for the app to function effectively. Conversely, we utilize the AAB format when we aim to publish our app to an Android store like Google Play. The AAB is a publishing format that encapsulates our app's compiled code and resources, deferring the generation and signing of APKs to Google Play.

.NET MAUI deployment

Application deployment in the context of .NET MAUI is not a consistent process but rather one distinguished by diversity due to the distinct requirements and distribution techniques of each platform. These include everything from meeting various security standards and compatibility requirements to adhering to specific user interface guidelines. As a result, the application deployment landscape becomes a kaleidoscope of unique and separate processes. Because each platform is unique, the flexibility of .NET MAUI is enhanced, allowing developers to create apps that are truly cross-platform and can cater to the distinct needs and expectations of users on each platform. As a result, there is a wider and more inclusive reach, a better user experience, and higher satisfaction.

iOS deployment crafting the IPA File

When distributing a .NET MAUI app for iOS, we generate an **.ipa** file. This iOS app archive file is a repository that securely houses our iOS app and its related resources. A significant step in the distribution process is that our .NET MAUI app on iOS must be provisioned using a provisioning profile. This profile establishes a connection between us, as developers, and our apps, clearly defining which devices the app can be installed on.

Mac Catalyst deployment the APP and PKG files

For Mac Catalyst, our deployment strategy requires generating a **.app** or a **.pkg** file. The **.app** file is a self-contained application that can be executed without additional installation, offering a direct and efficient user experience. Alternatively, the **.pkg** file is an installer package we create for distribution purposes, allowing us to perform more complex installations, such as directing files to specific locations or executing scripts during installation.

Role of integrated development environments

IDEs have revolutionized creating, testing, and deploying software applications. Before the era of IDEs, a regular text editor with no language support or highlighted syntax, like VS Code has today, was used. There was only a black screen and your code to write at the time. Students in those days did not have a **personal computer (PC)**. Therefore, we used to write code in a notebook and type it in the next lecture.

Combining several tools inside a single interface creates an environment that speeds up workflows while improving productivity and quality.

IDEs are sophisticated software applications that provide a full set of tools to help with the creation, testing, and debugging of code. Microsoft Visual Studio and JetBrains Rider are three of the most popular C# IDEs.

Microsoft Visual Studio is a feature-rich, capable IDE built primarily for Windows application development. It has a wide range of debugging tools, built-in templates for various applications, and a sophisticated code editor with code refactoring, syntax highlighting, and other features. Microsoft's Visual Studio Code is a lighter, open-source IDE. It is cross-platform, which means it can run on Windows, macOS, and Linux systems.

Visual Studio Code is highly customizable, and there is a vibrant community of developers and users that create and share plug-ins to increase its capabilities.

JetBrains Rider is yet another popular IDE for C# development produced by JetBrains, the same company that created IntelliJ IDEA and PyCharm. Rider includes advanced capabilities like as deep code analysis, automatic error-checking, and easy integration with a variety of popular tools and frameworks.

While these IDEs have their unique strengths, for this book, we will be using Visual Studio 2022. As the most comprehensive suite for development, Visual Studio 2023 offers all the tools we need to create robust, high-quality applications using C#.

Consolidating essential tools

A critical component is a compiler or interpreter, which is critical in converting the high-level code written by the developer into a language that a computer can understand and execute. This phase is critical because it puts the developer's instructions into action.

A debugger is also included with an IDE. As a diagnostic tool, the debugger assists developers in locating, tracing, and correcting any faults, defects, or errors that may arise in the code. This tool is critical for ensuring the functioning and performance of the software in development.

Furthermore, IDEs often include a host of other functionality. Built-in libraries for additional functionality, auto-completion for speedier coding, a file navigator for improved codebase management, and integrated testing tools for evaluating the code's functionality are examples of such features. These IDE components work together to make software development more effective and productive.

Code editing and management

The integrated source code editor in an IDE is a strong tool that offers advanced functionality considerably beyond those of a conventional text editor. Syntax highlighting is a visual technique that distinguishes code items such as keywords, variables, or comments by utilizing distinct colors or fonts. This feature improves readability and can help to reduce coding errors by making it easier for developers to discover faults.

Code completion, often known as autocomplete, is another advanced feature available in many IDEs. This tool saves time by predicting and proposing the rest of a line or block of code as the developer begins to input it. It operates based on the syntax of the language and the context in the code, and it can also suggest methods, variables, or class names, minimizing the possibility of typing errors and enhancing coding speed.

Refactoring tools are another useful feature that is built into many IDEs. These tools assist developers in reorganizing existing code without altering its exterior behavior. This is an important component of maintaining the general quality of the code over time. By finding duplicate code, suggesting more efficient techniques, and automating many of the changes, refactoring can assist improve code readability, reduce complexity, and build a more efficient, maintainable codebase.

Furthermore, several IDEs feature code navigation capabilities to help developers navigate big codebases more easily. These tools can quickly discover definitions, references, and instances of symbols, making complex codebases easier to comprehend and edit. Furthermore, some IDEs integrate version control, making it easier to manage changes over time, communicate with other developers, and avoid disagreements. Version control is an important tool in modern software development techniques since it allows numerous developers to collaborate on the same project without overwriting each other's modifications.

Finally, many IDEs have integrated testing tools that can perform unit tests, integration tests, and even automated UI tests, providing rapid feedback on code quality and assisting in the detection of issues before they reach production.

Overall, the extensive code editing and management features available in IDEs improve developers' productivity and efficiency while also assisting in the maintenance of high-quality code.

Debugging and testing

IDEs often provide a built-in debugger that allows developers to step through their code, monitor variables, and understand the flow of execution. It significantly reduces the time and effort required to identify and fix bugs. Moreover, most IDEs integrate with unit testing frameworks to help ensure that individual pieces of code are functioning as intended.

Integration and extensions

IDEs can integrate with a wide array of other tools that assist in the development, such as version control systems like Git for tracking changes to code. Furthermore, IDEs often support extensions or plugins, add-ons that provide additional functionality, such as support for different programming languages or tools for developing user interfaces.

> **Tip: Code linters are tools that analyze source code to flag programming errors, bugs, stylistic issues, and suspicious constructs. They help maintain code quality, enforce coding standards, and prevent bugs.**

Collaboration and deployment

Many modern IDEs offer features that support team collaboration, like **Live Share**. Some also provide capabilities for deploying applications, whether that is packaging an application for distribution, pushing a web application to a server, or deploying a cloud application.

In essence, IDEs play a central role in modern software development. By providing an all-in-one toolset tailored for coding, testing, debugging, and deploying applications, IDEs enable developers to work more efficiently and effectively, freeing them up to focus on the logic and structure of their applications.

.NET Framework vs. .NET Core

Over time, Microsoft's .NET initiative has evolved to embrace open-source development and become cross-platform, with the introduction of .NET Core and later .NET 5/6/7/8. With the introduction of .NET Core, a significant shift happened. Unlike its predecessor, .NET Core gained independence from the Windows operating system, broadening its reach to other platforms like macOS and Linux. However, it is important to note that this freedom comes with a cost-migrating from .NET Framework 4.x to .NET Core requires both time and development resources. *Table 1.1* depicts the main differences between .NET Framework and .NET Core:

Feature	.NET Framework	.NET Core (1/2/3/5/6/7/8)
Platform dependency	Windows only	Cross-platform (Windows, macOS, Linux)
Open source	No, proprietary	Yes, community-supported
Performance	Stable, but generally slower	Faster due to optimizations
Application types	Console Apps, WinForms, ASP.NET, WPF, Web Forms, MVC	Console Apps, ASP.NET Core, Cloud-based internet-connected applications, Cloud Native Apps and Microservices
APIs available	More extensive API set due to being more established	Smaller API set, but rapidly expanding
Support for microservices	Limited	Excellent, designed with microservices in mind
Deployment	System-wide	It can be packaged with the application, allowing side-by-side installations, that is the ability to install multiple versions of the same software on the same machine.
Updates and maintenance	Slower, controlled by Microsoft	Faster, powered by open-source community contributions
Runtime environment	.NET CLR	.NET **Core Common Language Runtime (CoreCLR)**

Table 1.1: .NET Framework x .NET Core

Overview of C# and .NET ecosystem

Since Microsoft first introduced the C# programming language in the early 2000s, the C# ecosystem and the .NET Framework have developed in a mutually beneficial partnership. With features that take advantage of the CLR and **Base Class Library** (**BCL**), C# was created especially as the flagship language for the .NET platform. From its beginnings with the C-style syntax, it has evolved to include sophisticated features like LINQ for data querying, async/await for asynchronous programming, and, more recently, pattern matching and record types. These features all work in tandem with the .NET runtime and libraries.

An example of how a programming language and its platform can complement one another's development is the relationship between C# and .NET. It changed to accept new concepts like cloud-native development, containerization, and cross-platform mobile applications as .NET evolved from a Windows-only framework to an open-source, cross-platform ecosystem. This co-evolution is still going strong today, with platform improvements in areas like memory management, performance optimization, and cross-platform support broadening what developers can do with it and C#'s language innovations frequently generating new runtime capabilities in .NET. The end result is a unified technology stack in which the platform and language work together to give developers power and productivity across a variety of application areas.

Installing and configuring Visual Studio

When writing C# code, you technically have the freedom to use command lines and any text editor, even something as basic as Microsoft's Notepad. However, to truly unlock productivity and achieve quicker, more efficient results, it is recommended to use an IDE.

Before starting, please check the Microsoft website for the installation and use requirements. The requirements for VS 2022 are recommended using an ARM64 or x64 quad-core processor. At least 4GB RAM, preferably 16GB for professional solutions, suggests a minimum of 2 vCPU and 8GB RAM, but ideally 4 vCPU and 16GB RAM. The installation needs 20-50GB of free space on disk. An SSD is recommended for faster performance. A video card that supports WXGA (1366x768) or higher resolution is advised.

To install the Microsoft Visual Studio IDE, follow these steps:

1. Open the URL **https://visualstudio.microsoft.com/** in your browser and download Visual Studio Community. This version is free for individuals. For more licensing information, look at the URL **https://visualstudio.microsoft.com/en-us/subscriptions/**.

   On this URL, there is a menu for downloading where you can choose the **Visual Studio** version to download, like this (see *Figure 1.1*):

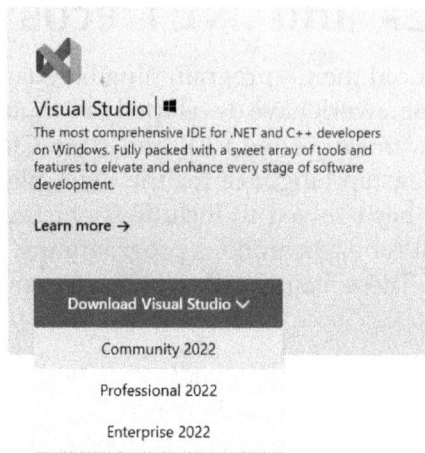

Figure 1.1: Visual Studio download menu

2. Please select these components to install. They will be used in this book.

    On Visual Studio Installer, there are workloads to install. Please check these options:

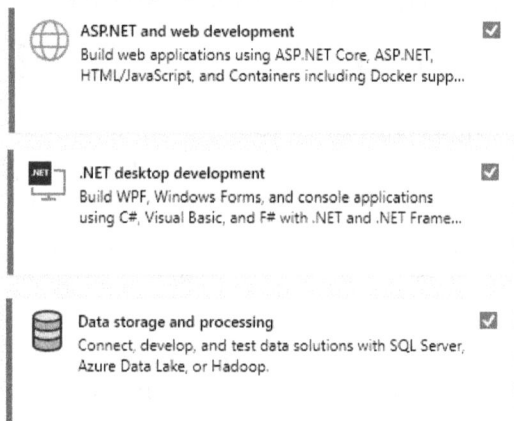

Figure 1.2: Workloads to select the installation

3. Start the installation and wait for it to be completed.

    After the installation, open the Visual Studio, and you will be ready to start, as shown in the following figure:

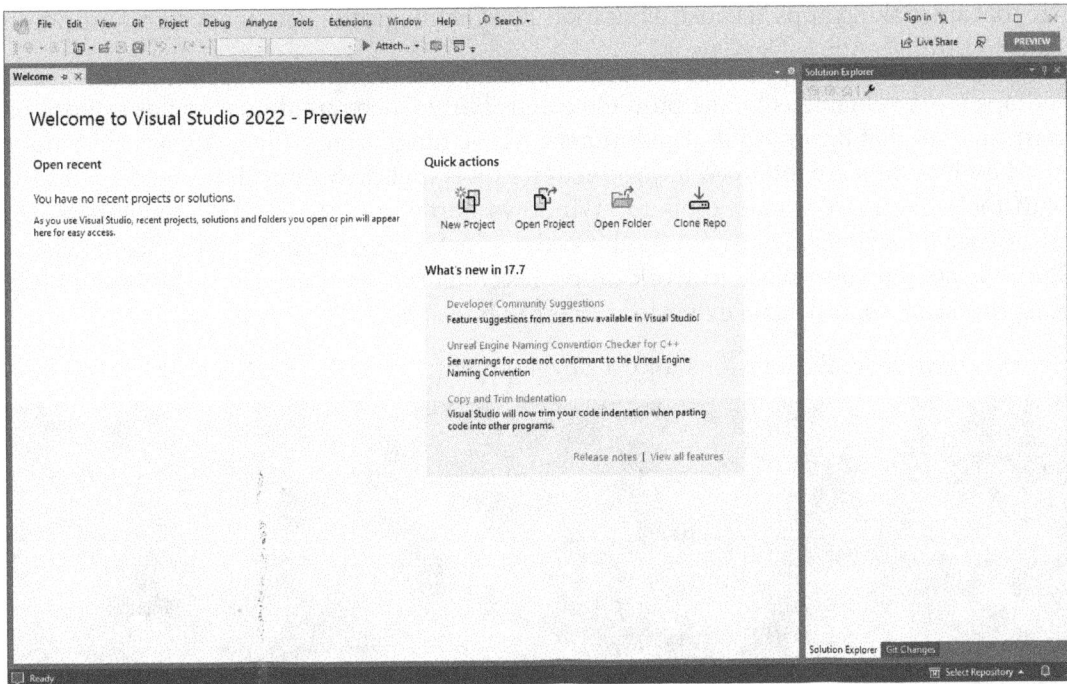

Figure 1.3: Initial screen of Microsoft Visual Studio

Exploring Visual Studio Code for C# development

Visual Studio gives us the best programming experience possible. It is Microsoft's most popular IDE and works perfectly with the .NET Framework. This means that coders can quickly and accurately make everything from desktop apps to web services. The powerful IntelliSense feature guesses what you are typing and gives you ideas that are relevant to the current situation. This cuts down on coding mistakes and development time by a large amount.

Visual Studio's analysis tools are especially useful for working with C# code. We can set breakpoints, go line by line through the code, look at variables, and analyze expressions while the program is running. Finding and fixing problems is much faster with this all-in-one debugging suite than with other environments. This is especially true for complex C# programs that use all the .NET tools and services.

When dealing with C# solutions, Visual Studio's project management tools shine. It is easy to find your way around the most complicated codebases because the solution explorer shows the clear structure of projects, files, and dependencies. Adding third-party libraries is easy with the built-in NuGet package manager. Visual Studio is great for teams of any size that are making apps because it has tools like Git integration and team communication features through Azure DevOps.

Perhaps most valuable is Visual Studio's extensibility. There are thousands of extensions in the market that improve C# development. These range from code analyzers that make sure best practices are followed to productivity tools that do boring chores automatically. With tools like the designer tools for Windows Forms and WPF apps, developers can make user interfaces visually while the code is instantly generated underneath. Visual Studio is also the best place to work on professional projects because it has both strong built-in features and flexible extensions that can be added.

Here we have several extensions for C# development:

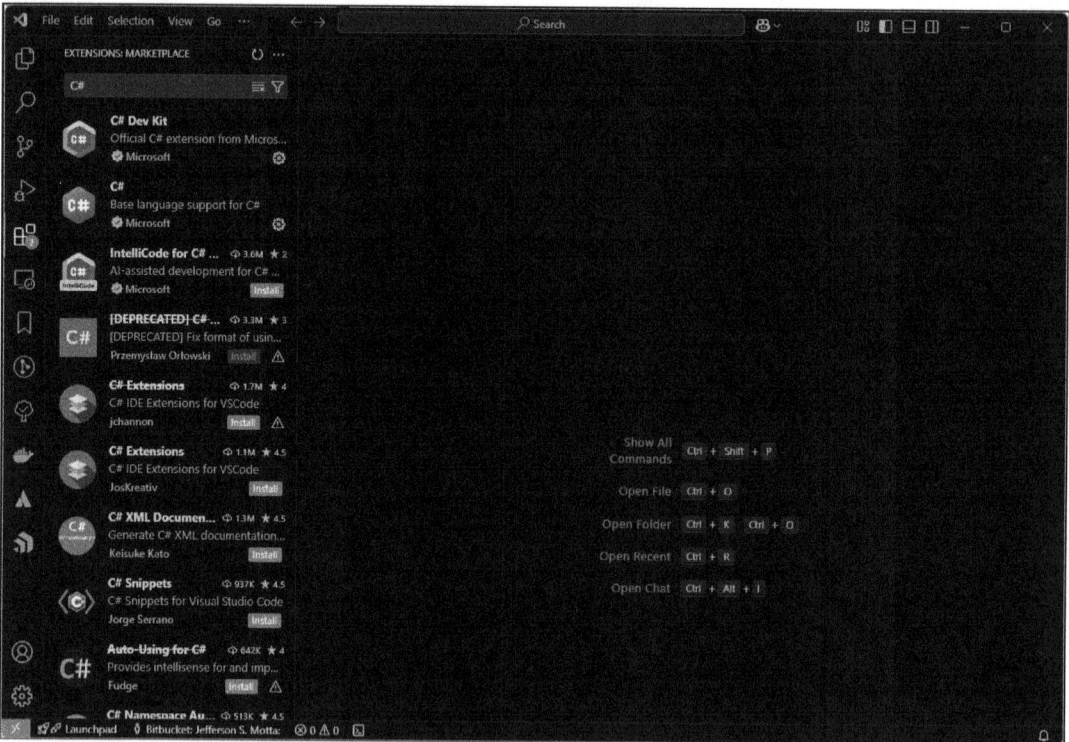

Figure 1.4: Visual Studio Code C# Extensions

Conclusion

From the Windows-only, proprietary, and reliable .NET Framework to the cross-platform, open-source, and rapid .NET Core, Microsoft's .NET project has come a long way. More work and time are needed to convert from the .NET Framework to NET Core, but the benefits of designing contemporary applications like microservices and cloud-based solutions are worth it. In the next chapter, we will discover that C# is a modern language from Microsoft with OOP features. We will also learn syntax, types, operations, namespaces, and memory management fundamentals.

Key terms

- **C#**: It is a modern, open-source, object-oriented programming language from Microsoft.

- **.NET**: A comprehensive software development platform that offers managed code, interoperability, and web services for a wide variety of applications.

- **IDE**: An acronym for integrated development environment, which includes a set of tools for creating, testing, and debugging code.

- **Visual Studio**: It is a powerful IDE designed to build Windows applications using C# and.NET.

- **Roslyn**: Also known as the .NET Compiler Platform, Roslyn provides APIs for code analysis and refactoring.

- **ASP.NET**: It is a particularly built framework for developing web applications using C# and.NET.

- **.NET MAUI**: A solution for developing mobile applications that can run on different platforms using C# and.NET.

- **Unity**: A game development engine that uses C# as its scripting language to create 2D and 3D video games.

- **.NET MAUI**: A framework for developing native device apps for mobile, tablet, and desktop platforms using C# and.NET.

Questions

1. What is the programming language's name created to combine the most significant characteristics of languages such as Java and C++?

2. What is the name of the software development framework that pioneered the concept of language interoperability, allowing multiple high-level languages to communicate with one another seamlessly?

3. What is the name of the Windows desktop application UI framework that leverages XAML for declarative layout and hardware acceleration for graphics rendering?

4. What is the name of the web framework that you may use to create interactive online applications?

Answers

1. **C# (C Sharp)** is a programming language designed to bring together the best features of other languages such as Java and C++.

2. When it comes to facilitating communication across different high-level programming languages, the .NET Framework was the first to introduce the notion.

3. **Windows Presentation Foundation (WPF)** is a UI framework for Windows desktop apps that makes use of XAML for declarative layout and hardware acceleration for graphics rendering.

4. The web framework known as ASP.NET may be used to build dynamic websites and web-based programs.

Join our book's Discord space

Join the book's Discord Workspace for Latest updates, Offers, Tech happenings around the world, New Release and Sessions with the Authors:

https://discord.bpbonline.com

CHAPTER 2
C# Fundamentals

Introduction

This chapter introduces you to the fundamentals of C#, a modern, object-oriented, and flexible programming language from the ground up. Due to its scalability, stability, and user-friendly syntax, Microsoft's C#, developed as part of the .NET program, has earned a prominent position in software development.

The bulk of the chapter's first section examines the structural conventions and rules that govern the formulation of programs written in C#. Next, we will discuss data types and how data may be stored and processed in C#. We will examine every data type, from integers and floats to strings and Booleans, to learn about their characteristics and applications.

Next, operators and expressions are covered, crucial to the ability to do calculations, data manipulation, and decision-making inside C# programming. In this lesson, we will look at the various operators available, such as arithmetic, logical, and comparison operators, and use them to build expressions that execute more involved operations. The following section digs into namespaces, a vital part of structuring code and preventing naming conflicts in more significant projects, and C# statements, the fundamentals of any C# program. These concepts provide the framework for learning how C# programs are structured and how control flows through them.

We will also go into the difference between value and reference types, an important distinction to make when working with C#'s storage mechanisms for information. We will detail how they vary when each is appropriate and what happens when you choose one over the other.

Type conversion methods will also be covered as an intricate but crucial issue. Converting data between different formats is frequently essential as part of processing user input or carrying out specific tasks.

C#'s strong type, automated garbage collection, and support for encapsulation, inheritance, and polymorphism will be discussed, along with other notable features.

After finishing this chapter, you will have a solid foundation in the basics of C# and be ready to create a variety of applications.

Structure

This chapter covers the following topics:

- Basics of C# syntax
- Working with variables in C#
- Storing and manipulating data in C#
- Understanding C# operators
- Fundamental C# data types
- Understanding C# namespaces
- Introduction to C# statements, expressions, and operators
- Using value and reference types in C#
- C# type conversion techniques
- C# keywords and identifiers

Objectives

In this first chapter, we lay the groundwork by delving into the core syntax of C#. This syntax is critical to understand since it serves as the template for the structural backbone of C# programs. In addition, we discuss the different data types, such as integers, floats, strings, and Booleans. When you finish this chapter, you will have a good basis for your future programming work since you can construct and manipulate variables of different data types.

Our focus now shifts to expressions and operators. It makes C# such a powerful programming language, allowing for calculations, data manipulations, and sophisticated judgments. In this part, you will broaden your programming vocabulary by learning to utilize C# operators and expressions to perform various operations and calculations.

Then, we go into the intricacies of C# statements, which are the foundation of any C# program. Writing and executing these statements to guide the execution of your program is critical for designing dynamic, user-friendly software.

We also go through how to use namespaces to organize your code. If you learn to avoid them today, you can ensure that your future large-scale projects will have clean, well-organized, and efficient code. We also review C#'s value and reference types, highlighting their key differences. A solid understanding of how C# manages memory storage and access is required for creating code smoothly.

Type conversion techniques, a vital concept permitting adaptable data processing, are thoroughly investigated. We will teach you how to convert values from one type to another using implicit, explicit, and conversion methods to assist you deal with user input and perform specified tasks.

After completing this chapter, you should be able to understand the principles of C#. We want you to be able to develop usable applications with what you learn here, not only grasp their syntax and capabilities. By the end of this chapter, you will have advanced significantly in your growth as a C# programmer, having gained critical information and skills.

Basics of C# syntax

The programming language syntax refers to the rules and guidelines defining the structure and composition of valid statements and expressions. It determines how programs are written, organized, and understood by both humans and computers. Syntax provides a way to express instructions and algorithms precisely and unambiguously.

The composition of C# syntax used several programming languages, including C, C++, and Java. His syntax is designed to be readable, expressive, and intuitive. It comprises keywords, operators, punctuation, and rules for constructing statements and expressions.

Features of C# language

The syntax of C# is designed to promote readability, maintainability, and efficient coding practices. It enables us to write structured and expressive code that makes it easier to understand, debug, and maintain software projects.

Here are the features of C#:

- **Declarations**: C# requires explicitly declaring variables, classes, and other program elements before they can be used. It helps maintain code clarity and reduce ambiguity.

- **Strong typing**: C# enforces strong typing, meaning variables must be declared with a specific data type and cannot be implicitly converted to incompatible types.

- **Curly braces**: C# uses curly braces (**{ }**) to define code blocks, such as class definitions, method bodies, and control structures. It helps in grouping related code and improving code readability.

- **Semicolons**: C# uses semicolons (**;**) to terminate statements. It is necessary to include a semicolon at the end of each statement to indicate its completion.

- **Object-oriented programming (OOP)**: C# is an object-oriented language that supports concepts such as classes, objects, inheritance, encapsulation, and polymorphism. OOP principles are reflected in the syntax of C#.

- **Comments**: C# provides single-line (**//**) and multi-line (**/* */**) comments to add explanatory notes and documentation within the code. The compiler ignores comments and helps enhance code understanding and collaboration.

- **Control structures**: C# supports control structures such as conditionals (if, else), loops (for, while, do-while), and switch statements. These control structures allow for logical flow control and decision-making within the program.

- **Libraries and namespaces**: C# allows importing libraries and organizing code using namespaces. Namespaces allow grouping related classes and avoiding naming conflicts, while libraries offer pre-built functionality for everyday tasks.

- **Type safety**: C# is a statically typed language, meaning variables must be declared with their specific types at compile-time. It ensures type safety and helps catch errors early in the development process.

- **Garbage collection**: C# incorporates automatic memory management through a garbage collector. It frees us from explicitly managing memory, as the garbage collector automatically deallocates memory for objects no longer in use.

- **Language interoperability**: The C# design was made to work seamlessly with other languages within the .NET ecosystem, such as Visual Basic.NET and F#. It allows us to leverage existing code and libraries written in different languages.

- **Exception handling**: C# provides robust exception handling mechanisms, allowing us to effectively catch and handle runtime errors. It helps maintain program stability and facilitates graceful error recovery.

- **Language-Integrated Query (LINQ)**: C# includes LINQ, which provides a unified syntax for querying and manipulating data from various data sources, such as databases, XML, and collections. LINQ simplifies data access and manipulation tasks.

- **Asynchronous programming**: C# offers powerful support for asynchronous programming through the async/await keywords. It enables us to write efficient and responsive applications that handle concurrent tasks without blocking the main execution thread.

- **Generics**: C# supports generics, allowing us to write reusable code that can work with different data types. Generics enhances code flexibility and performance by providing type-safe algorithms and data structures.

- **Delegates and events**: C# includes delegates and events, enabling event-driven programming implementation. Delegates allow us to pass methods as parameters, while events provide a convenient way to handle and respond to notifications or user actions.

Working with variables in C#

In programming, we work with data using variables. A variable is the name of a storage location that holds a value. It is like a container storing data types such as numbers, text, or complex objects. Variables are an essential concept in programming as they allow us to store and manipulate data during the execution of a program.

Think of a variable as a labeled box or memory space in which you can store information. Each variable has a unique name to refer to and access its value. By assigning values to variables, we can store data and retrieve it later, perform calculations, make decisions based on the stored data, and modify the values as needed.

When using variables in a program, we typically follow a three-step process: declaration, initialization, and usage, which is explained as follows:

- **Declaration**: We declare a variable by specifying its data type (for example, integer, string, Boolean) and giving it a name. This step informs the programming language that we intend to use a variable with a specific type and name.

- **Initialization**: After declaration, we can assign an initial value to the variable. This step is optional, but it is often helpful to give variables an initial value so they are ready to be used.

- **Usage**: Once a variable is declared and initialized, we can access its value and perform operations. We can read the value of a variable, modify it, or use it in calculations and logical conditions throughout the program.

Example:

```
1. // Declaration
2. int age;
3. // Initialization
4. age = 25;
5.  // Assignment to a new variable named "newAge"
6. int newAge = age;
```

In this code, we declare a variable named **age** of type integer. We then initialize it with a value of **25**. Finally, we create a new variable named **newAge** and assign it the value stored in the **age** variable. Now, **age** and **newAge** hold the value **25** and can be used independently.

The code may be simplified by utilizing the **var** keyword during definition, as long as the variable is also initialized with its value, as seen in the following code snippet:

```
1.  // Declaration with initialization
2.  var age = 25;
3.  // Assignment to a new variable named "newAge"
4.  var newAge = age;
```

The **var** keyword is often used when the type can be easily inferred or when the exact type is not essential or known at the time of declaration. It can save some typing and make the code more concise, especially when working with complex or anonymous types.

Remember that variables provide flexibility and dynamism in programming by allowing us to store and manipulate data. They enable us to write more expressive and powerful programs by working with values that can change and adapt during runtime.

Storing and manipulating data in C#

Storing and manipulating data is a fundamental aspect of programming that involves managing and operating on different types of information within a program. It allows us to create dynamic, interactive, and meaningful applications. In C# programming, data can be stored in variables, arrays, collections, databases, files, and other data structures.

In C#, data is stored in variables. A variable refers to a named memory location that holds a value of a specific data type. Variables in C# are declared by specifying a data type and an optional initial value.

In the following code, we declare **age**, **name**, and **salary**:

```
1.  // Declaring and initializing an integer
2.  int age = 30;
3.  // Declaring and initializing a string
4.  string name = "Paul";
5.  // Declaring and initializing a double
6.  double salary = 8000.50;
```

In the preceding example, we declare variables of different types (**int**, **string**, and **double**) and assign them initial values. These variables can then store and retrieve data throughout the program.

After creating the variables, data manipulation involves performing operations, calculations, transformations, and modifications on the stored data. C# provides a rich set of operators, functions, and libraries to manipulate data effectively.

Understanding C# operators

In programming, operators are symbols or keywords that perform operations on one or more operands (values or variables) to produce a result. Operators allow programmers to manipulate and combine data, perform calculations, make comparisons, and control the flow of execution within a program. They are an essential component of programming languages and are used extensively to perform various tasks.

Here we have the operations available in C#:

- **Mathematical operations**: C# supports arithmetic operations such as addition, subtraction, multiplication, and division.

    For example:

    ```
    1.  int a = 5;
    2.  int b = 10;
    3.  // Addition
    4.  int sum = a + b;
    5.  // Subtraction
    6.  int diff = a - b;
    7.  // Multiplication
    8.  int product = a * b;
    9.  // Division
    10. int quotient = b / a;
    ```

- **String manipulation**: C# provides various string manipulation methods to concatenate, format, split, replace, and manipulate strings.

    For example:

    ```
    1.  string greeting = "Hello";
    2.  string name = "Paul";
    3.  // String concatenation
    4.  string message = greeting + ", " + name;
    5.  // Convert to uppercase
    6.  string upperName = name.ToUpper();
    7.  // Split the message by space
    8.  string[] words = message.Split(' ');
    9.  // Replace part of the string
    10. string replacedMessage = message.Replace("Paul", "Jaimes");
    11.
    12. // Output
    13. Console.WriteLine("upperName:" + upperName);
    14. Console.WriteLine("words:" + words);
    ```

```
15. Console.WriteLine("words 0:" + words[0]);
16. Console.WriteLine("words 1:" + words[1]);
17. Console.WriteLine("replacedMessage:" + replacedMessage);
```

This code generates the output as given in the following figure:

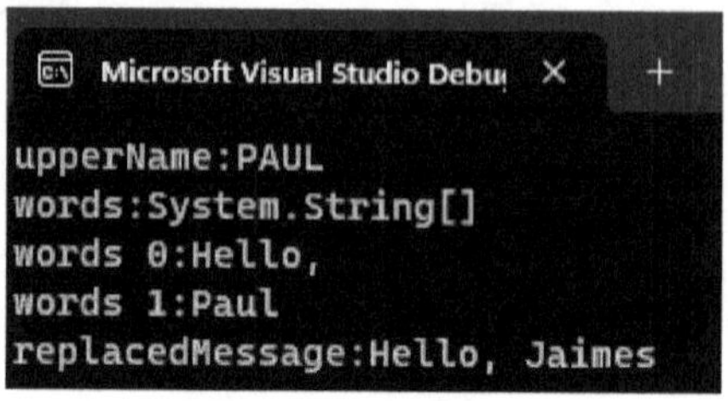

Figure 1.1: Console output

- **Logical operators**: C# supports the following logical operators as shown in *Table 2.1*:

Logical operator	Operator
AND	&&
OR	||
NOT	!

Table 2.1: Logical operators

- **Comparison operators**: Comparison operators compare values and return a Boolean result (true or false) based on the comparison. They are used to evaluate conditions and make decisions in programming. Examples of comparison operators in C# include (refer to *Table 2.2*):

Logical operator	Operator
Equal to	==
Not equal to	!=
Greater than	>
Less than	<
Greater than or equal to	>=
Less than or equal to	<=

Table 2.2: Comparison operators

- **Ternary operator**: The ternary operator (?:) is a shorthand conditional operator in C#. It allows you to write compact if-else statements. It evaluates a condition and returns one of two expressions based on the result of the condition.

For example:

```
1. int nextMonth = DateTime.Now.Month == 12 ? 1 : DateTime.Now.Month + 1;
```

In this example, the variable **nextMonth** gets the next month's number if the current **DateTime**. Now, the month is **12**, so the next month's number is **1**. Otherwise, the current month number is added to **1**.

- **Bitwise operators**: Bitwise operations in programming manipulate individual bits of binary data. They include AND, OR, XOR, NOT, left shift, and right shift. These operations perform low-level bit manipulation, handle flags, and bitwise comparisons, and optimize specific algorithms.

Bitwise operations are performed at the binary level and provide efficient ways to extract, modify, or combine specific bits within integer values. They are instrumental in scenarios involving data encoding, cryptography, bitmasks, and other situations requiring precise bit-level control.

The supported bitwise in C# is shown in *Table 2.3:*

Logical operator	Operator
AND	&
OR	|
NOT	~
XOR	^
Left shift	<<
Right shift	>>

Table 2.3:Bitwise logical operators

Sample of bitwise used to create a hash number:

```
1.  public static int GetStableHashCode(this string str)
2.  {
3.      unchecked
4.      {
5.          int hash1 = 5381;
6.          int hash2 = hash1;
7.
8.          for(int i = 0; i < str.Length && str[i] != '\0'; i += 2)
9.          {
10.             hash1 = ((hash1 << 5) + hash1) ^ str[i];
11.             if (i == str.Length - 1 || str[i+1] == '\0')
12.                 break;
13.             hash2 = ((hash2 << 5) + hash2) ^ str[i+1];
14.         }
```

```
15.
16.              return hash1 + (hash2*1566083941);
17.      }
18. }
```

The keyword **unchecked** in this sample is used to disable arithmetic overflow checking during arithmetic operations. C# uses arithmetic overflow checking by default, which means it throws an exception if an arithmetic operation returns a value outside the data type's range.

The operation result is shortened in an **unchecked** context by eliminating any high-order bits that do not fit in the destination type. In the case of addition, for example, it wraps from the maximum to the most negligible value.

Source code from:

https://stackoverflow.com/questions/46082180/implementing-string-gethashcode-manually

- **Data structures and collections**: C# offers various data structures and collections, such as arrays, lists, dictionaries, and sets, that enable efficient storage, retrieval, and manipulation of multiple data elements. These data structures provide methods and properties for manipulating the stored data. For example:

```
1.  // Array declaration and initialization
2.  int[] numbers = { 1, 2, 3, 4, 5, 6, 7, 8, 9 };
3.   // List declaration
4.  List<int> numberList = new List<int>();
5.  // Adding elements to the list
6.  numberList.AddRange(numbers);
7.  // Accessing elements by index
8.  int firstNumber = numberList[0];
9.  // Removing an element from the list
10. numberList.Remove(4);
```

- **Control flow and conditional statements**: Control flow and conditional statements allow us to make decisions and perform operations based on specific conditions. They enable conditional data manipulation and branching within the program.

For example:

```
1. int age = 22;
2. if (age >= 18)
3. {
4.     Console.WriteLine("You are an adult!");
5. }
```

```
6. else
7. {
8.     Console.WriteLine("You are a minor!");
9. }
```

In this code, different messages are displayed based on the condition (**age >= 18**), manipulating the output based on the data stored in the age variable.

Fundamental C# data types

In C# programming, we build blocks for storing and manipulating different kinds of data in a program. Understanding these data types is essential to working with variables and performing operations on them effectively.

Here are some fundamental C# data types:

- **Numeric types**: C# provides various numeric types such as **int**, **double**, **decimal**, **float**, and others, as shown below. These types represent whole numbers, floating-point numbers, and decimal values.

  Value range of numeric types, as shown in *Table 2.4:*

Type	Min value	Max value
sbyte	-128	127
byte	0	255
short	-32,768	32,767
ushort	0	65,535
int	-2,147,483,648	2,147,483,647
uint	0	4,294,967,295
long	-9,223,372,036,854,775,808	
ulong	0	
float	$\pm 1.5 \times 10^{-45}$	$\pm 3.4 \times 10^{38}$
double	$\pm 5.0 \times 10^{-324}$	$\pm 1.7 \times 10^{308}$
decimal	$\pm 1.0 \times 10^{-28}$	$\pm 7.9 \times 10^{28}$

  Table 2.4: Numeric type range

The **double** data type represents double-precision floating-point numbers. It has a precision of approximately 15-16 digits. It can accurately represent numbers with about 15 to 16 significant digits. However, beyond that range, the precision decreases, and the representation may become less accurate due to the limitations of floating-point arithmetic.

On the other hand, the **decimal** data type represents decimal numbers with high precision. It has approximately 28-29 digits of precision. It can accurately represent numbers with about 28 to 29 significant digits. The **decimal** type is designed for financial and monetary calculations or any scenario that requires high precision and accuracy, as it can maintain the exact representation of decimal numbers without the rounding errors that may occur with other numeric types.

The difference in precision between **double** and **decimal** is significant. While **double** provides a broader range of values and is suitable for general-purpose floating-point calculations, **decimal** is preferred for situations where precise decimal representation and accurate arithmetic operations are crucial, such as financial calculations, currency conversions, or when maintaining exact decimal values is essential.

Here we have the vars types:

- **Boolean type**: The **bool** type represents Boolean values, which can be true or false. It is helpful for logical conditions and decision-making in your code.

- **Character type**: The **char** type represents single characters, such as letters, digits, or symbols, and is enclosed in single quotes (' ').

- **String type**: The **string** type represents a sequence of characters and is used to store text data. Strings are enclosed in double quotes (" ").

- **Enumerations type**: Enumerations (**enum**) allow you to define a named set of constants, providing more expressive and readable code.

- **Nullable type**: C# also supports nullable versions of value types using the **?** symbol. For example, **int?** represents an **int** that can also have a null value.

- **Pointer type**: Pointer types in C# are used for working with unmanaged memory, which is memory outside the control of the runtime environment. They are primarily used in unsafe code blocks and allow direct memory manipulation. The * symbol represents a pointer-type declaration.

- **DateTime type**: The **DateTime** type in C# is used for working with dates and times. It represents a specific point in time, including the date, time, and time zone information. It provides various methods and properties to perform operations on dates and times, such as parsing, formatting, arithmetic calculations, and comparisons.

- **DateOnly type**: Reflects a given date without regard to time. It is great for storing important occasions like birthdays and anniversaries. **DateOnly**, unlike **DateTime**, cannot be offset by a time zone and always represents the date set. It also serializes less data because the time component is not included. A **DateOnly** structure can be modified by adding or removing days, months, or years.

- **TimeOnly type**: It is a new struct introduced in .NET 8. It reflects the current time of day, as read from a clock, with a value ranging from 00:00:00 (midnight) to 23:59:59.9999999. It is very beneficial when you want to represent the time of day without using a date. This type is a perfect match for SQL Server's time type. With EF Core 8.0, time is scaffolded as **TimeOnly**, ideal for mapping database time types.

- **TimeSpan type**: The `TimeSpan` type represents a duration of time or elapsed time between two points. It measures time intervals and can represent durations in days, hours, minutes, seconds, milliseconds, and ticks. It allows performing operations like addition, subtraction, comparison, and formatting of time intervals.

- **GUID type**: The **Globally Unique Identifier** (`GUID`) type represents a unique identifier. It is a 128-bit value typically displayed as a sequence of alphanumeric characters. `GUID` values are commonly used for various purposes like generating unique identifiers, identifying resources, or ensuring uniqueness in distributed systems.

- **Structs type**: Structs in C# define lightweight data structures containing fields and methods. They are value types commonly used to represent small, self-contained pieces of data. Structs are allocated on the stack, providing efficient memory usage and performance benefits for small data structures.

- **Classes type**: Classes in C# define reference types containing fields, properties, methods, etc. They allow encapsulating data and behavior into reusable entities. Classes support concepts like inheritance, polymorphism, and object-oriented programming principles. Objects of classes are created on the heap and accessed through references.

- **Record type**: Record types in C# provide a concise and convenient way to define immutable data structures with built-in equality and value-based semantics. They are handy when dealing with data transfer objects, data models, or any scenario where representing data values is the primary concern.

- **Interfaces type**: Interfaces in C# define a contract that classes can implement. They specify a set of methods, properties, events, or indexers that a class must provide. Interfaces allow for achieving abstraction, modularity, and code reuse. Classes can implement one or more interfaces, providing the necessary implementation for the defined members. Interfaces enable the usage of polymorphism and facilitate loose coupling between components.

Understanding C# namespaces

C# namespaces hierarchically organize related classes, interfaces, enums, and other types. They help in avoiding naming conflicts and provide a way to identify types within an application or library uniquely.

The primary purpose of namespaces is to create a logical separation of code, making it easier to manage and maintain large projects. They also improve code readability and enhance code reusability. To understand namespaces, let us consider an example. Suppose we are building a production application comprising various modules such as customer management, account management, and product stock. We can organize the code related to these modules using namespaces.

Below is a sample of empty classes that are a reference type with fields, properties, methods, etc. Encapsulates data and behavior into reusable things. It supports inheritance, polymorphism, and OOP. On the heap, class objects are created and accessed via references. In this sample, **public class Customer** is named **Customer** with **public** access modifier, capable of being accessed anywhere in the code:

```
1.  // Customer Management Module
2.  namespace ProductionApplication.CustomerManagement
3.  {
4.      public class Customer
5.      {
6.
7.      }
8.
9.      public class DeliveryAddress
10.     {
11.
12.     }
13. }
14.
15. // Account Management Module
16. namespace ProductionApplication.AccountManagement
17. {
18.     public class Account
19.     {
20.
21.     }
22.
23.     public enum AccountType
24.     {
25.
26.     }
27. }
28.
29. // Product Stock Module
30. namespace ProdutctionApplication.ProductStock
31. {
32.     public class ProductStock
33.     {
34.
35.     }
```

```
36.
37.    public interface IBaseProduct
38.    {
39.
40.    }
41. }
```

Although it is possible to declare multiple namespaces in the same file, it is recommended to separate namespaces based on the file content.

To use these namespaces in your code, we can include the appropriate directives at the beginning of your **.cs** files

The following example is an application program that runs in a console window and allows us to interact using text input and output. Its core architecture includes the **Main** method as the execution point, namespaces to structure code, and avoiding naming conflicts using directives to use types from other namespaces. It also includes classes that define the objects' data and behaviors, as well as statements, expressions, and operators that describe the program's logic and data manipulation.

Example:

```
1. using ProductionApplication.CustomerManagement;
2. using ProductionApplication.AccountManagement;
3. using ProductionApplication.ProductStock;
4.
5. public class Program
6. {
7.     public static void Main()
8.     {
9.         var customer = new Customer();
10.        var account = new Account();
11.        var product = new ProductStock();
12.
13.        // Do something
14.    }
15. }
```

If our development team chooses not to specify using directives in each **.cs** file and believes it would benefit the project process, we may create a global using directive. It may be accomplished by creating a special file, such as **globalUsings.cs**, in which using declarations can be made globally applicable:

```
1. global using ProductionApplication.CustomerManagement;
2. global using ProductionApplication.AccountManagement;
3. global using ProductionApplication.ProductStock;
```

There is a recent way to declare namespaces. The file-scoped namespaces use a less verbose format than typical files containing only one **namespace**. In this case, you can declare only one **namespace** per file:

```
1.  namespace ProdutctionApplication.Products;
2.
3.  public class Product
4.  {
5.
6.  }
7.
8.  public interface IBaseProduct
9.  {
10.
11. }
```

Introduction to C# statements, expressions, and operators

In C#, statements, expressions, and operators are fundamental building blocks of the language. They are crucial in defining program logic, performing computations, and manipulating data.

Statements in C# are the individual units of code that perform specific actions. They can include variable declarations, assignments, control flow structures (such as if-else statements and loops), method calls, and more. Statements are executed sequentially, and each statement typically ends with a semicolon (;) to denote its completion.

Expressions in C# are combinations of values, variables, operators, and method calls that produce a result. Expressions can be as simple as a single variable or constant or complex, involving multiple operators and operands. C# offers a rich set of operators for performing arithmetic, logical, bitwise, and comparison operations on expressions. Expressions are often used within statements to compute values, make decisions, and control program flow.

Operators in C# are symbols or keywords to perform operations on one or more operands. They allow us to manipulate values and variables in meaningful ways. C# provides a wide range of operators, including arithmetic operators (**+, -, *, /**), assignment operators (**=, +=, -=**), comparison operators (**==, !=, >, <**), logical operators (**&&, ||, !**), bitwise operators (**&, |, ^**), and more. As we have seen above, each operator has its own rules and behaviors.

Let us consider an example to illustrate the concepts of statements, expressions, and operators:

```
1.  // Statement: Variable declaration and assignment
```

```
2. int y = 20;
3. int x = 5;
4.   // Statement: Variable declaration and expression evaluation
5. int sum = x + y;
6.   // Statement: Conditional statement
7. if (sum > 20)
8. {
9.       // Statement: Method call
10.     Console.WriteLine("Sum is greater than 20.");
11. }
12. else
13. {
14.     Console.WriteLine("Sum is not greater than 20.");
15. }
```

In the above example, we declare and assign values to variables **x** and **y**. Then, we calculate the sum of **x** and **y** using the addition operator (**+**) and assign the result to the variable **sum**. It is an expression that involves both variables and an operator.

Next, we use an if-else statement to check if the sum exceeds 20. The condition **sum > 20** is an expression involving the comparison operator (**>**). Depending on the result of the condition, different statements are executed.

Using value and reference types in C#

In C#, variables and objects can be categorized into two main types: **value** types and **reference** types. These types determine how the data is stored and accessed in memory and have different characteristics regarding assignment, copying, and passing to methods.

Here we have the reference types:

- **Value types**: Value types store their data directly in memory, and each value type variable holds its copy of the data. When you assign a value type variable to another, a new copy of the data is made. Modifying one variable does not affect the other.

  Example:

  ```
  1. int x = 10;
  2.   // y gets a copy of the value of x
  3. int y = x;
  4.   // Modifying x doesn't affect y
  5. x = 20;
  6. // Output: 20
  7. Console.WriteLine(x);
  ```

```
8.  // Output: 10
9.  Console.WriteLine(y);
10. Console.ReadKey();
```

- **Reference types**: Reference types store a reference to the data in memory rather than the actual data itself. Objects, records, classes, arrays, and strings are examples of reference types in C#. Multiple variables can refer to the same underlying object.

When you assign a reference type variable to another, both variables point to the same object in memory. Modifying one variable affects the other because they both reference the same data.

Example:

```
1.  int[] arrNumber1 = { 1, 2, 3 };
2.  // arrNumber2 points to the same array as arrNumber1
3.  int[] arrNumber2 = arrNumber1;
4.  // Modifying arrNumber1 also modifies arr2
5.  arrNumber1[0] = 10;
6.  Console.WriteLine(arrNumber1[0]); // Output: 10
7.  Console.WriteLine(arrNumber2[0]); // Output: 10
8.  Console.ReadKey();
```

Passing reference types as method arguments means passing the reference to the object, not a copy of the object. Therefore, changes made to the object within the method are also reflected outside the method.

Following is a demonstration of modifying an array value:

```
1.  int[] myArray = { 1, 2, 3 };
2.  // Modifies the original array
3.
4.  ModifyArray(myArray);
5.
6.  // Output: 100
7.  Console.WriteLine(myArray[0]);
8.  Console.ReadKey();
9.
10.   void ModifyArray(int[] array)
11.   {
12.       array[0] = 100;
13.   }
```

It is important to note that assigning a value type to a reference type variable or vice versa involves boxing and unboxing operations to convert between the two types.

This is an example:

```
1. // Boxing
2. int valType = 123; // Value type
3. object refType = valType; // Boxing
4.
5. // Unboxing
6. int unboxed = (int)refType; // Unboxing
```

- **Boxing and unboxing**: Boxing converts a value type to an object type, while unboxing is the reverse process of extracting the value type from the object. Boxing is done implicitly when a value type is assigned to an object variable, and unboxing is done explicitly by casting the object back to the value type.

  Boxing creates a new object on the **heap**, which adds overhead, and unboxing involves type-checking and extracting the value, which can lead to performance costs.

  The **heap** is a region of memory used for dynamic memory allocation. It is where objects are allocated and deallocated during runtime.

C# type conversion techniques

In C#, type conversion allows you to convert a value from one data type to another. C# provides several techniques for performing type conversions, including implicit conversion, explicit conversion, and conversion methods.

- **Implicit conversion**: Implicit conversion occurs when the compiler automatically converts a value from one type to another without requiring explicit casting or conversion methods. It is possible when there is no data loss or potential precision loss.

  Example:

```
1. int x = 10;
2. long y = x; // Implicit conversion from int to long
```

- **Explicit conversion (casting)**: Explicit conversion, also known as **casting**, is performed when you explicitly convert a value from one type to another that may result in data loss or precision loss. It requires the use of casting operators.

  Example:

```
1. double x = 10.5;
2. // Explicit conversion from double to int using casting
3. int y = (int)x;
4. // Decimals from x, output 0,5
5. Console.Write(x-y);
6. Console.ReadKey();
```

- **Conversion methods**: Some types in C# provide conversion methods to convert between different types. These methods include:

- **Parse**: They convert a string representation of a value to another type.

  Example:

  ```
  1.  var number = int.Parse("10");
  ```

- **TryParse**: Similar to parse but returns a Boolean indicating the success or failure of the conversion.

  Example:

  ```
  1.  string str = "10";
  2.  if (int.TryParse(str, out var result))
  3.  {
  4.      // Output 10
  5.      Console.WriteLine(result);
  6.  }
  ```

- **Convert**: It provides various static methods for converting one type to another, as shown in conversion classes.

- **Type conversion classes**: C# provides several built-in classes for specific type conversions.

- **Convert class**: It provides methods for converting base data types.

  Example:

  ```
  1.  var x = Convert.ToInt32("123");
  2.  var y = Convert.ToByte("1");
  ```

- **BitConverter class**: It converts the base data types to an array of bytes and vice versa.

  This is especially beneficial in the following scenarios:

  - **Data serialization**: When you need to save or transmit data in a format other systems can utilize or recognize, you may need to convert the data to a byte array. This is referred to as serialization. Deserialization refers to converting byte arrays back to their original data formats.

  - **Networking**: Data is transported across networks through packets of bytes in networking. The **BitConverter** class can convert data into byte arrays before sending it over the network and then back into its original form at the receiving end.

  - **File I/O**: When reading or writing to binary files, byte arrays are frequently used. For this purpose, the **BitConverter** class provides an easy mechanism to convert data to and from byte arrays.

o **Cryptography**: Data is frequently worked with at the byte level in cryptography. Data can be converted into byte arrays using the **BitConverter** class for cryptographic operations.

Example:

```
1. byte[] byteArray = BitConverter.GetBytes(123);
```

- **Enum class**: It helps to convert values between enums and their underlying types.

Example:

```
1.  // Sunday as an underlying integer value
2.  int enumValue = 6;
3.  // Convert integer to enum
4.  DaysOfWeek day = (DaysOfWeek)enumValue;
5.  Console.WriteLine($"Converted value: {day}"); // Output Sunday
6.  // Convert enum to integer
7.  int intValue = (int)day;
8.  Console.WriteLine($"Converted value: {intValue}");  // Output 6
9.  Console.ReadKey();
10.
11. enum DaysOfWeek
12. {
13.     Monday,
14.     Tuesday,
15.     Wednesday,
16.     Thursday,
17.     Friday,
18.     Saturday,
19.     Sunday
20. }
```

C# keywords and identifiers

In programming languages, keywords are reserved words that have predefined meanings and functionalities within the language. They serve as building blocks for constructing valid programs by providing specific instructions, defining control structures, specifying data types, and performing various operations.

Keywords are an essential part of the language syntax and are used to create statements, expressions, and declarations that define the behavior and logic of a program. Since keywords have predefined meanings, they cannot be used in the program as identifiers (variable names, function names, class names, etc.).

In C#, keywords are specific to the C# programming language and have reserved meanings. They are part of the C# language specification and cannot be redefined or used for any other purpose in the code. C# keywords are case-sensitive, meaning they must be written precisely as the language specifies.

C# keywords

A list of C# keywords is as follows: `abstract`, `as`, `base`, `bool`, `break`, `byte`, `case`, `catch`, `char`, `checked`, `class`, `const`, `continue`, `decimal`, `default`, `delegate`, `do`, `double`, `else`, `enum`, `event`, `explicit`, `extern`, `false`, `finally`, `fixed`, `float`, `for`, `foreach`, `goto`, `if`, `implicit`, `in`, `int`, `interface`, `internal`, `is`, `lock`, `long`, `namespace`, `new`, `null`, `object`, `operator`, `out`, `override`, `params`, `private`, `protected`, `public`, `readonly`, `ref`, `return`, `sbyte`, `sealed`, `short`, `sizeof`, `stackalloc`, `static`, `string`, `struct`, `switch`, `this`, `throw`, `true`, `try`, `typeof`, `uint`, `ulong`, `unchecked`, `unsafe`, `ushort`, `using`, `virtual`, `void`, `volatile`, `while`, `yield`.

Note: It is not recommended, but we can use keywords as variable names by adding @ in the name, like var `@class` = "class name";.

These keywords have predefined meanings in the C# programming language and cannot be used as identifiers.

An identifier identifies a variable, method, class, or programming element within your code. Identifiers are user-defined names assigned to different program elements to make your code more readable and understandable.

Guidelines for identifiers

Before writing code, we must review the criteria for establishing identifiers in C#. A variable, function, class, module, or any other user-defined entity is identified by a name. We can guarantee that our code is clean, consistent, and legible by following certain rules and standards. The following are the most important things to know while defining identifiers in C#:

- **Valid characters**: Identifiers include letters (uppercase and lowercase), digits, and underscores. However, they must begin with a letter or an underscore.

- **Case sensitivity**: C# is case-sensitive, so uppercase and lowercase letters are treated as distinct characters. For example, `myVariable` and `myvariable` are different identifiers.

- **Length**: Identifiers can be of any length, but using descriptive names that are not excessively long is recommended to maintain code readability.

- **Reserved keywords**: C# has reserved keywords, listed above, with special meanings in the language and cannot be used as identifiers.

- **Meaningful names**: It is good practice to choose meaningful and descriptive names for your identifiers. It helps in understanding the purpose or functionality of the associated program element.

- **Camel case**: It is common to use camel case notation for identifiers in C#. In the camel case, the first letter of the identifier starts in lowercase, and subsequent words begin in uppercase. For example, `myVariable`, `resultSum`, or `professionalName`.

- **Namespace and class naming**: Namespaces and class names are typically written in Pascal's case, where each word starts with an uppercase letter. For example, `System.Text`, or `MyNameClass`.

Sample of identifiers, as seen in *Table 2.5:*

Identifiers
variableName
MethodName
ClassName
ConstantName
parameterName
PropertyName
InterfaceName
NamespaceName
EnumName

Table 2.5: Identifiers samples

Conclusion

The chapter thoroughly introduces the fundamentals of C#, an innovative, object-oriented, and versatile programming language, exposing its many facets. An in-depth investigation of essential C# concepts such as syntax, data types, operators, expressions, and statements are undertaken, as well as a review of extra features such as namespaces, among others.

The content goes beyond basic description to conduct an analytical comparison of value and reference categories. It explains how these differences significantly influence data storage and manipulation operations, giving the reader a better grasp of C#'s dynamic nature.

Imbibing the information provided by this book should provide the reader with a solid foundation in C# fundamentals, driving them toward the development of a wide range of applications. The reader is also expected to master the comprehension and use of C#'s various data structures and collections and, control flow, and conditional expressions.

This resource introduces you to fundamental principles and digs into advanced features like generics, delegates, events, LINQ, asynchronous programming, and much more.

These subjects prepare the reader to face challenges in the C# realm.

However, this is not the conclusion of the adventure. Readers are encouraged to continue researching these topics and honing their skills. The content emphasizes the importance of hands-on experience and encourages practice through building C# programs. Because programming is both an art and a science, this advice ensures that the reader applies their theoretical knowledge in real-world circumstances, allowing them to understand the width and depth of what C# offers.

In the next chapter, we will understand the C# control flow, interactions statements, loopings, nullable types, and more.

Remember that learning C# is a marathon, not a sprint. It does not matter how much you cover; what matters is that you comprehend each idea thoroughly. This content is intended to act as a stepping stone toward becoming fluent in C#, and readers are urged to utilize it as a foundation to grow further. Continue exploring, learning, and coding.

Join our book's Discord space

Join the book's Discord Workspace for Latest updates, Offers, Tech happenings around the world, New Release and Sessions with the Authors:

https://discord.bpbonline.com

CHAPTER 3
Harnessing the Code

Introduction

Welcome to an action-packed chapter covering essential topics in C# programming. We will explore control flow using selection and conditional statements, iterate through data with iteration statements, and learn about type conversion and type casting. Additionally, we will gain an overview of exception handling, implement robust error management, and uncover the power of nullable types. Finally, we will discuss looping constructs like for, while, and do-while and understand the significance of unchecked and checked operators. By the end of this chapter, you will have a comprehensive understanding of these concepts, enabling you to write efficient and error-resistant code in C#.

Structure

This chapter covers the following topics:

- Control flow in C# with selection statements
- Iteration statements in C#
- Understanding data type conversion in C#
- Looping constructs in C#
- Understanding and using nullable types in C#
- Unchecked and checked operators in C#

- Overview of exception handling in C#
- Implementing robust exception handling

Objectives

We will learn how to control code flow in C# using selection statements such as if and switch. Understanding selection statements enables you to run specific code blocks based on conditions and how to use iteration statements such as for, while, and do-while to create loops for repeated code execution will also be explored. These loops are helpful when you need to repeat tasks or wait for a condition to be met. You must first understand data type conversions to work with different data types effectively. Use loop constructs to iterate through arrays and collections efficiently for data processing. Furthermore, use nullable types to represent the absence of a value for value types and use checked and unchecked operators to control the behavior of integer arithmetic operations. Finally, understanding exception handling to managing errors at runtime, recovering gracefully, and ensuring code stability and reliability will also be learned.

Control flow in C# with selection statements

In C#, control flow refers to the order in which statements are executed in a program. Selection statements are essential to control flow, allowing you to decide based on certain conditions. Several selection statements are available in C# to control the flow of execution, namely if, if-else, if-else if-else, and switch statements.

If statement

The **if** statement evaluates a Boolean/logical expression and executes a code block when the condition is true. Here are some examples of syntax with different ways to validate the condition. Here are some syntax examples:

```
1.  if (myCondition)
2.  {
3.      // Do Something
4.  }
5.
6.  if (x == 25)
7.  {
8.      // Do Something
9.  }
10.
11. if (y == z)
12.     // Do Something
13. }
```

```
14.
15. if (myObject.MyFlag)
16. {
17.     // Do Something
18. }
19.
20. if (myObject.MyText.Equals(PmyConstant))
21. {
22.     // Do Something
23. }
```

The expression must be true to be executed, and in some cases, it could be negative validation, like this sample:

```
1. if (myCondition == false)
2. {
3.     // Do Something
4. }
5. // This is the same thing:
6. if (!myCondition)
7. {
8.     // Do Something
9. }
```

if-else statement

The if-else statement extends the **if** statement by providing an alternative block of code to execute when the condition is false. Here is the syntax:

```
1. if (myCondition)
2. {
3.   // Do something when the condition is true
4. }
5. else
6. {
7.   // Do something else if the condition is false
8. }
```

Using the if-else statement inverse, when in the sample, the variable **myCondition** is tested to be false:

```
1.  if (!myCondition)
2.  {
3.      // Do something when the condition is true
```

```
       but when the variable myCondition is false
4.  }
5.  else
6.  {
7.      // Do something then myCondition variable is true
8.  }
```

Although this is correct, it is usual to prioritize the true condition in the if statement to avoid unnecessary CPU processing steps.

If-else if-else statement

The if-else if-else statement allows you to check multiple conditions and execute different code blocks accordingly. Here is the syntax:

```
1.  if (myCondition1)
2.  {
3.      // Do something if myCondition1 is true
4.  }
5.  else if (myCndition2)
6.  {
7.      // Do something if myCondition2 is true
8.  }
9.  else
10. {
11.     // Do something if myCondition1 and myCondition2 is false
12. }
```

switch statement

The **switch** statement provides a way to get one of many code blocks to be executed based on the value of a variable or an expression. It is useful when you have multiple cases to handle.

Here is the basic syntax:

```
1.  switch (myExpression)
2.  {
3.      case myValue1:
4.          // Code to be executed if myExpression matches myValue1
5.          break;
6.      case myValue2:
7.          // Code to be executed if myExpression matches myValue2
8.          break;
```

```
9.      // ...
10.     default:
11.         // Code to be executed if myExpression doesn't match any case
12.           break;
13. }
```

It is allowed to have multiple tests in the **case** clause with the same return/result. Here is an example:

```
1.  switch (myExpression)
2.  {
3.      case "A":
4.      case "E":
5.      case "I":
6.      case "O":
7.      case "U":
8.          // Code to be executed if myExpression
9.          // matches these values
10.         break;
11.     case "W":
12.     case "Y":
13.         // Code to be executed if myExpression
14.         // matches W or Y
15.         break;
16.     // ...
17.     default:
18.         // Code to be executed if myExpression
19.         // doesn't match any case
20.         break;
21. }
```

In **switch** arguments, it is possible to use the clause **when** together with the expression of the **case**, shown as follows:

```
1.  switch (isDirectory)
2.  {
3.      case true when myFile != null
4.                  && myCondition == 0:
5.      // Do somenthing when isDirectory is true
6.      // and myFile is
7.      // different from null
8.      // and myCondition is equals 0
9.        break;
```

```
10.    case true when myCondition == 1
11.    // Do somenthing when isDirectory is true
12.    // and myCondition is equals 1
13.    break;
14.    case false:
15.    // Do something is isDirectory is false
16.    default:
17.    // Do something if isDirectory is true
18.    // and myFile is null or myCondition
19.    // is different than 0
20. }
```

Using the **switch** statement can be used to return a single value:

```
1. string Weekend(DayOfWeek dayOfWeek)
2. {
3.     return dayOfWeek switch
4.     {
5.         DayOfWeek.Sunday => "Sunday",
6.         DayOfWeek.Saturday => "Saturday",
7.         _ => "It's not weekend!"
8.     };
9. }
```

Major languages use a similar process to control the flow of the processing code. They may vary in syntax, but the underlying mental process of understanding remains the same.

Iteration statements in C#

In C#, iteration statements are used to execute the block of code repeatedly based on a specific condition or a predefined number of iterations. This technique is used to process a list of data or produce similar events with distinguished data, like sending e-mails or writing data from a processed list.

In the following sections, we see some of the iteration statements available in C#.

Foreach statement

The **foreach** statement is used to iterate over elements in an array or a collection. It automatically retrieves each element in the array or collection without explicitly using an index.

These are the syntax examples:

```
1. foreach (var item in collection)
```

```
2. {
3.      // Do something
4. }
5.
6. foreach(var primeNumber in new[] { 2, 3, 5, 7, 11, 13, 17, 19, 23,
   29 })
7. {
8.      // Do something
9. }
```

Goto statement

The **goto** statement allows you to transfer control to a labeled statement within the same method or block of code. However, the use of **goto** is generally discouraged as it can make code harder to read and maintain.

This is the syntax:

```
1. myLabel:
2.
3. // Code block
4.
5. goto myLabel;
```

This is an example:

```
1. tryAgain:
2. try
3. {
4.      var stream = new FileStream(filePath, FileMode.Open, FileAccess.
   Read);
5.      stream.Close();
6.      stream.Dispose();
7. }
8. catch
9. {
10.    Thread.Sleep(1_000);
11.    goto tryAgain;
12.}
```

Yield statement

The **yield** statement is used in iterator methods to provide a simplified way of creating enumerators. It allows you to return a sequence of values one at a time without building an entire collection beforehand.

Here is the basic syntax:

```
1.  IEnumerable<valueType> GetNumbers()
2.  {
3.      yield return value1;
4.  }
```

The **yield** allows to execute code and returns the value at any moment because the **yield** return does not stop code execution like a simple **return**. We use the **yield** break command inside a block with **yield return** to finish a process.

Let us see an example in the following code:

```
1.  foreach (int number in GetNumbers())
2.  {
3.      Console.WriteLine(number);
4.  }
5.  Console.ReadKey();
6.  IEnumerable<int> GetNumbers()
7.  {
8.      Console.WriteLine("Code execution 1");
9.      yield return 1;
10.     Console.WriteLine("Code execution 2");
11.     yield return 2;
12.     Console.WriteLine("Code execution 3");
13.     yield return 3;
14.     Console.WriteLine("Code execution 3");
15.     yield return 4;
16.     Console.WriteLine("Code execution 4");
17.     yield return 5;
18.     Console.WriteLine("Code execution 5");
19. }
```

This will result in this output as shown in *Figure 3.1*:

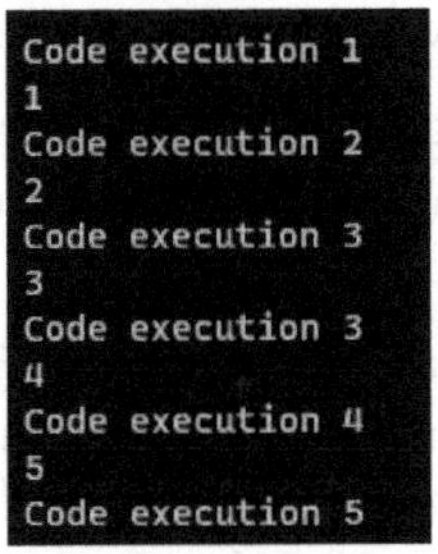

Figure 3.1: Console output

In C#, iteration statements allow for the repetition of code execution. These iteration statements provide flexibility and control flow within loops, allowing for efficient and concise code implementation in C#.

In this chapter, we will see the loop iterations too.

Understanding data type conversion in C#

Data type conversion in C# is essential for manipulating and transforming data. C# provides various mechanisms for converting between different data types. Implicit conversions occur automatically when the conversion is safe and does not result in data loss. Explicit conversions, also known as casting, are used when there is a potential data loss, and the conversion needs to be explicitly specified.

C# supports both built-in and user-defined conversions. Built-in conversions include numeric conversions (**int** to **float**), reference conversions (base class to derived class), and boxing/unboxing (*Chapter 2, C# Fundamentals* in the section *Using value and reference types in C#*) conversions. User-defined conversions can be defined in classes using operator overloading or explicit conversion methods.

Handling conversions requires caution to avoid unexpected results or exceptions. The Convert class provides methods for converting between different data types, offering additional control and error handling.

It is essential to be aware of pitfalls, such as data loss, precision issues, and compatibility between different data types the **System.Convert** class, type casting, and explicit conversion methods (for example., **float.Parse()**, **float.TryParse()**) are valuable tools for performing data type conversions effectively and safely in C#.

The critical difference is that the **Parse** methods throw an exception when the conversion fails. In contrast, **TryParse** methods return a Boolean value indicating the success or failure of a conversion without throwing an exception. It allows for safer input data handling, especially when the conversion is uncertain, or input validation is required.

As seen in *Chapter 2, C# Fundamentals* in section *C# type conversion techniques*, we have several ways to convert data types.

The following points show some methods from convert class:

- **ChangeType (Object, Type, IFormatProvider)**: This function returns an object of the specified type equivalent to the provided object. The parameter allows for culture-specific formatting information.

- **FromBase64CharArray (Char[], Int32, Int32)**: This function converts a portion of a Unicode character array, which represents binary data using base-64 digits, into a corresponding 8-bit unsigned integer array. The parameters indicate the subset of the input array and the number of elements to be converted.

- **FromBase64String (String)**: This function converts the provided string, which represents binary data using base-64 digits, into an equivalent 8-bit unsigned integer array.

- **FromHexString (ReadOnlySpan<Char>)**: This function converts the given span, which represents binary data using hexadecimal characters, into an equivalent 8-bit unsigned integer array.

- **FromHexString (String)**: This function converts the provided string, which represents binary data using hexadecimal characters, into an equivalent 8-bit unsigned integer array.

- **GetTypeCode (Object)**: This function returns the TypeCode corresponding to the specified object.

- **IsDBNull (Object)**: This function will provide a boolean value that indicates whether the given object is of the DBNull type.

- **ToBase64CharArray (Byte[], Int32, Int32, Char[], Int32)**: This function takes a segment of an array of 8-bit unsigned integers and converts it into a corresponding subset of a Unicode character array. The conversion is done by encoding it with base-64 digits. The parameters of the function define the starting positions in the input and output arrays, as well as the number of elements from the input array that should be converted.

- **ToBase64String (Byte[], Int32, Int32, Base64FormattingOptions)**: This function converts a specified portion of an array consisting of 8-bit unsigned integers into its string representation. The resulting string is encoded using base-64 digits. The function's parameters include the offset in the input array indicating the subset to convert, the number of elements to be converted, and a flag indicating whether line breaks should be included in the resulting string.

- **ToBase64String (ReadOnlySpan<Byte>, Base64FormattingOptions)**: This function converts the 8-bit unsigned integers within the specified read-only span into their corresponding string representation, encoded with base-64 digits. Optionally, you can specify whether to include line breaks in the returned value.

- **ToBoolean (Boolean)**: This function returns the specified Boolean value; no actual conversion takes place.

- **ToBoolean (Byte)**: This function converts the value of the specified 8-bit unsigned integer into an equivalent Boolean value.

- **ToBoolean (Char)**: This method will always throw an InvalidCastException.

- **ToBoolean (DateTime)**: Invoking this method will consistently throw an InvalidCastException.

- **ToByte (Boolean)**: This function converts the specified Boolean value into the equivalent 8-bit unsigned integer.

- **ToByte (Byte)**: This function returns the specified 8-bit unsigned integer without performing any actual conversion.

- **ToByte (Char)**: This function converts the value of the specified Unicode character into the equivalent 8-bit unsigned integer.

- **ToChar (Boolean)**: Invoking this method will consistently throw an InvalidCastException.

- **ToChar (Byte)**: This function converts the value of the specified 8-bit unsigned integer into its equivalent Unicode character.

- **ToChar (Char)**: This function returns the specified Unicode character value without performing any actual conversion.

- **ToDateTime (Boolean)**: Invoking this method will consistently result in throwing an InvalidCastException.

- **ToDateTime (Byte)**: This method will always throw an InvalidCastException.

- **ToDateTime (Char)**: Invoking this method will consistently throw an InvalidCastException.

- **ToDecimal (Boolean)**: This function converts the specified Boolean value into the equivalent decimal number.

- **ToDecimal (Byte)**: This function converts the value of the specified 8-bit unsigned integer into the equivalent decimal number.

- **ToDecimal (Char)**: Invoking this method will consistently throw an InvalidCastException.

- **ToDouble (Boolean)**: Converts the specified Boolean value into the equivalent double-precision floating-point number.

- **ToDouble (Byte)**: This function converts the value of the specified 8-bit unsigned integer into the equivalent double-precision floating-point number.

- **ToDouble (Char)**: Calling this method will always result in throwing an InvalidCastException.

- **ToHexString (Byte[])**: This function converts an array of 8-bit unsigned integers into its corresponding string representation, encoded with uppercase hexadecimal characters.

- **ToHexString (Byte[], Int32, Int32)**: This function takes a segment of an array of 8-bit unsigned integers and converts it into its corresponding string representation. The conversion is done by encoding the values with uppercase hexadecimal characters. The parameters of the function define the starting position in the input array and the number of elements from the array that should be converted.

- **ToHexString (ReadOnlySpan<Byte>)**: This function converts a span of 8-bit unsigned integers into its corresponding string representation, encoded with uppercase hexadecimal characters.

- **ToInt16 (Boolean)**: This function converts the specified Boolean value into the equivalent 16-bit signed integer.

- **ToInt16 (Byte)**: Translates the given 8-bit unsigned integer into its corresponding 16-bit signed integer.

- **ToInt16 (Char)**: Translates the given Unicode character into its corresponding 16-bit signed integer.

- **ToInt32 (Boolean)**: Translates the given Boolean value into its corresponding 32-bit signed integer.

- **ToInt32 (Byte)**: Translates the 8-bit unsigned integer into its corresponding 32-bit signed integer.

- **ToInt32 (Char)**: Translates the Unicode character into its corresponding 32-bit signed integer.

- **ToInt64 (Boolean)**: Translates the given Boolean value into its corresponding 64-bit signed integer.

- **ToInt64 (Byte)**: Translates the 8-bit unsigned integer into its corresponding 64-bit signed integer.

- **ToInt64 (Char)**: Translates the Unicode character into its corresponding 64-bit signed integer.

- **ToSByte (Boolean)**: Translates the given Boolean value into its corresponding 8-bit signed integer.

- **ToSByte (Byte)**: Translates the given 8-bit unsigned integer into its corresponding 8-bit signed integer.

- **ToSByte (Char)**: Translates the Unicode character into its corresponding 8-bit signed integer.

- **ToSingle (Boolean)**: Translates the given Boolean value into its corresponding single-precision floating-point number.

- **ToSingle (Byte)**: Translates the 8-bit unsigned integer into its corresponding single-precision floating-point number.

- **ToSingle (Char)**: Calling this method always throws InvalidCastException.

- **ToString (Boolean)**: Translates the given Boolean value into its corresponding string representation.

- **ToString (Boolean, IFormatProvider)**: Translates the given Boolean value into its corresponding string representation.

- **ToString (Byte)**: Translates the 8-bit unsigned integer into its corresponding string representation.

- **ToUInt16 (Boolean)**: Translates the Boolean value into its corresponding 16-bit unsigned integer.

- **ToUInt16 (Byte)**: Translates the 8-bit unsigned integer into its corresponding 16-bit unsigned integer.

- **ToUInt16 (Char)**: Translates the Unicode character into its corresponding 16-bit unsigned integer.

- **ToUInt32 (Boolean)**: Translates the Boolean value into its corresponding 32-bit unsigned integer.

- **ToUInt32 (Byte)**: Translates the 8-bit unsigned integer into its corresponding 32-bit unsigned integer.

- **ToUInt32 (Char)**: Translates the given Unicode character into its corresponding 32-bit unsigned integer.

- **ToUInt64 (Boolean)**: Translates the Boolean value into its corresponding 64-bit unsigned integer.

- **ToUInt64 (Byte)**: Translates the 8-bit unsigned integer into its corresponding 64-bit unsigned integer.

- **ToUInt64 (Char)**: Translates the Unicode character into its corresponding 64-bit unsigned integer.

- **TryFromBase64Chars (ReadOnlySpan<Char>, Span<Byte>, Int32)**: Attempts to translate the specified span, which contains a base-64 encoded string, into a span of 8-bit unsigned integers.

- **TryFromBase64String (String, Span<Byte>, Int32)**: Attempts to translate the specified base-64 encoded string into a span of 8-bit unsigned integers.

- **TryToBase64Chars (ReadOnlySpan<Byte>, Span<Char>, Int32, Base64FormattingOptions)**: Attempts to translate the 8-bit unsigned integers within the given read-only span into their corresponding base-64 encoded string representation. There is an option to include line breaks in the output if desired.

- **TryToBase64Chars (ReadOnlySpan<Byte>, Span<Char>, Int32, Base64FormattingOptions)**: Attempts to translate the 8-bit unsigned integers within the given read-only span into their corresponding base-64 encoded string representation. You can decide if you want to include line breaks in the resulting string.

A complete list with all methods can be accessed at Microsoft Learn:

https://learn.microsoft.com/en-us/dotnet/api/system.convert?view=net-8.0

Example of conversion text, arrays, and base-64 string:

```
1.  byte[] byteArray = { 0x43, 0x23, 0x4A, 0x53, 0x4D };
2.  string text = System.Text.Encoding.UTF8.GetString(byteArray);
3.  var arrayFromText = System.Text.Encoding.Default.GetBytes(text);
4.
5.  string textFromArray = System.Text.Encoding.UTF8.
    GetString(arrayFromText);
6.  string base64 = Convert.ToBase64String(byteArray);
7.  var fromBase64 = Convert.FromBase64String(base64);
8.
9.  Console.WriteLine(text);
10. Console.WriteLine(base64);
11.
12. if (text.Equals(textFromArray))
13. {
14.     Console.WriteLine("text equals to textFromArray");
15. }
16. if (arrayFromText.SequenceEqual(byteArray))
17. {
18.     Console.WriteLine("arrayFromText sequence equal to byteArray");
19. }
20. if (fromBase64.SequenceEqual(byteArray))
21. {
22.     Console.WriteLine("fromBase64 sequence equal to byteArray");
23. }
24. Console.ReadKey();
```

This code generates the output as shown in *Figure 3.2*:

```
C#JSM
QyNKU00=
text equals to textFromArray
arrayFromText sequence equal to byteArray
fromBase64 sequence equal to byteArray
```

Figure 3.2: Console output

Looping constructs in C#

Looping constructs in C# provide a powerful way to repeatedly execute a block of code, allowing for efficient and flexible control flow in your programs. The three primary looping constructs in C# are the for loop, the while loop, and the do-while loop.

For loop

The **for** loop is a widely used looping construct that allows you to repeat a code block for a specific number of iterations. It consists of three parts: initialization, condition, and iteration. The loop executes as long as the condition is true, and the iteration statement is executed after each iteration. The **for** loop is ideal when you know the exact number of iterations in advance or when you need precise control over the loop variable.

Here are some syntax examples:

```
1.  for (var i = 0; i < 10; i++)
2.  {
3.      // Do something 10 times
4.  }
5.
6.  for (var i = 0; i < myList.Count; i++)
7.  {
8.      // Do something for each item in myList
9.  }
10.
11. for (var i = 1; i < spreadSheet.Count(); i++)
12. {
13.     // Do something with data rows
14. }
```

While loop

The **while** loop executes multiple times a code block if a given condition remains true. It evaluates the condition before each iteration. The code block is executed only if the condition is valid (true). If the condition becomes invalid and false, the loop is exited, and the program continues with the following statement after the loop. The **while** loop is useful when the exact number of iterations is unknown, and you want the loop to continue until a specific condition is satisfied.

Here are some syntax examples:

```
1.  while (myCondition)
2.  {
3.      // Do something while
```

```
4.     // myCondition is true
5. }
6.
7. var reader = cmd.ExecuteReader();
8. while (reader.Read())
9. {
10.    // Process each record while
11.    // reader.Read() has records
12.    // to read from DataSource
13.    ProcessRecord(reader);
14.}
```

Tip: When executing (myCondition) like, you must set myCondition to false at some point. Otherwise, the process will be in an infinite loop.

Do-while loop

The do-while loop is similar to the while loop, but with a slight difference: it executes the entire code block at least once before evaluating the condition. After each iteration, it evaluates the condition. If the condition is valid (true), the loop continues; otherwise, it is exited. The do-while loop is suitable to ensure that the code block executes at least once, regardless of the condition.

This is a syntax example:

```
1. do
2. {
3.    // The code will be executed
4.    // and continue only if myCondition
5.    // remains true in the
6.    // while condition
7. } while (myCondition);
```

The primary distinction between the while and do-while loops is that the while loop will execute the code block only if the condition is true. In contrast, the do-while loop will always execute the code block at least once and continue to repeat it as long as the condition remains true.

Let us see the difference.

Once the **myCondition** starts with false, the code inside the while will not be executed:

```
1. var myCondition = false;
2. while (myCondition)
3. {
```

```
4.    Console.WriteLine("This will not be printed");
5. }
6. Console.ReadKey();
```

Otherwise, in do-while, even if **myCondition** starts false, the code will be executed at least once, but the loop will not continue because **myCondition** is false:

```
1. var myCondition = false;
2. do
3. {
4.     Console.WriteLine("This will be printed");
5. } while (myCondition);
6. Console.ReadKey();
```

Understanding and using nullable types in C#

In C#, a nullable type is a value type with a **null** value. Value types, such as **int**, **float**, and **bool**, cannot commonly be assigned the value **null**. However, with the introduction of nullable types in C# 2.0, assigning **null** to value types became possible by appending a question mark (**?**) to the type declaration.

Here is an example of declaring a nullable type:

```
1. int? myNullableInt = null;
```

MyNullableInt is a nullable integer that can hold a valid integer value or be assigned **null**.

Nullable types are helpful in scenarios where you need to represent the absence of a value in addition to the range of valid values. For example, when working with a database, a column may allow **null** values, and using a nullable type can help handle such cases more effectively.

To work with nullable types, C# provides a set of operators and methods specifically designed for handling null values. The most commonly used operators are the null-coalescing operator (**??**) and the null-conditional operator (**?.**).

The null-coalescing operator allows you to provide a default value if a nullable type is null.

Here is an example:

```
1. int? myNullableInt = null;
2. int value = myNullableInt ?? 10;
3. // If myNullableInt is null, assign 10 to the value
```

In this case, the value will be assigned 10 because **myNullableInt** is **null**.

The null-conditional operator is used to safely access members or invoke methods on nullable types without causing a null reference exception.

Here is an example:

```
1. string? myNullableString = GetString();
2. int length = myNullableString?.Length ?? 0;
3. // If myNullableString is null, assign 0 to length
```

In this case, **myNullableString?.Length** will return the length of the string if **nullableString** is not null, and it will return null if **myNullableString** is null. The null-coalescing operator is then used to assign 0 to the length if the result is null.

In addition to these operators, C# provides methods like **GetValueOrDefault()**, **HasValue**, and **Value** to work with nullable types. These methods allow you to retrieve the value of the nullable type or provide a default value if it is null.

It is worth noting that nullable types also have their own boxing and unboxing behavior. When a nullable value type is boxed, a null value is represented as an actual null reference, and a non-null value is boxed as the underlying value type.

C# 8 introduced a feature, **nullable reference types**, which allows you to annotate reference types as nullable or non-nullable to catch potential null reference exceptions at compile-time. This feature enhances the type system to make it more expressive and helps prevent null reference errors.

Lifted operators

By **lifting** the existing operators from the non-nullable form, lifted operators can operate on nullable types. For instance, if you:

```
1. int? x = 10;
2. int? y = 10;
3. int? z = x + y;
```

That + operator is lifted. It does not exist on Nullable<int>, but the C# compiler acts as if it does, generating code to do the addition and handle nulls correctly.

When one or both operands are null, these operators, also referred to as lifted operators, produce null; otherwise, the operator calculates the result using the contained values of its operands.

Here is an example:

```
1. int? x = 10;
2. int? y = null;
3. int? z = null;
4. Console.WriteLine($"{x} >= null is {x >= null}");
5. Console.WriteLine($"{x} < null is {x < null}");
```

6. `Console.WriteLine($"{x} == null is {x == null}");`
7. `Console.WriteLine($"null >= null is {y >= z}");`
8. `Console.WriteLine($"null == null is {y == z}");`

This will generate the output shown in *Figure 3.3*:

```
10 >= null is False
10 < null is False
10 == null is False
null >= null is False
null == null is True
```

Figure 3.3: *Console output*

Identifying a nullable value type

To identify a nullable value type in C#, you can add the **?** operator after the type name. For example, **int?** means that the value can either be an integer or null.

A nullable value type variable can also be examined, and its value obtained using the read-only features listed below: Nullable<T>. When a nullable value type instance contains the value of its underlying type, it is indicated with the **HasValue** keyword. Nullable<T>. If **HasValue** is true, **Value** returns the value of the underlying type.

Here is an example:

```
1.  int? calc1 = 0;
2.  int calc2 = 0;
3.
4.  DoSomething();
5.
6.  Console.WriteLine($"Calc 1:");
7.  Validate(typeof(int?), calc1);
8.
9.  Console.WriteLine($"Calc 2:");
10. Validate(typeof(int), calc2);
11.
12. Console.ReadKey();
13.
14. void Validate(Type type, int? value)
15. {
16.     if (IsNullable(type))
17.     {
18.         Console.WriteLine($"value type is null!");
19.     }
```

```
20.    if (!value.HasValue)
21.    {
22.        Console.WriteLine($"value is null!");
23.    }
24.    else
25.    {
26.        Console.WriteLine($"value is not null: {value}");
27.    }
28. }
29.
30. void DoSomething()
31. {
32.    calc1 = null;
33.    calc2 = 10;
34. }
35. bool IsNullable(Type type) =>
36.        Nullable.GetUnderlyingType(type) != null;
```

This will generate the output shown in *Figure 3.4*:

```
Calc 1:
value type is null!
value is null!
Calc 2:
value is not null: 10
```

Figure 3.4: Console output

In lines *1* and *2*, we declare the type of the variables.

In lines *32* and *33*, we change the values.

In line *16*, we validate if the type is nullable.

To summarize, nullable types in C# provide a way to represent the absence of a value for value types. They allow you to work with null values safely and concisely, using operators like null-coalescing and null-conditional. Nullable reference types, introduced in C# 8, provide further compile-time checks for null reference exceptions in reference types.

Unchecked and checked operators in C#

In C#, the **unchecked** and **checked** operators are used to control the behavior of integer arithmetic operations when overflow or underflow occurs. By default, C# performs arithmetic operations on integers, enabling overflow checking. However, the **unchecked** and **checked** operators provide a way to explicitly specify whether to turn overflow on or off, checking for a specific block of code.

Unchecked operator

The **unchecked** operator turns off overflow, checking for a code block and allowing arithmetic operations to wrap around when overflow or underflow occurs. It means that if the result of an arithmetic operation exceeds the maximum or minimum value that the data type can represent, it will wrap around and continue from the opposite end of the range.

The following code demonstrates the **unchecked** wrap to the next number, that is, the first negative one:

```
1. int x = int.MaxValue;
2. int y = unchecked(x + 1);
3. Console.WriteLine(y);   // Output: -2147483648 (int.MinValue)
4. Console.ReadKey();
```

In the above example, the **unchecked** operator disables overflow checking for the addition operation. Since the result of the addition exceeds the maximum value that can be stored in an integer, it wraps around to the minimum value (**int.MinValue**).

Checked operator

The **checked** operator enables overflow checking for a code block, ensuring that if an arithmetic operation causes an overflow or underflow, an exception of type **System. OverflowException** is thrown.

The following code throws an error while adding one to the max value:

```
1. int x = int.MaxValue;
2. int y = checked(x + 1);   // Throws System.OverflowException
```

The operators can be used at the beginning of a code block. Here is an example:

```
1. unchecked
2. {
3.     // do math
4. }
5. checked
6. {
7.     // do math
8. }
```

Overview of exception handling in C#

Exception handling is an essential aspect of programming in C# as it allows us to gracefully handle and recover from runtime errors or exceptional conditions that may occur during the execution of a program. In C#, exception handling is implemented using a combination of **try**, **catch**, and, **finally** blocks.

The following code demonstrates the try catch commands:

```
1.  try
2.  {
3.      // Do something
4.  }
5.  catch
6.  {
7.      // Handle exception
8.  }
9.  finally
10. {
11.     // Complete when completing the task if it fails or not
12. }
```

The **try** block encloses the code that might throw an exception. When an exception arises within the **try** block, the runtime looks for an appropriate **catch** block to handle that exception. Multiple **catch** blocks can be specified, each targeting a specific exception type or related exceptions.

The **catch** block associated with the specific exception type is executed to handle an exception. The **catch** block contains code that traps the exception, such as logging an error message, displaying a user-friendly error message, or taking corrective actions. If a **catch** block cannot handle the exception, it can rethrow it using the **throw** statement.

The exception-related syntax sample:

```
1.  try
2.  {
3.      // Do something
4.  }
5.  catch (ApplicationException ec)
6.  {
7.      // Handle Application exception
8.  }
9.  catch (SqlNullValueException se)
10. {
11.     // Handle SqlNullValue exception
12. }
13. catch (Exception ex)
14. {
15.     // Handle the default exception
16. }
17. finally
```

```
18. {
19.     // Complete the task if it fails or not
20. }
```

In addition to catching specific exceptions, it is possible to catch a more general exception type like **Exception**, which is the base class for all exceptions in C#. However, it is generally recommended to catch specific exceptions whenever possible to provide more targeted error handling and improve code readability.

```
1.  var filePath = "C:\\MyFile.docx";
2.  while (!CheckIsOpen(filePath))
3.  {
4.      Thread.Sleep(1_000);
5.  }
6.  static bool CheckIsOpen(string file)
7.  {
8.      try
9.      {
10.         var stream = new FileStream(file, FileMode.Open, FileAccess.
    Read);
11.         stream.Close();
12.         stream.Dispose();
13.         return true;
14.     }
15.     catch (FileNotFoundException f)
16.     {
17.         Console.WriteLine("File not found!");
18.         Console.ReadKey();
19.     }
20.     catch (Exception ex)
21.     {
22.       Console.WriteLine("Error: " + ex.Message);
23.       Console.ReadKey();
24.     }
25.     return false;
26. }
```

A **finally** block can be used to ensure that specific code is executed regardless of whether an exception is fired. The **finally** block is executed after the end of the **try** block and any associated **catch** blocks, regardless of whether an exception occurred or not. It is commonly used to release resources acquired in the **try** block, such as closing files or database connections.

C# also allows the creation of custom exception types by deriving them from the **Exception** class or one of its subclasses. It allows us to define their exception hierarchy and handle specific types of exceptions in a more specialized manner.

When an exception is thrown and not caught, it propagates up the call stack until it reaches an appropriate catch block or until it reaches the top level of the application. If an exception reaches the top level without being caught, it typically results in the termination of the program and an error message or stack trace is displayed.

Best practices

To code with excellence is necessary to do it with good practice. Let us see the best practices:

- **Only catch exceptions you can handle**: Catching exceptions you cannot handle appropriately can lead to unexpected behavior or obscure issues. Catching exceptions at an appropriate granularity level and handling them meaningfully is essential.

- **Use specific exception types**: Catching specific exception types allows for more targeted error handling. By catching specific exceptions, you can provide specialized error messages or perform specific actions based on the type of exception encountered.

- **Log exceptions**: Logging exceptions can be beneficial for troubleshooting and diagnosing issues in production environments. Logging the details of exceptions, including the stack trace and relevant context information, can significantly assist in identifying the root cause of errors.

- **Clean up resources in the finally block**: The **finally** block should be used to release any resources that were required and used in the try block, ensuring that they are appropriately cleaned up regardless of whether an exception occurred or not. It includes closing files, database connections, or releasing other system resources.

- **Use exception filters**: Exception filters provide the capability to catch exceptions selectively, taking into account additional conditions specified within the catch block. It can be helpful when handling exceptions differently based on specific criteria.

In conclusion, exception handling is essential to C# programming for handling unexpected errors or exceptional conditions. By using **try**, **catch**, and **finally**, blocks, we can gracefully handle exceptions, recover from errors, and ensure the proper release of resources. Following best practices in exception handling can significantly enhance the reliability and robustness of C# applications and not waste capital and human resources when the app crash and the end-user need to restart their process job.

Implementing robust exception handling

Implementing robust exception handling in C# is essential for creating reliable and stable software. Exception handling allows you to gracefully handle and recover from unexpected errors or exceptional conditions during program execution. It helps prevent application crashes and provides a way to communicate and handle errors in a structured manner.

In C#, exception handling is done using try-catch-finally blocks.

Here is a general structure of how exception handling is implemented:

```
1.  try
2.  {
3.      // Code that suspects to throw an exception
4.  }
5.  catch (ExceptionType1 ex)
6.  {
7.      // Handle except for type ExceptionType1
8.  }
9.  catch (ExceptionType2 ex)
10. {
11.     // Handle except for type ExceptionType2
12. }
13. catch (Exception ex)
14. {
15.     // General Handle
16. }
17. finally
18. {
19.     // Code that will always be executed,
20.     // if an exception occurred or not
21. }
```

In the **try** block, you place the code that may throw an exception. If an exception occurs, the execution of the **try** block is immediately halted, and the control is transferred to the appropriate **catch** block based on the exception type.

Here are two examples of implementing robust exception handling in C#:

Here is an example of file I/O exception handling:

```
1.  try
2.  {
3.      // Open a file to read
```

```
4.      using FileStream fileStream = File.Open("C:\\myFile.txt",
5.      FileMode.Open, FileAccess.Read);
6.      // Read file contents
7.      byte[] buffer = new byte[1024];
8.      fileStream.Read(buffer, 0, buffer.Length);
9. }
10. catch (FileNotFoundException ex)
11. {
12.     Console.WriteLine($"File not found: {ex.Message}");
13. }
14. catch (IOException ex)
15. {
16.     Console.WriteLine($"An I/O error occurred: {ex.Message}");
17. }
18. catch (Exception ex)
19. {
20.     Console.WriteLine($"An unexpected error occurred: {ex.
    Message}");
21. }
22. finally
23. {
24.     // Clean up resources or perform necessary
25.     // actions
26. }
```

In this example, we attempt to open a file and read its contents. If the file is not found, a **FileNotFoundException** is thrown, caught in the first catch block. If any I/O error occurs, an **IOException** is thrown and caught in the second **catch** block. Finally, any unexpected exceptions are caught in the last **catch** block, providing a fallback handling mechanism.

Here is an example of database exception handling:

```
1. try
2. {
3.      // Open a database connection
4.      using SqlConnection myConnection =
5. new SqlConnection(myConnectionString);
6.      myConnection.Open();
7.
8.      // Execute a database query
9.      using SqlCommand myCommand =
10.        new SqlCommand("SELECT * FROM Produtcs", myConnection);
```

```
11.     using SqlDataReader myReader =
12.         myCommand.ExecuteReader();
13.
14.     // Process the query results
15.     while (myReader.Read())
16.     {
17.         // Process each row
18.     }
19. }
20. catch (SqlException ex)
21. {
22.     Console.WriteLine($"A SQL error occurred: {ex.Message}");
23. }
24. catch (Exception ex)
25. {
26.     Console.WriteLine($"An unexpected error occurred: {ex.
    Message}");
27. }
28. finally
29. {
30.     // Clean up resources or perform necessary
31.     // actions, such as closing the connection
32. }
```

In conclusion, implementing robust exception handling is crucial in C# for developing reliable and stable software. Exception handling allows you to gracefully handle and recover from unexpected errors or exceptional conditions during program execution. By using try-catch-finally blocks, you can effectively handle different types of exceptions and ensure proper execution of your code.

In the example of file I/O exception handling, we demonstrated how to handle specific exceptions like **FileNotFoundException** and **IOException**, as well as a catch-all **Exception** block for any other unexpected errors. This approach provides a structured way to handle different exceptions and allows for appropriate error messaging or recovery actions.

By implementing robust exception handling, you can prevent application crashes, enhance the stability of your software, and improve the user experience. It is essential to properly handle exceptions to communicate errors effectively and ensure that your program continues running smoothly, even in unexpected issues.

Remember to clean up any resources or perform necessary actions in the final block to ensure proper resource management, regardless of whether an exception occurred.

Conclusion

This chapter explored key concepts in C# programming, such as control flow, iteration, data type conversion, nullable types, and exception handling. These concepts are fundamental for writing efficient and error-resistant code in C#. By mastering these concepts, you can enhance the control and flexibility of your programs.

Control flow statements allow you to make decisions and direct the execution of code based on specific conditions. Iteration statements enable you to repeat code blocks based on conditions or a predetermined number of iterations. Data type conversion is essential for working with different data types, ensuring compatibility, and enabling efficient data manipulation.

Nullable types provide a way to represent the absence of a value for value types, offering greater flexibility and handling scenarios where a value may be optional. Exception handling is essential for gracefully handling errors and failures at runtime, allowing for robust and reliable software.

By applying these concepts, you can tackle real-world programming scenarios effectively. For example, you can use control flow and iteration to navigate through arrays or collections, convert data types to perform calculations or data manipulation, utilize nullable types to handle optional data, and implement exception handling to handle unforeseen errors gracefully.

You should keep progressing on your learning journey and practice these concepts in your coding exercises and projects. By doing so, you will further improve your skills in C# programming. Remember, consistent practice leads to mastery. Keep exploring, experimenting, and expanding your knowledge to become a proficient C# developer.

In the next chapter, C# fundamentals will be covered, and it will begin with an introduction to C# function writing, covering function declaration, arguments, return types, and function calls.

Join our book's Discord space

Join the book's Discord Workspace for Latest updates, Offers, Tech happenings around the world, New Release and Sessions with the Authors:

https://discord.bpbonline.com

CHAPTER 4
Functions In-depth

Introduction

This chapter looks into C# functions, the key to creating maintainable and efficient code. You will learn about function basics like declaration, invocation, and diverse argument types. The chapter also introduces advanced topics like lambda expressions and higher-order functions, which elevate code modularity.

A section on exception handling enhances your code's robustness against unexpected conditions. The importance of unit testing in C# is also covered, helping ensure code quality and reliability. Additionally, you will get hands-on experience with Visual Studio's debugging tools, significantly reducing debugging time.

By the chapter's end, you will have a strong understanding of C# functions and debugging techniques, equipping you for complex tasks and making you a proficient C# developer. This foundational knowledge serves as a stepping stone in your journey to C# expertise.

Structure

This chapter covers the following topics:

- Basics of function writing in C#
- Using lambda expressions in C# functions
- Debugging techniques during development

- Implementing unit testing in C#
- Understanding C# methods and parameters
- Introduction to .NET debugging tools
- Writing testable code, the best practices
- Using testing frameworks, the NUnit and xUnit
- Working with return types and void methods
- Understanding and applying recursion in C#

Objectives

This chapter comprehensively reviews several essential aspects of C# programming. Beginning with an introduction to C# function writing, it covers function declaration, arguments, return types, and function calls, allowing users to define and use functions confidently. The chapter also looks at how to employ lambda expressions to create short and expressive inline methods, which improves code performance.

In addition, the chapter looks into numerous debugging techniques, such as creating breakpoints, walking through code, analyzing variables, and dealing with exceptions. This knowledge gives you practical skills for efficient and effective software debugging. The chapter then walks through implementing unit testing in C# with various testing frameworks and tools, enabling them to build tests that improve product dependability and robustness.

Finally, it goes over fundamental ideas linked to C# methods and parameters, such as value, reference, output, and parameter array types, reinforcing readers' understanding and ability to apply these concepts successfully in their C# programming work.

Basics of function writing in C#

Functions are essential for organizing and structuring code in C#. They provide repeatable instructions that make writing modular, reusable programs possible. Any C# programmer must have a foundational understanding of function writing. The core ideas of writing functions in C#, such as function declaration, parameters, return types, and function calls, will be discussed in this article. You will have a strong foundation in building and utilizing functions by the time you are through, enabling you to build robust and maintainable C# programs.

Function declaration

A function is declared in C# using the function keyword, the return type, the function name, and two pairs of parentheses. Indicated by the return type is the data type of any value that the function might return. For instance, the return type would be **int** if a function returned an integer value. A function's return type is void if it does not provide a value.

Here is a straightforward function declaration with an integer return value:

```
1.  public int Add(int a, int b)
2.  {
3.      int sum = a + b;
4.      return sum;
5.  }
```

The function in the example above is called **Add** and has two integer input arguments, **a** and **b**. The sum of **a** and **b** is computed inside the function body and is kept in the **sum** variable. The calculated **sum** is then returned to the calling code using the **return** keyword.

Function parameters

Function parameters are used in programming to pass values into functions. These arguments are defined in the parentheses that follow the function name and serve as placeholders for the real values that will be used when the function is executed or called. If the function takes multiple parameters, they are separated by commas within these parentheses. Parameters describe what kind of data a function requires to fulfill its work, and when the function is called, these placeholders are supplied with specific values known as arguments. The method **Add** requires two **int** type parameters, **a** and **b**, keeping with the preceding illustration. The values represented by these parameters are those that will be added together. We would supply the real values for these parameters when invoking the function:

```
1.  int result = Add(2, 8);
```

In this instance, inputs **2** and **8** are used to call the method **Add**. The function's parameters **a** and **b** are given the values **2** and **8**, respectively. After that, the function computes the sum and returns the outcome.

Function calls and return types

Return types define the kind of value that a function will return. The **Add** function's return type in the above example is **int**, indicating that it returns an integer value.

We can assign a function's output to a variable or use it as part of an expression to do anything with it. For instance:

```
1.  int result = Add(2, 8);
2.  Console.WriteLine(result);
```

In this instance, the result variable is given with the returned value from the **Add** function, which is then reported to the console by using the **Console.WriteLine** command.

It is also possible to call functions without storing the return value in a variable:

```
1. Console.WriteLine(Add(2, 8));
```

This code directly passes arguments **2** and **8** to the **Add** function and displays the returned value to the console.

Functions are crucial building elements in C# for writing modular, reusable programming. Understanding the fundamentals of function writing will help us organize our code more efficiently, make it easier to read, and encourage code reuse. We looked at the declaration of functions, including the parameters, return type, and function name. We also spoke about calling functions and using the results of those calls. With this information, we may start developing and using our functions to create C# applications that are effective and easy to maintain. Practice and experimentation will improve our ability to write functions, resulting in more reliable and scalable applications.

Functions as parameters

In C#, passing functions as parameters enables strong and adaptable code architecture. This feature facilitates the development of higher-order functions and encourages code reuse and abstraction. It is made feasible by delegates and functional programming ideas. In this explanation, we will explore the idea of functions supplied as parameters, look at how they are used, and see how they improve the adaptability of C# applications.

Delegates can be used to represent functions in C#. A delegate type defines a method signature, enabling it to store a reference to a method with a matching signature. Delegates enable C# to provide functions as parameters alongside any other data type.

Let us consider an example to illustrate this concept:

```
1.  ProcessNumbers(5, 3, Multiply);
2.
3.  // Function that takes two integers and a function as parameters
4.  static void ProcessNumbers(int a, int b,
5.  Func<int, int, int> operation)
6.  {
7.      int result = operation(a, b);
8.      Console.WriteLine("Result: " + result);
9.  }
10.
11. // Function that multiplies two integers
12. static int Multiply(int x, int y)
13. {
14.     return x * y;
15. }
```

Three functions are present in the previous example: `Main`, `ProcessNumbers`, and `Multiply`.

The `Multiply` function multiplies the input values of the two integer parameters, **x** and **y**.

The third parameter operation, type `Func<int, int, int>`, is passed to the `ProcessNumbers` function along with two integers, **a** and **b**. This `Func` delegate represents a function that accepts two integers as input and outputs an integer. The operation function is called inside the `ProcessNumbers` function with arguments **a** and **b**, and the outcome is saved in the result variable. We output the outcome to the console at the end.

We use the `ProcessNumbers` function in the `Main` method, passing it the numbers 5 and 3 for **a** and **b**, respectively. We also include the `Multiply` function as an additional operation parameter. Essentially, we are saying to process these numbers by applying the specified operation to them. The `Multiply` function is used here as the specified operation.

The software will print the following when it is run:

1. Result: 15

Programming may be pretty flexible when functions are passed as parameters. It enables us to create generic functions loosely tied to particular implementations and may be used with various actions. A function can dynamically change its behavior based on the parameters it accepts by accepting functions as parameters.

When working with collections or performing operations on numerous components, the ability to provide functions as parameters is especially helpful. We might, for instance, have a function that applies a certain operation to each element of a list (such as filtering or modifying data). We can reuse the same code for several operations by supplying the operation function as a parameter.

Additionally, giving functions as parameters enables the development of higher-order functions. A higher-order function accepts and/or returns one or more functions. Higher-order functions are powerful functional programming building blocks that expressively construct complex actions.

Finally, giving functions as parameters in C# adds a new degree of freedom and abstraction to our code. It enables us to develop generic and reusable functions that alter their behavior based on the specified functions. Using delegates and functional programming techniques, we may create more modular, manageable, and expressive code. Understanding and utilizing the power of functions supplied as parameters broaden our programming toolkit and enable us to develop efficient and adaptive C# programs.

Passing objects as parameter

`Form`, `Label`, and `TextBox` objects can be passed as parameters to functions in C# WinForms, allowing us to edit and interact with these UI elements.

Here is an example of how to use `Form`, `Label`, and `TextBox` objects as parameters:

```
1. using System;
2. using System.Windows.Forms;
3.
4. public partial class MainForm : Form
5. {
6.     public MainForm()
7.     {
8.         InitializeComponent();
9.     }
10.
11.     private void MainForm_Load(object sender, EventArgs e)
12.     {
13.         // Create a label and textbox objects
14.         Label myLabel = new Label();
15.         myLabel.Text = "Enter your name:";
16.         myLabel.Location = new System.Drawing.Point(20, 20);
17.         TextBox myTextBox = new TextBox();
18.         myTextBox.Location = new System.Drawing.Point(20, 50);
19.
20.         // Add Label and textbox to the form
21.         Controls.Add(myLabel);
22.         Controls.Add(myTextBox);
23.
24.         // Call a function that uses the label and textbox as
    parameters
25.         ProcessInput(myLabel, myTextBox);
26.     }
27.
28.     private void ProcessInput(Label label, TextBox textBox)
29.     {
30.         // Access and manipulate the label and textbox objects
31.         string name = textBox.Text;
32.         label.Text = "Hello, " + name + "!";
33.     }
34. }
```

In this example, we have a **MainForm** class derived from the WinForms **Form** class. A **Label** and a **TextBox** object are included in the **MainForm**.

We construct a **Label** object named **myLabel** in the **MainForm_Load** event handler and set its parameters, such as text and location. Likewise, we create a **TextBox** object called **myTextBox** and provide its location.

Next, we use the **Controls** to add the **myLabel** and **myTextBox** objects to the **MainForm** (the form's) **Controls** collection method **Add** should be called. It adds the label and textbox to the form, allowing the user to see them.

We call the **ProcessInput** function after adding the UI components to the form and supply the **myLabel** and **myTextBox** objects as parameters.

The **Label** and **TextBox** objects are passed as parameters to the **ProcessInput** function. We may access and alter the properties of these objects within this function. In this scenario, we use the **Text** property to extract the text input in the textbox and concatenate it with a greeting message, which is then set to the label's **Text** property.

We may execute operations on the label and textbox objects and alter their properties by sending them as parameters to the **ProcessInput** function.

This example shows how to interact with UI components in a WinForms application using functions with parameters. This technique may be extended to perform different operations on different controls, making our code more modular and adaptable.

We learned the fundamentals of C# function writing in this topic. We learned to define, call, and use functions with various parameters and return types. We also considered using delegates and functional programming techniques to pass functions as parameters. Finally, we looked at an example of providing objects as parameters to WinForms functions. If we understand these notions, we can develop modular, reusable, and adaptive programming in C#. Functions are critical building blocks in developing successful and maintainable C# programs.

Using lambda expressions in C# functions

Lambda expressions can be used to build delegates or expression tree types. Lambda expressions, introduced in C# 3.0, are a compact way to define a method that can be supplied as an argument or returned as a value from another function.

A lambda expression's basic grammar is as follows:

```
1. (input parameters) => expression
```

For example:

```
1. x => x * x
```

In this case, **x** is the input parameter, and **x * x** is the expression.

Lambda expressions are used extensively in LINQ queries and are commonly used in functional programming scenarios. They are a powerful tool in our C# programming toolbox that enables us to write more expressive and efficient code.

Identifying lambda expressions

Lambda expressions in programming come in two main types: expression lambdas and statement lambdas. Expression lambdas are concise and usually consist of a single expression that returns a value. They are written in the form **arguments => expression**, where the **=>** symbol separates the arguments and the expression. Expression lambdas are generally used for simple operations that can be represented in a single line of code. When executed, they evaluate the expression and return its value, making them ideal for operations like sorting or filtering data.

Statement lambdas, on the other hand, contain a block enclosed, in curly braces, and can have multiple statements. They are written as **arguments => { statements; }**. Unlike expression lambdas, they can perform more complex operations, including loops, conditional statements, and other code structures that may span multiple lines. Statement lambdas do not necessarily have to return a value, making them suitable for tasks that require more extensive computation or have side effects, like modifying external variables.

Lambdas expression

A lambda expression is a lambda expression that includes an expression on the right side of the lambda operator **=>**.

Here is an illustration:

```
1. Func<int, int> square = x => x * x;
```

x is a parameter in the preceding lambda expression, and **x * x** is an expression.

Lambdas statement

A lambda expression with a statement or series of statements on the right side of the lambda operator is known as a **statement lambda**.

Here is an illustration:

```
1. Action<string> greet| = name =>
2. {
3.     string greeting = $"Hello, {name}!";
4.     Console.WriteLine(greeting);
5. };
6. greet("World");  // Outputs: Hello, World!
```

The parameter **name** is in the lambda expression above, and the code block is a series of statements.

Understanding the different types of lambda expressions

Func and **Action** are special types of delegates that can be easily created using lambda expressions. A delegate is essentially a reference to a method, serving as a type-safe function pointer. **Func** and **Action** delegates allow you to define inline methods, often as arguments to other methods, without having to declare a named method.

A delegate of the **Func** type represents a function that accepts up to 16 input parameters and returns a value.

Here is an illustration:

```
1. Func<int, int, int> add = (x, y) => x + y;
2. int result = add(5, 10);
3. Console.WriteLine(result);  // Outputs: 15
```

(x, y) are arguments in the above lambda expression, **x + y** is an expression, and **add** is a **Func** type delegate that takes two integers as input and returns an integer.

The Action

A delegate of the **Action** type represents a method that accepts up to 16 input parameters and returns null.

Here is an illustration:

```
1. Action<string> print = message => Console.WriteLine(message);
2. print("Hello, World!"); // Outputs:Hello, World!
```

The **message** is a parameter in the lambda expression above, as is **Console.WriteLine(message)** is an expression, and **print** is an **Action** type delegate that accepts a string as input and returns null.

LINQ lambda expressions

Lambda expressions are widely used in LINQ to define inline methods concisely.

Here is an illustration:

```
1. List<int> numbers = new List<int> { 2, 3, 4, 5, 6 };
2. var evenNumbers = numbers.Where(n => n % 2 == 0);
```

The **n => n% 2 == 0** is a lambda expression that defines an inline method to determine whether an integer is even. This approach is then used to filter the list of integers in the **Where** clause.

Lambda expressions scope

Variables from the enclosing method and instance variables from the encompassing class are accessible to lambda expressions. It is referred to as closure.

Here is an illustration:

```
1. int factor = 10;
2. Func<int, int> multiplier = n => n * factor;
3. Console.WriteLine(multiplier(5));  // Outputs: 50
```

In this scenario, the lambda expression **n => n * factor** gets access to the enclosing method's local variable **factor**.

Anonymous lambda functions

Lambda expressions and anonymous functions are powerful C# features that allow us to design more compact and expressive code. They enable us to define inline functions without having to declare them, which increases the flexibility of our code and reduces boilerplate.

Anonymous functions are similar to lambda expressions in C# but have different syntax and limitations. They were introduced before lambda expressions in C# 2.0.

Here is how to write an anonymous function:

```
1. Func<int, int> doubleNumber = delegate(int x) { return x * 2; };
2. Console.WriteLine(doubleNumber(4));  // Outputs: 8
```

This code generates an anonymous function that multiplies the input by two. The **anonymous** function is assigned to the delegate **doubleNumber**. This delegate can then be used to call the anonymous function.

Unlike lambda expressions, **Anonymous** functions can only be transformed to delegate types, not expression types. It means anonymous functions cannot be utilized in expression trees, a frequent LINQ query requirement.

In addition, lambda expressions are frequently shorter than anonymous functions. They are especially useful when the function body is a single expression, allowing us to skip braces and the **return** keyword.

The identical function is defined using a lambda expression here:

```
1. Func<int, int> doubleNumber = x => x * 2;
2. Console.WriteLine(doubleNumber(4));  // Outputs: 8
```

Sample using local lambda Func

In our example, we utilize a local lambda function, **calculateAge**, to compute the person's age based on their birth date. The **calculateAge** function is a **Func<DateTime, int>**

delegate, which is a type that represents a function that accepts a **DateTime** as input and returns an **int**:

```
1.  using System.Data.SqlClient;
2.  namespace Book;
3.  public class Person
4.  {
5.      public string Name { get; set; }
6.      public string LastName { get; set; }
7.      public string Address { get; set; }
8.      public int Age { get; set; }
9.      public string Occupation { get; set; }
10.
11.     public static Person GetPersonFromSqlDataReader(SqlDataReader
    reader)
12.     {
13.         // Define a local lambda function for the age calculation
14.         Func<DateTime, int> calculateAge = birthDate =>
15.         {
16.             return birthDate.Date >
17.                     DateTime.Today.AddYears((DateTime.Today.Year -
    birthDate.Year) - 1)
18.                 ? (DateTime.Today.Year - birthDate.Year) - 1
19.                 : DateTime.Today.Year - birthDate.Year;
20.         };
21.
22.         return new Person
23.         {
24.             Name = Convert.ToString(reader["Name"]),
25.             LastName = Convert.ToString(reader["LastName"]),
26.             Address = Convert.ToString(reader["Address"]),
27.             Age = calculateAge(Convert.ToDateTime(reader["BirthDate"
    ])),
28.             Occupation = Convert.ToString(reader["Occupation"])
29.         };
30.     }
31. }
```

Lambda expressions and anonymous functions are essential in C#, allowing us to build flexible, compact, and expressive code. These powerful capabilities have many applications, such as simplifying difficult procedures, improving code readability, and encouraging functional programming paradigms. They are useful in LINQ queries, event handling, and building `Func` or `Action` delegates. We may improve their coding productivity and fluency in C# by knowing these features and understanding how and when to utilize them effectively. It makes it a vital component of mastering this language.

Debugging techniques during development

Debugging is locating, isolating, and correcting problems or errors in our code. Visual Studio, Microsoft's IDE, offers a comprehensive range of tools for simplifying and streamlining debugging in C# and .NET programs. Let us look at some of the most important techniques and features:

- **Tipping points**: Breakpoints are an important debugging tool in Visual Studio. A breakpoint is a line at which the running program should halt execution, allowing us to check the state of our program.

  Setting a breakpoint is as simple as clicking in the left margin adjacent to the line of code or placing the cursor on the line and pressing *F9*. Breakpoints are managed in the Breakpoints window (Debug I Windows I Breakpoints).

- **Conditional breakpoints**: Conditional breakpoints are activated only when a specific condition is met. Right-click a breakpoint and select Condition to set a conditional breakpoint. The condition for that breakpoint will then be specified.

- **Hit count breakpoints**: Hit count breakpoints are a breakpoint that only activates after a particular number of times the breakpoint line has been run. When troubleshooting loops or recurrent function calls, this can be handy.

- **Tracepoints**: Tracepoints are a breakpoint extension that sends a message to the output window instead of (or in addition to) breaking execution. It is handy for tracing and logging during debugging without interfering with program execution, as shown in *Figure 4.1*:

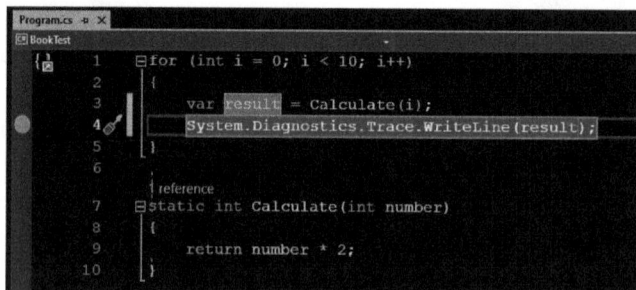

Figure 4.1: Breakpoint with tracepoint

Stepping through code

We can step through our code one line at a time in Visual Studio. It allows us to watch the execution flow of our program as well as the values of variables at each step:

1. **Step into (F11)**: Runs the next line of code before pausing. If the line invokes a method, it will *step into* that method and debug from there.

2. **Step over (F10)**: Run the following line of code before pausing. If the line invokes a method, it is executed entirely before pausing at the next line in the current method.

3. **Step out (Shift+F11)**: This command executes the remainder of the current method before pausing at the next line in the calling method.

Examining variables

Understanding variables and their current states is critical when debugging applications. Visual Studio includes a number of tools that make variable analysis both easy and efficient. These tools provide real-time insights to streamline the debugging process, whether you want to monitor the value of all local variables or just a few. Here are some key features you can use:

- **Watch window**: Allows us to watch one or more variables. As our program runs, the values of these variables will be shown and updated.

- **Immediate window**: This window allows us to query variable values or run code while our program is paused.

- **Hover over**: We can see the current value of a variable in our code by hovering over it.

Debugging windows

Visual Studio IDE provides an extensive set of debugging windows or panels to assist developers in diagnosing issues, monitoring application state, and understanding code flow. These debugging panels offer various functionalities that enable real-time analysis, variable tracking, and much more, making the debugging process more efficient and comprehensive. Each window serves a specific purpose, and collectively, they offer a robust environment for tackling a wide array of debugging needs. Here are the Visual Studio main windows for debugging:

- **Call stack window**: Displays the current call stack, indicating which methods were invoked to get to the current point of execution.

- **Exception settings window**: This window lets us select which exceptions will cause the debugger to halt execution.

- **Output window**: Displays numerous output messages from our program, such as tracepoint messages and debug output.

- **Diagnostic tools window**: Displays CPU and memory consumption and events such as errors and UI delays.

The debugging window is shown in the following figure:

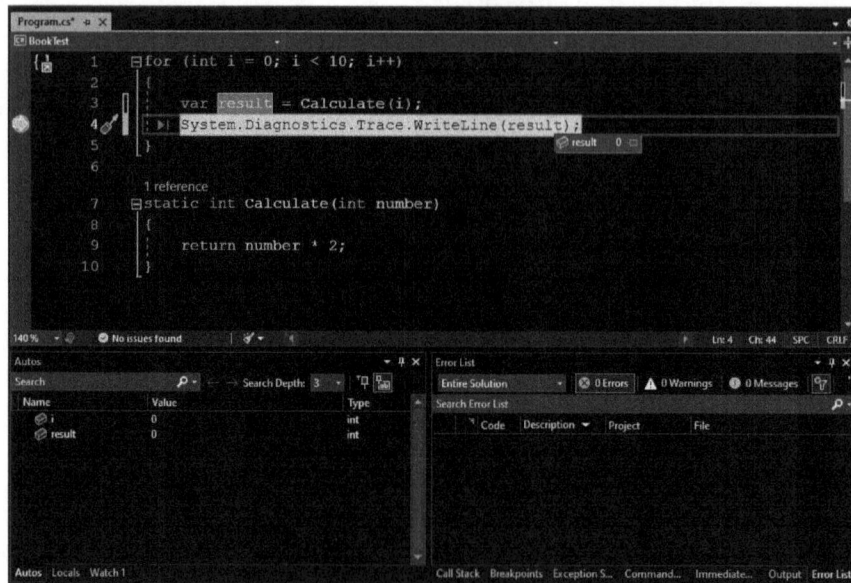

Figure 4.2: Debugging window

Handling exceptions

When an unhandled exception occurs, Visual Studio suspends execution. The IDE displays the exception message and indicates the line that threw the error. To control which exceptions will break execution, review the exception's properties or view the exception settings.

This offers important details like:

- What went wrong is explained in the exception message.

- The editor highlights the precise line of code where the exception was thrown. This makes it possible for engineers to identify the issue's origin fast.

Furthermore, Visual Studio has a comprehensive debugging environment that lets us to investigate variables, stack traces, and other program state when an exception occurs.

Debugging multi-threaded applications

Debugging multi-threaded apps is possible in Visual Studio. We can see the status of each thread in the Threads window (Debug | Windows | Threads), and we can switch between threads to study their separate execution statuses.

By doing this, the Threads window will open, displaying a list of all the threads that are active in our program at the moment. Every thread is recognized by:

- **Thread ID**: The thread's distinct identification.

- **Name**: If this is set, the thread's descriptive name (such as Main Thread or Worker Thread) will be displayed.

- **Status**: The thread's present condition, such as Running, Waiting, or Stopped.

- **Call stack**: Shows the thread's stack trace, which helps you see what code is running in that thread right now.

Remote debugging

Remote debugging in Visual Studio allows us to execute and debug a program on one machine from a debugger on another.

There are two primary parts to the remote debugging process.

Using the Visual Studio IDE to manage the debugging session, the developer works in the Visual Studio Debugger (Local Machine). It offers a variety of tools, including changeable inspection, watch windows, and breakpoints.

The Remote Debugging Monitor (Remote Machine), also known as `msvsmon.exe`, is installed on the remote machine, which also executes the application that has to be debugged. The connection between the remote application and the local Visual Studio instance is made possible by this monitor.

Visual Studio acts as though it is debugging the application locally after the connection between the local IDE and the remote debugger is made. This allows you to fully access the application's execution, variables, threads, and call stacks despite the fact that it is running on a distant computer.

Attach to Process

At times, we may need to troubleshoot an already running operation. It may be a Windows service or an **Internet Information Service (IIS)** web application. In Visual Studio, we may attach the debugger to a running process (Debug | Connect to Process).

Figure 4.3 shows the window to attach a process to the current debug:

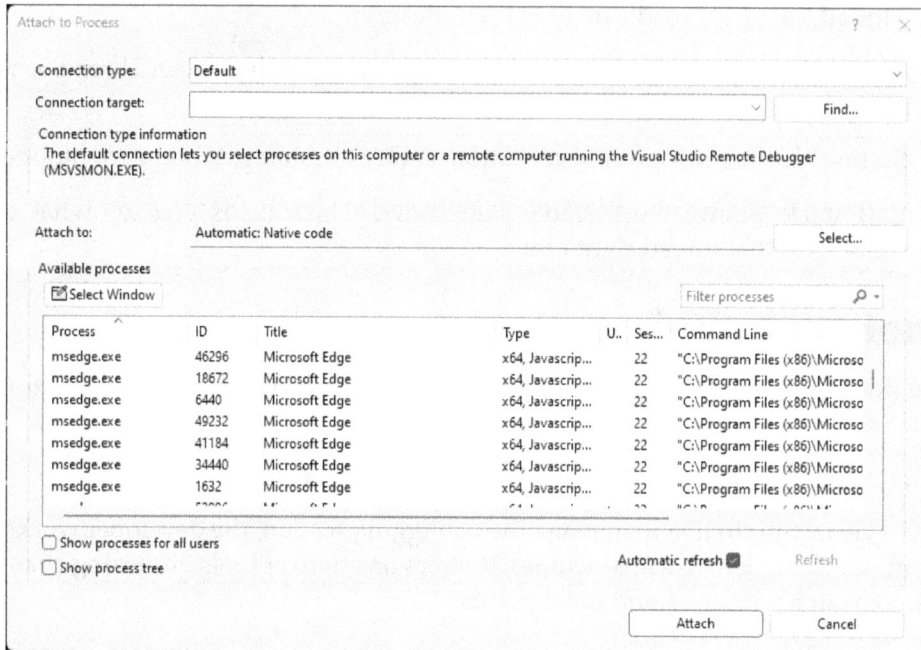

Figure 4.3: Attach to Process

Tips for debugging

The debug mode displays extra debugging information and eliminates various compiler optimizations that may cause the debugger to become confused. Release mode offers fewer debugging options but is faster.

Keyboard shortcuts for debugging can substantially accelerate the debugging process. Learn to use keyboard shortcuts to set breakpoints, step through code, and do other basic operations.

To output debug information to the output window, use **Debug.WriteLine**. Without interrupting the program, this might be handy for tracing variable values or program execution flow.

Debugging is an essential skill for each developer, regardless of their specialization. With many sophisticated tools and capabilities at our disposal, particularly in environments like Visual Studio, debugging is no longer just a reactive process for verifying code quality and enhancing functionality.

Among these tools, debugging techniques and approaches play an important role. They enable us to thoroughly examine our code, swiftly discovering and correcting faults, flaws, or potential bottlenecks. Understanding and implementing these strategies can considerably improve the efficiency of our C# and .NET programs, optimizing their operation and output.

However, the importance of debugging extends beyond the area of individual development. Teamwork and communication are essential components of any development project, and debugging approaches are no exception. When all team members have broad debugging skills, the working atmosphere becomes more cohesive and efficient. Misunderstandings and miscommunications are decreased, and each team member may contribute more effectively to detecting, understanding, and resolving problems.

In this manner, debugging approaches become a shared language, improving mutual comprehension and increasing team efficiency. By recognizing this aspect of debugging, we can improve not just our competency but also our team's overall efficiency.

Implementing unit testing in C#

Unit testing is a must-do in modern software development. It entails testing individual units of our code, typically at the function or method level, to ensure they perform as expected. We can effectively implement and run unit tests in C# by leveraging the features of Visual Studio and the .NET platform.

Unit testing frameworks MSTest, NUnit, and xUnit are three unit testing frameworks that operate well with Visual Studio. These are listed as follows:

2. **MSTest: Microsoft Test Framework (MSTest)**, included with Visual Studio and requires no extra downloads. It provides a ready-to-use collection of attributes for marking test methods, organizing and cleaning up tests, and verifying the outputs of the methods under test.

3. **NUnit**: NUnit is an open-source .NET testing framework. It includes a broad range of testing features and is extremely adaptable, allowing us to design simple and complicated tests.

4. **xUnit**: xUnit.net is a community-focused, free, open-source unit testing tool for .NET. It uses cutting-edge technologies to unit test C#, F#, VB.NET, and other .NET languages. xUnit.net is part of the .NET Foundation and works with ReSharper, CodeRush, TestDriven .NET, and Xamarin.

Making unit tests

The first step in establishing unit tests after selecting a testing framework is to create a new test project in Visual Studio. We will write our tests in the test project. It refers to the project we are testing for us to access and test its methods and classes.

Here is an example of an MSTest unit test:

```
1. [TestClass]
2. public class MyTests
3. {
4.     [TestMethod]
```

```
5.     public void TestAddition()
6.     {
7.         // Arrange
8.         var a = 5;
9.         var b = 10;
10.
11.        // Act
12.        var result = a + b;
13.
14.        // Assert
15.        Assert.AreEqual(15, result);
16.    }
17. }
```

TestClass and **TestMethod** are attributes supplied by MSTest to represent the test class and test methods in this example. MSTest provides the **Assert** class, which has methods for validating test results.

The comments **//Arrange**, **//Act**, and **//Assert** define the structure of a unit test. The Arrange part prepares the environment for the test, the Act section executes the code under test, and the **Assert** section ensures that the outcome is as expected.

Unit test execution and management

We can run our unit tests using Visual Studio's test explorer after we have written them. The Test Explorer allows us to run all of our tests, a subset of our tests, or specific tests. We may also organize and filter tests and see the outcomes of each test run.

Build our solution and open the Test Explorer (Test | Test Explorer) to run our tests. Our tests should now be visible in the Test Explorer, and we can execute them by clicking Execute All or right-clicking on individual tests and selecting Run Selected Tests.

After completing our tests, the Test Explorer will display a green checkmark next to each successful test and a red cross next to each failed test. If a test fails, we can click on it to view more information, such as the exception thrown (if any) and the values of any assert statements.

Best practices for unit testing

There are some key practices to remember while writing unit tests:

- Create short, focused testing. Each test should focus on a different part of our code.

- For our tests, use simple, descriptive names. Each test's name should indicate what it is testing and what the expected outcome is.

- Maintain the independence of our testing. Each test should be able to run independently of the others and should not be executed in any particular order.

- All paths via our code should be tested. Ensure that all feasible execution pathways via the code under test are covered. It usually means that each if and otherwise branch in our code should have at least one test.

- For external dependencies, use a mock or stub. Use a mock or a stub in our tests if the code under test interacts with an external system (such as a database or a web service). It enables us to isolate the code under test while ensuring our tests run rapidly.

Any C# developer must be able to perform unit testing. We can catch and repair errors early in development by writing and running unit tests and ensuring our code works as planned. Visual Studio and .NET provide robust tools for implementing unit tests, which can significantly boost our productivity and code quality.

Understanding C# methods and parameters

In C#, methods are operations that execute a particular purpose. They are defined in classes or structs by giving them a name, setting the return type, and any parameters. Parameter types in C# include value parameters (the default), reference parameters, output parameters, and parameter arrays.

Creating a method

In C#, a method declaration begins with a method header that provides the access level, return value, and method name. It likewise has a method body surrounded by braces.

Here is an example of a straightforward method:

```
1. public class MyClass
2. {
3.     // A simple method
4.     public void Greet()
5.     {
6.         Console.WriteLine("Hello, world!");
7.     }
8. }
```

In this case, the **public** is an access modifier, **void** is the return type, **Greet** is the method name, and **Console** is the execution environment. The method body is **WriteLine("Hello, world!")**.

Arguments and method parameters

Methods employ parameters to pass values or variable references. Arguments are the values supplied to the method.

Here is an illustration:

```
1. public void SayHello(string name)
2. {
3.     Console.WriteLine($"Hello, {name}!");
4. }
```

In this example, the **string name** is a parameter, and we might supply **Alice** as an input when calling this method.

Parameters of value

In C#, value parameters are the default type of parameter. They transmit a copy of the argument to the method, ensuring that changes to the parameter within the method do not affect the original argument.

Here is an illustration:

```
1. public void ChangeValue(int value)
2. {
3.     value = 10;
4. }
5. ...
6. int number = 5;
7. ChangeValue(number);
8. Console.WriteLine(number);   // Outputs: 5
```

Even when the value was changed to 10 within the method, the number remained at 5.

Parameters of reference

Reference parameters pass a pointer to the memory location of the argument. As a result, modifications to the parameter affect the original argument. The **ref** keyword denotes reference parameters.

Here is an illustration:

```
1. public void ChangeValue(ref int value)
2. {
3.     value = 10;
4. }
5. ...
```

```
6.  int number = 5;
7.  ChangeValue(ref number);
8.  Console.WriteLine(number);   // Outputs: 10
```

The number is modified within the method because a reference to it was supplied rather than a copy of its value.

Parameters for output

Output parameters are similar to reference parameters in that the beginning value is not required. These are the arguments for methods that must return more than one value. The **out** keyword denotes output parameters:

```
1.  public void GetDimensions(out int width, out int height)
2.  {
3.      width = 1024;
4.      height = 768;
5.  }
6.  ...
7.  int width, height;
8.  GetDimensions(out width, out height);
9.  Console.WriteLine($"Width: {width}, Height: {height}");   // Outputs:
    Width: 1024, Height: 768
```

Arrays of parameters

When the exact amount of arguments is unknown, parameter arrays are utilized. The keyword **params** denote a parameter array:

```
1.  public void PrintNames(params string[] names)
2.  {
3.      foreach (var name in names)
4.      {
5.          Console.WriteLine(name);
6.      }
7.  }
8.  ...
9.  PrintNames("Alice", "Bob", "Charlie");   // Outputs: Alice, Bob,
    Charlie
```

Values of return

The **return** keyword is used by methods to return a value. The method header specifies the **return** type:

```
1.  public int Multiply(int a, int b)
2.  {
```

```
3.      return a * b;
4. }
5. ...
6. int result = Multiply(5, 10);
7. Console.WriteLine(result);  // Outputs: 50
```

Methods of overloading

Methods in C# can be overloaded, which means they can have the same name but different parameters. The compiler selects the suitable method based on the amount, types, and sequence of parameters.

Here is an illustration:

```
1. public void Display(string message)
2. {
3.      Console.WriteLine(message);
4. }
5.
6. public void Display(string message, int times)
7. {
8.      for (int i = 0; i < times; i++)
9.      {
10.          Console.WriteLine(message);
11.     }
12.}
```

Using classes to simplify functions with many parameters

It is commonplace in programming to come across functions that require many parameters to execute their purposes. However, as the number of parameters increases, controlling and maintaining these functions becomes more complex and error-prone. This complexity is increased when the functions must be called from numerous locations, which can lead to confusion and inaccurate data being sent.

One solution to this problem and simplifying the function signature is encapsulating these parameters in a single object using classes or structures. This strategy has various advantages, including greater readability, increased maintainability, and simplified data validation.

Here is an illustration:

Assume you have the following function with the following signature:

```
1.  void ProcessData(int param1, string param2, double param3, string
      param4, bool param5, DateTime param6, string param7, double param8,
      int param9, string param10)
2.  {
3.      // Processing logic...
4.  }
```

As you can see, this function takes ten parameters, which can make it difficult to work with. Let us look at how we can improve this by introducing a class.

First, we make a class that has all of the parameters:

```
1.  public class ProcessingData
2.  {
3.      public int Param1 { get; set; }
4.      public string Param2 { get; set; }
5.      public double Param3 { get; set; }
6.      public string Param4 { get; set; }
7.      public bool Param5 { get; set; }
8.      public DateTime Param6 { get; set; }
9.      public string Param7 { get; set; }
10.     public double Param8 { get; set; }
11.     public int Param9 { get; set; }
12.     public string Param10 { get; set; }
13. }
```

The function is then modified to accept an instance of the **ProcessingData** class rather than the individual parameters:

```
1.  void ProcessData(ProcessingData data)
2.  {
3.      // You can access the parameters as properties of the data
      object
4.      // For example: data.Param1, data.Param2, etc.
5.      // Processing logic...
6.  }
```

This technique of replacing multiple parameters with a single object is called Parameter Object or Parameter Object Pattern. This pattern is commonly used to increase code readability and maintainability when dealing with functions or methods with an extensive list of parameters.

Mastering the understanding of methods and parameters is critical when writing in C#. They not only help with code structure and organization, but they also improve readability and encourage code reuse.

The Parameter Object Pattern, in particular, can be a powerful ally in the promotion of clean and maintainable code. We reduce complexity and possible points of failure by encapsulating numerous arguments into a single object. This is especially important when working in a team context because code must be understandable by different people with varying skill sets. Team members can comprehend, debug, and extend the code more successfully when there are fewer parameters to manage and clearer code structures.

The extensive toolset given by Visual Studio and .NET makes it even easier to manage, debug, and comprehend how methods and parameters work, speeding the development process and increasing productivity. We can create software that is not only functional but also efficiently planned and easy to maintain by combining strong coding principles like the Parameter Object Pattern with these robust tools, considerably boosting the overall quality of the deliverables.

Introduction to .NET debugging tools

Debugging is an essential task in software development. It is the process of finding, isolating, and correcting software defects. Various tools and features in the .NET framework make debugging easier and more efficient. Visual Studio has access to robust debugging tools.

Debugger for Visual Studio

One of the most important tools for debugging .NET programs is the Visual Studio Debugger. It has various bug-tracking functions, including step-by-step code execution, creating breakpoints, analyzing variables at runtime, and viewing the call stack.

Here are the actions while debugging:

1. **Breakpoints**: One of the most often used debugging tools is breakpoints. They enable us to pause code execution at a specific line of code to inspect our program's current state. Set a breakpoint in Visual Studio by clicking in the margin close to the line of code or pressing *F9*.

2. **Taking code steps**: Once our code execution has been paused at a breakpoint, we may use the step into, step over, and step out commands to execute our code line by line and observe how it is behaving. It is essential for understanding our code's flow and pinpointing a fault's location.

3. **Examining variables**: Visual Studio's Locals and Watch panels allow us to inspect variable values at runtime. The Locals box displays all variables in the current scope, but the Watch window allows us to specify specific variables to monitor.

4. **Stack of calls**: The Call Stack window displays the sequence of method calls that resulted in the current line of execution. It can be quite useful for understanding how our code came to its current state, particularly when troubleshooting complex applications with multiple levels of function calls.

Advanced debugging options

Navigating the complex landscape of debugging can be daunting, but leveraging advanced debugging options can significantly streamline the process. Whether dealing with conditional logic, handling exceptions, or debugging in a multithreaded environment, advanced tools and configurations are at your disposal to enhance your debugging experience. This introduction will guide you through some sophisticated options, from conditional breakpoints and exception configurations in Visual Studio to specialized .NET and Windows debugging tools. Each option offers unique capabilities that can make your debugging sessions more efficient and insightful, enabling you to diagnose issues more effectively and improve the quality of your code.

- **Breakpoints with conditions**: Conditional breakpoints enable us to provide a condition for a breakpoint, causing it to break only when that condition is met. It is very useful when dealing with loops or repeated code and wishes to interrupt execution only when a specific condition is fulfilled.

- **Exception configuration**: We may modify how the debugger responds to different types of exceptions in Visual Studio. We can tell the debugger to stop when an exception is thrown or goes unhandled.

- **Multithreaded application debugging**: When troubleshooting a multithreaded application, the Threads window in Visual Studio allows us to inspect and switch between distinct threads.

- **.NET debugging instruments**: Aside from the Visual Studio debugger, there are several .NET debugging tools that can be used separately or in conjunction with Visual Studio.

- **Cordbg**: CLR Debugger is a command line tool for debugging .NET applications. It includes basic debugging features such as breakpoints and code stepping.

- **Windows debugging tools**: WinDbg is a Windows debugger that can be used for various tasks. It can be used to debug .NET programs with the appropriate extensions. It supports greater in-depth and low-level debugging than the Visual Studio debugger.

SOS debugging extension

The **SOS debugging extension (SOS.dll)** provides information about the internal CLR environment to help us debug managed programs in Visual Studio and the **Windows debugger (WinDbg)**.

In the world of C# development, debugging is more than simply a talent; it is a heroic attempt. It is a mission to uncover the hidden bugs, similar to a hero facing the unknown. Understanding the various .NET debugging tools is thus a critical step toward becoming a master on this heroic path.

Visual Studio's robust and user-friendly debugger is a valuable tool in our armory. However, the.NET ecosystem provides a plethora of extra tools, all of which are meant to help us debug more efficiently and effectively. As we use these tools and gain expertise, we develop into seasoned debuggers capable of tracing and fixing bugs. This proficiency leads to more dependable, higher-quality code and more robust applications.

When working with huge firms, the power of debugging develops enormously. Our mastery of debugging tools, as well as our experience, are tested and honed in these environments. Collaborative debugging in such contexts not only speeds up issue identification and resolution but also encourages learning and information sharing, boosting the team's overall capability.

In essence, debugging is a cycle of constant learning and improvement, especially in a collaborative context. The more we learn about the tools and gain experience, the better we become, moving us closer to becoming actual debugging heroes.

Writing testable code, the best practices

Writing testable code is a must for modern software development. We improve code maintainability, robustness, and readability by arranging it to support testing. Several ideas, including the **Single Responsibility Principle (SRP)**, **dependency injection (DI)**, and prioritizing composition over inheritance, govern the construction of testable code.

The principle of single responsibility

The SRP states that a class should have only one reason to change. This design approach contributes to a clean, well-organized codebase that is simple to comprehend, alter, and test. As an example:

```
1.  public class Customer
2.  {
3.      public string Name { get; set; }
4.
5.      // This method could be moved to a CustomerRepository class
6.      public void SaveToDatabase()
7.      {
8.          // Save to database...
9.      }
10. }
```

Dependency injection

DI is a mechanism in which an object receives other objects on which it depends. It makes testing easier by allowing dependencies to be mocked or stubbed out.

A basic C# service layer implementation is shown in the code snippet that follows. It demonstrates the guidelines of SOLID architecture and allows for more flexibility and testability by using dependency injection to separate the **CustomerService** class from the underlying **ICustomerRepository** interface:

```
1.  public class CustomerService
2.  {
3.      private readonly ICustomerRepository _customerRepository;
4.
5.      public CustomerService(ICustomerRepository customerRepository)
6.      {
7.          _customerRepository = customerRepository;
8.      }
9.
10.     public void SaveCustomer(Customer customer)
11.     {
12.         _customerRepository.Save(customer);
13.     }
14. }
```

The **CustomerService** class in this example relies on an **ICustomerRepository** for data persistence. It does not, however, directly instantiate a **CustomerRepository**; instead, an implementation of the **ICustomerRepository** is passed as a constructor parameter. When testing, we can inject a **mock** or **fake** repository to isolate the **CustomerService** class from the database.

Avoid using static methods

While static methods are convenient, they make testing our code more difficult because we cannot mock or stub them out. Prefer instance methods over static ones whenever possible.

The main arguments against static methods are:

- **Impedes dependency injection**: The inability to inject static methods as dependencies into classes violates the **Inversion of Control (IoC)** principle and makes it more difficult to isolate code for testing.

- **Global state risks**: Static approaches frequently rely on or alter global state, which may result in unanticipated consequences or subtle errors that are challenging to identify.

- **Decreased testability**: Isolating the class being tested is a prerequisite for unit testing. Because static methods cannot be stubbed out or mocked, tests must use actual implementations, which might add needless dependencies and complexity.

- **Hinders polymorphism**: Static approaches restrict flexibility and conformity to the **Open/Closed Principle (OCP)** of SOLID design by not supporting overriding or polymorphism.

.NET unit testing

Unit testing develops small tests to validate behavior in the smallest portions of code, often methods in C#. MSTest, NUnit, and xUnit are the unit testing frameworks in the .NET environment. Mock frameworks such as Moq or NSubstitute can also be used to construct bogus dependencies for testing.

Unit testing is easier to integrate into our development workflow with Visual Studio's built-in support for running and maintaining unit tests.

Stubbing and mocking

When testing a class or method, it is common practice to separate it from its dependencies. Isolation is frequently achieved through mocking or stubbing. A mock or stub implements the same interface as a dependency but with reduced, controlled behavior suited for testing.

The usage of mocking and stubbing in unit testing is demonstrated in the example that follows. We can isolate the **CustomerService** class's behavior and confirm that it interacts with its dependency as intended by using a mock object for the **ICustomerRepository** interface. By avoiding real implementations of external dependencies, this method guarantees that the test is just concerned with the logic inside the class being tested:

```
1.  [TestMethod]
2.  public void TestCustomerServiceSave()
3.  {
4.      // Arrange
5.      var mockRepo = new Mock<ICustomerRepository>();
6.      var service = new CustomerService(mockRepo.Object);
7.      var customer = new Customer { Name = "Alice" };
8.
9.      // Act
10.     service.SaveCustomer(customer);
11.
12.     // Assert
13.     mockRepo.Verify(r => r.Save(customer), Times.Once());
14. }
```

In this example, we will utilize Moq to mock up an **ICustomerRepository**. The **Save** function is then called exactly one more.

Prefer composition to inheritance

Inheritance can cause a strong connection between base and derived classes, making testing more challenging. Choosing composition over inheritance helps to keep classes isolated and testable.

Unit testing is quickly becoming an essential component of software development. It not only ensures the code's quality and integrity, but it also dramatically decreases support and maintenance expenses for businesses worldwide. When done correctly, it produces more dependable, efficient, and simple software to maintain.

Embracing the discipline of designing testable code, adhering to its principles, and employing proper testing tools can significantly improve code quality, making our development process more efficient and predictable. The .NET environment, in conjunction with Visual Studio capabilities, provides a rich collection of tools and technologies that we can use to effectively integrate testing into our development workflow. This results in a more robust, high-quality codebase that will endure the test of time.

Professionals who can adequately manage these technologies are in high demand in the market. Their ability to develop testable code and use unit testing significantly improves cost-effective and dependable software creation. As a result, their involvement in today's software development process is becoming increasingly important, providing a competitive advantage to teams and companies who recognize and respect this skill.

Using testing frameworks, the NUnit and xUnit

Testing frameworks such as NUnit and xUnit in C# with .NET and Visual Studio are critical to modern software development. These frameworks help ensure our codebase's quality, stability, and maintainability by allowing us to develop automated tests for our applications. Let us look at these testing frameworks and see how they may be used effectively in a C# and .NET development environment using Visual Studio.

NUnit

NUnit is a popular and frequently used testing framework for C#. It includes many tools and capabilities that make developing and running unit tests easier. Here are some of NUnit's important features:

- **Attribute-based testing**: NUnit uses attributes to identify and categorize test methods, making arranging and grouping related tests simple.

  Tests add method in **MathOperations** class, ensuring correct sum with NUnit:

  ```
  1. using NUnit.Framework;
  2. public class MathOperations
  ```

```
3. {
4.     public int Add(int a, int b)
5.     {
6.         return a + b;
7.     }
8. }
9. [TestFixture]
10.public class MathOperationsTests
11.{
12.     [Test]
13.     public void Add_TwoPositiveIntegers_ReturnsSum()
14.     {
15.         MathOperations math = new MathOperations();
16.         int result = math.Add(3, 5);
17.         Assert.AreEqual(8, result);
18.     }
19.}
```

- **Assertions**: NUnit provides a variety of assertion techniques that allow us to validate the expected results of our tests. These assertions assist us in determining whether a specific test passed or failed.

  In the following, we see that the test divide method to ensure **Divide_ByZero_Exception** is thrown with zero divisors:

```
1. using NUnit.Framework;
2. using System;
3. [TestFixture]
4. public class MathOperationsTests
5. {
6.     [Test]
7.     public void Divide_ByZero_ThrowsDivideByZeroException()
8.     {
9.         MathOperations math = new MathOperations();
10.         Assert.Throws<DivideByZeroException>(() => math.
    Divide(10, 0));
11.     }
12.}
```

NUnit allows us to define test fixtures that set up the testing environment before running the tests and clean it up afterward. As a result, the experiments are separated and repeatable.

NUnit offers parameterized tests, allowing us to execute the same test with different input data and test diverse situations with minimal code duplication.

NUnit supports parallel test execution, which makes the testing process faster and more efficient.

xUnit

xUnit is yet another popular testing framework for C# and .NET applications. It adheres to the **Arrange, Act, Assert (AAA)** paradigm, which provides a simple and straightforward way to arrange our test methods. Among xUnit's key characteristics are:

- **Theory**: The theory feature of xUnit allows us to construct parameterized tests straightforwardly, making it simple to test many inputs and scenarios:

```
1. using Xunit;
2. public class MathOperations
3. {
4.     public int Subtract(int a, int b)
5.     {
6.         return a - b;
7.     }
8. }
9. public class MathOperationsTests
10. {
11.     [Theory]
12.     [InlineData(8, 3, 5)]
13.     [InlineData(10, 6, 4)]
14.     [InlineData(15, 8, 7)]
15.     public void Subtract_TwoIntegers_
    ReturnsDifference(int expected, int a, int b)
16.     {
17.         MathOperations math = new MathOperations();
18.         int result = math.Subtract(a, b);
19.         Assert.Equal(expected, result);
20.     }
21. }
```

- **Extensibility**: xUnit is intended to be extensible. We can customize the framework by creating unique test data sources, test case discoverers, and test execution behaviors.

- **Asynchronous support**: xUnit includes support for testing asynchronous code, allowing us to test async methods and available actions easily.

  Here is an illustration:

```
1.  using Xunit;
2.  using System.Threading.Tasks;
3.  public class FileProcessor
4.  {
5.      public async Task<bool> ProcessFileAsync(string filePath)
6.      {
7.          // Simulate async file processing
8.          await Task.Delay(1000);
9.          return true;
10.     }
11. }
12. public class FileProcessorTests
13. {
14.     [Fact]
15.     public async Task ProcessFileAsync_ValidFilePath_
    ReturnsTrue()
16.     {
17.         FileProcessor fileProcessor = new FileProcessor();
18.         bool result = await fileProcessor.ProcessFileAsync("test.
    txt");
19.         Assert.True(result);
20.     }
21. }
```

- **Parallel test execution**: xUnit, like NUnit, supports parallel test execution, which can greatly reduce the time required to run test suites.

- **Integration with Visual Studio**: Visual Studio provides good support for both the NUnit and xUnit testing frameworks. We may build test projects, define test cases, and run tests directly from the IDE. The Test Explorer window displays and manages our tests and extensive information on test results and code coverage.

- **Test-Driven Development**: NUnit and xUnit are both excellent choices for TDD approaches. TDD entails writing tests before developing production code. These frameworks make TDD easier by allowing us to easily design and run tests to check that their code fulfills the intended specifications.

- **Continuous integration**: Incorporating testing frameworks such as NUnit and xUnit into a CI pipeline is simple. Many CI/CD solutions, including Azure DevOps, Jenkins, and GitHub Actions, include functionality for running unit tests against these frameworks. It ensures that our tests are automatically conducted with each code commit, assisting in the early detection of errors and maintaining code quality.

NUnit and xUnit are powerful testing frameworks that greatly assist in delivering reliable and high-quality C# and .NET applications. Using these frameworks in conjunction with Visual Studio and incorporating them into our CI process can foster a robust testing culture and confidently build software.

NUnit sample

Write a sample NUnit test in C# and review each step:

1. **Setting up NUnit**: Before we begin, please ensure that NUnit is installed in our project. To add the NUnit framework to our test project, utilize NuGet Package Manager or the .NET CLI.

2. **Creating a class to test**: Assume we have a basic math class that does some fundamental arithmetic operations.

   Following the unit tests **MathOperations** are validating **Add** and **Subtract** methods:

```
1.  public class MathOperations
2.  {
3.      public int Add(int a, int b)
4.      {
5.          return a + b;
6.      }
7.
8.      public int Subtract(int a, int b)
9.      {
10.         return a - b;
11.     }
12. }
```

3. **Writing NUnit tests**: Let us make a NUnit test class to put the **MathOperations** class through its paces. The **[TestFixture]** attribute should be added to NUnit test classes.

   The following code defines unit tests for the **MathOperations** class, verifying that its **Add** and **Subtract** methods return correct results for specific integer inputs using NUnit:

```
1.  using NUnit.Framework;
2.
3.  [TestFixture]
4.  public class MathOperationsTests
```

```
5.  {
6.      private MathOperations math;
7.
8.      [SetUp]
9.      public void SetUp()
10.     {
11.         // This method runs before each test.
12.         math = new MathOperations();
13.     }
14.
15.     [Test]
16.     public void Add_TwoPositiveIntegers_ReturnsSum()
17.     {
18.         // Arrange
19.         int a = 5;
20.         int b = 3;
21.
22.         // Act
23.         int result = math.Add(a, b);
24.
25.         // Assert
26.         Assert.AreEqual(8, result);
27.     }
28.
29.     [Test]
30.     public void Subtract_TwoPositiveIntegers_ReturnsDifference()
31.     {
32.         // Arrange
33.         int a = 10;
34.         int b = 4;
35.
36.         // Act
37.         int result = math.Subtract(a, b);
38.
39.         // Assert
40.         Assert.AreEqual(6, result);
41.     }
42. }
```

4. **Understanding the NUnit test**: Let us go over each component of the NUnit test:

   a. **[TestFixture]**: This attribute indicates that the class is a test fixture serving as a container for test methods. A test fixture is a set of conditions or data on which a test relies for proper operation. Setting up relevant objects, establishing a specified state of the program, or preparing input data and expected results for a test are all examples. Its objective is to verify that tests execute consistently and reliably.

   b. **[SetUp]**: This attribute designates a method as a setup method, executed before each test method. In this example, we use it to initialize the math object before each test to ensure that each test gets a new instance.

   c. **[Test]**: This attribute identifies a method as a test method, where the actual testing occurs.

   d. **Arrange**: In this phase, we will set up the necessary data and create the test objects.

   e. **Act**: This is the stage in which we invoke the method being tested with the arranged data.

   f. **Assert**: In this part, we use one of NUnit's assertion techniques to validate the predicted outcome. If the assertion fails, the test is considered a failure.

5. **Running the NUnit test**: To execute the NUnit test, use Visual Studio's Test Explorer or a test runner like ReSharper or NUnit Console Runner. The test runner will discover, execute, and report the results of all the test methods in the test class.

   If everything is implemented successfully, both NUnit tests in this example should pass, indicating that the Add and Subtract methods in the MathOperations class behave as intended.

NUnit provides a comprehensive collection of characteristics and assertion methods for writing expressive and dependable tests for our C# code. We can use NUnit to generate a complete set of tests to validate the accuracy of our application and to support TDD methods. TDD is a software development approach in which tests are written before the actual code. It follows a cycle: write a test, write code to make it pass, and then rework the code for optimization. This promotes simple designs and builds trust in the software's functionality.

Using the NUnit testing framework in C#, a widely used and trusted industry technology, allows us to build robust and dependable test suites. As a result, complete verification of code behavior is facilitated, confirming its accuracy and functionality.

The value of NUnit extends beyond individual individuals or teams. Its widespread acceptance and application in the global market indicate its critical significance in modern software development processes. By using NUnit for unit testing, we can ensure that their code passes stringent inspections, resulting in high-quality, dependable software solutions.

Furthermore, the adoption of NUnit improves code maintainability and minimizes the risk of reoccurring bugs, resulting in lower software maintenance costs. It demonstrates that investment in good testing infrastructure, such as NUnit, pays dividends by improving the software development life cycle's overall efficiency, quality, and reliability.

Understanding and effectively employing NUnit, as a result, not only supplements an individual's or a team's coding practice but also aligns them with industry standards, strengthening their competitive edge in the ever-changing software market.

xUnit sample

Write a sample xUnit test in C# and review each step:

1. **Setting up xUnit**: Make sure you have xUnit installed in our project before we begin. To add the xUnit framework to our test project, utilize NuGet Package Manager or the .NET CLI.

2. **Creating a class to test**: Assume we have a basic math class that does some fundamental arithmetic operations.

   The **MathOperations** class provides two methods, **Add** and **Subtract**, to perform basic addition and subtraction of integers:

```
1.  public class MathOperations
2.  {
3.      public int Add(int a, int b)
4.      {
5.          return a + b;
6.      }
7.
8.      public int Subtract(int a, int b)
9.      {
10.         return a - b;
11.     }
12. }
```

3. **Writing xUnit tests**: Let us make a xUnit test class to put the **MathOperations** class through its paces. To define test traits or characteristics, xUnit test classes should be annotated with the **[Trait]** attribute:

```
1.  using Xunit;
2.
3.  [Trait("Category", "Math")]
4.  public class MathOperationsTests
```

```
5. {
6.     private MathOperations math;
7.
8.     public MathOperationsTests()
9.     {
10.         // This constructor runs before each test.
11.         math = new MathOperations();
12.     }
13.
14.     [Fact]
15.     public void Add_TwoPositiveIntegers_ReturnsSum()
16.     {
17.         // Arrange
18.         int a = 5;
19.         int b = 3;
20.
21.         // Act
22.         int result = math.Add(a, b);
23.
24.         // Assert
25.         Assert.Equal(8, result);
26.     }
27.
28.     [Fact]
29.     public void Subtract_TwoPositiveIntegers_ReturnsDifference()
30.     {
31.         // Arrange
32.         int a = 10;
33.         int b = 4;
34.
35.         // Act
36.         int result = math.Subtract(a, b);
37.
38.         // Assert
39.         Assert.Equal(6, result);
40.     }
41. }
```

4. **Understanding the xUnit test**: Let us go over each component of the xUnit test:

- **[Trait("Category", "Math")]**: This property allows us to classify the test class as **"Math"**. This classification can help with filtering and organizing tests.

- **Constructor**: This constructor is executed before each test method. In this example, we use it to initialize the math object before each test to ensure that each test gets a new instance.

- **[Fact]**: This attribute identifies a method as a test method where real testing occurs.

- **Arrange**: In this phase, we will set up the necessary data and create the test objects.

- **Act**: This is the stage in which we invoke the method being tested with the arranged data.

- **Assert**: In this section, we use the Assert to validate the intended outcome. xUnit has an equivalent technique. If the assertion fails, the test is considered a failure.

5. **Running the xUnit test**: To execute the xUnit test, use Visual Studio's Test Explorer or a test runner like ReSharper or the xUnit CLI runner. The test runner will discover, execute, and report the results of all the test methods in the test class.

If everything is implemented successfully, both xUnit tests in this example should pass, indicating that the Add and Subtract methods in the `MathOperations` class behave as expected.

xUnit offers a straightforward and clear approach to designing C# tests, and its interaction with Visual Studio and other test runners makes it simple to run tests and retrieve test results. Through automated testing, we can confirm the validity of their code and maintain a high level of code quality with xUnit.

Using the xUnit testing framework, which is well-known for its robustness and user-friendly interface, allows us to quickly create expressive, reliable tests. It is a tool that helps to reinforce the core quality and integrity of our codebase by fully utilizing unit testing procedures.

Adopting xUnit's features is more than just a tactical coding decision; it is a strategic step toward cultivating a thorough testing culture. This method supports the consistent creation and maintenance of reliable, high-quality software, which is critical in today's competitive market.

The impact of xUnit extends beyond isolated testing situations; it is a critical pillar in the global software development community. Its widespread use across a wide range of industries and project sizes demonstrates its critical role in defining industry standards and best practices.

Using xUnit's features not only improves individual developer skill sets but also aligns development teams with global standards, strengthening their competitive position. In an era where software reliability and speed are critical, xUnit stands out as a valuable ally, promising efficiency, precision, and quality in software development.

xUnit extensibility sample

Let us get into xUnit's amazing extension feature by creating a custom property, **SkipIfAttribute**, and a custom test case discoverer, **SkipIfTestCaseDiscoverer**. These modifications will allow us to skip tests depending on specified situations, increasing flexibility and control over our testing process.

The subsequent procedures demonstrate xUnit's potent extensibility by walking you through the creation of a custom **SkipIfAttribute** and a **SkipIfTestCaseDiscoverer**. With the help of these features, conditional test skipping based on predetermined criteria will be possible, providing a flexible and effective approach to test suite management. Before putting the test case discoverer into practice, let us define the characteristic.

1. **Create the SkipIfAttribute**: The first step is to define the **SkipIfAttribute**, which will allow us to identify test methods that may be skipped. The property will have two properties: **ShouldSkip**, a Boolean value indicating if the test should be skipped, and **Reason**, a statement explaining why the test should be skipped.

    Here is an illustration:

    ```
    1. using System;
    2.
    3. [AttributeUsage(AttributeTargets.Method, AllowMultiple = false)]
    4. public class SkipIfAttribute : Attribute
    5. {
    6.     public bool ShouldSkip { get; private set; }
    7.     public string Reason { get; private set; }
    8.     public SkipIfAttribute(bool shouldSkip, string reason)
    9.     {
    10.        ShouldSkip = shouldSkip;
    11.        Reason = reason;
    12.    }
    13. }
    ```

2. **Develop the SkipIfTestCaseDiscoverer**: We will then construct the **SkipIfTestCaseDiscoverer** a custom test case discoverer responsible for discovering and executing tests with the **SkipIfAttribute**. The discoverer will examine the attribute's **ShouldSkip** property and conditionally build test cases for skipped tests:

```
1.  using System.Collections.Generic;
2.  using Xunit.Abstractions;
3.  using Xunit.Sdk;
4.
5.  public class SkipIfTestCaseDiscoverer : IXunitTestCase
    Discoverer
6.  {
7.      public IEnumerable<IXunitTestCase> Discover(ITestFramework
    DiscoveryOptions discoveryOptions, ITestMethod testMethod,
    IAttributeInfo factAttribute)
8.      {
9.          bool shouldSkip = factAttribute.GetNamedArgument<bool>
    ("ShouldSkip");
10.         string reason = factAttribute.GetNamedArgument<string>
    ("Reason");
11.
12.         if (shouldSkip)
13.         {
14.             yield return new XunitTestCase(testMethod, reason,
    new object[] { });
15.         }
16.     }
17. }
```

3. **Incorporating the custom extensions into tests**: In our test classes, we can now use the custom **SkipIfAttribute** and **SkipIfTestCaseDiscoverer** attributes. By tagging individual test methods with the **SkipIfAttribute**, we can specify whether these tests should be skipped based on the circumstances we establish:

```
1.  using Xunit;
2.
3.  public class MathOperations
4.  {
5.      public int Divide(int dividend, int divisor)
6.      {
7.          if (divisor == 0)
8.              throw new DivideByZeroException();
9.          return dividend / divisor;
10.     }
11. }
12.
13. [TestCaseDiscoverer("SkipIfTestCaseDiscoverer", "TestProject")]
14. public class MathOperationsTests
```

```
15. {
16.     private MathOperations math;
17.
18.     public MathOperationsTests()
19.     {
20.         math = new MathOperations();
21.     }
22.
23.     [Theory]
24.     [InlineData(10, 2, 5)]
25.     [InlineData(15, 3, 0)]
26.     public void Divide_ValidDivisor_ReturnsQuotient(int
    dividend, int divisor, int expectedQuotient)
27.     {
28.         int result = math.Divide(dividend, divisor);
29.         Assert.Equal(expectedQuotient, result);
30.     }
31.
32.     [SkipIf(true, "Skipping this test because it is no longer
    relevant.")]
33.     [Fact]
34.     public void Divide_ByZero_ThrowsDivideByZeroException()
35.     {
36.         Assert.Throws<DivideByZeroException>(() => math.Divide
    (10, 0));
37.     }
38. }
```

Using xUnit's extensibility capability, we can develop unique attributes and discoverers that dramatically improve our testing capabilities. We may selectively skip tests based on specified criteria by creating the **SkipIfAttribute** and **SkipIfTestCaseDiscoverer**, making our testing process more adaptive and efficient. It enables us to customize our testing suite to meet our projects' needs better, resulting in a more regulated and effective testing experience.

Working with return types and void methods

Methods are key building blocks of programs in C# and .NET, responsible for encapsulating logic and performing particular actions. When working with methods, it is critical to understand the method's return type, which determines whether the method returns a value or executes a task without returning anything. Return types in C# can be data types or the void keyword, which indicates that the method does not return any value.

Methods with return types

Return types are methods that compute and return specific values to the caller. To define a method with a return type, use the **return** keyword within the method's body to indicate the data type of the value the method will return.

Example:

```
1. public int Add(int a, int b)
2. {
3.      return a + b;
4. }
```

In this example, we have a function called **Add** that takes two integers as parameters and returns the total of their values. The method's return type is int because it returns an integer value.

Void methods

On the other hand, do not return any value to the caller. They are used when the method's primary purpose is to conduct action or change the state of an object without returning a result to the caller.

Example:

```
1. public void DisplayMessage(string message)
2. {
3.      Console.WriteLine(message);
4. }
```

The **DisplayMessage** method in this example takes a **string** parameter and shows it on the console. We use the **void** keyword as the return type because the method does not return any value.

Using return types and void methods together

Methods are frequently used jointly, with some methods returning values and others acting as void methods. Methods with return types are handy when we need to compute and acquire precise results, but void methods are useful when we do not need to return data.

Example:

```
1. public int Multiply(int a, int b)
2. {
3.      return a * b;
4. }
5.
```

```
6. public void PrintResult(int result)
7. {
8.     Console.WriteLine("The result is: " + result);
9. }
```

We have a **Multiply** function that returns the product of two integers and a **PrintResult** method that takes an integer parameter and prints the result to the console. The **Multiply** method returns the calculated value, whereas the **PrintResult** method displays the result without returning anything.

Returning tuples

Tuple is a C# return type used to package many values and return them as a single entity from a method. Let us write a method that sums and averages an array of integers and returns the results as a tuple.

Example:
```
1. using System;
2.
3. public class MathOperations
4. {
5.     public Tuple<int, double> CalculateSumAndAverage(int[] numbers)
6.     {
7.         int sum = 0;
8.         foreach (int num in numbers)
9.         {
10.            sum += num;
11.        }
12.
13.        double average = (double)sum / numbers.Length;
14.
15.        return Tuple.Create(sum, average);
16.    }
17.}
```

In this example, we have a **MathOperations** class with a **CalculateSumAndAverage** method. This method accepts an array of integers as input and computes the sum and average of the array's elements. The method produces a **Tuple <int, double>**, with the first element containing the total and the second containing the average.

Let us apply the method from the **Main** method:
```
1. int[] numbers = { 10, 20, 30, 40, 50 };
2.
```

```
3. MathOperations math = new MathOperations();
4. var result = math.CalculateSumAndAverage(numbers);
5.
6. Console.WriteLine($"Sum: {result.Item1}");
7. Console.WriteLine($"Average: {result.Item2}");
```

The output is as follows:

```
1. Sum: 150
2. Average: 30
```

In this example, we make an array of integer numbers and then call the **CalculateSumAndAverage** method with the array as an argument. The technique yields a **Tuple<int, double>**, which we save in the result variable. The **Item1** and **Item2** properties (or named properties if using a tuple with named members) allow us to access the individual elements of the tuple.

Using a tuple allows us to bundle several method return values, making it easier and more efficient to interact with numerous values as a single unit. Remember that using bespoke classes or structures for greater readability and type safety may be more expressive and manageable when returning many values.

Return type named tuples

C# data structures give a straightforward and expressive approach to designing and using data structures without explicitly creating special classes or structs. Let us sample named tuples from a data source, including employee information.

Example:

```
 1. List<(string FirstName, string LastName, int Age)> employees =
    GetEmployeeData();
 2.       foreach (var employee in employees)
 3.       {
 4.         Console.WriteLine($"Name: {employee.FirstName} {employee.
    LastName}, Age: {employee.Age}");
 5. }
 6.
 7. public static List<(string FirstName, string LastName, int Age)>
    GetEmployeeData()
 8. {
 9.       List<(string, string, int)> employeeData = new List<(string,
    string, int)>
10.       {
11.             ("John", "Doe", 30),
12.             ("Jane", "Smith", 25),
```

```
13.                ("Michael", "Johnson", 35),
14.        };
15.        return employeeData;
16. }
```

We use a named tuple to describe the employee information in this example, which includes their first name, last name, and age. **GetEmployeeData** produces a **List<(string FirstName, string LastName, int Age)>** containing employee information.

We call **GetEmployeeData** in the **Main** method to acquire a list of employees and then use a foreach loop to print their information to the console. The named tuple members **FirstName**, **LastName**, and **Age** provide a straightforward and sensible way to retrieve the specific values.

The output is as follows:

```
1. Name: John Doe, Age: 30
2. Name: Jane Smith, Age: 25
3. Name: Michael Johnson, Age: 35
```

Named tuples are a stylish approach to interacting with structured data that can increase code readability and maintainability. They are handy when dealing with small data structures or transient data sources, where defining bespoke classes would be a needless burden. C#'s named tuples provide a powerful tool for representing and accessing data compactly.

Asynchronous return type

Asynchronous programming is an essential component of modern C# development, allowing for more responsive and efficient resource utilization. To specify and handle asynchronous actions in C#, the async and await keywords are utilized.

Let us see how it works, consider the following simple example:

```
1. public async Task<string> GetWebsiteContentAsync(string url)
2. {
3.     using (HttpClient client = new HttpClient())
4.     {
5.         string content = await client.GetStringAsync(url);
6.         return content;
7.     }
8. }
```

GetWebsiteContentAsync is an asynchronous method in this example that returns a **Task<string>**. This implies that the function will ultimately return a string, but the job wrapper indicates that the method will not block but will instead continue running and returning control to the caller method until the job is accomplished. The await keyword is used to wait for a job to finish asynchronously.

This function could be referred to as:

```
1. public async Task LoadContent()
2. {
3.     string url = "https://example.com";
4.     string content = await GetWebsiteContentAsync(url);
5.     Console.WriteLine(content);
6. }
```

We call **GetWebsiteContentAsync** in **LoadContent** and wait for the response. This implies that the execution of **LoadContent** will proceed only when **GetWebsiteContentAsync** has finished, but it will not block other activities or threads in the interim, increasing the responsiveness of your application.

Using awaiter and GetResult with asynchronous methods

Consider the following asynchronous approach for retrieving material from a website:

```
1. public async Task<string> GetWebsiteContentAsync(string url)
2. {
3.     using (HttpClient client = new HttpClient())
4.     {
5.         string content = await client.GetStringAsync(url);
6.         return content;
7.     }
8. }
```

To access the result of the asynchronous action, instead of utilizing the **await** keyword, you might use the **GetAwaiter()** and **GetResult()** methods.

Here is how it is done:

```
1. public void LoadContent()
2. {
3.     string url = "https://example.com";
4.     Task<string> contentTask = GetWebsiteContentAsync(url);
5.     string content = contentTask.GetAwaiter().GetResult();
6.     Console.WriteLine(content);
7. }
```

We call **GetWebsiteContentAsync(url)** without waiting in the **LoadContent** function. This produces a **Task<string>** that represents the currently running activity. Then we call **GetAwaiter()**. **GetResult()** methods are used to get the operation's result once it has been completed.

It should be noted, however, that `GetAwaiter()`. The `GetResult()` method is a blocking process. This indicates that it will halt code execution until the expected operation is completed. In most circumstances, await is suggested to avoid blocking, especially for UI threads or server tasks, in order to keep the application responsive. The `GetAwaiter()` method. The `GetResult()` method should be used with caution, as it might cause the current thread to be blocked, and it is mostly used when dealing with old code that does not support asynchrony.

Mastering and employing return types in C# is critical for developing powerful, functioning applications. Methods can provide computed values, data, or status information to the caller, facilitating result retrieval and interpretation. We may develop code that is better organized and simpler to maintain by carefully picking the proper return types and appropriately implementing them within functions, which improves the overall quality of our software projects.

Asynchronous programming in C# is a classic example of the significance of return types. The async keyword denotes asynchronous methods, which often yield **Task** or **Task<T>** types. These return types signify continuing work and can increase application speed and responsiveness dramatically.

Acquiring knowledge of return types, including the usage of asynchronous programming, enables us to write expressive and dependable code that is suited to the demands of our applications. This is true whether we are delivering basic data types, complex objects, or using sophisticated capabilities like tuples or Tasks. As a consequence, the software project's quality improves significantly, and the user experience improves, especially when dealing with resource-intensive processes or tasks that might otherwise hinder the application's responsiveness.

Understanding and applying recursion in C#

Recursion is a fundamental programming technique that is utilized in a wide range of computer languages, including C# and .NET. Recursion, in its most basic form, refers to the process by which a function calls itself to solve a problem. It is a really useful tool, especially when dealing with situations that can be broken down into smaller, easier, equivalent problems. This article examines the notion of recursion and how it can be utilized effectively in C# and the .NET framework.

Learning the recursion

As previously stated, recursion is a technique in which a function calls itself in its specification. It works well for issues that can be reduced into simpler sub-problems, which can then be divided further until a base case or termination condition is reached. This terminating condition is essential in any recursive solution to avoid infinite loops and system crashes.

Recursion in C#

Recursion is implemented in the C# programming language by implementing a method that calls itself to execute a specific task. Consider the most basic example of a recursive function-the factorial of a number:

```
1. public static int Factorial(int number)
2. {
3.     if (number == 1)
4.         return 1;
5.     else
6.         return number * Factorial(number - 1);
7. }
```

Factorial is a recursive function in this code sample that calls itself to compute the factorial of an integer. The function begins by determining whether the provided integer is equal to one (the default scenario). If this is the case, the method returns 1. If it is not, the function invokes itself with the lowered number and multiplies the result by the original amount.

Understanding the recursive call stack

When we call a recursive function, the system must maintain track of all the function calls we have performed and the status of local variables for each call. A call stack is used to handle this.

Each recursive call pushes a fresh stack frame onto the call stack. This frame contains the local variable values and the return address (where the control should return after execution). When the base case is fulfilled, the procedure returns and the stack frames are popped off individually with each recursive call return.

Tail recursion

Tail recursion is a recursion type in which the recursive function's final operation is the recursive call. It is significant because it enables certain optimizations, such as the compiler or interpreter reusing the current stack frame for the following recursive call, so conserving memory.

A tail-recursive **Factorial** function is as follows:

```
1. public static int Factorial(int number, int result = 1)
2. {
3.     if (number == 1)
4.         return result;
5.     else
6.         return Factorial(number - 1, number * result);
7. }
```

Because the C# compiler does not optimize tail recursion by default in .NET, we may not observe significant performance advantages when using tail recursion in C#.

Iteration vs. recursion

In some circumstances, recursion or iteration can be used to solve difficulties. The decision between these two strategies is usually dictated by the nature of the problem and the performance consequences.

While recursion can make code more understandable and accessible, it also has drawbacks. Each recursive call adds a new layer to the stack, increasing memory consumption. If the recursion is too deep, a **StackOverflowException** may occur. On the other hand, Iteration consumes a constant amount of memory and is generally faster. It may, however, result in more complex and difficult-to-read code.

Using recursion in .NET includes many data structures and techniques ideal for recursion practice. For example, recursion can be used to explore trees, graphs, or linked lists.

The binary tree data structure is a common example. A binary tree is a tree-like data structure in which each node has no more than two offspring, the left and right children. Recursion is commonly used to solve the challenge of traversing a binary tree in depth-first order (pre-order, in-order, or post-order).

Here is an illustration:

```
1. public class Node
2. {
3.     public int Value { get; set; }
4.     public Node Left { get; set; }
5.     public Node Right { get; set; }
6. }
7.
8. public void Traverse(Node node)
9. {
10.     if (node == null)
11.         return;
12.
13.     // Pre-order traversal: Node -> Left -> Right
14.     Console.WriteLine(node.Value);
15.     Traverse(node.Left);
16.     Traverse(node.Right);
17. }
```

Recursion is a strong approach for simplifying the coding of complicated issues. However, if not handled appropriately, it might result in excessive memory utilization and potential stack overflow faults. Understanding and controlling recursion in C# and .NET is critical to learning both platforms. Remember that while recursion can greatly simplify our code, we should always be conscious of performance and memory utilization trade-offs.

Conclusion

We have covered several important topics of C# programming in this chapter. We began by going through the essentials of function writing, including declaration, parameters, return types, and function calls. It gave you a great foundation for understanding how to design well-structured and useful functions, which are the building blocks of any C# application.

Next, we went over how to use lambda expressions in C# functions, which is a great tool for creating short inline methods that improve code performance and readability. This understanding allows you to pass methods as arguments or return them as values from other functions more efficiently.

We also looked into practical debugging approaches with Visual Studio. We learned how to set breakpoints, step through code, analyze variables, and handle exceptions, all necessary for quickly discovering and correcting programming issues.

We also looked at unit testing in C# and other testing frameworks and tools. This information enables you to develop robust tests that improve the dependability of your software products and ensure high-quality results.

Finally, we reviewed the fundamental notions of C# methods and parameters, such as value, reference, output, and parameter array types. It strengthens your comprehension of these concepts, allowing you to effectively apply them in your C# programming.

You have considerably widened your C# programming skills by understanding these topics. You may now develop modular, reusable, and adaptive code in C#, allowing you to create more effective and maintainable programs. As we continue our C# adventure, remember that these fundamental parts will serve as a foundation for more sophisticated concepts. Continue to practice and enjoy the process of becoming a better C# programmer.

In the next chapter, we will look into OOP in C#, covering foundational concepts like classes and objects to advanced topics like inheritance and polymorphism, along with C#-specific features such as records and extension methods, and real-world applications like interfacing with PostgreSQL and building data-driven apps.

CHAPTER 5

Building Apps with OOPs

Introduction

This chapter will dig into the complex realm of **object-oriented programming** (OOP) in C#, a cornerstone of modern software development. This chapter gives a thorough introduction and hands-on approach to the core principles, techniques, and applications of OOP in the C# programming language.

We will begin by looking at how to create classes and objects, which are the foundation of OOP. Then, we will go through how to store data in fields and modify it with methods. Encapsulation and abstraction will also be explored, two key OOP ideas that aid in creating resilient and secure programs.

We will also look at more complex concepts like inheritance and polymorphism, which allow for code reuse and dynamic behavior. We will examine how constructors, static, and instance members play a part in initializing and managing object states.

Furthermore, this chapter focuses on C# features such as records, which give a succinct approach to define classes, and extension methods, which extend the capabilities of existing types. We will also see how C# and .NET can communicate with PostgreSQL, a prominent open-source relational database, allowing us to represent and interact with data efficiently.

We will apply these principles to real-world scenarios like building a library system and generating data-driven apps to ensure that these principles are fully grasped. This hands-on approach is intended to provide you with applicable skills that you can instantly put into practice and theoretical understanding.

Structure

This chapter covers the following topics:

- Creating classes and objects in C#
- Using properties for data access in C#
- Storing data with fields in C#
- Writing and calling methods in C#
- Understanding encapsulation and abstraction
- Implementing inheritance in C#
- Understanding polymorphism in C#
- Creating and using constructors in C#
- Working with static and instance members in C#

Objectives

This chapter's goals are multifaceted. We want to help you learn the construction and use of classes and objects in C#, which is essential for designing real-world applications. You will learn to use fields to store data and properly portray information from databases. The emphasis will next change to developing and invoking methods in C#, demonstrating how to do certain activities inside your apps. We will introduce the notion of extension methods in C# to enhance the functionality of existing types. We will review advanced inheritance and polymorphism ideas, allowing you to design reusable, dynamic code. To initialize and maintain the state of your objects, we will walk you through the use of constructors, static and instance members, properties, and records. Finally, we will highlight encapsulation and abstraction, two C# fundamentals that improve your code's modularity and maintainability.

Creating classes and objects in C#

In this section, we will explore constructing a class, creating an object, and applying these principles in actual applications within the .NET framework using Visual Studio. This issue is critical because it is the foundation of OOP, a frequently used programming paradigm due to its ability to manage and scale complicated projects.

Recognizing classes and objects

A class in OOP is a blueprint or template for constructing objects. It specifies the characteristics (attributes) and methods (actions) an object derived from that class must have.

An object is a class instance with a state (properties) and behavior (methods). A class's objects might have various values for its attributes yet have the same set of methods.

Creating a C# class

Begin by launching Visual Studio and creating a new C# project. In the Solution Explorer, right-click the project name and choose Add, then Class. Give our class a name, such as **Person**.

Here is an example of a straightforward **Person** class:

```
1. public class Person
2. {
3.     // Properties
4.     public string Name { get; set; }
5.     public int Age { get; set; }
6.
7.     // Method
8.     public void Introduce()
9.     {
10.        Console.
    WriteLine($"Hello, I am {Name} and I am {Age} years old.»);
11.    }
12. }
```

This class has two attributes (**Name** and **Age**) and one method (**Introduce**).

Object creation in C#

The new keyword generates an object (a class instance).

Here is how we can make a **Person** class object:

```
1. Person person1 = new Person();
```

This code generates a new **Person** class instance and assigns it to the variable **person1**.

We now have an object and can give values to its attributes and invoke its methods:

```
1. person1.Name = "John";
2. person1.Age = 25;
3.
4. person1.
    Introduce(); // Outputs: "Hello, I am John and I am 25 years old."
```

Application in practice

Assume we are creating a system for a library. We would make a **Book** class with attributes like **Title**, **Author**, **ISBN**, and methods like **Borrow**, **Return**, and so on.

```
1.  public class Book
2.  {
3.      // Properties
4.      public string Title { get; set; }
5.      public string Author { get; set; }
6.      public string ISBN { get; set; }
7.      public bool IsBorrowed { get; set; }
8.
9.      // Methods
10.     public void Borrow()
11.     {
12.         if (!IsBorrowed)
13.         {
14.             IsBorrowed = true;
15.             Console.WriteLine($"{Title} has been borrowed.»);
16.         }
17.         else
18.         {
19.             Console.WriteLine($"{Title} is currently out on loan.»);
20.         }
21.     }
22.
23.     public void Return()
24.     {
25.         if (IsBorrowed)
26.         {
27.             IsBorrowed = false;
28.             Console.WriteLine($"{Title} has been returned.»);
29.         }
30.         else
31.         {
32.             Console.WriteLine($"{Title} wasn't borrowed.");
33.         }
34.     }
35. }
```

We might apply this class in the following ways:

```
1.  Book book1 = new Book();
2.  book1.Title = "Moby Dick";
3.  book1.Author = "Herman Melville";
4.  book1.ISBN = "1234567890";
5.  book1.IsBorrowed = false;
6.
7.  book1.Borrow();  // Outputs: "Moby Dick has been borrowed."
8.  book1.Return();  // Outputs: "Moby Dick has been returned."
```

We encapsulate the intricacies of each book and its actions by utilizing classes. As a result, our code is modular, reusable, and maintainable.

Mastering creating classes and objects in C# is a crucial component of OOP. These fundamental ideas promote better structured, scalable, and reusable programming. In this section, we looked at class formation and object generation using real-world examples like the **Person** and **Book** classes.

We used Visual Studio to demonstrate how classes are blueprints for objects, each with attributes and shared functions. These ideas emphasized the need for encapsulation in reducing complicated processes and enhancing code management.

Understanding and using these ideas is critical for any C# programmer. They not only serve as the foundation for OOP, but they also result in cleaner, more maintainable code by allowing for the modeling of real-world things, making the code more understandable and well-aligned with the problem domain.

Record object

Records introduced in C# 9.0 are perfect for data modeling because they reduce the boilerplate code associated with class-based data objects.

A record in C# is an object that is immutable by default. Immutability means that it cannot be modified once an item is formed. When we update a property of an immutable object, a new instance is produced while the old object remains unaffected.

In C#, records are created using value rather than reference semantics. As classes do, two record objects are equal if their attributes have the same values rather than referring to the same object instance.

Immutability is vital in multi-threaded programming because it improves thread safety. We do not have to worry about one thread modifying the data while another thread tries to read it, which might lead to inconsistencies. Complementing a record in C# and .NET is a reference type comparable to a class that allows simple syntax for expressing value semantics.

SqlDataReader's usage in conjunction with C# records is a good application. Because records are immutable, they can precisely represent individual rows of data, as each database row is simply a set of constant values. Each record object represents a row from the **SqlDataReader**, and each record attribute corresponds to a column in the row.

In .NET, we may read a forward-only stream of rows from a SQL Server database using the SqlDataReader class. This approach is constructive for row-by-row data processing from a database, such as for extracting massive amounts of data without putting all of the data into memory at once.

Defining and using records

Making a record is quite similar to making a class:

1. Let us start with a basic **Person** record:

   1. `public record Person(string Name, int Age);`

2. A record instance can be constructed by creating a class instance:

   1. `var person1 = new Person("John", 25);`

   One important aspect of records is value-based equality. In contrast to classes, where two objects are regarded equal if they reference the same object, two records are considered equal if their attributes are equal:

   1. `var person2 = new Person("John", 25);`
   2. `Console.WriteLine(person1 == person2);` *// Outputs: "True"*

3. Next, let us create a book **record**:

   1. `public record Book(string Title, string Author, string ISBN);`

4. Use it:

   1. `var book1 = new Book("Moby Dick", "Herman Melville", "1234567890");`
   2. `var book2 = new Book("Moby Dick", "Herman Melville", "1234567890");`
   3.
   4. `Console.WriteLine(book1 == book2);` *// Outputs: "True"*

SqlDataReader reading

SqlDataReader is a class that reads data from a database using SQL commands. Here is a basic example using a hypothetical **Books** table:

1. `using System.Data.SqlClient;`
2.

```
3.  IEnumerable<Book> ReadRecords(string connectionString)
4.  {
5.      using var connection = new SqlConnection(connectionString);
6.      try
7.      {
8.          connection.Open();
9.          using var command = new SqlCommand("SELECT Title, Author,
    ISBN FROM dbo.Books", connection);
10.         {
11.             using var reader = command.ExecuteReader();
12.             while (reader.Read())
13.             {
14.                 string title = reader.GetString(0);  // Assumes that
    Title is in the first column
15.                 string author = reader.GetString(1); // Assumes that
    Author is in the second column
16.                 string isbn = reader.GetString(2);   // Assumes that
    ISBN is in the third column
17.                 var book = new Book(title, author, isbn);
18.                 yield return book;
19.             }
20.         }
21.     }
22.     finally
23.     {
24.         connection.Close();
25.     }
26. }
```

The following code demonstrates the use of **ReadRecords** and walking through the book items:

```
1.  var books = ReadRecords("Your Connection String");
2.
3.  foreach (Book book in books)
4.  {
5.      Console.WriteLine($"Title: {book.Title}, Author: {book.
    Author}, ISBN: {book.ISBN}");
6.  }
```

These codes connect to the database, run an SQL statement to select all rows from the **Books** table, and produce and print a **Book** record for each row.

Understanding record x class

Remember, C# records are immutable types. They are simply syntactic sugar that enables more succinct code and provides extra features such as value-based equality. Records are largely intended for ease and immutability rather than performance.

There is no discernible difference in execution speed between a record and a class. Both are reference types, and the .NET runtime treats them similarly.

There may be a tiny performance difference when comparing records and classes. Records use value-based equality, which implies that when two records are compared, all of their characteristics are compared. This differs from reference types such as classes, which utilize reference equality by default (i.e., they merely check whether they point to the same object). As a result, comparing records might be time-consuming if there are numerous attributes to compare.

As usual, the decision between records and classes should be based on your software's needs, such as whether you want immutable types rather than performance factors. If performance becomes problematic, analyze your application to identify and improve bottlenecks.

Throughout this investigation, we learned much about using **SqlDataReader** to retrieve data from an SQL Server database and create records for each data row. We have figured out how to use records, a new feature introduced with C# 9.0 that allows us to efficiently describe immutable data using value semantics.

A significant distinction was identified between records and classes, particularly in terms of their opposing behaviors towards equality and immutability. Books and library systems have been demonstrated to portray real-world creatures and settings using records effectively.

The takeaways from this conversation highlight the strength and adaptability of C# and .NET when developing a wide range of applications. We have seen how these technologies encapsulate object-oriented ideas and facilitate data modeling firsthand. Because of this combination of characteristics, they are a top choice for us looking to create robust, scalable, and maintainable software programs. Adopting these current, well-designed tools can dramatically improve our C# programming experience and productivity.

Using properties for data access in C#

Data access is critical to every software program since it allows us to collect and change data from various sources such as databases, files, APIs, etc. Property encapsulation in C# and .NET provides an easy and effective solution to ensure data integrity, security, and maintainability. This article goes into the realm of C# properties and how they may be used to improve data access in .NET applications.

Properties in C#

Properties are unique members in C# that encapsulate read and write access to a class's private fields. They promote the notion of encapsulation by allowing controlled access to an object's internal state. Properties give a straightforward interface for reading and modifying the values of class fields while providing some abstraction over the underlying data. We may use properties to add logic such as validation, access restriction, or event triggering when a value changes.

Property syntax in C#

The syntax for defining a property in C# is as follows:

```
1. public dataType PropertyName
2. {
3.     get { /* return value; */ }
4.     set { /* logic to set the value; */ }
5. }
```

The get block obtains the property's value, and the set block is used to set the value. Properties can be read-only (without the set block) or write-only (without the get block).

Using properties to access data

In C# and .NET programs, properties are frequently utilized for data access. They give a clean and consistent approach to accessing an object's internal data while retaining the benefits of encapsulation. Here are two examples of how to utilize properties for data access:

Simple user class as an example:

```
1. public class User
2. {
3.     // Private fields
4.     private string username;
5.     private string email;
6.
7.     // Properties
8.     public string Username
9.     {
10.         get { return username; }
11.         set { username = value; }
12.     }
13.
14.     public string Email
```

```
15.    {
16.        get { return email; }
17.        set { email = value; }
18.    }
19. }
```

This example has a simple **User** class with private **username** and **email** fields. We may access and edit these values while regulating access using the property logic by giving public properties **Username** and **Email**.

Banking application as an example:

```
1.  public class BankAccount
2.  {
3.      private double balance;
4.
5.      public double Balance
6.      {
7.          get { return balance; }
8.          private set
9.          {
10.             if (value >= 0)
11.                 balance = value;
12.         }
13.     }
14.
15.     public void Deposit(double amount)
16.     {
17.         Balance += amount;
18.     }
19.
20.     public void Withdraw(double amount)
21.     {
22.         if (amount <= Balance)
23.             Balance -= amount;
24.         else
25.             throw new InvalidOperationException("Insufficie
    nt funds.");
26.     }
27. }
```

We have a **BankAccount** class with a private field balance in this example. Because the **balance** property only gives a getter, it is read-only to the outside world. The **balance** can be changed using the **Deposit** and **Withdraw** methods, ensuring that the **balance** is not set to zero.

The benefits of using properties for data access:

- **Encapsulation**: Encapsulation is enabled through properties that hide implementation details while offering a controlled interface to access and alter data.

- **Validation**: The property setter may include logic to ensure that only valid data is recorded.

- **Readability**: Properties give a more explicit and understandable syntax for accessing and setting data.

- **Debugging**: We may use properties to add breakpoints and debug data access, which can be difficult with direct field access.

- **Compatibility**: Properties are entirely compatible with serialization and data-binding frameworks.

Properties are a crucial C# and .NET feature, allowing more efficient data access and management. They encourage encapsulation and validation and give a systematic manner to interact with an object's internal state. By efficiently employing attributes, we may design strong, maintainable, and secure apps with a clear separation between data access and the rest of the application logic.

Storing data with fields in C#

One of the fundamental parts of .NET and C# programming is how we store and modify data. Fields, a type of variable that belongs to a class or struct, are essential for data storage. They serve as the basis for classes and structs, providing them with features that may be used to represent real-world objects.

Fields

Fields are variables defined directly in a class or struct in C#. They represent the status of the thing. Fields can be of any type or instance or static fields. Instance fields are associated with a specific object (an instance of the class), whereas static fields are associated with the class as a whole and not with any specific object.

```
1. public class MyClass
2. {
3.     public int myInstanceField;       // An instance field
4.     public static int myStaticField; // A static field
5. }
```

Fields and encapsulation

Encapsulation is a fundamental notion of object-oriented programming. The goal is to combine the data (fields) and the methods that operate on the data into a single unit, the class. Furthermore, the class should control how its fields are accessed and updated.

It is commonly accomplished in C# by designating private fields and providing public methods (getters and setters) or properties to access and edit them. It allows us to conceal the internal state of our objects while simultaneously adding checks to avoid incorrect actions.

Here is an example of a class having a **private** and **public** field:

```
1. public class MyClass
2. {
3.     private int myField;   // Private field
4.
5.     public int MyField     // Public property
6.     {
7.         get { return myField; }
8.         set { myField = value; }  // You could add checks here
    before setting the value
9.     }
```

Using fields to store data from a database

Fields are frequently used in .NET to model data from databases. Each object represents a data row, and each field is a column.

Here is an example of how fields may be used to keep data retrieved from a database in memory:

```
1. public class Employee
2. {
3.     public string Name;
4.     public int Age;
5. }
6. // Suppose we have an Employee object that we've read from a
    database
7. Employee employee = GetEmployeeFromDatabase();
8.
9. Console.WriteLine($"Name: {employee.Name}, Age: {employee.Age}");
```

Fields can also be used to hold data that will be stored in a database:

```
1. public class Employee
2. {
```

```
3.      public string Name;
4.      public int Age;
5. }
6.
7. // Create a new Employee object
8. Employee newEmployee = new Employee();
9. newEmployee.Name = "John Doe";
10.newEmployee.Age = 30;
11.
12.// Write this object to the database
13.WriteEmployeeToDatabase(newEmployee);
```

Fields in C# and .NET, in this sense, give us a versatile mechanism to store and alter data, whether that data is in memory as part of our program's state or saved persistently in a database. They serve as the foundation for our classes and structs and are required for representing and manipulating real-world objects in our programming.

Getters and setters

The keywords get and set are used in C# to specify getter and setter methods in properties. These methods are used to read (**get**) and write (**set**) a private field's value. You may use access modifiers like **public**, **private**, **protected**, **internal**, or a combination (**protected internal**) to govern how getter and setter methods can be accessed outside the class.

Here is a rundown of the various getter and setter access levels:

- **public get; public set;**

  When you auto-implement a property, the default access level is **public get; public set;**. Both the getter and setter methods are accessible from any location.

- **public get; private set;**

  It is a standard pattern for read-only properties: **public get; private set;**. Anybody may view the value, but it can only be changed inside the class.

- **private get; private set;**

  This indicates that the getter and setter functions are only available inside the class. This is similar to having a **private** field but with the extra advantage of utilizing properties (such as the ability to include logic in the getter and setter if necessary).

- **public get; protected set;**

  The value can be read from anywhere, but it can only be changed inside the class or any class inheriting it. **public get; protected set;** The value can be read from anywhere, but it can only be edited within the class itself or any class that inherits it.

- **internal get; private set;**

  The value may be read from anywhere inside the same assembly but can only be updated within the class.

- **protected get; protected set;**

  The getter and setter methods may be accessible both inside and in any class that inherits from it.

Remember that the getter and setter do not have to have the same access level. The ability to grant them varying degrees of access enables fine-grained control over how a property is accessed and updated.

Modified getter and setter

Getters may also be used to return values that have been changed. For example, if you have a string property that stores a monetary amount, you may modify the getter to format the value before returning it.

Consider the case of storing a decimal number indicating a monetary amount. It might be formatted into a currency string using the getter:

```
1.  public class Product
2.  {
3.      private decimal price;
4.
5.      public string Price
6.      {
7.          get { return $"${price:0.00}"; }
8.          set { price = decimal.Parse(value, NumberStyles.Currency); }
9.      }
10. }
```

The **Price** property in this example holds a **decimal** number. When you access the **Price** property, the getter provides this value as a **string** with a dollar sign and two **decimal** places. The setter parses the input text into a **decimal**, removing non-numeric characters, like the dollar sign or commas.

Getter and setter with lambda expression

Fields in C# offer a versatile method for reading, writing, and calculating the values of **private** fields. Properties may be considered methods that, like **public** data members, are accessible but include code to verify and return **private** field values. A property specified as a **private set** is read-only outside of the class or struct in which it is declared.

Here is an example:

```
1.  public class Product
2.  {
3.      private string name;
4.
5.      public string Name
6.      {
7.          get => name;
8.          private set => name = value;
9.      }
10.
11.     public Product(string name)
12.     {
13.         this.Name = name;
14.     }
15. }
```

In this **Product** class, we have a **private** field **name** and a **public** property **Name** with getter and setter functions that employ lambda expressions. The **get => name;** function equals the **get return name;** function. It retrieves the private field name's value. Similarly, **private set => name = value;** is the same as **private set name = value;** it gives the private field name a value. The private set restricts access to the **Name** attribute to the **Product** class.

You can utilize the **Product** class by creating a new **Product** object and printing the name:

```
1.  Product product = new Product("Apple");
2.  Console.WriteLine(product.Name); // Outputs: "Appl
```

This code generates a new **Product** object named **Apple** and prints it. Outside the **Product** class, the **Name** property may be read but not set because its setter is private.

Using PostgreSQL and fields

Using fields in C# and .NET to store data while communicating with a PostgreSQL database is essential to designing data-driven applications. This contact is facilitated via ADO.NET and the Npgsql package, a .NET data provider for PostgreSQL.

Let us look at how we can use Npgsql to read data into memory and publish data to a PostgreSQL database.

Data storage in memory

The **NpgsqlCommand** and **NpgsqlDataReader** classes are used to read data into memory.

Here is an example:

```
1.  using System.Collections.Generic;
```

```
2.  using Npgsql;
3.  public class Employee
4.  {
5.      public string Name { get; set; }
6.      public int Age { get; set; }
7.  }
8.
9.  IEnumerable<Employee> GetEmployees()
10. {
11.     var connectionString = "Your Connection String";
12.     using var connection = new NpgsqlConnection(connectionString);
13.     connection.Open();
14.
15.     using var command = new NpgsqlCommand("SELECT Name, Age FROM
    Employees", connection);
16.     using var reader = command.ExecuteReader();
17.
18.     while (reader.Read())
19.     {
20.         string name = reader.GetString(0);  // Assumes that Name is
    in the first column
21.         int age = reader.GetInt32(1);  // Assumes that Age is in the
    second column
22.
23.         yield return new Employee { Name = name, Age = age };
24.     }
25. }
```

This code sample establishes a connection to a PostgreSQL database using the connection string given. When the connection is established, it creates an SQL statement to get all entries from the **Employees** database, with an emphasis on the **Name** and **Age** columns.

After running the command, a data reader object loops over the result set row by row. The **Name** and **Age** values are retrieved from each record (assuming they are in the first and second columns of the result set, respectively) and used to create a new **Employee** object.

Each **Employee** object is returned as part of an enumerable collection using the **yield return** expression. Because it does not need to put all data into memory simultaneously, this strategy allows for more memory-efficient data retrieval, making this code ideal for handling massive datasets.

Finally, the database connection is immediately disconnected when the program leaves the statement scope. The **utilizing** keyword guarantees that resources are correctly disposed away when they are no longer required, eliminating memory leaks.

This sample shows how to connect with a database in C# by using object-oriented concepts to encapsulate the data obtained into useful C# objects.

Data entry into the database

The **NpgsqlCommand** class may be used to write data to a PostgreSQL database. Here is how to insert a new employee into the **Employees** table:

```
1.  public class Employee
2.  {
3.      public string Name { get; set; }
4.      public int Age { get; set; }
5.      public Employee(string name, int age)
6.      {
7.          Name = name;
8.          Age = age;
9.      }
10. }
11.
12. string connectionString = "Your Connection String";
13. using var connection = new NpgsqlConnection(connectionString);
14. connection.Open();
15.
16. List<Employee> employees = new List<Employee>
17. {
18.     new Employee("John Doe", 30),
19.     new Employee("Jane Smith", 35),
20.     new Employee("Mike Johnson", 40),
21.     new Employee("Emily Davis", 25),
22.     new Employee("Daniel Miller", 45),
23.     new Employee("Sarah Brown", 28)
24. };
25. foreach (Employee employee in employees)
26. {
27.     WriteEmploye(employee, connection);
28.
29. }
30.
31. static void WriteEmploye(Employee newEmployee, NpgsqlConnection
    connection)
32. {
33.     using var command = new NpgsqlCommand("INSERT INTO Employees
```

```
    (Name, Age) VALUES (@Name, @Age)", connection);
34.     command.Parameters.AddWithValue("Name", newEmployee.Name);
35.     command.Parameters.AddWithValue("Age", newEmployee.Age);
36.     command.ExecuteNonQuery();
37. }
```

The primary purpose of this code is to successfully manage and store employee data in a PostgreSQL database.

It begins by creating an **Employee** class that has two properties: **Name** and **Age**. This class contains an employee's information and provides a method for handling employee data. An instance of the **Employee** class is produced for each employee, and these instances are kept in a **List<Employee>**.

Using the Npgsql data provider, the power of C# is used to manage database connections and execute commands. It is made more accessible by using statements, which guarantee that resources are appropriately disposed of when they are no longer required, and by parameterized SQL statements, which give a secure way to put data into the database.

The code calls the **WriteEmployee** function in the main loop on each **Employee** object in the list. This technique creates and runs a SQL statement that adds the employee's information into the database. In this context, using object attributes (**newEmployee. Name** and **newEmployee.Age**) emphasizes the ease and efficiency of C#'s object-oriented approach to data management and manipulation.

In summary, this code shows how to leverage C#'s object-oriented features, data structures like lists and resource management skills to perform a typical task like maintaining and storing data systematically.

We looked at fields that are important to C# and .NET development. Fields, variables included within a class or struct, constitute the foundation of object-oriented programming by encapsulating an object's state. These fields can take several forms, including instance fields, which are linked to a particular object or instance of the class, and static fields, which are related to the class as a whole rather than any individual instance.

Encapsulation, a key idea in OOP, was investigated. Encapsulation allows the combining of data represented by fields and the corresponding methods that alter this data into a cohesive entity, a class. We illustrated how this system might manage field access and modification by designating **private** fields and giving **public** access and modification methods (getters and setters). By doing so, we can protect the internal state of our objects from unauthorized access and guarantee that any changes to these fields are screened to avoid inappropriate activities.

We investigated the critical function of fields in storing and changing data from a PostgreSQL database. We used ADO.NET, a set of classes in the .NET base class library, in conjunction with the Npgsql package, a .NET data provider for PostgreSQL. We could model data using these techniques, where each object represents a row of data, and each field represents a column. Using concrete examples, we examined how these fields may be used to read data into memory and write data into a database. This method enabled us to build robust, data-driven apps.

To summarize, our in-depth examination of fields in C# and .NET programming offered a thorough grasp of these crucial variables within a class or struct. We learned how to use encapsulation effectively to limit access to specific fields and protect data integrity, particularly when interacting with a PostgreSQL database. This understanding enables us to create more secure, dependable, and efficient data-driven applications. DDD is a design philosophy that stresses the use of data (historical or real-time) to guide decision-making throughout the design process, and data-driven applications are software systems that use input data to respond to and manage information. They rely on data as their primary purpose and logic to deliver a dynamic user experience, improve decision-making processes, and enable real-time customization and personalization. These applications are widely employed in various industries, from corporate analytics to customer relationship management.

Writing and calling methods in C#

Methods are essential to C# programming because they allow us to structure our code into reusable blocks that perform specific tasks. This section will walk you through the process of writing and calling methods in C# using the .NET framework, replete with code samples to assist in demonstrating the topics.

Defining method in C#

To build a method in C#, we must first define its return type, name, and parameters within a class.

Here is an easy example:

```
1. SayHello("John");
2.
3. static void SayHello(string name)
4. {
5.     Console.WriteLine("Hello, " + name + "!");
6. }
```

SayHello is a method in the code above that accepts a string as an argument and writes a greeting to the console. This function has a **void** return type, meaning that it returns nothing.

You will also note that we call the **SayHello** function in our **Main** method and provide the string **John** to it.

Method return types

MakeGreeting produces a string in this version, which is subsequently written to the console in the **Main** function.

Here is an example:

```
1.  string greeting = MakeGreeting("John");
2.  Console.WriteLine(greeting);
3.
4.  static string MakeGreeting(string name)
5.  {
6.      return "Hello, " + name + "!";
7.  }
```

Passing multiple parameters

Multiple arguments can be sent to methods. Create a method that receives two integers and returns their total, for example:

```
1.  int sum = AddNumbers(5, 10);
2.  Console.WriteLine(sum);
3.
4.  static int AddNumbers(int num1, int num2)
5.  {
6.      return num1 + num2;
7.  }
```

AddNumbers accepts two numbers as parameters and returns their total in this example.

Optional parameters

In C#, we may utilize optional arguments in our methods. The method specification specifies the default value for an optional argument. The default value will be used if the caller does not specify a value for the optional argument.

```
1.  GreetPerson("John"); // prints "Hello, John!"
2.  GreetPerson("John", "Goodbye"); // prints "Goodbye, John!"
3.
4.  static void GreetPerson(string name, string greeting = "Hello")
5.  {
6.      Console.WriteLine(greeting + ", " + name + "!");
7.  }
```

The greeting parameter in the **GreetPerson** method is optional, with **Hello** as the default value.

Overloading methods

In C#, method overloading allows a class to have many methods with the same name but distinct arguments. The quantity, type, or kind (value, ref, out) of arguments used by overloaded methods might vary.

```
1.  DisplayValue(10);    // prints "The integer value is: 10"
2. DisplayValue(3.14f); // prints "The float value is: 3.14"
3.
4. static void DisplayValue(int num)
5. {
6.     Console.WriteLine("The integer value is: " + num);
7. }
8.
9. static void DisplayValue(float num)
10. {
11.     Console.WriteLine("The float value is: " + num);
12. }
```

We have overloaded the **DisplayValue** method in the above example to accommodate integer and float values.

C# and the .NET framework provide a highly flexible and powerful environment for method definition and use, making it simpler to develop clean, manageable, and reusable code. As you continue to study, be careful to investigate additional topics like the **params** keyword, **out** and **ref** arguments, and async methods.

Default parameters values

In C#, you may give default values for method arguments. It is called optional parameters or default parameters. If you do not supply a value for an optional parameter when calling the method, the method utilizes the default value indicated in the method declaration.

Here is a basic example:

```
1. public void DisplayGreeting(string name, string greeting = "Hello")
2. {
3.     Console.WriteLine($"{greeting}, {name}!");
4. }
```

In this code, the name is a mandatory argument, while the greeting is an optional parameter with the value **Hello** by default. This procedure might be referred to as:

```
1. DisplayGreeting("Alice");  // Outputs: "Hello, Alice!"
2. DisplayGreeting("Bob", "Good morning");  // Outputs: "Good morning, Bob!"
```

Because we did not give a value for greeting in the initial call, the method uses the default value **Hello**. We did offer a value **Good morning** in the second call, so the procedure utilizes it instead of the default.

It is vital to notice that in the method declaration, optional arguments must come after all necessary parameters. Furthermore, once a parameter is declared optional, all following arguments in the method declaration must also be optional.

Polymorphism and OOP parameters

Classes can be used as arguments in methods in C#. It is a typical approach in OOP, where we frequently send objects to methods to alter or execute specific actions on them.

Assume we have a base class called **Person** and two derived classes called **Professor** and **Student**:

```
1. public class Person
2. {
3.     public string Name { get; set; }
4.     public int Age { get; set; }
5. }
6.
7. public class Professor : Person
8. {
9.     public string Subject { get; set; }
10.}
11.
12.public class Student : Person
13.{
14.     public string Major { get; set; }
15.}
```

We can write a method that accepts as an argument a **Person** object. We may give objects of the types **Professor** and **Student** to the procedure because they are derived from **Person**:

```
1. public void DisplayPersonInfo(Person person)
2. {
3.     Console.WriteLine($"Name: {person.Name}, Age: {person.Age}");
4.     if (person is Professor professor)
5.     {
6.         Console.WriteLine($"Subject: {professor.Subject}");
7.     }
8.     else if (person is Student student)
9.     {
10.        Console.WriteLine($"Major: {student.Major}");
```

```
11.      }
12. }
```

We begin the **DisplayPersonInfo** method by printing the **Name** and **Age** fields shared by all **Person** objects. The is operator is then used to determine whether the person object is of the type **Professor** or **Student**, and if so, we output the extra values **Subject** and **Major**.

It is a basic example of how to utilize classes as arguments in methods and use object polymorphism in C#.

Creating extension methods

Extension methods are a C# feature that enables the addition of methods to existing .NET types without having to build a new derived type, recompile, or edit the original type. Extension methods are static, although they are called **instance methods** on the extended type.

To define an extension method, use the following syntax:

Define it as a **static** method in a **static class**.

Employ the **this** keyword for the first parameter in the method definition. The type of this initial argument specifies the type that the method will operate upon.

Simple example:

```
1. public static class IntegerExtensions
2. {
3.     public static bool IsGreaterThan(this int i, int value)
4.     {
5.         return i > value;
6.     }
7. }
```

IsGreaterThan is an extension method defined in the **IntegerExtensions** static class in this code. This function accepts an integer and determines if it is bigger than the specified number. This procedure would be referred to as:

```
1. int x = 10;
2. bool result = x.IsGreaterThan(5); // result is true
```

Even though **IsGreaterThan** is a static method, it may be invoked as an instance method on int.

Practical example

Here is a more accurate example. Consider adding a method to the string class that capitalizes the initial letter of a string. We can use the following extension method:

```
1. public static class StringExtensions
2. {
3.     public static string CapitalizeFirstLetter(this string str)
4.     {
5.         if (string.IsNullOrEmpty(str))
6.         {
7.             return str;
8.         }
9.         return $"{str[..1].ToString().ToUpper()}{str[1..]}";
10.    }
11. }
```

Here is how to utilize this extension method:

```
1. string str = "hello";
2. str = str.CapitalizeFirstLetter(); // str is now "Hello"
```

When we use **CapitalizeFirstLetter** in this example, it looks to be a method of the **string** class, but it is defined in our **StringExtensions** class.

It is important to note that extension methods cannot override existing methods. When resolving method calls, the compiler always favors instance methods over extension methods.

Collections example

In this example, we extend the **IEnumerable<T>** interface by adding a function that prints each item in a collection:

```
1. public static class CollectionExtensions
2. {
3.     public static void Print<T>(this IEnumerable<T> collection)
4.     {
5.         foreach (T item in collection)
6.         {
7.             Console.WriteLine(item);
8.         }
9.     }
10. }
```

This extension method may be used with any type that implements **Ienumerable<T>**:

```
1. List<int> numbers = new List<int> { 1, 2, 3, 4, 5 };
2. numbers.Print(); // prints 1, 2, 3, 4, 5, each on a new line
```

The extension function works with any collection type, including arrays, lists, and dictionaries.

Finally, extension methods are a valuable feature in C# that allows us to extend the functionality of existing classes. They can make our code more precise and more user-friendly. They should, however, be utilized with caution to avoid making the code more incomprehensible.

Overloading extension method

Extension methods in C# can be overloaded in the same manner that ordinary methods can. In C#, an extension method is a **static** method that extends an existing type with additional functionality even if we cannot access its source code.

Here is an illustration:

```
1. public static class StringExtensions
2. {
3.     public static string AppendNumber(this string str, int number)
4.     {
5.         return str + number.ToString();
6.     }
7.
8.     public static string AppendNumber(this string str, double
    number)
9.     {
10.         return str + number.ToString();
11.     }
12. }
```

In the above code, we defined two extension methods called **AppendNumber**. They are both extensions of the string type. The first technique requires an **int** argument, whereas the second requires a **double**. These methods have different signatures since they have different argument types. Hence they are regarded as two distinct methods.

These approaches might be referred to as follows:

```
1. string original = "The number is: ";
2. string withInt = original.AppendNumber(10); // "The number is: 10"
3. string withDouble = original.
   AppendNumber(20.5); // "The number is: 20.5"
```

When we use the **AppendNumber** method, the C# compiler will select the proper method based on the kind of argument we supply. If we supply an **int**, the first **AppendNumber** method is used, and if we pass a **double**, the second one is used.

As a result, in C#, extension method overloading allows us to declare numerous extension methods with the same name but distinct arguments, providing flexibility in how these methods might be utilized.

Extension changing type return

An extension method is a sort of **static** method in C# that may be called as if it were an instance method based on the type of its first parameter. It is handy for adding functionality to existing classes or types without modifying their source code.

Here is an example of an extension method that can take a **decimal** number and return a money-formatted string. **this** keyword indicates that the method extends the **decimal** type in the method signature:

```
1. decimal amount = 1234.56m;
2. string formattedAmount = amount.ToMoneyFormat();
3. Console.WriteLine(formattedAmount); // Outputs: $1,234.56
4. static class DecimalExtensions
5. {
6.     public static string ToMoneyFormat(this decimal amount)
7.     {
8.         return String.Format("{0:C}", amount);
9.     }
10. }
```

In this example, we construct a static class **DecimalExtensions** and an extension function **ToMoneyFormat()**. The **ToMoneyFormat()** function uses the **String.Format()** method to format a decimal amount into a currency string. Then, in the **Main()** function of the **Program** class, we utilize this method to format a **decimal** value as a currency string and send it to the console. It is worth noting that we may call **ToMoneyFormat()** as if it were a method on the **decimal** type itself, even though it is a static function in a distinct class.

We have descended into the depths of C# methods, characterized as customizable code segments designed to execute specific tasks. The research looked into their construction, invocation, value return mechanisms, parameter provision, overloading capabilities, and unique extensions, which were made possible by C#'s varied syntax and characteristics.

A class captured the core of methods, return types, names, and arguments. We discovered that methods might have a **void** return type, which indicates no return, or hold value or reference types, which indicate the return of a value or an object.

We looked at how parameters are handled in methods. A method may have several parameters, some of which are required while others are optional. Including default values for optional parameters in the method definition is critical.

Overloading and extending techniques were investigated. Overloading offers methods with the same names but different kinds or amounts of parameters, whereas extension allows for an expansion in the functionality of an existing type without any change or inheritance from the original type. It is made feasible using extension methods, which are static methods that use the keyword **this** in the first parameter to signify the type being expanded.

C# methods offer a robust and extensible foundation for structuring and organizing code, improving its neatness, readability, and reusability. They extend .NET's capabilities and encourage interaction with new types and classes. As we progress through C#, a better knowledge of the **params** keyword, **out** and **ref** parameters, and asynchronous methods become increasingly important.

This synthesis thoroughly examined C# methods, emphasizing their definition, call mechanisms, overloading, and extensions. Classes have been used to demonstrate polymorphism, manage collections as arguments in methods, and define default and optional parameters. Method efficiency sets the path for clean, maintainable, and reusable C# code, which is the foundation of professional programming.

Understanding encapsulation and abstraction

Encapsulation and abstraction are two of the four essential concepts of OOP, with inheritance and polymorphism being the other two. While all four are necessary for developing well-structured software, this essay will concentrate on understanding encapsulation and abstraction, particularly in the context of .NET development.

Encapsulation

Encapsulation combines data and the procedures that act on it into a single unit known as an object. This encapsulation approach conceals an object's internal state and functionality from the outside world. Encapsulation improves program modularity and maintainability by concealing inherent complexity.

Classes and structs are often used in .NET to encapsulate data and behavior. In C#, here is a simple example of encapsulation using a class:

```
1.  public class Car
2.  {
3.      // private data members
4.      private string model;
5.      private int year;
6.
7.      // public method to access and modify private data members
8.      public void SetModel(string model)
9.      {
10.         this.model = model;
11.     }
12.
13.     public string GetModel()
```

```
14.    {
15.        return this.model;
16.    }
17.
18.    public void SetYear(int year)
19.    {
20.        this.year = year;
21.    }
22.
23.    public int GetYear()
24.    {
25.        return this.year;
26.    }
27. }
```

The **Car** class in this example encapsulates the data member's **model** and **year** and the methods **SetModel**, **GetModel**, **SetYear**, and **GetYear**. The data members are made **private**, making them available only within the **Car** class, preventing unauthorized access.

Abstraction

Abstraction, on the other hand, is the idea of simplifying complicated systems by modeling them so that only the essential qualities are captured. By minimizing information specifics, it enables a better level of generality. It conceals extraneous details and displays only what is required.

Interfaces and abstract classes are used in OOP to accomplish abstraction. Abstract classes in C# are defined using the **abstract** keyword and can include abstract (method declaration without implementation) and non-abstract methods.

In C#, here is an example of an abstract class:

```
1. public abstract class Animal
2. {
3.     public abstract void Speak();
4. }
```

In this example, **Animal** is an abstract class with an abstract function **Speak()**. This method is defined but not implemented in the abstract class, requiring all derived classes to supply their implementation of the **Speak** method, as seen in the following example:

```
1. public class Dog : Animal
2. {
3.     public override void Speak()
4.     {
```

```
5.          Console.WriteLine("The dog barks.");
6.     }
7. }
8.
9. public class Cat : Animal
10. {
11.     public override void Speak()
12.     {
13.          Console.WriteLine("The cat meows.");
14.     }
15. }
```

In this case, the **Dog** and **Cat** classes each provide their version of the **Speak** method. In this approach, the **Animal** class abstracts the notion of speaking while the derived classes implement it in detail.

Understanding these two principles is critical for becoming a skilled .NET programmer since they are essential for writing modular and maintainable code. Encapsulation enables us to group data and methods into objects and secure them from unauthorized access, which is critical for managing complexity and preventing problems. On the other hand, abstraction enables us to hide specifics and describe actions at a higher, more conceptual level, allowing us to reason about our software's behavior.

Encapsulation and abstraction contribute to system resilience by protecting users from the system's inherent intricacies and providing a simple interface to engage with. Understanding and effectively implementing these concepts will allow you to build more efficient and maintainable code, which is essential for effective .NET programming.

To summarize, we looked at encapsulation and abstraction, two key concepts in OOP. Encapsulation, which focuses on combining data and processes into objects and safeguarding them from external access, and abstraction, which focuses on simplifying complex systems by expressing them with only essential properties, have been intensively investigated. We used classes, structs, interfaces, and abstract classes in C# to correctly display these ideas. We also realized that encapsulation and abstraction are more than just theoretical notions; they are tools that improve our code's modularity, maintainability, and readability. We empower ourselves to construct efficient, resilient, and high-quality .NET programs by knowing and using these concepts.

Implementing inheritance in C#

In OOP, inheritance is a fundamental notion that allows one class to inherit the characteristics and behaviors of another. In C# and the .NET framework, inheritance is a vital technique that promotes class hierarchy and helps code reusability. This article will discuss the specifics of implementing inheritance in C# and show how it can be used in practice with two sample code samples.

Understanding inheritance

In C#, inheritance allows us to construct a new (derived) class based on an existing (base) class. The derived class inherits the parent class's non-private elements (fields, properties, methods), allowing us to enhance or change the base class's functionality without duplicating code. After the derived class declaration, use the (colon) : symbol followed by the base class name.

```
1. class BaseClass
2. {
3.     // Base class members
4. }
5.
6. class DerivedClass : BaseClass
7. {
8.     // Derived class members
9. }
```

Example 1 of creating a simple inheritance hierarchy

Let us look at a real-world example of inheritance in C#. Assume we wish to simulate many automobiles with certain common traits. We may design specialized vehicle types derived from an introductory class named **Vehicle**.

```
1. class Vehicle
2. {
3.     public string Make { get; set; }
4.     public string Model { get; set; }
5.     public int Year { get; set; }
6.
7.     public void Start()
8.     {
9.         Console.WriteLine("Engine started!");
10.    }
11.
12.    // Other common methods and properties related to vehicles
13. }
14.
15. class Car : Vehicle
16. {
17.     public int NumberOfDoors { get; set; }
18. }
19.
```

```
20. class Motorcycle : Vehicle
21. {
22.     public bool HasSidecar { get; set; }
23. }
```

The **Car** and **Motorcycle** classes in this example derive from the **Vehicle** class. Consequently, the properties **Make**, **Model**, **Year**, and procedure **Start()** are passed down to them. Furthermore, **Car** has the additional property **NumberOfDoors**, and **Motorcycle** has the additional property **HasSidecar**.

Example 2 of abstract classes and overriding

Using abstract classes and method overriding is another crucial feature of inheritance. An abstract class cannot be created directly but can serve as a template for derived classes.

Here is an illustration:

```
1.  abstract class Shape
2.  {
3.      public abstract double CalculateArea();
4.
5.      public void DisplayInfo()
6.      {
7.          Console.WriteLine("This is a shape.");
8.      }
9.  }
10.
11. class Circle : Shape
12. {
13.     public double Radius { get; set; }
14.
15.     public override double CalculateArea()
16.     {
17.         return Math.PI * Radius * Radius;
18.     }
19. }
20.
21. class Square : Shape
22. {
23.     public double SideLength { get; set; }
24.
25.     public override double CalculateArea()
26.     {
```

```
27.        return SideLength * SideLength;
28.    }
29. }
```

The **Shape** is an abstract class with an abstract function **CalculateArea()** in this example. The derived classes, **Circle** and **Square**, must implement the **CalculateArea()** function to offer their specialized area computation. We also override the **DisplayInfo()** function in the derived classes to tailor their behavior.

Inheritance is a strong C# and .NET feature that encourages code reuse and creates class hierarchies. It enables us to write flexible and maintainable code by declaring a base class and deriving additional classes. In this post, we discussed inheritance and provided two practical instances of its use in C#. The examples illustrated how inheritance may be used to simulate real-world relationships and build modular and adaptable code architectures. We may develop more efficient and structured C# applications within the. NET by efficiently exploiting inheritance.

Understanding polymorphism in C#

One of the essential notions of OOP is polymorphism. The name comes from the Greek terms *poly* and *morphe*, which indicate *many* and *form*, respectively. Polymorphism in programming allows things to take on several forms, improving flexibility and enabling more flexible programming approaches.

Recognizing polymorphism

Polymorphism's key benefit is that it allows a single interface to represent several types of objects. For example, a single function can process many objects by calling the relevant methods based on the object's class.

In C#, there are two forms of polymorphism.

Static/compile time polymorphism

It occurs during the compilation process. Overloading is an example of static polymorphism in which numerous methods with the same name but different arguments might exist.

It occurs during execution (i.e., during run time). A method in a derived class with the same name and type signature as a method in its base class is an example of dynamic polymorphism.

Overloading polymorphism

Overloading, static polymorphism, is having many methods with the same name but distinct arguments in a class. Based on the parameters' number, types, and sequence, the compiler selects which method to call.

Here is an illustration:

```
1.  Calculator calc = new Calculator();
2.
3.  Console.WriteLine(calc.Add(1, 2)); // Outputs: 3
4.  Console.WriteLine(calc.Add(1.0f, 2.0f)); // Outputs: 3.0
5.  Console.WriteLine(calc.Add(1, 2, 3)); // Outputs: 6
6.  public class Calculator
7.  {
8.      public int Add(int a, int b)
9.      {
10.         return a + b;
11.     }
12.
13.     public float Add(float a, float b)
14.     {
15.         return a + b;
16.     }
17.
18.     public int Add(int a, int b, int c)
19.     {
20.         return a + b + c;
21.     }
22. }
```

This example has three **Add** methods, each with its arguments. The proper procedure is picked at compilation time based on the inputs supplied.

Polymorphism with overriding

In C#, the **virtual** and **override** (dynamic polymorphism) keywords can regulate method overriding, a polymorphism type. The **override** keyword can override a virtual method in a base class by methods in derived classes.

Here is an illustration:

```
1.  Animal myAnimal = new Animal();
2.  Animal myPig = new Pig();
3.  Animal myDog = new Dog();
4.
5.  myAnimal.Sound();  // Outputs: The animal makes a sound
6.  myPig.Sound();  // Outputs: The pig says: wee wee
7.  myDog.Sound();  // Outputs: The dog says: bow wow
8.  public class Animal
```

```
9.  {
10.     public virtual void Sound()
11.     {
12.         Console.WriteLine("The animal makes a sound");
13.     }
14. }
15.
16. public class Pig : Animal
17. {
18.     public override void Sound()
19.     {
20.         Console.WriteLine("The pig says: wee wee");
21.     }
22. }
23.
24. public class Dog : Animal
25. {
26.     public override void Sound()
27.     {
28.         Console.WriteLine("The dog says: bow wow");
29.     }
30. }
```

In this scenario, the **Animal** class's sound function is designated as virtual, allowing it to be overridden in derived classes such as **Pig** and **Dog**. The actual type of the object decides which **Sound** method is invoked at runtime.

Finally, this part combines the fundamentals of polymorphism and constructors in C#. Polymorphism encourages the development of simple, clear interfaces that can support a wide range of inputs and circumstances. It is a solid OOP feature that improves code scalability and maintainability. Parallel to that, the part looks into constructors, shedding light on their significance in object initialization and the flexibility in parameter specification. It emphasizes the inheritability of constructors from base classes using the **base** keyword, supported with real code examples. The combined grasp of polymorphism and constructors, both essential components of C#, enables us to design and configure objects with unprecedented flexibility and efficiency. Finally, understanding these principles considerably improves the quality of our C# and .NET programming and design.

Creating and using constructors in C#

A constructor is a subroutine or function in object-oriented programming associated with an object class. It initiates an object's state and is called automatically when a class object is created. Constructors are essential in C# for preparing objects for usage.

Constructor default

In C#, a default constructor accepts no parameters. If no constructors are given in the class, C# will provide it automatically. This constructor returns the item to its default state.

Consider the following scenario:

```
1. public class Employee
2. {
3.     public string Name { get; set; }
4.     public int Age { get; set; }
5.
6.     // Default constructor
7.     public Employee()
8.     {
9.         Name = "Not Specified";
10.        Age = 0;
11.    }
12. }
13.
14. // Creating an object of the Employee class
15. Employee emp = new Employee();
16. Console.WriteLine(emp.Name); // Outputs: Not Specified
17. Console.WriteLine(emp.Age);  // Outputs: 0
```

The **Employee** class in the above example contains a default constructor that sets **Name** and **Age** to their default values. The default constructor is used when we use the **new** keyword to create an object **emp** of the **Employee** class.

Parameterized builder

A parameterized constructor takes arguments. These options aid in the initialization of an object when it is created. C# will not give a default constructor if we provide a parameterized constructor. If we require it, we must expressly give it.

An example of a parameterized constructor is as follows:

```
1. // Creating an object of the Employee class
2. Employee emp = new Employee("John", 30);
```

```
3. Console.WriteLine(emp.Name); // Outputs: John
4. Console.WriteLine(emp.Age);  // Outputs: 30
5. public class Employee
6. {
7.     public string Name { get; set; }
8.     public int Age { get; set; }
9.     // Parameterized constructor
10.    public Employee(string name, int age)
11.    {
12.        Name = name;
13.        Age = age;
14.    }
15. }
```

In this example, the **Employee** class has a parameterized constructor that accepts name and age as inputs. We now supply these options when constructing an **Employee** object. The arguments are then used to initialize the object's **Name** and **Age** attributes.

Using inheritance constructors

Base class constructors are not inherited by derived classes when it comes to inheritance. The derived class, on the other hand, can invoke the constructor of the base class.

Consider the following example:

```
1. // Creating an object of the Employee class
2. Employee emp = new Employee("John", 30);
3. Console.WriteLine(emp.Name); // Outputs: John
4. Console.WriteLine(emp.Age);  // Outputs: 30
5.
6. public class Person
7. {
8.     public string Name { get; set; }
9.
10.    // Base class constructor
11.    public Person(string name)
12.    {
13.        Name = name;
14.    }
15. }
16.
17. public class Employee : Person
18. {
```

```
19.     public int Age { get; set; }
20.
21.     // Derived class constructor
22.     public Employee(string name, int age) : base(name)
23.     {
24.         Age = age;
25.     }
26. }
```

The employee is a derived class derived from the **Person** base class in the preceding example. Employee's constructor calls the **Person** constructor and initializes the **Name** property using the **base** keyword.

Constructor with inheritance

When you have a class hierarchy (classes that inherit from each other) in C#, the derived class can use the constructor from the base class with the base keyword, which is useful when you want to inherit the behavior of the base class constructor while also adding some additional functionality or behavior in your derived class constructor.

Here is an illustration:

```
1.  Employee employee = new Employee("John Doe", "Developer");
2.
3.  Console.WriteLine($"Name: {employee.Name}, Position: {employee.
    Position}");
4.  // Outputs: Name: John Doe, Position: Developer
5.
6.  public class Person
7.  {
8.      public string Name { get; }
9.
10.     // Base class constructor
11.     public Person(string name)
12.     {
13.         Name = name;
14.     }
15. }
16.
17. public class Employee : Person
18. {
19.     public string Position { get; }
20.
```

```
21.    // Derived class constructor
22.    public Employee(string name, string position) : base(name) //
    Using base keyword
23.    {
24.        Position = position;
25.    }
26. }
```

The **Employee** is a class that inherits from the **Person** class in this example. The constructor of the **Person** class accepts a **string** parameter **name** and assigns it to the **Name** field. The constructor of the **Employee** class accepts two string inputs, **name** and **position**. The **Employee** constructor calls the **Person** constructor with the **name** parameter through the **base** keyword and then assigns the **position** argument to the **Position** property. So, when we create an **Employee** object in the **Main** function, we set both the **Name** and **Position** attributes, which we can then report to the console.

This discourse thoroughly dissects the complexities of constructors in the C# language, emphasizing their significance as critical subroutines for object state setup. We enable you to comprehend its diverse uses by digging into several constructor types—default, parameterized, and inherited—supported by relevant examples. The **base** keyword is also highlighted, emphasizing its value in invoking base class constructors from a derived class. This powerful approach enables the base class's behaviors to be seamlessly inherited and the incorporation of extra features in the derived class constructor. This investigation leads readers to conclude that using constructors in C#, mainly inherited constructors, is critical for developing efficient, well-structured, scalable object-oriented applications.

Working with static and instance members in C#

It is critical to grasp various class members when working in C#, especially using the .NET. It involves knowing the difference between static and instance members. This understanding may greatly aid in creating clean, efficient, and maintainable code.

Understanding instance members

Instance members are members of a class instance, not the class itself. When we create a new object or instance of a class, it has its own set of instance members.

A field, a variable that belongs to a class instance, is a frequent example of an instance member. Consider the **Person** class, which has a **string** field name. Each **Person** object we make can have a unique name.

```
1. Person person1 = new Person("Alice");
2. Person person2 = new Person("Bob");
```

```
3.
4. Console.WriteLine(person1.name); // Outputs "Alice"
5. Console.WriteLine(person2.name); // Outputs "Bob"
6.
7. public class Person
8. {
9.     public string name; // Instance member
10.
11.     public Person(string _name)
12.     {
13.         this.name = _name;
14.     }
15. }
```

Another sort of instance member is instance methods, which are methods that act on a class instance.

```
1. Person person = new Person("Alice");
2. person.SayHello(); // Outputs "Hello, my name is Alice."
3.
4. public class Person
5. {
6.     public string name;
7.
8.     public Person(string _name)
9.     {
10.         this.name = _name;
11.     }
12.
13.     public void SayHello() // Instance method
14.     {
15.         Console.WriteLine($"Hello, my name is {this.name}.");
16.     }
17. }
```

Understanding static members

Static members, as opposed to instance members, pertain to the class itself rather than an instance of the class. As a result, they are shared by all instances of that class.

For example, a static field may be used to count the number of instances of a class that have been generated. Because all instances share the field, increasing the count each time a new instance is generated will represent the total number of instances.

Here is an example:

```
1. Person person1 = new Person("Alice");
2. Person person2 = new Person("Bob");
3. Console.WriteLine(Person.count); // Outputs "2"
4.
5. public class Person
6. {
7.     public string name;
8.     public static int count = 0; //Static member
9.
10.    public Person(string _name)
11.    {
12.        this.name = _name;
13.        count++;
14.    }
15. }
```

Similarly, static methods belong to the class rather than any class instance. They can only interact with the class's static members:

```
1. Person person1 = new Person("Alice");
2. Person person2 = new Person("Bob");
3.
4. Person.ShowCount(); // Outputs "The total number of persons is 2."
5.
6. public class Person
7. {
8.     public string name;
9.     public static int count = 0;
10.
11.    public Person(string _name)
12.    {
13.        this.name = _name;
14.        count++;
15.    }
16.
17.    public static void ShowCount() // Static method
18.    {
19.        Console.
    WriteLine($"The total number of persons is {count}.");
20.    }
21. }
```

Static vs. instance members

We should utilize instance members when each class instance has to keep its state. Each person, for example, needs a name.

Static members, on the other hand, should be used when we need to retain a state shared by all class instances or to conduct operations that do not depend on the state of any specific instance. For example, our **Person** class keeps track of the total number of **Person** instances via a static count property and a static **ShowCount** function.

Understanding the distinction between static and instance members in C# is essential for designing effective and efficient code. Static members belong to the class and are shared by all instances, whereas instance members are unique to each class. The best option depends on whether you must keep a state unique to each instance or shared by all instances.

Conclusion

As this chapter draws to a conclusion, we have completed a thorough examination of OOP in the context of C#. We have been through the fundamental ideas and approaches, revealing how to build and use classes, objects, properties, fields, methods, constructors, static and instance members, records, and extension methods. Our path next took us through more complicated OOP constructs, such as inheritance, polymorphism, encapsulation, and abstraction.

We worked using C# and .NET to communicate with PostgreSQL, a widely used open-source relational database. We demonstrated the use of records for data modeling and manipulation in this way. We used concrete examples such as building a library system and developing data-driven applications to ground these notions in reality.

The ultimate goal of this chapter is to provide readers with a powerful combination of theoretical understanding and practical skills to construct robust, scalable, and stable OOP systems in C#. This foundation is then built upon by exploring advanced OOP principles, interoperability with PostgreSQL databases through ADO.NET and Npgsql, and adding new types via extension methods.

An in-depth grasp of OOP and its more complex aspects is a must-have skill for any programmer, especially those who work as part of a team. This understanding enables developers to build durable, scalable, and easy-to-maintain software systems and promotes practical team cooperation, paving the way for more efficient and harmonious software development activities.

In the next chapter, we get into C# and .NET, concentrating on key programming ideas such as interfaces, inheritance, and polymorphism. It also delves into C#'s value and reference types, which are critical for memory management and efficiency.

Join our book's Discord space

Join the book's Discord Workspace for Latest updates, Offers, Tech happenings around the world, New Release and Sessions with the Authors:

https://discord.bpbonline.com

CHAPTER 6

Mastering Interfaces and Inheriting Classes

Introduction

C# and .NET, well-known for their comprehensive capabilities and tools, offer a framework for writing clean, efficient, and dependable code. This comprehensive content takes you on a trip, enabling you to dig further into the complicated world of C# programming, exposing its essential ideas and principles, such as interfaces, inheritance, and polymorphism.

The importance of interfaces in creating a contract for classes, inheritance as a cornerstone of OOP that allows for code reuse, and polymorphism, which allows objects to take on multiple forms, are all crucial topics that will be fully covered. Understanding these core C# programming principles will provide an excellent basis for expanding your programming talents.

Furthermore, this content delves into the complexities of value types and reference types, two C# pillars with significant implications for memory management and speed. We look at the fundamental distinctions between the two kinds, their interactions with memory, and the effects of these interactions on the performance of your programs. You can create more efficient and high-performing apps if you grasp these ideas.

As we near the end of this in-depth examination, you will have a better knowledge of how to use C# to create software systems. The systems you will be able to build will be robust, scalable, and maintainable, allowing them to withstand the test of time and satisfy user demands indefinitely. This material acts as a solid guide that paves the road to harnessing the power of C# and .NET in your quest to become a skilled programmer.

Structure

The chapter covers the following topics:

- Understanding the concept of interfaces in C#
- Implementing interfaces in C#
- Class inheritance in C#
- Polymorphism in C# via interfaces
- Reusability and extensibility through interfaces and inheritance
- Memory management of the reference types and value types
- Understanding virtual, override, and new keywords
- Abstract classes vs. interfaces
- Role of interfaces in enforcing contracts
- Understanding System.Object and the inheritance hierarchy in C#

Objectives

The general goal of this chapter is to build a thorough understanding of C# programming language fundamentals, with a concentration on object-oriented ideas and memory management. We want to understand the concept and implementation of interfaces in C# and how they provide a structure that enforces specific contracts while facilitating polymorphism, reusability, and extensibility of code. We will look at class inheritance and see how it helps with code organization and reuse. Furthermore, we will investigate the usage of interfaces to implement polymorphism, allowing for a more flexible and dynamic approach to software design.

In this context, we will examine essential concepts in memory management, such as reference types and value types, to ensure that system resources are used efficiently. The role of specific C# keywords like **virtual**, **override**, and **new** will be thoroughly examined, particularly in connection to inheritance and method overloading. We will compare abstract classes and interfaces to understand their distinct responsibilities in C# programming and when using one over the other is preferable. Finally, the research will highlight the significance of the **System.Object** class and the inheritance structure in C# provide a comprehensive understanding of the language's object-oriented nature.

Understanding the concept of interfaces in C#

Interfaces in C# are an essential component of the OOP paradigm, which profoundly changed how programmers think about and arrange their programs. The origins of OOP may be traced back to biological metaphors.

History of OOP and its relationship to biology

The intricate architecture of biological systems inspired the concept of object-oriented programming. In biology, an organism comprises several organs, each with a unique role but functioning together to maintain the organism's existence. Similarly, in OOP, a program is composed of several objects or components, each with its own set of attributes (data) and actions (methods).

Each organ in the body may be compared to an OOP class, with each organ or class serving a distinct purpose. The heart, for example, has its methods to do specific jobs, similar to how a class in OOP has its methods to perform specific functions. Objects in OOP belong to a class and share similar features and behaviors specified by the class, much as various kinds of cells (blood cells, nerve cells, etc.) create distinct organs while adhering to a common framework.

Introduction to OOP with C# interfaces

In OOP and C#, an interface is analogous to a contract or protocol that specifies an object's capabilities without specifying how those capabilities are implemented. An interface in programming, like the interface between various organs in the body, where blood vessels convey oxygen and nutrition, establishes a communication contract between distinct portions of a software system.

An interface in C# might have declarations of methods, attributes, indexers, or events. However, it does not implement these elements; instead, it just describes an object's actions. Any interface-implementing class or struct must offer an implementation for its members. It is a technique for ensuring that an object follows a specified contract while keeping a high degree of abstraction.

Interfaces are vital for establishing abstraction, encapsulation, and polymorphism in C#, all fundamental ideas in OOP. They may improve code's readability, flexibility, and maintainability, adding to its quality.

They enable developers to construct loosely linked systems where changes in one element do not dramatically influence or damage other system sections. Because of this loose coupling, the code is simpler to expand, alter, and maintain over time. It makes the system more adaptable and scalable, and it aids in managing the complexity of substantial software systems.

Impact on teamwork and testing

Using interfaces in a big team helps speed development by enabling various developers to work on different portions of the system simultaneously. While one developer works on the interface, another works on the class that implements the interface. Because the developers conform to the interface's contract, their work may proceed in parallel without significant dispute.

Furthermore, interface-based systems are easy to test for **quality assurance (QA)** teams. Because the interface offers a contract that the implementing classes must meet, testing may be focused on whether each class meets the contract, enhancing testing accuracy and efficiency. Interfaces may also make fake objects easier to employ in unit testing, boosting test coverage and robustness.

While interfaces may not inherently speed up a system, they can contribute to improved code organization and structure, leading to more efficient code execution. Their primary advantage is enhanced design, maintainability, and testability, which are critical for the success of large-scale projects.

Knowing and using C# and OOP interfaces is critical for developing robust, scalable, and maintainable software systems. They are a must-have tool in every programmer's toolbox, with significant implications for team collaboration, testing, and overall software quality.

Interfaces and .NET

.NET has many tools that make creating robust and maintainable interfaces easier. These are some ways .NET may help us create robust interfaces:

- **Clear definitions of interfaces**: Interfaces are explicitly specified in .NET languages such as C# using the **interface** keyword. This simple syntax aids us in rapidly identifying and comprehending interfaces in the software.

- **Interface implementation**: A class or struct may implement several interfaces in .NET. It allows for a great degree of flexibility in the design of software systems. It assists in the achievement of separation of concerns since distinct functionality may be described in separate interfaces.

- **Implementation of an explicit interface**: In .NET, we may explicitly implement an interface, which means that the interface's elements are not available as public members of the class but only when the class instance is converted to the interface. It prevents name conflicts and allows us to conceal interface members that should not be utilized outside of the context of the interface.

- **Interface inheritance**: .NET enables interfaces to inherit from other interfaces, allowing for a hierarchical structure that may help vast codebases be simpler to explore and manage.

- **Strongly typed system**: .NET is a strongly typed system, which implies that during build time, the compiler examines the data type of variables and expressions. It lowers runtime errors and improves the interfaces' reliability and resilience.

- **Development tools**: .NET also provides powerful development tools (e.g., Visual Studio, .NET CLI) with features such as IntelliSense for auto-completion and suggestions, refactoring options, and tools for analyzing dependencies, making creating and maintaining interfaces easier.

- **Unit testing and mocking frameworks**: .NET offers strong support for unit testing and mocking frameworks (such as NUnit, xUnit, and Moq), which may interact effectively with interfaces to test system behavior. It stimulates the creation of testable code and the creation of robust, dependable interfaces.

- **Dependency injection (DI)**: .NET built-in support for dependency injection enables a class to accept dependencies from an external source rather than constructing them. DI works well with interfaces, resulting in loosely linked, readily tested, and maintainable code.

- **Interface-based**: .NET programming emphasizes programming to an interface rather than an implementation. It enables us to alter the concrete classes that the application employs without having to update the code that employs them. It makes the application more modular, versatile, and changeable.

Remember that building maintainable interfaces involves technology, design ideas, and practices. *Robert C. Martin's* acronym, SOLID principles, is essential for writing stable and resilient interfaces. They stand for the SRP, the Open-Closed Principle, the Liskov Substitution Principle, the Interface Segregation Principle, and the Dependency Inversion Principle. Each of these principles gives guidelines on building interfaces and implementing classes in a resilient, changeable, and understandable manner.

Implementing interfaces in C#

In today's fast-paced retail environment, adaptability and scalability are critical to the success of any store. Businesses must constantly update their offerings to fulfill their clients' ever-changing wants and stay ahead of the competition. Implementing a flexible and extensible system becomes a significant priority in online shopping, where clients want various items and services.

In this situation, utilizing interfaces in C# appears to be a helpful technique. Interfaces enable us to set contracts that products or services must follow while allowing for the seamless integration of new offers into the existing system.

Let us look at a hypothetical online bookstore that sells books and electronics. We will design product interfaces to reflect the items' common attributes and behaviors. For example, the **IProduct** interface will define attributes such as **Name** and **Price** shared by all items:

```
1. // Product interface represents common properties of all products
2. public interface IProduct
3. {
4.     string Name { get; set; }
5.     decimal Price { get; set; }
6. }
```

The store will also have a unique function where club members can borrow books. To manage this capability, we provide the **IRentable** interface, which includes a property for the rental time and a method to make the renting process more manageable.

```
1. // Rentable interface represents products that can be rented
2. public interface IRentable
3. {
4.     int RentalPeriodInDays { get; set; }
5.     void Rent();
6. }
```

Let us now create classes that comply with these interfaces. As club members can rent books, the **Book** class will implement the **IBook** and **IRentable** interfaces.

```
1. // Book class implementing IBook and IRentable interfaces
2. public class Book : IBook, IRentable
3. {
4.     public string Name { get; set; }
5.     public decimal Price { get; set; }
6.     public string Author { get; set; }
7.     public int RentalPeriodInDays { get; set; }
8.
9.     public void Rent()
10.    {
11.        Console.
    WriteLine($"Book {Name} by {Author} has been rented.»);
12.    }
13. }
```

Similarly, the **IElectronic** class will implement the **Electronic** interface, defining attributes particular to electronic items.

```
1. // Electronic class implementing IElectronic interface
2. public class Electronic : IElectronic
3. {
4.     public string Name { get; set; }
5.     public decimal Price { get; set; }
6.     public string Brand { get; set; }
7. }
```

Our online store benefits significantly from the use of interfaces. The company may grow its catalog with new products, such as computer rentals, by designing classes that implement appropriate interfaces. This method ensures a flexible and scalable architecture, allowing for the easy integration of numerous goods and services.

Professionals with experience dealing with interfaces are critical to the store's growth and evolution. They can introduce new items quickly, such as computer rentals, with minimal code modifications and improved code quality. Their knowledge enables the development team to produce with agility, propelling the store's core business to tremendous success and customer happiness.

Class inheritance in C#

Inheritance is a basic OOP notion frequently utilized in programming languages such as C#. It enables one class to inherit the characteristics (attributes and methods) of another, resulting in a class hierarchy representing a is-a relationship between them. It means that the properties of a derived class, also known as a subclass or child class, can be inherited by a base class, also known as a **superclass** or **parent class**. This method encourages code reuse, improves code organization, and allows system flexibility.

Consider a car factory that manufactures many sorts of vehicles, such as sports cars, luxury cars, trucks, and utility vehicles, to demonstrate the concept of inheritance. Each type of vehicle has unique qualities, but they all have some things in common.

Vehicle is the base class

Let us begin by defining an introductory class named **Vehicle**, which will contain all cars' features, such as the number of wheels, gasoline tank capacity, and vehicle brand. This class may also include standard car methods like **Start** and **Stop**:

```
1. public class Vehicle
2. {
3.     public int NumberOfWheels { get; set; }
4.     public double FuelTankCapacity { get; set; }
5.     public string Brand { get; set; }
6.
7.     public void Start()
8.     {
9.         Console.WriteLine("Vehicle started.");
10.    }
11.
12.    public void Stop()
13.    {
14.        Console.WriteLine("Vehicle stopped.");
15.    }
16. }
```

Now that we have our base class, **Vehicle** with common characteristics and functions, we can use inheritance to construct specialized classes for other types of vehicles. For example, we will make classes for **SportsCar**, **LuxuryCar**, **Truck**, and **UtilityVehicle**, each representing a different sort of vehicle with its own set of features.

Derived class: SportsCar

A sports car is a vehicle that is noted for its speed and performance. It will inherit the attributes and methods of the **Vehicle** base class and sports car-specific characteristics.

Here is an illustration:

```
1.  public class SportsCar : Vehicle
2.  {
3.      public int Horsepower { get; set; }
4.
5.      public void Drift()
6.      {
7.          Console.WriteLine("Performing a drift!");
8.      }
9.  }
```

The derived class LuxuryCar

A luxury car is a high-end vehicle distinguished by its premium amenities and comfort. It will also inherit from the **Vehicle** base class and may contain luxury-oriented properties and specific methods.

Here is an illustration:

```
1.  public class LuxuryCar : Vehicle
2.  {
3.      public string InteriorMaterial { get; set; }
4.
5.      public void MassageSeats()
6.      {
7.          Console.
    WriteLine("Enjoying a relaxing massage while driving!");
8.      }
9.  }
```

The derived class Truck

A truck is a large vehicle used to deliver cargo. It will provide truck-specific traits and functions to the **Vehicle** base class.

Here is an illustration:

```
1.  public class Truck : Vehicle
2.  {
3.      public double CargoCapacity { get; set; }
4.
5.      public void TransportCargo()
6.      {
7.          Console.WriteLine("Transporting cargo to its destination.");
8.      }
9.  }
```

The derived class UtilityVehicle

A utility vehicle is a multipurpose vehicle that can be used for various practical purposes. It will derive from the **Vehicle** base class and will be able to inherit its utility-focused attributes and methods.

Here is an illustration:

```
1.  public class UtilityVehicle : Vehicle
2.  {
3.      public int LoadCapacity { get; set; }
4.
5.      public void PerformUtilityTask()
6.      {
7.          Console.WriteLine("Completing a utility task.");
8.      }
9.  }
```

In our vehicle factory example, we used class inheritance to successfully construct a hierarchy of linked classes that share common qualities and functionalities and allow each specialized class to add unique features. This inheritance structure has various benefits that substantially impact the development process.

Code reusability and organization

Inheritance encapsulates the common characteristics and methods in the base class **Vehicle**, and each specialized class, such as **SportsCar**, **LuxuryCar**, **Truck**, and **UtilityVehicle**, inherits these features. It enhances code reusability because there is no need to duplicate code for shared functionalities. Furthermore, the code becomes more ordered and manageable, making it more maintainable in the long run.

Easy maintenance

Due to inheritance, changes or improvements made in the base class are automatically propagated to all derived classes. For example, suppose we update the **Vehicle** class to incorporate a new method for evaluating fuel efficiency. This update will be available to all vehicles, including sports cars, luxury cars, trucks, and utility vehicles. This streamlines maintenance operations minimizes the likelihood of introducing defects, and enhances the application's overall stability.

Agile expansion

Our automobile factory's software is well-prepared for future growth into additional vehicle categories, such as jet skis and boats, thanks to the flexibility given by class inheritance. We can efficiently add additional vehicle kinds by creating new classes that inherit from the fundamental **Vehicle** class, such as **Jet ski** and **Boat**, with little changes to the current code. This agility enables the automobile manufacturer to adjust to market needs and diversify its product options swiftly.

Team collaboration

Class inheritance promotes successful collaboration among multiple programming teams in a large-scale development project. Each team can be in charge of creating a particular sort of vehicle, utilizing the interface provided by the base class. This modularity allows teams to work independently, which reduces possible disputes and streamlines the development process.

Class inheritance in C# provides various advantages for developing our vehicle factory application. It encourages code reuse, improves maintainability, and establishes a clear is-a relationship between various vehicle kinds. The factory can easily and quickly construct jet skis, boats, or other vehicle varieties as needed because the system is well-organized and ready for future growth. Furthermore, class inheritance allows for seamless collaboration among diverse programming teams, resulting in a more efficient and unified development approach.

Polymorphism in C# via interfaces

Polymorphism is a basic idea in object-oriented programming that permits diverse objects to be considered objects of the same supertype. This notion improves application flexibility and maintainability, making adapting and evolving in response to business demands easier. Interfaces are an efficient approach to implement polymorphism in C#.

Understanding polymorphism

Let us begin by defining polymorphism. It comes from the Greek words *poly* and *morph*, which mean *many* and *forms*, respectively. In programming, it refers to an object's ability to take on several forms. OOP often uses polymorphism when a parent class refers to a child class object.

Polymorphism is highly advantageous to the maintainability and extensibility of programs. It gives an approach for arranging code so that when adding a new type, we frequently need to add new methods to the new type rather than altering old types or functions. This ability to innovate and adapt to changing requirements is crucial for many businesses, especially in fast-paced industries such as e-commerce.

Polymorphism via interfaces

When a class implements an interface, it enters into a contract to promise to perform certain functions. A class may implement many interfaces, and an object of that class can be considered an object of the interface type. It is when polymorphism enters the picture.

A sample e-commerce application

Take, for example, an e-commerce application with many sorts of items. All goods in this context will share characteristics like **Name** and **Price** and actions like **DisplayDetails()** and **ApplyDiscount()**.

An **IProduct** interface is defined as follows:

```
1. public interface IProduct
2. {
3.     string Name { get; }
4.     decimal Price { get; }
5.     void DisplayDetails();
6.     void ApplyDiscount(decimal discountAmount);
7. }
```

Then we have many classes implementing this interface, such as **Book**, **Electronics**, and **Clothing**:

```
1.  public class Book : IProduct
2.  {
3.      public string Name { get; private set; }
4.      public decimal Price { get; private set; }
5.
6.      public Book(string name, decimal price)
7.      {
8.          Name = name;
9.          Price = price;
10.     }
11.
12.     public void DisplayDetails()
13.     {
14.         Console.WriteLine($"Book: {Name}, Price: {Price}");
```

```
15.      }
16.
17.      public void ApplyDiscount(decimal discountAmount)
18.      {
19.          Price -= discountAmount;
20.      }
21. }
```

This is the class **Electronics**:

```
1.  public class Electronics : IProduct
2.  {
3.      public string Name { get; private set; }
4.      public decimal Price { get; private set; }
5.
6.      public Electronics(string name, decimal price)
7.      {
8.          Name = name;
9.          Price = price;
10.     }
11.
12.     public void DisplayDetails()
13.     {
14.         Console.WriteLine($"Electronics: {Name}, Price: {Price}");
15.     }
16.
17.     public void ApplyDiscount(decimal discountAmount)
18.     {
19.         Price -= discountAmount;
20.     }
21. }
```

Using the **IProduct** interface reference, we may handle all products polymorphically:

```
1.  IProduct book = new Book("Clean Code", 50.00m);
2.  IProduct electronics = new Electronics("Laptop", 1500.00m);
3.
4.  book.ApplyDiscount(5.00m);
5.  electronics.ApplyDiscount(100.00m);
6.
7.  book.DisplayDetails();  // Outputs: Book: Clean Code, Price: 45.00
8.  electronics.
    DisplayDetails();  // Outputs: Electronics: Laptop, Price: 1400.00
```

Even though they are instances of **Book** and **Electronics**, they are considered **IProduct** in the preceding example. It is polymorphism at the interface level.

Advantages

We made the system more adaptive and maintainable by utilizing polymorphism via interfaces. If a new product type is required, we build a new class that implements **IProduct** and provides the relevant implementations. The old code will be left alone, consistent with the OCP of SOLID principles in OOP: Software entities (classes, modules, functions, etc.) should be extensible but not modifiable.

To summarize, polymorphism in C# via interfaces is a valuable tool for creating programs that are simple to maintain, flexible to changing business requirements, and scalable. We may promote consistency and uniformity in huge codebases by defining a standard interface and ensuring that all classes implementing the interface follow the same pattern.

Reusability and extensibility through interfaces and inheritance

As we continue to evolve and enhance our software development techniques, we must focus on the concepts that enable our codebases to scale efficiently in size and complexity. Reusability and extensibility are essential characteristics that assist scaling, and they can be efficiently accomplished in C# and .NET via interfaces and inheritance.

Reusability is an essential component of any software development lifecycle. It refers to developing code once and reusing it in multiple portions of the program or even in different apps to reduce redundancy. Reusability speeds up the development process and improves software reliability because repeated code is usually well-tested and validated.

Reusability is frequently done in object-oriented programming through inheritance. This notion allows a new class (derived class) to inherit the attributes and methods of an existing class (base class). As a result, the code developed in the base class can be reused in the derived class, encouraging uniformity and considerably minimizing code duplication.

On the other hand, extensibility measures a system's capacity to add new features or components with minimal impact on existing components. Extensibility enhances a system's adaptability, guaranteeing it can manage future requirements or modifications without requiring a significant rewrite.

Interfaces are critical in C# and .NET for enabling extensibility. A contract for classes is defined by an interface, which specifies a set of methods and properties that a class must implement if it subscribes to the interface. It does not, however, implement these methods or attributes, leaving that to the implementing classes.

This interface feature offers a greater level of abstraction, allowing programmers to change or add to the behavior of classes without affecting other sections of the code that utilize the interface. It also supports multiple inheritances (through interface implementation), something C# does not directly offer due to the complexities it frequently brings, such as the diamond problem. We may add new functionalities to our classes while maintaining the system flexible and adaptive by using interfaces.

In conclusion, the ideas of reusability and extensibility, aided by inheritance and interfaces, are the foundations of robust, scalable, and maintainable software architecture. As we learn more about C# and .NET, we will see how these notions work together to facilitate the building of sophisticated systems while keeping code clean, organized, and flexible. We can considerably improve the lifetime and adaptability of our software systems by understanding and adequately adopting these concepts, guaranteeing they can fulfill the changing requirements of the digital age.

Let us see a sample:

As we know, the **interface** keyword in C# defines an interface. Let us make a simple interface, **ILivingBeing**, that represents the skills of a basic living form:

```
1. public interface ILivingBeing
2. {
3.     void Breathe();
4.     void Grow();
5. }
```

We define two methods in the **ILivingBeing** interface: **Breathe** and **Grow**. We do not, however, give any implementation specifics.

Let us now implement an interface in C#. A class that desires to utilize an interface must **implement** it by implementing each method given in the interface. It is important to note that a class may implement numerous interfaces.

Create two classes, **Plant** and **Animal**, both of which implement the **ILivingBeing** interface:

```
1. public class Plant : ILivingBeing
2. {
3.     public void Breathe()
4.     {
5.         Console.WriteLine("Plant is breathing through stomata...");
6.     }
7.
8.     public void Grow()
9.     {
10.        Console.WriteLine("Plant is growing...");
11.    }
12. }
```

```
13.
14. public class Animal : ILivingBeing
15. {
16.     public void Breathe()
17.     {
18.         Console.WriteLine("Animal is breathing through lungs...");
19.     }
20.
21.     public void Grow()
22.     {
23.         Console.WriteLine("Animal is growing...");
24.     }
25. }
```

Plant and **Animal** implement the **ILivingBeing** interface here with their implementations of **Breathe** and **Grow**.

Leveraging polymorphism with interfaces

Interfaces in C# provide polymorphism, meaning a method can execute multiple behaviors depending on the object it operates on. Any object that implements a specific interface can be considered an instance of that interface.

Here is an example of how to use it:

```
1. ILivingBeing livingBeing1 = new Plant();
2. livingBeing1.Breathe();
3. livingBeing1.Grow();
4.
5. ILivingBeing livingBeing2 = new Animal();
6. livingBeing2.Breathe();
7. livingBeing2.Grow();
```

In this case, **livingBeing1** and **livingBeing2** are of the **ILivingBeing** type but contain **Plant** and **Animal** instances, respectively. **Breathe** and **Grow** can be used in any instance that implements **ILivingBeing**.

Interface inheritance

In C#, an interface can inherit from another interface, allowing sophisticated, multi-tiered interfaces to be built from simpler ones. Let us make a more specialized interface, **IMammal**, that extends **ILivingBeing**:

```
1. public interface IMammal : ILivingBeing
2. {
```

```
3.      void FeedMilk();
4.  }
5.
6.  public class Human : IMammal
7.  {
8.      public void Breathe()
9.      {
10.         Console.WriteLine("Human is breathing through lungs...");
11.     }
12.
13.     public void Grow()
14.     {
15.         Console.WriteLine("Human is growing...");
16.     }
17.
18.     public void FeedMilk()
19.     {
20.         Console.WriteLine("Human is feeding milk to the child...");
21.     }
22. }
```

In the preceding example, **IMammal** derives from **ILivingBeing** and adds a new method, **FeedMilk**. The **Human** class implements the **IMammal** interface and includes **Breathe**, **Grow**, and **FeedMilk** implementations.

Finally, interfaces in C# are an excellent way to write clean, modular, and maintainable code. It provides a high level of abstraction and encapsulation, both essential OOP concepts. They also support polymorphism, which increases flexibility and encourages code reuse, making our systems more robust and scalable.

Memory management of the reference types and value types

Understanding how variables are saved and handled in memory is critical in programming, especially when working with the C# language. This concept is based on the division of variables into two types: value types and reference types. Let us look into these two sorts to understand better how they work, their differences, and their unique traits.

Value types

First, consider value kinds. Value types are variables that hold data directly. Their value is saved in stack memory, a section that adheres to the **last in, first out (LIFO)** rule, allowing quick access. This category of variables includes numeric kinds (such as integers and floats), enums, structures (**structs**), and boolean (**bool**) types.

The distinguishing feature of value types is that when a value type variable is assigned to another variable, the system copies the original value and stores it in a new memory address. The mechanism essentially copies the data, and the two variables work independently. They have the same values but are stored in different locations in memory. As a result, adjustments to one do not affect the other. It is referred to as pass-by-value behavior.

Reference types

We do, however, have reference types. Rather than storing the data directly, reference types store the address, or reference, to the location where the value is stored on the heap memory, a more flexible and considerable portion suitable for long-term storage or larger data structures.

Reference types include classes, interfaces, delegates, arrays, and strings. When one variable of the reference type is assigned to another variable, this causes both variables to refer to the same place in memory. They both refer to the same data. Because they both access the same underlying data, changes to one variable are mirrored in the other. It is referred to as pass-by-reference behavior.

Understanding the distinction between value types and reference types is essential for good C# programming. This knowledge influences memory management decisions, performance considerations, and potential bug avoidance. With this understanding, developing more efficient, effective, and robust C# programs is possible.

Nullable interfaces in C#

Nullable interfaces are possible in C#. A nullable interface can be given the null value. It is useful when we wish to represent whether or not a variable has a value. To create an interface nullable with C# 8.0 and later, use the nullable operator **?**.

Here is an example of how to use nullable interfaces with vegetables, fruits, and greens:

```
1. public interface IVegetable
2. {
3.     string Name { get; }
4. }
5.
6. public interface IFruit : IVegetable
7. {
8.     bool HasSeeds { get; }
9. }
10.
```

```csharp
11. public interface IGreen : IVegetable
12. {
13.     bool IsGreen { get; }
14. }
15.
16. public class Banana : IFruit
17. {
18.     public string Name => "Banana";
19.     public bool HasSeeds => false;
20. }
21.
22. public class Lettuce : IGreen
23. {
24.     public string Name => "Lettuce";
25.     public bool IsGreen => true;
26. }
27.
28. public class ShoppingList
29. {
30.     public List<IVegetable> Items { get; } = new List<IVegetable>();
31.
32.     public void AddItem(IVegetable? item)
33.     {
34.         if (item == null)
35.         {
36.             throw new ArgumentNullException(nameof(item));
37.         }
38.
39.         Items.Add(item);
40.
41.         switch (item)
42.         {
43.             case IFruit fruit:
44.                 Console.WriteLine($"Added fruit: {fruit.
    Name}, Has seeds: {fruit.HasSeeds}");
45.                 break;
46.             case IGreen green:
47.                 Console.WriteLine($"Added green: {green.
    Name}, Is green: {green.IsGreen}");
48.                 break;
```

```
49.              default:
50.                  Console.WriteLine($"Added vegetable: {item.Name}");
51.                  break;
52.          }
53.      }
54. }
55.
56. // Using the shopping list
57. var shoppingList = new ShoppingList();
58. shoppingList.AddItem(new Banana());
59. shoppingList.AddItem(new Lettuce());
```

Interfaces in this code include **IVegetable**, **IFruit**, and **IGreen**. **Banana** and **Lettuce** are two classes that implement these interfaces. **ShoppingList** is a class with a list of items, each of which is an **IVegetable**. The list can contain any object that implements **IVegetable**.

The **AddItem** function accepts an **IVegetable?**. It means it can accept either an **IVegetable** or **null**. If **null** is given, an exception is fired. If an **IVegetable** is passed, it is added to the list, and a message is written to the console depending on whether the **IVegetable** is an **IFruit** or an **IGreen**.

Finally, regarding quality software development, having a solid understanding of value types and reference types in C# is critical. Understanding how these kinds function, how they are kept in memory, and how they interact with one another forms the foundation for designing fast, maintainable, and robust code.

Value types, with their direct storage of data and independence from one another, provide a measure of safety by eliminating undesired side effects caused by changes in separate portions of our code. On the other hand, reference types provide significant tools for creating complex data structures and enabling more profound interaction between objects due to their common access to data.

The correct use and manipulation of these types are essential in object-oriented programming. They not only help with memory management and application speed, but they also add to code clarity. This understanding enables developers to avoid defects and errors caused by inappropriate data processing, resulting in more effective debugging and code reviews.

Furthermore, knowing whether the implementing classes are value types or reference types might influence the design and interaction of the systems inside our product while working with interfaces in C#. Because interfaces create a class's contract, understanding the subtleties of value types and reference types can help us better design these contracts and anticipate how they will be used and interacted with.

Being aware of value types and reference types will lead to the production of high-quality software in the long run. It is an integral part of learning C# and object-oriented programming in general, and it will surely help you on your way to becoming a software developer. The breadth of your knowledge of these essential concepts will determine your software programs' quality, efficiency, and dependability.

Understanding virtual, override, and new keywords

In interfaces, virtual, override, and new are terms used in OOP, a programming paradigm that uses **objects** to create applications and programs. These objects, built on classes and interfaces, allow for more complicated but structured systems.

Key virtual

In a base class, `this` keyword is used to declare that a method, property, indexer, or event can be overridden in classes that derive from it. Simply put, it says, *Hey, if any class inherits from me, it can change the behavior of this method/property/indexer/event*. It is a mechanism to give default behavior in derived classes that can be selectively replaced.

Key override

This keyword is used in a derived class to modify or extend the behavior of a base class method, property, indexer, or event. *I know I stole this method from my base class, but I want to do it differently*, it says. This keyword requires the virtual keyword to declare the method in the base class.

Key new

This keyword is used to hide a method, property, indexer, or event inherited from the base class in a derived class.

In C#, an interface is analogous to a class contract. *Any class implementing me must provide an implementation for these methods/properties/indexers/events*, it says. It does not, however, give any functionality. It just specifies the shape of the classes.

Let us look at a real-world example. Consider a car manufacturing plant. The process of making a car can be viewed as a method.

The base class is analogous to a basic car blueprint. It states that all automobiles (derived classes) must have a production process (method). It is stated as a virtual method so that other sorts of cars (such as sports cars or a truck) can modify (or override) the process to meet their requirements.

The **new** keyword comes into play when a particular type of car, such as an electric vehicle, refuses to use the fundamental manufacturing process. It wishes to define its procedure. As a result, it conceals the original method and employs its new way.

The interface is analogous to factory instructions that specify how the manufacturing process should be carried out. Any factory-built car (class) must adhere to these criteria (implement the interface).

Let us look at these ideas with a basic example. Assume we are creating a system for a car manufacturing plant that includes a database for storing information about various types of automobiles.

First, let us develop an **IDbConnection** interface to represent a database connection:

```
1. public interface IDbConnection
2. {
3.     void Connect();
4.     void Disconnect();
5. }
```

Assume we have two classes that implement this interface, **SqlServerConnection** and **MySqlConnection**:

```
1. public class SqlServerConnection : IDbConnection
2. {
3.     public void Connect()
4.     {
5.         // Connect to SQL Server
6.     }
7.
8.     public void Disconnect()
9.     {
10.         // Disconnect from SQL Server
11.     }
12. }
13.
14. public class MySqlConnection : IDbConnection
15. {
16.     public void Connect()
17.     {
18.         // Connect to MySQL
19.     }
20.
21.     public void Disconnect()
22.     {
23.         // Disconnect from MySQL
24.     }
25. }
```

Let us make an introductory class called **Vehicle** and a derived class called **Car**. We will suppose all cars have a **Manufacture** method. However, we would like to change how this way is implemented for a **Car**. So, in the base class, we use the virtual keyword, and in the derived class, we override:

```
1.  public class Vehicle
2.  {
3.      public virtual void Manufacture(IDbConnection connection)
4.      {
5.          // Basic manufacturing implementation
6.          connection.Connect();
7.          // Vehicle manufacturing
8.          connection.Disconnect();
9.      }
10. }
11.
12. public class Car : Vehicle
13. {
14.     public override void Manufacture(IDbConnection connection)
15.     {
16.         // Car-specific manufacturing implementation
17.         connection.Connect();
18.         // Car manufacturing
19.         connection.Disconnect();
20.     }
21. }
```

Assume we have another class, **Truck**, that likewise inherits from **Vehicle**, but we want to hide the parent class **Manufacture** implementation in this case. We will utilize the **new** keyword:

```
1.  public class Truck : Vehicle
2.  {
3.      public new void Manufacture(IDbConnection connection)
4.      {
5.          // Truck-specific manufacturing implementation
6.          connection.Connect();
7.          // Truck manufacturing
8.          connection.Disconnect();
9.      }
10. }
```

We may now use the proper **Manufacture** implementation depending on the type of vehicle we are producing:

```
1. Vehicle vehicle1 = new Car();
2. vehicle1.Manufacture(new SqlServerConnection());
3.
4. Vehicle vehicle2 = new Truck();
5. vehicle2.Manufacture(new MySqlConnection());
```

In the preceding example, **vehicle1.Manufacture(new   SqlServerConnection())** will use the **Car** class's **Manufacture** implementation, but **vehicle2.Manufacture(new MySqlConnection())** will use the **Truck** class's **Manufacture** implementation.

Here is another example of how these keywords could be applied to classes and interfaces:

```
1. public interface IVehicle
2. {
3.     void Drive();
4. }
5.
6. public class Vehicle : IVehicle
7. {
8.     public virtual void Drive()
9.     {
10.         Console.WriteLine("The vehicle drives.");
11.     }
12. }
13.
14. public class Car : Vehicle
15. {
16.     public override void Drive()
17.     {
18.         Console.WriteLine("The car drives.");
19.     }
20. }
21.
22. public class Truck : Vehicle
23. {
24.     public new void Drive()
25.     {
26.         Console.WriteLine("The truck drives.");
27.     }
28. }
```

In this example, the **vehicle** is an introductory class that offers a virtual implementation of the **Drive** method required by the **IVehicle** interface. This implementation is overridden by the **Car** class, which provides its version. The **Truck** class likewise has its implementation but hides the base class method, not override it.

Understanding and properly implementing the approaches associated with the virtual, override, new keywords, and interface implementation are vital for developers and solution architects. These methods promote the creation of sturdy, well-structured, and fluid systems.

Understanding and employing these strategies facilitates collaboration and code comprehension in big teams, as each team member can readily grasp the system's structure, improving overall code quality and efficiency.

Such strategies are also helpful in smaller teams or projects with tight deadlines. Efficient inheritance and interface implementation can result in a better-organized codebase and shorter development cycles, allowing the team to fulfill project deadlines while delivering high-quality software.

Furthermore, it is critical to recognize that the efficient application of these strategies can considerably impact the financial elements of software development. Well-structured, maintainable code facilitates adjustments and upgrades, resulting in less time spent implementing new features or making necessary changes. This efficiency helps to keep expenses under control, which is critical because more excellent development time frequently translates into higher expenditures, reducing revenues.

Mastering these strategies is therefore critical for developing high-quality software and practical team cooperation, fulfilling project deadlines, and assuring the financial feasibility of the software development process.

Abstract classes vs. interfaces

Understanding the distinctions between abstract classes and interfaces is essential when working with object-oriented programming languages such as C#. While all of these constructs allow us to build methods and attributes that all classes must have, they are utilized in different settings and have different rules and capabilities.

In C#, an abstract class is a type of class that cannot be instantiated on its own. It is frequently used as a basis class for additional classes. Abstract classes can define abstract methods that are declared but not implemented; these methods must be implemented in any non-abstract child class. An abstract class may also provide default behavior through implemented methods that descendant classes may utilize or override. This functionality allows us to exchange code amongst numerous closely related classes.

Conversely, an interface is an entirely abstract set of members that any class can implement, not simply those descended from a specific parent. Any methods stated in an interface are automatically considered abstract, and any class that uses the interface must implement the relevant methods. C# interfaces accomplish complete abstraction and multiple inheritance, which are not native C# features. Unlike abstract classes, interfaces cannot contain fields, attributes, or methods with any implementation.

When deciding between an abstract class and an interface, consider whether you need to provide default behavior, in which case an abstract class is preferable, or if you need to ensure that specific methods or properties exist in the implementing classes, in which case an interface is preferable. Generate an abstract class if you intend to generate several component versions. Abstract classes make it straightforward to version your components. When a modification is made to a base class, all classes that inherit from that class are immediately updated to reflect the change.

With these ideas in mind, let us use a real-world scenario incorporating living beings—animals and plants—to demonstrate these principles:

```
1.  // Abstract class LivingBeing
2.  public abstract class LivingBeing
3.  {
4.      public abstract void Grow();
5.  }
6.
7.  // Class Animal inherits from LivingBeing
8.  public class Animal : LivingBeing
9.  {
10.     public override void Grow()
11.     {
12.         Console.WriteLine("Animals grow by eating food and exercising.");
13.     }
14. }
15.
16. // Class Plant inherits from LivingBeing
17. public class Plant : LivingBeing
18. {
19.     public override void Grow()
20.     {
21.         Console.WriteLine("Plants grow by photosynthesis.");
22.     }
23. }
```

LivingBeing is an abstract class with an abstract method **Grow()** in the preceding example. This function is then implemented in the **Animal** and **Plant** derived classes.

Let us look at an interface sample now:

```
1. // Interface
2. public interface ILivingBeing
3. {
4.     void Grow();
5. }
6.
7. // Class Animal implements ILivingBeing
8. public class Animal : ILivingBeing
9. {
10.     public void Grow()
11.     {
12.         Console.
    WriteLine("Animals grow by eating food and exercising.");
13.     }
14. }
15.
16. // Class Plant implements ILivingBeing
17. public class Plant : ILivingBeing
18. {
19.     public void Grow()
20.     {
21.         Console.WriteLine("Plants grow by photosynthesis.");
22.     }
23. }
```

ILivingBeing is an interface that declares the **Grow()** method in this scenario. This interface is implemented by the **Animal** and **Plant** classes, which define the **Grow()** method.

Finally, abstract classes and interfaces can enforce that specified methods exist in certain classes. The primary distinction is that an abstract class can provide some default behavior that can be shared across several classes. In contrast, an interface guarantees that a method will be present in the classes that implement it without providing any implementation details.

The impact of knowing when to use abstract classes versus interfaces in C#

Understanding when to use abstract classes and interfaces in C# is more than just a theory; it may substantially impact your software solutions' quality, flexibility, and maintainability. The right decision can result in code that is easier to comprehend, more efficient to maintain, and more adaptable to changing requirements.

Abstract classes are ideal when there is a clear, hierarchical relationship between classes and you want them to share standard functionality and behavior. This method promotes a solid organizational structure in your software, making it more readable and manageable.

Conversely, interfaces are an effective tool for developing pluggable software components, enforcing specified behaviors across unrelated classes, and permitting a form of multiple inheritance. It can result in highly adaptable systems that can easily adjust to changing business requirements without extensive refactoring.

Both constructs are critical in developing durable, scalable, and efficient software. Teams that adhere to robust design principles will create systems that are more standardized, secure, and capable of continuous evolution and easy maintenance.

When teams emphasize understanding and accurately executing these principles, the result is better-suited software to satisfy business goals. This commitment to quality and consistency may give a significant competitive advantage by allowing for quicker feature delivery, more efficient use of resources, and the ability to adapt rapidly and effectively to changes in the business environment.

In summary, using abstract classes and interfaces with care is much more than good programming practice. It is a strategic decision with substantial business implications.

Role of interfaces in enforcing contracts

An interface defines a contract in OOP context, specifically in C#. This contract is a set of defined methods, attributes, and events that the implementing classes or structs must implement.

In this context, **contract** refers to an agreement on how software components should interact. It specifies the syntax of the interaction, stating what inputs are necessary and what outputs are expected, but does not detail how the process operates inside. This abstract nature allows for flexibility, allowing multiple classes to implement the same interface in various ways while retaining a consistent framework for dealing with those classes.

The concept is analogous to a real-world contract in that it states what each party should do and what duties each party has. Contracts in C# are defined through interfaces. In C#, an interface is a reference type that defines a set of members but does not implement these members. Any class or struct that implements the interface must support the interface's members.

In practice, consider a vehicle production situation. We have several types of vehicles, such as cars, trucks, and motorbikes, which may be taxed differently. This circumstance might be represented using C# interfaces as follows:

```
1. public interface IVehicle
2. {
```

```csharp
3.      string Model { get; set; }
4.      double Price { get; set; }
5.      double GetTaxRate();
6. }
7.
8. public class Car : IVehicle
9. {
10.     public string Model { get; set; }
11.     public double Price { get; set; }
12.
13.     public double GetTaxRate()
14.     {
15.         // Specific implementation for cars.
16.         return this.Price * 0.18;
17.     }
18. }
19.
20. public class Truck : IVehicle
21. {
22.     public string Model { get; set; }
23.     public double Price { get; set; }
24.
25.     public double GetTaxRate()
26.     {
27.         // Specific implementation for trucks.
28.         return this.Price * 0.15;
29.     }
30. }
31.
32. public class Motorcycle : IVehicle
33. {
34.     public string Model { get; set; }
35.     public double Price { get; set; }
36.
37.     public double GetTaxRate()
38.     {
39.         // Specific implementation for motorcycles.
40.         return this.Price * 0.10;
41.     }
42. }
```

IVehicle is an interface that defines a contract in this example. The contract states that any **IVehicle** must have a model, a price, and a means to calculate the tax rate. Then, because **Car**, **Truck**, and **Motorcycle** implement this interface, they must give an implementation for the **GetTaxRate()** method, each with its unique characteristics.

This structure enables client code to interact with any object that implements the **IVehicle** interface, regardless of vehicle implementation specifics. It is an example of polymorphism, a key concept in object-oriented programming. Furthermore, leveraging interfaces to establish contracts enables the development of more modular and reusable programs.

Understanding how to correctly build and implement contracts in interfaces is critical to maintaining a system's and its data's integrity. Such contracts ensure that objects interact consistently with one another, offering a transparent and trustworthy structure that drives the evolution of a solution. Developers may ensure the system works as expected under various conditions by correctly applying contracts and preventing unpredictable behaviors that might lead to data inconsistencies or system failure.

Furthermore, leveraging these contracts might give developers a competitive advantage. In a team environment where work is separated into squads, interfaces can help maintain a consistent coding standard across the system. It aids in the coordination of activities, the reduction of misconceptions and miscommunications, and the speeding up of the development process. It is advantageous in the setting of a business system, where data integrity and system stability are crucial for ongoing operations.

As a result, the system is more durable, maintainable, and scalable, allowing it to respond to changes in business requirements or technology improvements, ultimately boosting operational profitability. As a result, interfaces and the contracts they enforce are practical tools that developers may use to design high-quality, dependable, and efficient software systems.

Understanding System.Object and the inheritance hierarchy in C#

The term OOP refers to a programming paradigm in which code is written with the idea of objects in mind—which can comprise both data (in the form of fields, also known as **attributes** or **properties**) and code (in the form of procedures, also known as **methods**). This idea facilitates the creation of complicated code structures while encouraging code reuse and modularity.

In .NET, which contains the C# language, all classes are, directly or indirectly, inheritors of the base class **System.Object**. All classes use the same methods and attributes defined in the **System.Object** class. This idea is an essential component of the inheritance hierarchy.

Now consider how a string object in C# can compute the sum of two strings representing numbers. First, we must determine whether the strings can be transformed into numbers.

We transform the strings into numbers and then add the numbers if they can. We throw an exception or return an error message if they cannot be transformed. Here is an example of code that accomplishes this:

```
1.  public static double SumStringsAsNumbers(string str1, string str2)
2.  {
3.      if (double.TryParse(str1, out double num1) && double.TryParse
    (str2, out double num2))
4.      {
5.          return num1 + num2;
6.      }
7.      else
8.      {
9.          throw new ArgumentException("Both arguments must be
    convertible to a double.");
10.     }
11. }
```

This method accepts two strings as arguments. Each string is converted to a double using the **double.TryParse** method. If both conversions succeed, the numbers are added together, and the sum is returned. An exception is thrown if either conversion fails. Because the string class in C# derives from **System.Object**, it can access the base class's many proper methods and attributes.

Let us go diving into this situation. It is critical to realize that in C#, every type derives directly or indirectly from **System**, whether a user-defined class, a struct, or a predefined type like **int** or **double.Object**. It is why, in C#, every type contains system-defined functions such as **ToString()**, **GetHashCode()**, and **Equals(object obj).Object type**.

Inheritance

One of the essential notions of OOP is inheritance. It is a way to create a new class based on an existing one. The base class members are passed down to the new class, a derived class. This existing class is referred to as a base class. Inheritance enables code reuse and can aid in establishing relationships between classes.

We do not see inheritance in action in our string-to-number conversion example, but every class, including string, derives directly or indirectly from **System.Object**. For example, every string object can call the **ToString()** function specified in **System.Object**.

Polymorphism

Polymorphism is another important OOP notion. It permits objects from various classes related through inheritance to be considered to belong to the same superclass. This results in more adaptable and readily maintainable programming. Both value types (like structs) and reference types (like classes) are ultimately derived from **System.Object** in the .NET environment, allowing for some polymorphism when working with different types.

For example, we can have a method that accepts an **Object** parameter. Because all types originate from **Objects**, such a method might accept any parameter. However, utilizing an **Object** as a type should be done cautiously, as it can result in more difficulty in comprehending and maintaining code.

To explain this, let us edit the prior example:

```
1.  public static double SumObjectsAsNumbers(object obj1, object obj2)
2.  {
3.      if (obj1 is string str1 && double.TryParse(str1, out double num1) &&
4.          obj2 is string str2 && double.TryParse(str2, out double num2))
5.      {
6.          return num1 + num2;
7.      }
8.      else
9.      {
10.         throw new ArgumentException("Both arguments must be convertible to a double.");
11.     }
12. }
```

Polymorphism is used here by accepting any object type and testing whether it is a string that can be turned into a number. As a result, our method can now handle a broader range of inputs.

But keep in mind that with great power comes great responsibility. When using an **Object** as a type, you must frequently utilize type checking and casting, making your code more complex and error-prone if not appropriately handled.

Conclusion

Interfaces, inheritance, and polymorphism are three concepts that are very important in the field of C# programming, and the chapter that you have just finished reading provides an in-depth investigation into each of these subjects. This chapter aims to provide a comprehensive knowledge of these concepts to shed light on their crucial role in constructing and developing resilient, scalable, and efficient software systems. In addition, it highlights the importance of these concepts when it comes to adjusting software systems to suit the ever-changing requirements of businesses.

In addition, this chapter explores the contrast between value types and reference types, a subject that is of utmost importance in the context of the C# programming environment.

By understanding these two separate categories, you can comprehend how they interact with memory management and the consequences for the system's overall performance. Understanding when and how to utilize each type may lead to more efficient code, improving the program's overall performance.

In summary, this chapter is a valuable resource. Its mission is to make it easier for developers to create robust, adaptable, and easy-to-maintain software systems. In doing so, it hopes to contribute to the landscape of effective and efficient programming approaches. You are well on your approach to unlocking the enormous potential of C# and the .NET platform in general if you internalize and put into practice the ideas included in this content.

In the next chapter, we will look at text handling in C# within the .NET framework. Focusing on the **System.String** class and associated types like DateTime, TimeSpan, encoding, and regex explore these classes' architectural basis and practical implementation. It will also discuss common challenges and pitfalls in working with strings, dates, and times, equipping developers with the knowledge to navigate these complexities.

Join our book's Discord space

Join the book's Discord Workspace for Latest updates, Offers, Tech happenings around the world, New Release and Sessions with the Authors:

https://discord.bpbonline.com

CHAPTER 7
.NET Toolbox

Introduction

Strings are essential in many of our applications. They are one of the most fundamental data types in the .NET framework, providing numerous ways to interact with the text. We will investigate how strings are implemented in .NET. They are considered the finest methods for manipulating them. And about date and time formats, various encodings, or the complexities of regular expressions, this is the beginning. This chapter gets into the system in-depth, string class, with associated types such as DateTime, TimeSpan, encoding, and regex. We will explain the architectural foundations and rationale behind these classes' design choices and walk you through their practical implementation in various contexts. In addition, we will discuss common problems and potential dangers we, as developers, face when working with strings, dates, and times in C#. By this chapter's end, you will better understand text handling in C# and the larger .NET environment.

Structure

This chapter covers the following topics:

- Understanding System.String and string manipulation techniques
- Working with dates and times in .NET
- Regular expressions in .NET
- Understanding and using .NET collection types

- Working with arrays and tuples
- Understanding nullable types in C#
- Manipulating strings with StringBuilder
- Parsing dates, times, and numbers in .NET
- Understanding .NET format strings
- Using System.Guid and other common .NET types

Objectives

We are going to go into mastering the system in this chapter. String class, as well as the manipulation of dates, times, and strings within .NET; the use of regular expressions; the working with collections, arrays, and tuples; the comprehension of the notion of nullable types and StringBuilder; the parsing of data; the comprehension of .NET format strings; and the exploration of the use of system. In addition to other common .NET types, **Globally Unique Identifier (GUID)** is supported.

Understanding System.String and string manipulation techniques

In .NET, the `System.String` class represents strings. It is one of the framework's most frequently used classes, and understanding its architecture can provide significant insights into its behavior and performance characteristics.

The `System.String` architecture is broken down as follows:

- **Immutable**: One of the most essential properties of a `System.String` is its immutability. It means that a string cannot be modified once it is formed. All operations that appear to modify a string (for example, concatenation and replacement) return a new string.

- **Interning**: The .NET runtime improves string storage through a technique known as interning. When a string is interned, its value is saved in memory in a specific table. When a new string with an identical value is produced, the runtime does not allocate new memory; instead, it simply refers to the string in the intern table. This method is particularly applicable to string literals.

- **Storage**: In .NET, strings are stored as a series of UTF-16 code units. Every character is represented by two bytes (16 bits).

- **Length**: Each string object knows its length (the number of characters it contains). This data is saved as a field within the string object, which makes operations like Length highly efficient.

- **Memory layout**: The **System.String** object in memory comprises a few overhead bytes for the object header, followed by the string length, and finally, the string data (sequence of characters). The string data is saved within the string object inline.

The **System** is the sixth method. The **String** class includes a plethora of methods for performing various operations such as searching (**IndexOf**, **LastIndexOf**), editing (**Replace**, **Remove**), checking (**StartsWith**, **EndsWith**), splitting (**Split**), and many more.

- **Null vs. empty**: A string can be empty or null. A legitimate string instance with no characters is an empty string (**""**). However, a null string (**null**) denotes the lack of a string. There is also a static member **String.Empty** symbolizes an empty string to encourage better practice over **""**.

  String comparisons can be complicated due to varied requirements (case-sensitive, culture-specific, and so on). To tackle these cases, **System.String** includes methods such as compare, equals, and overloads that receive StringComparison enumerations to indicate the appropriate comparison method.

- **String concatenation**: The + operator or the concat method can concatenate strings. Due to the immutability of strings, repeated concatenations might be wasteful. **StringBuilder** is recommended in such cases.

- **Interpolation and formatting**: For string formatting, the **System.String** class provides static methods such as format. String interpolation (**$"Hello name"**) in newer versions of C# provides a more understandable approach to incorporating expressions into string literals.

- **Internals and reference source**: The .NET reference source is available online if you want to go deeper into the architecture and behavior of **System.String**. It displays the class's actual source code, allowing you to view how functions are implemented.

In conclusion, the **System.String** class in .NET provides a versatile and efficient way to work with text. Its architectural and design decisions, such as immutability, offer benefits and drawbacks that developers should consider when manipulating strings in performance-sensitive applications.

The importance of the System.String

We are reintroducing a **System.String** (or simply string) represents text as a sequence of Unicode characters. This fundamental data type is a programming pillar, particularly in applications involving user interaction, data storage, and communication.

Understanding the importance of text processing extends far beyond its technical applications.

Here are some uses of **System.String**:

- **Text processing's universality**: Text processing is used in almost every application, whether for user input, logging, configuration, or data storage.

- **Communication**: Strings are widely used to convey data between APIs, websites, and databases.

- **Data representation**: From dates and timings to serialized complex objects, strings may represent a wide range of data types in a human-readable manner.

- **Databases**: Most databases hold a large amount of data as text. Strings are essential for database queries, data storage, and retrieval.

Strings in databases, it is usual practice to use strings to save and retrieve data from databases. This is why:

- **Flexibility**: In textual form, strings can represent nearly any data type.

- **Readability**: Storing data as strings can improve the readability of raw database material. This can be useful for administrators or developers who need to check the database directly.

- **Search and query**: Using SQL's text manipulation methods, text-based data may be readily searched, filtered, and queried.

- **Interoperability**: Text data can be easily transferred across systems, languages, or applications, resulting in more excellent compatibility.

Memory

In C#, the `System.The` maximum array length limits string class since strings are essentially character arrays (`char[]`) behind the scenes.

Here is how the C# manages the memory string on the device.

Maximum character count

A string can theoretically hold up to `Int32.MaxValue` characters, or 2,147,483,647. However, you can never allocate a string of this length due to memory overhead and other system limits.

Memory restrictions

It is critical to recognize that it is theoretically feasible to allocate enormously big strings, but it is rarely a good idea. Such actions would be highly memory-intensive and drastically reduce an application's performance. When dealing with large amounts of text, you should often use streams or other solutions that do not require loading everything into memory.

The Unicode

The majority of the world's written languages are encoded using the Unicode character system, which is a character system encoding. Unicode's principal purpose is to unify the various character sets that have previously been used, making it easier to transmit and handle text data on a global scale.

Goals and features of Unicode

The following are the goals and features of Unicode:

- **Universal character set**: Unicode strives to give a unique code point (numeric value) for every character, regardless of platform, device, application, or language.

- **Unicode encodings**: Unicode can be represented in various encoding ways. The most common are:

    o **UTF-8**: Uses one byte for the first 128 characters (ASCII) and up to four bytes for additional characters. It is commonly used because it is compatible with ASCII and works well with Latin-based languages.

    o **UTF-16**: This format uses 16-bit units. It is, for example, the native encoding of Windows and .NET.

    o **UTF-32**: Uses 32-bit units to provide a set length for each character, which might simplify certain operations but consumes more memory.

- **Backward compatibility**: Unicode incorporates various character sets to ensure backward compatibility. For example, the first 128 Unicode code points correspond to the ASCII character set.

- **Depth**: Unicode has letters, numerals, symbols, diacritics, punctuation marks, and emojis. Text attributes such as case mappings, character properties, and deconstruction are also supported.

- **Logical order**: Unicode stores characters in a logical order (in which they are spoken) rather than visual order for scripts not written left-to-right (such as Arabic or Hebrew).

Importance of Unicode

Some points highlighting the importance of Unicode are listed as follows:

- **Globalization**: As the world becomes more interconnected, apps and services are increasingly required to support many languages and scripts. Unicode standardizes text encoding for practically all world languages.

- **Data integrity**: Because Unicode provides a distinct code point for each character, there is no ambiguity or overlap. It ensures that text is constant and unmodified between systems, platforms, or apps.

- **Standardization**: Because many technologies and protocols (such as HTML, XML, and JSON) rely on Unicode, it has become an essential standard in modern tech.

- **Historical preservation**: Unicode considers historical scripts, assisting in preserving humanity's linguistic heritage.

Assume we are developing a web application that will service users from all over the world. A user in Japan may enter text in Kanji, while another in Russia may enter text in Cyrillic, and yet another in India may enter text in Devanagari. Unicode allows your application to handle, save, and display text from these scripts without requiring various character encodings.

Finally, Unicode is a cornerstone of international software development, allowing for consistent text representation across platforms and languages. Its widespread use has substantially eliminated the challenges and inconsistencies associated with multiple-character encodings.

What is ASCII

American Standard Code for Information Interchange (**ASCII**) is a character encoding standard that gives each character a unique number, allowing them to be represented and controlled on computers. Letters, digits, symbols, and control characters are among the characters.

- **Early beginnings (1960s)**: The **American National Standards Institute** (**ANSI**) created ASCII in the early 1960s to replace other telegraphy codes such as Baudot and Murray. The goal was to provide a standardized text encoding technique for the rapidly growing computer and technology industries.

- **Standardization**: The initial version of ASCII, ASA X3.4-1963, was issued in 1963. It was changed several times, with the most prevalent version being the 1986 7-bit ASCII (or US-ASCII) standard.

- **7-bit character set**: Because the original ASCII employs 7 bits, it can represent 128 characters (from 0 to 127). Among these characters are:

  o **Control characters (0-31 and 127)**: These are non-printable characters that govern how text is processed. The carriage return and line feed are two examples.

  o **Printable characters (32-126)**: Letters (A-Z, a-z), digits (0-9), punctuation marks, and several special symbols are all included.

The importance of ASCII is listed as follows:

- ASCII is the foundation of several modern character encodings, including UTF-8 (a standard Unicode encoding). For instance, in order to preserve backward compatibility, the first 128 characters of UTF-8 are exactly the same as ASCII.

- **Computer pervasiveness**: ASCII was the de facto standard for early home computers and the internet. It enabled these systems to easily exchange, share, and process text data.

- **Protocol standard**: Many communication protocols used ASCII, particularly in the early days of networking and the internet. HTTP and SMTP, for example, utilize ASCII for many of its underlying processes.

- **Hardware language**: Many hardware devices (such as keyboards) and lower-level software functions still use ASCII.

- **String manipulation and programming**: ASCII is frequently encountered when dealing with text in programming, particularly in systems programming or older data formats. Understanding ASCII values is helpful for parsing bespoke binary files or working with outdated protocols.

In conclusion, while modern systems and applications have mostly gone beyond ASCII to more inclusive and comprehensive character sets (such as Unicode), ASCII's legacy and effect remain significant. A basic familiarity with ASCII is helpful for anyone in IT or software development, especially when working with older systems, specific hardware, or lower-level programming jobs.

ISO encoding

Strings are natively represented using Unicode (specifically, UTF-16). Therefore, you can directly include characters from various languages (Latin, Arabic, Japanese, Chinese, and many others) without any particular encoding conversion. It is one of the strengths of .NET's string handling.

When interacting with external data sources or systems that utilize different encodings, you may need to convert between these encodings and .NET's native UTF-16.

Here is an example of how you might handle strings in C# for different character sets:

Directly in code:
```
1. string latinText = "Hello, world!";
2. string arabicText = "مرحبا بك في C#";
3. string japaneseText = "C#へようこそ ";
4. string chineseText = "你好ç # ";
```

Reading from an external source with ISO-8859-1 encoding:
```
1. using System.Text;
2.
```

```
3. string filePath = @"path_to_your_file.txt";
4. Encoding gb2312 = Encoding.GetEncoding("GB2312");
5.
6. try
7. {
8.     using StreamReader reader = new StreamReader(filePath, gb2312);
9.     string content = reader.ReadToEnd();
10.    Console.WriteLine(content);
11. }
12. catch (Exception ex)
13. {
14.    Console.WriteLine("An error occurred: " + ex.Message);
15. }
```

In this example:

- We build a **GB2312** encoding instance.
- We then use a **StreamReader** to read the content of a file encoded in this manner.
- Finally, the content is written to the console.

String manipulation techniques

String manipulation is a fundamental programming feature. Working with strings in C# and in many other programming languages may be accomplished using a variety of different approaches and methods. Here are a few examples of standard string manipulation techniques:

- **Concatenation**: Combining two or more strings:
  ```
  1. string hello = "Hello, ";
  2. string world = "World!";
  3. string combined = hello + world; // "Hello, World!"
  ```
- **Substring extraction**: Taking a piece of a string and extracting it:
  ```
  1. string text = "Hello, World!";
  2. string sub = text.Substring(7, 5); // "World"
  ```
- **Searching**: Locating or determining the existence of a substring:
  ```
  1. string text = "Hello, World!";
  2. int position = text.IndexOf("World"); // 7
  ```
- **Replacing**: This function replaces all occurrences of a substring:
  ```
  1. string text = "Hello, World!";
  2. string replaced = text.
     Replace("World", "Universe"); // "Hello, Universe!"
  ```

- **Splitting**: Dividing a string into sections using delimiters:
    1. string text = "apple,banana,cherry";
    2. string[] fruits = text.
       Split(','); // ["apple", "banana", "cherry"]
- **Trimming**: Removing whitespace (or other characters) from a string's start and/or end:
    1. string text = "   trimmed   ";
    2. string result = text.Trim(); // "trimmed"
- **Case manipulation**: Changing a string's case to uppercase or lowercase:
    1. string text = "Hello";
    2. string upper = text.ToUpper(); // "HELLO"
    3. string lower = text.ToLower(); // "hello"
- **String comparison**: Checking strings for equality or order. It is possible in C# by using methods such as **string.Equals()**, string. Depending on the needs (case-sensitive, culture-specific, etc.), **compare()** and the **==** operator can be used:
    1. bool isEqual = StringComparer.OrdinalIgnoreCase.
       Equals(str1, str2); // true, because it ignores case
- **Padding**: Is the process of adding characters to a string until it reaches a certain length:
    1. string text = "42";
    2. string padded = text.PadLeft(5, '0'); // "00042"
- **Joining**: Combines an array or a list of strings into a single string using a given delimiter:
    1. string[] words = { "Hello", "World" };
    2. string joined = string.Join(" ", words); // "Hello World"
- **Formatting**: Use string interpolation or string to format values into a string template:
    1. string name = "Alice";
    2. string greeting = $"Hello, {name}!"; // Using string interpolation
    3. string formatted = string.Format("Hello, {0}!", name); // Using string.Format
- **Encoding and decoding**: As stated in encoding, converting strings to and from different **Encoding.GetEncoding()**:
    1. using System.Text;
    2. string originalString = "Hello, World!";
    3. Encoding.RegisterProvider(CodePagesEncodingProvider.Instance);

```
4.  Encoding win1252 = Encoding.GetEncoding("Windows-1252");
5.  byte[] encodedBytes = win1252.GetBytes(originalString);
6.  foreach (byte b in encodedBytes)
7.  {
8.      Console.Write($"{b:x2} «);
9.  }
10. Console.WriteLine();
11. string decodedString = win1252.GetString(encodedBytes);
12. Console.WriteLine(decodedString);
```

Note: To use Windows-1252, you need to add to your .NET project System. Text.Encoding.CodePages and before the use add to an instance like demonstrated in line 3.

Run this **dotnet** command on the terminal's project:

```
1.  dotnet add package System.Text.Encoding.CodePages
```

While Windows-1252 is supported on Windows-based systems, it may not be available by default on other platforms, particularly in specific versions or configurations of the .NET runtime. For example, to support non-Unicode encodings on specific Linux distributions with .NET, you may need to install additional libraries or packages.

Regular expressions is a powerful pattern-matching approach for performing sophisticated string operations like searching, replacing, splitting, and validation. In C#, **System.Text. RegularExpressions.Regex** provided the capability of regex.

Let us go through examples that utilize regex for different purposes:

- **Email validation**:
  ```
  1.  var emailPattern = @"^[\w-]+(\.[\w-]+)*@([\w-]+\.)+[a-zA-Z]
      {2,7}$";
  2.  var emails = new[] { "test@example.com", "invalid-
      email@", "sample@domain.org" };
  3.  foreach (var email in emails)
  4.  {
  5.      Console.WriteLine($"{email} is {(Regex.
      IsMatch(email, emailPattern) ? "valid" : "invalid")}");
  6.  }
  ```

- **Extracting numbers**:
  ```
  1.  var numberPattern = @"\d+";
  2.  var textWithNumbers = "I have 5 apples and 10 oranges.";
  3.  var matches = Regex.Matches(textWithNumbers, numberPattern);
  4.  Console.WriteLine("Numbers extracted:");
  ```

```
5. foreach (Match match in matches)
6. {
7.     Console.WriteLine(match.Value);
8. }
```

- **Replacing whitespace sequences:**

```
1. var whitespacePattern = @"\s+";
2. var spacedText = "This    has    irregular    spaces.";
3. var cleanedText = Regex.
   Replace(spacedText, whitespacePattern, " ");
4. Console.WriteLine($"Original: {spacedText}");
5. Console.WriteLine($"Cleaned: {cleanedText}");
```

Here is the console output:

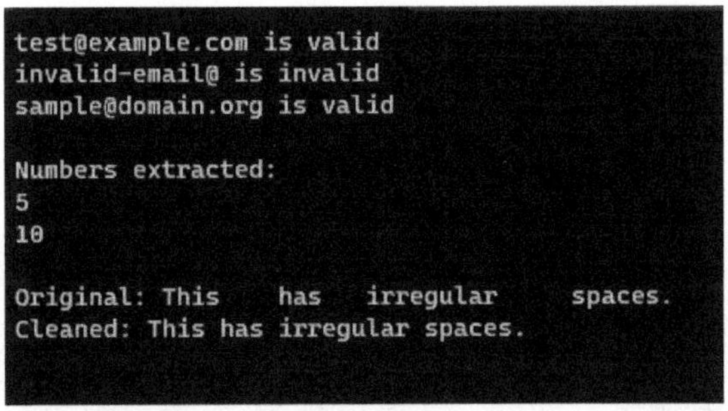

Figure 7.1: Console output

- **Escaping and unescaping:** The process of converting special characters in strings to their escaped versions and vice versa, which is frequently required when working with JSON, XML, or other formats.

```
1. using System.Net;
2.
3. string originalUrlString = "This is a query with special chars
   like & and spaces!";
4. string escapedUrlString = WebUtility.UrlEncode
   (originalUrlString);
5. Console.WriteLine($"Escaped URL: {escapedUrlString}");
6.
7. // URL Unescaping
8. string unescapedUrlString = WebUtility.UrlDecode
   (escapedUrlString);
9. Console.WriteLine($"Unescaped URL: {unescapedUrlString}");
```

Here is the console output:

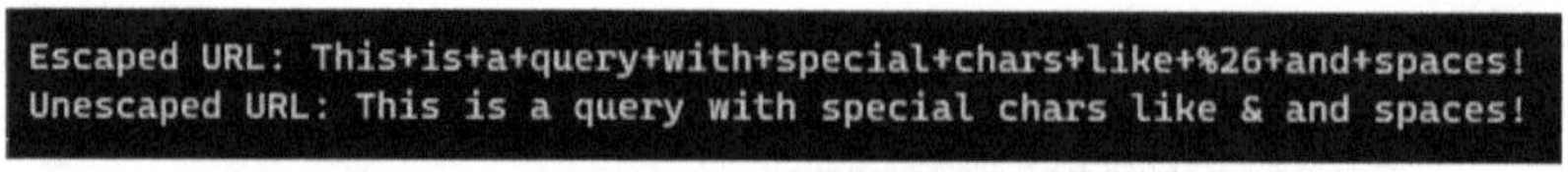

```
Escaped URL: This+is+a+query+with+special+chars+like+%26+and+spaces!
Unescaped URL: This is a query with special chars like & and spaces!
```

Figure 7.2: Console output

- **Length and character access**: Using the **Length** property to return how many characters are in a string or the indexer **[ ]** to access specific characters.

```
1.  string str = "Microsoft C#";
2.  char thirdCharacter = str[2]; // 0-based index, so [2] gets the
    third character
3.  Console.WriteLine($"The third character of the string '{str}'
    is: {thirdCharacter}");
4.  Console.WriteLine($"Characters in the string '{str}':");
5.  for (int I = 0; i < str.Length; i++)
6.  {
7.      Console.WriteLine(str[i]);
8.  }
```

Here is the console output:

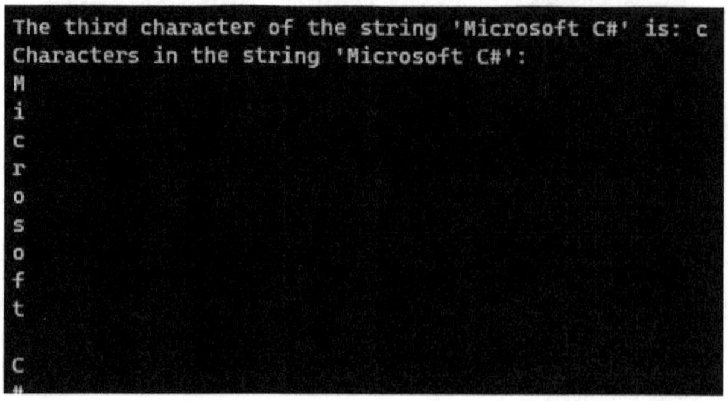

```
The third character of the string 'Microsoft C#' is: c
Characters in the string 'Microsoft C#':
M
i
c
r
o
s
o
f
t

C
#
```

Figure 7.3: Console output

The **String** class in C# provides a **Length** property to get the number of characters and an indexer for direct character access (with a 0-based index). It allows iteration through each character using loops.

StringBuilder: To reduce excessive string construction and copying, it is often recommended to utilize **StringBuilder** instead of the basic string methods in performance-critical cases where several string manipulations occur.

We present you the **System.String** class is a fundamental data type for working with text. You learned about the class's primary characteristics and design considerations, including immutability, interning, storage, and encoding. We also covered standard string manipulation methods and techniques like concatenation, searching, replacing, formatting, and encoding conversion. It also addresses the advantages and disadvantages of using **StringBuilder** in performance-critical settings with frequent string changes.

Finally, we briefly discussed Unicode, ASCII, ISO encoding, and regular expressions. This part aims to give you a basic grasp of how strings function in C# and how to utilize them successfully in various applications.

Working with dates and times in .NET

The system namespace in C# .NET includes the DateTime and TimeSpan classes, among others, for representing and manipulating dates and times. Let us understand and operate with dates and times in C#.

TimeSpan, on the other hand, denotes the length of time or the difference between two dates and times. TimeSpan, unlike DateTime, encapsulates a period rather than a precise point in time. Ticks are also used to represent TimeSpan values, with each tick representing 100 nanoseconds. So, when you think of a TimeSpan as 2 hours, 30 minutes, and 45 seconds, it is a count of ticks that add up to that time.

TimeSpan's strength resides in its adaptability. You can create a TimeSpan instance to represent any length of time, from milliseconds to days, months, or even years. TimeSpan, like DateTime, has characteristics that allow you to study or deconstruct the duration into days, hours, minutes, seconds, and milliseconds. TimeSpan also includes methods for adding and subtracting durations, comparing durations, and converting a duration into a human-readable string.

Calculating the difference between two DateTime values, waiting for a given length using tasks or threads, and scheduling tasks at specific intervals are all common activities with TimeSpan. TimeSpan has the unique property of representing both positive and negative durations. It is convenient when calculating differences between two dates where the order is essential. When you subtract an earlier date from a more current date, you get a positive TimeSpan, but when you reverse the order, you get a negative one.

To summarize, while DateTime and TimeSpan deal with the concept of time, they serve fundamentally different roles in .NET. DateTime grounds our programs in real-world moments, offering reference points. At the same time, TimeSpan assists us in managing and computing durations, intervals, and changes between those points. They form a comprehensive toolkit for practically any time-related activity you may need to execute in a.NET application.

- **The beginning of time in C#**: In contrast to some other systems and languages that use January 1, 1970, as their epoch or the start of time (commonly referred to as the Unix epoch), the DateTime structure in .NET utilizes a different reference date: January 1, 0001 (in the Gregorian calendar). It is commonly known as the *Calendar era*.

  For example, consider creating a new **DateTime** instance with zero ticks:

  ```
  1. DateTime time = new DateTime(0);
  2. Console.WriteLine(time);
  ```

The result is **01/01/0001 00:00:00** (depending on your date and time format settings).

- **C# with Unix timestamp**: While C# starts its calendar period on January 1, 0001, you may still encounter situations where you must work with Unix timestamps (which begin on January 1, 1970). Fortunately, changing from Unix timestamps to **DateTime** is simple:

```
1. // Convert DateTime to Unix timestamp
2. DateTime someDateTime = new DateTime(2023, 8, 11);
3. long unixTimestamp = (someDateTime.
   Ticks - new DateTime(1970, 1, 1).Ticks) / TimeSpan.
   TicksPerSecond;
4.
5. // Convert Unix timestamp back to DateTime
6. DateTime originalDate = new DateTime(1970, 1, 1).
   AddSeconds(unixTimestamp);
```

In summary, **Ticks** in C# are a high-precision time representation. While C# utilizes a calendar era beginning on January 1, 0001, converting to and from Unix timestamps (beginning on January 1, 1970) is a typical operation, especially when dealing with systems that use the Unix epoch as their time reference.

- **C# and UTC**: **Coordinated Universal Time** (**UTC**) is the primary time standard used to control clocks and time worldwide. UTC and **Greenwich Mean Time** (**GMT**) are nearly identical. However, GMT is no longer used for exact timekeeping.

The DateTime structure in C# provides properties that return the current date and time in UTC:

- **DateTime.UtcNow**: Gets the current date and time in UTC format.

When you construct a DateTime object, it has a **Kind** property that might be one of the following:

- **DateTimeKind.Local**: The time is local.
- **DateTimeKind.Utc**: The time is UTC.
- **DateTimeKind.Unspecified**: The time is neither local nor UTC.

Sample converting between UTC and Australia's local DateTime

Because of its enormous area, Australia has numerous time zones:

- **Australian Eastern Standard Time (AEST)**
- **Australian Central Standard Time (ACST)**
- **Australian Western Standard Time (AWST)**

And others, particularly considering daylight saving time changes. You can convert between UTC and local times in C# by using the **TimeZoneInfo** class:

```
1.  // Assuming your DateTime is in AEST
2.  DateTime aestDateTime = new DateTime(2023, 8, 11, 14, 0, 0,
    DateTimeKind.Unspecified); // 2:00 PM AEST
3.
4.  // Get the Australian Eastern Standard Time zone (considering
    daylight saving)
5.  TimeZoneInfo aestZone = TimeZoneInfo.FindSystemTimeZoneById("E.
    Australia Standard Time");
6.
7.  // Convert the AEST DateTime to UTC
8.  DateTime utcDateTime = TimeZoneInfo.ConvertTimeToUtc(aestDateTime,
    aestZone);
9.  Console.WriteLine(utcDateTime);  // This will show the UTC equivalent
    of the provided AEST date and time
```

From UTC to Australia's local time zone:

```
1.  DateTime utcTime = new DateTime(2023, 8, 11, 4, 0, 0,
    DateTimeKind.Utc); // 4:00 AM UTC
2.
3.  // Convert the UTC DateTime to AEST
4.  DateTime localTime = TimeZoneInfo.ConvertTimeFromUtc(utcTime,
    aestZone);
5.  Console.WriteLine(localTime); // This will show the AEST equivalent
    of the provided UTC date and time
```

Replace the string in **FindSystemTimeZoneById** with the proper time zone identification for other Australian time zones.

Note: The time zone identifiers might vary based on the operating system and its updates. Always ensure that you have the correct identifier for your target time zone. If in doubt, you can list all available time zones on your system using TimeZoneInfo. GetSystemTimeZones() and search for the appropriate Australian zones.

Conclusion: In this section, you learned how to manage dates and times in C# using the **DateTime** and **TimeSpan** classes. The distinction between these two classes was clarified, with details on how they represent time using ticks and how to switch between them. The course also discussed handling different time zones, emphasizing UTC and Australian zones, thanks to the **TimeZoneInfo** class. The vital practical applications discussed are crafting **DateTime** instances, finding the interval between dates, transitioning to and from Unix timestamps, and switching between UTC and local time representations. The overall purpose of this section was to provide learners with the information and tools they needed to work with dates and times in C# efficiently and precisely.

Regular expressions in .NET

Regular expressions (**regex** or **regexp**) are character sequences that create a search pattern. They are a powerful text processing tool. They can be used for data validation, scraping, wrangling, and string parsing, among other things.

Regular expressions provide developers with a flexible and fast approach to search, alter, and manipulate textual data in C# and the .NET platform. They are incorporated into the .NET via the `System.Text.RegularExpressions` namespace.

The development of regular expressions can be traced back to theoretical computer science, notably formal language theory. Its primary motivation for its development was to define and discover string patterns. As the world moved towards the computing age, this theoretical principle found practical application in text processing jobs.

Sophisticated regular expressions are resource-intensive backtracking: some regex patterns, particularly those with nested quantifiers, can lead the regex engine to try many permutations before evaluating whether or not a string matches. Backtracking is a procedure that might result in exponential time complexity for particular patterns on specific srings.

- **Ambiguity**: A complicated regex may match a given input in several ways. The regex engine attempts every feasible way, which can be computationally demanding.

- **Non-optimized patterns**: A regex may be constructed inefficiently, causing the regex engine to perform more work than is required.

The most difficulties in learning regular expressions:

- Regular expressions have a succinct and dense syntax that can intimidate newcomers.

- Regular expressions deal with abstract string patterns that might be difficult to understand and comprehend.

- **Language variations**: While the essential notions remain similar, the syntax and behavior of regex might differ slightly from different computer languages, which can be confusing.

- **Difficulties in debugging**: Errors in regular expressions may not always result in traditional errors or exceptions. Instead, they may not match the expected text, which can be more challenging to diagnose.

Sample usage in C# and .NET:

- **Validating an email address**:
  ```
  1. using System.Text.RegularExpressions;
  2.
  ```

```
3. string pattern = @"^[\w-\.]+@([\w-]+\.)+[\w-]{2,4}$";
4. bool isValid = Regex.IsMatch("example@email.com", pattern);
```

- **Extracting all URLs from a text**:
  ```
  1. string pattern = @"https?://([\w-]+\.)+[\w-]+(/[\w- ./?%&=]*)?";
  2. MatchCollection matches = Regex.Matches("Visit https://www.
     example.com for more info.", pattern);
  ```

- **Replacing specific words**:
  ```
  1. string result = Regex.Replace("Hello World", "World", "C#");
  2. // result: "Hello C#"
  ```

- **Splitting a string by multiple delimiters**:
  ```
  1. string[] result = Regex.
     Split("apple,orange;banana:grape", "[,;:]");
  2. // result: ["apple", "orange", "banana", "grape"]
  ```

- **Matching dates in MM/DD/YYYY format**:
  ```
  1. string pattern = @"^(0[1-9]|1[0-2])/(0[1-9]|1\d|2\
     d|3[01])/\d{4}$";
  2. bool isValidDate = Regex.IsMatch("08/11/2023", pattern);
  ```

Regex, the developer's fear

Regex are helpful for text processing, but their thick syntax and subtle behavior can make them difficult to design and maintain. Many developers mention discomfort or even pain while using regex.

Some of the causes behind this sentiment:

- **Steep learning curve**: Regular expression syntax is succinct but not always obvious. The learning curve can be considerable, especially for individuals who do not use regex regularly. When symbols are concatenated, they can have a variety of meanings, giving regex the sense of its language.

- **Difficulties in debugging**: Debugging might be difficult when a regex does not work as planned. Unlike traditional programming, where errors might be more informative, regex mistakes frequently show as *no matches* or *unexpected matches*. It can make determining the root cause difficult.

- **Readability issues**: Regular expressions can grow complex and lengthy. Without sufficient comments or pattern breakdowns, it is difficult for another developer (or even the original creator) to grasp the meaning or rationale behind a given regex pattern after some time.

- **Performance pitfalls**: As previously stated, specific regex patterns can be exceedingly wasteful on particular inputs, resulting in performance issues. Unless developers know the complexities of regex engine behavior, they may mistakenly construct patterns that cause excessive backtracking, costing many CPU resources.

- **Variations across platforms and languages**: While essential regex concepts are similar, there are differences in regex support, features, and behavior across different programming languages and platforms. A pattern in one setting may not work or act differently in another, resulting in inconsistencies.

- **Overkill for simple jobs**: Regex might be overkill for simple string manipulation jobs. However, the allure of a one-liner solution might drive developers to use regex even when more straightforward string functions would work, resulting in excessive complexity.

- **Maintenance issues**: Because of the difficulties with readability and platform variances, keeping regex patterns in codebases may be difficult. Future developers may hesitate to touch or edit an existing regex pattern for fear of breaking it.

- **Fear of the unknown**: Regex may be unfamiliar to many developers. Infrequent exposure paired with the opaque nature of regex might make it seem intimidating, resulting in an avoidance attitude.

Despite these problems, regular expressions remain an essential tool. They can perform sophisticated text processing jobs with brevity that would be difficult with regular string operations. The key for developers is understanding when to use regex, thoroughly annotate their patterns, and guarantee that they are extensively tested against various inputs.

Conclusion: This section examined the idea and actual applications of regular expressions (regex) in the C# and .NET environments. Regex are character sequences that are designed to establish a specific search pattern and are used in a variety of text-processing operations. It includes data validation, scraping, wrangling, and complex string processing. Regex derives from formal language theory and has a succinct yet complex syntax smoothly incorporated into the .NET via the `System.Text.RegularExpressions` namespace.

Furthermore, we investigated the numerous obstacles and roadblocks developers frequently face while working with regex. Among these challenges are the intimidating learning curve, arduous debugging processes, readability concerns, potential performance bottlenecks, inconsistencies across different platforms and languages, the tendency to overcomplicate simple tasks, looming maintenance concerns, and general apprehension stemming from unfamiliarity with regex. The section highlights the necessity of best practices in navigating these hurdles, such as determining whether regex is the most appropriate tool, painstakingly documenting patterns, and thoroughly testing to verify correctness and speed.

To put theory into practice, we provided various examples of how to use regex in C# and .NET. We demonstrated the tremendous variety and power of regex in addressing varied text-processing requirements by using actual scenarios such as email validation, URL extraction from texts, word replacements, string splitting based on numerous delimiters, and date formatting in the MM/DD/YYYY format.

Understanding and using .NET collection types

In computer science and computing, a collection is a grouping of data elements that allows them to be considered a single unit for specific actions. The word collections in .NET refers to classes specially designed to contain, manage, and manipulate a group of objects.

Collections are used for the following purposes:

- **Data grouping**: Collections offer a logical approach to organizing groupings of items. Whether it is an essential list of names or a more sophisticated hierarchy of items, collections make it easy for developers to work with such groupings.

- Unlike arrays, which have a fixed size once initialized, some collections can expand and decrease as needed. It enables flexibility when the quantity of items is unknown ahead of time.

- **Specialized operations**: Depending on the collection type, various operations such as indexing, searching, sorting, or queueing can be implemented effectively.

Benefits of using collections:

- **Efficiency**: Certain collections, such as dictionaries, have quick lookup times for items, which can be vital in performance-sensitive applications.

- **Flexibility**: With a wide range of collection types available, developers can select the one that best meets their requirements.

- Type safety is provided by generic collections, which ensure that only objects of a specific type may be added to the collection, reducing runtime errors.

- In conjunction with technologies like LINQ, collections enable complex actions on data sets, such as filtering, sorting, grouping, and aggregation.

- **Data reading collections and text list manipulation**: Collections are essential in data processing operations. For example, when reading data from a database or a file, the resulting set of records can be kept in a collection for further processing. When combined with LINQ, collections give strong capabilities for manipulating text lists, filtering out extraneous material, transforming data into a desired format, and even analyzing trends and frequencies.

- **Artificial intelligence and neural networks role**: Collections may be used to handle massive volumes of data in the context of artificial intelligence, particularly in neural networks. Layers, neurons, and weights make up neural networks. Collections may be used to represent and modify each of these. As an example:

Neuron layers can be kept in a list or an array.

Matrixes or multi-dimensional arrays can hold the weights that link neurons.

Using collections, managing the structure and state of neural networks becomes more practical and systematic. It is also worth mentioning that collection efficiency guarantees that neural network activities like feed-forward and backpropagation run swiftly and efficiently.

Finally, collections are the foundation for data-centric operations in many applications, providing efficiency, flexibility, and usability. Collections are essential in modern software development, from simple data processing to powering complicated artificial intelligence models.

.NET collection types

To meet the different storage and retrieval needs of applications, the .NET provides a multitude of collection types. Knowing how and when to utilize these collections is critical for .NET developers like us. we bring various .NET collection types and how to manage them, focusing on the LINQ.

There are various collection types available in C# and .NET, but we will concentrate on the ones that are most typically used:

- **Non-generic collections (in System.Collections)**:
    o **ArrayList**: Like List<T>, but not type-safe because it holds an object.
    o **Dictionary<TKey, TValue> HashTable**: A non-generic variant of Dictionary<TKey, TValue>.
    o **Queue**: A non-generic form of Queue<T>.
    o **Stack**: A non-generic form of Stack<T>.
    o **BitArray**: A boolean array used to manage individual bits.

    Here is a sample of use:

```
1.  using System.Collections;
2.
3.  // ArrayList
4.  var arrayList = new ArrayList { "apple", 42, true };
5.  Console.WriteLine($"ArrayList: {string.Join(", ", arrayList.
    Cast<object>())}");
6.
7.  // Hashtable
8.  var hashTable = new Hashtable
9.          {
```

```
10.            { "key1", "value1" },
11.            { "key2", 42 }
12.        };
13. Console.WriteLine($"Hashtable: key1={hashTable["key1"]},
    key2={hashTable["key2"]}");
14.
15. // Queue
16. var queue = new Queue();
17. queue.Enqueue("apple");
18. queue.Enqueue(42);
19. Console.WriteLine($"Queue (after two enqueues): {string.Join(",
    ", queue.Cast<object>())}");
20. var dequeuedValue = queue.Dequeue();
21. Console.WriteLine($"Dequeued from Queue: {dequeuedValue}");
22.
23. // Stack
24. var stack = new Stack();
25. stack.Push("apple");
26. stack.Push(42);
27. Console.WriteLine($"Stack (after two pushes): {string.Join(",
    ", stack.Cast<object>())}");
28. var poppedValue = stack.Pop();
29. Console.WriteLine($"Popped from Stack: {poppedValue}");
30.
31. // BitArray
32. var bitArray = new BitArray(new[] { true, false, true });
33. Console.Write("BitArray: ");
34. foreach (bool bit in bitArray)
35. {
36.     Console.Write(bit + " ");
37. }
```

This is the output:

```
ArrayList: apple, 42, True
Hashtable: key1=value1, key2=42
Queue (after two enqueues): apple, 42
Dequeued from Queue: apple
Stack (after two pushes): 42, apple
Popped from Stack: 42
BitArray: True False True |
```

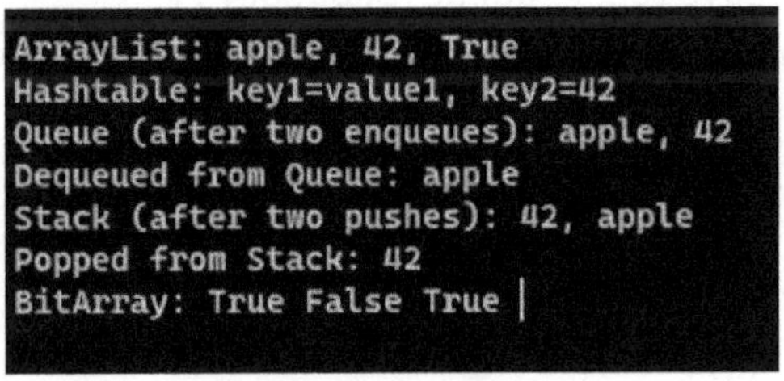

Figure 7.4: Console output

- **Generic collections (in System.Collections.Generic)**: Contains the collection class List<T>, a versatile and type-safe dynamically resizing list. Unlike arrays, the List<T> automatically adjusts its size as elements are added or removed. Because it is generic, it ensures type safety, which means it enforces the storage of elements of a specific datatype, resulting in improved performance and fewer runtime errors.

  o **Dictionary<TKey, TValue>**: A collection of keys and values.

    ▪ FIFO collection in Queue<T>.

    ▪ LIFO collection with Stack<T>.

  o **HashSet<T>**: Create a data structure with no duplicate values.

  o **LinkedList<T>**: A linked list with two elements.

  o **SortedSet<T>**: A set with automatically sorted values.

    ▪ SortedList<TKey, TValue> and SortedDictionary<TKey, TValue> store key-value pairs with automated key sorting. Their internal implementations differ, resulting in a wide range of performance characteristics.

Here is a sample of use:

```
1. var dictionary = new Dictionary<string, string>
2.          {
3.                { "key1", "value1" },
4.                { "key2", "value2" }
5.          };
6. Console.WriteLine($"Dictionary: {string.
   Join(", ", dictionary)}");
7.
8. // Queue<T>
9. var queue = new Queue<int>();
10. queue.Enqueue(1);
11. queue.Enqueue(2);
12. Console.WriteLine($"Queue (after two enqueues): {string.
    Join(", ", queue)}");
13. int dequeuedValue = queue.Dequeue();
14. Console.WriteLine($"Dequeued from Queue: {dequeuedValue}");
15.
16. // Stack<T>
17. var stack = new Stack<int>();
18. stack.Push(3);
19. stack.Push(4);
```

```
20. Console.WriteLine($"Stack (after two pushes): {string.Join(",
    ", stack)}");
21. int poppedValue = stack.Pop();
22. Console.WriteLine($"Popped from Stack: {poppedValue}");
23.
24. // HashSet<T>
25. var hashSet = new HashSet<int> { 5, 6, 6 }; // Adding
    duplicate value 6, but HashSet will filter it out
26. Console.WriteLine($"HashSet: {string.Join(", ", hashSet)}");
27.
28. // LinkedList<T>
29. var linkedList = new LinkedList<string>();
30. linkedList.AddLast("firstElement");
31. linkedList.AddLast("secondElement");
32. Console.WriteLine($"LinkedList: {string.Join(", ", linkedList)
    }");
33.
34. // SortedSet<T>
35. var sortedSet = new SortedSet<int> { 8, 7, 9 }; // The set
    will sort the values automatically
36. Console.WriteLine($"SortedSet: {string.Join(", ", sortedSet)
    }");
37.
38. // SortedList<TKey, TValue> and SortedDictionary<TKey, TValue>
39. var sortedList = new SortedList<string, string>
40.         {
41.             { "b", "valueB" },
42.             { "a", "valueA" }
43.         };
44. Console.WriteLine($"SortedList: {string.Join(", ", sortedList)
    }");
45.
46. var sortedDictionary = new SortedDictionary<string, string>
47.         {
48.             { "b", "valueB" },
49.             { "a", "valueA" }
50.         };
51. Console.WriteLine($"SortedDictionary: {string.Join(", ",
    sortedDictionary)}");
```

This is the output:

```
Dictionary: [key1, value1], [key2, value2]
Queue (after two enqueues): 1, 2
Dequeued from Queue: 1
Stack (after two pushes): 4, 3
Popped from Stack: 4
HashSet: 5, 6
LinkedList: firstElement, secondElement
SortedSet: 7, 8, 9
SortedList: [a, valueA], [b, valueB]
SortedDictionary: [a, valueA], [b, valueB]
```

Figure 7.5: Console output

- **Concurrent collections (in System.Collections.Concurrent)**: These are thread-safe collections designed for concurrent access scenarios:

  o **ConcurrentDictionary<TKey, TValue>**: A thread-safe variant of Dictionary<TKey, TValue>.

  o ConcurrentQueue<T> is a thread-safe Queue<T>.

  o The thread-safe variant of Stack<T> is ConcurrentStack<T>.

  o **ConcurrentBag<T>**: A thread-safe, unsorted collection of items.

  o **ThreadSafeCollection<T>**: A thread-safe collection that may be used as a buffer.

Here is a sample of use:

```csharp
1. using System.Collections.Concurrent;
2.
3. // ConcurrentDictionary<TKey, TValue>
4. var concurrentDictionary = new ConcurrentDictionary<string,
   string>();
5. concurrentDictionary.TryAdd("key1", "value1");
6. concurrentDictionary.TryAdd("key2", "value2");
7. Console.WriteLine($"ConcurrentDictionary: {string.
   Join(", ", concurrentDictionary)}");
8.
9. // ConcurrentQueue<T>
10. var concurrentQueue = new ConcurrentQueue<int>();
11. concurrentQueue.Enqueue(1);
12. concurrentQueue.Enqueue(2);
13. concurrentQueue.TryDequeue(out int queueResult);
14. Console.
    WriteLine($"Dequeued from ConcurrentQueue: {queueResult}");
15.
16. // ConcurrentStack<T>
```

```
17. var concurrentStack = new ConcurrentStack<int>();
18. concurrentStack.Push(3);
19. concurrentStack.Push(4);
20. concurrentStack.TryPop(out int stackResult);
21. Console.WriteLine($"Popped from ConcurrentStack: {stackResult}"
    );
22.
23. // ConcurrentBag<T>
24. var concurrentBag = new ConcurrentBag<int>();
25. concurrentBag.Add(5);
26. concurrentBag.Add(6);
27. concurrentBag.TryTake(out int bagResult);
28. Console.WriteLine($"Taken from ConcurrentBag: {bagResult}");
29.
30. // BlockingCollection<T> can be a thread-safe buffer/
    collection.
31. // It wraps around an IProducerConsumerCollection<T> (like
    ConcurrentQueue by default)
32. var blockingCollection = new BlockingCollection<int>(5); //
    Bounded capacity of 5 items
33. blockingCollection.Add(7);
34. blockingCollection.Add(8);
35. Console.WriteLine($"BlockingCollection (after two additions):
    {string.Join(", ", blockingCollection)}");
36.
37. // Let's retrieve from the BlockingCollection
38. int blockingResult = blockingCollection.Take();
39. Console.WriteLine($"Taken from BlockingCollection:
    {blockingResult}");
```

This is the output:

```
ConcurrentDictionary: [key1, value1], [key2, value2]
Dequeued from ConcurrentQueue: 1
Popped from ConcurrentStack: 4
Taken from ConcurrentBag: 6
BlockingCollection (after two additions): 7, 8
Taken from BlockingCollection: 7
```

Figure 7.6: Console output

- **Immutable collections (in System.Collections.Immutable)**: These collections cannot be altered once established. Any update will result in a new instance with the desired changes:

- o **ImmutableArray<T>**: An array's immutable version.

- o List<T> is an immutable variant of List<T>.

- o Dictionary<TKey, TValue> is an immutable variant of Dictionary<TKey, TValue>.

- o **ImmutableHashSet<T>**: An immutable HashSet<T>.

- o **Queue<T>**: An immutable variant of Queue<T>.

- o **ImmutableStack<T>**: A variant of Stack<T> that is immutable.

Here is a sample of use:

```
1.  using System.Collections.Immutable;
2.
3.  // ImmutableArray<T>
4.  ImmutableArray<int> immutableArray = ImmutableArray.
    Create(1, 2,
    3, 4);
5.  Console.WriteLine($"ImmutableArray: {string.Join(", ",
    immutableArray)}");
6.
7.  // ImmutableList<T>
8.  ImmutableList<int> immutableList = ImmutableList.Create(5, 6,
    7, 8);
9.  Console.WriteLine($"ImmutableList: {string.Join(", ",
    immutableList)}");
10.
11. // ImmutableDictionary<TKey, TValue>
12. var builder = ImmutableDictionary.CreateBuilder<string,
    string>();
13. builder.Add("key1", "value1");
14. builder.Add("key2", "value2");
15. ImmutableDictionary<string, string> immutableDictionary =
    builder.ToImmutable();
16. Console.WriteLine($"ImmutableDictionary: {string.Join(", ",
    immutableDictionary)}");
17.
18. // ImmutableHashSet<T>
19. ImmutableHashSet<int> immutableHashSet = ImmutableHashSet.
    Create(9, 10, 11);
20. Console.WriteLine($"ImmutableHashSet: {string.Join(", ",
    immutableHashSet)}");
21.
```

```
22. // ImmutableQueue<T>
23. ImmutableQueue<int> immutableQueue = ImmutableQueue.Create(12,
    13, 14);
24. immutableQueue = immutableQueue.Enqueue(15); // Since it's
    immutable, to add, we get a new queue back
25. Console.WriteLine($"ImmutableQueue (after Enqueue):
    {string.Join(", ", immutableQueue)}");
26. var dequeuedValue = immutableQueue.Dequeue();
27. Console.WriteLine($"Dequeued value from ImmutableQueue:
    {dequeuedValue.Peek()}, is empty: {dequeuedValue.IsEmpty}");
28.
29. // ImmutableStack<T>
30. ImmutableStack<int> immutableStack = ImmutableStack.Create(16,
    17, 18);
31. immutableStack = immutableStack.Push(19); // Since it's
    immutable, to push, we get a new stack back
32. Console.WriteLine($"ImmutableStack (after Push): {string.
    Join(",
    ", immutableStack)}");
33. var poppedValue = immutableStack.Pop();
34. Console.WriteLine($"Popped value from ImmutableStack:
    {poppedValue.Peek()}, is empty: {poppedValue.IsEmpty}");
```

This is the output:

```
ImmutableArray: 1, 2, 3, 4
ImmutableList: 5, 6, 7, 8
ImmutableDictionary: [key1, value1], [key2, value2]
ImmutableHashSet: 9, 10, 11
ImmutableQueue (after Enqueue): 12, 13, 14, 15
Dequeued value from ImmutableQueue: 13, is empty: False
ImmutableStack (after Push): 19, 18, 17, 16
Popped value from ImmutableStack: 18, is empty: False
```

Figure 7.7: Console output

- **System collections specialized (in System.Collections.Specialized)**: This class houses specialized, strongly-typed collections tailored to specific use cases and designed for specific use cases. These collections, which are distinct from the standard generic and non-generic collections, include structures such as **NameValueCollection**, which can hold multiple string values for a single key; **HybridDictionary**, which dynamically switches between list and hashtable implementations based on size; and **BitVector32**, among others. They cater to niche scenarios where typical collections may fall short, but in most modern applications, **System.Collections.Generics** are preferred because they are type-safe and versatile.

- o **NameValueCollection**: A sorted collection of string keys and string values that may be retrieved using either the key or the index.

- o **StringCollection**: Represents a string collection.

- o **StringDictionary**: A hashtable with the key and value tightly typed as strings rather than objects.

- o **HybridDictionary**: A dictionary that converts from a ListDictionary to a HashTable when the number of items exceeds a certain threshold.

- o **ListDictionary**: A dictionary implemented using a singly linked list. Suitable for collections of less than ten components.

- o **OrderedDictionary**: A collection of key and value pairs that are ordered by key and accessible by key and index.

- o **Bit Manipulation**: BitVector32: This structure contains Boolean values and tiny integers in 32 bits of memory.

Here is a sample of use:

```
1. using System.Collections.Specialized;
2.
3. NameValueCollection nameValueCollection = new
   NameValueCollection();
4. nameValueCollection.Add("first", "John");
5. nameValueCollection.Add("second", "Doe");
6. Console.WriteLine($"NameValueCollection - first:
   {nameValueCollection["first"]}");
7.
8. // StringCollection
9. StringCollection stringCollection = new StringCollection();
10. stringCollection.AddRange(new[] { "John", "Doe" });
11. Console.WriteLine($"StringCollection - first item:
    {stringCollection[0]}");
12.
13. // StringDictionary
14. StringDictionary stringDictionary = new StringDictionary();
15. stringDictionary["name"] = "John Doe";
16. Console.WriteLine($"StringDictionary - name:
    {stringDictionary["name"]}");
17.
18. // HybridDictionary
19. HybridDictionary hybridDictionary = new HybridDictionary();
20. hybridDictionary["name"] = "John";
```

```
21. Console.WriteLine($"HybridDictionary - name:
    {hybridDictionary["name"]}");
22.
23. // ListDictionary
24. ListDictionary listDictionary = new ListDictionary();
25. listDictionary["name"] = "John";
26. Console.WriteLine($"ListDictionary - name:
    {listDictionary["name"]}");
27.
28. // OrderedDictionary
29. OrderedDictionary orderedDictionary = new OrderedDictionary();
30. orderedDictionary.Add("id", 1);
31. orderedDictionary.Add("name", "John");
32. Console.WriteLine($"OrderedDictionary - name:
    {orderedDictionary["name"]}");
33.
34. // BitVector32
35. System.Collections.Specialized.BitVector32 bitVector = new
    System.Collections.Specialized.BitVector32(0);
36. int bit1 = System.Collections.Specialized.BitVector32.
    CreateMask();
37. int bit2 = System.Collections.Specialized.BitVector32.
    CreateMask(bit1);
38. bitVector[bit1] = true;
39. bitVector[bit2] = false;
40. Console.WriteLine($"BitVector32 - Bit1: {bitVector[bit1]},
    Bit2: {bitVector[bit2]}");
```

This is the output:

```
NameValueCollection - first: John
StringCollection - first item: John
StringDictionary - name: John Doe
HybridDictionary - name: John
ListDictionary - name: John
OrderedDictionary - name: John
BitVector32 - Bit1: True, Bit2: False
```

Figure 7.8: Console output

- **Observable collections (in System.Collections.ObjectModel)**: A dynamic data collection that notifies you when items are modified (add/remove) or the entire list is refreshed. This feature is handy in WPF or Xamarin Forms data binding scenarios.

Here is a sample of use:

```
1. // ObservableCollection<T> (generic)
2. ObservableCollection<string> observableCollection = new
   ObservableCollection<string>() { "Apple" };
3. observableCollection.Add("Banana");
4. Console.WriteLine($"ObservableCollection: {string.Join(", ",
   observableCollection)}");
```

- **Memory and Span**: are novel structures for representing contiguous memory regions. Memory<T> provides a heap-allocated counterpart that can be used in asynchronous operations. In contrast, SpanT> provides a stack-only, sliceable region of any memory segment, allowing efficient manipulation without allocations. Both seek to improve performance by reducing unnecessary copying and allowing for more direct access to underlying data.

  o **Span**: A new feature in.NET Core that represents a continuous region of arbitrary memory with performance comparable to arrays. Helpful in slicing and working with buffers/memory that do not have allocations.

  o **Memory**: Like Span, except it may be kept on the heap and utilized throughout async operations.

  o **Lazy**: Allows for the use of lazy initialization. It enables the postponement of the formation of an extensive or resource-intensive object or the execution of a resource-intensive action, mainly when such creation or execution may not occur within the program's lifetime.

Here is a sample of use:

```
1. int[] numbers = new int[] { 0, 1, 2, 3, 4, 5, 6, 7, 8, 9 };
2.
3. ProcessSpan(numbers);
4. ProcessMemory(numbers);
5.
6. Lazy<ExpensiveResource> lazyResource =
   new Lazy<ExpensiveResource>();
7. lazyResource.Value.DoWork();
8.
9. static void ProcessSpan(int[] numbers)
10. {
11.     // Convert the array into a Span
12.     Span<int> span = numbers;
13.
14.     // Slice the span to get a subset. This does not allocate a
    new array.
```

```
15.     Span<int> slicedSpan = span.Slice(2, 5);   // start at 2nd
    element and take 5 elements: {2, 3, 4, 5, 6}
16.
17.     Console.WriteLine("Processing Span:");
18.     foreach (var number in slicedSpan)
19.     {
20.         Console.WriteLine(number);
21.     }
22. }
23. static void ProcessMemory(int[] numbers)
24. {
25.     // Convert the array into Memory
26.     Memory<int> memory = numbers;
27.
28.     // Slice the Memory to get a subset. This does not allocate
    a new array.
29.     Memory<int> slicedMemory = memory.Slice(5, 3);   // start at
    5th element and take 3 elements: {5, 6, 7}
30.
31.     Console.WriteLine("\nProcessing Memory:");
32.     foreach (var number in slicedMemory.Span)   // You access the
    span of the memory to enumerate it
33.     {
34.         Console.WriteLine(number);
35.     }
36. }
37.
38. public class ExpensiveResource
39. {
40.     public ExpensiveResource()
41.     {
42.         Console.WriteLine("ExpensiveResource is being
    initialized...");
43.     }
44.
45.     public void DoWork()
46.     {
47.         Console.WriteLine("ExpensiveResource is working...");
48.     }
49. }
```

This is the output:

```
Processing Span:
2
3
4
5
6

Processing Memory:
5
6
7
ExpensiveResource is being initialized...
ExpensiveResource is working...
```

Figure 7.9: Console output

- **Tuple and ValueTuple**: Are two tools for organizing multiple values. While both encapsulate heterogeneous data, the reference-type Tuple contains immutable, generically named elements such as Item1 and Item2. In contrast, the value-type ValueTuple supports mutable, descriptively named elements, which improves memory efficiency and code readability. The decision between them is based on specific requirements and performance criteria.

    o **Tuple**: A value collection that can hold up to seven items without nesting. Tuple was commonly used to group values before adding ValueTuple to avoid creating a specialized type.

    o **ValueTuple**: A value type version of a Tuple. ValueTuple, unlike Tuple, can have named elements and carry more than seven items without the need for cumbersome nesting.

Here is a sample of use:

```csharp
1.  // Creating a tuple with three elements
2.  Tuple<int, string, bool> tuple = new Tuple<int, string,
    bool>(1, "Hello", true);
3.
4.  // Accessing elements
5.  Console.WriteLine(tuple.Item1); // Outputs: 1
6.  Console.WriteLine(tuple.Item2); // Outputs: Hello
7.  Console.WriteLine(tuple.Item3); // Outputs: True
8.
9.  // Creating a ValueTuple with named elements
10. (int Id, string Name, bool IsActive) person = (1, "John",
    true);
11.
12. // Accessing elements by their names
```

```
13. Console.WriteLine(person.Id);        // Outputs: 1
14. Console.WriteLine(person.Name);      // Outputs: John
15. Console.WriteLine(person.IsActive);  // Outputs: True
```

This is the output:

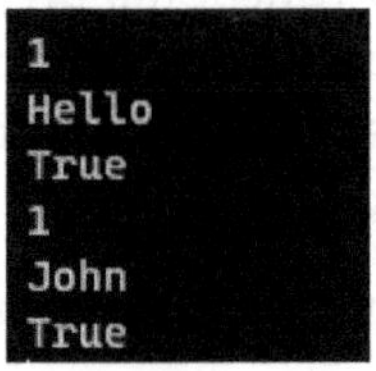

Figure 7.10: *Console output*

Working with arrays and tuples

Tuples are a method of storing many values in a single variable. They have been around for a while, but ValueTuples, a lightweight, value-based alternative to the standard reference-based tuples. A tuple is a data structure that represents a diverse set of components. The key notion is that you may group numerous items without declaring a new type.

There are several conveniences to using Tuples, let us see some ones:

- **Convenience and ease of use**: Before tuples, if you required a function to return several values, you had to either construct a new class/struct, utilize out arguments, or use collections (such as an array or list), which do not always express the structure and meaning of the given data.

- **Multiple return values**: Many algorithms and procedures provide more than one result by default. For example, when determining the minimum and maximum of a collection, both values result from a single computation. Such methods can use tuples to return both values semantically meaningfully.

- **Temporary data grouping**: Sometimes you need a lightweight approach to group data together for short-term use, particularly within a function, without defining a new class or struct.

Objectives of introducing Tuples in C#:

- **Improve productivity by introducing Tuples in C#**: Tuples decrease the boilerplate code required. Without tuples, developers frequently had to construct a slew of little classes merely to return several values from a method, resulting in a slew of extra, often single-use code.

- **Improve readability**: Using named Tuples, code may become considerably more self-explanatory. It is not particularly informative when a method returns a tuple (string, int). The goal becomes evident when it returns (string Name, int Age).

The importance of performance, Tuples are value types (structs), which implies they are allocated on the stack rather than the heap. It relieves the trash collector's workload and can increase performance, particularly in cases where numerous temporary tuples are produced.

Tuples are a frequent feature in many functional programming languages; therefore, they are aligned with them. Tuples have been a logical addition to support patterns prevalent in functional programming as C# has incorporated more functional capabilities over time (such as LINQ, local functions, and so on).

Tuples can make it easier to interoperate with other languages and systems that use them.

- **Anonymous Tuples**: The default names of the tuple elements are Item1, Item2, and so on when using the original Tuple class or without specifying names for the components in a ValueTuple.

```
1. var person = GetPerson();
2. Console.WriteLine($"Name: {person.Item1}, Age: {person.
   Item2}");
3.
4. (string, int) GetPerson()
5. {
6.     return ("Alice", 30);
7. }
```

The **GetPerson** function in this example produces a tuple with two components (a string and an int). The returned tuple is saved in the variable person. We then use the person to retrieve the Tuple's components **.Item1** and the individual **.Item2** will be used to print the name and age.

- **Named Tuples (ValueTuples)**: Tuples with names (or ValueTuples) were introduced. They improved the tuple notion by enabling you to name its elements. This results in simpler syntax and improved readability.

```
1. var person = (Name: "John", Age: 30);
2. Console.WriteLine(person.Name); // Outputs "John"
```

- **Tuples can be deconstructed**: You may divide the tuple's elements into different variables. It makes code more transparent and understandable, especially with individual tuple components.

```
1. var person = GetPerson();
2. (string personName, int personAge) = person;
3. (string personName, int personAge) GetPerson()
4. {
5.     return ("Jefferson", 22);
6. }
7. Console.WriteLine($"Name: {personName}, Age: {personAge}");
```

Conclusion: In summary, introducing tuples, particularly named tuples (ValueTuples) in C#, targeted increasing developer efficiency, improving code readability, and better supporting functional programming techniques. They offer a succinct and fast method of representing and manipulating grouped data without the overhead of custom-defined classes or structs.

Understanding nullable types in C#

It is common in software development to encounter situations where a value is missing or undefined, especially when working with databases or web services. Traditional C# value types (such as int, double, bool, and so on) lack a built-in way to represent a value's absence.

They are permanently assigned a default value, such as 0 for integers or false for booleans. In C#, this is where nullable types come into play.

Nullable types are a C# feature that allows value types to represent the absence of a value. A nullable type can hold either a value or null.

- **How to define a nullable type**: To define a nullable type, append a **?** to the type name:

  ```
  1. int? nullableInt = null;
  2. double? nullableDouble = null;
  3. bool? nullableBool = null;
  4. string? nullableString = null;
  ```

  Nullable types can also be represented using the **Nullable<T>** generic structure for unfamiliar people.

  ```
  1. Nullable<int> anotherNullableInt = null;
  ```

- **Checking for a value**: Before using the value of a nullable type, it is a good idea to use the **HasValue** property to see if it has a value.

  ```
  1. int? num = null;
  2.
  3. if (num.HasValue)
  4. {
  5.     Console.WriteLine($"Value is: {num.Value}");
  6. }
  7. else
  8. {
  9.     Console.WriteLine("No value present.");
  10. }
  ```

- **Using the ?? operator**: The **??** operator (null-coalescing operator) is a shorthand for working with nullable types. You can use this operator to return a default value if the nullable type is null.

  1. `int? number = null;`
  2. `int backupNumber = 100;`
  3. `int finalNumber = number ?? backupNumber;   // finalNumber will be 100`

- **Using the ?. operator (null-conditional operator)**: We may need to occasionally operate on a member of a nullable type, but only if the nullable type has a value. It is precisely what the **?.** operator does:

  1. `string lengthOfValue = nullableInt?.ToString().Length;`

  If **nullableInt** contains a value, it is converted to a string,, and its length is returned. If **nullableInt** is null, the expression as a whole will return null.

  Value types vs. reference types: reference types (class types) can naturally be null. So, why the need for nullable value types?

  Value types have a default value to which they revert; for example, an int has a default value of 0. Sometimes, 0 may be a valid value in your application, and you must distinguish between no value and the default value. This distinction is significant when reading from or writing to databases where a value may be missing.

- **DBNull**: While nullables (int?, double?, etc.) help represent missing or undefined values for value types in.NET.

  The DBNull class represents a value that does not exist. In a database, for example, a field could be either a date or a null value, indicating that the date is unknown or not applicable. This database null is not the same as the null in C#. When ADO. NET retrieves null database fields, they return DBNull.

  This distinction is primarily historical and relates to how databases handle the concept of NULL. NULL is not equal to anything in a database, not even itself. As a result, distinguishing between null (a concept in programming languages) and DBNull (a concept in database design) can be beneficial.

- **DBNull check**: The DBNull value is different from the language keyword null. The **Equals** method is used to determine whether an object is DBNull.

  Here is a sample:
  1. `object someValue = GetSomeValueFromDatabase();`
  2.
  3. `if (DBNull.Value.Equals(someValue))`
  4. `{`

```
5.       Console.WriteLine("The value is DB null.");
6. }
7. else
8. {
9.       Console.WriteLine($"The value is: {someValue}");
10. }
```

In summary, when working with databases in .NET, it is critical to understand the difference between null and DBNull and how to handle each correctly. Failure to distinguish between them can result in runtime errors or incorrect application logic.

Conclusion: This section explained the differences, applications, and advantages of null types, nullable types, and DBNull in C#. Readers can learn how to define, check, and use nullable types, which provide a way for value types to indicate the absence of a value. Furthermore, the distinction between null and DBNull, both related to dealing with non-existent database values, is clarified. Code examples are provided to highlight key points and aid in learning. This content is invaluable for software developers who work with C# and databases because it helps to prevent errors or logical issues when dealing with null or nullable values.

Manipulating strings with StringBuilder

StringBuilder has a mutable representation; as previously stated, StringBuilder's key advantage is that it represents a modifiable string of characters. It means that once a StringBuilder instance has been established, it can be updated without producing new string instances.

- **Internal implementation**: StringBuilder keeps an internal character array in which it stores the string. This internal array is directly updated as actions are performed (for example, adding or removing material).

- **Capacity management**: StringBuilder allocates a larger array and copies the contents when the current character array is full. Because the reallocation does not occur with every modification, the overall process is more efficient.

Benefits of using StringBuilder:

- **Memory efficiency**: Because regular strings are immutable, any alteration results in a new string object (a new memory allocation). It results in significant overhead in memory allocation and garbage collection, particularly in cases involving many string alterations. Because StringBuilder is mutable, it avoids this overhead by updating its internal array.

- **Faster execution**: Because of the lower memory allocations, StringBuilder operations are typically faster, especially in tight loops or cases involving repeated string manipulations. Memory allocation and data copying take less time than concatenating them.

- **Predictable growth**: If you have an estimate of the size, you can set the starting capacity of the StringBuilder to avoid repeated reallocations. Furthermore, suppose the StringBuilder's current capacity is exceeded. In that case, it does not simply increase by a single character space but often doubles its internal array size, minimizing the frequency of such expansions.

- **When to use StringBuilder**: it should be noted that StringBuilder is not always the ideal tool for the job. The overhead of constructing a StringBuilder instance may not be justified for single or significantly few string changes (such as concatenations or replacements). On the other hand, StringBuilder usually provides a clear performance advantage in instances involving repetitive manipulations, particularly within loops.

Consider the following string adding loop:

```
1.  using System.Text;
2.  string result = "";
3.  // Not optimized
4.  for (int i = 0; i < 10000; i++)
5.  {
6.      result += i.ToString();
7.  }
8.
9.  result = "";
10.
11. // Optimized with StringBuilder
12. StringBuilder sb = new StringBuilder();
13. for (int i = 0; i < 10000; i++)
14. {
15.     sb.Append(i);
16. }
17. result = sb.ToString();
```

In the first example, a new string object is generated with each loop iteration, resulting in 10,000 string objects created and then deleted. The internal character array is updated in the second example with StringBuilder, resulting in far fewer memory allocations.

Conclusion: While StringBuilder has advantages regarding memory use and execution speed in particular scenarios, assessing the nature of your string operations is critical before deciding on the right tool for the task.

Parsing dates, times, and numbers in .NET

Parsing dates, times, and numbers are common in .NET, mainly when working with user inputs, files, or databases. Understanding the underlying techniques and methodologies can help developers handle a wide range of data more efficiently. Let us now get into the subject.

Parsing refers to converting a string representation of data, such as dates, times, or numbers, into structured types or objects that the language or framework can natively understand and work within the context of .NET (and most programming environments).

When data is received as a string, it must often be transformed into a more structured format before it can be used effectively in computations, comparisons, or other operations. Parsing is the name given to this transformation process.

- **Parsing dates and times**: Date and time parsing methods are provided by the DateTime structure. The Parse method is one of the most commonly used methods.

  Here is a sample:

```
1.  string dateString = "2023-08-12 15:30:00";
2.  DateTime dateTime = DateTime.Parse(dateString);
3.  Console.WriteLine(dateTime);  // Output: 8/12/2023 3:30:00 PM
```

- **DateTime.TryParse**: `DateTime.TryParse` is the safe way to parse a string, as it does not throw exceptions. It instead returns a boolean indicating whether or not the parsing was successful.

  Here is a sample:

```
1.  string dateString = "2023-08-32";  // Invalid Date
2.  DateTime result;
3.  bool success = DateTime.TryParse(dateString, out result);
4.
5.  if (success)
6.  {
7.      Console.WriteLine(result);
8.  }
9.  else
10. {
11.     Console.WriteLine("Invalid Date Format");
12. }  // Output: Invalid Date Format
```

- **Parsing numbers**: NET provides structures like Int32, Double, and Decimal for numeric operations to convert string representations into their respective numeric types; these structures have methods like **Parse** and **TryParse**.

- **Int32.Parse**: This function translates a number's string representation to its 32-bit signed integer counterpart. If the string cannot be parsed, a FormatException is issued.

  Here is a sample:

```
1. string numberString = "12345";
2. int number = Int32.Parse(numberString);
3. Console.WriteLine(number);  // Output: 12345
```

- **Int32.TryParse**: Like **DateTime.TryParse**, this method tries to parse a string and returns a Boolean indicating the outcome.

  Here is a sample:
```
1. string numberString = "123abc";
2. int result;
3. bool success = Int32.TryParse(numberString, out result);
4.
5. if(success)
6. {
7.     Console.WriteLine(result);
8. }
9. else
10. {
11.     Console.WriteLine("Invalid Number Format");
12. }  // Output: Invalid Number Format
```

Understanding .NET format strings

When developing applications, formatting strings is a common requirement. It is critical to present data in a way that makes sense to users, whether you are displaying numbers, dates, or any other values. .NET gives many tools to help with this. Understanding string formatting will help you make the output of your application more readable and professional.

- **String formatting fundamentals**: String formatting in C# is primarily accomplished using the **String.Format** method. The method accepts a format string and one or more objects to be inserted into that string:
```
1. string formatted = String.Format("Hello, {0}!", "World");
2. Console.WriteLine(formatted); // Outputs "Hello, World!"
```

  Here, **{0}** is a format item. It gets replaced by the first object after the format string.

- **Formatting numbers**: Depending on the situation, numbers can be formatted in a variety of ways:
```
1. double value = 12345.6789;
2. Console.WriteLine(String.
   Format("{0:C}", value)); // Outputs "$12,345.68" (assuming U.S.
   culture)
```

3. `Console.WriteLine(String.Format("{0:N2}", value)); // Outputs "12,345.68"`

The **C** denotes currency formatting, and N2 denotes number formatting with two decimal places.

- **Date and time formatting**: Dates and timings may be formatted in several ways as well:

    1. `DateTime now = DateTime.Now;`
    2. `Console.WriteLine(String.Format("{0:MM/dd/yyyy}", now)); // Outputs "08/10/2023" (assuming the date is August 10, 2023)`
    3. `Console.WriteLine(String.Format("{0:dddd, MMMM d, yyyy}", now)); // Outputs "Thursday, August 10, 2023"`

In these examples, **MM/dd/yyyy** specifies the format in which the date should be shown.

1. `double value = 0.12345;`
2. `Console.WriteLine(String.Format("{0:0.00%}", value)); // Outputs "12.35%"`

- **Custom format strings**: Custom format strings can be used in addition to the regular formats for additional control:

    1. `double value = 0.12345;`
    2. `Console.WriteLine(String.Format("{0:0.00%}", value)); // Outputs "12.35%"`

Interpolated strings are a more readable approach to embedding expressions into string literals:

1. `string name = "John";`
2. `int age = 30;`
3. `string result = $"My name is {name} and I am {age} years old.»;`
4. `Console.WriteLine(result); // Outputs "My name is John and I am 30 years old."`

- **Composite formatting**: In string formatting, composite formatting refers to combining numerous values into a single string. Multiple arguments can be passed to the **String.Format** method:

    1. `string name = "Alice";`
    2. `int age = 28;`
    3. `string city = "New York";`
    4. `Console.WriteLine(String.Format("{0} is {1} years old and lives in {2}.", name, age, city));`

- **Format string alignment**: You can specify the alignment of values in the format item:
  1. `Console.WriteLine(String.Format("|{0,10}|", "test")); //` *Outputs "| test|"*
  2. `Console.WriteLine(String.` `Format("|{0,-10}|", "test")); // Outputs "|test        |"`

Format strings with enumerations can be used to format strings:

- The **D**, **G**, **X**, **F**, and additional format strings can be used to format enumerations:
  1. `enum Colors { Red = 1, Green = 2, Blue = 4 };`
  2. `Console.WriteLine(String.Format("{0:G}", Colors.` `Red)); // Outputs "Red"`
  3. `Console.WriteLine(String.Format("{0:D}", Colors.` `Red)); // Outputs "1"`
  4. `Console.WriteLine(String.Format("{0:X}", Colors.` `Red)); // Outputs "01"`

- **Escaping braces**: To include a brace **{** or **}** in the formatted string, use double braces **{{** or **}}**:
  1. `Console.WriteLine(String.Format("{{0}} is a format item, but {0}` `is replaced.", "this"));`
  2. `// Output :{0} is a format item, but this is replaced.`

- **The ":" in format strings**: The format specifier is introduced by the **:** in a format item. This specifier determines the format of the matching object argument:
  1. `Console.WriteLine(String.Format("{0:0.00}", 2.4)); // Outputs` *"2.40"*
  2. `Console.WriteLine(String.Format("{0:#.##}", 2.4)); // Outputs` *"2.4"*

`0:0.00` utilizes the 0 characters as a placeholder for mandatory digits, guaranteeing the output always has two decimal places, whereas `0:#.##` uses the # character as a placeholder for optional digits, displaying up to two decimal places only if they are non-zero. As a result, the former will always display two decimal places (2.40) for the input 2.4, but the latter will clip trailing zeroes, resulting in 2.4.

- **Strings in standard numeric format**: There are numerous common ways to format numbers, some of which are as follows:

  - **C or c**: Currency

  - **D or d**: Decimal

  - **E or e**: Scientific

  - **F or f**: Fixed-point

- **G or g**: General

- **N or n**: Number

- **P or p**: Percent

- **R or r**: Round-trip

- **X or x**: Hexadecimal

Here is a sample of these items:

```
1.  double sampleNumber = 12345.6789;
2.
3.  // C or c: Currency
4.  Console.WriteLine(String.Format("Currency: {0:C}",
    sampleNumber));  // Outputs "$12,345.68" for en-US culture
5.
6.  // D or d: Decimal (used for integral types only)
7.  Console.WriteLine(String.Format("Decimal: {0:D}", 12345));
    // Outputs "12345"
8.
9.  // E or e: Scientific
10. Console.WriteLine(String.Format("Scientific: {0:E}",
    sampleNumber));  // Outputs "1.234568E+004"
11.
12. // F or f: Fixed-point
13. Console.WriteLine(String.Format("Fixed-point: {0:F2}",
    sampleNumber));  // Outputs "12345.68"
14.
15. // G or g: General
16. Console.WriteLine(String.Format("General: {0:G}",
    sampleNumber));  // Outputs "12345.6789"
17.
18. // N or n: Number
19. Console.WriteLine(String.Format("Number: {0:N2}",
    sampleNumber));  // Outputs "12,345.68"
20.
21. // P or p: Percent
22. Console.WriteLine(String.
    Format("Percent: {0:P2}", 0.123456789));  // Outputs "12.35%"
23.
24. // R or r: Round-trip
25. Console.WriteLine(String.Format("Round-
    trip: {0:R}", sampleNumber));  // Outputs "12345.6789"
```

```
26.
27. // X or x: Hexadecimal (used for integral types only)
28. Console.WriteLine(String.
    Format("Hexadecimal: {0:X}", 255));  // Outputs "FF"
```

- **IFormatProvider and CultureInfo**: This interface can be used to define custom formatting. It is most typically used in conjunction with the **CultureInfo** class to format strings based on cultural conventions:

```
1.  double value = 1234567.89;
2.
3.  // en-US: United States
4.  Console.WriteLine(String.Format(new CultureInfo("en-
    US"), "{0:C}", value)); // Outputs "$1,234,567.89"
5.
6.  // de-DE: Germany
7.  Console.WriteLine(String.Format(new CultureInfo("de-
    DE"), "{0:C}", value)); // Outputs "1.234.567,89 €"
8.
9.  // fr-FR: France
10. Console.WriteLine(String.Format(new CultureInfo("fr-
    FR"), "{0:C}", value)); // Outputs "1 234 567,89 €"
11.
12. // ru-RU: Russia
13. Console.WriteLine(String.Format(new CultureInfo("ru-
    RU"), "{0:C}", value)); // Outputs "1 234 567,89 ₽"
```

String formatting in .NET allows developers to present data in a way that improves readability and fits a variety of application needs. .NET provides us with the tools we need to efficiently express information to consumers by combining standard and custom format specifiers and culture-specific formatting. Whether you are formatting numbers, dates, or custom objects, the framework provides adaptable ways to meet various display requirements. Like many other aspects of .NET, understanding string formatting is essential for developing polished and professional apps.

Using System.Guid and other common .NET types

System.Guid is a 128-bit (16-byte) number that uniquely identifies records, objects, or other data. The primary use of a GUID is to generate unique keys, which, given the large expanse of the 128-bit field, virtually guarantees that the identical value will not be generated elsewhere.

A typical GUID looks like this:

1. 6868f370-2903-4ac3-86a5-8b9ce5a3ec01

It is divided into five parts:

- 32-bit number (8 hex digits)
- 16-bit number (4 hex digits)
- 16-bit number (4 hex digits)
- 16-bit number (4 hex digits)
- 48-bit number (12 hex digits)

Other common types in .NET:

.NET type	Explanation
System.DateTime	Represents an instant in time, usually expressed as a date and time of day.
System.Boolean	Represents a Boolean value, which may either be true or false.
System.TimeSpan	Represents a time interval and is the difference between two DateTime values.
System.Byte	Represents an 8-bit unsigned integer, with values ranging from 0 to 255.
System.SByte	Represents an 8-bit signed integer, with values ranging from -128 to 127.
System.Double	Represents a double-precision floating-point number.
System.Decimal	Represents a decimal number with high precision, often used for financial calculations.
System.Char	Represents a single Unicode character.
System.Short	Represents a 16-bit signed integer.
System.UShort	Represents a 16-bit unsigned integer.
System.Int32	Represents a 32-bit signed integer.
System.Int64	Represents a 64-bit signed integer.
System.Int128	Represents a 128-bit signed integer.
System.UInt32	Represents a 32-bit unsigned integer.
System.UInt64	Represents a 64-bit unsigned integer.
System.UInt128	Represents a 128-bit unsigned integer.

Table 7.1: Some common types in .NET

About unsigned and signed integers

Unsigned integers only represent non-negative numbers using all available bits for the value. However, signed integers can represent positive and negative numbers by using one bit for the sign. Each can represent a different set of values, affecting future program behavior.

The System.Guid is a unique identifier in .NET that ensures distinctness across systems, databases, and entities, making it essential in distributed systems and database management.

Basic .NET types such as integers, characters, and booleans are foundational building blocks for developers, allowing for a wide range of data representation and manipulation in applications, emphasizing the .NET's richness and versatility in accommodating both specialized and general programming needs.

Conclusion

This chapter introduced the regular expressions in C# and .NET and provided an overview of the System.String class, the DateTime class, and the TimeSpan class. In the next chapter, we are going to talk about Data in Motion.

This chapter breaks down the most critical aspects of these classes and ideas, including their design choices and the real-world implementations of those decisions. In addition, it demonstrates how to utilize them in various scenarios involving text processing, the manipulation of dates and times, and pattern matching. Learners should be able to walk away from this content and understand how to use these tools in their own C# and .NET projects effectively and efficiently. Learners can improve their expertise and capabilities in working with strings, dates, times, and regular expressions in C# and .NET if they master the topics in this section.

Join our book's Discord space

Join the book's Discord Workspace for Latest updates, Offers, Tech happenings around the world, New Release and Sessions with the Authors:

https://discord.bpbonline.com

CHAPTER 8
Data in Motion

Introduction

In this chapter, we look at the fundamentals of file operations in .NET, from reading and writing text files to handling file and directory exceptions and guaranteeing safe file operations. We will also look at the importance of streams in .NET, which are the foundation for reading and writing data from diverse sources such as files, networks, and memory. We will also introduce you to serialization in .NET, a critical technique for transforming an object or data structure into a digital format that can be stored or sent. This chapter describes the many types of serialization: binary, **Extensible Markup Language (XML)**, **JavaScript Object Notation (JSON)**, and custom. It also offers examples for each. By the end of this article, you will have a firm grasp of how to use the `System.IO` namespace and related classes to conduct a wide range of file and stream operations in C# and be able to serialize and deserialize data in various formats. We will also discuss essential concerns and best practices to remember when working with data in motion.

Structure

This chapter covers the following topics:

- Basics of file operations in .NET
- Understanding streams in .NET
- Reading and writing text files in C#

- Introduction to serialization in .NET
- XML and JSON serialization in .NET
- Binary serialization in .NET
- Understanding file and directory classes in System.IO
- Working with paths, buffers, and memory streams
- Handling file and directory exceptions
- Secure file operations and file I/O permissions

Objectives

In this chapter, you will learn how to explore the **System.IO** namespace and use its classes to perform routine file and stream tasks in C#. You will learn all there is to know about serialization in .NET, including binary, XML, JSON, and custom serialization methods. You will also learn how to use the **XmlSerializer**, **JsonSerializer**, and **BinaryFormatter** classes to serialize and deserialize objects in various formats. We will also show you how to use attributes to manage and personalize the serialization and deserialization operations. Finally, we will teach you how to handle failures and exceptions during file interactions, stream operations, or the serialization process.

Basics of file operations in .NET

The .NET includes a complete set of classes for working with files and directories. These classes are primarily found in the **System.IO** namespace. This article will review the fundamentals of file operations in C#. We will concentrate on two essential tasks: reading from and writing to files, and we will look at two sample programs to comprehend these activities better.

System.IO namespace

The System.IO namespace contains types that allow synchronous and asynchronous reading and writing on data streams and files. This namespace's key classes include:

- **FileStream**: Used to read from and write to files in a file system.
- **StreamReader and StreamWriter**: These classes are used to read and write string data to a stream.
- **TextReader and TextWriter**: These are base classes for reading and writing strings, respectively.
- **BinaryReader and BinaryWriter**: These classes read and write non-character binary data.
- **File and FileInfo**: Used for creating, deleting, and relocating files.
- **Directory and DirectoryInfo**: These are used for directory operations.

Reading data from a file

There are several methods for reading from a file:

- **ReadAllText()** is used to read a file at once. **StreamReader** is used to read lines one by one.

  Example 1: Reading the entire text at once, we can put all the content of a file into a memory variable:

  ```
  1. using System;
  2. using System.IO;
  3.
  4. namespace FileOperations
  5. {
  6.     class Program
  7.     {
  8.         static void Main(string[] args)
  9.         {
  10.             string filePath = "example.txt";
  11.
  12.             if (File.Exists(filePath))
  13.             {
  14.                 string content = File.ReadAllText(filePath);
  15.                 Console.WriteLine("File content is:");
  16.                 Console.WriteLine(content);
  17.             }
  18.             else
  19.             {
  20.                 Console.WriteLine("File does not exist.");
  21.             }
  22.         }
  23.     }
  24. }
  ```

  File.ReadAllText() reads the whole text content of the file into a string variable in this example. It is adequate for tiny files but may be inefficient for larger files.

  Example 2: Line-by-line reading, we can process line by line from an entire file:

  ```
  1. using System;
  2. using System.IO;
  3.
  4. namespace FileOperations
  ```

```
5. {
6.     class Program
7.     {
8.         static void Main(string[] args)
9.         {
10.             string filePath = "example.txt";
11.
12.             if (File.Exists(filePath))
13.             {
14.                 using (StreamReader reader = new
    StreamReader(filePath))
15.                 {
16.                     string line;
17.                     while ((line = reader.ReadLine()) != null)
18.                     {
19.                         Console.WriteLine(line);
20.                     }
21.                 }
22.             }
23.             else
24.             {
25.                 Console.WriteLine("File does not exist.");
26.             }
27.         }
28.     }
29. }
```

In this example, we read the file line by line with **StreamReader**, which is more memory-efficient for huge files.

Creating a file

Writing to a file is also versatile:

- Using **File.WriteAllText()**, write all text at once.
- **StreamWriter** is used to write text incrementally.

Example 3: Writing all of the text at once:

```
1. using System;
2. using System.IO;
3.
4. namespace FileOperations
```

```
 5.  {
 6.      class Program
 7.      {
 8.          static void Main(string[] args)
 9.          {
10.              string filePath = "output.txt";
11.              string content = "Hello, World!";
12.
13.              File.WriteAllText(filePath, content);
14.
15.              Console.WriteLine("Text written to file.");
16.          }
17.      }
18. }
```

Example 4: Writing text incrementally:

```
 1.  using System;
 2.  using System.IO;
 3.
 4.  namespace FileOperations
 5.  {
 6.      class Program
 7.      {
 8.          static void Main(string[] args)
 9.          {
10.              string filePath = "output.txt";
11.
12.              using (StreamWriter writer = new StreamWriter(filePath))
13.              {
14.                  writer.WriteLine("Hello, World!");
15.                  writer.WriteLine("How are you?");
16.              }
17.
18.              Console.WriteLine("Text written to file.");
19.          }
20.      }
21. }
```

In this example, **StreamWriter** writes text incrementally, which can be more efficient for larger files.

Understanding streams in .NET

Streams are a crucial component of .NET's **input/output (I/O)** framework, offering an abstract method for reading and writing data. They are the basis for various higher-level data operations, including reading and writing to files, network interactions, and even interacting with data in memory. Understanding how to work with streams is essential for any .NET developer dealing with data transformation or transport.

Let us understand what exactly is a stream.

A Stream is just a series of bytes that may be read or written to. Streams are represented in .NET by the **Stream** base class in the **System.IO** namespace. This class defines the fundamental methods **Read**, **Write**, **Flush**, and **Close**, which are overridden by derived classes for specific types of streams. Streams can be classified in various ways, including readable, writable, seekable, and so on, and the .NET framework includes particular implementations such as **FileStream**, **MemoryStream**, **NetworkStream**, and others.

Stream operations

The fundamental operations that may be done on a stream are as follows:

- **Reading**: It is transferring data from a stream into a data structure.
- **Writing**: Copy data from a data structure to the stream.
- **Seeking**: Move up in the stream from where you started reading or writing.
- **Flushing**: Ensure that all data has been written to the underlying medium by clearing any buffered data.

Finally, any resources consumed by the stream should be released.

- **Taking a stream reading**: The **Read** method can read from a stream since it reads a block of bytes from the stream and writes the data into a buffer. Here is a C# example of reading a file with **FileStream**:

```
1. using System;
2. using System.IO;
3.
4. class Program
5. {
6.     static void Main()
7.     {
8.         using (FileStream fs = new FileStream("example.
   txt", FileMode.Open))
9.         {
10.            byte[] buffer = new byte[1024];
11.            int bytesRead = fs.Read(buffer, 0, buffer.Length);
```

```
12.              Console.WriteLine($"Read {bytesRead} bytes.»);
13.
14.              // Convert bytes to string and display.
15.              string content = System.Text.Encoding.UTF8.
    GetString(buffer, 0, bytesRead);
16.              Console.WriteLine(content);
17.          }
18.      }
19. }
```

- **Writing to a stream**: Reading is analogous to writing to a stream. The **Write** method uses a block of bytes to the stream from a buffer. Here is an example of writing text to a file:

```
1. using System;
2. using System.IO;
3.
4. class Program
5. {
6.     static void Main()
7.     {
8.         using (FileStream fs = new FileStream("example.
    txt", FileMode.Create))
9.         {
10.             string content = "Hello, World!";
11.             byte[] buffer = System.Text.Encoding.UTF8.
    GetBytes(content);
12.             fs.Write(buffer, 0, buffer.Length);
13.         }
14.     }
15. }
```

- **Seekable streams**: Not all streams allow for searching operations. Inspect the **CanSeek** attribute of a stream to verify if it supports seeking. You can modify your position in the stream using the **Seek** method if your system supports it.

  Here is how to use **Seek** to return to the start of a **FileStream** and reread it:

```
1. using (FileStream fs = new FileStream("example.txt", FileMode.
    Open))
2. {
3.     // Read from the beginning.
4.     byte[] buffer1 = new byte[5];
5.     fs.Read(buffer1, 0, buffer1.Length);
6.
```

```
7.     // Seek to the beginning.
8.     fs.Seek(0, SeekOrigin.Begin);
9.
10.    // Read again.
11.    byte[] buffer2 = new byte[5];
12.    fs.Read(buffer2, 0, buffer2.Length);
13. }
```

- **Asynchronous operations**: Asynchronous methods for executing read and write operations are also provided by .NET, which is helpful for I/O-bound workloads. These are the **ReadAsync** and **WriteAsync** functions.

Here is a simple example of asynchronous file reading:

```
1. using System;
2. using System.IO;
3. using System.Threading.Tasks;
4.
5. class Program
6. {
7.     static async Task Main()
8.     {
9.         using (FileStream fs = new FileStream("example.
   txt", FileMode.Open))
10.        {
11.            byte[] buffer = new byte[1024];
12.            int bytesRead = await fs.
   ReadAsync(buffer, 0, buffer.Length);
13.            Console.WriteLine($"Read {bytesRead} bytes.»);
14.
15.            string content = System.Text.Encoding.UTF8.
   GetString(buffer, 0, bytesRead);
16.            Console.WriteLine(content);
17.        }
18.    }
19. }
```

In summary, .NET streams are a versatile and powerful tool for dealing with I/O. They provide a uniform interface for dealing with various data sources and can be extended for specific implementations. Understanding streams is critical for tasks ranging from file I/O to network connections. You can make your .NET applications more resilient, scalable, and maintainable by harnessing the power of streams.

Reading and writing text files in C#

Reading and writing text files is a typical process in software development, and the System.IO namespace makes these activities simple. This namespace includes classes such as **StreamReader**, **StreamWriter**, **File**, and **TextReader** to perform file operations efficiently. This article will show you how to read from and write to text files in C# using various methods.

Reading text files

A text file is a kind of file that stores plain text information, which means it only contains readable letters, whitespace, and newlines. Text files, as opposed to binary files, which contain a series of bytes representing various types of data such as text, pictures, and executable code, are human-readable and can be modified using simple text editors.

The extension **.txt** commonly identifies a text file but has different endings, such as **.log** for log files, **.md** for markdown files, **.csv** for comma-separated value files, etc. The content of a text file is arranged as a sequence of lines, each ending with a newline character (**n** in Unix/Linux systems, **rn** in Windows).

Using StreamReader

StreamReader is a class that reads characters from byte streams with a specific encoding (by default, UTF-8). Here is an easy way to read a text file line by line:

```
1. using System;
2. using System.IO;
3.
4. class Program
5. {
6.     static void Main()
7.     {
8.         using (StreamReader reader = new StreamReader("example.txt"))
9.         {
10.             string line;
11.             while ((line = reader.ReadLine()) != null)
12.             {
13.                 Console.WriteLine(line);
14.             }
15.         }
16.     }
17. }
```

Using File class

The **File** class contains static methods for doing everyday file operations such as reading and writing to files. Here is how to read all text from a file at once:

```
1.  using System;
2.  using System.IO;
3.
4.  class Program
5.  {
6.      static void Main()
7.      {
8.          string text = File.ReadAllText("example.txt");
9.          Console.WriteLine(text);
10.     }
11. }
```

You can also read lines into a string array:

```
1.  using System;
2.  using System.IO;
3.
4.  class Program
5.  {
6.      static void Main()
7.      {
8.          string[] lines = File.ReadAllLines("example.txt");
9.          foreach (string line in lines)
10.         {
11.             Console.WriteLine(line);
12.         }
13.     }
14. }
```

Append text to an existing file: You may want to attach text to an existing file at times. It can be accomplished by using the **StreamWriter** or **File** class methods.

Using StreamWriter

This sample demonstrates how to use **StreamWriter** to write text:

```
1.  using System;
2.  using System.IO;
3.
4.  class Program
```

```
5.  {
6.      static void Main()
7.      {
8.          using (StreamWriter writer = new StreamWriter("example.
    txt", true))
9.          {
10.             writer.WriteLine("This line will be appended.");
11.         }
12.     }
13. }
```

Error handling

When dealing with file I/O, it is critical to include suitable error handling. To handle problems gracefully, you can catch exceptions such as **FileNotFoundException**, **IOException**, or the base **Exception** class:

```
1.  using System;
2.  using System.IO;
3.
4.  class Program
5.  {
6.      static void Main()
7.      {
8.          try
9.          {
10.             string text = File.ReadAllText("nonexistent.txt");
11.         }
12.         catch (FileNotFoundException e)
13.         {
14.             Console.WriteLine($"File not found: {e.Message}");
15.         }
16.         catch (IOException e)
17.         {
18.             Console.WriteLine($"I/O error: {e.Message}");
19.         }
20.         catch (Exception e)
21.         {
22.             Console.WriteLine($"Unexpected error: {e.Message}");
23.         }
24.     }
25. }
```

In summary, using the `System.IO` namespace, .NET provides many methods for reading and writing text files. The framework provides flexibility and ease of use for these basic tasks, whether you use `StreamReader` and `StreamWriter` or the `File` class. Error handling ensures that your program can respond appropriately to any problems during file I/O.

Introduction to serialization in .NET

Turning an item or data structure into a format that can be easily saved or transmitted and then reconstructed is known as **serialization**. It is a crucial concept in programming, mainly when dealing with distributed systems, file operations, or whenever an object needs to be flattened to be transferred across a network, stored in a file, or stored in a database. Serialization is well-supported in .NET, with a plethora of options available to developers. This article will provide an overview of serialization in the .NET environment using C#, covering the fundamentals and examples for simple and sophisticated scenarios.

Main types of serialization in .NET

.NET offers four main types of serialization. Here are the basic types:

- **Binary**: Serializes the object as binary data.
- **XML**: Converts the object to XML format.
- **JSON**: Converts the object to JSON format.
- **Custom**: Allows for the creation of a unique serialization procedure.

Binary serialization

Transforming an object into a binary stream is known as **binary serialization**. This method is not human-readable but is a quick way to serialize and deserialize data.

Binary serialization is typically used for:

- Object persistence on local storage.
- Communication between applications on the same platform.
- Fast, compact storage and transfer.

XML serialization

Transforming an object into a binary stream is known as **binary serialization**. This method is not human-readable but is a quick way to serialize and deserialize data.

XML serialization is widely used for the following purposes:

- Configuration documents.
- Data exchange between systems, particularly those that use XML-based communications protocols like SOAP Data storage in a legible format.

JSON serialization

JSON serialization is converting an object into a JSON structured string. JSON is less verbose than XML and can be read by humans and machines.

JSON serialization is helpful for:

- RESTful APIs, web services.
- Configuration documents.
- Modern web applications store and exchange data.

Custom serialization

Custom serialization gives us complete control over the serialization and deserialization processes.

Custom serialization should be used when:

- The default serialization techniques do not meet your requirements.
- Specific fields must be included or excluded.
- You wish to include additional functionality, such as encryption or compression.

These serialization types have advantages, disadvantages, and particularly beneficial scenarios. Various criteria, such as speed, readability, and cross-language support, influence their decision.

XML and JSON serialization in .NET

Turning an item or data structure into a format that can be easily saved or transmitted and then reconstructed is known as serialization. There are various methods for serializing objects in .NET, the most common of which are XML and JSON serialization. Both formats are extensively used for different reasons, each with advantages and disadvantages.

XML and JSON

XML and JSON are commonly used for data storage and exchange, particularly in online services and APIs. However, they each have benefits and drawbacks, making them more suited for various settings.

The advantages of XML:

- XML has a formal specification and has been around for a long time. It is widely used in various industries and has extensive platform tooling and support.
- **Self-descriptive**: Due to its tag structure, XML is self-descriptive. It is simpler to grasp what each piece of data represents, which is vital in complex applications.

- **Extensible**: You can specify your tags and structure, allowing for powerful type and validation using **Document Type Definitions (DTD)** or **XML Schema Definitions (XSDs)**.

- **Metadata support**: XML can carry metadata as attributes on tags, allowing for more complex data representation.

- Namespace support prevents name conflicts and allows for more elaborate hierarchical data structures.

- **Comments**: Because XML allows for comments, it is easy to incorporate annotations directly into the document.

- **Wide application**: Widely used in configurations, SOAP-based online services, document-based databases such as XHTML, and various other contexts.

XML readability, how easy is for humans and machines to read XML:

- **Human-readable**: Despite being more verbose, adding descriptive tags makes XML more readable. This verbosity, however, can make it challenging to filter through substantial XML files.

- **Machine-readable**: Almost every programming language includes extensive support for parsing XML.

JSON advantages, JSON is XML without the bloat:

- **JSON is lightweight**: JSON's syntax is easier to understand and write since it is more straightforward.

- **Fast**: Its simplified structure makes it often faster to read and write, minimizing client and server overhead.

- JSON includes intrinsic support for basic data types such as numbers, booleans, and null, allowing it to be more expressive with less effort.

- **JSON structures are easily mapped to programming structures**: JSON structures are easily mapped to arrays and objects in programming languages such as JavaScript, Python, and Java.

- JSON has native support in all modern browsers because it is developed from JavaScript, making it perfect for client-server communication in online applications.

- **APIs and NoSQL**: JSON is the most often used data format in RESTful APIs and many NoSQL databases such as MongoDB.

- **JSON readability**: **Human-readable**: Although it lacks some of the descriptive qualities of XML, its concise syntax makes it very straightforward to read.

- JSON is easier and faster for machines to understand and generate since it is less verbose and more structured.

Summary of comparisons, We need to compare and make the best for our team and project specifications:

- XML is more verbose than JSON, which can be advantageous (more descriptive) and disadvantageous (bigger size).

- **Standards and validation**: XML has a more structured standard and supports schema-based validation. JSON is less rigid and lacks built-in support for namespaces and validation than XML.

- **Data kinds**: JSON includes built-in support for fundamental data kinds, whereas XML describes data types using string data and properties.

- **Metadata**: XML's attribute capability allows for more detailed metadata, whereas JSON must embed metadata into the data structure.

- JSON is generally faster to read and write since it is less verbose.

- **Readability**: The verbosity of XML makes it more self-descriptive and more challenging to read in huge files. JSON is easy to read but may require external documentation to comprehend the data's structure and purpose.

- **Use cases**: XML is frequently preferable for document-based, hierarchical, and sophisticated structures containing metadata, whereas JSON is preferable for data structures and APIs where speed and simplicity are critical.

In summary, the choice between XML and JSON will be determined by your application's specific requirements, such as speed, complexity, and the data you need to process.

XML serialization sample

The **XmlSerializer** class in the **System** library can be used to serialize XML in .NET. The namespace **Xml.Serialization**. Following is a simple example of serializing and deserializing an object to and from XML:

```
1. using System;
2. using System.IO;
3. using System.Xml.Serialization;
4.
5. public class Person
6. {
7.     public string Name { get; set; }
8.     public int Age { get; set; }
9. }
10.
11. public class Program
12. {
13.     public static void Main()
```

```
14.    {
15.        Person person = new Person { Name = "Alice", Age = 30 };
16.
17.        // Serialize object to XML
18.        XmlSerializer serializer = new
    XmlSerializer(typeof(Person));
19.        using (StringWriter writer = new StringWriter())
20.        {
21.            serializer.Serialize(writer, person);
22.            string xmlString = writer.ToString();
23.            Console.WriteLine("Serialized XML:");
24.            Console.WriteLine(xmlString);
25.        }
26.
27.        // Deserialize object from XML
28.        string xmlInput = "<Person><Name>Alice</Name><Age>30</Age></
    Person>";
29.        using (StringReader reader = new StringReader(xmlInput))
30.        {
31.            Person deserializedPerson = (Person)serializer.
    Deserialize(reader);
32.            Console.WriteLine($"Deserialized Person: Name =
    {deserializedPerson.Name}, Age = {deserializedPerson.Age}");
33.        }
34.    }
35. }
```

XmlSerialization attributes: You can control the **XmlSerialization** process by utilizing attributes such as:

- **[XmlAttribute]**: The property is serialized as an attribute rather than an XML element.

- **[XmlElement]**: Allows you to provide the XML element's name.

- **[XmlIgnore]**: This attribute is ignored during serialization.

JSON serialization sample

JSON serialization in .NET can be done using the **System.Text.Json.JsonSerializer**:

```
1. using System;
2. using System.Text.Json;
3.
4. public class Person
```

```
 5. {
 6.     public string Name { get; set; }
 7.     public int Age { get; set; }
 8. }
 9.
10. public class Program
11. {
12.     public static void Main()
13.     {
14.         Person person = new Person { Name = "Alice", Age = 30 };
15.
16.         // Serialize to JSON
17.         string jsonString = JsonSerializer.Serialize(person);
18.         Console.WriteLine("Serialized JSON:");
19.         Console.WriteLine(jsonString);
20.
21.         // Deserialize from JSON
22.         Person deserializedPerson = JsonSerializer.Deserialize<Perso
    n>(jsonString);
23.         Console.
    WriteLine($"Deserialized Person: Name = {deserializedPerson.
    Name}, Age = {deserializedPerson.Age}");
24.     }
25. }
```

Attributes for JSON serialization: With `System.Text.Json`, you can use attributes like:

- **[JsonPropertyName("name")]**: To specify a different name for the JSON property.
- **[JsonInclude]**: This is new in .NET 9. It allows us to include non-public members in the serialization and deserialization process.

`JsonPropertyName` is especially useful when the property name in the C# class does not match the key name in the JSON object or when you wish to follow a specific naming convention in the JSON output.

Consider this class:

```
1. public class Person
2. {
3.     [JsonPropertyName("first_name")]
4.     public string FirstName { get; set; }
5.
6.     [JsonPropertyName("last_name")]
7.     [JsonInclude]
```

```
8.     private string LastName { get; set; }
9. }
```

If we serialize an object of this type to JSON without using **JsonPropertyName**, the default behavior is to use the class's property names, resulting in JSON that looks like this:

```
1. {
2.   "FirstName": "John",
3.   "LastName": "Doe"
4. }
```

Using **JsonPropertyName**, however, the JSON output will adhere to the supplied property names:

```
1. {
2.   "FirstName": "John",
3.   "LastName": "Doe"
4. }
```

Why we should use it: There are some reasons why we use and not use it:

- **Conventions for naming**: Different systems may use various naming standards. Your C# code may utilize PascalCasing while the API you are dealing with uses snake_case. **JsonPropertyName** bridges this gap.

- **Readability**: Certain property name patterns may be easier to grasp or more consistent with other data formats or standards humans are dealing with when reading JSON output.

- **Compatibility**: **JsonPropertyName** can ensure that serialization and deserialization function correctly when dealing with existing JSON data or third-party APIs where property names do not match your class property names.

- **Refactoring**: If you need to refactor your C# class properties but do not want the change to influence the serialized JSON, **JsonPropertyName** can decouple the two, allowing for independent adjustments.

- **Data contracts**: Specifying property names in a contract on how the JSON should look can ensure that both parties (e.g., a client and a server) agree on the format, regardless of their internal naming standards.

- **Selective serialization**: While it is not its primary purpose, you can use it with other attributes to further customize serialization behavior, making your data output more versatile.

To summarize, **JsonPropertyName** allows you to manage the naming of properties in JSON serialization and deserialization, improving readability, compatibility, and maintainability.

Binary serialization in .NET

Turning an item or data structure into a format that can be easily saved or transmitted and then reconstructed is known as serialization. Binary serialization is a type of serialization in which the state of an object is changed to a binary representation.

The .NET framework has support for binary serialization via the **System.Text.Json or System.Xml.XmlSerializer**. This classes allows you to serialize and deserialize an object graph (an object and its linked objects) into a binary stream.

Here is a simple example of binary serialization and deserialization:

Serializing:

```
1. using System;
2. using System.IO;
3. using System.Text.Json;
4.
5. class Person
6. {
7.     public string Name { get; set; }
8.     public int Age { get; set; }
9. }
10.
11. class Program
12. {
13.     static void Main()
14.     {
15.         Person person = new Person { Name = "Alice", Age = 30 };
16.
17.         string jsonString = JsonSerializer.Serialize(person);
18.         File.WriteAllText("person.json", jsonString);
19.
20.         Console.WriteLine("Serialization complete.");
21.     }
22. }
```

Deserializing:

```
1. using System;
2. using System.IO;
3. using System.Text.Json;
4.
5. class Person
6. {
```

```
7.      public string Name { get; set; }
8.      public int Age { get; set; }
9. }
10.
11. class Program
12. {
13.     static void Main()
14.     {
15.         string jsonString = File.ReadAllText("person.json");
16.
17.         Person person = JsonSerializer.Deserialize<Person>(jsonStri
   ng);
18.
19.         Console.WriteLine($"Name: {person.Name}, Age: {person.
   Age}");
20.     }
21. }
```

Important considerations

When working with serialization in .NET, there are several key points to keep in mind:

- **Serializable property**: To make a class serializable, add the **[Serializable]** property to it.

- **Binary formatter**: The **BinaryFormatter** class is responsible for serialization and deserialization.

- **Stream**: Serialization writes to a stream, while deserialization reads from it. It could be a file stream, a memory stream, or something else entirely.

- **Security**: When deserializing objects from an untrusted source, be cautious since this can lead to security flaws.

- **Versioning**: If the structure of the class changes (e.g., adding/removing properties), deserialization may fail.

- **Object graph**: The **BinaryFormatter** will recursively serialize the item and all associated objects, allowing it to handle complex object graphs.

- **Not all items can be serialized**: Some system objects and resources are incompatible with serialization.

- **Performance**: Binary serialization is more efficient in size and performance than other forms of serialization, such as XML and JSON, but it is less human-readable.

- **Platform dependency**: In general, binary serialization in .NET is not cross-platform. Usually, serialized objects can only be deserializable back into a .NET application.

Tip: **BinaryFormatter** **was deemed insecure for untrusted data and is not recommended for data transfer between trustworthy and untrusted systems. Always review the most recent documentation for the most up-to-date best practices.**

Understanding file and directory classes in System.IO

The **System.IO** namespace in .NET has some classes that allow you to communicate with the file system. The **File** and **Directory** classes are the most widely utilized for basic file and directory handling operations.

File class includes static methods for creating, deleting, opening, copying, and moving files. Here is an overview of some of the more popular methods:

```
1.  // Create
2.  File.Create("example.txt");
3.
4.  // Exists
5.  bool exists = File.Exists("example.txt");
6.
7.  // Read all text
8.  string content = File.ReadAllText("example.txt");
9.
10. // Write all text
11. File.WriteAllText("example.txt", "Hello World!");
12.
13. // File delete
14. File.Delete("example.txt");
```

Directory class offers static methods for creating, deleting, and moving directories and retrieving directory metadata:

```
1.  // Create
2.  Directory.CreateDirectory("NewFolder");
3.
4.  // Exists
5.  bool exists = Directory.Exists("NewFolder");
6.
7.  // Get files
```

```
8. string[] files = Directory.GetFiles("NewFolder");
9.
10. // Get directories
11. string[] dirs = Directory.GetDirectories("NewFolder");
12.
13. // Delete
14. Directory.Delete("NewFolder", true);
```

Always check if the file or directory exists before executing operations to avoid exceptions. For clarity, the preceding examples are kept simple and do not include such checks.

Working with paths, buffers, and memory streams

The **System.IO.Path** class in the .NET class allows you to manipulate paths without writing all of the functionality yourself—functions such as **Path.Combine**, **Path.DirectoryName** and **Path.GetFileName** can be used to create and parse file and directory paths.

Buffers are used in C# to store data transported from one location to another temporarily. The **byte[]** array is the most fundamental buffer in C#. .NET also includes the **Buffer** class, which includes static methods like **BlockCopy** for manipulating arrays.

A memory stream is a stream that reads or writes to a memory block. **MemoryStream** class in **System.IO** namespace exists in .NET for this purpose. Memory streams are handy when retaining the entire stream in memory, such as when the size is tiny, and you require quick, random access.

Following is an example of working with paths, buffers, and memory streams:

```
1. using System;
2. using System.IO;
3.
4. namespace PathBufferMemoryStreamExample
5. {
6.     class Program
7.     {
8.         static void Main(string[] args)
9.         {
10.            // Working with Paths
11.            string folder = @"C:\ExampleFolder";
12.            string fileName = "test.txt";
13.            string fullPath = Path.Combine(folder, fileName);
14.            Console.WriteLine($"Full Path: {fullPath}");
```

```
15.
16.                  // Create some data as a buffer
17.                  byte[] buffer = new byte[1024]; // 1 KB buffer
18.                  for (int i = 0; i < buffer.Length; i++)
19.                  {
20.                      buffer[i] = (byte)(i % 256);
21.                  }
22.
23.                  // Working with Memory Stream
24.                  using (MemoryStream memoryStream = new MemoryStream())
25.                  {
26.                      // Write the buffer to the memory stream
27.                      memoryStream.Write(buffer, 0, buffer.Length);
28.
29.                      // Reset the position of the stream to the beginning
30.                      memoryStream.Seek(0, SeekOrigin.Begin);
31.
32.                      // Read from the memory stream back into a new
    buffer
33.                      byte[] readBuffer = new byte[1024];
34.                      memoryStream.Read(readBuffer, 0, readBuffer.Length);
35.
36.                      // Verify that readBuffer is the same as buffer
37.                      for (int i = 0; i < buffer.Length; i++)
38.                      {
39.                          if (buffer[i] != readBuffer[i])
40.                          {
41.                              Console.WriteLine("Buffers are not equal!");
42.                              return;
43.                          }
44.                      }
45.
46.                      Console.WriteLine("Buffers are equal!");
47.                  }
48.          }
49.      }
50. }
```

In the example, we used **Path** to define a **Path.Combine**. After combining, a byte buffer was formed. To test the procedure, we used a **MemoryStream** to write the buffer to memory and then read it back into another buffer.

Handling file and directory exceptions

Exception handling in C# and .NET when dealing with files and directories is critical for developing solid and fault-tolerant programs. The **System.IO** namespace includes file and directory management classes, including **File**, **FileInfo**, **Directory**, and **DirectoryInfo**. Many of these methods may throw exceptions, which must be caught and handled correctly.

Typical exceptions

When working with file operations in programming, it is important to anticipate and handle exceptions that may arise. Here are some typical exceptions encountered in file handling:

- **FileNotFoundException**: Thrown while attempting to access a non-existent file.
- **DirectoryNotFoundException**: When a directory cannot be discovered.
- **UnauthorizedAccessException**: Thrown when the program lacks the required permissions.
- **IOException**: The base class for the majority of I/O exceptions, thrown for a variety of I/O failures.
- **PathTooLongException**: This exception is thrown when a path or fully qualified file name exceeds the system-defined maximum length.

Exception handling fundamentals

The try, catch, and finally, blocks are often employed for exception handling:

```
1. using System;
2. using System.IO;
3.
4. class Program
5. {
6.     static void Main()
7.     {
8.         string filePath = "somefile.txt";
9.         try
10.        {
11.            string text = File.ReadAllText(filePath);
12.            Console.WriteLine("File contents: ");
13.            Console.WriteLine(text);
14.        }
15.        catch (FileNotFoundException e)
16.        {
```

```
17.          Console.WriteLine($"File not found: {e.Message}");
18.      }
19.      catch (UnauthorizedAccessException e)
20.      {
21.          Console.WriteLine($"Access denied: {e.Message}");
22.      }
23.      catch (IOException e)
24.      {
25.          Console.WriteLine($"An I/O error occurred: {e.
   Message}");
26.      }
27.      finally
28.      {
29.          // This block will consistently execute, regardless of
   whether an exception was thrown or not.
30.          Console.WriteLine("Completed reading file.");
31.      }
32.  }
33.}
```

We can also validate specific methods before using them, like this sample:

```
1.  string filePath = "somefile.txt";
2.  if (File.Exists(filePath))
3.  {
4.      string text = File.ReadAllText(filePath);
5.      Console.WriteLine("File contents: ");
6.      Console.WriteLine(text);
7.  }
8.  else
9.  {
10.     Console.WriteLine("File does not exist.");
11. }
```

In summary, by correctly employing these components, you may create robust apps that handle files and directories gracefully under various scenarios.

Secure file operations and file I/O permissions

In C# and .NET, file operations and I/O are often performed using **System.IO** namespace classes such as **FileStream**, **StreamReader**, **StreamWriter**, **File**, and **Directory**. These classes include methods for reading and writing data to files and creating, deleting, and moving files and directories.

Any software system relies heavily on file operations and permissions. incorrectly specified permissions might result in illegal access or data loss, so it is critical to execute file activities securely. In C# and .NET, you can use a variety of classes and methods to securely handle file I/O, including setting permissions.

Key classes and methods they allow to get and set information:

- **System.IO.File**: For basic file operations like reading and writing.
- **System.IO.FileInfo**: For detailed file attributes.
- **System.IO.StreamReader/StreamWriter**: For reading and writing to files in a more controlled manner.
- **System.Security.AccessControl.FileSecurity**: For setting and getting file permissions.

Following is an example that demonstrates creating, writing, reading a file, and setting permissions in C#:

```
1.  using System;
2.  using System.IO;
3.  using System.Security.AccessControl;
4.  using System.Security.Principal;
5.
6.  namespace SecureFileOperations
7.  {
8.      class Program
9.      {
10.         static void Main(string[] args)
11.         {
12.             string filePath = "test.txt";
13.
14.             // Create and Write to File
15.             using (StreamWriter sw = new StreamWriter(filePath))
16.             {
17.                 sw.WriteLine("Hello, world!");
18.             }
19.
20.             // Secure the File
21.             FileSecurity fileSecurity = new FileSecurity();
22.             SecurityIdentifier everyone = new
        SecurityIdentifier(WellKnownSidType.WorldSid, null);
23.             fileSecurity.
```

```
              AddAccessRule(new FileSystemAccessRule(everyone,
         FileSystemRights.Read, AccessControlType.Allow));
24.            File.SetAccessControl(filePath, fileSecurity);
25.
26.            // Read the File Content
27.            string content = File.ReadAllText(filePath);
28.            Console.WriteLine($"File content: {content}");
29.
30.            // Show Permission
31.            fileSecurity = File.GetAccessControl(filePath);
32.            foreach (FileSystemAccessRule rule in fileSecurity.
         GetAccessRules(true, true, typeof(SecurityIdentifier)))
33.            {
34.                Console.WriteLine($"Identity:
         {rule.IdentityReference.Value}, Right: {rule.FileSystemRights},
         Type: {rule.AccessControlType}");
35.            }
36.        }
37.    }
38.}
```

These are the main points we need to care about in the file operations and permissions:

- **Security**: Improperly specified file permissions can allow unwanted access to sensitive data.

- **Data integrity**: Handling files securely helps to prevent data corruption.

- **Resource management**: Opening and closing file handles correctly ensures system resources are appropriately managed.

- **Auditing**: Setting permissions correctly can also help with security audits.

Remember to install any required packages or assemblies for the code to compile. For instance, **System.Security.AccessControl** may need to be installed using NuGet package manager.

Make sure that this application is run with the required permissions. To alter file permissions on Windows, you may need to execute it as an administrator.

Conclusion

This chapter introduced file operations, streams, and serialization in .NET using C#. It explained using the **System.IO** namespace to read and write text files, manage paths and buffers, and handle file exceptions. It also showed how to serialize and deserialize objects in XML, JSON, and binary formats using the **XmlSerializer**, **JsonSerializer**, and **BinaryFormatter** classes. It also digs into modifying these procedures through characteristics, which improves data management and communication in .NET apps.

In the next chapter, we get into **Entity Framework Core** (**EF Core**), a sophisticated ORM framework for .NET apps, streamlining data handling via .NET objects, not SQL queries. It includes database setup for SQL Server, PostgreSQL, SQLite, and MySQL, along with LINQ querying, change tracking, CRUD operations, DbContext, DbSet, data relationships, and inheritance.

Join our book's Discord space

Join the book's Discord Workspace for Latest updates, Offers, Tech happenings around the world, New Release and Sessions with the Authors:

https://discord.bpbonline.com

CHAPTER 9

Data Handling with EF Core

Introduction

This chapter covers **Entity Framework Core (EF Core)**, an advanced ORM framework for .NET applications. The framework simplifies data management by using .NET objects instead of SQL queries, increasing productivity. Database configuration with SQL Server, PostgreSQL, SQLite, and MySQL will be covered. The chapter also covers LINQ data querying, EF Core change tracking, and CRUD operations. DbContext and DbSet, EF Core's foundational classes, are covered, along with data relationships and inheritance.

The chapter covers advanced features like database migrations, which sync your schema and data model. You will also learn object-oriented principles applied to your data model through EF Core's inheritance features. Finally, we discuss performance options like lazy, eager, and caching. This chapter will teach you how to use EF Core in .NET applications for efficient database management and give you tips and best practices for optimizing your work with this powerful tool.

Structure

This chapter covers the following topics:

- Introduction to Entity Framework Core
- Querying data using LINQ

- Understanding EF Core change tracking
- Configuring a database using EF Core
- Performing CRUD operations using EF Core
- Understanding DBContext and DBSet in EF Core
- Navigating relationships with EF Core
- Migrations in Entity Framework Core
- Implementing inheritance with Entity Framework Core
- Performance considerations when using Entity Framework Core

Objectives

This chapter dives into Entity Framework Core, a free and open-source **Object-Relational Mapping (ORM)** framework for .NET. You will understand how to set up and configure databases using various providers, explore data querying with LINQ, and grasp how EF Core tracks changes to facilitate CRUD operations. Additionally, this chapter will compare EF Core with the lower-level ADO.NET and highlight its benefits, such as enhanced developer productivity and cross-database compatibility.

Introduction to Entity Framework Core

Entity Framework Core is a free and open-source ORM framework for Microsoft .NET applications. It adds an abstraction layer to the database interface, allowing us to work with databases using .NET objects rather than database tables, columns, and SQL queries. EF Core is a slimmer, more versatile, and cross-platform version of the earlier Entity Framework that runs .NET.

Core features of Entity Framework Core

Entity Framework key features include database abstraction, data modeling, query capabilities, caching, concurrency management, migrations, and transactions. These capabilities work together to provide a robust ORM architecture, allowing us to connect with databases through .NET objects rather than SQL queries. From designing data models using code-first or database-first techniques to querying data with LINQ, EF Core offers smooth data operations. It also has additional features, including built-in support for transactions and optimistic concurrency, first-level caching for speed optimization, and database migrations for schema maintenance, making it a complete solution for data access in .NET applications.

- **Database abstraction**: EF Core offers a layer of abstraction over the database, allowing us to interact with data as if working with in-memory objects. It removes the need to compose sophisticated SQL queries for many typical data tasks manually. The framework converts LINQ-to-Entities queries into database-specific SQL queries, executes them, and returns the results as objects.

- **Data model**: EF Core enables us to create the application's data model using .NET classes, either through a database-first or a code-first approach. You develop your classes first under the code-first model, and EF Core produces related tables in the database. EF Core may construct classes based on an existing database schema in the database-first method.

- **Querying with LINQ**: EF Core queries data using LINQ. It enables us to utilize strongly typed queries, which feature compile-time syntax verification and IntelliSense. Because the queries are written in C#, they are easy to debug, manage, and version.

- **Caching**: EF Core has first-level caching by default. When an entity is loaded into the application's DbContext, it is cached for faster subsequent access. It increases performance by lowering the number of database's roundtrips.

- **Concurrency handling**: EF Core has optimistic concurrency support. When an entity is read, EF Core remembers its original values. If a record in the database has changed since it was first read, EF Core throws a concurrency exception, letting the application address the issue correctly.

- **Migrations**: The Migrations feature helps you to maintain your database structure and data model in sync while keeping existing data in the database. It allows you to version your database schema and make incremental updates automatically.

- **Transactions**: EF Core provides strong transaction support. It assures that a sequence of actions is conducted as a single transaction using the Unit of Work pattern, conforming to the ACID principles.

- **Database provider extensibility**: EF Core works on Windows, Linux, and macOS. It also supports SQL Server, PostgreSQL, SQLite, and others. It makes it flexible for various project needs.

Why use Entity Framework Core

EF Core automates data model mapping and SQL query creation, increasing developer productivity, improving code maintainability, and simplifying cross-database interoperability.

- **Developer productivity**: EF Core increases developer productivity dramatically by automating the vast bulk of database-related code. We may conduct schema updates using capabilities like migrations instead of manually creating SQL scripts.

- **Maintainability**: EF Core automates data model mapping and SQL query generation, boosting developer productivity, code maintainability, and cross-database compatibility.

- **Strongly typed syntax**: Because EF Core supports LINQ querying, it benefits from compile-time syntax verification, which reduces runtime mistakes. This strict typing also improves the readability and self-explanation of the code.

- **Cross-database compatibility**: With a few code modifications, you may build your application in one database and deploy it in another. You could, for example, build in PostgreSQL and then deploy to SQL Server by simply changing the database provider.

Working with databases

EF Core has a modular and adaptable design, allowing it to interface with various database providers. It allows for database switching with few code modifications, resulting in a consistent and simplified development experience. A comparison of EF Core with four databases: SQL Server, PostgreSQL, SQLite, and MySQL:

- **SQL Server**:
  - **Pros**: Native interaction with the .NET stack, which provides sophisticated capabilities such as spatial data types, table partitioning, and window functions. Scalability and transaction support are ideal for enterprise-grade applications that demand high scalability and robust transaction support. Comprehensive tooling, offering an extensive array of tools for monitoring and administration, facilitating efficient database management.
  - **Cons**: Commercial versions typically have more significant license charges. It has platform constraints because it is primarily designed for Windows systems.
  - **Use case**: Excellent for enterprise-level applications that require scalability, dependability, and sophisticated functionality.

- **PostgreSQL**:
  - **Pros**: While being open-source and versatile, it also supports JSON, XML, geographical data formats, and advanced indexing algorithms. Full-text search enables efficient and powerful querying of text data for relevant results, while materialized views improve query performance by storing precomputed query results and reducing computational overhead.
  - **Cons**: For read-heavy workloads, extra tweaking and optimization may be required. Some enterprise-level functionalities present in SQL Server may be missing.
  - **Use case**: Suitable for applications requiring diverse features and data kinds, such as GIS.

- **SQLite**:
  - **Pros**: It is extremely light and serverless, ideal for mobile or standalone apps. A single database file simplifies setup and sharing. It uses extremely little memory and is highly quick for read-intensive processes.
  - **Cons**: It has limited concurrent capabilities due to the usage of file-level locking. Some complex capabilities, such as stored procedures and triggers, are missing.
  - **Use case**: It is perfect for mobile apps, embedded devices, and local storage needs that require simplicity and a tiny footprint.

- **MySQL**:
  - **Pros**: It is open source with a vast community and a wealth of internet information. Excellent replication and clustering capabilities. It comes with ACID compliance and transaction support, which is dependable.
  - **Cons**: Enterprise features may necessitate costly licensing. Some sophisticated indexing and data types seen in PostgreSQL are missing.
  - **Use case**: Ideal for online applications, particularly those that use the LAMP stack or applications that require robust replication functionality.

While each of the four databases has advantages and disadvantages, EF Core makes working with any of them a breeze. EF Core is a flexible tool in your development arsenal. It allows you to construct your application on one database and then move to another by changing the database provider and connection string. An example of database-agnostic development is PostgreSQL to SQL Server.

One of the remarkable aspects of EF Core is its ability to be database-agnostic, thanks to its extensible database provider model. It means you could develop your application locally using a PostgreSQL database for its open-source benefits and then deploy it on a SQL Server database for production, taking advantage of its scalability and robustness.

It would help if you changed the database provider and connection string to switch between PostgreSQL and SQL Server. For example, during development, you might configure your DbContext as follows for PostgreSQL:

```
1. protected override void OnConfiguring(DbContextOptionsBuilder
   options)
2.     => options.UseNpgsql("Host=my_host;Database=my_db;Username=my_
   user;Password=my_pw");
```

You can then switch to SQL Server for production:

```
1. protected override void OnConfiguring(DbContextOptionsBuilder
   options)
2.     => options.UseSqlServer(@"Server=myServerAddress;Database=
   myDataBase;User Id=myUsername;Password=myPassword;");
```

It makes EF Core not only a powerful ORM but also a flexible one, capable of meeting various development and production requirements.

EF Core is a cornerstone technology for .NET developers because it unifies several complex parts of database interaction into a unified, well-documented API. Whether developing a simple web application or an extensive corporate system, EF Core delivers the capabilities to make data access simple, quick, and resilient.

Steps to create a model

Let us study how to set up and build a small sample of a Farm:

Setup: First, install EF Core in your project:

```
1. dotnet add package Microsoft.EntityFrameworkCore.SqlServer
```

Model: A model is a group of classes that reflect the data structure you are dealing with in the EF Core context. These classes serve as a template for constructing database tables and are the entities on which your application will work. Entity classes, the context class inherited from DbContext, and any settings applied via data annotations, or the Fluent API are typically included in the model. These elements establish the form of your data, the relationships between tables, and the restrictions and rules you wish to apply. The model abstracts your database, letting you interact with it in a more .NET-idiomatic manner:

The **Farm** class models a farm entity with properties for its unique identifier, name, and a list of associated **Crop** objects, initializing an empty list for crops. The abstract **Crop** class serves as a base for different crop types, encapsulating common properties such as the crop's identifier, variety, planting and harvest dates, and a reference to the associated farm. Derived classes like **Vegetable**, **Rice**, and **Bean** extend the **Crop** class with specific properties such as **Type**, **Grade**, and **Color**, respectively. This approach allows for a structured, type-safe representation of farm data, facilitating efficient data manipulation and querying within a .NET application.

```
1. public class Farm
2. {
3.     public int FarmId { get; set; }
4.     public string Name { get; set; }
5.     public List<Crop> Crops { get; } = new List<Crop>();
6. }
7.
8. public abstract class Crop
9. {
10.     public int CropId { get; set; }
11.     public string Variety { get; set; }
12.     public DateTime PlantingDate { get; set; }
13.     public DateTime HarvestDate { get; set; }
```

```
14.     public int FarmId { get; set; }
15.     public Farm Farm { get; set; }
16. }
17.
18. public class Vegetable : Crop
19. {
20.     public string Type { get; set; }
21. }
22.
23. public class Rice : Crop
24. {
25.     public string Grade { get; set; }
26. }
27.
28. public class Bean : Crop
29. {
30.     public string Color { get; set; }
31. }
```

Database context (look at *Understanding DbContext and DbSet in EF Core* below):

The following sample code installs a farm with some crops and then conducts basic activities for the **Main** program using **Farm**:

```
1. using System;
2. using System.Linq;
3. using Microsoft.EntityFrameworkCore;
4.
5. public class Program
6. {
7.     public static void Main()
8.     {
9.         using (var db = new FarmingContext())
10.        {
11.            // Initialize a new Farm
12.            var farm = new Farm { Name = "Green Valley" };
13.            db.Farms.Add(farm);
14.
15.            // Add some crops
16.            var vegetable = new Vegetable { Type = "Carrot",
   Variety = "Nantes", PlantingDate = DateTime.
   Now.AddMonths(-2), HarvestDate = DateTime.Now.
   AddMonths(1), Farm = farm };
```

```
17.            var rice = new Rice { Grade = "Basmati", Variety =
    "White", PlantingDate = DateTime.Now.AddMonths(-3), HarvestDate =
    DateTime.Now.AddMonths(3), Farm = farm };
18.            var bean = new Bean { Color = "Black", Variety =
    "Black Bean", PlantingDate = DateTime.Now.AddMonths(-1), HarvestDate
    = DateTime.Now.AddMonths(2), Farm = farm };
19.
20.            db.AddRange(vegetable, rice, bean);
21.            db.SaveChanges();
22.
23.            // List all Farms
24.            Console.WriteLine("Farms:");
25.            var farms = db.Farms.Include(f => f.Crops).ToList();
26.            foreach (var f in farms)
27.            {
28.                Console.WriteLine($"- {f.Name}");
29.                foreach (var crop in f.Crops)
30.                {
31.                    Console.WriteLine($"  - {crop.Variety}
    ({crop.GetType().Name}),
    Planted on: {crop.PlantingDate}, Harvest on: {crop.HarvestDate}");
32.                }
33.            }
34.
35.            // Delete a crop
36.            Console.WriteLine("Deleting the first crop...");
37.            var firstCrop = db.Crops.First();
38.            db.Crops.Remove(firstCrop);
39.            db.SaveChanges();
40.        }
41.    }
42. }
```

It is a simple example that does not cover every aspect of EF Core or OOP, but it should provide a good starting point for modeling a farm that grows different crops using EF Core.

Querying data using LINQ

Querying data in EF Core with LINQ allows us to obtain, filter, and alter data in a highly typed, syntactically consistent way. LINQ allows you to construct queries in a manner comparable to writing standard C# code, making working in the .NET environment more natural. EF Core converts these LINQ searches into SQL queries for the database, obtains the data, and then maps the results to the .NET objects described in your model. Strong type provides compile-time checks, which reduces runtime errors and improves readability.

Learn to query data using LINQ in EF Core

To query data using LINQ in EF Core, you must first create a DbContext object with the DbSet attributes corresponding to the tables in your database. Once you have this, you can run queries using LINQ methods like **Where**, **Select**, **GroupBy**, and so on, or you may utilize LINQ query syntax. LINQ queries are delayed, so they are not run against the database until you iterate through the query result, commonly done with methods like **ToList()** or **FirstOrDefault()**.

Farm sample query example: Assuming you have a **Farming** database with **Farm**, **Crop**, and **Vegetable** classes. Here is an example of how to use LINQ to get data:

```
1. using System;
2. using System.Linq;
3. using Microsoft.EntityFrameworkCore;
4.
5. public class Program
6. {
7.     public static void Main()
8.     {
9.         using (var context = new FarmingContext())
10.        {
11.            // Fetch all Farms that grow more than 3 types of
    Vegetables
12.            var farmsWithMultipleVegetables = context.Farms
13.                .Include(f => f.Vegetables)
14.                .Where(f => f.Vegetables.Count > 3)
15.                .ToList();
16.
17.            // Fetch all Farms that are growing Carrots
18.            var farmsGrowingCarrots = context.Farms
19.                .Include(f => f.Vegetables)
20.                .Where(f => f.Vegetables.Any(v => v.Name ==
    "Carrot"))
21.                .ToList();
22.
23.            // Fetch the total quantity of all Crops grown in
    all Farms
```

```
24.              var totalCropQuantity = context.Crops
25.                  .Sum(c => c.Quantity);
26.
27.              // Output the results
28.              Console.WriteLine("Farms with multiple types of
   Vegetables:");
29.              foreach (var farm in farmsWithMultipleVegetables)
30.              {
31.                  Console.WriteLine(farm.Name);
32.              }
33.
34.              Console.WriteLine("\nFarms growing Carrots:");
35.              foreach (var farm in farmsGrowingCarrots)
36.              {
37.                  Console.WriteLine(farm.Name);
38.              }
39.
40.              Console.WriteLine($"\nTotal quantity of all Crops:
   {totalCropQuantity}");
41.          }
42.      }
43. }
```

Three queries are executed using LINQ in this example:

- The first search returns farms that cultivate more than three varieties of vegetables.
- The second query returns carrot-growing farms.
- The final query determines the total amount of crops cultivated across all farms.

The contain function is used for eager loading of linked entities. Therefore, in the first two searches, each **Farm** object will contain its connected **Vegetables** in the response.

EF Core and LINQ x ADO.NET

The simplicity of creation and maintenance is one of the significant advantages of utilizing EF Core with LINQ over ADO.NET. EF Core abstracts the database at a higher level, allowing us to interact with .NET objects rather than writing raw SQL queries. This ORM functionality automatically manages the mapping between database tables and your C# classes, saving us the time-consuming and error-prone process of manual data mapping. This can result in shorter development cycles and code that is easier to maintain. With LINQ, queries may be strongly typed directly in C# code, benefiting from compile-time syntax checking and IntelliSense support in IDEs such as Visual Studio.

Code reusability and abstraction: EF Core increases code reuse and provides a consistent programming style when used with LINQ. LINQ allows you to define and reuse queries across different program portions, making your code more modular and easier to manage. The abstraction layer offered by EF Core also allows for transferring database providers with little code modifications. It is a significant benefit over ADO.NET, which frequently requires rewriting SQL queries and data access code to suit database-specific syntax and functionality.

Advanced features and performance: Lazy loading, caching, migrations, and transaction support are among the advanced functionality included in EF Core that would otherwise need bespoke implementation in ADO.NET. While ADO.NET may provide more incredible speed in some cases, EF Core is constantly improving in this area. You also receive built-in support for things like optimistic concurrency, relationships, and data integrity restrictions with EF Core, which you must manage manually with ADO.NET. Furthermore, LINQ queries are converted into optimized SQL queries to ensure efficient data retrieval.

In summary, as compared to ADO.NET, EF Core combined with LINQ gives a more developer-friendly, maintainable, and versatile data access method. While ADO.NET's fine-grained control may be required in some circumstances, the benefits of EF Core make it a tempting alternative for most applications.

The following code is an ADO.NET example that replicates the capabilities of the previous EF Core + LINQ example. This example requires that you have comparable columns and connections in your database (**Farms**, **Crops**, and **Vegetables**). An ADO.NET sample that mirrors the capabilities of the previous EF Core + LINQ example is provided below. This example requires that you have comparable columns and connections in your database (**Farms**, **Crops**, and **Vegetables**).

```
1.  using System;
2.  using System.Data.SqlClient;
3.
4.  public class Program
5.  {
6.      public static void Main()
7.      {
8.          string connectionString = "Data Source=localhost;Initial
    Catalog=FarmingDB;Integrated Security=True";
9.
10.         using (SqlConnection conn = new
    SqlConnection(connectionString))
11.         {
12.             conn.Open();
13.
14.             // Query 1: Fetch all Farms that grow more than 3 types
```

of Vegetables

```
15.            string query1 = @"SELECT f.Name FROM Farms f
16.                        WHERE (SELECT COUNT(*) FROM Vegetables
    v WHERE v.FarmId = f.Id) > 3»;
17.            SqlCommand cmd1 = new SqlCommand(query1, conn);
18.            SqlDataReader reader1 = cmd1.ExecuteReader();
19.            Console.WriteLine("Farms with multiple types of
    Vegetables:");
20.            while (reader1.Read())
21.            {
22.                Console.WriteLine(reader1["Name"].ToString());
23.            }
24.            reader1.Close();
25.
26.            // Query 2: Fetch all Farms that are growing Carrots
27.            string query2 = @"SELECT f.Name FROM Farms f
28.                        INNER JOIN Vegetables v ON f.Id =
    v.FarmId
29.                        WHERE v.Name = 'Carrot'";
30.            SqlCommand cmd2 = new SqlCommand(query2, conn);
31.            SqlDataReader reader2 = cmd2.ExecuteReader();
32.            Console.WriteLine("\nFarms growing Carrots:");
33.            while (reader2.Read())
34.            {
35.                Console.WriteLine(reader2["Name"].ToString());
36.            }
37.            reader2.Close();
38.
39.            // Query 3: Fetch the total quantity of all Crops grown
    in all Farms
40.            string query3 = @"SELECT SUM(c.Quantity) FROM Crops c";
41.            SqlCommand cmd3 = new SqlCommand(query3, conn);
42.            int totalCropQuantity = (int)cmd3.ExecuteScalar();
43.            Console.WriteLine($"\nTotal quantity of all Crops:
    {totalCropQuantity}");
44.        }
45.    }
46.}
```

EF Core and LINQ comparisons

When comparing EF Core with LINQ to traditional ADO.NET approaches, several key differences highlight the benefits and trade-offs of each technology. They provide a more modern, intuitive, and streamlined approach to database interactions within .NET applications. Here, we explore the differences in readability and verbosity, abstraction levels, and the reusability and adaptability of the code:

- **Readability and verbosity**:
  - **ADO.NET**: You must create raw SQL queries and manually execute them with `SqlCommand`, which might result in more verbose and less understandable code.
  - **EF Core with LINQ**: Allows you to construct queries using LINQ methods or syntax, resulting in less verbose and more understandable code.
  - **ADO.NET type safety**: There is no compile-time type verification for SQL queries, making them more error-prone. Strongly typed queries provide compile-time checks, lowering the likelihood of mistakes.
  - **ADO.NET data mapping:** You manually map data from `SqlDataReader` to your objects, which can be time-consuming and error prone.
  - **EF Core with LINQ**: Provides automatic mapping between tables and objects, making data retrieval easier.

- **Abstraction**:
  - **ADO.NET**: Offers little to no database abstraction, forcing you to manage connections, commands, and readers.
  - **EF Core with LINQ**: Provides a high-level abstraction, automatically handling connections and transactions.

- **Reusability and adaptability**:
  - Since each query is a new SQL string that you cannot simply combine or reuse, ADO.NET is less versatile and modular.
  - **EF Core with LINQ**: Encourages code reuse and lets you create complicated queries by combining smaller ones.

In conclusion, while ADO.NET provides complete control, it does so at the expense of additional complexity and a more significant probability of mistakes. EF Core simplifies many of these operations when combined with LINQ, making code easier to develop, read, and maintain.

Understanding EF Core change tracking

EF Core has a robust feature called **change tracking** that automatically tracks the state of entities obtained from or connected with a database context. When you use EF Core to get entities, the framework knows whether those entities have been updated, added, or destroyed. When you are done with making changes, use the **SaveChanges()** function to commit them all at once. EF Core will construct the SQL statements required to update the database.

Change tracking vs. manual tracking in ADO.NET

Change tracking in ADO.NET is often done manually. You must remember what modifications were made to your data, commonly accomplished by preserving copies of the original data to compare against. When you are ready to save your changes, you construct SQL statements to handle inserts, updates, and deletes, which are then executed using a **SqlCommand**. This manual method is not only time-consuming, but it is also prone to mistakes.

Consider a basic **Farm** scenario in which a farm produces beans and rice. First, you would update your **DbContext** to remove the **DbSets** for **Rices** and **Beans** and add new **DbSets** for **Fruits** and **Eggs**.

EF Core sample:

```
1. using Microsoft.EntityFrameworkCore;
2.
3. public class FarmingContext : DbContext
4. {
5.     public DbSet<Farm> Farms { get; set; }
6.     public DbSet<Crop> Crops { get; set; }
7.     public DbSet<Vegetable> Vegetables { get; set; }
8.     // Removed DbSet<Rice> Rices { get; set; }
9.     // Removed DbSet<Bean> Beans { get; set; }
10.    public DbSet<Fruit> Fruits { get; set; }
11.    public DbSet<Egg> Eggs { get; set; }
12.
13.    protected override void OnConfiguring(DbContextOptionsBuilder options)
14.        => options.UseSqlServer(@"Server=localhost;Database=FarmingDB;Trusted_Connection=True;");
15. }
16.
17. public class Farm { /*... same as before ...*/}
18. public class Crop { /*... same as before ...*/}
```

```
19. public class Vegetable { /*... same as before ...*/}
20. public class Fruit { /*... new definition ...*/}
21. public class Egg { /*... new definition ...*/}
```

Generate migration and update database: Then, you would generate a new migration to capture these changes and apply it to update the database schema:

```
1. dotnet ef migrations add RemoveBeansAndRicesAddFruitsAndEggs
2. dotnet ef database update
```

Change tracking in EF Core

Note that EF Core's change tracking is generally not for table-level operations but more for row-level operations. It works by tracking changes to entities after they have been retrieved into the application, making it simple to persist those changes back to the database in a transactionally consistent manner. When you remove or add entities to your code, the change tracker knows what SQL commands to generate when **SaveChanges()** is called.

ADO.NET sample:

```
1. using System.Data.SqlClient;
2.
3. public class Program
4. {
5.     public static void Main()
6.     {
7.         string connectionString = "Data Source=localhost;Initial
   Catalog=FarmingDB;Integrated Security=True";
8.         using (SqlConnection conn = new
   SqlConnection(connectionString))
9.         {
10.            conn.Open();
11.
12.            string dropBeansTable = "DROP TABLE Beans;";
13.            string dropRicesTable = "DROP TABLE Rices;";
14.
15.            using (SqlCommand command = new
   SqlCommand(dropBeansTable, conn))
16.            {
17.                command.ExecuteNonQuery();
18.            }
19.
20.            using (SqlCommand command = new
   SqlCommand(dropRicesTable, conn))
```

```
21.            {
22.                command.ExecuteNonQuery();
23.            }
24.        }
25.    }
26.}
```

Managing and manipulating data within a .NET application and EF Core offers several advantages over traditional ADO.NET. It simplifies many common tasks, automates complex processes, and enhances code readability and maintainability. The following are key points illustrating the ease of use and flexibility provided by EF Core in comparison to ADO.NET:

- **Ease of use**: EF Core simplifies updating entities by altering the in-memory objects and executing **SaveChanges()**. ADO.NET requires you to build and execute SQL queries manually.

- **Automation**: Manual change tracking in ADO.NET is error-prone because you have to remember what changes were made and build SQL queries accordingly. EF Core automates this step.

- **Readability**: The EF Core code is more readable and maintainable. The ADO.NET code requires SQL expertise and can quickly get sophisticated as additional criteria are added.

- **Flexibility**: EF Core lets you alter the object model in code and quickly persist such changes. You would have to return to your SQL queries with ADO.NET to make comparable adjustments.

In summary, compared to the manual method required with ADO.NET, EF Core's change tracking simplifies keeping track of entity changes, minimizes the chance of mistakes, and provides a more straightforward and flexible way to handle data changes.

While EF Core's change tracking mechanism simplifies row-level **Create, Read, Update, Delete (CRUD)** operations, table-level changes like adding or removing tables are typically handled through the migration feature.

Configuring a database using EF Core

EF Core simplifies database setup and configuration by abstracting relational databases and letting us use .NET objects instead of SQL queries. No SQL code is needed to CRUD with EF Core. We can focus on business logic while it manages database connections and transactions. The setup includes adding the database provider package, writing connection strings, and using DbContext to describe the database connection. It reduces boilerplate code, making the codebase clean, manageable, and efficient.

Ensuring correct database setup and configuration for seamless development and robust production deployments is critical. An appropriately set up database enables faster iterations, better troubleshooting, and more straightforward cooperation among team members throughout development. In a manufacturing setting, the stakes are significantly higher. A properly designed database is critical for maintaining data integrity, security, and performance. Poor database configuration may cause many issues, from sluggish application performance to serious security concerns. By advocating best practices such as code-first migrations, seed data setup, and the separation of concerns between application logic and database operations, EF Core helps mitigate these challenges.

Setting up and configuring a database using EF Core in Visual Studio can differ depending on the database you use, PostgreSQL, MySQL, SQL Server, or Oracle. Below, you will find a guide for each:

Some prerequisites are as follows:

1. Check that your machine has the .NET Core SDK installed.
2. With the ASP.NET and web development workload, use Visual Studio 2022 or above.
3. Create a New Project Launch Visual Studio.
4. Create a new project should be selected.
5. Select ASP.NET Core Web Application as the template.
6. Give your project a name, then press the Create button.
7. Choose the application you wish to build (for example, Web API or MVC).

PostgreSQL database

To configure EF Core to work with a PostgreSQL database, follow these steps to ensure proper installation and setup. This guide will walk you through installing the necessary packages, updating your application settings, and configuring the DbContext to use PostgreSQL.

1. **Install NuGet package**: Install the `Npgsql.EntityFrameworkCore.PostgreSQL` package.

2. **AppSettings**: Refresh your app settings. To add the PostgreSQL connection string, use JSON.

   Copy the following code:

```
1. {
2.   "ConnectionStrings": {
3.     "DefaultConnection": "Host=my_host;Database=my_db;Username=my_
   user;Password=my_pw"
4.   }
5. }
```

3. **DbContext**: Replace **Program.cs** with PostgreSQL:

```
1. Services for copying code in C#.MyContext>AddDbContext(options =>
2.     options.UseNpgsql(Configuration.
   MySQL GetConnectionString("DefaultConnection"));
```

MySql database

To configure EF Core to work with a MySQL database, follow these steps to ensure proper installation and setup. This guide will walk you through installing the necessary packages, updating your application settings, and configuring the DbContext to use MySQL.

1. **Install NuGet package**: Install the **Pomelo.EntityFrameworkCore.MySql** package.

2. **AppSettings**: Refresh your app **settings.To** add the MySQL connection string, use JSON:

```
1. Services for copying code in C#.
   MyContext>AddDbContext(options =>
2.     options.UseNpgsql(Configuration.
   MySQL GetConnectionString("DefaultConnection"));
3. {
4.   "ConnectionStrings": {
5.     "DefaultConnection": "Server=my_server;Database=my_
   db;User=my_user;Password=my_pw;"
6.   }
7. }
```

3. **DbContext**: Update **Program.cs** to use MySQL:

```
1. services.AddDbContext<MyContext>(options =>
2.     options.UseMySql(Configuration.GetConnectionString("DefaultCo
   nnection"),
3.     new MySqlServerVersion(new Version(8, 0, 21))));
```

The Microsoft SQL Server

To configure EF Core to work with a Microsoft SQL Server database, follow these steps to ensure proper installation and setup. This guide will walk you through installing the necessary packages, updating your application settings, and configuring the DbContext to use SQL Server.

1. **Install NuGet package**: Install the **Microsoft.EntityFrameworkCore.SqlServer** package.

2. **AppSettings**: To add the SQL Server connection string, use JSON:

```
1. {
```

```
2.   "ConnectionStrings": {
3.     "DefaultConnection": "Server=my_server;Database=my_
   db;User Id=my_user;Password=my_pw;"
4.   }
5. }
```

3. **DbContext**: Replace **Program.cs** with SQL Server:

```
1. services.AddDbContext<MyContext>(options =>
2.     options.UseSqlServer(Configuration.GetConnectionString("Defa
   ultConnection")));
```

Oracle database

To configure Entity Framework Core to work with an Oracle database, follow these steps to ensure proper installation and setup. This guide will walk you through installing the necessary packages, updating your application settings, and configuring the DbContext to use Oracle.

1. **Install NuGet package**: Install the **Oracle.EntityFrameworkCore** package.

2. **AppSettings**: Update your **appsettings.json** to include the Oracle connection string:

```
1. {
2.   "ConnectionStrings": {
3.     "DefaultConnection": "User Id=my_user;Password=my_
   pw;Data Source=my_source;"
4.   }
5. }
```

3. **DbContext**: Update **Program.cs** to use Oracle:

```
1. services.AddDbContext<MyContext>(options =>
2.     options.UseOracle(Configuration.GetConnectionString("Defa
   ultConnection")));
```

Final steps

Now, follow these final steps:

1. Create your **DbContext** and **Models**.

2. **Run migrations to create the database schema**: Add-Migration InitialCreate followed by Update-Database.

3. It is a simplified guide but should get you started with setting up and configuring

a database using EF Core in Visual Studio for PostgreSQL, MySQL, SQL Server, and Oracle.

Performing CRUD operations using EF Core

EF Core provides a smooth method of interacting with your database by making CRUD activities in a Razor Page application simple. The DbContext-derived **FarmingContext** class serves as an intermediary between your application and the database. Each entity, such as **Farm** and **Fruit**, has **DbSet** characteristics included in it, which allow EF Core to track and manage these entities.

For example, the **Fruit** entity, which has characteristics like **Id**, **Name**, **Quantity**, and **FarmId**, represents the fruit data structure. This context can be used in a Razor Page application to search the database for fruits, add new fruits, edit current fruits, and remove fruits. Razor Pages and EF Core's simplicity make it easy to handle forms and bind data, which makes CRUD processes efficient and easy to understand. With the help of EF Core's strong change tracking and potent LINQ features, developers can create dynamic, responsive websites that communicate with databases in an extremely efficient way.

1. Here is how you might define your **FarmingContext** and **Fruit** entity:

```
1. using Microsoft.EntityFrameworkCore;
2.
3. public class FarmingContext : DbContext
4. {
5.     public DbSet<Farm> Farms { get; set; }
6.     public DbSet<Fruit> Fruits { get; set; }
7.
8.     protected override void OnConfiguring(DbContextOptions
    Builder options)
9.         => options.UseSqlServer(@"Server=localhost;Database=
    FarmingDB;Trusted_Connection=True;");
10. }
11.
12. public class Farm
13. {
14.     public int Id { get; set; }
15.     public string Name { get; set; }
16. }
17.
18. public class Fruit
19. {
20.     public int Id { get; set; }
```

```
21.    public string Name { get; set; }
22.    public int Quantity { get; set; }
23.    public int FarmId { get; set; }
24.    public Farm Farm { get; set; }
25. }
```

2. The **Fruit.cshtml.cs** code-behind file defines the page model class, including properties and methods for handling data operations. This class interacts with the **FarmingContext** to perform database operations such as retrieving, creating, updating, and deleting Fruit records. You can efficiently manage data flow between the user interface and the database by leveraging the page model's lifecycle methods (e.g., **OnGet**, **OnPost**). The **Fruit** entity, which includes properties like **Id**, **Name**, and **Quantity**, is seamlessly bound to the Razor Page's HTML form elements. This binding enables smooth data manipulation through form submissions, allowing users to add new fruits, edit existing ones, and delete records. The integration of EF Core with Razor Pages provides a robust and scalable solution for handling CRUD operations, ensuring a clean separation of concerns and enhancing the maintainability of the web application.

3. **Fruit.cshtml.cs** (Code-behind file):

```
1. using Microsoft.AspNetCore.Mvc.RazorPages;
2. using Microsoft.EntityFrameworkCore;
3. using System.Collections.Generic;
4. using System.Linq;
5. using System.Threading.Tasks;
6.
7. public class FruitModel : PageModel
8. {
9.     private readonly FarmingContext _context;
10.
11.    public FruitModel(FarmingContext ontexto)
12.    {
13.        _context = ontexto;
14.    }
15.
16.    public Ilist<Fruit> Fruits { get; set; }
17.
18.    public async Task OnGetAsync()
19.    {
20.        Fruits = await _context.Fruits.ToListAsync();
21.    }
22.
```

```
23.    // Create
24.    public async Task<IactionResult> OnPostCreateAsync(string
   name, int quantity)
25.    {
26.        var fruit = new Fruit { Name = name, Quantity =
   quantity };
27.        _context.Fruits.Add(fruit);
28.        await _context.SaveChangesAsync();
29.        return RedirectToPage();
30.    }
31.
32.    // Update
33.    public async Task<IactionResult> OnPostUpdateAsync(int id,
   string newName, int newQuantity)
34.    {
35.        var fruit = await _context.Fruits.FindAsync(id);
36.        if (fruit == null)
37.        {
38.            return NotFound();
39.        }
40.        fruit.Name = newName;
41.        fruit.Quantity = newQuantity;
42.        await _context.SaveChangesAsync();
43.        return RedirectToPage();
44.    }
45.
46.    // Delete
47.    public async Task<IactionResult> OnPostDeleteAsync(int id)
48.    {
49.        var fruit = await _context.Fruits.FindAsync(id);
50.        if (fruit == null)
51.        {
52.            return NotFound();
53.        }
54.        _context.Fruits.Remove(fruit);
55.        await _context.SaveChangesAsync();
56.        return RedirectToPage();
57.    }
58. }
```

4. Fruits.cshtml (Razor page):

```
1.  @page
2.  @model FruitModel
3.
4.  <h1>Fruits</h1>
5.
6.  <table>
7.      <thead>
8.          <tr>
9.              <th>ID</th>
10.             <th>Name</th>
11.             <th>Quantity</th>
12.             <th>Actions</th>
13.         </tr>
14.     </thead>
15.     <tbody>
16.         @foreach (var fruit in Model.Fruits)
17.         {
18.             <tr>
19.                 <td>@fruit.Id</td>
20.                 <td>@fruit.Name</td>
21.                 <td>@fruit.Quantity</td>
22.                 <td>
23.                     <form method="post">
24.                         <input type="hidden" name="id" value="@fruit.Id" />
25.                         <input type="text" name="newName" placeholder="New name" />
26.                         <input type="number" name="newQuantity" placeholder="New quantity" />
27.                         <button type="submit" asp-page-handler="Update">Update</button>
28.                         <button type="submit" asp-page-handler="Delete">Delete</button>
29.                     </form>
30.                 </td>
31.             </tr>
32.         }
33.     </tbody>
34. </table>
35.
```

```
36. <!-- Create new Fruit -->
37. <form method="post">
38.     <input type="text" name="name" placeholder="Fruit name" />
39.     <input type="number" name="quantity" placeholder="Quantity"
    />
40.     <button type="submit" asp-page-handler="Create">Create</
    button>
41. </form>
```

In this example, we:

- **Read**: Fetch all the **Fruit** entries and display them in a table.
- **Create**: Add a new **Fruit** by filling out a form at the bottom and clicking **Create**.
- **Update**: Edit an existing **Fruit** by filling out the new name and quantity and clicking **Update**.
- **Delete**: Remove an existing **Fruit** by clicking **Delete**.

This Razor page provides a user interface to perform all CRUD operations on the Fruit entity. Behind the scenes, EF Core translates these operations into corresponding SQL queries to interact with the database.

Understanding DBContext and DBSet in EF Core

EF Core's **DbContext** class acts as a link between your .NET application and the database. It is an essential component of EF Core that encapsulates database connections and transactions, functioning as the session for entity activities like CRUD. **DbContext** controls entity objects throughout the runtime, including modifications to those objects and the persistence of those changes to the database.

A **DbSet** is a collection of entities of a given kind that may be queried or updated. It acts as a portal for retrieving records from a database table. **DbSet** allows you to do actions such as adding, updating, removing, and querying data. Each entity class associated with a database table should have a **DbSet** field in the **DbContext** class.

Here is a simplified code block from the **Farm** sample:

```
1. public class FarmingContext : DbContext
2. {
3.     public DbSet<Farm> Farms { get; set; }
4.     public DbSet<Crop> Crops { get; set; }
5.     public DbSet<Vegetable> Vegetables { get; set; }
6.     public DbSet<Rice> Rices { get; set; }
7.     public DbSet<Bean> Beans { get; set; }
```

```
8.
9.     protected override void OnConfiguring(DbContextOptionsBuilder
   options)
10.        => options.UseSqlServer(@"Server=localhost;Database=
   FarmingDB;Trusted_Connection=True;");
11. }
```

The **FarmingContext** class in this example derives from **DbContext**, making it a specific context for dealing with farm-related things.

- **public DbSet<Farm> Farms { get; set; }**: **Farms** is a **DbSet** property that contains a collection of all **Farm** entities in the database. This property might be used to query or update the **Farm** table.

- **public DbSet<Crop> Crops { get; set; }**: **Crops**, on the other hand, is a **DbSet** representing the **Crop** table in the database.

- **public DbSet<Vegetable> Vegetables { get; set; }, public DbSet<Rice> Rices { get; set; }, and public DbSet<Bean> Beans { get; set; }**: These are more specialized **DbSets** for certain crops. They enable you to carry out crop-specific activities.

- **protected override void OnConfiguring(DbContextOptionsBuilder options)**: This function is used to specify the database to connect to. We are using SQL Server in this example, but changing to another supported database is simple. Understanding **DbContext** and **DbSet** is critical while working with EF Core since they are the foundational components for dealing with the database. Using these classes, you may handle transactions, query data, and persist in changes with simplicity and efficiency.

Navigating relationships with EF Core

Here, we have a C# example demonstrating the usage of EF Core to describe an essential agricultural environment provided in the following code block. This ecosystem demonstrates how entities for **Farms**, **Fruits**, **DistributionCenters**, and **Markets** may be integrated. The code intends to demonstrate different EF Core elements such as **DbContext**, **DbSet**, and navigation properties. By the conclusion of this example, you will learn how to construct entities, establish relationships between them, and combine them all using a **DbContext** class. This core understanding will allow you to navigate complicated relationships and effectively conduct CRUD operations in real-world apps.

The following code demonstrates the necessary classes and configurations to set up the data context and define the entity models for a farming application using EF Core. The **FarmingContext** class, which inherits from **DbContext**, serves as the primary context for the application, connecting the entity models to the database. The models include **Farm**,

Fruit, **DistributionCenter**, and **Market**, each with properties and relationships. This setup enables efficient database interactions, facilitating CRUD operations and complex queries within the application.

```csharp
1. using Microsoft.EntityFrameworkCore;
2.
3. public class FarmingContext : DbContext
4. {
5.     public DbSet<Farm> Farms { get; set; }
6.     public DbSet<Fruit> Fruits { get; set; }
7.     public DbSet<DistributionCenter> DistributionCenters
   { get; set; }
8.     public DbSet<Market> Markets { get; set; }
9.
10.     protected override void OnConfiguring(DbContextOptionsBuilder
   options)
11.         => options.UseSqlServer(@"Server=localhost;Database=
   FarmingDB;Trusted_Connection=True;");
12. }
13.
14. public class Farm
15. {
16.     public int Id { get; set; }
17.     public string Name { get; set; }
18.     public List<Fruit> Fruits { get; set; }
19. }
20.
21. public class Fruit
22. {
23.     public int Id { get; set; }
24.     public string Name { get; set; }
25.     public int Quantity { get; set; }
26.     public int FarmId { get; set; }
27.     public Farm Farm { get; set; }
28. }
29.
30. public class DistributionCenter
31. {
32.     public int Id { get; set; }
33.     public string Location { get; set; }
34.     public List<Market> Markets { get; set; }
```

```
35. }
36.
37. public class Market
38. {
39.     public int Id { get; set; }
40.     public string Name { get; set; }
41.     public int DistributionCenterId { get; set; }
42.     public DistributionCenter DistributionCenter { get; set; }
43. }
```

Explanation

Why navigating relationships is important. Navigating relationships in EF Core is essential for modeling real-world scenarios where entities have various dependencies, hierarchies, or associations. For example, in our farming model, farms produce fruits, which may be distributed through different distribution centers and sold in various markets. Understanding these relationships is crucial for any operation that involves more than one entity.

Learning how relationships are modeled

In the farming application, relationships between entities are modeled as follows:

- **One-to-many between farm and fruit**: A single **Farm** can produce multiple types of **Fruits**. We model this by having a **List<Fruit>** inside the **Farm** class and a **FarmId** inside the **Fruit** class.

- **One-to-many between the distribution center and market**: One **DistributionCenter** may supply several **Markets**. We represent this with a **List<Market>** inside the **DistributionCenter** class and a **DistributionCenterId** in the **Market** class.

Navigation properties

Fruit.Farm and **Farm.Fruits** are navigation properties the **Fruit.Farm** property allows us to navigate from a **Fruit** entity back to its parent **Farm**. Likewise, **Farm.Fruits** allow us to navigate from a **Farm** entity to all its **Fruit** children.

Similarly, **Market.DistributionCenter** and **DistributionCenter.Markets** are navigation properties for their respective entities.

Database context (FarmingContext): This is the core of our EF Core interaction. It inherits from **DbContext** and contains **DbSet<T>** properties that represent tables in the database. We define sets for **Farm**, **Fruit**, **DistributionCenter**, and **Market** to allow EF Core to perform CRUD operations on these entities.

These relationships and navigation properties let you query complex scenarios and relations between your entities, making developing, maintaining, and understanding your application easier.

Following is a simplified example of a Web API in C# that exposes endpoints to:

- List **Markets** by the type of **Fruits** they sell.
- List Distribution Centers by the **Farms** they source from.
- Return the total sales by **Fruit** type, segmented by Farm, Distribution Center, and Market.

We are using the EF Core model defined earlier for Farm, Distribution Center, and Market:

```
1.  using Microsoft.AspNetCore.Mvc;
2.  using Microsoft.EntityFrameworkCore;
3.  using System.Collections.Generic;
4.  using System.Linq;
5.  using System.Threading.Tasks;
6.
7.  [ApiController]
8.  [Route("api/[controller]")]
9.  public class FarmApiController : ControllerBase
10. {
11.     private readonly FarmingContext _context;
12.
13.     public FarmApiController(FarmingContext context)
14.     {
15.         _context = context;
16.     }
17.
18.     // 1. API to List Markets by Fruits
19.     [HttpGet("MarketsByFruits/{fruitName}")]
20.     public async Task<ActionResult<IEnumerable<Mark
    et>>> GetMarketsByFruits(string fruitName)
21.     {
22.         var markets = await _context.Markets
23.             .Where(m => m.DistributionCenter.Markets
24.             .Any(dc => dc.Fruits.Any(f => f.Name == fruitName)))
25.             .ToListAsync();
26.
27.         return Ok(markets);
28.     }
```

```
29.
30.     // 2. API to List DistributionCenters by Farms
31.     [HttpGet("DistributionCentersByFarms/{farmName}")]
32.     public async Task<ActionResult<IEnumerable<DistributionCenter>>>
    GetDistributionCentersByFarms(string farmName)
33.     {
34.         var centers = await _context.DistributionCenters
35.             .Where(dc => dc.Farms.Any(f => f.Name == farmName))
36.             .ToListAsync();
37.
38.         return Ok(centers);
39.     }
40.
41.     // 3. API to Return Total Sales by Fruit type
42.     [HttpGet("TotalSalesByFruit/{fruitName}")]
43.     public async Task<ActionResult<object>> GetTotalSalesByFruitType
    (string fruitName)
44.     {
45.         var totalSalesByFruit = await _context.Markets
46.             .Where(m => m.Fruits.Any(f => f.Name == fruitName))
47.             .Select(m => new
48.             {
49.                 MarketName = m.Name,
50.                 Farm = m.DistributionCenter.Farms.First(f =>
    f.Fruits.Any(fr => fr.Name == fruitName)).Name,
51.                 DistributionCenter = m.DistributionCenter.Location,
52.                 TotalSales = m.Fruits.Where(f => f.Name ==
    fruitName).Sum(f => f.Quantity)
53.             })
54.             .ToListAsync();
55.
56.         return Ok(totalSalesByFruit);
57.     }
58. }
```

At this point, you have gained a strong understanding of navigating complex relationships in EF Core through the examples of Farms, Fruits, Distribution Centers, and Markets. The accompanying web API further illustrates this by implementing endpoints that perform specialized queries, such as listing Markets by the Fruits they sell, Distribution Centers by the Farms they are connected to, and aggregating sales data. It showcases the power and flexibility of EF Core in handling intricate relationships between entities. It enables complex querying capabilities through Web API endpoints, which can be extremely valuable in real-world applications.

Migrations in Entity Framework Core

EF Core migrations maintain your database schema aligned with your entity model classes. A migration collects changes to your model, such as adding a new property to a class or modifying a data annotation, and generates code to update the database schema. These migrations may then be used to update the database, making it easier to handle schema changes.

Learning migrations makes developer's life easier

We had to manually write SQL scripts to alter the database schema before migration tools such as EF Core's migrations arrived. Keeping track of which scripts had been executed was complicated and error-prone, especially in collaborative situations. Migrations automate this process, providing various benefits:

- **Versioning**: Each migration creates a new database version. You have the option of moving ahead or rolling back to prior states.

- **Collaboration**: Migrations are code. Thus, they can be readily shared and versioned via source control, making teamwork easier.

- **Database-agnostic**: Migrations enable you to operate in a database-agnostic manner, allowing you to swap underlying databases easily.

- **Consistency**: Using migrations keeps the database in sync with the code, which reduces problems caused by schema incompatibilities.

Before migration technology

Before the advent of migration frameworks, we had to:
- To change the database, manually develop SQL scripts.
- Keep track of the scripts' order.
- Manually run these scripts in each environment (Dev, Test, and Production).

We hope for the safety of your project; no one else has made any incompatible modifications.

Sample for MySQL and SQLServer

The same project can be configured to use different databases. You can specify the database provider in the **OnConfiguring** method of your **DbContext**. Here is how you can set it up for both MySQL and SQL Server:

```
1.  public class FarmingContext : DbContext
2.  {
3.      private readonly string _databaseProvider;
4.
5.      public FarmingContext(string databaseProvider)
6.      {
7.          _databaseProvider = databaseProvider;
8.      }
9.
10.     public DbSet<Farm> Farms { get; set; }
11.     public DbSet<Fruit> Fruits { get; set; }
12.     public DbSet<DistributionCenter> DistributionCenters { get;
    set; }
13.     public DbSet<Market> Markets { get; set; }
14.
15.     protected override void OnConfiguring(DbContextOptionsBuilder
    options)
16.     {
17.         if (_databaseProvider == "SQLServer")
18.         {
19.             options.UseSqlServer(@"Server=localhost;Database=
    FarmingDB;Trusted_Connection=True;");
20.         }
21.         else if (_databaseProvider == "MySQL")
22.         {
23.             options.UseMySql(@"Server=localhost;Database=FarmingDB;
    User=root;Password=your_password;", new MySqlServerVersion(new
    Version(8, 0, 21)));
24.         }
25.     }
26. }
```

Challenges that migrations solve in EF Core

The following are the challenges that migrations solve in EF Core:

- **Schema evolution**: As your application changes, so must the underlying database schema. Migrations manage these changes automatically, allowing you to grow your database structure without requiring manual involvement.

- **Version control**: Migrations function as database version control. It enables better management of schema changes by allowing you to roll back to a prior state or step ahead to a new one.

- **Team collaboration**: Migrations allow numerous developers to work on a project simultaneously. Because migration files are part of your codebase, they may be submitted to source control repositories, enabling team members to discuss database changes effortlessly.

- **Environment synchronization**: Migrations aid in synchronizing several environments (development, staging, and production). To maintain consistency, use the same migrations across all environments.

- **Database provider ignorance**: EF Core supports a variety of database providers. Migrations allow you to move between databases, providing high project flexibility quickly.

- **Error reduction:** Manually updating databases increases the possibility of mistakes. Migrations mitigate this risk by creating the SQL required to change schema automatically.

Migrations create a historical record of all database schema changes, making it easier to understand how your database changed over time.

Understanding and using migrations in EF Core greatly simplifies the problematic and sometimes time-consuming process of database schema maintenance. It improves team cooperation and guarantees that database updates are properly versioned and deployed. The ability to effortlessly switch between multiple database providers increases its value even more. Understanding migrations is crucial for successful and efficient database administration in modern application development, not merely a suggested best practice. You are well-equipped to construct robust, scalable, and maintainable data-driven applications if you are familiar with EF Core and its migrations feature.

Implementing inheritance with Entity Framework Core

Along with encapsulation, polymorphism, and abstraction, inheritance is one of the four core OOP principles. Inheritance allows a subclass to inherit characteristics and behaviors (methods) from a superclass. This technique encourages code reuse and creates a natural hierarchy of parent and child classes.

EF Core supports inheritance, so you may model your domain classes with inheritance hierarchies and have those hierarchies accurately recorded in the database. EF Core has several techniques for modeling inheritance, but the most frequent are **Table-Per-Hierarchy** (**TPH**) and **Table-Per-Type** (**TPT**). The default is TPH, which entails storing all classes in the inheritance hierarchy in a single database table. In contrast, TPT uses a distinct table for each class in the inheritance tree.

In our **Farm** example, here is how to represent **ExoticFruit** as a subclass of **Fruit**.

Let us start by defining our **Fruit** and **ExoticFruit** classes:

```
1.  public class Fruit
2.  {
3.      public int Id { get; set; }
4.      public string Name { get; set; }
5.      public string Color { get; set; }
6.  }
7.
8.  public class ExoticFruit : Fruit
9.  {
10.     public string CountryOfOrigin { get; set; }
11.     public string UniqueFeature { get; set; }
12. }
```

In this example, **ExoticFruit** is a subclass of **Fruit**. It inherits the properties of **Fruit** and defines additional properties: **CountryOfOrigin** and **UniqueFeature**.

Now, update the **FarmingContext DbContext** class to include **ExoticFruits**:

```
1.  public class FarmingContext : DbContext
2.  {
3.      public DbSet<Farm> Farms { get; set; }
4.      public DbSet<Fruit> Fruits { get; set; }
5.      public DbSet<ExoticFruit> ExoticFruits { get; set; }
6.      // Other DbSets...
7.
8.      protected override void OnConfiguring(DbContextOptionsBuilder
    options)
9.          => options.UseSqlServer(@"Server=localhost;Database=
    FarmingDB;Trusted_Connection=True;");
10. }
```

When you run a migration, EF Core will use the TPH strategy by default. It will result in a table named **Fruits** with all the properties of **Fruit** and **ExoticFruit**. A discriminator column will be used to distinguish between **Fruit** and **ExoticFruit**.

To run the migration, you can use these commands:

```
1.  dotnet ef migrations add AddExoticFruits
2.  dotnet ef database update
```

After running the migration, you will have a single table that efficiently represents both **Fruit** and **ExoticFruit**, with the power of EF Core managing the complexities of inheritance for you.

Learn inheritance for concise, efficient, and clean code

Inheritance in object-oriented programming offers numerous benefits that contribute to writing concise, efficient, and clean code. By leveraging inheritance, we can achieve code reusability, ensuring that base classes contain shared traits and behaviors, which reduces code duplication across derived classes. This centralization of standard functionality in base classes also promotes consistency, as any bug fixes or updates in the base class automatically propagate to all subclasses, simplifying maintenance. Debugging and testing are streamlined when shared behaviors are tested once in the base class, allowing developers to focus on unique functionalities in derived classes. A well-structured inheritance hierarchy enhances readability, making understanding relationships between classes and the overall codebase easier. Additionally, inheritance facilitates polymorphism, enabling objects of different classes to be treated as instances of a common superclass. This simplifies the creation of generic code that can handle various data types.

- **Code reusability**: This is one of the significant benefits of inheritance. Base classes contain the traits and behaviors that derived classes share. Instead of duplicating code in several classes, declare it once in a base class to reduce repetition.

- **Consistency**: By centralizing standard functionality in a base class, you ensure consistent implementation across derived classes. If a bug is discovered in the shared functionality, fixing it in the base class fixes it for all subclasses, making the codebase easier to maintain.

- **Debugging and testing**: They are simplified when standard functionality is gathered in a base class. You can concentrate on testing the base class for shared behaviors and the derived classes for functionalities that are unique to them.

- **Readability**: A well-designed inheritance hierarchy makes the code more readable. When you look at a subclass, you can quickly understand its relationship to other classes, making it easier to understand the codebase.

- **Polymorphism**: Another fundamental OOP concept requires inheritance. It enables objects of diverse classes to be considered objects of a similar superclass, making creating generic code that deals with many data types simpler.

Adaptability for unpredictable future needs

Inheritance in object-oriented programming not only promotes concise and efficient code but also significantly enhances the adaptability of software systems to accommodate unpredictable future needs. This adaptability is crucial in dynamic environments where requirements frequently change, or new functionalities must be integrated. By leveraging inheritance, developers can ensure their systems remain extensible, agile, and robust.

- **Extensibility**: One of the main benefits of using inheritance is adding new features or behaviors to the system without affecting existing code. You can create new subclasses that inherit attributes and behaviors from existing classes, adding new functionalities as needed.

- **Overriding and extension**: If future requirements necessitate specialized behavior in a subclass, methods from the parent class can be overridden or extended. It preserves the integrity of the existing code while allowing for targeted changes.

- **Agility**: An inheritance-based architecture can be more agile in rapidly changing environments where new features or adjustments are frequently required. By leveraging the established base classes, new features can be rolled out quickly and with less room for error.

- **Robustness**: As the system evolves, inheritance provides a structured way to manage changes, making the system more robust. Well-designed base classes are strong pillars, ensuring system expansions or modifications are more reliable.

In conclusion, inheritance aids in keeping your code concise, clean, and efficient. It simplifies the development and maintenance processes, allowing you to quickly adapt to new or changing requirements, making your software more robust and future-proof.

Performance considerations when using Entity Framework Core

EF Core simplifies data access but might pose performance bottlenecks if not handled appropriately. When utilizing EF Core, paying attention to performance issues is critical for the success of your application from both a business and end-user standpoint.

Financial consequences

In a corporate setting, wasteful queries might result in slower application replies, requiring more processing resources. It frequently increases expenditures when growing the program to meet user expectations. Slow database operations can sometimes result in timeouts, hurting user experience and creating financial losses. These milliseconds may add up to much money for firms, especially those involved in e-commerce or financial trading. As a result, investing in work early to improve your EF Core processes can produce tremendous long-term benefits.

User experience and product quality

A successful user experience necessitates speed and reactivity. Poor performance might result in user or client loss. It is not just about software but how the program improves or degrades the user's engagement. Slow apps can cause user unhappiness, decrease productivity, and, eventually, harm your company's brand image. We may create apps that perform correctly and thrill the user with their responsiveness and speed by paying particular attention to how EF Core interacts with the database.

Steve Jobs and saving time

Steve Jobs had a view on saving time that is similar to the concept of software performance. He famously described a computer's efficiency as a *bicycle for the mind*, emphasizing how technology may drastically increase human capacities. Another time, Jobs stated that if the Mac could reduce boot time by even 10 seconds, it would save human lifetimes given the number of users and frequency of use. The concept may also be applied to application performance. Every millisecond saved by optimizing searches adds up, possibly saving lifetimes of aggregate human experience and increasing user productivity.

Optimizing EF Core performance is a financial and ethical consideration since it contributes to end-user well-being and productivity. As a result, performance concerns are more than simply a nice-to-have but a necessary part of responsible software development.

Actions to make EF Core efficient

Understanding the effects of various actions on performance is crucial when working with EF Core. Despite its ease of use and reliability, EF Core can occasionally cause inefficiencies if not handled cautiously. Some essential concerns are as follows:

- **Lazy vs. eager loading**: Lazy loading can cause performance concerns by causing N+1 query issues. Loading related data in one round-trip to the database may be more efficient.

- **Tracking vs. no-tracking**: Entity tracking is beneficial in instances where entities will be updated, although it incurs some expenses. To increase efficiency, use `.AsNoTracking()` for read-only operations.

- **Batch operations**: Rather than doing individual CRUD tasks, try batching numerous operations together. The `SaveChanges` function in EF Core records changes and conducts all **Create, Update, Delete** (**CUD**) activities in a single transaction, which makes it more efficient.

- **Filtering and paging**: As much filtering and sorting logic as feasible should be sent to the database level to prevent drawing superfluous data into your application.

- **Indexing**: Ensure that your database tables are correctly indexed. EF Core cannot compensate for a poorly indexed database.

- **Avoid SELECT * queries**: Select just the columns you need. It decreases the quantity of data transmitted from the database and the overhead associated with object creation.

- **Compiled queries**: Use compiled queries to increase speed if you have queries regularly performed with varied parameters.

Let us see each in detail. For the samples, we will consider this base code:

```
1. using Microsoft.EntityFrameworkCore;
2. using System.Collections.Generic;
3.
4. public class FarmingContext : DbContext
5. {
6.     public DbSet<Farm> Farms { get; set; }
7.     public DbSet<Crop> Crops { get; set; }
8.
9.     protected override void OnConfiguring(DbContextOptionsBuilder options)
10.         => options.UseSqlServer(@"Server=localhost;Database=FarmingDB;Trusted_Connection=True;");
11. }
12.
13. public class Farm
14. {
15.     public int Id { get; set; }
16.     public string Name { get; set; }
17.     public string Location { get; set; }
18.     public List<Crop> Crops { get; set; }
19. }
20.
21. public class Crop
22. {
23.     public int Id { get; set; }
24.     public string Name { get; set; }
25.     public int FarmId { get; set; }
26.     public Farm Farm { get; set; }
27. }
```

Lazy loading vs. eager loading

When using EF Core, you must frequently select how to load linked entities. It is accomplished through two primary mechanisms: lazy loading and eager loading. Both have advantages and disadvantages, and the optimal option typically relies on the unique needs of your application.

- **Loading slowly**: Lazy loading prevents related things from being loaded until they are explicitly accessed. It can shorten application startup time and reduce initial database load, but it might also result in extra database requests as you explore the object graph, possibly causing performance issues.

- **Excited loading**: In a single query, eager loading retrieves the principal entities and their linked entities. If you know, you will need the associated entities right away; this is typically more efficient because it decreases the number of database requests.

Let us look at how each works with our existing **Farm** example. Assume we are working with the same **DbContext** and entities.

Example: Lazy loading

```
1.  // Enable Lazy Loading by adding virtual keyword
2.  public class Farm
3.  {
4.      public int Id { get; set; }
5.      public string Name { get; set; }
6.      public string Location { get; set; }
7.      public virtual List<Crop> Crops { get; set; }
8.  }
9.
10. using (var context = new FarmingContext())
11. {
12.     var farm = context.Farms.First();
13.     var crops = farm.Crops; // Lazy Loading: This line triggers a
    separate query to load crops
14. }
```

Example: Eager loading

```
1.  using (var context = new FarmingContext())
2.  {
3.      var farm = context.Farms
4.                          .Include(f => f.
    Crops) // Eager Loading: Crops are loaded along with Farm
5.                          .First();
6.      var crops = farm.
    Crops; // No separate query, crops are already loaded
7.  }
```

The **Crops** property is designated with the virtual keyword in the slow-loading example. When you visit **farm.Crops** for the first time, EF Core will immediately load the corresponding **Crop** instances from the database, causing a separate query.

We used **the** **.Include()** function in the eager loading example to declare that the **Crops** should simultaneously be loaded from the database as the **Farm**. There is no need to run a separate query to retrieve the **Crops**.

Lazy loading may appear convenient, but it can cause performance issues known as the N+1 problem. Eager loading is generally more efficient for read-heavy workloads, but lazy loading may be appropriate when the associated entities are seldom visited. To make an informed choice between lazy and eager loading, you must first understand your application's requirements and profile its performance.

Tracking vs. no tracking

EF Core employs tracking to monitor entity instances throughout the life of a **DbContext** instance. When you query entities, they are automatically cached and watched for changes in the **DbContext**. Tracking is proper when you want to update or remove entities because EF Core automatically knows which entities to update in the database during a **SaveChanges()** call.

However, tracking has significant drawbacks. Turning off tracking improves efficiency if you are merely reading entities and do not intend to alter them.

In the context of our **Farm** example, here is how you can utilize tracking and no-tracking.

Example: With tracking

You can use tracking to get an entity and then edit it. When **SaveChanges()** is invoked, EF Core automatically identifies the changes and updates the database.

```
1. using (var context = new FarmingContext())
2. {
3.     // Query with tracking (default behavior)
4.     var trackedFarm = context.Farms.First(f => f.Id == 1);
5.
6.     // Modify the entity
7.     trackedFarm.Name = "Updated Farm Name";
8.
9.     // Save changes
10.    context.SaveChanges();
11. }
```

Example: With no-tracking

If you do not intend to update the object and require it for read-only reasons, you may turn off tracking to avoid some performance overhead.

```
1. using (var context = new FarmingContext())
2. {
```

```
3.      // Query without tracking
4.      var nonTrackedFarm = context.Farms.AsNoTracking().First(f =>
    f.Id == 1);
5.
6.      // Even if you modify the entity, it won't be saved back to the
    database
7.      nonTrackedFarm.Name = "Name Change Won't Persist";
8.
9.      // Save changes
10.     context.SaveChanges(); // No changes will be committed to the
    database
11. }
```

Batch operations

The execution of many operations in a single round-trip to the database improves speed by decreasing the number of individual database calls. You may conduct several CUD actions in a batch with EF Core. However, it does not allow batch queries out of the box. Batch modifications are commonly performed by changing numerous entities in your **DbContext** and then using **SaveChanges()** once.

Here is how you can use our **Farm** example context to do batch operations:

```
1.  using (var context = new FarmingContext())
2.  {
3.      // Adding multiple Farms
4.      var farm1 = new Farm { Name = "Green Farm", Location = "USA" };
5.      var farm2 = new Farm { Name = "Blue Farm", Location = "Canada"
    };
6.      context.Farms.AddRange(farm1, farm2);
7.
8.      // Updating multiple Crops
9.      var crop1 = context.Crops.Find(1);
10.     var crop2 = context.Crops.Find(2);
11.     crop1.Name = "UpdatedCrop1";
12.     crop2.Name = "UpdatedCrop2";
13.
14.     // Deleting a Crop
15.     var cropToDelete = new Crop { Id = 3 };
16.     context.Crops.Remove(cropToDelete);
17.
18.     // Executes Insert for farm1 and farm2, Update for crop1 and
    crop2, and Delete for cropToDelete in a single transaction
```

```
19.      context.SaveChanges();
20. }
```

In this example, we first populate the **Farms** DbSet with numerous **Farm** instances. Then, we get an update on two **Crop** entities before removing one. After that, we call **SaveChanges()**. These activities are combined into a single transaction and then executed against the database in a single round-trip.

Batching is crucial for maximizing speed when dealing with several tasks that may be grouped. Minimizing the number of database round-trips may significantly decrease latency and improve application performance.

Filtering and paging

Filtering and paging are crucial functions in EF Core when working with huge collections. They assist you in retrieving only the information you want, lowering processing overhead and data transport expenses. While filtering retrieves data based on certain conditions, paging divides a massive dataset into smaller, more manageable bits.

Example: Filtering and paging

```
1. using (var context = new FarmingContext())
2. {
3.      // Filtering: Get all farms located in "Texas"
4.      var texasFarms = context.Farms
5.                          .Where(f => f.Location == "Texas")
6.                          .ToList();
7.
8.      // Paging: Get the first page of farms with 5 farms per page
9.      int pageSize = 5;
10.     int pageNumber = 1; // Starting with the first page
11.     var pagedFarms = context.Farms
12.                         .Skip((pageNumber - 1) * pageSize)
13.                         .Take(pageSize)
14.                         .ToList();
15. }
```

Indexing

Indexing is a method of speeding up data retrieval processes in a database. Without an index, the database engine must scan the table for relevant entries, which can take a long time, especially with massive datasets. Indexes are especially beneficial when distinct columns are regularly utilized in search conditions or when unique restrictions must be maintained.

EF Core allows you to specify indexes on your entity model classes, which are subsequently produced in the database when migration is conducted. You can choose between single and composite indices.

Let us extend the **Farm** sample to show how to add an index to the **Farm** entity. We will add an index to the **Location** column to speed up queries that search by location.

```
1. using Microsoft.EntityFrameworkCore;
2. using System.Collections.Generic;
3.
4. public class FarmingContext : DbContext
5. {
6.     public DbSet<Farm> Farms { get; set; }
7.     public DbSet<Crop> Crops { get; set; }
8.
9.     protected override void OnConfiguring(DbContextOptionsBuilder
    options)
10.         => options.UseSqlServer(@"Server=localhost;Database=
    FarmingDB;Trusted_Connection=True;");
11.
12.     protected override void OnModelCreating(ModelBuilder
    modelBuilder)
13.     {
14.         // Defining an index on the Location column of the Farm
    entity
15.         modelBuilder.Entity<Farm>()
16.                 .HasIndex(f => f.Location)
17.                 .HasDatabaseName("Index_Location");
18.     }
19. }
```

The **OnModelCreating** function is altered in the preceding code to establish extra parameters that cannot be applied via data annotations. With **modelBuilder**, we added an index to the Farm table's **Location column.Entity<Farm>().f.Location => HasIndex(f). HasDatabaseName("Index_Location");**.

After adding this index, you will need to perform the Add-Migration and Update-Database commands to make the change permanent in the database.

The existence of the index speeds up lookups depending on location:

```
1. using (var context = new FarmingContext())
2. {
3.     // This query will benefit from the index on the Location column
4.     var texasFarms = ontexto.Farms
```

```
5.                          .Where(f => f.Location == "Texas")
6.                          .ToList();
7. }
```

By properly indexing columns frequently used in queries, you can dramatically improve the performance of data retrieval operations.

Avoiding SELECT * queries

SELECT * queries are wasteful because they obtain all columns from the database table, even those you do not require in your application. Not only does this waste bandwidth between your application and the database, but it also increases memory utilization and CPU stress when translating the results to objects.

By utilizing projection, EF Core allows you to select the columns you are interested in. You may significantly minimize the quantity of data that has to be transmitted from the database to your application by projecting queries.

Let us utilize the current **Farm** example to eliminate SELECT * queries by retrieving only the required data.

Projection in EF Core allows you to select specific columns from the database rather than fetching all columns with a SELECT * query. This practice can improve performance by reducing the data transferred from the database to the application and decreasing memory usage. Here is how you can use projection to select only the **Id** and **Name** columns from the **Farm** table:

```
1. using (var context = new FarmingContext())
2. {
3.     // Using projection to fetch only Id and Name fields from the
   Farm table
4.     var farms = context.Farms
5.                        .Select(f => new { f.Id, f.Name })
6.                        .ToList();
7. }
```

Instead of retrieving all columns from the **Farm** database, we retrieve the **Id** and **Name** fields in this query, making the query more efficient. This projection type ensures that just the data required by the program is retrieved, improving overall speed.

Compiled queries

The usage of compiled queries is one of the aspects of Entity Framework Core that may considerably improve speed. A compiled query is only translated into SQL once and then saved for further use. It implies that the same LINQ-to-Entities query may be repeated without incurring the expense of re-translation into SQL, providing a performance gain, particularly for frequently run queries.

Example: Using compiled queries

```
1.  using Microsoft.EntityFrameworkCore;
2.  using System;
3.  using System.Linq;
4.
5.  // Define a compiled query
6.  var findFarmsByLocation = EF.
    CompileQuery((FarmingContext db, string location) =>
7.      db.Farms.Where(f => f.Location == location));
8.
9.  using (var context = new FarmingContext())
10. {
11.     // Execute the compiled query
12.     var texasFarms = findFarmsByLocation(context, "Texas").ToList();
13.     var californiaFarms = findFarmsByLocation(context, "California").
    ToList();
14. }
```

In this example, we use **EF.CompileQuery** to construct a compiled query **findFarmsByLocation**. This built query accepts a **FarmingContext** and a location string as input and returns an **IQueryable<Farm>** with information about the farms in the specified location.

Once the query has been constructed, it may be reused with various parameters several times. We used it twice: once to get all Texas farms and then again to obtain all California farms. As the query is only translated into SQL once and cached, future executions are more efficient.

Compiled queries are a fantastic method to increase the efficiency of your EF Core-based applications, especially when dealing with queries that are conducted with various parameters numerous times.

Considerations of EF Core performance

When utilizing EF Core, performance concerns are more than simply a technical footnote; they are an essential aspect of responsible and productive program development. A thorough grasp of how to utilize EF Core efficiently, optimize queries, decrease database roundtrips, and implement best practices can set you apart as a professional who creates code and adds value to the company and end-users. With such a skill set, you become an essential addition to any development team or project, as performance tuning frequently immediately leads to cost savings, higher dependability, and improved user happiness.

The satisfaction that comes from mastering performance factors extends beyond the technical. It extends to a sense of accomplishment in knowing that your work has a concrete, good influence on people's lives by developing software that functions smoothly, with less waiting and aggravation for its users. Every millisecond saved and query improved provides a more fluid and productive interaction for the user, contributing to IT's ultimate goal of making human life more accessible, productive, and pleasurable.

When we consider that technology and software exist to increase our skills and improve our quality of life, it becomes evident that concentrating on performance is not simply a desirable ability but a need. By succeeding in this area, you exemplify the genuine essence of technology as an enabler, transforming you from a good to a great developer. Moreover, by doing so, you are perpetuating the idea that technology, when properly deployed, can be a great force for good.

Conclusion

This chapter introduced EF Core, a robust ORM framework for .NET applications. The chapter helped you set up and configure SQL Server, PostgreSQL, SQLite, and MySQL databases. LINQ, a powerful C# feature for type-safe queries, was also covered in the chapter.

EF Core's change tracking features automatically monitor entity states and create SQL commands for database updates. The importance of DbContext and DbSet for database connections and activities was explained. You learned how to browse entity relationships using navigation properties and foreign keys.

The chapter also showed how database migrations synchronize your database structure and data model. You learned how to implement inheritance in EF Core using table per hierarchy, type, and concrete type. The chapter concluded with speed concerns, including lazy loading, eager loading, and caching.

By the end of this chapter, you should know how to use EF Core to manage databases in .NET applications effectively. The chapter provided advice and best practices to maximize the use of this robust framework. In the next chapter, we will discuss LINQ.

Exercises

1. **What is the main topic of the chapter?**
    a. Data handling with EF Core
    b. Querying data using LINQ
    c. Setting up and configuring a database using EF Core
    d. Understanding EF Core change tracking

2. **What is EF Core?**

   a. An advanced ORM framework for .NET applications

   b. A free and open-source ORM framework for .NET

   c. A slimmer, more versatile, and cross-platform version of the earlier EF

   d. All of the above

3. **What are some of the key features of EF Core?**

   a. Database abstraction, data modeling, query capabilities, caching, concurrency management, and transactions

   b. Database abstraction, data modeling, query capabilities, caching, concurrency management, and migrations

   c. Database abstraction, data modeling, query capabilities, caching, concurrency management, migrations, and transactions

   d. Database abstraction, data modeling, query capabilities, caching, and concurrency management

4. **How does EF Core query data using LINQ?**

   a. It converts LINQ-to-SQL queries into database-specific SQL queries, executes them, and returns the results as objects.

   b. It converts LINQ-to-Entities queries into database-specific SQL queries, executes them, and returns the results as objects.

   c. It converts LINQ-to-Objects queries into database-specific SQL queries, executes them, and returns the results as objects.

   d. It converts LINQ-to-XML queries into database-specific SQL queries, executes them, and returns the results as objects.

5. **What are some benefits of using EF Core with LINQ over ADO.NET?**

   a. Increased developer productivity, improved code maintainability, and cross-database compatibility.

   b. Increased developer productivity, improved code readability, and cross-database compatibility.

   c. Increased developer productivity, improved code readability, and cross-platform compatibility.

   d. Increased developer productivity, improved code maintainability, and cross-platform compatibility.

6. **What are the two approaches to creating the data model using EF Core?**

   a. Code-first and database-first

   b. Model-first and code-first

    c. Database-first and schema-first

    d. Schema-first and model-first

7. **What is the difference between lazy loading and eager loading in EF Core?**

    a. Lazy loading loads related entities only when they are accessed, while eager loading loads them along with the main entity.

    b. Lazy loading loads related entities along with the main entity, while eager loading loads them only when they are accessed.

    c. Lazy loading loads only the main entity, while eager loading loads all the entities in the context.

    d. Lazy loading loads all the entities in the context, while eager loading loads only the main entity.

8. **What is the benefit of using migrations in EF Core?**

    a. Migrations allow you to version your database schema and make incremental updates automatically

    b. Migrations allow you to generate SQL scripts for creating and dropping database objects

    c. Migrations allow you to synchronize your data model with your code model

    d. All of the above

9. **How can you implement inheritance with EF Core?**

    a. By using the [Table] attribute on the derived classes

    b. By using the [Inheritance] attribute on the base class

    c. By using the HasDiscriminator method in the OnModelCreating method of the context class

    d. By using the IsA method in the OnModelCreating method of the context class

10. **What are some performance considerations when using EF Core?**

    a. Choosing an appropriate loading strategy (lazy, eager, or explicit)

    b. Using compiled queries to avoid query compilation overhead

    c. Using asynchronous methods to avoid blocking threads

    d. All of the above

Answers

1.	a.
2.	d.
3.	c.
4.	b.
5.	a.
6.	a.
7.	a.
8.	d.
9.	c.
10.	d.

Join our book's Discord space

Join the book's Discord Workspace for Latest updates, Offers, Tech happenings around the world, New Release and Sessions with the Authors:

https://discord.bpbonline.com

CHAPTER 10
LINQ Unleashed

Introduction

This chapter will get into LINQ. This powerful C# feature allows you to query and manipulate data from various sources using a consistent and expressive syntax. You will learn to utilize LINQ with various data types, including collections, databases, XML, and JSON. You will also learn how to make effective designs and versatile queries using LINQ operators, lambda expressions, and deferred execution. At the end of this chapter, you can utilize LINQ to perform typical data operations such as filtering, sorting, grouping, aggregation, and transformation.

Structure

This chapter covers the following topics:
- Understanding Language Integrated Query
- Writing simple LINQ queries
- Grouping and aggregation with LINQ
- Using LINQ with Entity Framework Core
- Understanding deferred execution in LINQ
- LINQ to XML and LINQ to JSON
- Using LINQ to manipulate collections and arrays

- Advanced LINQ operators
- Understanding lambda expressions with LINQ
- Implementing custom comparers and equality in LINQ
- What is new in .NET 9

Objectives

The goals of this chapter are to comprehend the benefits and principles of LINQ as a versatile tool for querying and manipulating data. This chapter will also help you comprehend its basic query and method syntax alongside standard operators such as **Where** and **OrderBy**. We will also learn to investigate its integration with EF Core for database abstraction to get into its deferred execution feature for improved query performance and flexibility. Finally, we will also understand how to handle XML and JSON data using LINQ syntax.

Understanding Language Integrated Query

LINQ was added to the .NET Framework 3.5 and C# 3.0. Querying data from a database or manipulating collections of objects in C# before LINQ was frequently verbose and necessitated the use of loops, conditionals, and temporary variables. LINQ sought to address these challenges by providing a uniform and convenient query experience for objects and data, regardless of data source, databases, XML files, or in-memory collections.

LINQ is essentially a set of C# language characteristics that allow for smooth data querying without the need to convert to a new language or syntax. It replaced the need to switch between SQL for databases, XML XPath for XML, and loops and conditionals for object collections while also combining these into a single, consistent, language-integrated method.

The benefits of using LINQ

LINQ is a powerful C# technology that offers numerous advantages for searching and manipulating data. Some of the reasons to utilize LINQ are:

- **A uniform syntax**: You can use consistent querying syntax regardless of the data source while working with LINQ. You can use the same LINQ query syntax whether you are querying an SQL database, an XML file, or an in-memory list. This is because LINQ is database-independent.

- **Safety of the type**: LINQ queries are type-safe, and errors can be caught during compile time instead of run time, typically when using SQL strings to query databases. In contrast, errors cannot be caught during run time with LINQ queries.

- **Support for IntelliSense**: Because LINQ is fully integrated into C#, **integrated development environments** (**IDEs**) like Visual Studio include support for

IntelliSense, which makes it much simpler to write queries in the correct format.

- **Readability and maintainability**: LINQ searches usually provide code that is easier to read and maintain. The syntax is intended to be expressive, allowing us to explain the operations performed on the data in a straightforward and easy-to-understand manner.

- **Composability**: Composing LINQ queries is simple, meaning you may use an existing query as the foundation for a brand-new query. It makes it much simpler to construct complicated searches incrementally.

LINQ and databases

LINQ can communicate with databases through its many providers, such as LINQ to SQL and EF, allowing you to construct LINQ queries translated to SQL queries. It means you may use database optimizations only to get the data you need into memory, which is typically more efficient than retrieving and filtering all the data.

Lists and collections in LINQ

LINQ may also query in-memory collections like lists, arrays, and others. It provides a quick and easy way to filter, sort, aggregate, and transform data.

Efficiency because of the increased degree of abstraction, LINQ queries may introduce some performance penalty when compared to manually optimized loops compared to arrays. For many typical jobs, however, the difference is often minimal and can be regarded as a reasonable trade-off for the benefits of readability, maintainability, and code reusability.

It allows us to conduct advanced queries on collections like lists, arrays, dictionaries, and other enumerable data structures. It provides a collection of standard query operators for filtering, sorting, projecting, and aggregating data. These operators allow us to do sophisticated data manipulation operations with a few lines of code, making it easier to work with collections. LINQ also enables postponed execution, which implies that the query does not run until the results are enumerated. This can boost performance by lowering the amount of data that must be processed.

Here is a sample code snippet in C# demonstrating LINQ's postponed execution:

```
1. // Sample list of integers
2. List<int> numbers = new List<int> { 1, 2, 3, 4, 5 };
3.
4. // LINQ query to filter even numbers (postponed execution)
5. var evenNumbersQuery = numbers.Where(n => n % 2 == 0);
6.
7. // At this point, the query hasn't been executed yet
8. Console.WriteLine("Query created but not executed yet.");
```

```
9.
10. // Enumerating the query triggers its execution
11. foreach (var number in evenNumbersQuery)
12. {
13.     Console.WriteLine(number);
14. }
```

In this example, the LINQ query, filters even numbers from the list, does not run until we enumerate the results. This postponed execution enables optimization and effective data handling.

Difficulties before LINQ

You had to manually build loops to filter, sort, and aggregate data before LINQ. It may result in verbose and difficult-to-read code. In addition, multiple query languages and methodologies would be used for different data types, resulting in inconsistencies and higher cognitive strain. SQL strings encoded in code were also vulnerable to errors and SQL injection attacks, and detecting these vulnerabilities frequently necessitated runtime debugging.

In summary, LINQ in C# and .NET has wholly altered how we interact with data by providing a standardized, safe method for all types of data, and easy to read when it comes to querying databases, XML, and in-memory collections. Even though there could be some performance drawbacks due to this change, the benefits of code quality, maintainability, and efficiency typically outweigh these drawbacks.

Writing simple LINQ queries

The code snippet below demonstrates the fundamentals of LINQ in C#. LINQ is a vital C# feature that lets us query collections in a type-safe, declarative manner. In this example, we will use a JSON array to store information about various clients. An **id**, a **customer_name**, and a profession identify each client.

The program does the following functions:
- Deserializes a JSON string into a collection of **Customer** objects.
- This list is filtered using LINQ to contain only customers whose names begin with the letter A.
- The **id** of each customer orders the filtered list.
- Each filtered customer's **id**, **customer_name**, and **profession** are printed.

```
1. using System.Text.Json;
2.
3. string jsonText = """"
4.
```

```
5.  [
6.    {"id": 1, "customer_name": "Alice", "profession": "Doctor"},
7.    {"id": 2, "customer_name": "Bob", "profession": "Engineer"},
8.    {"id": 3, "customer_name": "Charlie", "profession": "Lawyer"},
9.    {"id": 4, "customer_
      name": "David", "profession": "Secretary"},
10.   {"id": 5, "customer_name": "Eve", "profession": "Doctor"},
11.   {"id": 6, "customer_name": "Frank", "profession": "Engineer"},
12.   {"id": 7, "customer_name": "Grace", "profession": "Lawyer"},
13.   {"id": 8, "customer_
      name": "Hannah", "profession": "Secretary"},
14.   {"id": 9, "customer_name": "Isaac", "profession": "Doctor"},
15.   {"id": 10, "customer_name": "Jack", "profession": "Engineer"},
16.   {"id": 11, "customer_name": "Anna", "profession": "Lawyer"},
17.   {"id": 12, "customer_
      name": "Andrew", "profession": "Secretary"}
18. ]
19.
20.
21. """;
22.
23. List<Customer> customers = JsonSerializer.
    Deserialize<List<Customer>>(jsonText);
24.
25. var filteredCustomers = from c in customers
26.                         where c.customer_name.StartsWith("A")
27.                         orderby c.id
28.                         select c;
29.
30. foreach (var customer in filteredCustomers)
31. {
32.     Console.WriteLine($"ID: {customer.id}, Name: {customer.
    customer_name}, Profession: {customer.profession}");
33. }
34. class Customer
35. {
36.     public int id { get; set; }
37.     public string customer_name { get; set; }
38.     public string profession { get; set; }
39. }
```

The following result lists only customer in the provided JSON data whose name starts with **A**, and their details are printed according to the specified format:

```
ID: 1, Name: Alice, Profession: Doctor
ID: 11, Name: Anna, Profession: Lawyer
ID: 12, Name: Andrew, Profession: Secretary
```

Figure 10.1: Output result

In this example, we looked at how LINQ can be used for simple collection queries. We showed how to deserialize a JSON string into a collection of custom C# objects and then use LINQ to filter and sort these objects depending on specific criteria. The shown result is a filtered list of customers whose names begin with the letter A and are sorted by their IDs. It is a simple introduction to LINQ that demonstrates how it may simplify complex operations on collections, improving code readability and maintainability.

Grouping and aggregation with LINQ

The supplied code sample explains how to organize a collection of customer objects based on their professions using LINQ. LINQ is a powerful C# feature that allows you to query collections declaratively, akin to SQL queries. The following example shows how to use the LINQ group by clause to arrange the customer collection into multiple profession-based groups.

Customers in this example are probably a list or an enumerable collection of customer objects, each containing a property named profession. The LINQ query classifies these clients into distinct categories depending on their occupation attributes. The query then creates a new anonymous type for each profession, collecting both the profession and the number of clients.

The code sample below imports the necessary namespace for JSON serialization before defining a string representing a list of customer objects, each with its ID, name, and profession. This JSON string is deserialized into a list of **Customer** objects using **System.Text.Json**. It then groups the customers based on occupation and produces an anonymous type with two properties: occupation (representing the profession) and **Count**. Finally, it iterates through the grouped customers and prints each profession and the number of customers in that profession. The **Customer** class is defined after the code and represents the structure of each customer object, including attributes for ID, name, and profession.

```
1. using System.Text.Json;
2.
3. string jsonText = """
4.
5. [
6.    {"id": 1, "customer_name": "Alice", "profession": "Doctor"},
7.    {"id": 2, "customer_name": "Bob", "profession": "Engineer"},
8.    {"id": 3, "customer_name": "Charlie", "profession": "Lawyer"},
9.    {"id": 4, "customer_name": "David", "profession": "Secretary"},
```

```
10.     {"id": 5, "customer_name": "Eve", "profession": "Doctor"},
11.     {"id": 6, "customer_name": "Frank", "profession": "Engineer"},
12.     {"id": 7, "customer_name": "Grace", "profession": "Lawyer"},
13.     {"id": 8, "customer_name": "Hannah", "profession": "Secretary"},
14.     {"id": 9, "customer_name": "Isaac", "profession": "Doctor"},
15.     {"id": 10, "customer_name": "Jack", "profession": "Engineer"},
16.     {"id": 11, "customer_name": "Anna", "profession": "Secretary"},
17.     {"id": 12, "customer_name": "Andrew", "profession": "Secretary"}
18. ]
19.
20. """;
21.
22. List<Customer> customers = JsonSerializer.
    Deserialize<List<Customer>>(jsonText);
23.
24. var groupedCustomers = from c in customers
25.                        group c by c.profession into professionGroup
26.                        select new
27.                        {
28.                            Profession = professionGroup.Key,
29.                            Count = professionGroup.Count()
30.                        };
31.
32. foreach (var group in groupedCustomers)
33. {
34.     Console.WriteLine($"Profession: {group.
    Profession}, Count: {group.Count}");
35. }
36. class Customer
37. {
38.     public int id { get; set; }
39.     public string customer_name { get; set; }
40.     public string profession { get; set; }
41. }
```

The code is explained as follows:

- **from c in customers**: The query starts by iterating over each customer object in the customers' collection.

- **group c by c.profession**: This line groups the customer objects by profession property.

- **into professionGroup**: The grouped data is stored in a temporary variable named `professionGroup`.

- **select new { ... }**: A new anonymous type is created for each profession group. This type has two properties:

- **Profession = professionGroup.Key**: The key (`profession`) for each group.

- **Count = professionGroup.Count()**: The number of customers within each group.

Finally, a foreach loop iterates across the resultant **groupedCustomers** collection, printing to the console the profession and the number of customers in each profession.

Using LINQ to aggregate data collections like lists is simple and natural. The syntax and code are clear and straightforward to read and comprehend. To accomplish the same functionality without LINQ, you would likely have to create many loops and use extra data structures like dictionaries or hash maps. All of this is possible using LINQ with just a few lines of code.

Due to this, LINQ is declarative. It is easy to reason about what the code is doing, which simplifies both development and maintenance. It enables you to concentrate on the what rather than the how, allowing you to develop more expressive and succinct code.

The hard way to accomplish it without LINQ is that the code below highlights how tough it is to group using loops.

The following sample uses the **System**. We can use the **Text.Json** package to deserialize the string into a list of **Customer** objects. The JSON string provides customer information such as ID, name, and profession. Following deserialization, the code iterates through the list of customers, counting the number of instances of each profession using a **Dictionary**. Finally, it prints out each profession and its count. In addition, a **Customer** class is constructed with characteristics corresponding to the structure for correct deserialization.

```
1. using System.Text.Json;
2.
3. string jsonText = """"
4.
5. [
6.     {"id": 1, "customer_name": "Alice", "profession": "Doctor"},
7.     {"id": 2, "customer_name": "Bob", "profession": "Engineer"},
8.     {"id": 3, "customer_name": "Charlie", "profession": "Lawyer"},
9.     {"id": 4, "customer_name": "David", "profession": "Secretary"},
10.    {"id": 5, "customer_name": "Eve", "profession": "Doctor"},
11.    {"id": 6, "customer_name": "Frank", "profession": "Engineer"},
12.    {"id": 7, "customer_name": "Grace", "profession": "Lawyer"},
13.    {"id": 8, "customer_name": "Hannah", "profession": "Secretary"},
14.    {"id": 9, "customer_name": "Isaac", "profession": "Doctor"},
```

```
15.     {"id": 10, "customer_name": "Jack", "profession": "Engineer"},
16.     {"id": 11, "customer_name": "Anna", "profession": "Secretary"},
17.     {"id": 12, "customer_name": "Andrew", "profession": "Secretary"}
18. ]
19.
20. """;
21.
22. List<Customer> customers = JsonSerializer.Deserialize<List<Customer>
    >(jsonText);
23.
24. Dictionary<string, int> professionCounter = new Dictionary<string,
    int>();
25.
26. foreach (var customer in customers)
27. {
28.     if (professionCounter.ContainsKey(customer.profession))
29.     {
30.         professionCounter[customer.profession]++;
31.     }
32.     else
33.     {
34.         professionCounter.Add(customer.profession, 1);
35.     }
36. }
37.
38. foreach (var kvp in professionCounter)
39. {
40.     Console.WriteLine($"Profession: {kvp.Key}, Count: {kvp.Value}");
41. }
42.
43. public class Customer
44. {
45.     public int id { get; set; }
46.     public string customer_name { get; set; }
47.     public string profession { get; set; }
48. }
```

Following is the outcome of the code:

```
Profession: Doctor, Count: 3
Profession: Engineer, Count: 3
Profession: Lawyer, Count: 2
Profession: Secretary, Count: 4
```

Figure 10.2: The outcome of both codes is the same

Aggregation

Aggregation refers to gathering and presenting data in a summary in the context of databases or data processing. We aggregated the list of customers by their professions in both the LINQ and non-LINQ instances, summarizing the individual customer records into profession-based groupings. Then, inside each category, count the number of consumers to get a summary of the original list.

LINQ's group by and `Count()` functions simplify aggregation processes, resulting in simple and easy-to-understand code. Manually implementing the aggregation process, as shown in the non-LINQ example, requires more effort in handling data structures such as dictionaries and necessitates writing additional lines of code to accomplish equal functionality. Although both approaches achieve the purpose of data aggregation, their efficiency and clarity in performing such operations are apparent.

Using LINQ with Entity Framework Core

LINQ and EF Core are strong data-querying and manipulation technologies in the .NET environment. They combine the characteristics of relational database management systems and object-oriented programming, allowing us to interact with data more flexibly, safely, and resiliently.

EF Core offers many benefits for us as developers, making database interactions smoother and code more maintainable. Here is a breakdown of some key advantages:

- **Abstraction over database**: EF Core provides an abstraction over the database, allowing us to work with tightly typed **Common Language Runtime** (**CLR**) objects rather than dealing directly with database tables and SQL queries. It results in more transparent, more maintainable code.

- **Query expressiveness**: LINQ provides a fluid, expressive query syntax for data processing. You may use familiar C# syntax to filter, sort, aggregate, and alter data on the fly.

- **Compile-time checking**: With LINQ, query problems are discovered at compile time rather than runtime, making it easier to spot issues early in the development process.

- **Don't Repeat Yourself (DRY)**: LINQ with EF Core can decrease code duplication by centralizing data logic, making the code easier to maintain and extend.

- **Data provider agnostic**: EF Core supports different database providers, making it easy to swap databases without altering much code.

- **Cross-platform**: EF Core is part of the .NET framework, which is cross-platform and can be run on Windows, Linux, and macOS.

- **Community support**: As a member of the .NET ecosystem, you can access comprehensive community and official documentation, tutorials, and third-party tools.

In this example, we will build a basic C# console application that manages a vehicle reseller's inventory using EF Core and LINQ. We will also create a **Car** object and populate it with fields like **Manufacturer**, **Model**, **Price**, **Color**, **Type**, and **YearOfFabrication**. We will populate the database with 20 bogus records and show them in two alternative sequences:

- Manufacturer sorted

- Sorted by category

We will also summarize the prices and tally the number of automobiles by manufacturer and model.

Packages required: You must first install EF Core and Microsoft's SQL Server provider for EF Core. The following instructions will install these packages from the NuGet package manager console:

1. `Install-Package Microsoft.EntityFrameworkCore`
2. `Install-Package Microsoft.EntityFrameworkCore.SqlServer`

Here is a complete example:

```
1. using Microsoft.EntityFrameworkCore;
2. using System.ComponentModel.DataAnnotations;
3.
4. using CarContext db = new CarContext();
5.
6. // Create the database
7. db.Database.EnsureCreated();
8.
9. // Seed database
10.if (!db.Cars.Any())
11.{
12.    var carsToSeed = new List<Car>
13.{
14.new Car { Manufacturer="Tesla", Model="Model S", Price=80000,
   Color="Red", Type="Sedan", YearOfFabrication=2023 },
15.new Car { Manufacturer="Ford", Model="Focus", Price=20000,
```

```
        Color="Blue", Type="Hatchback", YearOfFabrication=2021 },
16. …
17. new Car { Manufacturer="Cadillac", Model="CTS", Price=45000,
        Color="Black", Type="Sedan", YearOfFabrication=2023 }
18. };
19.
20.
21.     db.Cars.AddRange(carsToSeed);
22.     db.SaveChanges();
23. }
24.
25. // Display cars sorted by Manufacturer
26. var carsByManufacturer = db.Cars.OrderBy(c => c.Manufacturer);
27. Console.WriteLine("Cars sorted by Manufacturer:");
28.
29. foreach (var car in carsByManufacturer)
30. {
31.     Console.WriteLine($"Manufacturer: {car.Manufacturer}, Model:
        {car.Model}, Price: {car.Price}, Color: {car.Color}, Type:
        {car.Type}, Year: {car.YearOfFabrication}");
32. }
33.
34. Console.WriteLine();
35.
36. // Display cars sorted by Type
37. var carsByType = db.Cars.OrderBy(c => c.Type);
38. Console.WriteLine("Cars sorted by Type:");
39. foreach (var car in carsByType)
40. {
41.     Console.WriteLine($"Manufacturer: {car.Manufacturer}, Model:
        {car.Model}, Price: {car.Price}, Color: {car.Color}, Type:
        {car.Type}, Year: {car.YearOfFabrication}");
42. }
43.
44. Console.WriteLine();
45.
46. // Summarize price and count by Manufacturer and Model
47. var summary = db.Cars.GroupBy(c => new { c.Manufacturer, c.Model })
48.     .Select(g => new
49.     {
50.         g.Key.Manufacturer,
```

```
51.          g.Key.Model,
52.          Count = g.Count(),
53.          TotalPrice = g.Sum(c => c.Price)
54.     });
55.
56. Console.WriteLine("Summary:");
57. foreach (var item in summary)
58. {
59.     Console.WriteLine($"Manufacturer: {item.
    Manufacturer}, Model: {item.Model}, Count: {item.
    Count}, Total Price: {item.TotalPrice}");
60. }
61.
62. public class Car
63. {
64.     [Key]
65.     public int Id { get; set; }
66.     public string Manufacturer { get; set; }
67.     public string Model { get; set; }
68.     public double Price { get; set; }
69.     public string Color { get; set; }
70.     public string Type { get; set; } // Sedan, SUV, etc.
71.     public int YearOfFabrication { get; set; }
72. }
73.
74. public class CarContext : DbContext
75. {
76.     public DbSet<Car> Cars { get; set; }
77.
78.     protected override void OnConfiguring(DbContextOptionsBuilder
    optionsBuilder)
79.     {
80.         optionsBuilder.UseSqlServer(@"Server=(localdb)\
    mssqllocaldb;Database=CarResellerDB;Trusted_Connection=True;");
81.     }
82. }
```

For simplicity, SQL Server LocalDB is used in this example. Change the connection string in **OnConfiguring()** if you use a different database.

When we run the program, we should see automobiles sorted by manufacturer and type and a breakdown of the count and total price by manufacturer and model.

The following sample connects with a database. It initially connects to it using the **CarContext** class derived from **DbContext**. Then, if the **Cars** table is empty, it creates the database and seeds it with car data. After seeding, it retrieves cars categorized by manufacturer and kind and displays them on the console. Finally, it includes an overview of the cars' overall numbers and prices, organized by manufacturer and model. The **Car** class describes the structure of a car object, with attributes such as **Manufacturer**, **Model**, **Price**, **Color**, **Type**, and **YearOfFabrication**, with **Id** designated as the primary key via the **[Key]** attribute. The **CarContext** class uses SQL Server to set up the database connection and defines the **Cars** table via the **DbSet**.

```
Manufacturer: Land Rover, Model: Discovery, Price: 52000, Color: Green, Type: SUV, Year: 2022
Manufacturer: Porsche, Model: Macan, Price: 60000, Color: Grey, Type: SUV, Year: 2023

Summary:
Manufacturer: Mazda, Model: 3, Count: 1, Total Price: 21000
Manufacturer: BMW, Model: 3 Series, Count: 1, Total Price: 41000
Manufacturer: Audi, Model: A4, Count: 1, Total Price: 40000
Manufacturer: Nissan, Model: Altima, Count: 1, Total Price: 23000
Manufacturer: Toyota, Model: Camry, Count: 1, Total Price: 24000
Manufacturer: Mercedes-Benz, Model: C-Class, Count: 1, Total Price: 42000
Manufacturer: Jeep, Model: Cherokee, Count: 1, Total Price: 34000
Manufacturer: Honda, Model: Civic, Count: 1, Total Price: 22000
Manufacturer: Cadillac, Model: CTS, Count: 1, Total Price: 45000
Manufacturer: Land Rover, Model: Discovery, Count: 1, Total Price: 52000
Manufacturer: Hyundai, Model: Elantra, Count: 1, Total Price: 20000
Manufacturer: Lexus, Model: ES, Count: 1, Total Price: 39000
Manufacturer: Ford, Model: Focus, Count: 1, Total Price: 20000
Manufacturer: Porsche, Model: Macan, Count: 1, Total Price: 60000
Manufacturer: Chevrolet, Model: Malibu, Count: 1, Total Price: 22000
Manufacturer: Tesla, Model: Model S, Count: 1, Total Price: 80000
Manufacturer: Subaru, Model: Outback, Count: 1, Total Price: 27000
Manufacturer: Volkswagen, Model: Passat, Count: 1, Total Price: 26000
Manufacturer: Volvo, Model: S60, Count: 1, Total Price: 37000
Manufacturer: Kia, Model: Sorento, Count: 1, Total Price: 29000
```

Figure 10.3: Console output

In summary, combining LINQ with EF Core provides a fast, expressive, and type-safe method of querying and manipulating data. They significantly increase productivity by allowing us to focus on business logic rather than data plumbing.

Understanding deferred execution in LINQ

Deferred execution in LINQ is a feature that postpones query execution until the results are enumerated. In other words, when you define a query with LINQ, it is not instantly executed. Instead, the query is only evaluated when you begin iterating the results (for example, in a foreach loop) or when you invoke a method that forces execution, such as **ToList()** or **ToArray()**.

Here is an example using LINQ to objects:

```
1. IEnumerable<int> numbers = new List<int> { 1, 2, 3, 4, 5, 6, 7, 8,
   9, 10 };
2. IEnumerable<int> evenNumbers = numbers.Where(n => n % 2 == 0);
```

```
3. // At this point, the query has not been executed.
4. // Execution happens here.
5. foreach (var n in evenNumbers)
6. {
7.     Console.WriteLine(n);
```

Advantages

Deferred execution can be more efficient since it eliminates needless processing. The query will only process the necessary elements if you have a vast data collection but only require a portion.

- **Composability**: You may create sophisticated searches by chaining together several actions. Deferring execution until the final question is enumerated makes it more efficient and, in many cases, more straightforward to comprehend and maintain.

- **Streaming**: Deferred execution works effectively. You do not have to load all of the data into memory since the query executes as you cycle over it.

- Deferred execution allows you to compose queries dynamically at runtime without executing them, allowing you to generate queries based on criteria.

- **Data source ignorance**: The same LINQ query may frequently be used against several data sources, such as collections, databases, or XML files. Deferred execution aids in query optimization for a given data source.

Making developers work faster and easier

We gain greatly from LINQ, which revolutionizes development. With delayed execution, we can decrease the code needed for complex data manipulation operations, speeding up development. Its clarity and succinctness in queries simplify code maintenance, keeping code understandable and manageable. LINQ's postponed execution allows developers to improve queries and test criteria, and add filters, reducing errors and improving code stability. It also uses deferred execution to let the engine or data source optimize queries automatically, improving efficiency without developer intervention. Finally, it separates issues, allowing developers to focus on data requirements rather than data gathering and management, simplifying code authoring, testing, and maintenance. Here is a list of benefits:

- **Less coding**: Developers use LINQ and delayed execution to write less code to accomplish complicated data manipulation tasks, which speeds up development.

- **Readability**: LINQ queries are frequently more readable and succinct than classic loop-based methods, simplifying maintenance.

- **Less error-prone**: Because queries are not performed immediately, developers have the opportunity to construct and revise queries progressively, testing criteria and adding filters, which can lead to fewer mistakes.

- **Optimization**: Deferred execution enables the LINQ engine or data source to optimize the query, making the entire operation more efficient without additional effort on the developer's behalf.

- **Separation of concerns**: Developers may concentrate on specifying what data is required rather than on how to collect and manage it. It makes it easy for the code to be written, tested and kept up to date.

To summarize, postponed execution in LINQ can result in more efficient, legible, and maintainable code, which enhances both the development process and the application's runtime performance.

Using deferred execution with EF Core

Here is how you may use the last **Car** example to show postponed execution by reading and filtering two lists of cars: **SUVs** and **Sedans**:

```
1.  // Create an IQueryable for SUVs
2.  var suvCarsQuery = db.Cars.Where(car => car.Type == "SUV");
3.
4.  // Create an IQueryable for Sedans
5.  var sedanCarsQuery = db.Cars.Where(car => car.Type == "Sedan");
6.
7.  // At this point, no query has been executed against the database
    yet.
8.  // Execution is deferred until you actually enumerate over the
    IQueryable.
9.
10. // Execute query and display SUVs
11. Console.WriteLine("List of SUVs:");
12. foreach (var suv in suvCarsQuery)  // The query gets executed here
13. {
14.     Console.WriteLine($"Manufacturer: {suv.Manufacturer}, Model:
    {suv.Model}, Price: {suv.Price}, Color: {suv.Color}, Year:
    {suv.YearOfFabrication}");
15. }
16.
17. Console.WriteLine();
18.
19. // Execute query and display Sedans
20. Console.WriteLine("List of Sedans:");
```

```
21. foreach (var sedan in sedanCarsQuery)  // The query gets executed
    here
22. {
23.     Console.WriteLine($"Manufacturer: {sedan.Manufacturer}, Model:
    {sedan.Model}, Price: {sedan.Price}, Color: {sedan.Color}, Year:
    {sedan.YearOfFabrication}");
24. }
25.
26. Console.WriteLine();
```

suvCarsQuery and **sedanCarsQuery** are **IQueryable<Car>** classes that carry the expression trees that describe the queries in this example. These queries are not run until the foreach loop is started to iterate over them. It is the core of LINQ's postponed execution.

The following result outputs lists of SUVs and sedans. Database-based lists show automobile manufacturer, model, price, color, and year of manufacture. Executing the IQueryable queries to the database to filter cars by type earlier in the code retrieves the data. Thus, the result will be a list of SUVs and sedans with their respective data:

```
List of SUVs:
Manufacturer: Subaru, Model: Outback, Price: 27000, Color: Green, Year: 2023
Manufacturer: Kia, Model: Sorento, Price: 29000, Color: Black, Year: 2022
Manufacturer: Jeep, Model: Cherokee, Price: 34000, Color: Brown, Year: 2021
Manufacturer: Land Rover, Model: Discovery, Price: 52000, Color: Green, Year: 2022
Manufacturer: Porsche, Model: Macan, Price: 60000, Color: Grey, Year: 2023

List of Sedans:
Manufacturer: Tesla, Model: Model S, Price: 80000, Color: Red, Year: 2023
Manufacturer: Honda, Model: Civic, Price: 22000, Color: Black, Year: 2022
Manufacturer: Toyota, Model: Camry, Price: 24000, Color: White, Year: 2021
Manufacturer: Nissan, Model: Altima, Price: 23000, Color: Silver, Year: 2020
Manufacturer: Chevrolet, Model: Malibu, Price: 22000, Color: Grey, Year: 2021
Manufacturer: Volkswagen, Model: Passat, Price: 26000, Color: Blue, Year: 2022
Manufacturer: Hyundai, Model: Elantra, Price: 20000, Color: Red, Year: 2020
Manufacturer: Audi, Model: A4, Price: 40000, Color: White, Year: 2023
Manufacturer: Mercedes-Benz, Model: C-Class, Price: 42000, Color: Black, Year: 2022
Manufacturer: BMW, Model: 3 Series, Price: 41000, Color: Blue, Year: 2021
Manufacturer: Lexus, Model: ES, Price: 39000, Color: Silver, Year: 2021
Manufacturer: Volvo, Model: S60, Price: 37000, Color: Blue, Year: 2022
Manufacturer: Cadillac, Model: CTS, Price: 45000, Color: Black, Year: 2023
```

Figure 10.4: Console output

LINQ to XML and LINQ to JSON

LINQ to XML and LINQ to JSON provide a powerful, unified, and flexible way to query, manipulate, and transform XML and JSON data using LINQ syntax in C#.

XML, the markup language

The markup language XML stores structured data. It employs tags like HTML to construct components and characteristics that represent the data. XML is extensively utilized in various applications, such as online services, document storage, and data transmission between disparate systems. It is customizable, enabling you to create categories and document structure.

Here is how an XML file containing information about car parts might look:

```
1.  <?xml version="1.0" encoding="UTF-8"?>
2.  <CarParts>
3.    <Part>
4.      <PartName>Engine</PartName>
5.      <PartNumber>ENG-001</PartNumber>
6.      <Manufacturer>Ford</Manufacturer>
7.      <Price>5000</Price>
8.    </Part>
9.    <Part>
10.     <PartName>Transmission</PartName>
11.     <PartNumber>TRN-002</PartNumber>
12.     <Manufacturer>Toyota</Manufacturer>
13.     <Price>2000</Price>
14.   </Part>
15.   <Part>
16.     <PartName>Brake Pad</PartName>
17.     <PartNumber>BRK-003</PartNumber>
18.     <Manufacturer>Honda</Manufacturer>
19.     <Price>200</Price>
20.   </Part>
21. </CarParts>
```

Learn what is **JavaScript Object Notation** (**JSON**) a lightweight data-interchange format that is simple for people and machines to read and write. Unlike XML, JSON has a less verbose syntax based on key-value pairs. It is frequently used in online applications for client-server communication and is native to JavaScript; thus, it is convenient for web-based services and applications.

Here is how a JSON file for the same information might look:

```
1.  {
2.    "CarParts": [
3.      {
4.        "PartName": "Engine",
5.        "PartNumber": "ENG-001",
6.        "Manufacturer": "Ford",
7.        "Price": 5000
8.      },
9.      {
```

```
10.        "PartName": "Transmission",
11.        "PartNumber": "TRN-002",
12.        "Manufacturer": "Toyota",
13.        "Price": 2000
14.    },
15.    {
16.        "PartName": "Brake Pad",
17.        "PartNumber": "BRK-003",
18.        "Manufacturer": "Honda",
19.        "Price": 200
20.    }
21.  ]
22.}
```

LINQ's user-friendliness

Both XML and JSON are standard data storage and exchange formats. However, manually parsing or manipulating various data types can be time-consuming and error prone. Through LINQ to XML and LINQ to JSON, LINQ provides a more elegant approach to interface with these formats.

LINQ allows you to do strongly typed, complicated queries, transformations, and manipulations on XML or JSON data. The queries are validated at build time, which reduces runtime mistakes and strengthens your code. As LINQ is declarative, you can focus on the what rather than the how, making the code easier to comprehend and maintain. This consistent querying experience enables us to transition between data sources such as databases, XML, and JSON with little cognitive strain.

Working with XML and JSON using LINQ

For LINQ users, standard querying, such as switching to XML or JSON, is intuitive. The same query syntax simplifies the procedure, whether the data source is a SQL database, in-memory collection, XML file, or JSON object. This continuity reduces the learning curve and streamlines the transfer of skills and best practices across data repositories, increasing productivity. LINQ's integration with tightly typed ensures that types are known at build time, improving auto-completion recommendations and compiler type-related fault identification. Thus, code becomes more durable and manageable, decreasing runtime errors. By precisely exploring and manipulating XML and JSON data, LINQ's high-level API improves code readability by freeing developers from complex details and focusing on task logic. With its dynamic querying, development is faster, and needs can be easily changed. Finally, LINQ's declarative grammar emphasizes what rather than how, making code shorter, clearer, and easier to debug and maintain. Here we see it in detail:

- **Experience with uniform querying**: If you have worked with LINQ before, transitioning from LINQ to XML or JSON feels intuitive. This is due to the query syntax remaining constant across data sources. The essential LINQ operators and method calls are the same whether you are searching an SQL database, an in-memory collection, an XML file, or a JSON object. It minimizes the learning curve and boosts productivity by allowing us to effortlessly transfer our existing skills and best practices between multiple data repositories.

- **Powerfully written**: Types are known at compile time in a tightly typed language like C#. LINQ extends this advantage to access XML and JSON data. It implies that the IDE will provide better auto-completion recommendations, and the compiler can detect type-related issues before the code executes. As a result, your code is more resilient and manageable, with fewer runtime errors and problems. For example, attempting to execute a string operation on an integer field would result in an error, which would not occur with flexibly typed query methods.

- **Readability**: Manually parsing XML and JSON might result in lengthy and difficult-to-read code. LINQ provides a more precise, higher-level API for searching and manipulating these formats. Using LINQ queries clarifies the intent of the code, boosting readability. You do not have to get bogged down in the specifics of XML trees or JSON key-value pairs; instead, you can concentrate on the logic of what you are trying to accomplish, which makes the code easier to comprehend and maintain.

- **Flexibility**: Traditional DOM operations may be inflexible and require much boilerplate code to achieve even simple tasks. LINQ provides XML and JSON data with dynamic and expressive querying capabilities. For example, with a few lines of code, you may filter, sort, group, or change data on the fly. This adaptability enables faster development and more straightforward adaptation to changing circumstances.

- **Declarative grammar**: Writing imperative code that defines how to conduct actions is standard in traditional XML and JSON manipulations. The declarative syntax of LINQ emphasizes what you wish to achieve while abstracting away the underlying mechanisms. Instead of constructing a loop to filter out specific components, you may utilize a single LINQ query. It produces shorter, more concise, and more intelligible code, which makes it simpler to debug and maintain.

These advantages make LINQ an indispensable tool for dealing with XML and JSON in C#, making your development process more effective, error-free, and pleasant.

LINQ to XML example

The LINQ to XML example takes a file containing car information and converts it into a list of **Car** objects in C#. The code sifts through the XML document using LINQ queries, selecting and picking out the components representing specific automobiles and their properties. These properties are then utilized to populate C# objects grouped in a list. Finally, the list is looped through to display the details of each automobile in the console. To do this in a concise and accessible manner, the example makes use of LINQ's expressive querying features.

Here, you can save the list of cars to an XML file and read it back using LINQ to XML:

```
1.  using System.ComponentModel.DataAnnotations;
2.  using System.Xml.Linq;
3.
4.  var carsToSeed = new List<Car>
5.  {
6.  new Car { Manufacturer="Tesla", Model="Model S", Price=80000,
       Color="Red", Type="Sedan", YearOfFabrication=2023 },
7.  new Car { Manufacturer="Ford", Model="Focus", Price=20000,
       Color="Blue", Type="Hatchback", YearOfFabrication=2021 },
8.  new Car { Manufacturer="Honda", Model="Civic", Price=22000,
       Color="Black", Type="Sedan", YearOfFabrication=2022 },
9.  new Car { Manufacturer="Toyota", Model="Camry", Price=24000,
       Color="White", Type="Sedan", YearOfFabrication=2021 },
10. new Car { Manufacturer="Nissan", Model="Altima", Price=23000,
       Color="Silver", Type="Sedan", YearOfFabrication=2020 },
11. new Car { Manufacturer="Chevrolet", Model="Malibu", Price=22000,
       Color="Grey", Type="Sedan", YearOfFabrication=2021 },
12. new Car { Manufacturer="Volkswagen", Model="Passat", Price=26000,
       Color="Blue", Type="Sedan", YearOfFabrication=2022 },
13. new Car { Manufacturer="Subaru", Model="Outback", Price=27000,
       Color="Green", Type="SUV", YearOfFabrication=2023 },
14. new Car { Manufacturer="Hyundai", Model="Elantra", Price=20000,
       Color="Red", Type="Sedan", YearOfFabrication=2020 },
15. new Car { Manufacturer="Kia", Model="Sorento", Price=29000,
       Color="Black", Type="SUV", YearOfFabrication=2022 },
16. new Car { Manufacturer="Jeep", Model="Cherokee", Price=34000,
       Color="Brown", Type="SUV", YearOfFabrication=2021 },
17. new Car { Manufacturer="Mazda", Model="3", Price=21000,
       Color="Red", Type="Hatchback", YearOfFabrication=2022 },
18. new Car { Manufacturer="Audi", Model="A4", Price=40000,
       Color="White", Type="Sedan", YearOfFabrication=2023 },
19. new Car { Manufacturer="Mercedes-Benz", Model="C-Class",
       Price=42000, Color="Black", Type="Sedan", YearOfFabrication=2022 },
20. new Car { Manufacturer="BMW", Model="3 Series", Price=41000,
       Color="Blue", Type="Sedan", YearOfFabrication=2021 },
21. new Car { Manufacturer="Land Rover", Model="Discovery",
       Price=52000, Color="Green", Type="SUV", YearOfFabrication=2022 },
```

```
22. new Car { Manufacturer="Porsche", Model="Macan", Price=60000,
       Color="Grey", Type="SUV", YearOfFabrication=2023 },
23. new Car { Manufacturer="Lexus", Model="ES", Price=39000,
       Color="Silver", Type="Sedan", YearOfFabrication=2021 },
24. new Car { Manufacturer="Volvo", Model="S60", Price=37000,
       Color="Blue", Type="Sedan", YearOfFabrication=2022 },
25. new Car { Manufacturer="Cadillac", Model="CTS", Price=45000,
       Color="Black", Type="Sedan", YearOfFabrication=2023 }
26. };
27.
28.
29. var carsToXML = new XElement("Cars",
30.     from car in carsToSeed
31.     select new XElement("Car",
32.         new XElement("Manufacturer", car.Manufacturer),
33.         new XElement("Model", car.Model),
34.         new XElement("Price", car.Price),
35.         new XElement("Color", car.Color),
36.         new XElement("Type", car.Type),
37.         new XElement("YearOfFabrication", car.YearOfFabrication)
38.     )
39. );
40.
41. carsToXML.Save("Cars.xml");
42.
43. public class Car
44. {
45.     [Key]
46.     public int Id { get; set; }
47.     public string Manufacturer { get; set; }
48.     public string Model { get; set; }
49.     public double Price { get; set; }
50.     public string Color { get; set; }
51.     public string Type { get; set; } // Sedan, SUV, etc.
52.     public int YearOfFabrication { get; set; }
53. }
```

The code given above will produce the **Cars.xml** file:

```
1. <?xml version="1.0" encoding="utf-8"?>
2. <Cars>
3.   <Car>
```

```
4.      <Manufacturer>Tesla</Manufacturer>
5.      <Model>Model S</Model>
6.      <Price>80000</Price>
7.      <Color>Red</Color>
8.      <Type>Sedan</Type>
9.      <YearOfFabrication>2023</YearOfFabrication>
10.   </Car>
11.   <Car>
12.     <Manufacturer>Ford</Manufacturer>
13.     <Model>Focus</Model>
14.     <Price>20000</Price>
15.     <Color>Blue</Color>
16.     <Type>Hatchback</Type>
17.     <YearOfFabrication>2021</YearOfFabrication>
18.   </Car>
19. ....
```

LINQ for XML reading

Reading XML with LINQ entails loading the XML document into memory and then searching for and extracting the data you want using LINQ queries. The XML is read into an XDocument object, which allows the XML to be represented as a tree-like structure of nodes. The tree may then be navigated and filtered using LINQ queries to retrieve relevant nodes and their values. Typically, extracted data is mapped to C# objects for future usage in the application. This method makes it simple to read portions of an XML document straightforwardly and expressively.

```
1. using System.ComponentModel.DataAnnotations;
2. using System.Xml.Linq;
3.
4. string xmlFilePath = "Cars.
   xml"; // Assuming the file is in the same directory as the executable
5.
6. XDocument xDocument = XDocument.Load(xmlFilePath);
7.
8. var carsFromXml = xDocument.Descendants("Car")
9.                             .Select(car => new Car
10.                            {
11.                                Manufacturer = car.
    Element("Manufacturer")?.Value,
12.                                Model = car.Element("Model")?.Value,
13.                                Price = double.Parse(car.
```

```
    Element("Price")?.Value ?? "0"),
14.                                 Color = car.Element("Color")?.Value,
15.                                 Type = car.Element("Type")?.Value,
16.                                 YearOfFabrication = int.Parse(car.
    Element("YearOfFabrication")?.Value ?? "0")
17.                         })
18.                         .ToList();
19.
20. // Display the cars read from the XML file
21. foreach (var car in carsFromXml)
22. {
23.     Console.WriteLine($"Manufacturer: {car.
    Manufacturer}, Model: {car.Model}, Price: {car.Price}, Color: {car.
    Color}, Type: {car.Type}, Year Of Fabrication: {car.
    YearOfFabrication}");
24. }
25.
26.
27. public class Car
28. {
29.     [Key]
30.     public int Id { get; set; }
31.     public string Manufacturer { get; set; }
32.     public string Model { get; set; }
33.     public double Price { get; set; }
34.     public string Color { get; set; }
35.     public string Type { get; set; } // Sedan, SUV, etc.
36.     public int YearOfFabrication { get; set; }
37. }
```

LINQ to JSON example

Reading a JSON document into a format that can be readily queried using LINQ expressions in C# is what LINQ to JSON is all about. It allows you to comb through the JSON structure and retrieve specific information. The JSON document is typically deserialized into a C# object or a dynamic structure that reflects the JSON data's deep hierarchy. When the data is in this state, LINQ queries are used to explore, filter, and alter it. The generated data can be utilized directly within the program or changed further. This technique simplifies working with JSON data by utilizing LINQ's familiar and expressive syntax.

We can serialize your list of car parts into a JSON string and save it to a file like this:

```
1. using System.Text.Json;
```

```
2.
3.
4.  var carParts = new List<CarPart>
5.  {
6.      new CarPart { PartName = "Engine", PartNumber = "ENG-
    001", Manufacturer = "Ford", Price = 5000 },
7.      new CarPart { PartName = "Transmission", PartNumber = "TRN-
    002", Manufacturer = "Toyota", Price = 2000 },
8.      new CarPart { PartName = "Brake Pad", PartNumber = "BRK-
    003", Manufacturer = "Honda", Price = 200 }
9.  };
10.
11. string jsonString = JsonSerializer.Serialize(carParts);
12. File.WriteAllText("CarParts.json", jsonString);
13.
14. public class CarPart
15. {
16.     public string PartName { get; set; }
17.     public string PartNumber { get; set; }
18.     public string Manufacturer { get; set; }
19.     public int Price { get; set; }
20. }
```

The code given above will produce the **CarParts.json** file.

```
1.  {
2.    "CarParts": [
3.      {
4.        "PartName": "Engine",
5.        "PartNumber": "ENG-001",
6.        "Manufacturer": "Ford",
7.        "Price": 5000
8.      },
9.      {
10.       "PartName": "Transmission",
11.       "PartNumber": "TRN-002",
12.       "Manufacturer": "Toyota",
13.       "Price": 2000
14.     },
15.     {
16.       "PartName": "Brake Pad",
17.       "PartNumber": "BRK-003",
```

```
18.       "Manufacturer": "Honda",
19.       "Price": 200
20.     }
21.   ]
22. }
```

Reading from JSON using System.Text.Json

Using **System.Text.Json** to read from a JSON-formatted text into a string and then using the library's **JsonSerializer** is how JSON works. To transform the string into C# objects, use the **Deserialize** method. This method allows you to convert JSON data into native C# types quickly and effectively, making it easier to manage and use the data inside your application.

We can read this JSON file back into a C# object like so:

```
1. string jsonString = File.ReadAllText("CarParts.json");
2. List<CarPart> carParts = JsonSerializer.
   Deserialize<List<CarPart>>(jsonString);
3.
4. foreach (var part in carParts)
5. {
6.     Console.WriteLine($"Part Name: {part.
   PartName}, Manufacturer: {part.Manufacturer}");
7. }
```

Using LINQ to manipulate collections and arrays

Filtering, sorting, grouping, and aggregating may be performed directly on data structures like arrays, lists, dictionaries, and other enumerable collections using LINQ, eliminating the need for complex loops or conditional statements.

LINQ provides a uniform querying experience across several data sources, such as in-memory collections, databases, and XML files, allowing you to transfer your abilities between data types seamlessly. It adds SQL-like query operations to C#, allowing you to create declarative, highly typed code.

LINQ, in short, provides a high-level, abstract interface for interacting with data, allowing you to build more evident, more efficient, and maintainable code.

These are the fundamental operations on collections and arrays:

- **Filtering**: We may use **Where** methods to filter collection items depending on a criterion.

```
1. // Filter cars that are priced above $30,000
2. var expensiveCars = cars.Where(car => car.Price > 30000).
   ToList();
3. foreach (var car in expensiveCars)
4. {
5.     Console.WriteLine($"{car.Manufacturer} {car.Model} - ${car.
   Price}");
6. }
```

- **Projection**: The **Select** function lets you project each piece in a sequence onto a new form, which typically reduces the amount of data you have to work with. For example, if an array of objects requires one property from each, you may use **Select** to extract that property.

```
1. // Select only the models of the cars
2. var carModels = cars.Select(car => car.Model).ToList();
3. foreach (var model in carModels)
4. {
5.     Console.WriteLine(model);
6. }
```

- **Sorting with OrderBy and OrderByDescending**: Collections may be sorted using **OrderBy** and **OrderByDescending**. You may combine several **ThenBy** or **ThenByDescending** methods to create more sophisticated sorting criteria.

```
1. // Sort cars by price in ascending order
2. var carsByPrice = cars.OrderBy(car => car.Price).ToList();
3. // Sort cars by price in descending order
4. var carsByPriceDesc = cars.OrderByDescending(car => car.Price).
   ToList();
```

- **Setup procedures**: Methods such as **Union**, **Intersect**, and **Except** provide set-based operations, enabling you to locate items shared by two collections, elements unique to each collection, and so on.

```
1. // Union of two lists
2. var allCarModels = carModels1.Union(carModels2).ToList();
3.
4. // Intersection of two lists
5. var commonCarModels = carModels1.Intersect(carModels2).
   ToList();
```

- **Conversion**: To convert a collection to a specific type, utilize methods such as **ToArray**, **ToList**, **ToDictionary**, and **ToLookup**.

```
1. // Convert to array
2. var carArray = cars.ToArray();
```

- **Lazy assessment**: LINQ employs deferred execution, meaning the query is not executed until you iterate over the sequence. It makes LINQ more efficient since it reduces the work done beforehand.

- **Chaining**: To build complicated queries more legibly and manageable, you may chain numerous LINQ methods together.

  Lazy evaluation and chaining sample:

```
1. // The query doesn't execute here
2. var query = cars.Where(car => car.Price < 30000)
3.                 .OrderBy(car => car.Price)
4.                 .Select(car => new { car.Manufacturer, car.
   Model });
5.
6. // The query executes when you enumerate the results
7. foreach (var car in query)
8. {
9.     Console.WriteLine($"{car.Manufacturer} {car.Model}");
10. }
```

- **Complex condition filtering**: Assume you wish to locate all automobiles built in 2021 or after that are either Tesla-made or priced under $30,000.

```
1. var complexFilter = cars.Where(car => (car.
   YearOfFabrication >= 2021) && (car.
   Manufacturer == "Tesla" || car.Price < 30000)).ToList();
2.
3. foreach (var car in complexFilter)
4. {
5.     Console.WriteLine($"{car.Manufacturer} {car.Model} - ${car.
   Price}");
6. }
```

Considerations about LINQ operations

One LINQ query may locate elements in a collection that fulfill specified criteria instead of nested loops. It saves lines and makes code more transparent. Filtering, grouping, and joining are more manageable and cleaner using LINQ.

LINQ is a robust C# data processing tool. Abstraction makes code clearer, readable, and maintainable. Its performance trade-offs are generally outweighed, making it a crucial tool for C# programming.

Advanced LINQ operators

Advanced LINQ operators provide more advanced features for manipulating collections and data sequences than simple filtering, sorting, and projection. Aggregation procedures like **Sum** and **Average**, set operations like **Union** and **Intersect**, and even relational operations like **Join** and **GroupJoin** are among the sophisticated capabilities. You may use these operators to do key-based grouping, combine several collections in various ways, and even transform query results into new types, such as arrays or dictionaries. Advanced LINQ operators enable us to design more powerful, expressive, and flexible queries, improving their ability to handle and analyze data effectively.

The following are the primary advanced operations:

- **GroupBy**: This assists in sorting data into groups based on a particular property. It is handy for complicated datasets that require data to be aggregated based on one or more attributes.

```
1. // Group cars by manufacturer
2. var carsGroupedByManufacturer = cars.GroupBy(car => car.
   Manufacturer);
3. foreach (var group in carsGroupedByManufacturer)
4. {
5.     Console.WriteLine($"Manufacturer: {group.Key}");
6.     foreach (var car in group)
7.     {
8.         Console.WriteLine($"    Model: {car.
   Model}, Price: ${car.Price}");
9.     }
10. }
```

- **Aggregation**: **Sum**, **Average**, **Min**, **Max**, and **Count** are aggregation functions that may be used to conduct mathematical computations over a sequence of variables.

```
1. // Calculate the total price of all cars
2. var totalPrice = cars.Sum(car => car.Price);
3. // Calculate average price of all cars
4. var averagePrice = cars.Average(car => car.Price);
```

- **Joins**: For querying relational data structures, LINQ includes **Join** and **GroupJoin**. You can combine records from two or more collections using a related key.

```
1. // List of manufacturers
2. var manufacturers = new List<Manufacturer> {
3.     new Manufacturer { Name = "Tesla", Country = "USA" },
4.     new Manufacturer { Name = "Ford", Country = "USA" },
5.     // ...
6. };
```

```
7.
8. // Join lists to get full data
9. var carWithCountry = cars.Join(manufacturers,
10.                                car => car.Manufacturer,
11.                                manufacturer =>
   manufacturer.Name,
12.                                (car, manufacturer) => new {
   car, manufacturer.Country });
```

- **Operations on elements**: Methods such as **First**, **Last**, **SingleOrDefault**, and **ElementAt** can locate a specific element in a collection depending on a condition or location.

```
1. // Get the first Tesla car
2. var firstTesla = cars.First(car => car.Manufacturer == "Tesla");
```

- **Paging**: We may build simple paging with **Skip** and **Take**. For example, you might skip the first ten pieces and use the following 20 as your second page of data.

```
1. // Skip the first 2 cars and then take the next 3
2. var pagedCars = cars.Skip(2).Take(3).ToList();
```

- **Query syntax**: LINQ queries over C#, and .NET collections are more declarative and SQL-like. Query syntax expresses complicated inquiries more clearly than chained method calls. When you have many filtering, sorting, or grouping actions, it lets you organize them like SQL queries. Use keywords like **from**, **select**, **where**, **group**, and **orderby** to express data activities. Query and method syntax are compatible, so you may switch between them as needed.

```
1. var luxuryCars = from car in cars
2.                  where car.Price > 50000
3.                  select car.Model;
```

LINQ allows us to conduct complicated data operations on collections and arrays in a straightforward and accessible manner. For example, with a few lines of code, you can filter automobiles priced above $30,000, sort them by price, and group them by manufacturer. **Where**, **OrderBy**, and **GroupBy** methods provide elegant, declarative searches that may be chained together for increased versatility. It not only makes our code more legible and manageable, but it also enables rigorous compile-time verification, which increases overall code dependability.

Professionals who can use LINQ to manipulate collections and arrays are highly appreciated in development teams for their ability to build transparent, efficient, and maintainable code. This knowledge translates into long-term business profitability by drastically lowering the costs of code creation, deployment, and maintenance. Code that is well-structured and easy to update reduces the likelihood of mistakes and promotes future additions, making the whole software development life cycle more efficient. As a result, knowing LINQ makes you a more productive developer and a strategic asset in achieving cost-efficiency and sustainability for your firm.

Understanding lambda expressions with LINQ

Lambda expressions help to make LINQ queries more concise and expressive. A lambda expression is a kind of anonymous function that may own variables inside its scope. Building inline methods without first needing to identify them is possible thanks to this handy approach.

Anatomy of a lambda expression

The syntax for a lambda expression is:

```
1. (input parameters) => expression or statement block
```

The code given above demonstrates a lambda function with input and body.

- The input parameters are akin to the arguments of a method.
- The => is the lambda operator.
- The expression or statement block is the lambda's body, a single expression or code block.

Sample filtering a list of integers using Where

Assume you have a list of integers and wish to locate all values bigger than 5. To filter this list, utilize LINQ's **Where** function in combination with a lambda expression.

```
1. List<int> numbers = new List<int> { 1, 2, 3, 4, 5, 6, 7, 8, 9, 10 };
2.
3. var filteredNumbers = numbers.Where(x => x > 5);
4.
5. foreach (int number in filteredNumbers)
6. {
7.     Console.WriteLine(number);
8. }
```

The lambda expression in this case is **x => x > 5**. It accepts an integer x as input and returns a boolean indicating whether or not x is bigger than 5.

The following results show integers bigger than 5 from the list **numbers**. Specifically, it will print the numbers 6, 7, 8, 9, and 10 on a new line in the console. The code filters the initial list **numbers** using LINQ's **Where** method, which chooses elements bigger than 5. The code then iterates through the filtered sequence and uses a foreach loop to print each number to the console, displaying the requested numbers.

Figure 10.5: Console output

Sample, transforming a list of strings using **Select**.

Consider a collection of strings representing names that you wish to change to uppercase. To do this, utilize LINQ's **Select** function in conjunction with a lambda expression.

```
1. List<string> names = new List<string> { "Alice", "Bob", "Charlie",
   "David" };
2.
3. var upperCaseNames = names.Select(name => name.ToUpper());
4.
5. foreach (string name in upperCaseNames)
6. {
7.     Console.WriteLine(name);
8. }
```

This is the console output we will have:

Figure 10.6: Console output

LINQ queries written in C# with lambda expressions are more expressive and easier to read. They allow you to define inline logic without first declaring explicitly named methods or delegates, making your code more succinct. You will be able to use the full potential of LINQ in your C# programs if you have a solid grasp of how to make efficient use of lambda expressions.

Implementing custom comparers and equality in LINQ

Custom comparers in LINQ can be developed for various reasons, such as filtering, sorting, and grouping. It is significant because you may wish to compare or equate objects based on custom rules not supported by their default comparison or equality methods.

Implementing a case-insensitive string comparer in LINQ query, let us say we have a list of strings and want to filter out unique names without considering their case:

```
1.  List<string> names = new List<string> { "Alice", "Bob", "ALICE",
    "Charlie", "bob" };
2.
3.  var uniqueNames = names.Distinct(new CaseInsensitiveComparer()).
    ToList();
4.
5.  foreach (var name in uniqueNames)
6.  {
7.      Console.WriteLine(name);
8.  }
9.  class CaseInsensitiveComparer : IEqualityComparer<string>
10. {
11.     public bool Equals(string x, string y)
12.     {
13.         return x.Equals(y, StringComparison.OrdinalIgnoreCase);
14.     }
15.
16.     public int GetHashCode(string obj)
17.     {
18.         return obj.ToLowerInvariant().GetHashCode();
19.     }
20. }
```

Explanation of the code:

- **CaseInsensitiveComparer** is a custom comparer that implements **IEqualityComparer<string>**. It overrides the **Equals** and **GetHashCode** methods.

- **Equals** perform a case-insensitive comparison of two strings.

- **GetHashCode** returns the hash code of the string in a case-insensitive manner.

We use this comparison in the **Distinct** method to get unique names without considering their case; refer to the following figure:

Figure 10.7: Console output

Custom comparer for complex type

When working with bespoke objects, we often need to sort them by criteria that the default sorting algorithms do not provide. Custom comparers help here. Custom comparers let us design our own comparison logic to order objects as needed.

Suppose we have a list of **Person** objects with **Name** and **Age** properties. Let us sort these **Person** objects by age and then by name if ages are equal. This is difficult with C#'s default sorting methods. Custom sorting logic is easy to construct with a custom comparer.

The **Person** class in the example has **Name** and **Age** attributes. A custom comparer class, **PersonComparer**, also implements the **IComparer<Person>** interface. We must define comparison logic using a **Compare** method for this interface.

The **PersonComparer** class compares two **Person** objects' names and ages. Compares two people's ages. If ages are equal, names are compared further. This logic sorts **Person** objects by age first, then by name if ages are the same.

Using our specific comparison logic, we may arrange **Person** instances using **OrderBy** LINQ and a **PersonComparer** instance. This produces a sorted list that satisfies our needs.

Powerful custom comparers allow flexible and controlled sorting of bespoke object collections. They allow developers to adjust sorting behavior for their apps, making sorting efficient and customizable.

Suppose we have a list of **Person** objects, and you want to sort them by their age and name:

```
1.  List<Person> people = new List<Person>
2.      {
3.          new Person { Name = "Alice", Age = 30 },
4.          new Person { Name = "Bob", Age = 25 },
5.          new Person { Name = "Charlie", Age = 25 },
6.          new Person { Name = "David", Age = 35 }
7.      };
8.
9.  var sortedPeople = people.OrderBy(p => p, new PersonComparer()).
    ToList();
10.
11. foreach (var person in sortedPeople)
12. {
13.     Console.WriteLine($"Name: {person.Name}, Age: {person.Age}");
14. }
15.
16. class Person
17. {
18.     public string Name { get; set; }
```

```
19.    public int Age { get; set; }
20. }
21.
22. class PersonComparer : IComparer<Person>
23. {
24.    public int Compare(Person x, Person y)
25.    {
26.        int ageComparison = x.Age.CompareTo(y.Age);
27.        if (ageComparison == 0)
28.        {
29.            return x.Name.CompareTo(y.Name);
30.        }
31.        return ageComparison;
32.    }
33. }
```

Explanation of the code:

- **Person** is a simple class with **Name** and **Age** properties.

- **PersonComparer** is a custom comparer that implements **IComparer<Person>**. It overrides the **Compare** method.

- Inside **Compare**, we first compare the **Age**. If they are the same, we compare the **Name**.

- We use this custom comparer in the **OrderBy** LINQ method to sort the list of people by age and then by name if the age is the same.

Using custom comparers like these allows you to encapsulate complex comparison or equality logic in a reusable way, making your LINQ queries more expressive and easier to maintain.

This result sample below creates a **Person** class with attributes for name and age and a **PersonComparer** class that implements **IComparer<Person>** to compare **Person** instances based on age first, then name if a tie occurs. The people list starts with four **Person** objects with various names and ages. The list is then sorted using **OrderBy** and a custom comparer **PersonComparer**, yielding a new list of **sortedPeople**, sorted first by age and then name. Finally, the sorted list is iterated to print each person's name and age:

```
Name: Bob, Age: 25
Name: Charlie, Age: 25
Name: Alice, Age: 30
Name: David, Age: 35
```

Figure 10.8: Console output

While LINQ provides a solid and expressive vocabulary for searching and manipulating data, it is critical to understand that the possibilities are not limitless. The success of a LINQ-based solution is heavily influenced by factors such as software specifications, performance considerations, and underlying data structures. Furthermore, the development team's ability to create bespoke solutions using custom comparers and equality logic is critical.

Custom comparers help design domain-specific sorting, filtering, and grouping rules. However, implementation must be done cautiously to ensure consistency with the overall program design and needs. To fully use the potential of custom comparers and LINQ queries, the team must have a solid understanding of both the issue domain and the LINQ framework.

As a result, while LINQ and custom comparers provide a comprehensive set of functionalities, their utility is limited by the software's particular specifications and the team's competence in a judicious application.

What is new in .NET 9

LINQ offers terrific new features in .NET 9 that significantly improve data querying. The first is **CountBy**, which makes tasks like frequency analysis easier, enabling you to count elements in your collection according to a particular feature. Then comes **AggregateBy**, which makes it simple to construct summaries or unique groupings without complicated code by allowing data to be grouped based on the value of a specified property. The **Index** property, which gives the index position directly within LINQ queries, is the final significant addition. This enhancement makes LINQ even more robust and user-friendly in .NET 9 by simplifying accessing and modifying element locations.

Here, we have a sample to illustrate the new feature **CountBy**:

```
1. List<Person> people =
2. [
3.     new("Steve", "Jobs"),
4.     new("Steve", "Carell"),
5.     new("Elon", "Musk")
6. ];
7.
8. foreach (var peopleWithSameFirstName in people.CountBy(p => p.
   FirstName))
9. {
10.     Console.WriteLine($"There are {peopleWithSameFirstName.
   Value} people with the name {peopleWithSameFirstName.Key}");
11. }
12.
13. public record Person(string FirstName, string LastName);
```

In this example, wé can state that there are two **Steve** and one **Elon** in the list because **CountBy** counts the number of times each **FirstName** appears:

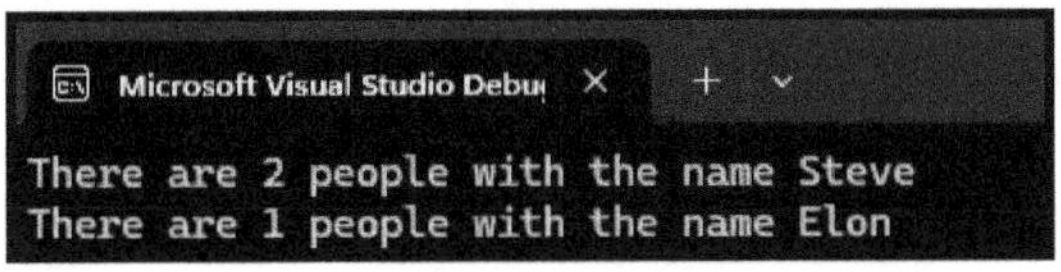

Figure 10.9: *Console output*

Here, we have a sample to illustrate the new feature **AggregateBy**:

```
1. List<Person> people = new()
2. {
3.     new("Steve", "Jobs", 10),
4.     new("Steve", "Carell", 100),
5.     new("Elon", "Musk", 10)
6. };
7.
8. var aggregateBy = people.AggregateBy(
9.     person => person.SomeNumber,   // Group by SomeNumber
10.    x => 0,                        // Start each aggregation with 0
11.    (x, y) => x + y.SomeNumber     // Add each person's SomeNumber
   to the sum
12. );
13.
14. foreach (var kvp in aggregateBy)
15. {
16.     Console.WriteLine($"Sum of SomeNumber for Key {kvp.Key} is
   {kvp.Value}");
17. }
18.
19. public record Person(string FirstName, string LastName, int
   SomeNumber);
```

To obtain the total **SomeNumber** for each distinct value in the list, **AggregateBy** groups individuals by **SomeNumber** and adds the values of each group.

Figure 10.10: *Console output*

Index sample:
```
List<Person> people =
[
new("Steve", "Jobs"),
new("Steve", "Carell"),
new("Elon", "Musk")
];

foreach (var (index, item) in people.Index())
{
Console.WriteLine($"Entry {index}: {item}");
}

public record Person(string FirstName, string LastName);
```

In this example, the index position of each **Person** object in the list can be retrieved thanks to **Index**, which makes it simple to print the index and item information, like **Entry 0: Steve Jobs**, and so forth.

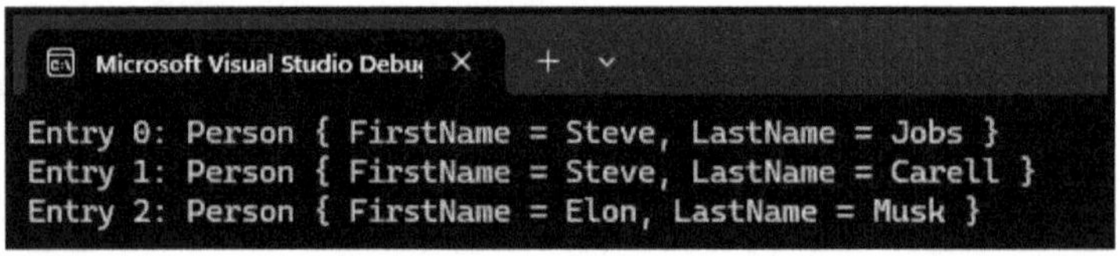

Figure 10.11: Console output

Thanks to these new enhancements, the custom extensions we previously used as workarounds are no longer necessary. Our code gets clearer, easier to understand, and more effective using the **CountBy**, **AggregateBy**, and **Index** features. Instead of battling clumsy hacks, we can now create attractive solutions. As we embrace the potential of these streamlined functions, this change increases our productivity and makes us feel happy and satisfied. Let us rejoice in the ease and joy these features have brought our growth process!

Conclusion

In this chapter, we demonstrated the revolutionary power of LINQ in the C# arena, demonstrating that it is an invaluable tool for data querying and manipulation across various forms, including collections, databases, and even XML and JSON. With an understanding of LINQ operators, the finesse of lambda expressions, and the strategic advantage of postponed execution, you are now ready to design queries as efficiently as they are elegant. The underlying conclusion is clear: LINQ not only makes your code perform better, but it also makes it easier to deal with, improving readability, maintainability, and productivity, all at once. In the next chapter, we will learn about ASP.NET Core, which is the future of web development

Exercise

Check if the following sentences are true or false:

1. LINQ stands for Language Integrated Query.

2. LINQ can only be used with SQL databases.

3. The query syntax and the method syntax are two ways to write LINQ queries.

4. The Where and OrderBy are examples of LINQ operators.

5. EF Core is an object-relational mapper that provides an abstraction over the database.

6. Deferred execution in LINQ postpones query execution until the results are enumerated.

7. LINQ to XML and LINQ to JSON are used to query, manipulate, and transform XML and JSON data, respectively.

8. LINQ can improve code readability, maintainability, and productivity.

9. LINQ can only be used with strongly typed CLR objects.

10. LINQ queries are executed immediately when they are defined.

Answers

1. True
2. False
3. True
4. True
5. True
6. True
7. True
8. True
9. False
10. False

Join our book's Discord space

Join the book's Discord Workspace for Latest updates, Offers, Tech happenings around the world, New Release and Sessions with the Authors:

https://discord.bpbonline.com

CHAPTER 11

ASP.NET Core the Future of Web Development

Introduction

This chapter introduces you to ASP.NET Core, a contemporary and robust framework for creating online apps and services. You will learn about ASP.NET Core's primary features and benefits, including cross-platform compatibility, high performance, modularity, and security. You will also gain hands-on experience designing a basic web application using ASP.NET Core, including understanding its structure, implementing functionality, testing, improving, and deploying it. You will also learn about Razor Pages, a page-based programming architecture that simplifies and speeds online user interface development. You will comprehend Razor syntax, Razor Pages structure, request handling logic, form submission and model binding, routing, URL creation, and Razor Pages use cases. By the conclusion of this chapter, you will have a basic understanding of ASP.NET Core and Razor Pages and will be able to develop your online apps and services using .NET.

Structure

This chapter covers the following topics:

- Introduction to ASP.NET Core
- Understanding Razor Pages in ASP.NET Core
- Introduction to the Model-View-Controller pattern
- Understanding middleware in ASP.NET Core

- History of middleware in ASP.NET Core
- Working with dependency injection in ASP.NET Core
- Understanding server-side vs. client-side in ASP.NET Core
- Improvements in .NET 9

Objectives

This chapter aims to offer a thorough grasp of ASP.NET Core, a high-performance, open-source required for constructing modern online applications. The goals include introducing the key capabilities and advantages of ASP.NET Core key and covering critical components such as middleware, dependency injection, and routing. The chapter then walks readers through building a basic web application with ASP.NET Core. Understanding the project structure, application development, testing, enhancement, and deployment procedures is part of this. The chapter also goes into Razor Pages in ASP.NET Core, a page-based programming style that simplifies web UI development. Readers will learn about Razor syntax, Razor Page structure, page handlers, form submission mechanisms, model binding, Razor Pages routing, and URL generation tactics, all essential for efficient online application development.

Introduction to ASP.NET Core

ASP.NET Core is a high-performance, open-source for developing modern, cloud-based, internet-connected apps. The first version in .NET Core was a redesigned version of ASP.NET from Microsoft that integrated the **Model-View-Controller** (**MVC**) and Web API into a unified development model. Developers can use it to create online applications and services, IoT apps, and mobile back-ends. The architecture of ASP.NET Core is modular, allowing for a great degree of flexibility and configurability. It allows for cross-platform development, which means that apps created with it can operate on Windows, Linux, and macOS. Another notable feature is its out-of-the-box support for dependency injection, which promotes simpler and more modular code. ASP.NET Core works well with popular client-side modules like Angular, React, and Bootstrap.

One of the most significant advantages of ASP.NET Core is its performance. It is one of the quickest web applications available, making it an excellent choice for high-traffic web applications. The .NET also provides improved support for asynchronous programming paradigms, which is essential when developing large applications. Another pillar is security, which includes built-in mechanisms to protect against typical threats such as **cross-site scripting** (**XSS**), **cross-site request forgery** (**CSRF**), and SQL injection. The lightweight and modular architecture of ASP.NET Core allows for the creation of cloud-optimized applications, with capabilities such as environment-based configuration and lightweight HTTP request processing. Furthermore, the community and Microsoft contribute to its ongoing development and expansion, ensuring it remains a cutting-edge tool for modern web development.

With the release of .NET 9, ASP.NET Core gained some essential features and advancements. Let us look at a few significant updates:

- **Blazor**: This full-stack web UI is designed to develop component or page-level apps. Blazor, now stable in .NET 9, provides various rendering choices. An example is static server rendering, which generates static HTML, interactive server rendering, and interactive WebAssembly rendering. The Interactive Auto rendering is a noteworthy feature. It initially renders and interacts with content using the server-side ASP.NET Core runtime before switching to the client-side .NET WebAssembly runtime after downloading the Blazor bundle and activating the WebAssembly runtime. This method usually results in the quickest app starting. Furthermore, by default, interactive render modes prerender content.

- **Minimal APIs**: A new addition allows us to create web APIs with minimal coding. These APIs employ the ASP.NET Core routing system to ease HTTP endpoint definition, emphasizing a lightweight, fast, and user-friendly approach.

- **SignalR**: It is a real-time messaging system that is required for the development of online applications. SignalR has been improved with the latest .NET 9 release, which includes streaming and server-to-server communication features.

- **Native AOT**: ASP.NET Core 8 supports native **ahead-of-time** (**AOT**) compilation, which can enhance web application performance, size, and startup time. gRPC, basic API, and worker service apps currently support native AOT. See ASP.NET Core support for native AOT for further information.

- **Identity API endpoints**: ASP.NET Core 8 introduces MapIdentityApi. This new extension method adds two API endpoints (`/login` and `/logout`) for leveraging ASP.NET Core Identity for authentication in **single-page apps** (**SPA**) or Blazor apps. Instead of using the regular Razor Pages UI, these endpoints provide JSON replies. See Identity API endpoints for further details.

- **Keyed services**: ASP.NET Core 8 introduces support for leveraging keys to register and retrieve dependency injection services. Keys enable the targeting of registration and service consumption. See keyed services for further details.

  ASP.NET Core 8 introduces new project templates for developing SPAs with an ASP.NET Core back-end. The JavaScript frameworks Angular, React, and React with Redux are used in these templates. These templates generate a Visual Studio solution that includes both a front-end and a back-end project. We recommend searching the web for SPA templates.

- **User override culture**: This feature allows developers to override the application's default culture settings, making it a valuable tool for multi-language and multi-cultural applications.

These developments demonstrate ASP.NET Core's dedication to offering a diverse, efficient, and robust foundation for modern online development.

These features will be expanded in *Chapter 14, Mastering Web Services*.

Creating a basic web application with ASP.NET Core

Creating a basic web application with ASP.NET Core involves several key steps, from setting up the environment to deploying the application. Here is an overview:

Setting up the environment

Creating a web application with ASP.NET Core begins with setting up the environment, a crucial step to ensure a smooth development process. This initial phase involves installing the .NET Core SDK, which provides the necessary tools and libraries for building ASP. NET Core applications. Additionally, selecting an appropriate IDE or code editor, such as Visual Studio, Visual Studio Code, or JetBrains Rider, is essential. These tools facilitate code writing, debugging, and project management. The setup is completed by creating a new ASP.NET Core project, using either the command line interface or the chosen IDE, laying the foundation for your web application development journey:

- **Install the necessary tools**: Before you begin, you must install the .NET Core SDK, which contains everything you need to create and run ASP.NET Core apps. A code editor or an IDE like Visual Studio, Visual Studio Code, or JetBrains Rider is also helpful.

- **Create a new project**: Using a command-line interface or an IDE, create a new ASP.NET Core project. You might choose an ASP.NET Core Web App or ASP. NET Core Web API project template for a basic web application.

To create a new project using CLI, follow these steps:

1. Start the command line.
2. Use PowerShell or command prompt on Windows.
3. You can use the **run** command (refer to the following figure):

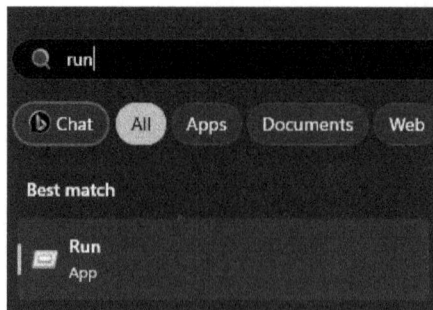

Figure 11.1: *Types run in the Windows menu*

4. **You can also create an empty folder and start the terminal prompt**: Open terminal (**Abrir no Terminal** in the image below—Portuguese), refer to the following figure:

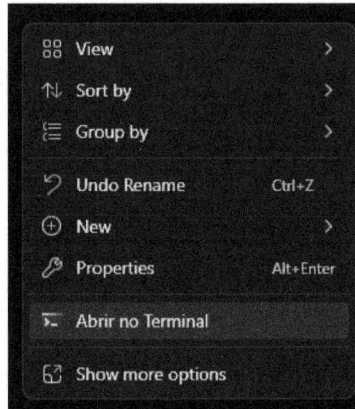

Figure 11.2: Context menu file explorer

Here is the terminal prompt:

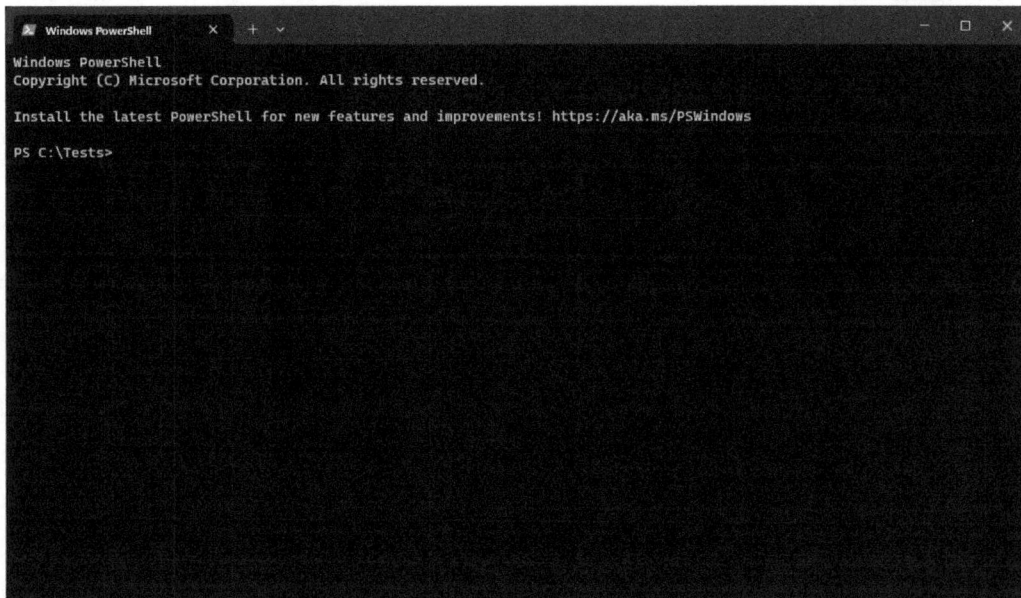

Figure 11.3: Prompt terminal

5. Terminal is available on macOS and Linux, too.

6. **Visit your favorite directory**: Change to your project directory with **cd** if you have not started by the Windows 11 File Explorer context menu. Following the example:

    1. `cd yourdirectory`

7. **Make the project**: To start a project, type dotnet new, followed by the template name. Web App, MVC, and Web API are ASP.NET Core templates for Razor Pages, MVC, and Web API projects.

8. To create an MVC or Razor Pages web app, use:

MVC:

1. `dotnet new mvc -n MyNewApp`

Adding the Razor Pages:

1. `dotnet new razor -n MyNewApp`

9. Here, **-n MyNewApp** names your project. Change **MyNewApp** to your project name.

10. Find the project directory, once the project is created, enter its directory

1. `cd MyNewApp`

11. **Optional**: **run** the project with:

1. `dotnet run`

12. This command launches the app on a local development server. It is usually **http://localhost:5000** or **https://localhost:5001** in the command line (refer to the following figure):

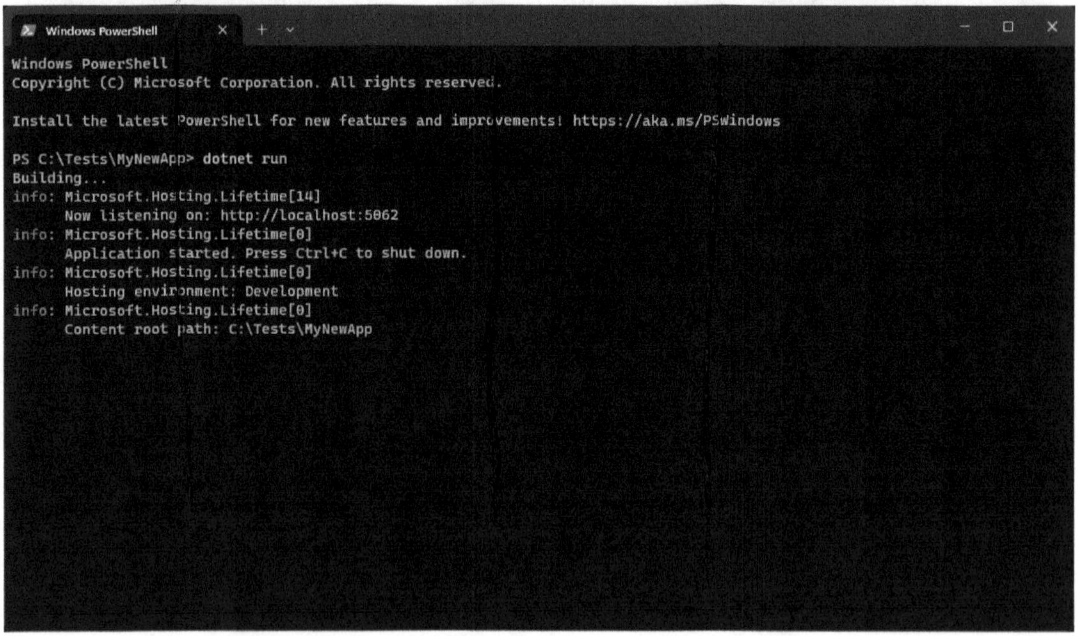

Figure 11.4: dotnet run result

13. **Continue development**: Start developing your app. Open and edit the project in your preferred code editor or IDE.

14. Additional advice to list all available templates use:

1. `dotnet new --list`

Following is the output of the command:

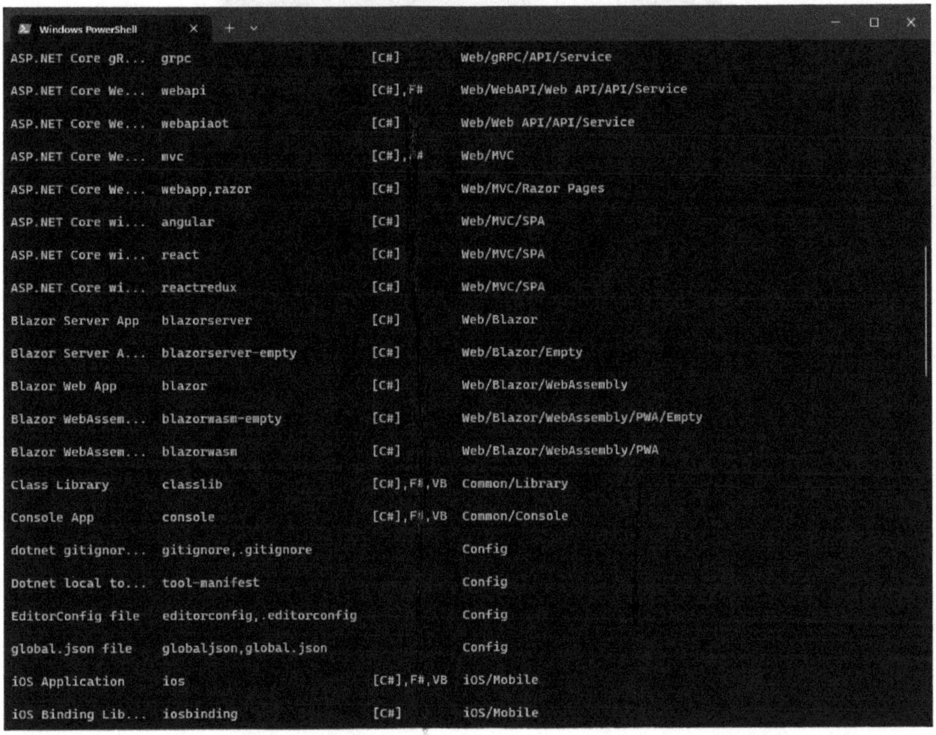

ASP.NET Core gR...	grpc	[C#]	Web/gRPC/API/Service
ASP.NET Core We...	webapi	[C#],F#	Web/WebAPI/Web API/API/Service
ASP.NET Core We...	webapiaot	[C#]	Web/Web API/API/Service
ASP.NET Core We...	mvc	[C#],F#	Web/MVC
ASP.NET Core We...	webapp,razor	[C#]	Web/MVC/Razor Pages
ASP.NET Core wi...	angular	[C#]	Web/MVC/SPA
ASP.NET Core wi...	react	[C#]	Web/MVC/SPA
ASP.NET Core wi...	reactredux	[C#]	Web/MVC/SPA
Blazor Server App	blazorserver	[C#]	Web/Blazor
Blazor Server A...	blazorserver-empty	[C#]	Web/Blazor/Empty
Blazor Web App	blazor	[C#]	Web/Blazor/WebAssembly
Blazor WebAssem...	blazorwasm-empty	[C#]	Web/Blazor/WebAssembly/PWA/Empty
Blazor WebAssem...	blazorwasm	[C#]	Web/Blazor/WebAssembly/PWA
Class Library	classlib	[C#],F#,VB	Common/Library
Console App	console	[C#],F#,VB	Common/Console
dotnet gitignor...	gitignore,.gitignore		Config
Dotnet local to...	tool-manifest		Config
EditorConfig file	editorconfig,.editorconfig		Config
global.json file	globaljson,global.json		Config
iOS Application	ios	[C#],F#,VB	iOS/Mobile
iOS Binding Lib...	iosbinding	[C#]	iOS/Mobile

***Figure 11.5**: dotnet new–list result*

15. Practice learning the template's project structure and files, like **`wwwroot`**, **`Controllers`**, **`Models`**, **`Views`**, and pages.

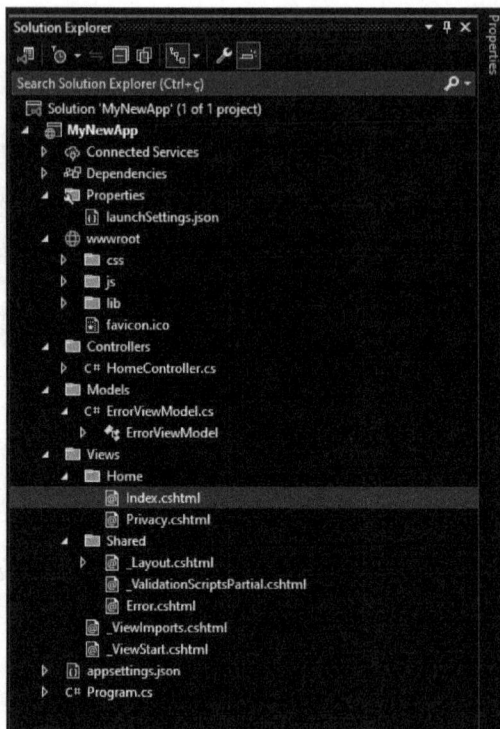

Figure 11.6: Solution Explorer MVC

This is the **Solution Explorer** we will have now:

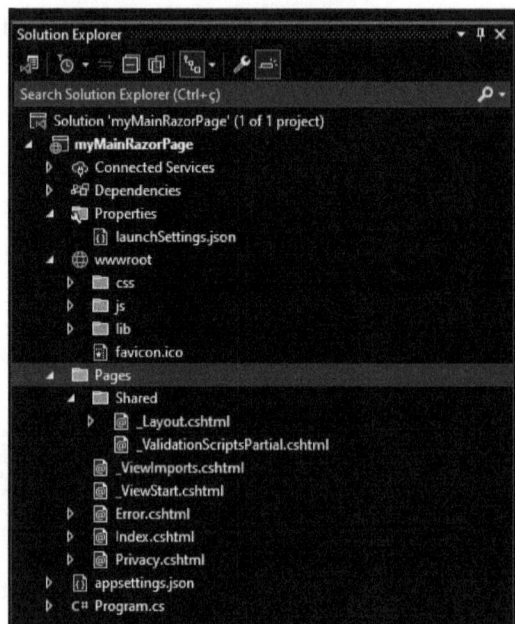

Figure 11.7: Solution Explorer Razor Pages

16. Creating a project using the CLI bootstraps ASP.NET Core development quickly and efficiently, providing a solid foundation.

Understanding the structure

Understanding the structure of your project is critical to productive development when diving into ASP.NET Core. This level entails familiarity with the default project layout, which is critical for adequately browsing and arranging your application's components. The **Controllers** directory handles HTTP requests, the **Models** folder handles data representation, and the **Views** section handles user interfaces in MVC applications. Furthermore, the **wwwroot** directory contains static files such as CSS, JavaScript, and pictures. The **Program.cs** file, which is the foundation of any ASP.NET Core application, configures services and the request pipeline, which are critical for the functionality and performance of your program. This fundamental understanding of the project structure is essential for developing a solid and scalable web application.

- **Project structure**: Familiarize yourself with the default project structure. Key folders include:

- **Controllers**: Contains classes that handle HTTP requests.

- **Models**: Holds data models that represent the data of your application.

- **Views (for MVC applications)**: Contains the UI pages, typically Razor views (**.cshtml** files).

- **wwwroot**: Stores static files like HTML, CSS, and JavaScript.

- **Startup class**: Understand the **Program.cs** file, which configures services and the app's request pipeline.

Developing the application

An ASP.NET Core application's development phase is where your project begins to take shape and come to life. This critical stage entails establishing routes and controllers, both required for handling HTTP requests and routing traffic inside your application. Creating views using Razor syntax becomes a critical chore for people employing the MVC paradigm, combining server code with HTML for dynamic web page production. Data model development is significant since these models act as the backbone of your program, representing and controlling the data it processes. This phase is distinguished by creating and refining code, often in C#, and utilizing ASP.NET Core's rich features to create a functional, user-centric web application. It is a stage that blends creativity and technological prowess to lay the groundwork for a strong and flexible web presence.

- **Routing and controllers**: Define routes in the **Program.cs** or use attribute routing in controller classes. Implement controller actions to handle different HTTP requests.

- **Views and Razor syntax (for MVC)**: Create views using razor, a syntax for embedding server-based code into webpages.

- **Data models**: Define models representing the data your application will handle. These models are typically plain C# classes (POCOs).

Testing the application

Testing is essential in developing an ASP.NET Core application since it ensures your program works as planned and is bug-free. Throughout this phase, the application is launched locally using the Kestrel server supplied with ASP.NET Core, which provides an easy way to test and debug throughout development. Debugging tools in your favorite IDE are essential for discovering and addressing issues. This stage involves discovering mistakes and ensuring the program fits the desired requirements and behaves correctly under various scenarios. Testing is an iterative process essential for providing a dependable and high-quality online application and lays the groundwork for a successful deployment.

- **Run the application locally**: Test your application by running it locally. ASP.NET Core includes a built-in development server (Kestrel), which makes it easy to run and test our application during development.

- **Debugging**: Use the debugging tools provided by your IDE to troubleshoot and resolve issues.

Enhancing the application

Enhancing an ASP.NET Core application is a thrilling phase in which you take your project beyond its basic functionality and instill it with advanced features and optimizations. This stage entails investigating and integrating middleware, which serves as a powerful tool in the request processing pipeline of the app, providing features like authentication, error handling, and static file serving. It is also an excellent opportunity to use ASP.NET Core's built-in dependency injection, which allows for better management of services and their dependencies. This phase is distinguished by application refinement, which includes improving performance, scalability, and security. Enhancing your application, whether by adding new features, optimizing current ones, or improving the overall architecture, is critical for establishing a robust, efficient, and user-friendly web solution.

Middleware: Understand and use middleware to add features to your app's request-handling pipeline. Middleware can handle authentication, error handling, and static file serving.

Services and dependency injection: Utilize ASP.NET Core's built-in dependency injection to manage services and their dependencies.

Deploying the application

The deployment phase of an ASP.NET Core application marks a crucial milestone in its lifecycle, shifting it from development to a live environment where users may interact with it. This stage involves publishing the program to a hosting environment, ranging from traditional web servers such as IIS to newer cloud-based services such as Azure. This procedure necessitates careful evaluation of many aspects, including configuration and environment settings. This level emphasizes the significance of securely handling vital information such as database connections and API keys for various deployment settings. Deploying an ASP.NET Core application entails more than just making it available to users; it also entails ensuring it runs consistently, scales effectively, and maintains security in a real-world environment. This phase completes the development process by showcasing your application to end users and marking the start of its operational existence.

Publishing: You can publish your application to a hosting environment once it is ready. This might be a web server running IIS, Linux with NGINX, or a cloud service like Azure.

Configuration and environment settings: Securely set up environment-specific settings like database connection strings and API keys.

Throughout this process, you will write code primarily in C# and utilize ASP.NET Core's extensive libraries and features to build your web application. Remember, this is a basic overview, and ASP.NET Core offers much more functionality and flexibility that can be incorporated as you grow more comfortable with it.

Understanding Razor Pages in ASP.NET Core

This is a page-based programming model that simplifies and accelerates the development of web user interfaces. It is an extension of the ASP.NET Core.

Understanding the Razor syntax

Razor syntax is a markup used primarily in ASP.NET for embedding server-based code into web pages. It is a mix of HTML and C# (or VB.NET) that enables the creation of dynamic web pages. Razor reduces the number of characters and keystrokes necessary in a file, allowing for a quick and fluid coding approach. It does not employ a new markup language, unlike other template syntaxes. Its design focuses on enabling an intuitive coding experience. Razor syntax is characterized by using the **@** symbol to transition from HTML to C# and back, allowing developers to write C# code within HTML markup, seamlessly integrating server code with the front end.

```
1.  @{ var welcomeMessage = "Hello, Razor!"; }
2.  <h1>@welcomeMessage</h1>
```

Razor Pages structure

Each web page in Razor Pages is linked to a C# class (**MyPage** page model) that performs server-side processing. The structure is organized around page model pairs: the Razor Page (**MyPage.cshtml** file) contains the HTML markup and Razor syntax for dynamic content rendering. In contrast, the associated page model (**MyPage.cs** file) provides server-side logic such as form submission and data processing. This separation of priorities promotes clean code and makes complex interactions easier to handle, especially in page-focused applications. Razor Pages are often arranged in folder structures that group each page and its model, providing a more natural and organized approach than traditional MVC views and controllers.

```
1. // Index.cshtml.cs
2. public class IndexModel : PageModel
3. {
4.     public string Message { get; set; }
5.
6.     public void OnGet()
7.     {
8.         Message = "My application description page.»;
9.     }
10.}
```

Handling requests with page handlers

Page handlers are methods within a page model that process HTTP requests like GET, POST, PUT, and so on and are used to manage requests. Each handler is usually called after the HTTP verb it handles, such as **OnGet** for GET requests or **OnPost** for POST requests, to provide a clean and structured approach to managing different sorts of requests on the same page. These handlers can also be customized with extra suffixes to handle specific cases, providing fine-grained control over the request-handling logic while maintaining code structure and maintainability. This method simplifies web application development by tightly integrating the user interface and management of user interactions within the same Razor Page.

```
1. public void OnGet()
2. {
3.     ViewData["Message"] = "Welcome to my Razor Pages tutorial!»;
4. }
```

Let us see the HTTP methods GET, POST, and PUT, each serving a specific role in web communication:

- The GET technique is used to request information from a specific resource. It is the most often used HTTP request method for retrieving data from a server at the specified site. The request is delivered via the URL when using GET. Therefore, all query strings (if any) are displayed in the URL. It should be noted that GET queries should only be used to retrieve data and not to modify it. They are regarded as safe and idempotent (i.e., several identical requests should have the same impact as a single one).

- To create/update a resource, the POST method sends data to a server. The HTTP request body preserves the POST data sent to the server. This method is frequently utilized when submitting form input or uploading a file. Unlike GET requests, POST requests do not append data to the URL; instead, they include the data in the request's body and can thus contain more information. POST requests are neither safe nor idempotent, which means they can change the server's state (such as adding or changing a resource).

- The PUT method sends data to the server to create or replace a resource. The distinction between POST and PUT requests is that PUT requests are idempotent, which means that calling the same PUT request many times will always result in the same result. On the other hand, repeatedly calling a POST request can have various results. POST can be used to create/initialize new resources or update an existing one without specifying the resource to be updated. In contrast, PUT is often used to update an existing resource.

Each method is a critical component of the HTTP specification, detailing how clients (such as browsers) and servers communicate.

Form submission and model binding

Razor Pages simplifies web UI development by mixing server-side functionality with HTML markup. Razor Pages uses model binding to give a more straightforward approach to handling user input when dealing with form submissions. Model binding, in essence, automatically converts data from an HTTP request to action method arguments or Razor Page model properties. This procedure allows the developer to work directly with highly typed objects, eliminating the requirement for the developer to extract and convert request data manually.

Consider a simple Razor Page form submit scenario to demonstrate this notion. Assume we have a **Customer** model that has the properties name and email. Create a form with input tags for each of these properties on the associated Razor Page, ensuring their name attributes match the model's property names. You define a **Customer** property in the Razor Page code behind (the **cshtml.cs** file) and adorn it with the **[BindProperty]** attribute. This instructs the model binder to populate this property with data from the form submission. The **OnPost** method is called after the form is submitted, and the **Customer** property is automatically filled with the information supplied by the user in the form. After that, the method can perform the business logic, such as saving the data to a database.

```
1.  using Microsoft.AspNetCore.Mvc;
```

```
2.  using Microsoft.AspNetCore.Mvc.RazorPages;
3.
4.  namespace MyAppRazorPage.Pages;
5.
6.  public class Customer
7.  {
8.      public string Name { get; set; }
9.      public string Email { get; set; }
10. }
11.
12. public class CustomerPageModel : PageModel
13. {
14.     [BindProperty]
15.     public Customer Customer { get; set; }
16.
17.     public void OnGet()
18.     {
19.         // Initialization code if needed
20.     }
21.
22.     public IActionResult OnPost()
23.     {
24.         if (!ModelState.IsValid)
25.         {
26.             return Page();
27.         }
28.
29.         // Handle the customer data, e.g., save to the database
30.         // ...
31.
32.         return RedirectToPage("./Success");
33.     }
34. }
```

In the corresponding Razor Page (**cshtml** file), you would have the following:

```
1.  @page
2.  @model MyAppRazorPage.Pages.CustomerPageModel
3.
4.  <form method="post">
5.      <label asp-for="Customer.Name" class="control-label">Name</
    label>
```

```
6.      <input asp-for="Customer.Name" type="text" class="form-
   control" /><br />
7.
8.
9.      <label asp-for="Customer.Email" class="control-label">Email</
   label>
10.     <input asp-for="Customer.Email" type="email" class="form-
   control" /><br />
11.
12.
13.     <span asp-validation-for="Customer.Name" class="text-danger"></
   span>
14.     <span asp-validation-for="Customer.Email" class="text-danger"></
   span><br />
15.
16.     <button type="submit" class="btn btn-primary">Submit</button>
17. </form>
```

Following is the output of the code:

Name

John Doe

Email

The Email field is required.

Submit

Figure 11.8: Customer page validating the email address

This example demonstrates the ease of use and strength of model binding in Razor Pages, allowing developers to handle form submissions quickly.

Razor Pages routing and URL generation

Razor Pages provides a page-based coding style that makes creating web user interfaces more accessible and more productive. The routing system, which takes URLs and maps them to pages, is the most essential part of Razor Pages. Each page in Razor Pages is a self-contained Razor Page file (**.cshtml**) with the option of a code-behind file. The routing system uses these page files to identify which page should handle a request. By default, Razor pages routing is determined by the file path and name of the Razor Page in the project. For example, a Razor Page at **/Pages/Products/Details.cshtml** will handle queries to **/Products/Details**. The URL format and page organization are simplified with this convention-based routing.

Razor Pages' URL creation is meant to function in tandem with its routing mechanism. The ASP.NET Core contains numerous URL-generating methods, such as **Url.Page()**, which can be used to build URLs for pages in razor files and code-behind files. These approaches are intelligent enough to recognize routing patterns and generate accurate URLs based on page names and routes. For example, in a Razor file, you can use **@Url.Page("/Products/ Details," new id = productId)** to produce a link to the Details page for a product. This method ensures the URLs are consistent with the routing setup, making the application easy to manage and traverse. Furthermore, Razor Pages allows custom routes, allowing developers to design more complex URL patterns that meet their requirements.

```
1. // In the main Program.cs
2. app.UseEndpoints(endpoints =>
3. {
4.     endpoints.MapRazorPages();
5. });
```

Creating the Razor Page sample

Now, we will demonstrate how to create a Razor Page sample in ASP.NET Core to display product details. This tutorial covers both the UI element (the Razor Page itself) and the related code-behind file.

1. First, you will have a Razor Page to display product details. This file will be at **/ Pages/Products/Details.cshtml**.

   Details.cshtml:
```
1. @page "{id}"
2. @model DetailsModel
3.
4. <h2>Product Details</h2>
5.
6. <p>Product ID: @Model.ProductId</p>
```

2. Next, you create the code behind file (**Details.cshtml.cs**) for the Razor Page containing the page model.

   Details.cshtml.cs:
```
1. using Microsoft.AspNetCore.Mvc.RazorPages;
2.
3. public class DetailsModel : PageModel
4. {
5.     public int ProductId { get; private set; }
6.
7.     public void OnGet(int id)
```

```
8.    {
9.        ProductId = id;
10.   }
11. }
```

3. This code-behind file defines a **DetailsModel** class that retrieves the product ID from the URL and makes it available to the Razor Page.

4. Finally, generate another Razor Page or its code-behind file. You can generate a URL to the Details page using the **URL.Page()**.

   Example in a Razor file:

```
1. @{
2.     var productId = 123; // This would typically be dynamic
3. }
4.
5. <a href="@Url.Page("/Products/
   Details", new { id = productId })">View Product Details</a>
```

5. This snippet generates a link to the Details page for a product with a specific ID.

6. If you use Visual Studio IDE, the **Details.cshtml.cs** is created automatically.

7. On the **Pages** folder, right-click on it and select **Add** | **Razor Page** (refer to the following figure):

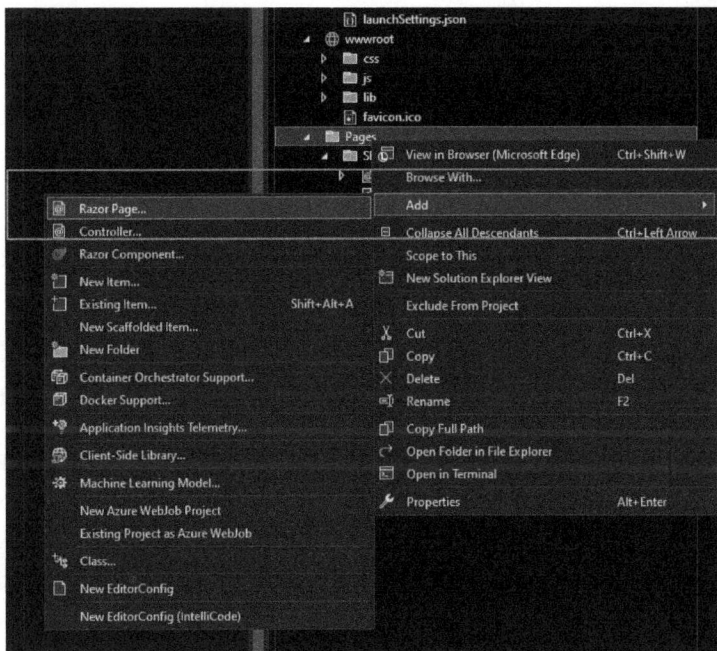

Figure 11.9: Menu new Razor Pages

8. Select **Razor Pages – Empty**, and insert the name you desire, in our case, URL (refer to the following figure):

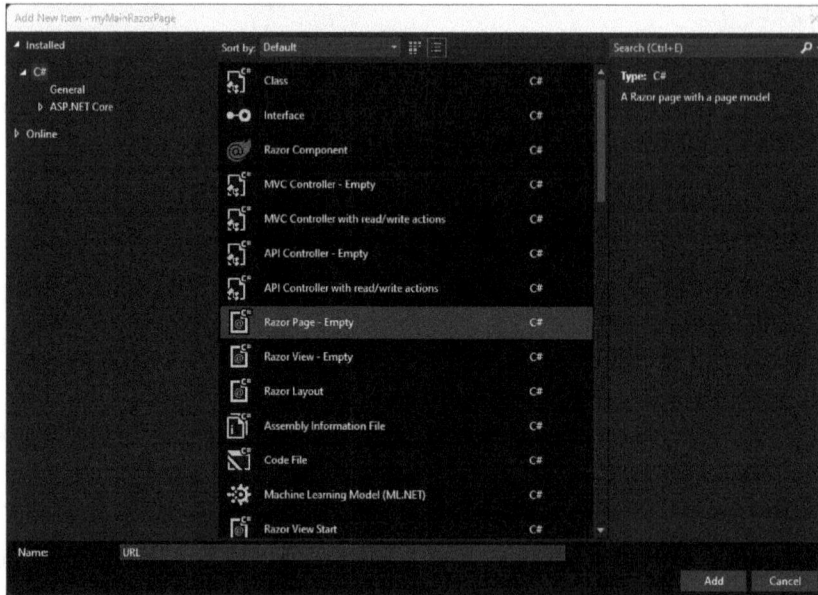

Figure 11.10: *Menu new Razor Pages*

9. The file is created with both Razor Page and CS (refer to the following figure):

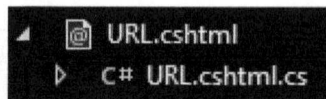

Figure 11.11: *Menu new Razor Pages*

Use cases

Razor Pages provides a unique and efficient approach to developing online apps. Each use case demonstrates the tool's versatility and adaptation to various development demands. Razor Pages offers a streamlined and accessible way for creating simple web apps and complicated CRUD activities. This section will look at scenarios where Razor Pages thrive, such as form handling, rapid prototyping, content management, etc. These use cases demonstrate not just the use of Razor Pages in real-world applications but also their role in promoting a more organized and efficient development process. Whether you are a seasoned developer or new to the profession, understanding these circumstances can improve your ability to use Razor Pages effectively in your projects. Let us get into these various applications to fully comprehend the potential and benefits of using Razor Pages in ASP.NET Core:

- **Simple web applications**: Razor Pages helps create simple, page-focused online applications. This technique excels when the primary objective is to show and manage content over multiple pages without requiring sophisticated interactions or extensive client-side dependencies. Razor Pages' simple structure, for example, benefits websites such as modest business pages, personal portfolios, and basic informational webpages. This enables developers to swiftly set up and manage each page separately, making creating, maintaining, and updating content-focused online applications simple.

- **CRUD operations**: Implementing CRUD operations in online applications is a typical requirement, and Razor Pages provides a streamlined way for this. Each activity may be controlled efficiently on its page, simplifying the development process. Razor Pages, for example, can be used in a customer management system to establish different pages for adding new customers, viewing customer details, changing customer information, and deleting customers. This explicit separation of concerns makes the software more manageable and intuitive, especially for applications with simple data management requirements.

- **Forms and data entry**: Razor Pages are ideal for applications requiring substantial form and data entry. The Razor Pages supports form validations, model binding, and managing POST requests, all required for data entry applications. This is especially beneficial when users must input and submit data, such as online surveys, application forms, or registration systems. Razor Pages make it easier to collect and handle data on the server side, resulting in a more seamless and secure user experience.

- **Rapid prototyping and development**: Razor Pages is a good alternative for quickly developing prototypes or small projects. Its ease of use and simplicity allow for rapid development and iteration. We can rapidly create pages, incorporate back-end logic, and tweak or extend features. This makes Razor Pages a perfect tool for startups, hackathons, and other situations where web development speed and agility are critical.

- **Content-driven websites**: Razor Pages provides an organized and efficient method for designing websites where content is king, such as blogs, news portals, or educational platforms. Each page in the application can represent a distinct type of content, category, or feature, allowing developers to organize and manage content properly. This page-centric architecture is well-suited to the requirements of content-driven websites, where clarity and organization of content are critical.

- **Admin and dashboard interfaces**: Razor Pages is ideal for developing administrative interfaces and dashboards that necessitate a clean separation of distinct administrative responsibilities. The .NET enables the building of different pages for each administration area, whether it is managing users, content, or data. This results in interfaces that are not only well-organized but also easy to maintain and traverse, improving administrators' overall user experience.

- **Learning and teaching web development**: The simplicity of Razor Pages makes it an excellent educational tool. It provides a softer learning curve for web development newbies, allowing them to grasp the foundations of constructing online apps without becoming overwhelmed by the complexities of more advanced frameworks. Similarly, instructors can utilize Razor Pages to introduce students to concepts such as server-side processing, form handling, and web application structure.

- **Integrating with microservices**: Razor Pages can be used as a lightweight and manageable front-end solution in microservices architecture. It can communicate with multiple back-end services while also serving as the user interface layer for microservices. This is especially beneficial when multiple microservices are responsible for different areas of the application, and a simple, robust front end is required to aggregate these services into a cohesive user experience.

- **Migration from legacy systems**: Migrating legacy web applications to ASP.NET Core can be challenging. When opposed to using a complete MVC design, Razor Pages provides a more straightforward method for such migrations. Its simplicity and resemblance to standard online forms make it easy for teams to migrate legacy apps to a more contemporary, efficient, and secure.

- **SEO-friendly web applications**: Razor Pages is a good solution for applications where **search engine optimization** (**SEO**) is a priority. Because the pages are rendered on the server, they are more SEO-friendly than client-side-produced applications. This makes Razor Pages ideal for public-facing websites that rely heavily on search engine presence and ranking, such as corporate websites, e-commerce platforms, and informational portals.

Razor Pages simplify web application development and give flexibility and speed. The basic structure and syntax have been covered.

Razor Pages' easy routing architecture, robust Tag Helpers, and single-file HTML/C# integration show their intelligence. It provides an easy-to-use but sophisticated web development environment for novices and experts.

Comparing ASP.NET Core to the MVC paradigm shows its adaptability, making it suited for various online applications. Razor Pages' focus is appealing for constructing tiny websites and complex online applications.

Razor Pages in ASP.NET Core showcase the growth of web development with its perfect balance of simplicity, flexibility, and power. Razor Pages is a powerful and versatile solution for current web developers to fulfill the demands of the changing digital ecosystem..

Introduction to the Model-View-Controller pattern

The .NET 9, the MVC pattern, and ASP.NET Core represent a significant evolution in web development. Let us investigate these ideas and their developments.

Model-View-Controller pattern in web development pattern

We will concentrate on three critical components: the Model, the View, and the Controller, combined as the MVC pattern. This section explains the responsibilities and interactions of various components in current web applications. We will look at the *Model*, which is at the heart of any online application and houses data and business logic, highlighting its importance in data management and application rules. Next, we focus on the *View*, the user interface layer that displays data to users, emphasizing its importance in rendering and user experience. Finally, we look at the *Controller*, which connects the Model and View by orchestrating user input processing and output display. Understanding these principles is critical for aspiring or experienced web developers since they are the foundation for solid, efficient, and scalable web applications. This book describes the functionality of each component and emphasizes its relevance in constructing harmonious, maintainable, and user-friendly online applications.

Let us examine each one.

Model

The Model in the MVC pattern encapsulates an application's data and business logic. It is in charge of managing the application's data, logic, and rules. In an e-commerce application, for example, the Model would include data structures for items (such as Products) with properties such as name, price, and description. It also includes business logic such as discounts, stock availability, and tax calculations. To store and retrieve data, the Model interacts with the database, ensuring that the data representation in the application is consistent with the business rules and logic.

Sample of a model:

The Model component would represent the data structures and business logic associated with books and bookstore activities. Here is an example of a simple **Book** model in an ASP. NET Core application written in C#:

```
1.  public class Book
2.  {
3.      public int Id { get; set; }
4.      public string Title { get; set; }
5.      public string Author { get; set; }
6.      public string ISBN { get; set; }
7.      public decimal Price { get; set; }
8.      public string Genre { get; set; }
9.      public string Description { get; set; }
10.     public DateTime PublishDate { get; set; }
```

```
11.     public int StockQuantity { get; set; }
12.     // Business Logic: Determines if the book is a best-seller
13.     public bool IsBestseller()
14.     {
15.         // logic to determine if the book is a best-seller
16.         // This could be based on sales, ratings, etc.
17.         return true; // Placeholder return value
18.     }
19.     // Business Logic: Calculates the discount price of the book
20.     public decimal CalculateDiscountPrice(decimal
    discountPercentage)
21.     {
22.         return Price - (Price * discountPercentage / 100);
23.     }
24. }
```

This book model includes **Id**, **Title**, **Author**, **ISBN**, **Price**, **Genre**, **Description**, **PublishDate**, and **StockQuantity**, which represent a book's attributes.

Business logic is represented by **IsBestseller()** and **CalculateDiscountPrice(decimal discountPercentage)**. **IsBestseller()** can identify whether a book is a best-seller based on various factors, whereas **CalculateDiscountPrice** can compute a discounted price depending on a percentage.

Controllers in the MVC application would utilize this model to communicate with databases (for storing and retrieving book data) and views to display book information to users. The business logic methods encapsulate actions unique to the bookstore's domain, ensuring that data management and business rules are centered within the model.

View

The user interface component in the MVC architecture is the View. It shows the user the data from the Model and represents how that data is presented and formatted. Views are typically HTML templates with embedded Razor syntax in ASP.NET in the context of a web application. For example, a View in our e-commerce application might display a well-structured and styled list of products with their names, prices, and images. The View contains no business logic or data manipulation; it simply renders the data provided by the Model in the manner specified by the controller.

Sample View for the **Book** model:

Creating a View for the **Book** model in an ASP.NET Core MVC application entails creating an HTML template that displays the **Book** object's properties. The View will employ Razor syntax, which allows C# code to be embedded in HTML for dynamic content rendering.

Here is a basic example of how a View for displaying details of a single book may look:

```
1. @model YourAppNamespace.Models.Book
2.
3. @{
4.     ViewBag.Title = «Book Details»;
5. }
6.
7. <h2>Book Details</h2>
8.
9. <div>
10.     <h3>@Model.Title</h3>
11.     <p><strong>Author:</strong> @Model.Author</p>
12.     <p><strong>ISBN:</strong> @Model.ISBN</p>
13.     <p><strong>Genre:</strong> @Model.Genre</p>
14.     <p><strong>Published:</strong> @Model.PublishDate.
    ToString("dd MMM yyyy")</p>
15.     <p><strong>Description:</strong> @Model.Description</p>
16.     <p><strong>Price:</strong> $@Model.Price</p>
17.     <p><strong>In Stock:</strong> @Model.StockQuantity</p>
18.     <p><strong>Bestseller:</strong> @(Model.
    IsBestseller() ? "Yes" : "No")</p>
19. </div>
20.
21. <!-- Add a link to go back to the list or perform other actions -->
22. <p>
23.     <a href="@Url.Action("Index", "Books")">Back to List</a>
24. </p>
```

According to this view:

- **@model YourAppNamespace.Models.Book** indicates that this view expects a type **Book** model from your application's namespace.

- **ViewBag.Title** is used to set the page title dynamically.

- **@Model** displays the Book's properties (**Title**, **Author**, **ISBN**, and so on) The **@** symbol is used to embed C# code within HTML.

- **@Model.PublishDate**, the date is formatted using **ToString("dd MMM yyyy")**.

The model's **IsBestseller** technique determines whether the book is a bestseller.

There is a link to return to the book list or other relevant pages.

This view is a simple depiction that focuses on displaying book details. In a real-world application, you might wish to add extra capabilities like editing, deleting, or adding books, as well as customizing them to match the style of your program.

Controller

In the MVC pattern, the Controller is a connection point between the Model and the View. It processes user input and returns the output display. The Controller accepts requests (similar to HTTP requests in a web application), interacts with the Model to retrieve data or perform actions, and then selects the appropriate View to display the response. In our e-commerce application, for example, when a user requests to view a specific product, the controller receives the request, retrieves the product details from the Model, and then sends this data to the Product Details View to be displayed to the user. The controller centralizes decision-making and manages the Model and View data flow.

Example: In an online bookstore web application:

- The Controller may include logic for handling user requests, such as adding a book to a shopping cart, retrieving book details, etc.

- The Model could represent data structures for books, such as title, author, and price, as well as business logic, such as discount calculation.

- The View would be the HTML or web pages displaying these books and their details.

Sample Controller for the View and Model

This sample demonstrates that a CRUD controller for a **Book** model entails building methods to handle each activity. The controller communicates with the model to handle data and choose which view to render. Here is an example of a **BooksController**, complete with a function for displaying a list of books:

```
1.  using Microsoft.AspNetCore.Mvc;
2.  using YourAppNamespace.Models;
3.  using System.Collections.Generic; // For using List<>
4.  // Include other necessary namespaces
5.
6.  public class BooksController : Controller
7.  {
8.      private readonly IBookRepository _
    bookRepository; // Assuming an interface for data operations
9.
10.     // Constructor injection for the repository
11.     public BooksController(IBookRepository bookRepository)
12.     {
13.         _bookRepository = bookRepository;
14.     }
15.
```

```
16.    // GET: Books
17.    public IActionResult Index()
18.    {
19.        var books = _bookRepository.
    GetAllBooks(); // Retrieves all books from the repository
20.        return View(books); // Passes the list of books to the view
21.    }
22.
23.    // GET: Books/Details/5
24.    public IActionResult Details(int id)
25.    {
26.        var book = _bookRepository.GetBookById(id);
27.        if (book == null)
28.        {
29.            return NotFound();
30.        }
31.        return View(book);
32.    }
33.
34.    // GET: Books/Create
35.    public IActionResult Create()
36.    {
37.        return View();
38.    }
39.
40.    // POST: Books/Create
41.    [HttpPost]
42.    [ValidateAntiForgeryToken]
43.    public IActionResult Create([Bind("Title,Author,ISBN,Price,
    Genre,Description,PublishDate,StockQuantity")] Book book)
44.    {
45.        if (ModelState.IsValid)
46.        {
47.            _bookRepository.AddBook(book);
48.            return RedirectToAction(nameof(Index));
49.        }
50.        return View(book);
51.    }
52.
53.    // GET: Books/Edit/5
```

```
54.    public IActionResult Edit(int id)
55.    {
56.        var book = _bookRepository.GetBookById(id);
57.        if (book == null)
58.        {
59.            return NotFound();
60.        }
61.        return View(book);
62.    }
63.
64.    // POST: Books/Edit/5
65.    [HttpPost]
66.    [ValidateAntiForgeryToken]
67.    public IActionResult Edit(int id, [Bind("Id,Title,Author,ISBN,
       Price,Genre,Description,PublishDate,StockQuantity")] Book book)
68.    {
69.        if (id != book.Id)
70.        {
71.            return NotFound();
72.        }
73.
74.        if (ModelState.IsValid)
75.        {
76.            _bookRepository.UpdateBook(book);
77.            return RedirectToAction(nameof(Index));
78.        }
79.        return View(book);
80.    }
81.
82.    // GET: Books/Delete/5
83.    public IActionResult Delete(int id)
84.    {
85.        var book = _bookRepository.GetBookById(id);
86.        if (book == null)
87.        {
88.            return NotFound();
89.        }
90.        return View(book);
91.    }
92.
```

```
93.     // POST: Books/Delete/5
94.     [HttpPost, ActionName("Delete")]
95.     [ValidateAntiForgeryToken]
96.     public IActionResult DeleteConfirmed(int id)
97.     {
98.         _bookRepository.DeleteBook(id);
99.         return RedirectToAction(nameof(Index));
100.       }
101.    }
```

ASP.NET Core effectively uses the MVC pattern:

- **Structured Model Classes** (**SMCs**) are C# classes that represent the data model and include database binding and validation rules.

- **Database support**: SQL Server, MySQL, PostgreSQL, and non-relational databases such as MongoDB are all supported.

- In ASP.NET Core, for example, you can define a model class for a Book that includes attributes for validation and database binding. A controller can then use this model to interact with a database and pass data to the view for rendering.

.NET 9 advancements include the following: ASP.NET Core and MVC enhancements:

- **Server-side Blazor rendering**: Enables dynamic web page rendering with Razor components outside ASP.NET Core.

- **System.Text.Json serialization/deserialization**: Improved data handling with more type support.

- **Native AOT compilation**: Improves performance by compiling code in advance.

- **Sections in Blazor**: You can define reusable content blocks for increased modularity.

- **Route short-circuiting**: Improves performance by eliminating redundant request processing.

For example, a Blazor application written in .NET 9 can dynamically update UI components with server-side rendering. It can also use route short-circuiting to process web requests more efficiently.

We will see route short-circuiting later in this chapter and in Blazor in *Chapter 15, Blazor for UI Development*.

Creating and using View components

View components in Razor Pages provide a powerful method to encapsulate and reuse aspects of your application's UI, especially in the context of a bookshop. They function as mini-controllers, managing a portion of the rendering process with logic and data retrieval. As a result, they are great for genre-based book listings, user-specific suggestions, or a dynamic best-seller section.

In a bookshop application, for example, you could construct a **BestsellerBooksViewComponent** to control the display of bestselling books.

First, in a separate **components** directory, build a class that extends **ViewComponent**:

```
1.  public class BestsellerBooksViewComponent : ViewComponent
2.  {
3.      private readonly IBookRepository _bookRepository; // Assuming
    an interface for book data operations
4.
5.      public BestsellerBooksViewComponent(IBookRepository
    bookRepository)
6.      {
7.          _bookRepository = bookRepository;
8.      }
9.
10.     public async Task<IViewComponentResult> InvokeAsync()
11.     {
12.         var bestsellerBooks = await _bookRepository.
    GetBestsellerBooksAsync(); // Retrieves bestselling books
13.         return View("BestsellerBooks", bestsellerBooks); // Uses a
    specific view to render the books
14.     }
15. }
```

With the advancements brought by .NET 9, integrating the MVC pattern in ASP.NET Core provides a powerful and efficient way of building modern web applications. Using server-side Blazor, improved serialization/deserialization and performance enhancements such as AOT compilation and route short-circuiting improve web applications' capabilities and efficiency.

Understanding middleware in ASP.NET Core

Middleware in ASP.NET Core is a critical concept for building web applications. It is a software component assembled into an application pipeline to handle requests and responses. Each middleware component in ASP.NET Core has a specific purpose and is responsible for a specific task in the request-response pipeline.

Understanding what a pipeline is

The term pipeline in ASP.NET Core refers to the request processing pipeline, a key element in how .NET handles incoming HTTP requests. This pipeline is made up of many middleware components. Each component has a distinct function and can change or examine the HTTP request and response.

- **Processing in sequence**: The pipeline processes Each incoming HTTP request sequentially. The request is routed through the pipeline by various middleware components in the sequence specified in the application's launch configuration.

- **Middleware components**: Each middleware component can process the request, provide a response, or forward the request to the next component in the pipeline. This results in a more adaptable and modular approach to managing requests.

- **Control over request flow**: Middleware components can decide whether to send a request further down the pipeline or to short-circuit it, which means to stop further processing and return a response immediately.

- **Configurable**: We can configure the pipeline in an ASP.NET Core application's **Startup** class. This setting specifies which middleware components should be included and in what order.

Pipeline workflow example

It is a request that passes through logging, authentication, routing, and static file middleware, then returns a response, ensuring secure, efficient processing. Let us see step-by-step:

1. **First component**: It is a logging middleware that logs the request details.

2. **Next steps**: It may go via authentication middleware to confirm that the user is authenticated.

3. **Further processing**: Following authentication, it could pass via a routing middleware to decide which controller and action method to call.

4. **Final stages**: If the request is for a file, such as an image or CSS, static file middleware may provide it at the end of the pipeline.

5. **Response**: Finally, the application's response is sent back through the pipeline, where middleware might check or modify it before sending it to the client.

The importance of ASP.NET Core is that the pipeline in ASP.NET Core provides flexibility, modular design, and efficient handling of HTTP requests for robust web applications. Let us see each stage:

- **Control and flexibility**: The pipeline architecture provides excellent flexibility and control over processing requests. This is critical for authentication, error handling, logging, and static file serving.

- **Custom middleware**: We can create custom middleware, which allows for specialized request processing logic tailored to specific application needs.

- **Cross-cutting concerns**: It manages cross-cutting concerns—those features of a program that influence other parts—in a centralized and non-intrusive manner, such as logging and error handling.

The pipeline in ASP.NET Core is a robust and adaptable method for controlling how an application reacts to HTTP requests. It enables us to build an application out of modular components (middleware), each of which handles a different part of request and response processing. This style provides web applications that are clean, maintainable, and efficient.

Why we need middleware

It is essential for constructing efficient and manageable web applications due to its modularity and flexibility. It serves as a series of interconnected components within an application pipeline, each dedicated to handling specific tasks in processing HTTP requests and responses. This architecture promotes a clean separation of concerns, where each middleware component focuses on a distinct aspect of request processing, such as logging, authentication, or error handling, and enhances the application's modularity. Middleware facilitates adaptable and scalable application development by enabling developers to add or remove functionalities easily. Furthermore, it offers a streamlined approach to customizing request-response processing, allowing for the integration of specific functionalities tailored to an application's unique needs. This level of customization and modular design is pivotal in building modern web applications that are both efficient and maintainable.

The ASP.NET Core request pipeline comprises a series of request delegates called one after the other in a sequential formation. The principle is illustrated in the following figure. Following the black arrows is the path that leads to the execution.

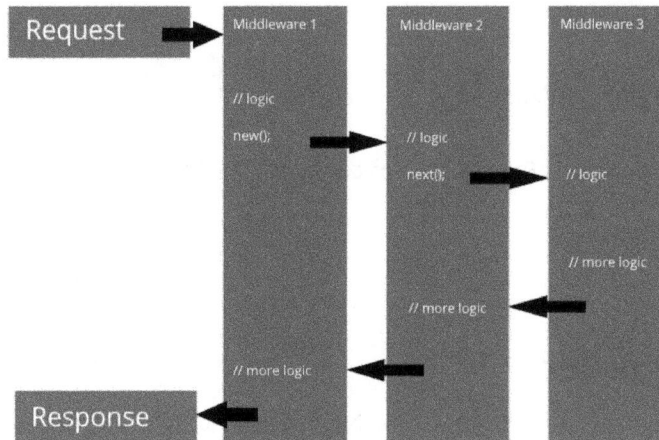

Figure 11.12: Middleware workflow

Delegates can operate before and after each other. Early pipeline calls to exception-handling delegates allow them to capture subsequent pipeline exceptions.

The most straightforward All ASP.NET Core requests are handled by one request delegate. This example lacks a request pipeline. After each HTTP request, a single anonymous function is called.

```
1.  var builder = WebApplication.CreateBuilder(args);
2.  var app = builder.Build();
3.
4.  app.Run(async context =>
5.  {
6.      await context.Response.WriteAsync("Hello world!");
7.  });
8.
9.  app.Run();
```

Combine request delegates with **Use**. The next parameter represents the pipeline delegate. Not invoking the next parameter short-circuits the pipeline. As the following example shows in *lines 4 to 9,* you can usually act before and after the next delegate:

```
1.  var builder = WebApplication.CreateBuilder(args);
2.  var app = builder.Build();
3.
4.  app.Use(async (context, next) =>
5.  {
6.      // Do work that can write to the Response.
7.      await next.Invoke();
```

```
8.      // Do other work that doesn't write to the Response.
9. });
10.
11. app.Run(async context =>
12. {
13.     await context.Response.WriteAsync("Hello from 2nd delegate.");
14. });
15.
16. app.Run()
```

Middleware order

The following diagram depicts the ASP.NET Core MVC and Razor Pages request processing pipeline. You can observe how a typical app orders middleware and adds new ones. You can arrange or insert custom middleware as needed for your situations.

The following figure represents the path of the middleware until the endpoint:

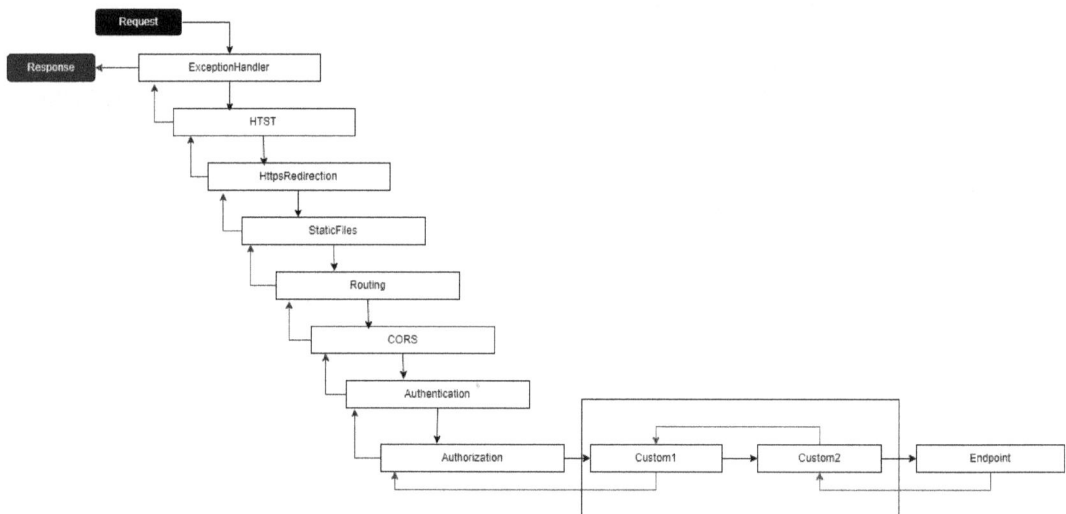

Figure 11.13: Middleware order

The order of the program middleware **addition.cs** file specifies the request to middleware component order and response reverse order. The sequence is crucial for security, performance, and usefulness in the following sample from *lines 20 to 43*:

```
1. using Microsoft.AspNetCore.Identity;
2. using Microsoft.EntityFrameworkCore;
3. using WebMiddleware.Data;
4.
5. var builder = WebApplication.CreateBuilder(args);
```

```
6.
7. var connectionString = builder.Configuration.GetConnectionString("Def
   aultConnection")
8.     ?? throw new InvalidOperationException("Connecti
   on string 'DefaultConnection' not found.");
9. builder.Services.AddDbContext<ApplicationDbContext>(options =>
10.     options.UseSqlServer(connectionString));
11. builder.Services.AddDatabaseDeveloperPageExceptionFilter();
12.
13. builder.Services.AddDefaultIdentity<IdentityUser>(options => options.
    SignIn.RequireConfirmedAccount = true)
14.     .AddEntityFrameworkStores<ApplicationDbContext>();
15. builder.Services.AddRazorPages();
16. builder.Services.AddControllersWithViews();
17.
18. var app = builder.Build();
19.
20. if (app.Environment.IsDevelopment())
21. {
22.     app.UseMigrationsEndPoint();
23. }
24. else
25. {
26.     app.UseExceptionHandler("/Error");
27.     app.UseHsts();
28. }
29.
30. app.UseHttpsRedirection();
31. app.UseStaticFiles();
32. // app.UseCookiePolicy();
33.
34. app.UseRouting();
35. // app.UseRateLimiter();
36. // app.UseRequestLocalization();
37. // app.UseCors();
38.
39. app.UseAuthentication();
40. app.UseAuthorization();
41. // app.UseSession();
42. // app.UseResponseCompression();
```

```
43. // app.UseResponseCaching();
44.
45. app.MapRazorPages();
46. app.MapDefaultControllerRoute();
47.
48. app.Run();
```

History of middleware in ASP.NET Core

Middleware in ASP.NET Core is an essential improvement over the previous ASP.NET Core, signaling a paradigm shift in web application development. ASP.NET initially relied on a system of HttpModules and HttpHandlers to process requests and responses. While effective at the time, this technique had certain drawbacks regarding modularity and adaptability.

HttpModules were event handlers responding to HTTP application lifecycle events, whereas HttpHandlers handled individual endpoint requests. As web technologies matured, however, there was an increasing demand for more flexibility and adaptability to address the complex requirements of current web applications.

As a reaction to these changing expectations, ASP.NET Core introduced the concept of middleware.

Middleware met this requirement nicely, providing a more modular and configurable solution than the earlier HttpModules and HttpHandlers. In ASP.NET Core, each piece of middleware is a standalone component that can be joined in various ways to create a customized request-processing pipeline. This design increased the flexibility and efficiency of online applications and aligned with current software development trends, emphasizing modularity and cross-platform compatibility.

Goals of middleware

Middleware in ASP.NET Core's central purpose is to provide a highly efficient and modular framework for managing HTTP requests and answers within a web application. This efficiency is realized by a streamlined, pipeline-based approach in which each middleware component is in charge of a specific task, such as authentication, logging, or error handling. Because of this modularity, each component is focused and specialized, resulting in better-organized and more maintainable code.

The middleware design lets developers quickly replace, delete, or reorganize components, allowing them to adjust the request-processing pipeline to their application's specific needs. This strategy simplifies development and improves application performance by removing extraneous processing and focusing only on the components essential to each request.

Another essential purpose of ASP.NET Core middleware is to promote reusability and ease of configuration. Middleware components are designed to be reusable across several applications, allowing us to use built-in middleware for everyday activities or create our bespoke middleware for more particular requirements. This reusability cuts development time in half and maintains uniformity across projects.

Furthermore, the ease of configuration is a crucial feature of ASP.NET Core middleware. The .NET enables developers to configure the middleware components easily using the app's starting class. This method streamlines the setup process and provides clear visibility into how requests are processed within the application, making it easier to identify problems and understand how the program behaves. Overall, the goals of middleware in ASP.NET Core are to provide a strong, versatile, and developer-friendly environment for developing modern web applications.

Steps of pipeline workflow

Pipeline operations streamline data processing and web queries. Usually, a request reaches the logging middleware, which methodically logs it. An authentication middleware verifies the user's identity after this. A routing middleware determines the controller and action method after authentication. When pictures or CSS are needed, a static file middleware is used. Finally, the application's answer returns through the pipeline for middleware examination and change before delivery to the client. This method illustrates modern software's complex orchestration:

- **First component**: Initially, a request is sent to a logging middleware, which records the specifics of the request once it has been received.

- **Next steps**: It may then be processed by an authentication middleware to guarantee that the user is recognized as legitimate.

- **Further processing**: It could involve going through a routing middleware after authentication to determine which controller and action method to can upon.

- **Final stages**: Static file middleware may provide static resources at the very end of the pipeline if the request is for a file such as an image or CSS.

- **Response**: At long last, the response generated by the application is sent back through the pipeline. It allows the middleware to inspect or modify the response once more before providing it to the client.

Avoiding middleware with route short-circuiting

Route short-circuiting allows an endpoint to bypass middleware between the RoutingMiddleware and the EndpointMiddleware. It means the endpoint can avoid middleware that is not necessary for its execution. Short-circuit routing is used in your application on one or more endpoints.

For example, if an endpoint does not require authorization or **Cross-Origin Resource Sharing (CORS)** support, you can utilize short-circuit routing to bypass the middleware that provides these functionalities. It can help your application perform better by decreasing the number of middleware components performed for each request.

Short-circuiting is also utilized in other contexts, such as microservices-based applications, where the circuit breaker design is employed to prohibit an application from doing a potentially failure-prone operation. Short-circuiting occurs in a request pipeline when a middleware component decides not to call the next piece of middleware in the pipeline. It is convenient as it eliminates unnecessary work.

Code sample:

```
1.  ...
2.
3.  app.UseRouting();
4.
5.  ShortCircuitsConfig(app);
6.
7.
8.  if (!app.Environment.IsDevelopment())
9.  {
10.     app.UseExceptionHandler("/Error");
11.     app.UseHsts();
12. }
13.
14. ...
15.
16. static void ShortCircuitsConfig(WebApplication app)
17. {
18.     app.MapGet("/Redirect/Contoso",
19.         (context) =>
20.         {
21.             context.Response.Redirect("https://www.contoso.com/");
22.             return Task.CompletedTask;
23.         }
24.     ).ShortCircuit(200);
25.
26.     app.MapGet("/KeyPage",
27.         (context) =>
28.         {
29.             context.Response.Redirect("https://www.contoso.com/
    KeyPage");
```

```
30.                  return Task.CompletedTask;
31.              }
32.      ).ShortCircuit(200);
33.
34.      app.MapGet("/",
35.          (context) =>
36.          {
37.                  context.Response.Redirect("https://www.contoso.com/
     Info");
38.                  return Task.CompletedTask;
39.          }).ShortCircuit(200);
40.
41.      app.MapGet("/robots.txt",
42.          () => @"
43.            User-agent: *
44.            Disallow: /
45.          ").ShortCircuit(200);
46. }
```

In the above code:

- In *line 5*, we call **ShortCircuitsConfig** to concentrate all **ShortCircuits**.
- In *lines 18* and *26*, demonstrate the redirect and a **KeyPage** to redirect the context.
- In *line 34*, we redirect when there are no parameters in the URL call.
- In *line 41*, demonstrates that we can return text for a specific file in the URL call.

Note that we can process content for CSS, for example:

```
1.    app.MapGet("/css/pages.css",
2.           () => MyCode.GetCssPage()).ShortCircuit(200);
```

In *line 2*, **MyCode.GetCssPage()** could read the content for the **pages.css** file from a database.

This section highlights the critical role of middleware in ASP.NET Core as a foundational element for managing requests and responses within web applications. Middleware, functioning within a configurable pipeline, enables the efficient processing, alteration, or redirection of these requests and responses. This pipeline is structured as a sequence of middleware components designated for specific tasks such as authentication, logging, or routing. It possesses the autonomy to either pass the request along or terminate it. The versatility of middleware is paramount in web development, offering developers the ability to tailor request processing, leverage reusable functionalities, and handle various concerns in a unified manner. The configuration of this middleware, which is pivotal for the application's security, performance, and functionality, is conducted in the Startup class of an ASP.NET Core application, where the sequence and inclusion of middleware components are determined.

Working with dependency injection in ASP. NET Core

In the fast-paced world of web development, the ability to build clean, manageable, and scalable code is critical. **Dependency injection** (**DI**) in ASP.NET Core stands out as a critical architectural pattern that enables developers to fulfill these aims. This introductory guide is designed to explain the concepts and practical applications of DI within the ASP. NET Core, a key component of the .NET ecosystem.

ASP.NET key, known for its outstanding performance and scalability, incorporates dependency injection as a key feature, radically changing how we approach application design. This book will investigate the essence of DI, its significance, and how it integrates effortlessly into the ASP.NET Core architecture.

This approach is critical for promoting a modular codebase where components may be developed, tested, and maintained independently.

Basics of DI

Any modern software developer must understand the concepts of DI. DI is more than a coding method; it is a fundamental idea that guides the development of scalable, maintainable, and testable programs. The principle of loose coupling, which fundamentally affects how classes interact with their dependencies, lies at the heart of DI.

Let us now understand what exactly is DI. It is a design pattern in which a class obtains its dependencies from outside sources rather than constructing them internally. To put it simply, rather than a class instantiating its dependencies, these are injected into it, generally through the constructor, a property, or a method.

Dependency injection fundamentals

DI has a number of noteworthy benefits that can enhance the quality and maintainability of code:

- **Inversion of control (IoC)**: This principle decouples classes from their dependents by transferring control of creating and managing dependencies from the class to a separate framework or container.

  DI supports separating concerns by allowing a class to focus on its primary functionality rather than developing and managing dependencies.

- **Interchangeability and testability**: Dependencies can be readily swapped or mocked with DI, improving code testability. This is especially useful in unit testing circumstances.

- **Promoting loose coupling with DI decoupling classes**: By injecting dependencies, classes are not required to explicitly know their dependencies' specific implementations. The code becomes more modular and adaptable as a result of this decoupling.

- **Increasing flexibility and maintainability**: modifications in dependence implementation or configuration do not require modifications in the dependent class. This separation makes maintenance easier and increases the flexibility to extend or modify programs with minimum impact.

- **Better design practices**: DI encourages developers to design for interfaces rather than specific implementations, following the *program to an interface, not an implementation* approach.

Let us write a basic C# example that shows how to use DI. In this case, we will design a message-logging application, but the logging mechanism (dependency) will be injected into the class that requires it rather than the class that creates it directly.

First, we will develop an interface for our logging service, followed by an implementation. Following that, we will design a class that requires logging and inject the logging service into it.

```
1.  // Step 1: Define the logging service interface
2.  public interface ILoggerService
3.  {
4.      void Log(string message);
5.  }
6.
7.  //Step 2: Implement the interface
8.
9.  public class ConsoleLoggerService : IloggerService
10. {
11.     public void Log(string message)
12.     {
13.         Console.WriteLine($"Log: {message}");
14.     }
15. }
16.
17. //Step 3: Create a Class that requires logging
18.
19. public class Processor
```

```
20. {
21.     private readonly IloggerService _logger;
22.
23.     public Processor(IloggerService logger)
24.     {
25.         _logger = logger;
26.     }
27.
28.     public void Process(string data)
29.     {
30.         // Processing data...
31.         _logger.Log($"Processing data: {data}");
32.     }
33. }
34.
35. //We have an IloggerService dependence in the Processor class. The
    constructor is used to inject this dependency.
36.
37. //Step 4: Injecting the Dependency
38. //You may manually inject the dependencies in a basic console
    application like this:
39.
40.
41. IloggerService logger = new ConsoleLoggerService();

42. Processor processor = new Processor(logger);

43.

44. processor.Process("Some Data");
```

This is the console output we will get:

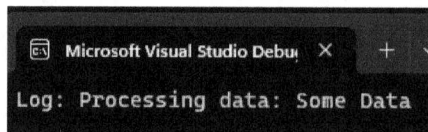

Figure 11.14: Console output

The **ConsoleLoggerService** is manually constructed in this example and provided to the **Processor** class via its constructor. The ASP.NET Core built-in dependency injection container often handles this injection in more complicated applications, particularly those created using ASP.NET Core.

Learning the foundations of dependency injection is necessary to become an expert software engineer. It improves not only the design and architecture of your applications but also the testability and maintainability of your code. By learning and utilizing DI, you better understand the concepts of modern software architecture, laying the groundwork for designing robust and scalable systems.

Managing dependent object life cycles with DI.

Managing the life cycle of dependent objects is critical in DI. It governs how and when these objects' instances are generated, shared, and destroyed. It is commonly controlled by service lifetimes in .NET's DI.

Understanding .NET Core service lifetime DI supports the following service lifetimes:

- **Transient**: A new instance is created every time the service is requested. This is appropriate for stateless, lightweight services.

- **Scoped**: In ASP.NET Core applications, a single instance of the service is created per scope, which is often a web request. It is appropriate for services that keep a request's state.

- **Singleton**: Only one service instance is produced over the application's lifetime. It is appropriate for thread-safe stateful services intended to be shared across the application.

Let us create an example to demonstrate these notions. We will build a basic C# console application with three different services: transient, scoped, and singleton.

1. Setting up DI in a console application:

```
1. Install-Package Microsoft.Extensions.DependencyInjection
```

2. Create service interfaces and implementations:

```
1. public interface ITransientService
2. {
3.     Guid GetOperationID();
4. }
5.
6. public interface IScopedService
7. {
8.     Guid GetOperationID();
9. }
10.
11. public interface ISingletonService
12. {
13.     Guid GetOperationID();
14. }
```

```
15.
16. public class TransientService : ITransientService
17. {
18.     private Guid _operationID;
19.
20.     public TransientService()
21.     {
22.         _operationID = Guid.NewGuid();
23.     }
24.
25.     public Guid GetOperationID() => _operationID;
26. }
27.
28. public class ScopedService : IScopedService
29. {
30.     private Guid _operationID;
31.
32.     public ScopedService()
33.     {
34.         _operationID = Guid.NewGuid();
35.     }
36.
37.     public Guid GetOperationID() => _operationID;
38. }
39.
40. public class SingletonService : ISingletonService
41. {
42.     private Guid _operationID;
43.
44.     public SingletonService()
45.     {
46.         _operationID = Guid.NewGuid();
47.     }
48.
49.     public Guid GetOperationID() => _operationID;
50. }
```

3. Add this code to the **Program.cs**:

```
1. using Microsoft.Extensions.DependencyInjection;
2.
```

```
3.  var services = new ServiceCollection();
4.  services.AddTransient<ITransientService, TransientService>();
5.  services.AddScoped<IScopedService, ScopedService>();
6.  services.AddSingleton<ISingletonService, SingletonService>();
7.
8.  var serviceProvider = services.BuildServiceProvider();
9.
10. // Simulate two separate requests
11. using (var scope1 = serviceProvider.CreateScope())
12. {
13.     var scopedService1 = scope1.ServiceProvider.GetRequiredServ
    ice<IScopedService>();
14.     Console.WriteLine($"Scoped Service 1 ID: {scopedService1.
    GetOperationID()}");
15.
16.     var transientService1 = scope1.ServiceProvider.GetRequiredS
    ervice<ITransientService>();
17.     Console.
    WriteLine($"Transient Service 1 ID: {transientService1.
    GetOperationID()}");
18. }
19.
20. using (var scope2 = serviceProvider.CreateScope())
21. {
22.     var scopedService2 = scope2.ServiceProvider.GetRequiredServ
    ice<IScopedService>();
23.     Console.WriteLine($"Scoped Service 2 ID: {scopedService2.
    GetOperationID()}");
24.
25.     var transientService2 = scope2.ServiceProvider.GetRequiredS
    ervice<ITransientService>();
26.     Console.
    WriteLine($"Transient Service 2 ID: {transientService2.
    GetOperationID()}");
27. }
28.
29. var singletonService = serviceProvider.GetRequiredService<ISing
    letonService>();
30. Console.WriteLine($"Singleton Service ID: {singletonService.
    GetOperationID()}");
31.
32. Console.ReadKey();
```

Explanation:

In this example, we create a transitory, a scoped, and a singleton service. When a service is instantiated, it generates a unique `Guid`.

Every time a request is made, the `TransientService` generates a new `Guid`.

Once per scope (in this case, per simulated web request), the `ScopedService` generates a new `Guid`.

The `SingletonService` generates a single `Guid` that remains constant during the application's lifetime.

When you launch this application, you will see separate IDs for each transient service instance, the same ID for the scoped service within each scope, and the same ID for the singleton service throughout the application.

In DI, managing the life cycle of services is critical to ensuring that services are given and disposed of properly. It gives us control over how instances are shared and used across an application, balancing performance, memory management, and thread safety.

Overview of routing in ASP.NET Core

An overview routing in ASP.NET Core is a key notion that connects incoming requests to the proper controller actions or Razor Pages. It is a critical component that governs how an application replies to a client's request. The routing system in ASP.NET Core is designed to be highly flexible, allowing us to construct custom routes that best suit the architecture of their application.

Routing in ASP.NET Core is fundamentally about mapping a URL pattern to a specific request handler. This handler could be a controller action or a Razor Page in MVC applications. Routes are commonly defined in the `Configure` function of an ASP.NET Core application's `Program.cs` file.

Types of routing

ASP.NET Core supports two primary types of routing:

- **Conventional routing**: This type of routing was utilized in previous versions of ASP.NET. It entails defining routes in the `Program.cs` file following a particular pattern. Conventional routes are simple and are frequently used in applications with a fixed URL structure.

- **Attribute routing**: Introduced in later versions, attribute routing allows for finer-grained control over the routing process. Developers can define routes directly on controllers and actions by using attributes. This method provides more flexibility, particularly in complicated applications with changeable URL patterns.

Utilizing route parameters

In ASP.NET Core routing, route parameters are potent tools. They enable URLs to contain variable portions that the application can use to process requests dynamically. Parameters are usually defined within the route template and can be required or optional.

Advanced routing options

Advanced routing features distinguish ASP.NET Core in the dynamic web development environment. These include route limitations for personalized control, route grouping for efficient organization, and custom middleware for request processing enhancement. This toolkit improves ASP.NET Core routing precision and versatility.

ASP.NET Core includes the following advanced routing features:

- **Custom route constraints**: Based on custom logic, these allow for more sophisticated control over matching routes.

- **Route grouping**: This feature allows you to organize routes into groups, making complex routing settings more straightforward to manage.

- **Integration of custom middleware**: Routing can be coupled with custom middleware to provide enhanced functionality and control over the request processing pipeline.

Let us look at a simple example of convention-based and attribute routing in an ASP.NET Core application written in C#.

Example of conventional routing: The **Program.cs** file defines convention-based routing. Here is a sample:

```
1.  ...
2.
3.  builder.Services.AddControllersWithViews();
4.
5.  ...
6.
7.  app.UseRouting();
8.
9.  app.UseEndpoints(endpoints =>
10. {
11.     // Define a route
12.     endpoints.MapControllerRoute(
13.         name: "default",
14.         pattern: "{controller=Home}/{action=Index}/{id?}");
15. });
```

A default route is created in this example using the pattern **controller=Home/action=Index/id?**. This means that if a user navigates to the website's root, they will be sent to the **Home** controller's **Index** action. The **id?** section indicates that the id parameter is not required.

Attribute routing example:

Controllers and actions define attribute routing directly. Here is a simple example:

```
1.  using Microsoft.AspNetCore.Mvc;
2.
3.  public class HomeController : Controller
4.  {
5.      // route to the index page
6.      [Route ("")]
7.      [Route("Home")]
8.      [Route("Home/Index")]
9.      public IActionResult Index()
10.     {
11.         return View();
12.     }
13.
14.     // route with a parameter
15.     [Route("Home/Details/{id}")]
16.     public IActionResult Details(int id)
17.     {
18.         // logic to handle the details view
19.         return View();
20.     }
21. }
```

The **Index** method in this example can be accessed via three different paths (**Home/Index**, **Home**, or the root " "). The **Details** function is configured to need an id argument in the URL, such as **Home/Details/1**.

Summary: Routing is a versatile and essential part of web application development in ASP.NET Core. It implements the mechanism for routing incoming requests to the appropriate handlers, ensuring that the application behaves as intended. Routing is a vital ability for developers to grasp, even as ASP.NET Core evolves.

Understanding ASP.NET Core security

Understanding ASP.NET Core security in the context of a more extensive .NET application necessitates a holistic strategy that includes authentication, authorization, data protection, secure communication, and threat mitigation features.

Authorization and authentication

In computing systems, authorization and authentication are critical security operations. Authentication is validating a user's or system's identification, typically using credentials like usernames and passwords, biometric data, or security tokens. It is equivalent to proving your worth. After authentication, authorization takes effect, determining what an authorized user or system can perform based on specified rules, roles, or policies. This could include allowing or limiting access to specific system resources or actions. In a business network, for example, authentication may be used to authenticate an employee's identity. In contrast, authorization may be used to determine which files or programs the employee may access or edit. Both steps are necessary for ensuring secure and regulated access to systems and data. Let us understand this further:

- **Authentication**: In ASP.NET Core, authentication is the process of identifying a user. This is often accomplished through several methods, such as username/ password, tokens, or external identity providers. Let us look at some examples:

  o **Example 1**: **Authentication using cookies**: When a user registers in a cookie-based authentication scenario, a cookie is issued and sent to the user's browser. The cookie is then sent back to the server with each request, allowing the server to identify the user.

    ```
    1. builder.Services.
       AddAuthentication(CookieAuthenticationDefaults.
       AuthenticationScheme)
    2.     .AddCookie(options =>
    3.     {
    4.         options.LoginPath = "/login";
    5.         options.ExpireTimeSpan = TimeSpan.FromMinutes(30);
    6.     });
    ```

- **Authorization**: In ASP.NET Core, authorization governs what a user can do. It is frequently implemented through the use of roles or policies.

  o **Example 2**: **Role-based authorization**: This example shows how to limit access to a specific action method to users with a specific role:

    ```
    1. [Authorize(Roles = "Administrator")]
    2. public IActionResult AdminDashboard()
    3. {
    4.     return View();
    5. }
    ```

- **Data protection**: ASP.NET Core has a data protection layer for safeguarding data like authentication cookies, anti-forgery tokens, and application secrets.

  o **Data protection API sample**: This API can be used in your application to encrypt and decrypt data:

```
1. ...
2.
3. builder.Services.AddDataProtection();
4.
5. ...
6.
7. static void SomeMethod(IDataProtectionProvider provider)
8. {
9.     var protector = provider.CreateProtector("MyPurpose");
10.    string protectedPayload = protector.
   Protect("Hello World!");
11.    string unprotectedPayload = protector.
   Unprotect(protectedPayload);
12.}
```

- **Secure communication**: It is essential to ensure secure communication between the client and the server. This is often accomplished through HTTPS, which encrypts the data sent back and forth.

  o **Sample**: Enforcing HTTPS

  You may enforce HTTPS in ASP.NET Core, guaranteeing that every communication is encrypted.

```
1. ...
2.
3. app.UseHttpsRedirection();
4.
5. ...
```

- **Threat mitigation**: ASP.NET Core includes technologies that help to protect against attacks like XSS, CSRF, and SQL injection.

  o **Anti-CSRF tokens as a sample**: In forms, ASP.NET Core produces anti-CSRF tokens automatically.

```
1. <form asp-action="Create">
2.     <input type="hidden" asp-antiforgery="true" />
3.     <!-- Form fields here -->
4.     <input type="submit" value="Create" />
5. </form>
```

- **Summary**: Design with security in ASP.NET Core requires a layered strategy that addresses several areas of security, such as authentication and authorization, as well as data protection and secure communication. Each component is critical in establishing a secure application environment within the .NET. Its complete security strategy ensures that ASP.NET Core applications are fast and resistant to various threats.

Basics of error handling in ASP.NET Core

Error management in ASP.NET Core is essential for creating robust and user-friendly web applications. When something goes wrong, efficient error handling guarantees the program can manage it gracefully, delivering helpful feedback to the user, logging the error for analysis, and maintaining the application's stability. Let us start with this topic's fundamentals, including a few sample implementations.

Understanding error handling in ASP.NET Core

Error management in ASP.NET Core is critical to developing dependable, user-friendly web applications. It entails anticipating, catching, and managing exceptions that arise during execution.

- **Types of errors**:
  - **Compile-time errors**: Detected by the compiler before the application runs (e.g., syntax errors).
  - **Runtime errors**: Occur during application execution (e.g., null reference, file not found).

- **Exception handling**:
  - An exception is a type of object that contains information about an error.
  - The .NET provides a rich set of built-in exceptions (e.g., `NullReferenceException`, `IOException`).

- **The try-catch-finally block**:
  - **try**: Encloses code that might throw an exception.
  - **catch**: Specifies how to handle the exception.
  - **finally**: Code that executes regardless of whether an exception was thrown.

Error handling mechanisms in ASP.NET Core

ASP.NET Core includes comprehensive error-handling tools for adequately managing and responding to application issues. This section discusses fundamental tactics for ensuring smooth application execution, such as custom error pages, logging exceptions, and global exception handling.

- **Developer exception page**:
  - They are used in development for detailed error information.

   o They are enabled with `app.UseDeveloperExceptionPage()` in `Program.cs`.

- **Custom error pages**:
  - o In production, it is better to use custom error pages.
  - o It is configured using the `app.UseExceptionHandler("/Error")`, where `"/Error"` is the route to the error handling action.

- **Logging exceptions**:
  - o Essential for diagnosing issues.
  - o ASP.NET Core integrates with various logging frameworks, such as Serilog, Nlog, and Log4Net.

- **Global exception handling**:
  - o Use middleware for global exception handling.
  - o Catches exceptions not handled by other components.

- **Use of statusCode pages**:
  - o For handling HTTP errors like 404.
  - o Enabled with `app.UseStatusCodePages()`.

Sample implementations

With these sample solutions, we will investigate practical error-handling features in ASP. NET Core. These examples show how to use try-catch blocks and configure global error handling in middleware, putting the topics addressed into context.

- **Sample 1**: Try-catch-finally in C#:

```
1. public void SampleMethod()
2. {
3.     try
4.     {
5.         // Code that might throw an exception
6.     }
7.     catch (SpecificException ex)
8.     {
9.         // Handle specific exception
10.    }
11.    catch (Exception ex)
12.    {
13.        // Handle all other exceptions
14.    }
15.    finally
```

```
16.    {
17.         // Code that runs regardless of exceptions
18.    }
19. }
```

- **Sample 2**: Global exception handling in ASP.NET Core middleware

```
1. ...

2.

3. if (app.Environment.IsDevelopment()) app.
   UseDeveloperExceptionPage(); otherwise app.UseExceptionHandler("/
   Error"); // Other options...

4.

5. app.UseRouting();

6.

7. app.
   MapControllerRoute( name: "default", pattern: "controller=Home/
   action=Index/id? ");

8.

9. ...
```

- **Recommended practices**: By stressing specific tactics such as precise exception catching, extensive logging, and user-friendly error reporting, these practices enable more resilient and maintainable code, which is essential for any professional .NET application development.
  - In **catch** blocks, always utilize particular exception types.
  - Unless required, avoid catching general exception types.
  - Keep detailed records of exceptions.
  - Exceptions should never be swallowed silently in catch blocks without being logged.
  - Create user-friendly personalized error pages.

Summary

Error management in ASP.NET Core is a complicated process requiring meticulous preparation and execution. Developers may design robust and reliable programs by understanding many failures, employing the proper error handling techniques, and following best practices. The sample code provides an example of handling errors in a

.NET context successfully.

Understanding server-side vs. client-side in ASP.NET Core

Understanding server-side versus client-side in ASP.NET Core necessitates understanding web application architecture and the server and client responsibilities in this context.

Server-side in ASP.NET Core

Understanding the idea of server-side processing is critical in web development, particularly inside the ASP.NET Core. Many robust online applications rely on this strategy, in which most of the application's actions, such as data retrieval, processing, and rendering, are performed on the server. It is not only about where the processing takes place but also about the languages and frameworks that enable it, the performance implications, and the level of control it provides over the program.

Server-side processing with ASP.NET Core often entails the usage of C# or other .NET-supported languages, using their strength and adaptability to execute complicated activities. ASP.NET Core MVC and Razor Pages stand out in this environment, providing standardized methods for developing and managing online applications. These frameworks have a substantial impact on server performance, which in turn determines the overall scalability and speed of the application. Furthermore, server-side processing in ASP.NET Core provides better control over the application's behavior and security, which are crucial in today's digital world. This introduction lays the groundwork for delving further into each of these aspects, revealing how they work together to establish the server-side paradigm in ASP.NET Core.

In resume:

- **Processing**: Server-side processing in ASP.NET Core means that all the logic, including data retrieval, manipulation, and rendering, happens on the server.
- **Languages**: Typically involves C# or other .NET-supported languages.
- **Frameworks**: Examples include ASP.NET Core MVC, and Razor Pages.
- **Performance**: The server's performance impacts the application's scalability and speed.
- **Control**: Offers more control over the application's behavior and security.

Sample: ASP.NET Core MVC

Description: A MVC used for building web apps.

Sample code:

```
1. public class HomeController : Controller
2. {
3.     public IActionResult Index()
4.     {
5.         return View();
6.     }
7. }
```

Client-side in ASP.NET Core

Client-side processing is a critical notion in the various worlds of online application development, particularly in ASP.NET Core. This technique focuses on running scripts directly in the user's browser, using the capabilities of various scripting languages. It is a departure from standard server-side processing, focusing on the end-user's engagement with the program.

To develop dynamic and interactive online experiences, client-side processing mainly employs JavaScript and contemporary adaptations such as TypeScript or Blazor WebAssembly. These languages are frequently used with sophisticated frameworks such as Blazor, Angular, React, or Vue, each providing capabilities and benefits to the development process.

One of the most essential characteristics of client-side processing is its dependency on the client's device and browser capabilities, directly influencing the application's speed. This method provides a considerable benefit in terms of interaction, improving user experience by making apps more responsive and engaging. It transfers part of the processing work from the server to the client, allowing for speedier interactions and a more pleasant user experience.

This introduction lays the groundwork for further investigation into how client-side processing in ASP.NET Core leverages the power of these languages to offer rich, responsive, and interactive online applications that adjust the user experience to the capabilities of the client's device and browser.

In resume:

- **Processing**: Client-side processing involves running scripts in the user's browser.
- **Languages**: Typically JavaScript, but can include TypeScript or Blazor WebAssembly.
- **Frameworks**: Blazor, Angular, React, or Vue with ASP.NET Core.
- **Performance**: Depends on the client's device and browser capabilities.
- **Interactivity**: Enhances user experience by making applications more responsive.

Sample: Blazor WebAssembly

Description: A client-side web that allows developers to build interactive web UIs using C# instead of JavaScript.

Sample code:

```
1.  @page "/counter"
2.
3.  <h1>Counter</h1>
4.
5.  <p>Current count: @currentCount</p>
6.
7.  <button class="btn btn-primary" @onclick="IncrementCount">Click me</
    button>
8.
9.  @code {
10.     private int currentCount = 0;
11.
12.     private void IncrementCount()
13.     {
14.         currentCount++;
15.     }
16. }
```

The decision between server-side and client-side data processing is critical in the fast-paced world of web development. Server-side processing provides better protection and control, but it depends on server resources, affecting performance and scalability. Client-side processing, on the other hand, offloads duties to the user's browser, boosting interaction while being dependent on the client's device capabilities. Each strategy has complexities: the server side is often more superficial due to centralization, whereas the client side suffers browser compatibility issues. The best technique depends on the application's demands: server-side is better for robust control and processing. At the same time, the client side is suitable for generating responsive user interfaces with less server reliance.

Making wise architectural choices while developing web apps with ASP.NET Core requires an awareness of the distinctions between server-side and client-side processing. These methods have an impact on user experience, development complexity, security, and performance:

- **Data processing location**:
    o **Server-side**: On the server, it is often more secure.
    o **Client-side**: In the user's browser, reducing server load.
- **Performance and scalability**:

- o **Server-side**: Affected by server resources.
  - o **Client-side**: Dependent on the client's device capabilities.

- **Development complexity**:
  - o **Server-side**: Potentially simpler as it is centralized.
  - o **Client-side**: This can be complex due to browser compatibility issues.

- **Use cases**:
  - o **Server-side**: Ideal for applications requiring server-side solid control and processing.
  - o **Client-side**: Suitable for interactive, responsive UIs with less server dependency.

In ASP.NET Core, we must understand the distinction between server-side and client-side processing. It impacts web application design and performance, development processes, security considerations, and user experience. Using the .NET environment, developers can construct powerful, efficient, and user-friendly online apps by efficiently merging both methodologies.

Improvements in .NET 9

ASP.NET Core 9.0 includes several cutting-edge features and improvements designed to enhance our development experiences. Among the most significant changes is the new solution template for .NET MAUI, which simplifies the development of native and Blazor web client apps. This template allows us to use the same user interface on several platforms, such as the Web, Mac, Windows, iOS, and Android. This feature makes it easier to create flexible apps by optimizing code reuse.

SignalR now supports polymorphic hub methods and has an ActivitySource to improve hub method call tracing. Trimming and native ahead-of-time compilation support for SignalR client and server situations are the latest additions to the Native AOT journey, which offers notable performance advantages for real-time online interactions.

Updates have also been made to minimal APIs, most notably with the **TypedResults** class. Factory methods for returning strongly typed HTTP status code-based answers are now included in this class. Combined with improved OpenAPI compatibility, these enhancements make it easier to generate and customize API documentation, allowing us to quickly and easily design reliable and thoroughly documented APIs.

Here we have a sample of minimal API with **TypedResults** class:

```
1. app.MapGet("/todos", async (TodoDbContext db) =>
2. {
3.     var todos = await db.Todos.ToListAsync();
4.     return TypedResults.Ok(todos);
```

```
5.  });
6.  app.MapGet("/todos/{id}", async (int id, TodoDbContext db) =>
7.  {
8.      var todo = await db.Todos.FindAsync(id);
9.      return todo != null ? TypedResults.Ok(todo) : TypedResults.
    NotFound();
10. });
11. app.M
```

After retrieving every to-do item from the database, the GET **/todos** endpoint uses **TypedResults** to return a 200 OK **response.Ok()**, which incorporates the to-do list. Based on its ID, the GET **/todos/{id}** endpoint retrieves a specific to-do item; if the item is located, it returns a 200 OK response with the item; if the ID is not found, **TypedResults** returns a 404 Not Found response.**NotFound()**. Users can add a new to-do item to the database using the POST **/todos** endpoint. The location of the new resource with **TypedResults** is shown in the 201 Created response that is returned once the item has been successfully saved.

To guarantee consistent and self-describing HTTP answers, the **TypedResults** class is essential. It improves the quality and clarity of the API's output by offering strongly typed methods for producing these responses. This uniformity enhances client interactions and helps with API description. The API benefits from the simplicity and effectiveness of simple APIs while maintaining robustness and ease of maintenance by utilizing **TypedResults**, which guarantees type safety and clarity in all responses.

Support for polymorphic types in SignalR hubs

This feature allows us to define a method in our hub that takes a base class type, resulting in more straightforward and versatile code. This technique makes handling different derived types easy without creating separate methods for each type.

Here we have a sample:

```
1.  using Microsoft.AspNetCore.SignalR;
2.  using System.Text.Json.Serialization;
3.  public class MyHub : Hub
4.  {
5.      public void Method(JsonPerson person)
6.      {
7.          if (person is JsonPersonExtended)
8.          {
9.              // Handle JsonPersonExtended
10.         }
11.         else if (person is JsonPersonExtended2)
```

```
12.         {
13.             // Handle JsonPersonExtended2
14.         }
15.         else
16.         {
17.             // Handle base JsonPerson
18.         }
19.     }
20. }
21.
22. [JsonPolymorphic]
23. // Here we define the other types we like
24. [JsonDerivedType(typeof(JsonPersonExtended),
    nameof(JsonPersonExtended))]
25. [JsonDerivedType(typeof(JsonPersonExtended2),
    nameof(JsonPersonExtended2))]
26. public class JsonPerson
27. {
28.     public string Name { get; set; }
29.     public Person Child { get; set; }
30.     public Person Parent { get; set; }
31. }
32.
33. public class JsonPersonExtended : JsonPerson
34. {
35.     public int Age { get; set; }
36. }
37.
38. public class JsonPersonExtended2 : JsonPerson
39. {
40.     public string Location { get; set; }
41. }
42.
43. public class Person
44. {
45.     public string Name { get; set; }
46.     public int Age { get; set; }
47.     public string Location { get; set; }
48. }
```

The **Method** will dynamically identify the type of **JsonPerson** it works with when a client submits a JSON object to the hub. Consider a JSON payload such as this:

```
1.  {
2.    "Name": "John",
3.    "Child": {
4.      "Name": "Jane",
5.      "Age": 5,
6.      "Location": "Home"
7.    },
8.    "Parent": {
9.      "Name": "Doe",
10.      "Age": 30,
11.      "Location": "City"
12.    },
13.    "Age": 40
14. }
```

We may now handle various data structures in real-time applications thanks to SignalR hubs' support for polymorphic types. As our example shows with **JsonPerson** and its extensions, we may design more adaptable and maintainable code that effectively handles various derived types by allowing a base class type for method parameters. In addition to making complex logic easier to build, this feature improves an application's responsiveness and adaptability to interact with various client-side payloads easily. In the end, this enhancement enables us to design more resilient and adaptable real-time systems that can change to meet the changing demands of their users.

Conclusion

This chapter presented an in-depth exploration of ASP.NET Core, an open-source designed for building modern web applications with high performance. It starts with an introduction to ASP.NET Core, getting into its key features like cross-platform development, enhanced security, cloud-readiness, and new advancements in version 8. The chapter then guided you through creating a basic web application. Additionally, it sheds light on Razor Pages, a page-based model that streamlines web UI development, detailing aspects like Razor syntax, structure, page handlers, form submission, and URL generation. The chapter aims to equip you with a solid understanding of ASP.NET Core and Razor Pages, enabling you to apply these tools in your projects effectively.

In the next chapter, we will learn about Razor Pages, an ASP.NET Core feature, and how

CHAPTER 12

Building Powerful Websites with Razor

Introduction

In this chapter, you will learn about Razor Pages, an ASP.NET Core feature that uses a page-centric approach to revolutionize website design. Razor Pages provides a faster development process by combining C# and HTML in a single file, stressing clear separation of concerns and easy data management. You will learn how to create and manage Razor Pages within a .NET Core framework and how to use Razor syntax, Tag Helpers, layouts, and partials to build dynamic and responsive websites. The chapter discusses essential topics such as form management, user input processing, data validation, and performing CRUD operations with Razor Pages. By the end of this chapter, you will be able to create Razor Pages, understand their lifecycle, work with forms, use Tag Helpers for streamlined HTML creation, embed C# code with Razor syntax, and use layouts and partials for consistent UI elements, all culminating in the creation of a CRUD application using Razor Pages.

Structure

This chapter covers the following topics:

- Creating Razor Pages in ASP.NET Core
- Understanding the lifecycle of a Razor Page
- Working with forms in Razor Pages

- Form validation in ASP.NET Core Razor Pages
- Understanding Tag Helpers in Razor Pages
- Razor syntax and its usage in Razor Pages
- Creating layouts and partials in Razor Pages
- Building a CRUD operation using Razor Pages

Objectives

Our goals in this chapter are multifarious and focused on Razor Pages in ASP.NET Core. We intend to present and explore Razor Pages, a page-centric approach to web development. Understanding the construction and maintenance of these pages within the .NET Core framework and learning the use of Razor syntax, Tag Helpers, layouts, and partials for creating dynamic and responsive websites are all part of this. We will also review essential subjects like form management, processing user inputs, data validation, and performing CRUD activities. To reinforce these concepts, the chapter finishes with a hands-on project: creating a CRUD application using Razor Pages in conjunction with EF Core, allowing you to put your theoretical understanding into practice.

Creating Razor Pages in ASP.NET Core

Developing online applications using Razor Pages in ASP.NET Core and .NET entails utilizing a page-based programming paradigm that provides a simpler and more focused alternative to MVC. Razor Pages are an ASP.NET Core component that uses the C# programming language for backend functionality and HTML and Razor syntax for frontend rendering.

Razor Pages in ASP.NET Core combine the capabilities of C# with HTML to provide a streamlined approach to web development. They combine server-side programming with HTML using the simple @ syntax. Each page is supported by a separate Page Model containing the business logic. Routing is intuitively mapped depending on the directory placement of the page, simplifying navigation and URL formats.

Following are the basics of Razor Pages:

- **Razor syntax**: Combines C# with HTML. The C# code is embedded within HTML using @ syntax.

- **Page Model**: Each Razor Page has a corresponding Page Model (C# class) where backend logic is written.

- **Routing**: By default, the routing in Razor Pages is based on the page's location in the project's directory structure.

Sample: Basic Razor Page project

Open the command prompt; create the directory you would like to create the project and run the **dotnet** command, where **MyRazorPagesApp** is the name you would like to give to the project:

```
1. dotnet new razor -n MyRazorPagesApp
```

Project structure of the solution:

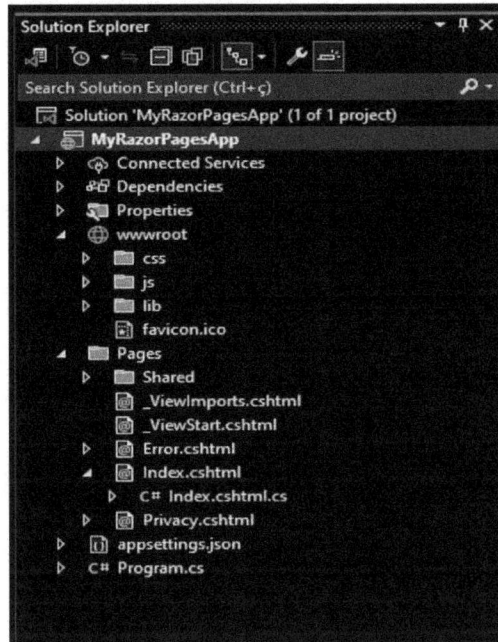

Figure 12.1: Solution Explorer in Visual Studio

Here is the files of the project in this sample:

/Pages

Index.cshtml: The Razor view file.

Index.cshtml.cs: The Page Model for Index.

Following is the code for **Index.cshtml**:

```
1. @page
2. @model IndexModel
3. @{
4.     ViewData[«Title»] = «Home page»;
5. }
6.
7. <div class="text-center">
8.     <h1 class="display-4">Welcome</h1>
```

```
9.     <p>Learn about <a href="https://learn.microsoft.com/aspnet/
core">building Web apps with ASP.NET Core</a>.</p>
10. </div>
```

Following is the code for **Index.cshtml.cs**:

```
1.  using Microsoft.AspNetCore.Mvc;
2.  using Microsoft.AspNetCore.Mvc.RazorPages;
3.
4.  namespace MyRazorPagesApp.Pages;
5.
6.  public class IndexModel : PageModel
7.  {
8.      private readonly ILogger<IndexModel> _logger;
9.
10.     public IndexModel(ILogger<IndexModel> logger)
11.     {
12.         _logger = logger;
13.     }
14.
15.     public void OnGet()
16.     {
17.
18.     }
19. }
```

Following are the steps to creating a page **Contact.cshtml**:

1. Right-mouse click on **Pages** | **Add** | **Razor Page**, as shown in the following figure:

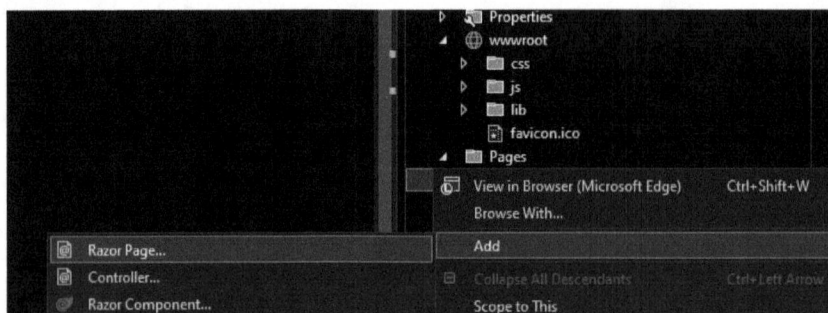

Figure 12.2: Menu to add new Razor Page

2. Select **Razor Page – Empty**, as shown in the following figure:

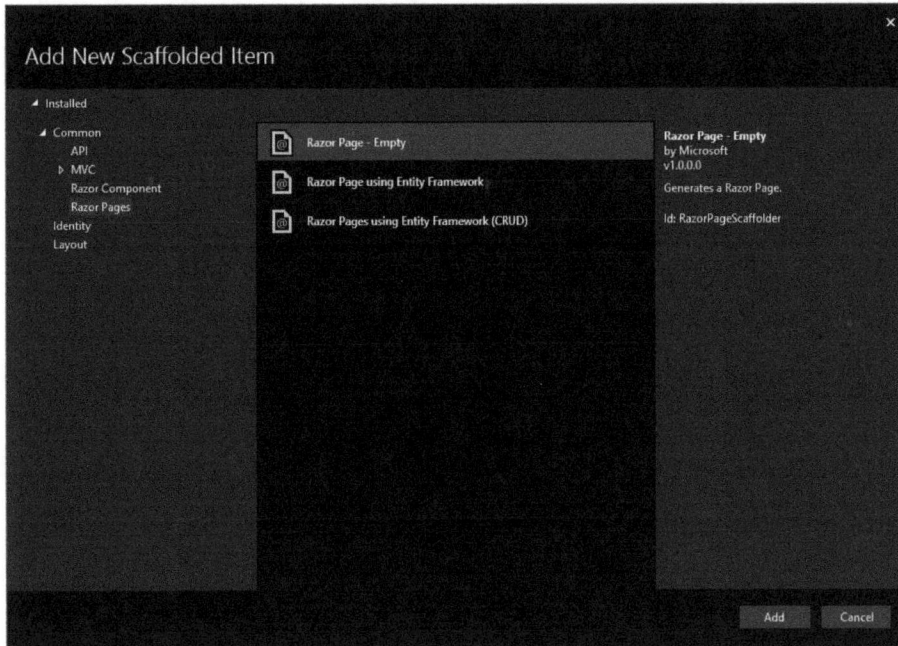

Figure 12.3: Selecting the type of Razor Page

3. Give a name to the page, in this case, **Contact**, as shown in the following figure:

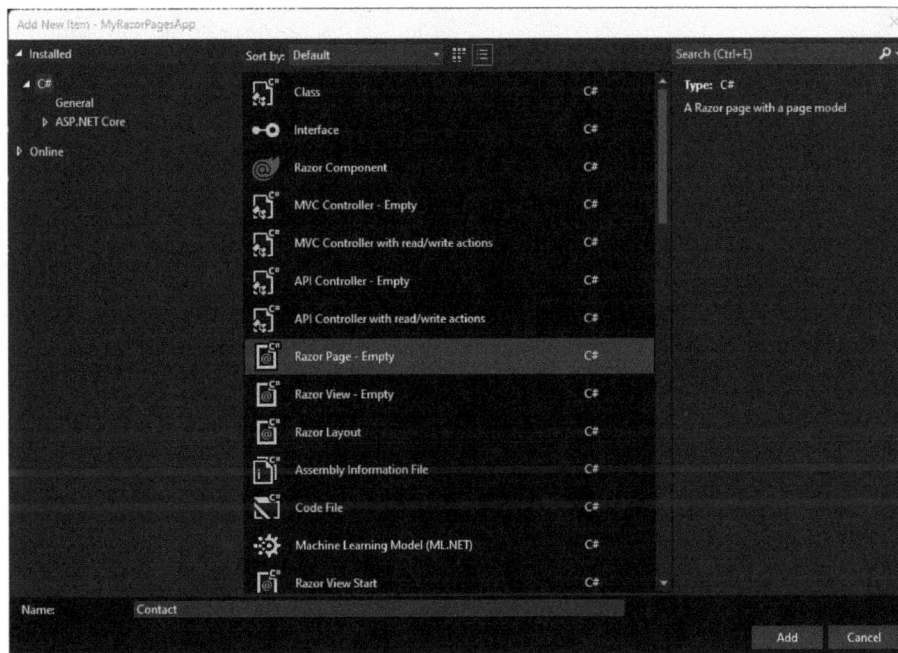

Figure 12.4: Adding the name to the page

4. Add this code to **Contact.cshtml**, as follows, as shown in the following figure:

```
1.  @page
2.  @model MyRazorPagesApp.Pages.ContactModel
3.  @{
4.  }
5.
6.  <form method="post">
7.      <label asp-for="Name"></label><br />
8.      <input asp-for="Name" /><br /><br />
9.      <label asp-for="Message"></label><br />
10.     <textarea asp-for="Message"></textarea><br /><br />
11.     <button type="submit">Submit</button>
12. </form>
```

Running the project we will have this screen:

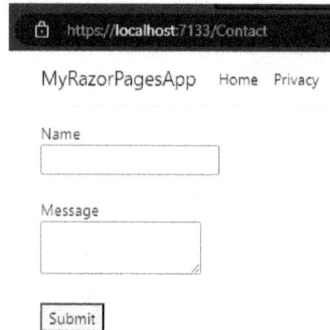

Figure 12.5: Sample running the app

In **Contact.cshtml.cs**, the model properties and the file will look like:

```
1.  using Microsoft.AspNetCore.Mvc;
2.  using Microsoft.AspNetCore.Mvc.RazorPages;
3.
4.  namespace MyRazorPagesApp.Pages;
5.
6.  public class ContactModel : PageModel
7.  {
8.      [BindProperty]
9.      public string Name { get; set; }
10.
11.     [BindProperty]
12.     public string Message { get; set; }
13.
```

```
14.    public void OnPost()
15.    {
16.        // Handle form submission
17.    }
18. }
```

Here we have a simple contact form shown in this example. The frontend (**Contact. cshtml**) contains form elements tied to Page Model properties (**Contact.cshtml.cs**). The Page Model's **OnPost** function handles form submission. Following are the main points:

- **Recommended practices**: Keep logic in Page Models, and views focused on markup to keep code organized.

- **Validation**: Use data annotations to validate forms.

- **Security**: Use anti-forgery tokens in forms to protect against CSRF attacks.

In ASP.NET Core, Razor Pages provides a streamlined approach to web page development, stressing a clear separation of concerns and ease of usage. These examples demonstrate how to construct and manage Razor Pages in a .NET Core application.

Understanding the lifecycle of a Razor Page

Understanding the lifecycle of a Razor Page in .NET entails investigating how the .NET Core processes these pages from the time they are requested by a user to the time the answer is returned. Razor Pages, an ASP.NET Core feature, makes developing web apps more accessible and productive. Let us break down the Razor Page lifecycle and illustrate it with two instances.

Lifecycle of a Razor Page

Every razor page has a lifecycle, here is how it works:

- **Request processing**: We must grasp the Razor Page lifecycle in ASP.NET Core web development. When the server receives and evaluates a user's request, request processing starts this lifecycle. The ASP.NET Core middleware intercepts the request and then routes it to the appropriate Razor Page based on its URL. This phase ends with creating a Razor Page instance and preparing for processing. This initial phase is crucial to Razor Page functionality in ASP.NET Core because it sets the tone for how the application interacts with the user.

  o **Request received**: When a user submits a request to the server, the ASP.NET Core middleware intercepts it first.

  o **Routing**: The middleware determines which Razor Page should handle the request based on the URL.

  o **Page creation**: A Razor Page instance is generated.

- **Page Model implementation**: The Page Model implementation step of an ASP. NET Core Razor Page's lifecycle affects how a web application handles user interactions. The user's request data, including form values and query parameters, is methodically connected to Page Model characteristics during model binding. The application needs to comprehend user input appropriately. This phase also executes request-specific handler methods like `OnPostAsync` for POST, `OnPutAsync` for PUT, and `OnDeleteAsync` for DELETE. The Razor Page's lifecycle in ASP.NET Core relies on these methods, which enable user-driven replies and actions.

  o **Model binding**: Request data (such as form values and query parameters) is bound to Page Model attributes.

  o **Handler methods**: If the request is a POST, PUT, or DELETE, the relevant handler methods are called, such as `OnPostAsync`, `OnPutAsync`, or `OnDeleteAsync`.

- **Page rendering**: Page rendering is a significant phase in the lifecycle of a Razor Page within the ASP.NET Core, where the Razor engine comes into play, demonstrating its ability to generate HTML content dynamically. It is the stage at which the actual visual representation of a web page takes shape. It is a complex procedure in which the Razor engine combines the `.cshtml` file, which is the Razor Page itself, with the data wrapped in the Page Model. This combination yields fully formed, data-driven HTML content suited to the request and circumstance. After this rendering, the final step is critical. The response, which consists of this produced HTML, is sent back to the client. This stage completes the request-processing cycle by delivering a visually and functionally complete web page to the user, showing the effectiveness and efficiency of the Razor Page lifecycle in ASP.NET Core.

  o **Razor engine renders**: HTML content by merging the Razor Page (`.cshtml` file) with data from the Page Model.

  o **Response sent**: As the response, the rendered HTML is returned to the client.

Example 1 contact form

The contact form example in ASP.NET Core Razor Pages demonstrates how a standard online form works within the lifecycle of a Razor Page. Let us split this sample into its scenario and the steps in its lifespan:

- **Scenario**: In this example, a user interacts with a contact form on a website. This form collects user input, such as a user's name, email address, and message. The following are the essential actions in this scenario:

  o **User submission**: The user fills out and submits the contact form.

  o **Operations on the server**: The server receives this data, validates it to verify if it satisfies particular requirements (such as the correct email format), and then saves it, typically in a database.

- **Lifecycle steps/contact request**: This contact form request has numerous steps in its lifecycle:

  1. **Form submission**: The user completes and submits the form on the webpage. In most cases, the submission is sent to a specified URL, in this case, /Contact.

  2. **Page association**: When ASP.NET Core receives this request, it correlates it with the **Contact.cshtml** Razor Page and its associated **ContactModel**. This relationship is critical since it tells which Page Model to use.

  3. **Model binding**: The .NET connects the form's user input (name, email, and message) to the **ContactModel** appropriate properties. This procedure converts the data entered by the user into model properties.

  4. **OnPostAsync execution**: The method in **ContactModel** occurs once the model binding is complete. This function is intended to handle POST requests commonly used for form submissions.

  5. **Validation and processing**: The input is validated within the **OnPostAsync** method (for example, to see if an email address has a correct format). Following validation, the data is handled, for example, by saving it in a database.

  6. **Rendering**: After processing, the page is rendered with a success message. **Contact.cshtml** handles this rendering and confirms that the form was successfully submitted.

Following is the source code for **Contact.cshtml**:

```
1.  @page
2.  @model MyRazorPagesApp.Pages.ContactModel
3.  @{
4.  }
5.
6.  <form method="post">
7.      <input type="text" asp-for="Name" /><br />
8.      <span asp-validation-for="Name"></span><br />
9.      <br />
10.     <input type="email" asp-for="Email" /><br />
11.     <span asp-validation-for="Email"></span><br />
12.     <br />
13.     <textarea asp-for="Message"></textarea><br />
14.     <span asp-validation-for="Message"></span><br />
15.     <br /><br />
16.     <button type="submit">Submit</button>
17. </form>
18.
19. @if (Model.MessageSent)
```

```
20. {
21.     <p>Your message has been sent successfully!</p>
22. }
```

Source code for **ContactModel.cs** (Page Model):

```
1.  using Microsoft.AspNetCore.Mvc;
2.  using Microsoft.AspNetCore.Mvc.RazorPages;
3.  using System.ComponentModel.DataAnnotations;
4.
5.  namespace MyRazorPagesApp.Pages;
6.
7.  public class ContactModel : PageModel
8.  {
9.
10.     [BindProperty]
11.     public string Name { get; set; }
12.
13.     [BindProperty]
14.     [EmailAddress]
15.     public string Email { get; set; }
16.
17.     [BindProperty]
18.     public string Message { get; set; }
19.
20.     public bool MessageSent { get; set; }
21.
22.     public void OnGet()
23.     {
24.     }
25.
26.     public async Task<IActionResult> OnPostAsync()
27.     {
28.         if (!ModelState.IsValid)
29.         {
30.             return Page();
31.         }
32.
33.         // Process the data here (e.g., save it to the database)
34.         // For this example, we'll  simulate that the message is
    sent
35.         MessageSent = true;
```

```
36.
37.          // You can redirect to another page or  return to the same
   page
38.          return Page();
39.    }
40. }
```

The solution has these files:

- **Contact.cshtml**: This is the Razor Page on which the form is defined. It has input areas for name, email, message, and a submit button. A success message is displayed if **MessageSent** is valid once the form is submitted.

- **ContactModel.cs**: This is the **Contact.cshtml** Page Model class. It includes properties related to form inputs as well as the **OnPostAsync** method. When the form is submitted, this method is called. It validates the model state before processing the data (similar to storing it in a database). To simulate successful processing, we set **MessageSent** to true in our example.

This code is a simple example that lacks sophisticated features such as database integration and extensive error handling that would be required for a commercial application.

This example depicts a common use-case situation in online applications where user input is captured, evaluated, and acknowledged. It emphasizes the smooth and quick handling of user interactions, data validation, server-side processing, and response rendering, all part of the Razor Page lifecycle in ASP.NET Core.

Example 2 data display page

The second example focuses on a data display page, which exemplifies another popular scenario in web development with ASP.NET Core Razor Pages. This example involves showing the user a list of items. Let us take a closer look at the situation and the stages involved in its lifetime.

- **Scenario**: In this case, the user wants to see a list of products. The following are the crucial actions:

  o **How it works**: A user intends to view a product list, most commonly on an e-commerce or retail website.

  o **Server response**: The server retrieves and displays this product data from a storage system (such as a database).

- **Steps in the lifecycle**: Request for / Products: The procedure begins when the user navigates to the products page, often by clicking a link or typing a URL pointing to **/Products**. Let us look at the steps now:

1. **Routing**: When the ASP.NET Core receives the request, it routes it to the proper Razor Page. In this case, the **Products.cshtml** page is linked to **ProductsModel**. The routing system ensures that requests are routed to the appropriate page and model.

2. **OnGetAsync execution**: The **ProductsModel OnGetAsync** method is called when a page displays data. This method is intended to handle GET requests, which are used to retrieve and display data.

3. **Data fetching**: The fetching of product data from a database occurs within the **OnGetAsync** function. It could entail accessing a database to retrieve a list of items along with their specifications.

4. **Rendering**: After retrieving the data, the **Products.cshtml** file is rendered. Razor Page handles the rendering. It generates HTML text that shows the product list dynamically. This rendering combines the product data with the HTML markup defined in **Products.cshtml**.

- Finally, the user is either shown the product list on the same page or moved to the products page if they were previously on another page. The result is a web page displaying a list of products in response to the user's request.

Understanding the lifecycle of a Razor Page is critical for developing .NET web apps that are resilient and efficient. It guarantees that we accurately handle requests, process data efficiently, and render results optimally. The examples highlight how the Razor Page lifecycle is essential to handling web requests and responses in .NET Core applications.

Following is the code sample for **Products.cshtml** (Razor Page):

```
1.  @page
2.  @model MyRazorPagesApp.Pages.ProductsModel
3.  @{
4.  }
5.
6.  <h2>Product List</h2>
7.
8.  <ul>
9.  @foreach (var product in Model.Products)
10. {
11.     <li>@product.Name - $@product.Price</li>
12. }
13. </ul>
```

The code sample for **ProductsModel.cs** (Page Model) is as follows:

```
1.  using Microsoft.AspNetCore.Mvc.RazorPages;
2.  using System.Collections.Generic;
3.
4.  public class Product
5.  {
6.      public string Name { get; set; }
7.      public decimal Price { get; set; }
8.  }
9.
10. public class ProductsModel : PageModel
11. {
12.     public List<Product> Products { get; private set; }
13.
14.     public void OnGet()
15.     {
16.         // In a real application, you would fetch this data from a
    database
17.         Products = new List<Product>
18.         {
19.             new Product { Name = "Laptop", Price = 999.99M },
20.             new Product { Name = "Smartphone", Price = 499.99M },
21.             new Product { Name = "Tablet", Price = 299.99M }
22.         };
23.     }
24. }
```

Following is the explanation of the given code:

- **Products.cshtml**: This Razor Page uses a straightforward structure to display products. It iterates through the **ProductsModel** products list, displaying the name and price of each product.

- **ProductsModel.cs**: The Page Model class for **Products.cshtml** is **ProductsModel.cs**. It has a **Product** property that includes a list of product objects. This list is initialized with some example data via the **OnGet** function. In a practical application, you would query your database for product info here.

This code provides an essential structure for showing a product list on a Razor Page. A full-fledged application would include more complicated logic for data access and error management and possibly use a service layer to fetch data from a database.

This ASP.NET Core Razor Pages data display page demonstrates a regular read-only web interaction. It demonstrates how user data requests are handled flawlessly, from routing to data gathering and presentation. This procedure demonstrates the Razor Page lifecycle's efficiency and efficacy in managing data-driven web pages, stressing its utility in developing dynamic and responsive web applications.

Working with forms in Razor Pages

Working with forms in Razor Pages using .NET is an essential skill for web developers creating dynamic, data-driven websites. Razor Pages, introduced in ASP.NET Core, provides a page-based programming model that simplifies and accelerates the development of web user interfaces. Let us get into this topic in depth with extensive explanations and examples.

Razor Pages, a feature of ASP.NET Core, improves web page creation. It uses the MVC architecture for simplicity and efficiency but integrates the controller directly into the page. Integration makes development more seamless and natural. The famous code-behind, or **.cshtml.cs** file, manages the page's events and data processing, while the **.cshtml** file handles the user interface's HTML content and Razor syntax. The versatile, open-source .NET complements Razor Pages. Known for its robustness, security, and scalability, .NET can run online, mobile, and desktop applications, making it essential for us.

Each Razor Page usually has two parts:

- **.cshtml file**: This HTML markup file uses Razor syntax for the user interface.

- **.cshtml.cs file**: This script, known as the **code-behind**, contains C# code for managing the page's events and data.

Consider a more complex example of a customer form for a hospital used for capturing customer details in a hospital setting.

The code for **Customer.cshtml** is as follows:

```
1.  @page
2.  @model MyRazorPagesApp.Pages.CustomerModel
3.  @{
4.  }
5.
6.  <form method="post">
7.      <label asp-for="Customer.Name">Name:</label>
8.      <input asp-for="Customer.Name" />
9.
10.     <label asp-for="Customer.Age">Age:</label>
11.     <input asp-for="Customer.Age" type="number" />
12.
13.     <label asp-for="Customer.AppointmentDate">Appointment Date:</label>
14.     <input asp-for="Customer.AppointmentDate" type="date" />
```

```
15.
16.    <button type="submit">Register</button>
17. </form>
```

The code for **Customer.cshtml.cs** is as follows:

```
1.  using Microsoft.AspNetCore.Mvc;
2.  using Microsoft.AspNetCore.Mvc.RazorPages;
3.
4.  namespace MyRazorPagesApp.Pages
5.  {     public class Customer
6.      {
7.          public string Name { get; set; }
8.          public int Age { get; set; }
9.          public DateTime AppointmentDate { get; set; }
10.     }
11.     public class CustomerModel : PageModel
12.     {
13.         [BindProperty]
14.         public Customer Customer { get; set; }
15.
16.         public void OnPost()
17.         {
18.             // Handle form submission, such as registering the customer
19.             // and scheduling the appointment
20.         }
21.     }
```

This example shows how to use Razor Pages in .NET to develop a customer form for a hospital. This form is intended to collect vital information from hospital clients, such as their name, age, and appointment date. Let us dissect the example:

- **(Customer.cshtml) HTML markup**: The form's HTML markup is defined in the **.cshtml** file, which uses Razor syntax to bind form fields to model parameters dynamically.

  The **<form method=post></form>** tag specifies that the form will be submitted via the HTTP POST method. It is a standard procedure for forms that communicate information to the server.

  o **Input fields**: The customer's name, age, and appointment date are all input fields. The asp-for Tag Helper associates each input field with a Customer model property. It implies that input values are immediately transferred to these properties when you submit the form.

o **Name**: A text input area where the customer's name can be entered.

o **Age**: A number input box for the age of the customer.

o **Appointment date**: An input area where you can enter the appointment date.

o **Submit button**: To send the form, click the `<button type=submit>Register</button>`.

- **(Customer.cshtml.cs) code-behind**: The C# code that handles form submission is contained in the `.cshtml.cs` file.

  Model binding for Customers: The `Customer` class is a simple model representing the customer, containing properties for `Name`, `Age`, and `AppointmentDate`. The `[BindProperty]` element links this model to the form, allowing form data to be automatically mapped to model attributes upon form submission.

  When the form is submitted, the `OnPost` method is activated. The logic for managing the form data after submission is written here. You could, for example, store this information in a database or use it to book an appointment.

  o **Customer type**: This class is the model, and its characteristics correspond to the form fields. It includes the following:

  o **Name**: A string property that stores the name of the customer.

  o **Age**: An integer parameter that represents the customer's age.

  o **Appointment date**: The appointment date's `DateTime` property.

Discovering how it works:

When a user completes the form and clicks the register button, the form data is delivered to the server using HTTP POST. The Razor Page Model binding links the input data to the `Customer` model properties automatically. This model can then be used by the `OnPost` method to execute different tasks, such as saving the data to a database or processing it for other purposes.

This example shows how Razor Pages in .NET may ease the process of developing and processing forms, making it a handy tool for us, mainly when dealing with client data in a hospital context.

Form validation in ASP.NET Core Razor Pages

Form validation is essential to web development because it ensures that user input is correct and valuable before processing. Form validation in ASP.NET Core Razor Pages is handled using a combination of C# model classes and Razor syntax. Here is a detailed look into form validation in this context, with two examples.

Understanding model validation in ASP.NET Core Razor Pages entails several fundamental principles, each essential in ensuring that data given via forms is correct and safe to handle. Let us break each aspect down:

- **Annotations to data**: Annotations to data are attributes that are applied to model properties to define how data should be validated. These annotations act as declarative validation rules, allowing you to add standard validation logic within our model classes easily. Here are some examples of popular data annotations in ASP.NET Core:

    o **[Required]**: Makes sure a property has a value; it cannot be null or empty.

    o **[StringLength]**: This property specifies a string's maximum (and possibly minimum) length.

    o **[EmailAddress]**: Checks that a property value is in the correct email format.

    o **[Range]**: Defines a numeric range for the value of a property.

    o **[RegularExpression]**: Ensures that the value of a property fits a regular expression pattern.

    These annotations are used by the client side to validate and help validate data on the server side.

- **The model state**: The `ModelState` property of an ASP.NET Core Page Model or controller represents the state of the form submission. It includes the outcomes of model binding (mapping request data to model characteristics) and validation.

- **Learn how models work**:

    o Model state stores the success or failure of the validation checks defined by data annotations.

    o Model state includes error messages that can be presented in the view if validation fails.

    o **Model binding feedback**: It also gives feedback on the binding process, indicating whether or not particular submitted data might be tied to model characteristics.

- **Tag assistants**: Razor Pages uses HTML Tag Helpers to make attaching model properties to form fields and showing validation messages easier. Some of the most typical Tag Helpers for validation are:

    o **Asp-validation-for**: A span or div element that is linked to a model property to display validation messages for that property.

    o **Bindings**: Binding an input, select, or textarea element to a model property with asp-for enables model binding and client-side validation.

    o **Helpers**: Tag Helpers add server-side characteristics to HTML components, increasing the maintainability and readability of Razor views.

- **Client-side validation vs. server-side validation**: Validation in online applications can occur on both the client and server sides, with each providing a distinct purpose:
  - ○ **Client-side validation**: Validation performed in the user's browser, typically using JavaScript. It gives the user rapid feedback, which improves the user experience. It can, however, be circumvented or disabled. Therefore, it should not be relied on for data integrity or security.
  - ○ **Server-side validation**: It occurs after the form data is submitted on the server. Server-side validation is critical for data security and integrity because it assures that data is legitimate, safe, and compliant with business standards, regardless of client-side validation status.

In summary, model validation in ASP.NET Core Razor Pages is a comprehensive approach that combines data annotations for declarative validation rules, model state for tracking validation results and binding feedback, Tag Helpers for easy validation message integration in views, and a set of client-side and server-side validation to ensure both a good user experience and robust data integrity.

Sample validation, code for **Registration.cshtml**:

```
1.  @page
2.  @model MyRazorPagesApp.Pages.RegistrationModel
3.  @{
4.  }
5.
6.  <form method="post">
7.      <div>
8.          <label asp-for="User.FullName"></label><br />
9.          <input asp-for="User.FullName" /><br />
10.         <span asp-validation-for="User.FullName"></span>
11.     </div>
12.     <div>
13.         <label asp-for="User.Email"></label><br />
14.         <input asp-for="User.Email" /><br />
15.         <span asp-validation-for="User.Email"></span>
16.     </div>
17.     <div>
18.         <label asp-for="User.Password"></label><br />
19.         <input asp-for="User.Password" /><br />
20.         <span asp-validation-for="User.Password"></span>
21.     </div>
22.     <div>
23.         <label asp-for="User.DateOfBirth"></label>
```

```
24.          <input asp-for="User.DateOfBirth" type="date" />
25.          <span asp-validation-for="User.DateOfBirth"></span>
26.     </div>
27.
28.
29.     <br />
30.     <button type="submit">Register</button>
31. </form>
```

Code sample for **Registration.cshtml.cs**:

```
1.  using Microsoft.AspNetCore.Mvc;
2.  using Microsoft.AspNetCore.Mvc.RazorPages;
3.  using System.ComponentModel.DataAnnotations;
4.
5.  namespace MyRazorPagesApp.Pages;
6.
7.  public class User
8.  {
9.      [Required]
10.     [Display(Name = "Full Name")]
11.     public string FullName { get; set; }
12.
13.     [Required]
14.     [EmailAddress]
15.     [Display(Name = "Email Address")]
16.     public string Email { get; set; }
17.
18.     [Required]
19.     [StringLength(100, MinimumLength = 6)]
20.     [DataType(DataType.Password)]
21.     public string Password { get; set; }
22.
23.     [Required]
24.     [AgeValidation(16)]
25.     public DateTime DateOfBirth { get; set; }
26.
27. }
28. public class RegistrationModel : PageModel
29. {
30.     public User User { get; set; }
```

```
31.     public void OnGet()
32.     {
33.     }
34.
35.     public void OnPost()
36.     {
37.         if (!ModelState.IsValid)
38.         {
39.             // Handle the validation failure
40.             return;
41.         }
42.         // Process the data
43.     }
44.
45. }
```

The code for **AgeValidation** for *line 24* given above is as follows:

```
1. using System.ComponentModel.DataAnnotations;
2.
3. public class AgeValidationAttribute : ValidationAttribute
4. {
5.     public int MinimumAge { get; }
6.
7.     public AgeValidationAttribute(int minimumAge)
8.     {
9.         MinimumAge = minimumAge;
10.     }
11.
12.     protected override ValidationResult IsValid(object value,
    ValidationContext validationContext)
13.     {
14.         if (value is DateTime dateOfBirth)
15.         {
16.             var age = DateTime.Today.Year - dateOfBirth.Year;
17.             if (age >= MinimumAge)
18.                 return ValidationResult.Success;
19.         }
20.         return new ValidationResult($"You must be at least
    {MinimumAge} years old.»);
21.     }
22. }
```

The code examples above demonstrate a complete form validation example in an ASP. NET Core Razor Pages application. This example focuses on a user registration form with fields for complete name, email, password, and birth date.

Breakdown of the code:

- **Registration page (Registration.cshtml)**:
  - o Using HTML and Razor terminology, the Razor page defines the structure of the user registration form.
  - o The `asp-for` Tag Helper associates each input field with a different feature of the User model. This guarantees that the data supplied in the form is linked to the correct property.
  - o The `asp-validation-for` Tag Helper is utilized to display validation messages for each field. It displays error messages if the input does not fulfill the model's validation criteria.

- **Registration.cshtml.cs Page Model**: The user class represents the data model with characteristics matching the form fields. The following data annotations are used to validate each property:
  - o **[Required]**: Denotes that a field is required.
  - o **[EmailAddress]**: Checks to see if the input is valid.
  - o **[StringLength]**: Checks that the password is within a specific length range.
  - o **[DataType(DataType.Password)]**: Indicates that the field is a password, which allows for proper handling and validation.
  - o **[AgeValidation(16)]**: A custom validation attribute that ensures the user is over 16.

  The logic to handle form submission is contained in the `RegistrationModel` class, which derives from `PageModel`. `ModelState` is checked by the `OnPost` function. Use `IsValid` to see if the form data has passed all validation checks. If validation fails, the form is re-rendered with error warnings; if validation succeeds, the data can be processed.

- **AgeValidation custom validation attribute**:
  - o `AgeValidationAttribute` is a custom validation attribute used to validate the user's age.
  - o It takes as a parameter a minimum age and estimates the user's age depending on their date of birth. A validation error is generated if the user is under the specified minimum age.

If you run the code as it is, the validation will not occur because the property **User** is not properly bound, so add the bin, like follows, and the code will not execute the validation:

```
1.    [BindProperty]
2.    public User User { get; set; }
```

Following is the screen we will have when running the project:

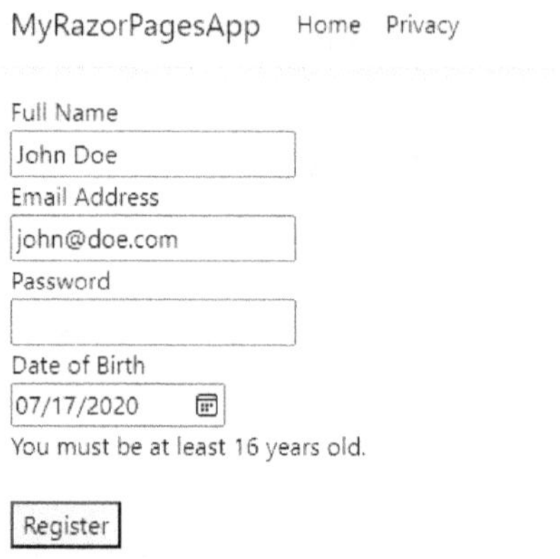

Figure 12.6: Sample validating date of birth

This example shows how to use ASP.NET Core Razor Pages to do form validation. The application ensures that user inputs are correctly formatted, meet specified criteria, and are suitable for further processing by combining data annotations for standard validation rules, a custom validation attribute for specific business logic (age validation in this case), and Razor syntax for integrating these validations into the user interface. It not only improves data quality and security but also improves user experience by providing instant feedback on any input errors.

Understanding Tag Helpers in Razor Pages

Tag Helpers are intended to make Razor markup more natural with HTML while allowing server-side rendering. Let us get into this topic in depth.

Tag Helpers is a feature in ASP.NET Core. It is a technique to generate HTML components in Razor files (`.cshtml`) using server-side code. Tag Helpers add server-side logic to HTML markup in Razor files, making designing and maintaining robust and dynamic web pages more accessible.

Let us look at the advantages of Tag Helpers in Razor Pages, specifically their straightforward syntax, IntelliSense support, modularity, reusability, and contribution to cleaner Razor views:

- **Intuitive HTML-like syntax**: Tag Helpers are intended to look and feel like ordinary HTML. They use common HTML tags and properties, making them more approachable, particularly for those familiar with HTML.

    o **Benefit**: This familiarity reduces the learning curve for front-end engineers switching to Razor Pages because the syntax is similar to HTML. We can write and understand code more naturally, improving the overall development experience. It connects frontend and server-side programming, allowing for more seamless integration.

- **Rich IntelliSense support**: IntelliSense is a code-completion that helps function in development environments such as Visual Studio. IntelliSense fully supports Tag Helpers, which provides auto-completion, tooltips, and documentation while coding.

  o **Benefit**: This feature dramatically increases productivity by lowering the manual coding and minimizing errors. We receive quick feedback and ideas as they type, allowing them to write more precise and efficient code. It is handy for avoiding typos and learning the available attributes and intended values for each Tag Helper.

- **Reusability and modularity**: Tag Helpers advocate for a modular approach to coding. They can be defined once and utilized across several views. This modularity is critical in the development of components that contain functionality.

  o **Benefit**: reusability results in less repetitious code, and programs are easier to maintain and update. It encourages us to write code that is more ordered and structured. When a change is required, upgrading a single Tag Helper can affect all views where it is used, improving maintainability.

- **Clean razor opinions**: Instead of regular Razor syntax or HTML Helpers, Tag Helpers keeps Razor views more transparent and understandable. Traditional Razor syntax frequently necessitates inline C# code, which can clog the HTML structure.

  o **Benefit**: The C# code is cleanly packed into attributes with Tag Helpers, preserving the clean structure of HTML. This separation of concerns results in easier maintenance and understanding of code because C# code blocks do not disrupt the HTML structure. It is easier for us to explore and update the views, making the codebase more approachable, especially for those with a front-end development background.

The following are key Tag Helpers available in ASP.NET Core:

- **The Form Tag Helper**: Generates HTML form elements. It extends the conventional HTML **<form>** element by introducing new server-side routing and validation properties.

```
1.  <form method="post">
2.
3.      <label asp-for="FullName"></label><br />
4.      <input asp-for="FullName" /><br />
5.      <span asp-validation-for="FullName"></span>
6.
7.      <label asp-for="Email"></label><br />
```

```
8.     <input asp-for="Email" /><br />
9.     <span asp-validation-for="Email"></span>
10.
11.    <button type="submit">Log in</button>
12. </form>
```

- **Link Tag Assist**: To make links, use the Link Tag Helper. It makes it easier to create URLs to action methods within controllers.

```
1. <a asp-action="Details" asp-controller="Home" asp-route-id="@
   Model.Id">View Details</a>
```

- **Custom Tag Helpers**: The Grid Tag Helper is not an ASP.NET Core Razor Pages or MVC built-in feature, but you can develop custom Tag Helpers to simulate a grid-like structure. The following is an example of how to create a simple custom Grid Tag Helper in ASP.NET Core. This example illustrates how you could begin developing your own Tag Helper:

```
1. using Microsoft.AspNetCore.Razor.TagHelpers;
2. using System.Text;
3.
4. [HtmlTargetElement("grid")]
5. public class GridTagHelper : TagHelper
6. {
7.     public IEnumerable<dynamic> Items { get; set; }
8.     public string CssClass { get; set; }
9.
10.    public override void Process(TagHelperContext context,
    TagHelperOutput output)
11.    {
12.        output.TagName = "div"; // Replacing <grid> with <div>
13.        output.Attributes.SetAttribute("class", CssClass);
14.
15.        var content = new StringBuilder();
16.        content.Append("<table>");
17.
18.        // Assuming each item in Items is an object with
    properties
19.        foreach (var item in Items)
20.        {
21.            content.Append("<tr>");
22.            foreach (var prop in item.GetType().GetProperties())
23.            {
24.                content.Append($"<td>{prop.GetValue(item)}
```

```
                     </td>");
25.                  }
26.                  content.Append("</tr>");
27.          }
28.
29.          content.Append("</table>");
30.          output.Content.SetHtmlContent(content.ToString());
31.      }
32. }
```

o Register the Custom Tag Helper like follows:

```
1.  @addTagHelper *, [YourAssemblyName]
```

In your **_ViewImports.cshtml** file, add a directive to include your custom Tag Helper.

Replace **[YourAssemblyName]** with the name of your project or assembly where the Grid Tag Helper is defined.

o Using the Grid Tag Helper in a Razor Page, now you use can use the grid like this:

```
1.  <grid items="@Model.YourDataList" css-class="your-css-
    class">
2.  </grid>
```

Items are the collection you want to display in the grid, and CSS-class is a CSS class that can be used to decorate the grid.

To summarize, Tag Helpers in ASP.NET Core Razor Pages improve the development experience by providing a syntax that blends well with standard HTML, robust IntelliSense support for efficient coding, promoting code modularity and reusability, and maintaining cleaner and more readable Razor views. These advantages add up to a more efficient, maintainable, and developer-friendly environment for web application development.

Razor syntax and its usage in Razor Pages

Razor is a markup syntax that allows server-side code to be included in web pages written in C#. This syntax is elegant and succinct, intending to reduce the code required for complicated tasks. In ASP.NET Core apps, it is primarily used in Razor Pages and MVC views.

```
1.  <p>@DateTime.Now.ToString()</p>
```

Razor renders the current date and time within a paragraph tag in this snippet.

Let us go deeper into the Razor syntax features that considerably improve the building of web apps in ASP.NET using C#.

Features of Razor syntax

Razor syntax in C# is a versatile and robust web development tool that effortlessly integrates server-side functionality with HTML. Code expressions for inserting dynamic information, code blocks for sophisticated logic, layouts for consistent UI, partial views for modularity, and Tag Helpers for efficient HTML creation are among the features available. These components form a solid foundation for creating efficient and attractive web applications.

- **Expressions in code**: Razor's code expressions are an essential feature that allows C# code to be embedded within HTML markup. This enables dynamically inserting values into the HTML rendered to the client. This is how they work:

  The **@** sign is used to insert a C# expression into HTML. For instance, **@DateTime**. The current date and time would now be inserted into the HTML.

  Code expressions are widely used to display data from variables, results from function calls, or to perform simple logic directly within HTML.

  - **HTML encoding**: To guard against XSS threats, Razor automatically HTML encodes expressions. It means that special characters like and **>** are shown correctly.

- **Code sections**: Razor code blocks enable more complicated C# functionality to be expressed within a Razor file. These blocks are contained within @...

  They are used to declare variables, write loops, conditionals, and other C# logic that may alter the HTML output.

  Variables and functions specified within a code block can be accessed from the same view or page.

  Control flow: Code blocks are excellent for managing the flow of HTML markup generation, such as dynamically producing a list or table based on data.

- **Designs**: Layouts are a valuable feature in Razor that allows you to create consistent and reusable view layouts.

  A layout often includes the typical HTML structure (headers, footers, and navigation bars) shared across multiple pages.

  - **Usage**: A view can define its layout, and the Razor engine will render the view within it, ensuring a consistent look across several pages.

  - **Sections**: Razor layouts support the creation of sections, which allow individual views to put content into specific portions of the layout.

- **Partial perspectives**: In Razor, partial views are analogous to components that can be reused across several views.

  They serve the purpose of dividing complex views into smaller, more manageable, and reusable components.

  o **Integration**: Using particular Razor syntax, such as **@Html**, a partial view can be rendered within another view.**Partial("PartialViewName")**.

  o **Use cases**: Excellent for reusable form components, headers, footers, and UI elements.

- **Tag Helpers**: Tag Helpers are an important Razor feature that improves the production and rendering of HTML elements.

  They enable server-side programming to participate in creating and rendering HTML components using a natural, HTML-like syntax.

  We can customize Tag Helpers to encapsulate reusable UI logic.

  Examples include built-in Tag Helpers for forms (**<form>**), links (**<a>**), and more, allowing for a smooth connection with server-side functionality.

  By combining these capabilities, Razor syntax provides a productive environment for generating dynamic, data-driven web pages in ASP.NET applications. It effortlessly bridges the gap between HTML and C#, allowing us to create rich and interactive online interfaces quickly.

  The sample Razor file below demonstrates these features. We will use a fictional example of a simple web page displaying a product list. This example will showcase code expressions, code blocks, layouts, partial views, and Tag Helpers.

```
1.  @* Layouts: Using a shared layout for a
    consistent look and feel *@
2.  @layout "_Layout"
3.
4.  @* Code Blocks: Declaring a variable and a simple logic *@
5.  @{
6.      var productList = new List<string> { "Apple", "Banana",
    "Cherry" };
7.  }
8.
9.  @* Main content area *@
10. <div>
11.     <h2>Our Products</h2>
12.
13.     @* Code Expressions: Looping through the products and
        displaying them *@
```

```
14.     <ul>
15.     @foreach(var product in productList)
16.     {
17.         <li>@product</li> @* Displaying each product in the
    list *@
18.     }
19.     </ul>
20.
21.     @* Partial Views: Including a partial view for a common
    component, like a footer *@
22.     @Html.Partial(«_Footer»)
23.
24.     @* Tag Helpers: Using a form tag helper for a simple search
    form *@
25.     <form asp-action="Search" method="post">
26.         <input asp-for="SearchTerm" />
27.         <button type="submit">Search</button>
28.     </form>
29. </div>
```

- **Layouts**: **@layout** _Layout specifies the layout for this view. The **_Layout** file would generally contain the HTML structure shared across pages, such as headers, footers, and navigation.

- **Code blocks**: **@...** is a C# code block. In this case, **productList** is a list of strings initialized with some values. If necessary, this block can contain more complicated logic.

- **Code expressions**: A foreach loop is utilized within the **<ul>** to iterate across **productList**. Each product name is enclosed in a **<li>** tag. The **@product** tag is an example of C# code embedded into HTML.

  @Html.Partial("_Footer") contains a partial view named **_Footer**. This partial view may include shared material, such as a footer area utilized on multiple pages.

  Form Tag Helpers: An example of a form tag helper is the **<form asp-action="Search" method="post">**. It makes HTML forms and their elements easier to create. The **asp-action** tag helper changes the form's action property to the URL of the search action method.

This sample captures the core of ASP.NET Razor syntax and demonstrates how it neatly integrates C# code with HTML to generate dynamic web pages. Each feature is critical to increasing efficiency and ensuring clean, maintainable code.

Razor Pages key features for programming model

Compared to the standard MVC paradigm, Razor Pages, a feature introduced in ASP. NET Core, is a more streamlined and straightforward approach to designing web user interfaces. It is built on Razor, a markup syntax for embedding server-side code into web pages, and it delivers a slew of benefits and capabilities explicitly tailored to web development demands.

In contrast to MVC, which divides an application into models, views, and controllers, Razor Pages are centered on a single Razor Page (**a.cshtml** file). This method simplifies the structure of a web application, particularly in cases when a page is a discrete unit of functionality.

Exploring the razor features:

- **Page template**: Each Razor Page is supported by a Page Model, a C# class file (**.cshtml.cs**) containing the server-side logic.

  This Page Model handles the page's data and actions, resulting in a clear separation of concerns. It is similar to combining a controller with a view model for a given page.

  The Page Model includes methods such as **OnGet** to handle initial page load and **OnPost** to handle form submissions.

- **Request processing**: Each page in Razor Pages handles its requests, removing the need for a single controller like in MVC.

  Since everything connected to a page (display logic, form processing, etc.) is included within its Page Model, this direct approach streamlines the process of building page-specific logic.

- **Routing**: Razor Pages includes a built-in routing system that is more user-friendly for page-focused apps.

  The routing mechanism maps URLs to Razor Pages in the **Pages** folder by default. For example, **/Products/List** corresponds to **Pages/Products/List.cshtml**.

  This convention-based routing is more straightforward than MVC's controller-action-based routing.

- **Handling forms**: Form submissions are simple in Razor Pages. The Page Model can define methods such as **OnPost** or **OnPostAsync** to manage form submissions.

  This method enables the direct handling of form data and validation logic within the page, reducing the interaction process with user input.

The advantages of using Razor Pages

Razor Pages in ASP.NET Core boosts productivity by emphasizing the user interface and encouraging a well-organized, maintainable codebase. It supports a variety of technologies, such as dependency injection and partial views, and is easier to grasp than MVC, especially for novices. Here are the topics:

- Productivity and simplicity are ideal for developers who prefer to focus on the user interface rather than the intricacies of a complete MVC application.

- Razor Pages promotes a better-ordered and maintainable codebase by aligning related functionalities and their models within the same page.

- It provides flexibility by supporting technologies such as dependency injection, layout pages, partial views, and view components.

- Compared to MVC, Razor Pages has a lower learning curve for novice developers.

Razor Pages is a sophisticated web application framework that provides a page-based approach that simplifies many elements of web development, from routing to form handling. As a result, it is an appealing option for both simple and complex web applications in the ASP.NET Core ecosystem.

Let us build a complete Razor Page with ASP.NET Core to demonstrate its essential capabilities. We will make a simple product listing page as an example.

Products.cshtml (Razor Page), this is the page for products:

```
1.  @page
2.  @model ProductsModel
3.
4.  <h2>Product List</h2>
5.
6.  @if (Model.Products.Any())
7.  {
8.      <ul>
9.          @foreach (var product in Model.Products)
10.         {
11.             <li>@product.Name - @product.Price</li>
12.         }
13.     </ul>
14. }
15. else
16. {
17.     <p>No products available.</p>
18. }
19.
20. <form method="post">
21.     <input type="submit" value="Reload Products" />
22. </form>
```

Products.cshtml.cs (Page Model), this is the page for products model:

```
1.  using Microsoft.AspNetCore.Mvc.RazorPages;
2.
3.  public class Product
4.  {
5.      public string Name { get; set; }
6.      public decimal Price { get; set; }
7.  }
8.
9.  public class ProductsModel : PageModel
10. {
11.     public List<Product> Products { get; private set; } = new
    List<Product>();
12.
13.     public void OnGet()
14.     {
15.         // Initialize with some data for demonstration purposes
16.         Products.Add(new Product { Name = "Apple", Price = 1.99M });
17.         Products.Add(new Product { Name = "Banana", Price = 0.99M });
18.     }
19.
20.     public void OnPost()
21.     {
22.         // Reload or refresh the product list could be fetched from
    a database
23.         Products.Add(new Product { Name = "Cherry", Price = 2.99M });
24.     }
25. }
```

Explanation of the Razor Page's key features

Following are the key points of each feature:

- **Products.cshtml**: The **@page** directive turns this file into a Razor Page.

  This page is linked to its Page Model (**Products.cshtml.cs**) via **@model ProductsModel**.

  The product list is displayed using HTML markup combined with Razor syntax.

  A product reloading form displaying a basic POST request.

- **Products.cshtml.cs**: **PageModel**, the root class for Razor Pages, is inherited.

  Product property used to store product details.

The `OnGet()` method initializes data when the page is first requested.

The `OnPost()` method handles form submissions (POST requests) to reload or refresh the product list.

- **Routing**: This page is sent to the `/Products` URL by default.

  Unless custom routes are wanted, no explicit routing setting is required.

- **Handling Forms**: A POST request is generated using the form on the Razor Page.

  The Page Model's `OnPost()` method reacts to this request, exhibiting direct form processing within the page.

This sample exemplifies Razor Pages' more straightforward approach. It shows how pages handle their logic and data, resulting in a more ordered and intuitive structure. This is particularly useful in circumstances where pages represent distinct functionality. As a result, Razor Pages is a robust and user-friendly framework for small and sophisticated online applications.

Best practices

Adhering to best practices when utilizing Razor syntax and Razor Pages in ASP.NET Core development will improve our web applications' maintainability, readability, and general quality. Here are some primary best practices explained:

- **The minimal logic principle**: Razor syntax is intended to embed C# code in HTML to display data. It is not designed to handle complicated business logic.
  - **Importance**: Keeping server-side code to a minimum within Razor files keeps the pages tidy and focused on display. Razor files with complex logic can be challenging to comprehend, maintain, and test.
  - **Implementation**: Any sophisticated logic should be separated into independent services or layers of business logic. Razor files should only contain the bare minimum of logic required for presentation, such as looping through a collection or basic conditional expressions.

- **Use Tag Helpers principle**: Tag Helpers allow server-side C# code to assist in producing and rendering HTML components, resulting in cleaner and more intuitive HTML.
  - Tag Helpers remove the complex, explicit syntax frequently required for HTML creation. They make the markup more readable and maintainable by closely approximating conventional HTML.
  - Use built-in Tag Helpers for typical activities like constructing forms (`<form>`), producing links (`<a asp-action="...">`), and so on. Custom Tag Helpers can also be created for reusable UI logic relevant to your application.

- **Make use of partial views and layouts**: Partial views and layouts reuse HTML structures and keep the application looking consistent.
    - **Importance**: They help to avoid repetition and make the application DRY. It is also easy to keep the UI consistent.
    - Use layouts for standard page elements such as headers, footers, and navigation bars.
    - Use partial views for reusable components such as widgets or sections on multiple pages.
- **Testability principle**: When business logic is separated from UI logic, an application's testability increases.
    - **Importance**: Testability ensures software quality and reliability. Business logic-heavy Razor files are more difficult to test.
    - **Implementation**: Maintain the Razor Pages or Views' focus on UI logic and implement business logic in distinct classes or services that can be tested separately using unit testing tools.

A broad perspective

Razor syntax and Razor Pages provide a robust and efficient framework for creating dynamic web pages in ASP.NET. By adhering to these best practices, we can create functional, user-friendly, clean, maintainable, and easily testable apps. It results in higher-quality software and shorter development cycles.

Let us create a simple ASP.NET Core application that lists products. This example will include a Razor Page for displaying products, a Page Model for handling logic, Tag Helpers, Partial Views, and Layouts for a consistent UI, and a service class to handle business logic.

- **Pages/Products/Index.cshtml**: Razor Page for displaying products.
- **Pages/Products/Index.cshtml.cs**: Page Model for the Products page.
- **Services/IProductService.cs**: Interface for product service.
- **Services/ProductService.cs**: Implementation of the product service.
- **Pages/Shared/_Layout.cshtml**: Common layout for the application.
- **Pages/Shared/_ProductListPartial.cshtml**: Partial view for displaying product list.
- **Sample codes**:
    - `IProductService.cs`—service interface, this is the product interface:

```
1. public interface IProductService
2. {
3.     IEnumerable<string> GetProductNames();
4. }
```

o **ProductService.cs**—service implementation:

```
1. public class ProductService : IProductService
2. {
3.     public IEnumerable<string> GetProductNames()
4.     {
5.         // Here, we'd generally interact with a database
6.         return new[] { "Apple", "Banana", "Cherry" };
7.     }
8. }
```

o **Index.cshtml**—Razor Page:

```
1. @page
2. @model IndexModel
3.
4. @{
5.     ViewData[«Title»] = «Product List»;
6. }
7.
8. <h2>Product List</h2>
9.
10.<partial name="_ProductListPartial" model="Model.
   ProductNames" />
11.
12.<form asp-page="Index" method="post">
13.    <input type="submit" value="Refresh List" />
14.</form>
```

o **Index.cshtml.cs**—Page Model:

```
1. public class IndexModel : PageModel
2. {
3.     private readonly IProductService _productService;
4.
5.     public IndexModel(IProductService productService)
6.     {
7.         _productService = productService;
8.     }
9.
10.    public IEnumerable<string> ProductNames { get;
   private set; }
11.
12.    public void OnGet()
13.    {
```

```
14.        ProductNames = _productService.GetProductNames();
15.    }
16.
17.    public void OnPost()
18.    {
19.        ProductNames = _productService.GetProductNames();
20.        // Additional logic for post request
21.    }
22. }
```

- o **_ProductListPartial.cshtml**—Partial view:

```
1. @model IEnumerable<string>
2.
3. <ul>
4. @foreach (var productName in Model)
5. {
6.     <li>@productName</li>
7. }
8. </ul>
```

- **Explanation of Razor minimal logic**: **Index.cshtml** has merely markup and minimal logic for presenting data. The **ProductService** handles the sophisticated logic.

  - o **Tag Helpers**: Used in the form element of **Index.cshtml** to produce clean and legible HTML.

  - o **Partial views and layouts**: The partial view **_ProductListPartial.cshtml** is used in **Index.cshtml** to display the product list, promoting DRY principles. The application's typical layout would be defined in **_Layout.cshtml**.

  - o **Testability**: Business logic is separated from UI logic and is housed in **ProductService**. It allows the business logic to be tested independently of the UI.

The sample supplied demonstrates a clean, maintainable, and tested approach to organizing an ASP.NET Core application using Razor Pages by adhering to these best practices. Using service classes for business logic and minimum logic in Razor files contributes to a fast development process and a high-quality application.

Razor syntax and Razor Pages in ASP.NET Core provide strong and efficient web development, combining the convenience of HTML and C# integration with a clean, page-focused approach. We can create robust, maintainable, and user-friendly web applications by following best practices such as keeping logic in Razor files to a minimum, leveraging Tag Helpers for intuitive HTML, utilizing Partial Views and Layouts for DRY code and consistent UI, and ensuring testability through separation of concerns. These approaches improve the development process and produce high-quality, scalable software, making Razor Pages a popular choice for modern web application development in the ASP.NET Core ecosystem.

Creating layouts and partials in Razor Pages

To generate reusable templates and components for their online applications, we can create layouts and partials in Razor Pages, a key component of web development using ASP.NET Core.

- **Purpose of layouts**: To properly understand layouts concerning Razor Pages, it is necessary to acknowledge their function as templates that offer a uniform appearance and behavior throughout a website. A more in-depth explanation is as follows:

  - **Uniform appearance**: Layouts standardize web page structure and appearance. Creating a professional and unified user experience requires this uniformity.

  - **Efficiency in design**: Layouts eliminate the need to repeat HTML structure (headers, footers, etc.) on every page, speeding up development.

  - **Ease of maintenance**: Changes to the site's common design elements in the layout file automatically update all pages that use it.

- **How layouts work**: Centralized common elements are usually in layouts are as follows:

  - **Header**: The header usually has the website's logo, main navigation, and other global components.

  - **Footer**: The footer usually contains copyright, contact, and other general information.

  - **Navigation menus**: Easy accessibility to website parts.

  - **Sidebars**: Optional sidebars provide navigation or information.

- **Layout file definition**: A Razor Pages layout file is usually **_Layout.cshtml**. The HTML and Razor syntax for some common elements are in this file.

- **Content placeholders**: The layout file has **@RenderBody()** Razor method. This technique injects Razor Page content as a placeholder.

  The layout file may contain:
```
1. <html>
2. <head>...</head>
3. <body>
4.    <header>...</header>
5.    <main>
6.       @RenderBody()
```

```
7.        </main>
8.        <footer>...</footer>
9.   </body>
10. </html>
```

- **Page-specific content injection**: Headers and footers are not included in Razor Pages. Instead, focus on that page's unique content.

  The Razor view engine injects this unique content into the layout's **@RenderBody()** method during rendering.

  The browser receives HTML with the Razor Page's layout and unique content.

  Razor Pages layouts provide a foundation for page content. This technique encourages DRY principles to reduce repetition and simplify website management. Knowing and using layouts may construct more efficient, maintainable, and visually consistent web apps.

Creating a layout

Defining a template that will act as the standard framework for various pages in our web application is the first step in creating a layout in Razor Pages.

Here is a step-by-step guide to creating and comprehending a default layout: The default layout is a master page or template that provides the HTML structure and elements shared by several pages in our application. It often contains features such as headers, footers, navigation bars, and other shared components. It enhances reusability and maintainability by allowing you to describe these common parts in a single location rather than repeating the same HTML and Razor code across multiple pages.

- **Naming and location**:
  - **_Layout.cshtml** is the most common name for this file.
  - In ASP.NET, the underscore (_) at the beginning of the file name implies a shared layout or partial view. It aids in distinguishing layout files from standard Razor Pages or MVC views.
  - The file is in the **Pages/Shared** directory for Razor Pages Applications.
  - A Pages folder is used for Razor Pages projects, and each Razor Page is often a combination of a **.cshtml** file for markup and a **.cshtml.cs** file for the Page Model. Layouts and other shared resources are stored in the **Pages/Shared** directory.
  - Storing the layout in a shared directory (**Pages/Shared**) makes it available to all views or pages in the application.
  - Since the layout is centralized, any page or view inside the application can be defined, often using a Razor directive in the page/view file.

- **Working on the application**:

    o **Setting the layout in Pages**: You can specify the layout in individual pages or views using a Razor directive like **@ Layout = "_Layout"**.

    o The program will use the default layout if no layout is specified on a page.

    o **Fallback to default layout**: If the layout is not defined page-by-page, ASP. NET Razor Pages will utilize the shared directory's **_Layout.cshtml**. This feature ensures that our pages have a consistent default structure.

    o In Razor Pages applications, the default layout (**_Layout.cshtml**) is a basic template that offers a uniform look and structure for various web application pages. Its centralized presence in **Pages/Shared** guarantees that it is easily accessible and utilized by all pages, advocating a DRY approach and improving maintainability.

- **Implementing layouts in Razor Pages**:

    o Implementing layouts involves two primary actions, which are specifying which layout to use and passing data to that layout. To specify a layout, a Razor Page includes the directive **@{ Layout = "_Layout"; }**, where **_Layout** refers to the layout file. It tells the Razor engine to render the page content within the designated layout.

    o Additionally, data can be passed from the Razor Page to the layout using **ViewData**. These dynamic properties allow data to be shared between the page and its layout, enabling dynamic content rendering and consistent data usage across different application parts.

    o Here is an example of a layout for a theater ticket seller that entails creating a **_Layout.cshtml** file that establishes the standard structure for our pages. In this situation, you should show the day's main movie at the top and three movies for ticket purchases in the body.

Here is an easy example.

_Layout.cshtml file code:

This file contains placeholders for inserting specific material from individual pages.

```
1. <!DOCTYPE html>
2. <html>
3. <head>
4.     <title>@ViewData["Title"] - Theater Ticket Seller</title>
5.     <!-- Add links to your CSS files and other head elements
   here -->
```

```
6.  </head>
7.  <body>
8.      <header>
9.          <h1>Main Movie of the Day</h1>
10.         <!-- Placeholder for the main movie -->
11.         @RenderSection("MainMovie", required: false)
12.     </header>
13.
14.     <div class="content">
15.         <h2>Available Movies for Tickets</h2>
16.         @RenderBody()
17.     </div>
18.
19.     <footer>
20.         <p>Copyright © @DateTime.Now.Year - Theater Ticket
    Seller</p>
21.     </footer>
22. </body>
23. </html>
```

- **MainMovie.cshtml, file code**: This is an example of a Razor Page that uses the layout and features the day's primary movie. The **@section** directive injects material into the relevant section of the layout.

```
1.  @{
2.      Layout = «_Layout»;
3.      ViewData[«Title»] = «Main Movie»;
4.  }
5.
6.  @section MainMovie {
7.      <h2>@Model.MainMovieTitle</h2>
8.      <!-- Details about the main movie -->
9.  }
```

- **MovieList.cshtml, file code**: This page displays a list of three movies for which tickets are available. It has the same layout as before but populates the main content section.

```
1.  @{
2.      Layout = «_Layout»;
3.      ViewData[«Title»] = «Available Movies»;
4.  }
```

```
5.
6. <div class="movie-list">
7.     @foreach (var movie in Model.AvailableMovies) {
8.         <div class="movie-item">
9.             <h3>@movie.Title</h3>
10.            <!-- Movie details and purchase button -->
11.        </div>
12.    }
13. </div>
```

- Following is the explanation of the rendering:

  o **@RenderSection("MainMovie", required: false)**: This line in the layout allows sites to add material to the `Main Movie` section. If the page lacks this part, the layout will still render correctly (required: false).

  o **@RenderBody()**: The primary content of each page will be rendered here.

    `Model.MainMovieTitle` and `Model.Movies` available: These are several methods for accessing data from the Page Model. Your data model and business logic would determine the actual implementation.

    This sample demonstrates the fundamental structure. You would need to include actual data passing, styling (CSS), and any more logic required by your application.

Understanding Razor Pages partials

Partials are critical in Razor Pages for designing fast and maintainable web applications. Understanding their purpose, benefits, and creation process is critical to adequately incorporating them into your initiatives.

Razor pages partials have some characteristics:

- **Functions of partials**:
  o **Reusable HTML content**: The primary use of partials is to encapsulate reusable HTML content. These sections of our website must be used on several pages, such as headers, footers, navigation bars, or other repetitive information.

  o **Inclusion in multiple pages**: Partials can be included in multiple pages or even within other partials. This inclusion is dynamic and programmatically controllable, providing for a flexible design and layout structure.

- **Benefits of using partials code reusability**:
  o By isolating common page elements into partials, you avoid duplicating HTML and Razor code across multiple pages. This reuse saves time and keeps our codebase cleaner and more organized.

- Maintenance is simplified because you only need to change a standard piece once in the partial view. This change is automatically applied to all pages that utilize the partial, making maintenance and changes much more manageable.

- **Making partial naming conventions**: Partials are often titled with an underscore (for example, **_MyPartial.cshtml**). The underscore indicates that the file is not an independent view but a component of another view. It aids in distinguishing partials from standard Razor Pages.

- **Location**: Partials are typically saved in the **Pages/Shared** directory Razor Pages apps. Still, they can also be placed in specialized folders if they are only relevant to specific portions of the application.

- **Structure of the content**: A partial view's content is identical to standard Razor Pages, except it is usually smaller and focused on a particular functionality or page fragment.

  A partial view includes only the HTML and Razor code required for its intended functionality and excludes layout specifications (such as **@RenderBody()**).

- **Utilization of partials**:

  - **Flexibility**: HTML can be used to render partials statically. Partially or dynamically via **HTML.PartialAsync**.

  - **Data passing**: By passing data to partials via model binding or **ViewData**, you can make them dynamic and adaptive to varied settings.

Razor Page's partials help develop dynamic, reusable, and maintainable online applications. They encapsulate repetitive HTML and Razor code, making it easier to reuse and maintain. Understanding how to generate and use partials efficiently is critical for any developer working with ASP.NET Core Razor Pages.

Using partials in Razor Pages

Partials in Razor Pages are an excellent tool for creating reusable and maintainable web application components. Understanding how to use them correctly can considerably improve efficiency and clarify our code.

Observe the following points:

- **Making a partial static rendering**: We can use the **@Html.Partial("_MyPartial")** method to incorporate a partial in your Razor Page or layout. The supplied partial view is rendered concurrently with the caller view.

  It is simple and is often used when the partial content does not require asynchronous processing.

- **Rendering asynchronously**: `@await` HTML is another option. Partials are rendered asynchronously using `PartialAsync("_MyPartial")`.

  It is convenient when the partial view's rendering includes I/O activities, such as database calls, because it does not interfere with the remainder of the page's rendering.

  Passing data to partials model binding, in which a model object is supplied to the partial view, allows partials to accept data. It is useful when the data shown is complex or heavily typed.

  `@Html.PartialAsync("_MyPartial", myModel)` provides `myModel` to the partial view.

  Passing `ViewData` to partials for less complex data or when a tightly typed model is not required.

  `ViewData` is a dictionary that can store data that the partial view can access. This technology allows for a more flexible, yet less structured, form of data transmission.

Best practices

Following best practices while constructing online applications with Razor Pages is critical, such as keeping layouts simple, generating modular partials, and utilizing a consistent naming strategy. These approaches help speed development, improve maintainability, and ensure scalability. Furthermore, using shared layouts for uniform branding, partials for standard UI components, and dynamically injecting content all contribute to efficient, consistent, and interactive user experiences. These tactics improve the coding process, overall quality, and user engagement of online apps.

- **Maintain simple layouts**: Layouts should not be overcomplicated. Complex layouts can be challenging to manage and comprehend. In general, a straightforward, well-structured layout is ideal.

- **Modular partitions**: Make your partials self-contained and modular. It means they should be self-contained and reusable in diverse situations without alteration.

- **Consistent naming convention**: For our partials (such as the leading underscore). It facilitates the easy identification and management of specific files inside our project.

Typical use cases

Layouts and partials are commonly used in Razor Pages to create shared layouts for consistent branding, develop reusable components such as navigation menus, footers, and forms, and dynamically inject content through partials based on user interactions, enhancing user engagement and interface consistency.

We have a variety of uses, here are a few:

- One typical use case is to design a shared layout that combines branding components consistently across all application pages.

  o Common UI elements such as navigation menus, footers, and forms can be generated as partials and reused across several pages to ensure consistency and reduce redundancy.

  o Partials can also dynamically inject material into pages based on user interactions or other runtime conditions. It improves the application's interactivity and usability.

  o Here is a sample of a CRM that shows the financial operators the billing address and, for call center operators, the delivery address on the page Recent Purchases.

The following are the requirements:

- **Base page (RecentPurchases.cshtml)**: The main Razor page displays recent purchases. It will include partial views based on the user's role.

- **Partial view for financial operators (BillingAddress.cshtml)**: This partial view displays the billing address. It should only be shown to financial operators.

- **Partial view for customer success operators (DeliveryAddress.cshtml)**: This partial view shows the delivery address and is intended for customer success operators.

- **C# model (Purchase.cs)**: A model representing a purchase, including billing and delivery addresses.

- **Role checking**: We will assume the application handles that role checking; for this example, we will use simple conditionals.

We start defining the models in a CRM system with Razor Pages in C#, which entails establishing classes that represent the system's essential entities. A **Purchase** model, for example, may represent each transaction, including details such as the purchase ID, date, billing, and delivery addresses. The address model captures address details such as street, city, and postal code and is utilized in the **Purchase** model to represent billing and delivery locations. Finally, the **User** model depicts persons interacting with the system, as defined by attributes such as their role (e.g., financial operator, customer success operator) and other personal information. These models form the application's backbone, structuring data and allowing interactions between the user interface and the database, maintaining data integrity, and applying business logic. Let us see:

```
1. public class Purchase
2. {
3.     public int Id { get; set; }
4.     public DateTime Date { get; set; }
5.     public Address BillingAddress { get; set; }
```

```
6.      public Address DeliveryAddress { get; set; }
7.      // Other properties like Amount, CustomerId, etc.
8.  }
9.  public class Address
10. {
11.     public string Street { get; set; }
12.     public string City { get; set; }
13.     public string PostalCode { get; set; }
14.     // Additional address details
15. }
16. public class User
17. {
18.     public int Id { get; set; }
19.     public string Name { get; set; }
20.     public string Role { get; set; }
21.     // Other user properties
22. }
```

Create a Razor Page for **Recent Purchases**. Within this page, you will use partial views to display the billing and delivery addresses.

- Code for **RecentPurchases.cshtml**:

```
1.  @page
2.  @model RecentPurchasesModel
3.  <h2>Recent Purchases</h2>
4.
5.  <!-- Other content -->
6.
7.  @if(UserIsFinancialOperator())
8.  {
9.      <!-- Include Partial for Billing Address -->
10.     @Html.Partial("_BillingAddressPartial", Model.Purchases)
11. }
12.
13. @if(UserIsCustomerSuccessOperator())
14. {
15.     <!-- Include Partial for Delivery Address -->
16.     @Html.Partial("_DeliveryAddressPartial", Model.Purchases)
17. }
```

- Code for **_BillingAddressPartial.cshtml**:

```
1.  @model IEnumerable<Purchase>
```

```
2.
3. <h3>Billing Addresses</h3>
4. @foreach(var purchase in Model)
5. {
6.     <p>@purchase.BillingAddress.Street,
   @purchase.BillingAddress.City</p>
7. }
```

- Code for **_DeliveryAddressPartial.cshtml**:

```
1. @model IEnumerable<Purchase>
2.
3. <h3>Delivery Addresses</h3>
4. @foreach(var purchase in Model)
5. {
6.     <p>@purchase.DeliveryAddress.Street,
   @purchase.DeliveryAddress.City</p>
7. }
```

- Code for Page Model **RecentPurchases.cshtml.cs**:

```
1. public class RecentPurchasesModel : PageModel
2. {
3.     public List<Purchase> Purchases { get; set; }
4.
5.     public void OnGet()
6.     {
7.         // Load recent purchases
8.         Purchases = /* Fetch from database or service */;
9.     }
10.
11.    public bool UserIsFinancialOperator()
12.    {
13.        // Implement our logic to determine if the current user
   is a financial operator
14.    }
15.
16.    public bool UserIsCustomerSuccessOperator()
17.    {
18.        // Implement our logic to determine if the current user
   is a customer success operator
19.    }
20. }
```

Following is the explanation:

- **Models (Purchase.cs, Address.cs, User.cs):**

  - **Purchase.cs:** This model represents a purchase transaction. It includes properties like `Id`, `Date`, `BillingAddress`, and `DeliveryAddress`. The `BillingAddress` and `DeliveryAddress` are instances of the `Address` model.

  - **Address.cs:** This model contains address details such as `Street`, `City`, and `PostalCode`. It is used in the `Purchase` model to represent both billing and delivery addresses.

  - **User.cs:** This model represents a user, like an employee or a customer. It includes properties like `Role`, which helps distinguish the type of user (e.g., financial operator, customer success operator).

- **Razor Pages:**

  - **RecentPurchases.cshtml:** This is the principal Razor Page showing recent purchases. It conditionally includes partial views based on the user's role. If the user is a financial operator, it shows billing addresses; if a customer success operator, it shows delivery addresses.

  - **_BillingAddressPartial.cshtml:** A partial view that displays billing addresses for each purchase.

  - **_DeliveryAddressPartial.cshtml:** A partial view showing delivery addresses for each purchase.

- **Page Model: RecentPurchasesModel:** The Page Model for `RecentPurchases.cshtml`, is responsible for loading recent purchases and includes methods to check the user's role (`UserIsFinancialOperator`, `UserIsCustomerSuccessOperator`).

Finally, this example shows how Razor Pages can use partials in a C# CRM system. By using models like `Purchase`, `Address`, and `User` and Razor Pages like `RecentPurchases.cshtml` and partial views `_BillingAddressPartial.cshtml` and `_DeliveryAddressPartial.cshtml`, the example shows how partial views can modularize and reuse webpage sections. In the `Recent Purchases` tab, these partials display billing addresses for finance operators and delivery addresses for customer success operators. This method improves code cleanliness, maintainability, and scalability in modern web development utilizing ASP.NET Core's Razor Pages.

In conclusion, partials in Razor Pages are an essential tool for web developers since they allow them to create reusable and maintainable components. You may design more efficient, clean, and scalable web applications by learning to render and send data to parties and following best practices. These components not only make creation and maintenance easier, but they also improve the user experience by presenting content consistently and dynamically.

Building a CRUD operation using Razor Pages

This section covers developing a CRUD activity using Razor Pages in .NET and C#. From project environment setup and data model definition to CRUD operation implementation and security, this book walks you through it. This thorough tutorial provides insights and practical examples to help you construct a solid and efficient web application, whether a newbie or an experienced developer learning .NET with Razor Pages.

1. **Setting up the project**:
   a. Create a new project, the ASP.NET Core 8 Web Application, in Visual Studio.
   b. Choose the **Web Application** template, which includes Razor Pages.
   c. Ensure you have the necessary NuGet packages for EF Core if you use a database.

2. **Creating the data model**: Define the data model in a C# class. This model represents the data structure in our database.

```
1. public class Item
2. {
3.     public int Id { get; set; }
4.     public string Name { get; set; }
5.     // Other properties
6. }
7.
```

   a. Create a **DbContext** class for EF Core to manage database operations.

```
1. public class ApplicationDbContext : DbContext
2. {
3.     public ApplicationDbContext(DbContextOptions<
        ApplicationDbContext> options)
4.             : base(options)
5.     {
6.     }
7.
8.     public DbSet<Item> Items { get; set; }
9. }
```

3. **Setting up the database**:
   a. Configure the database connection in **appsettings.json**.
   b. Use EF Core migrations to create the database schema.

4. **Creating Razor Pages**: Create Razor Pages for each CRUD operation. Typically, it would help if you had pages for listing items (Read), creating a new item (Create), editing an existing item (Update), and deleting an item (Delete).

5. **Implementing create operation**: In the `Create.cshtml.cs` file, create a method to handle the POST request, which saves the new item to the database.

```
1. public async Task<IActionResult> OnPostAsync()
2. {
3.     if (!ModelState.IsValid)
4.     {
5.         return Page();
6.     }
7.
8.     _context.Items.Add(Item);
9.     await _context.SaveChangesAsync();
10.
11.     return RedirectToPage("./Index");
12. }
```

The corresponding Razor Page **Create.cshtml** contains the HTML form for item submission.

6. The `Index.cshtml.cs` file fetches the items from the database.

```
1. public IList<Item> Items { get;set; }
2.
3. public async Task OnGetAsync()
4. {
5.     Items = await _context.Items.ToListAsync();
6. }
```

Index.cshtml displays these items in a list or table.

7. **Implementing update operation**: Similar to create but fetches the existing item and updates its properties before saving.

```
1. public async Task<IActionResult> OnPostAsync(int id)
2. {
3.     var itemToUpdate = await _context.Items.FindAsync(id);
4.
5.     if (itemToUpdate == null)
6.     {
7.         return NotFound();
8.     }
9.
```

```
10.     if (await TryUpdateModelAsync<Item>(
11.         itemToUpdate,
12.         "item",   // Prefix for form value.
13.         i => i.Name, i => i.OtherProperty))
14.     {
15.         await _context.SaveChangesAsync();
16.         return RedirectToPage("./Index");
17.     }
18.
19.     return Page();
20. }
```

8. **Implementing delete operation**: Retrieves the item to be deleted and removes it from the database.

```
1. public async Task<IActionResult> OnPostDeleteAsync(int id)
2. {
3.     var item = await _context.Items.FindAsync(id);
4.
5.     if (item != null)
6.     {
7.         _context.Items.Remove(item);
8.         await _context.SaveChangesAsync();
9.     }
10.
11.     return RedirectToPage("./Index");
12. }
```

Building a CRUD application with Razor Pages in .NET using C# requires knowledge of ASP.NET Core, Razor Pages, EF Core, and C#. Creating a secure and functional app requires each step. This tutorial gives a foundation, but for advanced situations, explore each topic.

Conclusion

As we get to the end of this chapter, we reflect on our extensive journey through Razor Pages in ASP.NET Core, a paradigm changes in web development that favors a page-based approach. We looked into combining HTML and C# to create dynamic web pages capable of advanced user interactions and data processing. The construction and execution of Razor Pages using tools such as the dotnet command and Visual Studio, as well as understanding the lifecycle within the ASP.NET Core, are among the key takeaways. We have also examined how forms are created and managed in Razor Pages, emphasizing the importance of data annotations, model binding, and validation in ensuring robust and secure user inputs. The chapter has taught you the fundamentals of Razor Pages, from creation to rendering, laying the groundwork for constructing rich, interactive online apps in ASP.NET Core.

In the next chapter, we will look into developing the MVC pattern.

Exercise

Choose true or false for the following questions:

1. Razor Pages is a feature of ASP.NET Core that simplifies web page development.

2. Razor Pages uses the MVC architecture to separate:
   a. The user interface
   b. The business logic

3. Each Razor Page has two parts: a .cshtml file for the HTML markup and a .cshtml. cs file for the C# code.

4. The @page directive at the top of a Razor Page indicates that the file is a Razor Page and specifies the URL pattern for the page.

5. The Page Model class contains the properties and methods that handle the page's events and data processing.

6. The OnGet method is executed when a page is requested using the HTTP GET method, which is typically used to display data.

7. The OnPost method is executed when a page is requested using the HTTP POST method to submit data.

8. The asp-for tag helper binds an input element to a model property.

9. The asp-validation-for tag helper displays validation messages for a model property.

10. Data annotations are attributes applied to model properties to define how data should be validated.

11. The ModelState property represents the state of the model binding and validation process.

12. Client-side validation is performed on the server using C# code.

13. Server-side validation is performed on the user's browser using JavaScript code.

14. Razor syntax is a combination of HTML and C# code used to generate HTML content dynamically.

15. The Razor engine renders HTML content by merging the Razor Page (.cshtml file) with data from the Page Model.

16. Routing in Razor Pages is based on the page's location in the project's directory structure.

17. The [BindProperty] attribute binds a model to a form, allowing form data to be automatically mapped to model properties.

18. The [EmailAddress] attribute checks that a property value is in the correct email format.

19. The [StringLength] attribute is used to specify a string's maximum and minimum length.

20. The [Required] attribute is used to make sure a property has a value.

Answers

1. True
2. False
3. True
4. True
5. True
6. True
7. True
8. True
9. True
10. True
11. True
12. False
13. False
14. True
15. True
16. True
17. True
18. True
19. True
20. True

Join our book's Discord space

Join the book's Discord Workspace for Latest updates, Offers, Tech happenings around the world, New Release and Sessions with the Authors:

https://discord.bpbonline.com

CHAPTER 13
Website Development Using MVC Pattern

Introduction

The MVC structure is introduced in this chapter of ASP.NET Core, a robust framework for constructing modern web applications. We will learn how to design Controllers and Views, utilize MVC routing, work with data using EF Core, implement form validation, and use ViewModel in MVC. By the end of this chapter, we will have a basic understanding of the MVC architecture and how to apply it effectively in our web development projects.

Structure

This chapter covers the following topics:

- Introduction to the MVC pattern in ASP.NET Core
- Creating Controllers and Views in MVC
- Understanding MVC routing
- Working with data in MVC
- Implementing form validation in MVC
- Understanding ViewModel in MVC
- Building a CRUD operation using MVC
- Using Entity Framework Core with MVC

- Producing and consuming APIs using MVC
- Testing in MVC applications

Objectives

In this chapter, we will learn how to leverage the MVC pattern in ASP.NET Core to create dynamic and robust web apps. We will examine the Model, View, and Controller components' roles and interactions and how they enable us to separate data, presentation, and logic concerns. We will also see how to use EF Core, an object-relational mapper, to simplify data access and manipulation. In addition, we will go over form validation, ViewModels, CRUD operations, and MVC API development. By the end of this chapter, we will have a basic understanding of the MVC framework and its benefits for web development.

Introduction to the MVC pattern in ASP.NET Core

The MVC pattern is a software engineering design paradigm that divides an application into three interconnected components: the Model, the View, and the Controller. This distinction allows for more effective code management, modular development, and a clear separation of concerns, which is helpful in web application development.

ASP.NET Core is a cross-platform, open-source framework for developing modern, cloud-enabled, and internet-connected apps. MVC is built as a framework in ASP.NET Core to create dynamic websites efficiently with a clean separation of concerns. The design aims for it to function with other ASP.NET Core capabilities, including EF Core for data access and identity for authentication.

The following highlights the role of MVC and the evolution of ASP.NET Core in modern web development:

- **MVC history with Microsoft and open-source—early days**: MVC as a concept extends back to the 1970s, but Microsoft's acceptance of MVC for online development occurred much later, with the release of ASP.NET MVC in 2009. ASP.NET MVC represented a substantial departure from the previous web forms method, providing a more structured and testable framework for developing web applications.

- **Move to ASP.NET Core**: Microsoft introduced ASP.NET Core in 2016 in response to the growth of the .NET and the demand for more modular and cross-platform solutions. ASP.NET Core was a complete overhaul of the ASP.NET framework aimed to be lighter, more flexible, and cloud-optimized.

- **Open-sourcing**: The open-sourcing of .NET Core, including ASP.NET Core, was a watershed moment in Microsoft's development journey. This change enabled community contributions, enhancing the framework's robustness and adaptability to the changing needs of modern web development.

Following are the benefits of using MVC in ASP.NET Core:

- **Clean architecture**: MVC allows for a clean separation of responsibilities by splitting an application into three layers: Model (business logic), View (UI logic), and Controller (input logic), making application management and maintenance much more accessible.

- **Testability**: Separation of concerns improves testability. The MVC architecture allows for independent component testing, resulting in more robust applications.

- **Asynchronous programming support**: ASP.NET Core MVC supports asynchronous programming techniques, essential for designing high-performance web applications.

- **Strong routing**: ASP.NET Core MVC includes a robust and flexible routing capability that allows developers to design and change human-friendly and search engine-friendly URLs.

- **Extensibility and scalability**: ASP.NET Core MVC is modular, highly expandable, and scalable. We can plug in additional components or replace existing ones with bespoke implementations to address unique requirements.

- **Cross-platform**: ASP.NET Core MVC apps can run on Windows, Linux, and macOS, allowing for a broader range of deployment platforms.

- **Community and ecosystem**: Because it is open-source and supported by Microsoft, ASP.NET Core MVC has a huge community and a rich ecosystem of tools, libraries, and resources.

It supports and interacts well with modern client-side frameworks such as Angular, React, and Vue.js, enabling the building of sophisticated, dynamic user interfaces.

Finally, ASP.NET Core MVC provides a robust framework for developing web apps. Its use of the MVC paradigm and the latest ASP.NET Core features makes it a fantastic alternative for us as developers looking to create scalable, maintainable, and tested online applications.

Creating Controllers and Views in MVC

Creating Controllers and Views in a MVC framework, particularly in the context of ASP.NET Core, necessitates a thorough grasp of their roles and interactions. This understanding is essential for creating an n-tier architecture, a frequent strategy used in complicated programs to promote scalability and maintainability.

MVC Controllers

Controllers are middlemen between the MVC architecture's user interface (Views) and the data (Model). A controller in ASP.NET Core is a class that extends the Controller introductory class. Controllers are primarily responsible for interpreting user inputs sent via HTTP requests, handling these inputs by executing appropriate business logic (often located in a separate business layer or service), and then selecting and populating Views with data to present a response to the user. Routing is used in this procedure to map incoming requests to controller actions based on URL patterns.

MVC Views

Views, on the other hand, are in charge of displaying the user interface. We commonly use the Razor View engine in ASP.NET Core to create Views, embedding C# code within HTML. The primary function of the view is to render the HTML content displayed in the user's browser. It gets data from the Controller to build the final HTML. In MVC, it Views solely present data and does not engage in business logic or data modification, adhering to the separation of concerns approach.

Controllers and Views interaction

The MVC framework relies heavily on the interaction between Controllers and Views. Controllers perform business logic and then pass the necessary data to Views. Data transport typically involves Models or ViewModels. When the Controller completes the request, it chooses a specific View to render the response. The View then generates the HTML content that is returned to the user using the data provided by the Controller.

MVC and n-tier architecture

Incorporating an n-tier design into an MVC application entails splitting the application into multiple levels, each with its responsibilities. A display layer often includes Views and sections of Controllers, while a **business logic layer** (**BLL**) and a **data access layer** (**DAL**) complement the architecture. The BLL includes the central business rules and logic and communicates with the DAL for data persistence requirements. The presentation layer's controllers communicate with the BLL to process data and then transfer it to the views for display.

This method has numerous advantages. It improves scalability by allowing each layer to be scaled separately based on demand. It also increases maintainability because changes in one layer, such as changing the data storage mechanism or updating business rules, have little effect on the other layers. This division of responsibilities guarantees that the application is more straightforward and adaptable to future developments.

ASP.NET Core MVC with n-tier implementation

N-tier architecture is a software development design approach that divides an application into discrete, logical tiers, each dedicated to a different component of the application's operation. This typically contains a presentation layer (which handles user interface and interaction), a business logic layer (which processes data and applies business rules), and a data access layer (which interacts with databases or other storage systems). This modular architecture improves maintainability, scalability, and flexibility because each layer runs independently and can be changed or scaled without affecting the others. It also allows for improved organization and responsibility allocation, making complicated applications more straightforward to manage, develop, and extend.

Implementing MVC with an n-tier architecture in an ASP.NET Core application entails developing controllers with defined routes and methods to handle various requests. These controllers communicate with the BLL to carry out business logic. For any data processing, the BLL communicates with the DAL. Views in the application are entirely responsible for displaying the user interface rendering HTML using data provided by the controllers.

Sample: Basic Razor MVC project

Open the command prompt; create the directory you would like to create the project and run the dotnet command, where **MyRazorMvcApp** is the name you would like to give to the project:

1. `dotnet new mvc -n MyRazorMvcApp`

Like the Razor Pages, this hierarchical approach to application architecture provides for a clear separation of responsibilities, with each layer having a separate duty, making the program more controllable, scalable, and maintainable in the long term.

Figure 13.1 shows the structure of the project:

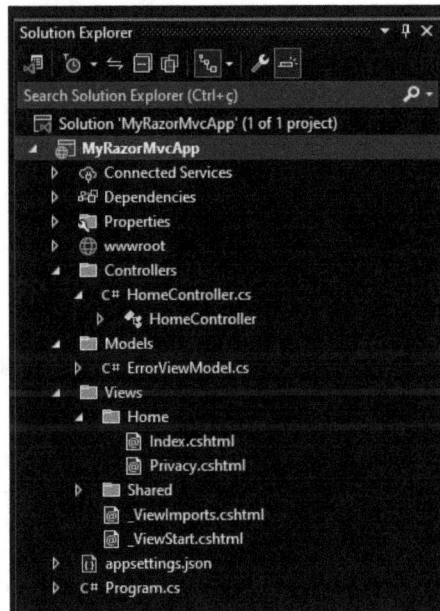

Figure 13.1: Solution Explorer in Visual Studio

Understanding MVC routing

MVC routing in ASP.NET Core is an essential part of web application development that we frequently use to handle requests efficiently. The routing idea in ASP.NET Core's MVC architecture is mapping incoming browser requests to particular controller actions. It is critical for designing SEO-friendly and user-friendly URLs since it defines how URLs map to specific action methods in our controllers.

MVC routing has a long history, dating back to the early versions of ASP.NET and evolving dramatically over time. Routing was initially stricter and less flexible, but the introduction of ASP.NET Core has made it more versatile and powerful. The application requirement to be more modular, testable, and manageable has spurred this evolution.

Using MVC routing in ASP.NET Core has various advantages. The MVC routing feature in ASP.NET Core provides a multitude of advantages that improve the construction of web applications, including the following:

- **Clean and readable URLs**: It aids in creating clear and user-friendly URLs that are easy to read and excellent for SEO.

- **Flexibility**: We can build routes in various ways, including describing patterns the routing engine should match against incoming requests.

- **Separation of concerns**: It follows the MVC paradigm, with a distinct separation of the application logic, data, and presentation. This division helps to organize and manage our application.

- **Control over URL structure**: We can completely control and customize the URL structure to meet our application's requirements.

- **Enhanced testability**: Testing becomes more simplified due to the clear separation of concerns and the ability to fake routing data.

The ideal way to integrate MVC routing into other ASP.NET Core projects.

Following these essential strategies will ensure that your ASP.NET Core applications have the best possible performance and clarity, allowing you to incorporate MVC routing properly:

- **Maintain consistency**: To ensure clarity in routing, ensure consistent naming standards across controllers and actions.

- **Use attribute routing**: Directly enables more exact route management on controllers and actions, making routes more straightforward to comprehend and manage.

- **Centralize route definitions**: If possible, centralize the route definitions in a single location to make managing and reviewing the routing system easier.

- **Thoroughly test routings**: Always guarantee that all routes are thoroughly tested, especially in complicated applications with several routes.

- **Optimize for performance**: Consider how routing affects application performance and optimize routes for efficiency.

- **Adapt to project demands**: Tailor the routing configuration to the project's demands, considering project size, complexity, and particular URL patterns.

For a hospital system, let us create a sample text schema for routing in an ASP.NET Core application. This requires structuring routes to handle various departments and functionalities. Consider the possibility that we have departments such as Emergency, Cardiology, Neurology, Pediatrics, and General Medicine, in addition to services such as Appointments, Patient Records, and Billing.

Routing schema for a hospital system:

```
1. HomeController
/ or /home: Home page of the hospital system
/home/about: About the hospital
/home/contact: Contact information

2. EmergencyController
/emergency: Emergency department home
/emergency/services: List of emergency services
/emergency/contact: Emergency contact information

3. CardiologyController
/cardiology: Cardiology department home
/cardiology/doctors: List of cardiologists
/cardiology/appointments: Making appointments in cardiology

4. NeurologyController
/neurology: Neurology department home
/neurology/doctors: List of neurologists
/neurology/research: Information on neurology research

5. PediatricsController
/pediatrics: Pediatrics department home
/pediatrics/activities: Childcare activities and schedules
/pediatrics/doctors: List of pediatricians

6. GeneralMedicineController
/general-medicine: General medicine department home
/general-medicine/services: Services offered in general medicine
/general-medicine/appointments: Appointment scheduling

7. AppointmentController
```

```
/appointments: Main appointment page
/appointments/book: Booking an appointment
/appointments/cancel: Canceling an appointment
/appointments/reschedule: Rescheduling an appointment

8. PatientRecordController
/patient-records: Accessing patient records
/patient-records/view/{patientId}: Viewing specific patient record
/patient-records/update/{patientId}: Updating patient records

9. BillingController
/billing: Billing and payment information
/billing/pay: Payment processing
/billing/history: Billing history

10. AdminController
/admin: Administrative controls
/admin/department-management: Management of hospital departments
/admin/staff-management: Staff management interface
```

This schema helps navigate a hospital's services and departments clearly and organizedly. Each controller handles the routing for a particular department or capability, ensuring that the application is well-organized and straightforward for us as developers and users. For an ASP.NET Core MVC application, the implementation of these routes would need the creation of controllers and actions that correspond to each route, as well as the possible utilization of attribute routing, which would result in code that is more understandable and easier to maintain.

Working with data in MVC

The MVC architecture contributes to the robustness and adaptability of ASP.NET Core, making it a preferred framework in web development. This architecture makes defining the boundaries between different concerns easier and makes interacting with data more streamlined. One of the most critical aspects of this is the EF Core. This chapter has a section, especially for EF Core, an **ORM** that allows us to deal with database entities by utilizing C# objects. This process significantly simplifies data access. This article will break down the technique of interacting with data in ASP.NET Core MVC into many complexities. In this detailed discussion, we will go into the core aspects of the MVC architecture, including the role and configuration of DbContext within the framework of EF Core.

Additionally, we will present a real C# example to explain these principles. Our primary focus will be on the modifications required in the **Program.cs** file to incorporate the **DbContext** component, an essential step in enabling data operations within an ASP.NET Core application.

The MVC architecture is essential in defining the structure and behavior of applications in ASP.NET Core. The Model serves a dual purpose in this system, comprising data representation and business logic. Models in ASP.NET Core are typically implemented as **Plain Old CLR Objects (POCO)** classes. These classes are simple in design, with characteristics corresponding to a database table's columns.

In contrast, a **Data Transfer Object (DTO)** performs a different function. While models are directly tied to database structure and may contain business logic, DTOs are simpler objects used purely for data transfer across layers or processes and do not contain any business logic. DTOs are especially useful in establishing a clear separation between the internal database model and the data presented to or received from the client, thereby improving data security, lowering the likelihood of inadvertently exposing sensitive data, and optimizing data transfer by carrying only necessary information. The user interface presenting the data is the view. We generally use Razor syntax to create views in ASP.NET Core. This syntax allows the embedding of C# code into HTML.

Controller: This component handles user input, interacts with the model, and chooses a view to render the output. Any classes derived from the Controller base class inherit from it as their ancestor.

Having to deal with data: When working with data in ASP.NET Core MVC, using EF Core, an ORM is standard practice. Interacting with your database through the use of strongly typed objects is something that EF Core makes possible.

Understanding POCO

POCO is a crucial paradigm in ASP.NET Core and the MVC architecture. POCOs are framework-agnostic and simple OOP without dependencies. It contrasts with the earlier .NET period, when objects were tightly connected with frameworks, restricting reusability and complicating unit testing. POCOs changed .NET development by making designs more decoupled, testable, and manageable. These objects, representing data structures and business entities, fit test-driven development, clean architecture, and domain-driven design.

POCOs are widely used as models in the MVC architecture of web development, notably in ASP.NET Core, to connect the application to databases using ORMs like EF Core. Their simplicity simplifies data handling and improves application maintainability and scalability. POCOs reflect the industry's changing demands and practices by promoting modular, testable, and adaptable software design patterns.

Listed features include:

- **Framework independent**: They are not dependent on any framework, which enables them to be extraordinarily reusable and susceptible to testing.

- **No conventions**: In contrast to some frameworks, POCOs do not have any conventions that need specified base classes or characteristics. This is because POCOs do not have these limitations.

- **Uncomplicated**: POCOs are often employed for data representation and do not possess any business logic or behavior associated with a particular framework.

- **The early .NET**: Before the widespread use of POCOs, many .NET objects tightly tied themselves to frameworks such as ASP.NET and Entity Framework, complicating testing and reusability.

- **Rise of Test-Driven Development**: The growing importance of **Test-Driven Development** (**TDD**) and design patterns like DI is driving an increase in demand for more testable objects, such as POCOs, that are disconnected from one another.

- **EF and ORM**: The EF, an ORM tool, significantly contributed to the widespread use of POCOs. This framework enabled us to deal with database data using plain .NET objects.

Incorporate into ASP.NET Core MVC:

- **Models and the MVC pattern**: The Model component of the MVC pattern frequently consists of POCO classes. These Models represent the application's data and the business rules that govern it. As Models, POCOs can boost the application's flexibility and maintainability because they are not dependent on any particular framework.

- **EF Core**: POCOs are widely used in conjunction with EF Core for database operations in web development with ASP.NET Core. Acting as a connection between the program and the database, they make it straightforward to manipulate data.

- **Application programming interface development**: We often use POCOs in ASP. NET Core APIs, or DTO, to define the transmitted or received data structure.

POCOs are great for unit testing in ASP.NET Core apps because of their decoupled nature, which makes them perfect for testing such applications. These tools allow the software to help us write tests without worrying about database connections or other framework requirements.

Examples in C# illustrate the difference between POCO and DTO:

In the context of a pharmaceutical laboratory managing experiments on diseases in mice, which involves defining two classes. One will be a simple POCO class, representing the domain model with its business logic, while the other will be a DTO, used solely for transferring data without business logic.

Let us assume the pharmaceutical laboratory needs to keep track of experiments, including details like experiment ID, name, disease under study, and results. The POCO class will include these fields and potential methods for business logic, while the DTO will consist of only the fields necessary for data transfer.

POCO example: `Experiment` class

```
1. public class Experiment
2. {
3.       public int ExperimentId { get; set; }
4.       public string Name { get; set; }
5.       public string Disease { get; set; }
6.       public string Results { get; set; }
7.
8.       public void AnalyzeData()
9.       {
10.          // Business logic for analyzing experiment data
11.      }
12.
13.      public void UpdateResults(string newResults)
14.      {
15.          // Business logic to update experiment results
16.          Results = newResults;
17.      }
18. }
```

In this POCO class, Experiment, we have properties common in an experiment and methods like **AnalyzeData()** and **UpdateResults()**, which contain business logic.

DTO example: **ExperimentDto** class.

```
1. public class ExperimentDto
2. {
3.       public int ExperimentId { get; set; }
4.       public string Name { get; set; }
5.       public string Disease { get; set; }
6.
7.       // Note: No business logic methods here, just data fields
8. }
```

The **ExperimentDto** class is a DTO. It has the properties to carry data between processes but does not contain business logic. In this case, it might transfer experiment data across network calls, such as in a web API, where only basic experiment information (without results) is needed.

These examples illustrate the primary difference between POCO and DTO in a C# context, especially within a domain like pharmaceutical research. The POCO class (**Experiment**) is a full-fledged object with properties and behaviors, while the DTO (**ExperimentDto**) is a lightweight object used only for data transportation.

To create a business class that operates on the DTO sample, let us design a class called **ExperimentAnalysisService**. This class will use the **ExperimentDto**, from the last sample for reading experiment data and providing analysis functionalities. The **ExperimentDto** will serve as a data carrier, while the **ExperimentAnalysisService** will encapsulate the business logic for analyzing the data.

Business class: The **ExperimentAnalysisService** class will use **ExperimentDto** to perform data analysis:

```
1.  public class ExperimentAnalysisService
2.  {
3.      public string AnalyzeData(ExperimentDto experiment)
4.      {
5.          if (experiment == null)
6.          {
7.              throw new ArgumentNullException(nameof(experiment),
    "Analysis requires experiment data.
8.          }
9.
10.         // Example analysis logic (can be replaced with actual
    analysis methods)
11.         var analysisResult = $"Analyzing Experiment:
    {experiment.Name} for disease: {experiment.Disease}.";
12.
13.         // Add more complex analysis logic here
14.
15.         return analysisResult;
16.     }
17.
18. }
```

In conclusion, we explored ASP.NET Core's complex MVC architecture in this session. First, we defined the responsibilities and functions of the Model, View, and Controller components, essential to building solid and scalable online applications.

The comparison also showed a fascinating POCO vs. the DTO class. This investigation detailed their data representation and transmission responsibilities, revealing when and how to employ these classes in different situations.

Finally, C# code samples concluded the presentation. These examples were carefully selected to show POCO, DTO, and DbContext class use. They helped you to understand and apply these approaches to their applications.

Implementing form validation in MVC

The MVC framework in ASP.NET Core provides a rigorous approach to form validation, ensuring that user input follows the anticipated structure and criteria. Validation may be conducted on both the client side (in the user's browser) and the server side (on the web server) with this framework.

Understanding the validation concept

In online applications, validation refers to determining if user data fulfills specific criteria before it is processed or accepted by the program. Consider a website form in which you must enter your email address. In this situation, validation would entail determining if what you supplied resembles a genuine email address (for example, it should have a @ sign and a domain ending in `.com`). This procedure ensures that the data is in the proper format and makes sense for the program's intended usage, which is critical for the application to run successfully and securely.

Why validate on client and server-side

Double-checking data is significant at the user's and server's end (client-side). This dual-layered technique is critical for ensuring the integrity and security of web applications because it comprehensively verifies the accuracy and safety of the data.

- **Client-side validation**: This happens directly in the user's browser. When you fill out a form and get immediate feedback like `This field is required` or `Enter a valid email address`, that is client-side validation. It is like a quick check-up that occurs on the spot, ensuring the basic requirements meet standards before the data travels anywhere else. This type of validation is excellent for improving the user experience because it provides instant feedback, helping users correct their mistakes immediately.

- **Server-side validation**: After the data passes the initial client-side checks, the server, where the application resides, receives it. Here, server-side validation kicks in. This is a more rigorous and secure check. It is like a final and thorough inspection to ensure that the data is correct in format, safe, and appropriate for the application to process. Unlike client-side validation, this is crucial because one cannot easily bypass or tamper with it. It is a vital safeguard, protecting the application from accepting harmful or malicious data.

In developing software, validation is essential, particularly in online applications, because it guarantees the data's consistency, quality, and maintainability. The following is a breakdown of how validation contributes to each of these parts:

- **Consistency**: To ensure consistency, we use validation to enforce specific standards and regulations on the data submitted or processed by the program. For instance, if a form requires a field for entering phone numbers, validation ensures it only accepts legitimate ones. The program achieves consistency by maintaining identical data formats throughout. When there is consistency in the data, it is much simpler to handle, process, and analyze the data. This is of utmost significance in large-scale applications or systems that interface with other services.

- **Quality**: When it comes to the correct operation of any program, having high-quality data is necessary. Validation contributes to the maintenance of this quality by filtering out erroneous, incomplete, or malicious data. An example of this is a form that only allows the entry of legitimate email addresses into an email field. During the validation process, incorrect data is prevented from being entered, guaranteeing that the data gathered and saved is accurate and valuable. This cannot be overstated, especially for applications largely dependent on data-driven decision-making.

- **Maintainability**: Applications with verified data are easier to maintain throughout their lifetime. Using consistently formatted and high-quality data reduces the chance of mistakes and faults that unexpected or malformed data inputs can cause. Additionally, implementing validation rules clearly defines how data should be processed. This makes it simpler for future developers to comprehend and work with the code. Because of this, upgrades, improvements, and troubleshooting are carried out more smoothly.

In a nutshell, validation serves as a gatekeeper for the data that is being sent to an application, making specific that only the data that is relevant, correct, and helpful is allowed. Consequently, this results in improved consistency, quality, and maintainability of the data and the program, all contributing to software projects' success and permanence.

Validation's role in improving UI for a better experience

Validation is critical in enhancing apps' **user interface** (**UI**), directly contributing to a better user experience. Validation in UI design guarantees that users enter the proper data in the intended format, reducing mistakes and frustrations caused by wrong entries. For example, when a user fills out a form, rapid validation feedback, such as flagging an incorrectly typed email address, allows them to amend it immediately. This saves time while also reducing confusion and increasing customer happiness. Validation inside the user interface also leads to a cleaner and more ordered design. The UI is free of error warnings and superfluous information requests by avoiding improper data submission. This simplified interaction, in which users are gently encouraged to supply the relevant information in the proper format, dramatically improves the application's overall usability and visual appeal.

Validation's influence on UX and overall satisfaction

Validation is critical in providing a smooth and efficient user experience from the user's **user experience** (**UX**) standpoint. It is more than looks; it is about functionality and overall happiness from using the app. Reasonable validation procedures in UX design contribute to the application's sense of trust and dependability. Users feel more assured When they are appropriately instructed and know their input is valid. This component of validation decreases user mistakes and annoyance and aids in the completion of tasks more effectively. Effective validation, for example, ensures that customers submit proper payment information in an e-commerce application, reducing transaction failures and improving the purchasing experience. Furthermore, careful validation methods may anticipate and prevent any problems from occurring, resulting in a more proactive and user-centric experience. In summary, validation is a critical component of UX design that verifies the correctness of user inputs and adds significantly to overall user pleasure and application effectiveness.

The cost of poor business validation

Inadequate or poorly executed validation may cost a firm much money regarding time, data accuracy, and consumer confidence. Businesses risk processing incorrect or incomplete data when validation methods are not robust. Errors that are both time-consuming and expensive might result from this. For example, erroneous client information in orders might result in unsuccessful delivery, requiring additional time and resources to fix these problems. Furthermore, poor validation can lead to security flaws, making the system vulnerable to data breaches or assaults, jeopardizing data integrity, and having legal and financial consequences.

Poor validation also influences the customer experience. Customers who experience numerous failures or difficulties using a company's services due to validation issues are prone to irritation. This can lower consumer satisfaction and loyalty, resulting in turnover. Customer loss can negatively affect revenue and market image, particularly in competitive marketplaces. Furthermore, the time and resources spent dealing with consumer complaints and correcting validation errors may have been spent on more productive tasks, resulting in opportunity costs.

The advantages of effective validation in business

On the other hand, a well-implemented validation plan may provide significant benefits to a corporation. Efficient validation processes assure data quality and dependability, which are essential for making sound business decisions. It simplifies operations and lowers the need for rework or data cleansing, saving time and money. For example, in an e-commerce platform, correct data validation promotes successful transactions and delivery, increasing consumer satisfaction and repeat business.

Furthermore, excellent validation procedures improve user experience by making interfaces more user-friendly and intuitive. Users are more inclined to continue using simple and dependable services, directly leading to customer satisfaction and retention. In terms of security, strong validation is an essential line of defense against data breaches and cyber assaults, protecting the company's data assets and reputation.

In a larger commercial context, the dependability and efficiency achieved by successful validation can contribute to increased market position and competitive advantage. Companies regarded for their reliability and outstanding user experience may attract more clients and frequently charge a higher price for their services. Furthermore, the time and money saved by effective data management may be allocated to efforts for innovation and growth, putting the organization farther ahead in its field.

Finally, the influence of validation on a firm is significant. While inadequate validation processes can result in considerable losses, good validation can increase efficiency, customer satisfaction, and overall corporate success.

Let us see an example of client-side validation.

Using a hospital emergency form, this sample will show how to build client-side validation in an ASP.NET Core MVC application. The form will ask for the patient's first and last name, date of birth, residence, city, and occupation. The date of birth field will have a special validation rule: it must be older than today and later than January 1, 1900. Furthermore, the form will alter dynamically depending on the patient's age. If the patient is under 18, the form will ask for extra information, such as a guardian's name and phone number. This example will use jQuery to improve the user experience using interactive and responsive validation procedures.

The goal is to construct a user-friendly form that checks data correctness and integrity before sending it to the server. By performing these validations on the client side, we want to improve the application's speed and user experience while decreasing server load and giving users rapid feedback.

Now, let us get started on the code for this hospital emergency form using the required validation rules:

- Code for **EmergengyViewModel**:

```
1. using System.ComponentModel.DataAnnotations;
2.
3. public class EmergencyViewModel
4. {
5.     [Required(ErrorMessage = "Name is required")]
6.     public string Name { get; set; }
7.
8.     [Required(ErrorMessage = "Last Name is required")]
9.     public string LastName { get; set; }
10.
11.     [Required(ErrorMessage = "Date of Birth is required")]
12.     [DataType(DataType.Date)]
13.     public DateTime DateOfBirth { get; set; }
14.
15.     [Required(ErrorMessage = "Address is required")]
16.     public string Address { get; set; }
17.
18.     [Required(ErrorMessage = "City is required")]
```

```
19.    public string City { get; set; }
20.
21.    [Required(ErrorMessage = "Profession is required")]
22.    public string Profession { get; set; }
23.
24.    public string GuardianName { get; set; }
25.
26.    [Phone]
27.    public string GuardianPhoneNumber { get; set; }
28. }
```

- Code for **Emergency.cshtml** with comments:

```
1. <script src="https://code.jquery.com/jquery-3.6.0.min.js"></script>
2. @{
3.     ViewData[«Title»] = «Emergency Room»;
4. }
5.
6. @model EmergencyViewModel
7.
8. <form id="emergencyForm">
9.     <!-- Name input -->
10.    <label for="name">Name:</label><br />
11.    <input type="text" id="name" name="Name" required /><br />
12.    <br />
13.
14.    <!-- Last Name input -->
15.    <label for="lastName">Last Name:</label><br />
16.    <input type="text" id="lastName" name="LastName" required /><br />
17.    <br />
18.
19.    <!-- Address input -->
20.    <label for="address">Address:</label><br />
21.    <input type="text" id="address" name="Address" required /><br />
22.    <br />
23.
24.    <!-- City input -->
25.    <label for="city">City:</label><br />
26.    <input type="text" id="city" name="City" required /><br />
```

```
27.    <br />
28.
29.    <!-- Profession input -->
30.    <label for="profession">Profession:</label><br />
31.    <input type="text" id="profession" name="Profession"
   required /><br />
32.    <br />
33.
34.    <!-- Date of Birth input -->
35.    <label for="dob">Date of Birth:</label><br />
36.    <input type="date" id="dob" name="DateOfBirth" required
   /><br />
37.    <div class="alert alert-danger col-md-4" id="dobMessage">
   </div>
38.    <br />
39.
40.    <!-- Guardian Information section -->
41.    <div id="guardianInfo" style="display:none;">
42.        <!-- Guardian Name input -->
43.        <label for="guardianName">Guardian Name:</label><br />
44.        <input type="text" id="guardianName"
   name="GuardianName" /><br />
45.        <br />
46.
47.        <!-- Guardian Phone Number input -->
48.        <label for="guardianPhone">Guardian Phone
   Number:</label><br />
49.        <input type="tel" id="guardianPhone"
   name="GuardianPhoneNumber" /><br />
50.        <br />
51.    </div>
52.
53.    <!-- Submit button -->
54.    <button id="submit" type="submit">Submit</button>
55. </form>
56.
57. <script>
58.    $(document).ready(function () {
59.        // Hide the Date of Birth error message and turn off
   the Submit button
60.            $('#dobMessage').hide();
```

```
61.            $('#submit').prop('disabled', true);
62.
63.            // Event handler for Date of Birth input change
64.            $('#dob').change(function () {
65.                var dob = new Date($(this).val());
66.                var today = new Date();
67.                var age = today.getFullYear() - dob.getFullYear();
68.
69.                // Hide the Date of Birth error message and enable
      the Submit button
70.                $('#dobMessage').hide();
71.                $('#submit').prop('disabled', false);
72.
73.                // Validate the Date of Birth
74.                if (dob > today || dob < new Date('1900-01-01')) {
75.                    $('#dobMessage').text('Invalid Date of Birth')
      .show();
76.                    $('#submit').prop('disabled', true);
77.                } else if (age < 18) {
78.                    // Show the Guardian Information section and
      make the Guardian Name and Guardian Phone Number inputs
      required
79.                    $('#guardianInfo').show();
80.                    $('#guardianName').prop('required', true);
81.                    $('#guardianPhone').prop('required', true);
82.
83.                } else {
84.                    // Hide the Guardian Information section
85.                    $('#guardianInfo').hide();
86.                    // Remove the required attribute from the
      Guardian Name and Guardian Phone Number inputs
87.                    $('#guardianName').removeProp('required');
88.                    $('#guardianPhone').removeProp('required');
89.                }
90.            });
91.        });
92. </script>
```

Stages of validation for the form:

1. **Validation of birth**: The form checks if the entered date of birth is after January 1, 1900. This validation ensures that the data is within a reasonable and valid range.

2. **Displaying guardian information fields**: When the form identifies the patient as under 18 years old based on their date of birth, it shows additional fields for entering the guardian's name and phone number. This step is crucial for gathering necessary contact information for minors.

3. **Mandatory guardian name field**: Once the system displays the guardian information fields for a minor, you must fill in the guardian's name on the form. This mandatory field ensures that a responsible adult's contact information is available for underage patients.

These validation stages ensure that the form collects accurate and appropriate information based on the patient's age, adhering to necessary data collection standards and legal requirements for minors.

This is how the form will works:

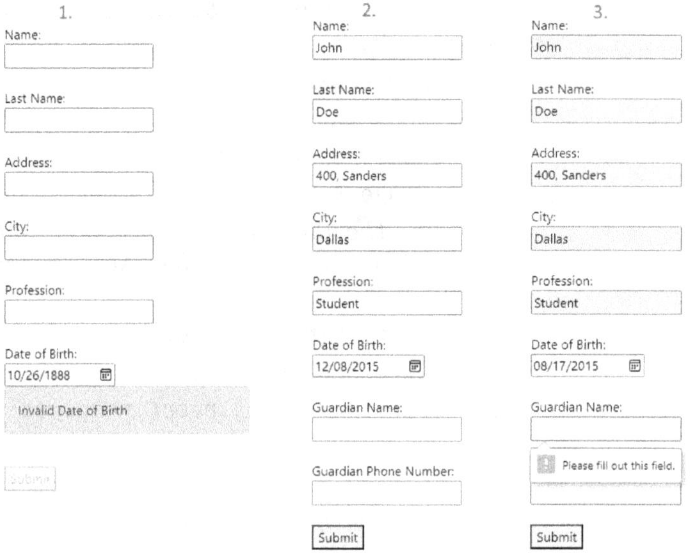

Figure 13.2: Forms

Ensure to validate data on the server side; client-side validation is not a substitute. Server-side validation is essential for maintaining data integrity and security since it is the primary defense against incorrect or malicious data inputs that can bypass the initial line of protection.

Client-side validation saves server round trips, which is essential for fast, responsive apps. It also improves data quality by avoiding errors at the source. It also makes the program more responsive and user-friendly because users get quick feedback on their inputs without a server response.

In conclusion, client-side validation is essential for responsive, efficient, and user-friendly online apps. Robust server-side validation comprehensively addresses data integrity and user experience. It shows that online development now prioritizes utility, usability, and user engagement.

Let us see an example of server-side validation.

1. Create the validation for the date of birth:

```
1. public class DateOfBirthValidation : ValidationAttribute
2. {
3.     protected override ValidationResult IsValid(object value,
   ValidationContext validationContext)
4.     {
5.         DateTime dob = (DateTime)value;
6.         if (dob < DateTime.
   Now && dob > new DateTime(1900, 1, 1))
7.         {
8.             return ValidationResult.Success;
9.         }
10.        else
11.        {
12.            return new ValidationResult("Invalid Date of Birth.
   Date must be older than today and after 01/01/1900.");
13.        }
14.    }
15. }
```

2. Create the validation for the guardians:

```
1. public class GuardianValidation : ValidationAttribute
2. {
3.     protected override ValidationResult IsValid(object value,
   ValidationContext validationContext)
4.     {
5.         var emergencyFormModel =
   (EmergencyModel)validationContext.ObjectInstance;
6.
7.         DateTime dob = emergencyFormModel.DateOfBirth;
8.         var age = DateTime.Now.Year - dob.Year;
9.         if (dob > DateTime.Now.AddYears(-age)) age--;
10.
11.        // Check if the age is less than 18
12.        if (age < 18)
13.        {
14.            // Retrieve the GuardianName and
   GuardianPhoneNumber from the model
```

```
15.
16.             if (string.IsNullOrWhiteSpace(emergencyFormModel.
    GuardianName) ||
17.               string.IsNullOrWhiteSpace(emergencyFormModel.
    GuardianPhoneNumber))
18.             {
19.               return new ValidationResult("Guardian name and
    phone number are required for patients under 18 years of
    age.");
20.             }
21.         }
22.
23.     // If the age is 18 or above, or if guardian details
    are provided for minors, validation is successful
24.         return ValidationResult.Success;
25.     }
26. }
```

3. Add the validation to the respective fields:

```
1.  ...
2.
3.      [Required(ErrorMessage = "Date of Birth is required")]
4.      [DataType(DataType.Date)]
5.      [DateOfBirthValidation]
6.      public DateTime DateOfBirth { get; set; }
7.
8.      [GuardianValidation]
9.      public string GuardianName { get; set; }
10.
11.     [Phone]
12.     [GuardianValidation]
13.     public string GuardianPhoneNumber { get; set; }
```

4. Add the **HttpPost** method to the Controller:

```
1.  [HttpPost]
2.  public IActionResult Emergency(EmergencyModel model)
3.  {
4.      if (ModelState.IsValid)
5.      {
6.          // Process the valid model here (e.g., save data,
    send response)
7.          return RedirectToAction("SuccessPage");
```

```
8.          }
9.
10.          // If the model state is not valid, return the same
      view with the model to show validation errors
11.          return View(model);
12.      }
```

5. Now, we revamp a new version of the form to use the ASP controls:

```
1. <script src="https://code.jquery.com/jquery-3.6.0.min.js">
   </script>
2. @{
3.      ViewData[«Title»] = «Emergency Room»;
4. }
5.
6. @model EmergencyModel
7.
8. <form id="emergencyForm" asp-action="Emergency"
   asp-controller="Home" method="post">
9.      <!-- Name input -->
10.      <label for="name">Name:</label><br />
11.      <input asp-for="Name" type="text" id="name"
   class="form-control" /><br />
12.      <span asp-validation-for="Name" class="text-danger">
   </span><br />
13.
14.      <!-- Last Name input -->
15.      <label for="lastName">Last Name:</label><br />
16.      <input asp-for="LastName" type="text" id="lastName"
   class="form-control" /><br />
17.      <span asp-validation-for="LastName" class="text-danger">
   </span><br />
18.
19.      <!-- Address input -->
20.      <label for="address">Address:</label><br />
21.      <input asp-for="Address" type="text" id="address"
   class="form-control" /><br />
22.      <span asp-validation-for="Address" class="text-danger">
   </span><br />
23.
24.      <!-- City input -->
25.      <label for="city">City:</label><br />
26.      <input asp-for="City" type="text" id="city" class="form-
```

```
      control" /><br />
27.     <span asp-validation-for="City" class="text-danger"></
    span><br />
28.
29.     <!-- Profession input -->
30.     <label for="profession">Profession:</label><br />
31.     <input asp-
    for="Profession" type="text" id="profession" class="form-
    control" /><br />
32.     <span asp-validation-for="Profession" class="text-
    danger"></span><br />
33.
34.     <!-- Date of Birth input -->
35.     <label for="dob">Date of Birth:</label><br />
36.     <input asp-
    for="DateOfBirth" type="date" id="dob" class="form-
    control" /><br />
37.     <span asp-validation-for="DateOfBirth" class="text-
    danger"></span><br />
38.     <span class="alert alert-danger col-md-4" id="dobMessage"></
    span>
39.
40.     <!-- Guardian Information section -->
41.     <div id="guardianInfo" style="display:none;">
42.
43.         <!-- Guardian Name input -->
44.         <label for="guardianName">Guardian Name:</label><br />
45.         <input asp-
    for="GuardianName" type="text" id="guardianName" class="form-
    control" /><br />
46.         <span asp-validation-for="GuardianName" class="text-
    danger"></span><br />
47.
48.         <!-- Guardian Phone Number input -->
49.         <label for="guardianPhone">Guardian Phone Number:</
    label><br />
50.         <input asp-
    for="GuardianPhoneNumber" type="tel" id="guardianPhone"
    class="form-control" /><br />
51.         <span asp-validation-
    for="GuardianPhoneNumber" class="text-danger"></span><br />
52.         <br />
```

```
53.    </div>
54.
55.    <!-- Submit button -->
56.    <button id="submit" type="submit"
    class="btn btn-primary">Submit</button>
57.
58. </form>
59.
```

The complete source code can be found in the GitHub repository of this book.

To understand the server-side validation process more clearly, it is helpful to temporarily turn off the client-side validation. Submitting the form without client-side validation triggers server-side validation, which identifies and reports any errors or issues with the form data back to the user. The screenshot provided appears to show a form after server-side validation has occurred. It displays messages for each field that did not pass validation, such as an invalid date of birth and missing required information for the guardian's name and phone number. Users would see this if client-side validation was not present to catch these errors before the form submission.

This is the result for the current form:

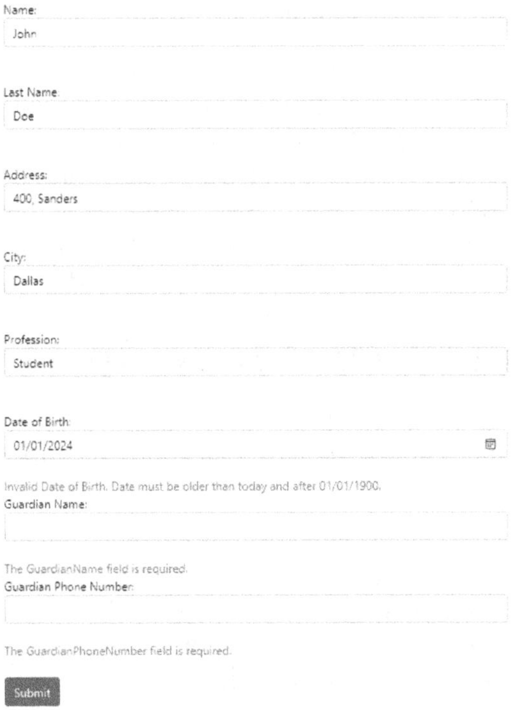

Figure 13.3: Emergency form

Key points in this form:

- **Custom validation**: The `DateOfBirthValidation` attribute is a custom validator ensuring that the date of birth is older than the current day and later than January 1, 1900.

- **Guardian validation**: We could add conditional validation in the Controller based on the patient's age for the guardian's name and phone number. Alternatively, we could implement a custom validation attribute that considers the patient's age and whether guardian information is required.

- **ModelState**: The `ModelState.IsValid` property in the controller action method checks whether the model passed from the view meets all validation criteria defined in the model.

- **Handling validation results**: If the model state is invalid, the same View is returned, displaying the validation error messages. If it is valid, the form is processed accordingly.

In this overview, we have stressed the importance of form validation in MVC applications on both the client and server sides. Ensuring user data meets requirements before application processing is essential for various reasons. Maintains data consistency, quality, and maintainability while improving security and user experience. we provided a realistic example of client-side validation using jQuery and server-side validation using custom attributes and model states—these examples aid app development.

Further, client-side validation occurs in the user's browser, providing a fast response. This quick response helps users fix issues, decrease server queries, and speed up the service. However, client-side validation does not guarantee security. Server-side validation on the web server checks for dangerous data and protects the application. It fixes mistakes that slip past client-side validation. we also investigated custom validation, where you can write rules for specific fields or the entire model. It makes validation more flexible and context-specific, including conditional validation depending on model fields or characteristics.

Understanding ViewModel in MVC

The concept of ViewModel is at the heart of this design, particularly in the realms of C# and .NET. Let us dig deeper into this idea to understand its importance and applicability in MVC.

ViewModel, as the name implies, is an all-encompassing model designed exclusively for the view. It represents the information we wish to show on our website or user interface. The Model represents the domain data (business logic and data access) in the MVC design, the View is the user interface, and the Controller manages the input. The ViewModel serves as a connector between the Model and the View.

ViewModel essential architecture.It is used for a variety of purposes. It primarily enables us to shape the data most conveniently for our perspectives. ViewModels are developed exclusively for the view, as opposed to business models, which are designed to represent business entities and logic. This division results in more manageable and cleaner code.

Making a ViewModel

Creating a ViewModel is simple. In our view, we define a class representing the data we want to display or the actions we want to accomplish. This class can include business model characteristics, computed fields, or even lists of objects to be shown in drop-down lists or grids.

ViewModel binding to Views

We tie our ViewModel to our view when we define it. It is commonly done in MVC with C# using Razor syntax. Razor can show the data and manage user interaction after passing the ViewModel from our controller to the view.

Benefits of using ViewModel:

- **Separation of concerns**: ViewModel allows us to keep our business logic and presentation layers separate.

- **Flexibility**: We can customize our ViewModel to meet the specific needs of our view, such as formatting, grouping, or merging data from multiple business entities.

- **Simplified testing**: ViewModels are more straightforward to unit test since they are independent of the business logic.

Here is an example. We will create a page that displays details about a patient, including personal information, cardiac health details, and a list of appointments or treatments:

- We start with the models for the application:

```
1. namespace MyCardiologyApp.Models;
2.
3. public class Patient
4. {
5.     public int Id { get; set; }
6.     public string Name { get; set; }
7.     public int Age { get; set; }
8.     public string Gender { get; set; }
9. }
10.
11. public class CardiacRecord
12. {
13.     public int Id { get; set; }
```

```
14.    public int PatientId { get; set; }
15.    public string Diagnosis { get; set; }
16.    public string TreatmentPlan { get; set; }
17. }
```

- We create **PatientCardiologyViewModel.cs**:

```
1. namespace MyCardiologyApp.Models;
2. public class PatientCardiologyViewModel(Patient patient,
   List<CardiacRecord> cardiacRecords)
3. {
4.     public string Name { get; set; } = patient.Name;
5.     public int Age { get; set; } = patient.Age;
6.     public string Gender { get; set; } = patient.Gender;
7.     public List<CardiacRecord> CardiacRecords { get; set; } =
   cardiacRecords;
8. }
```

- We create the **CardiologyController.cs**:

```
1. using Microsoft.AspNetCore.Mvc;
2. using MyCardiologyApp.Models;
3.
4. public class CardiologyController : Controller
5. {
6.     public IActionResult PatientDetails(int id)
7.     {
8.         // Assume these methods get the data from the database
9.         var patient = GetPatientById(id);
10.        var cardiacRecords = GetCardiacRecordsByPatientId(id);
11.
12.        var viewModel = new PatientCardiologyViewModel(patient,
   cardiacRecords);
13.
14.        return View(viewModel);
15.     }
16.
17.     // Methods to get data from the database (for illustration
   purposes)
18.     private Patient GetPatientById(int id)
19.     {
20.         // Fetch the patient from the database
21.         // For simplicity, returning a dummy patient
22.         return new Patient { Id = id, Name = "Jane Doe", Age =
```

```
                45, Gender = "Female" };
23.      }
24.
25.      private List<CardiacRecord>
     GetCardiacRecordsByPatientId(int id)
26.      {
27.          // Fetch the cardiac records from the database
28.          // For simplicity, returning dummy records
29.          return
30.          [
31.              new CardiacRecord { Id = 1, PatientId = id,
     Diagnosis = "Hypertension", TreatmentPlan = "Medication A" },
32.              new CardiacRecord
33.              {
34.                  Id = 2, PatientId = id, Diagnosis =
     "Arrhythmia", TreatmentPlan = "Medication B and regular
     monitoring"
35.              }
36.          ];
37.      }
38. }
```

- So, we create the **PatientDetails.cshtml** inside Views\Cardiology:

```
1.  @{
2.      ViewBag.Title = «Patient Details»;
3.  }
4.
5.  <h2>Patient Details</h2>
6.
7.  <div>
8.      <h3>Personal Information</h3>
9.      <p><strong>Name:</strong> @Model.Name</p>
10.     <p><strong>Age:</strong> @Model.Age</p>
11.     <p><strong>Gender:</strong> @Model.Gender</p>
12. </div>
13.
14. <div>
15.     <h3>Cardiac Records</h3>
16.     @if (Model.CardiacRecords != null && Model.CardiacRecords.
     Any())
17.     {
18.         <table>
```

```
19.              <tr>
20.                  <th>Diagnosis</th>
21.                  <th>Treatment Plan</th>
22.              </tr>
23.              @foreach (var record in Model.CardiacRecords)
24.              {
25.                  <tr>
26.                      <td>@record.Diagnosis</td>
27.                      <td>@record.TreatmentPlan</td>
28.                  </tr>
29.              }
30.          </table>
31.      }
32.      else
33.      {
34.          <p>No cardiac records were found for this patient.</p>
35.      }
36. </div>
```

So, this is what we did here. We begin by defining the basic models of our database with two classes, **Patient** and **CardiacRecord**. The **Patient** class holds personal details like ID, name, age, and gender, while **CardiacRecord** stores medical information such as diagnosis and treatment plans. We then introduce **PatientCardiologyViewModel** in the **MyCardiologyApp.Models** namespace to integrate patient details with their cardiac records. This model takes a **Patient** object and a list of **CardiacRecords** as input, encapsulating them into a single-ViewModel. Next, we create **CardiologyController**, where the **PatientDetails** method retrieves patient and cardiac record data, likely from a database, and passes it to the **PatientCardiologyViewModel**. This integration lets us comprehensively view each patient's personal and medical data. Finally, we craft **PatientDetails.cshtml** in the Views\Cardiology folder for the front-end. This view utilizes the model to display the patient's personal information and cardiac records, offering a clear and organized presentation of patient details and their medical history.

Finally, understanding and utilizing ViewModels in MVC apps is critical for designing robust, scalable, and maintainable web applications. We improve our apps' overall design and performance by separating the concerns of the business logic and the presentation layer. Remember that the correct ViewModel implementation might be a game changer in your MVC application development journey.

Building a CRUD operation using MVC

In software development, let us examine the essential ideas of CRUD operations and MVC architecture.

CRUD is an acronym that stands for create, read, update, and delete. These are the four basic operations performed on data in each database application. Anyone who works with databases or develops apps that interface with databases must understand CRUD. These operations are defined as follows:

- **Create**: This process entails inserting new data into the database, for example, creating a new user account or adding a product to the inventory of an online business.

- **Reading**: Data entails accessing a database to obtain particular information. It might be anything from displaying a single item to presenting a list of data depending on specific criteria.

- **Updating**: This process involves changing existing data, for example, adjusting the pricing of a product or editing a user's profile information.

- **Delete**: As the name implies, this action removes data from the database. It might entail removing a discontinued product from a catalog or deactivating a user account.

MVC and CRUD in ASP.NET Core

The MVC architectural pattern is implemented by ASP.NET Core MVC, a web application framework. This framework is particularly well-suited for developing online applications that execute CRUD activities because of its organized approach, simplicity of database interaction, and extensive data handling features.

Model: In the MVC design, the Model represents the application's data and business logic, primarily handling CRUD activities. The model defines the data structure, manages data validation, and interacts directly with the database to perform CRUD operations.

The View is the application's user interface. It presents info to the user and lets the user interact with it. Views are used in CRUD activities to render forms for generating and modifying data and to show data for reading and confirmations for removals.

- **Controller**: The Controller is a go-between for the Model and the View. It processes user requests, performs CRUD operations on the Model, and feeds data to the View. Each CRUD operation is associated with a distinct controller action.

- **Routing in MVC**: Routing is used in ASP.NET Core MVC to map incoming browser requests to particular controller actions. It is critical for CRUD activities since it controls how the user navigates within the application to create, read, update, and remove data.

- **Entity Framework Core**: Often used in conjunction with ASP.NET Core MVC, Entity Framework Core is an **Object-Relational Mapper** (**ORM**) that facilitates CRUD operations. It enables us to interact with data as objects and properties rather than writing complicated SQL queries.

- **Validation and security**: It is critical to ensure data validation and security procedures are in place when performing CRUD processes. It involves verifying user input, avoiding SQL injection, and ensuring users have the necessary permissions.

Example of CRUD:

In this example, we will demonstrate a CRUD of a **Product**:

1. Start creating the connection in the **application.json** at the root of the project. Like this:

```
1. "ConnectionStrings": {
2.     "DefaultConnectionApp": "Server=(localdb)\\
   mssqllocaldb;Database=MyEfCoreDbApp;Trusted_Connection=True;"
3.   },
```

2. Create the Model **Product** like this:

```
1. using System.ComponentModel.DataAnnotations;
2. using Microsoft.EntityFrameworkCore;
3.
4. namespace MyEfCoreApp.Models;
5.
6. public class Product
7. {
8.     /// <summary>
9.     /// Gets or sets the product ID.
10.    /// </summary>
11.    [Key]
12.    [Required]
13.    public int Id { get; set; }
14.    /// <summary>
15.    /// Gets or sets the product name.
16.    /// </summary>
17.    [Required]
18.    [StringLength(100)]
19.    [Display(Name = "Products Name")]
20.    public string Name { get; set; }
21.    /// <summary>
22.    /// Gets or sets the product price.
23.    /// </summary>
24.    [Precision(18, 2)]
25.    [Display(Name = "Products Price")]
26.    public decimal Price { get; set; }
```

```
27. }
```

3. Create the **ApplicationDbContext** like this:

```
1. namespace MyEfCoreApp.DbContexts;
2.
3. using Microsoft.EntityFrameworkCore;
4. using MyEfCoreApp.Models;
5.
6. public class ApplicationDbContext : DbContext
7. {
8.     public ApplicationDbContext(DbContextOptions
   <ApplicationDbContext> options) : base(options)
9.     {
10.    }
11.    public DbSet<Product>? Products { get; set; }
12.
13.    protected override void OnModelCreating(ModelBuilder
   modelBuilder)
14.    {
15.        // Specifying that the Products entity maps to a table
   named "Products" in the database
16.        modelBuilder.Entity<Product>().ToTable("Products");
17.    }
18. }
```

4. Add the **ApplicationDbContext** to the **builder.Services** in **Program.cs**, like this:

```
1. builder.Services.AddDbContext<ApplicationDbContext>(options =>
2.     options.UseSqlServer(builder.Configuration.
   GetConnectionString("DefaultConnectionApp")));
```

5. Create the **ProductsController** like this:

```
1. using Microsoft.AspNetCore.Mvc;
2. using Microsoft.EntityFrameworkCore;
3. using MyEfCoreApp.DbContexts;
4. using MyEfCoreApp.Models;
5.
6. namespace MyEfCoreApp.Controllers;
7.
8. public class ProductsController(ApplicationDbContext context) :
   Controller
```

```
9.  {
10.      // GET: Products
11.      public async Task<IActionResult> Index()
12.      {
13.          return View(await context.Products.ToListAsync());
14.      }
15.
16.      // GET: Products/Create
17.      public IActionResult Create()
18.      {
19.          return View();
20.      }
21.
22.      // POST: Products/Create
23.      [HttpPost]
24.      [ValidateAntiForgeryToken]
25.      public async Task<IActionResult>
      Create([Bind("Id,Name,Price")] Product product)
26.      {
27.          if (!ModelState.IsValid) return View(product);
28.
29.          context.Add(product);
30.          await context.SaveChangesAsync();
31.          return RedirectToAction(nameof(Index));
32.      }
33.
34.      // GET: Products/Edit/5
35.      public async Task<IActionResult> Edit(int? id)
36.      {
37.          if (id == null)
38.          {
39.              return NotFound();
40.          }
41.
42.          var product = await context.Products.FindAsync(id);
43.          return product == null ? NotFound() : View(product);
44.      }
45.
46.      // GET: Products/Details/5
47.      public async Task<IActionResult> Details(int? id)
```

```
48.      {
49.          if (id == null)
50.          {
51.              return NotFound();
52.          }
53.
54.          var product = await context.Products.FindAsync(id);
55.          return product == null ? NotFound() : View(product); …
```

The complete source code can be found in the GitHub repository of this book.

6. Create the folder **Products** inside **View** and add these files: **Index.chsml**, **Create.cshtml**, **Edit.cshtml**, **Delete.cshtml** and **Details.cshtml**:

Index.cshtml, this view displays a list of products and provides links to the other operations:

```
1.  @model IEnumerable<Product>
2.
3.  <h2>Products</h2>
4.
5.  <p>
6.      <a asp-action="Create">Create New</a>
7.  </p>
8.  <table class="table">
9.      <thead>
10.     <tr>
11.         <th>
12.             @Html.DisplayNameFor(model => model.Name)
13.         </th>
14.         <th>
15.             @Html.DisplayNameFor(model => model.Price)
16.         </th>
17.         <th></th>
18.     </tr>
19.     </thead>
20.     <tbody>
21.     @foreach (var item in Model) {
22.         <tr>
23.             <td>
24.                 @Html.DisplayFor(modelItem => item.Name)
25.             </td>
26.             <td>
```

```
27.                        @Html.DisplayFor(modelItem => item.Price)
28.                </td>
29.                <td>
30.                    <a asp-action="Edit" asp-route-id="@item.
    Id">Edit</a> |
31.                    <a asp-action="Details" asp-route-id="@item.
    Id">Details</a> |
32.                    <a asp-action="Delete" asp-route-id="@item.
    Id">Delete</a>
33.                </td>
34.            </tr>
35.        }
36.    </tbody>
37. </table>
```

We demonstrate running the code in the following figure:

Products

Create New

Name	Price			
Aspirin	1,00	Edit	Details	Delete
Surgical tape	1,50	Edit	Details	Delete

Figure 13.4: View Index

Create.cshtml, this view contains a form for creating a new product.

```
1.  @model Product
2.
3.  <h2>Create</h2>
4.
5.  <form asp-action="Create">
6.      <div class="form-group">
7.          <label asp-for="Name" class="control-label"></label>
8.          <input asp-for="Name" class="form-control" />
9.          <span asp-validation-for="Name" class="text-danger"></
    span>
10.     </div>
11.     <div class="form-group">
12.         <label asp-for="Price" class="control-label"></label>
13.         <input asp-for="Price" class="form-control" />
14.         <span asp-validation-for="Price" class="text-danger"></
    span>
```

```
15.    </div>
16.    <input type="submit" value="Create" class="btn btn-
   primary" />
17. </form>
18.
19. <div>
20.    <a asp-action="Index">Back to List</a>
21. </div>
```

We demonstrate running the code in the following figure:

Create

Name

Price

Create

Back to List

Figure 13.5: View Create

7. **Edit.cshtml**, this view is similar to Create, but it pre-populates the form with the existing product data.

```
1.  @model Product
2.
3.  <h2>Edit</h2>
4.
5.  <form asp-action="Edit">
6.      <input type="hidden" asp-for="Id" />
7.      <div class="form-group">
8.          <label asp-for="Name" class="control-label"></label>
9.          <input asp-for="Name" class="form-control" />
10.         <span asp-validation-for="Name" class="text-danger"></
   span>
11.     </div>
12.     <div class="form-group">
13.         <label asp-for="Price" class="control-label"></label>
14.         <input asp-for="Price" class="form-control" />
15.         <span asp-validation-for="Price" class="text-danger"></
   span>
16.     </div>
17.     <input type="submit" value="Save" class="btn btn-
   primary" />
18. </form>
```

```
19.
20. <div>
21.     <a asp-action="Index">Back to List</a>
22. </div>
```

We demonstrate running the code in the following figure:

Edit

Name

Aspirin

Price

1,00

Save

Back to List

Figure 13.6: View Edit

8. **Delete.cshtml**, this view confirms the deletion of a product.

```
1.  @model Product
2.
3.  <h2>Delete</h2>
4.
5.  <h3>Are you sure you want to delete this?</h3>
6.  <div>
7.      <h4>Product</h4>
8.      <hr />
9.      <dl class="row">
10.         <dt class="col-sm-2">
11.             @Html.DisplayNameFor(model => model.Name)
12.         </dt>
13.         <dd class="col-sm-10">
14.             @Html.DisplayFor(model => model.Name)
15.         </dd>
16.         <dt class="col-sm-2">
17.             @Html.DisplayNameFor(model => model.Price)
18.         </dt>
19.         <dd class="col-sm-10">
20.             @Html.DisplayFor(model => model.Price)
21.         </dd>
22.     </dl>
23.
24.     <form asp-action="Delete" method="post">
```

```
25.          <input type="hidden" asp-for="Id" />
26.          <input type="submit" value="Delete" class="btn btn-
     danger" /> |
27.          <a asp-action="Index">Back to List</a>
28.     </form>
29. </div>
```

We demonstrate running the code in the following figure:

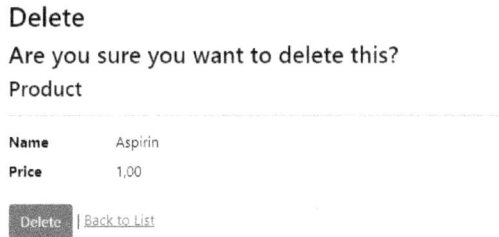

Delete

Are you sure you want to delete this?

Product

Name	Aspirin
Price	1,00

[Delete] | <u>Back to List</u>

Figure 13.7: View Delete

9. **Details**, this view shows the details of a single product, but it is not part of the CRUD:

```
1.    @model Product
2.
3.    <h2>Details</h2>
4.
5.    <div>
6.         <h4>Product</h4>
7.         <hr />
8.         <dl class="row">
9.             <dt class="col-sm-2">
10.                 @Html.DisplayNameFor(model => model.Name)
11.             </dt>
12.             <dd class="col-sm-10">
13.                 @Html.DisplayFor(model => model.Name)
14.             </dd>
15.             <dt class="col-sm-2">
16.                 @Html.DisplayNameFor(model => model.Price)
17.             </dt>
18.             <dd class="col-sm-10">
19.                 @Html.DisplayFor(model => model.Price)
20.             </dd>
21.         </dl>
```

```
22. </div>
23. <div>
24.     <a asp-action="Edit" asp-route-id="@Model.Id">Edit</a> |
25.     <a asp-action="Index">Back to List</a>
26. </div>
```

We demonstrate running the code in the following figure:

Details

Product

Name	Aspirin
Price	1,00

Edit | Back to List

Figure 13.8: View Details

Each view uses the ASP.NET Core MVC tag helpers to produce the relevant connections and form actions. These points of view should be included.

10. Now, open the prompt and run these commands:

```
1. dotnet ef migrations add InitialCreate --context
   ApplicationDbContext

2. dotnet ef database update
```

The **--context** is optional. Use it only if you have more than one DbContext in the application.

In *line 2*, we create and update the database.

Now, the application is ready to run.

Finally, understanding the MVC architecture and successfully using each component—Models, Views, and Controllers—is required to develop CRUD activities in ASP.NET Core MVC. The framework's organized approach and robust tools like EF Core make data management more accessible for online applications. The key to a successful implementation is meticulous data model preparation, intuitive user interface design, and robust routing, validation, and security methods.

Using Entity Framework Core with MVC

EF Core is a lightweight, extensible, and cross-platform version of EF, the widely used .NET ORM framework. It connects our C# code to the database, allowing us to manipulate data in the database with highly typed C# objects. Compared to typical database access methods such as SQL queries, this approach provides a higher level of abstraction, making data access more straightforward and more manageable.

Entity Framework Core's key features

EF Core is comprehensive and fully equipped to meet our data manipulation requirements in C# and .NET-based applications. The key features of EF Core include the following:

- **Cross-platform compatibility**: EF Core is compatible with a variety of systems. EF Core provides a uniform experience and is compatible with .NET Core, a cross-platform, high-performance framework, whether you are creating on Windows, macOS, or Linux.

- **Support for LINQ**: Using LINQ to query the database is one of the most powerful capabilities of EF Core. It enables us to create database queries in C# syntax, offering type safety IntelliSense support in IDEs and lowering the possibility of runtime errors.

- **Performance enhancements**: EF Core enhances performance over its predecessor, offering improved query generation, better memory utilization, and increased overall performance, especially in large-scale applications.

- **Code-first and database-first**: EF Core supports both code-first and database-first techniques. Database-first generates C# classes from an existing database schema, while code-first enables us to create their database schema using C# classes.

- **Migrations**: EF Core has a sophisticated migration system that allows you to evolve your database structure over time. This functionality tracks model changes and applies them to your database schema in a controlled manner.

- **Modularity and extensibility**: EF Core's design focuses on modularity, allowing you to maintain a lightweight application by including only the necessary components. It also has some extension points for customizing its behavior and integrating third-party libraries.

- **Multiple database providers**: EF Core supports a variety of database providers, including SQL Server, MySQL, SQLite, PostgreSQL, and others. It allows you to move between databases with few changes to your code.

- **Tracking and no-tracking queries**: EF Core offers options for tracking changes made to your entities, which is helpful for data updates. It also allows for no-tracking queries for read-only operations, which improves performance by lowering overhead.

- **Concurrency control**: Includes support for dealing with concurrency conflicts in a multi-user environment, assuring data consistency and integrity.

- **Caching and batch updates**: EF Core includes first-level caching and improved batch update functionality, reducing database round trips.

Benefits of using EF Core

EF Core provides several critical advantages in ASP.NET MVC applications. For starters, it simplifies data access and saves boilerplate code. We can concentrate on business logic rather than database processes. The ability of EF Core to transform LINQ queries into SQL, reducing the need for human SQL code, is mainly responsible for this efficiency. Furthermore, its code-first approach simplifies database schema upgrades, making managing and evolving database structures easier.

Another significant advantage of utilizing EF Core in ASP.NET MVC applications, mentioned earlier in the key features, is its support for diverse database providers. This adaptability enables us to move between databases with little code changes. Furthermore, EF Core improves performance with lazy, eager, and explicit loading capabilities, which manage data retrieval effectively and reduce server stress. Furthermore, its built-in caching method increases application speed by avoiding unnecessary database requests, resulting in more responsive and scalable ASP.NET MVC applications.

Key concepts of DbContext, DbSet, Migrations

The EF framework is built on three key components: DbContext, DbSet, and Migrations. Each serves a distinct and critical function in bridging the gap between your application's data models and the database itself, thereby speeding up database operations and schema management. Let us dive into these components to learn about their functions and how they work together to improve database management in a code-first approach.

Our gateway to database operations with DbContext

Entity Framework often uses the DbContext class. It acts as a conduit between your domain or entity classes and the database, making database administration more manageable. It provides techniques to query, insert, update, and delete data while successfully managing database connection and operation management complications. It enables us to concentrate on business logic rather than the intricacies of database access. It makes DbContext an essential tool for any developer working with Entity Framework in a C# environment.

Managing entity collections with DbSet

DbSet is a property of DbContext that represents a collection of entities of a given kind that corresponds to a table in the database. Entity Framework is notified of its responsibilities to maintain an entity class concerning the database by declaring a DbSet. DbSet has features for reading, inserting, modifying, and removing entities. A `DbSet<Student>` in your DbContext, for example, simplifies actions such as adding new students, retrieving students based on criteria, and modifying student information, resulting in a streamlined interface for managing entity collections.

Changing our database schema with Migrations

Migrations are essential to Entity Framework, allowing you to manage and propagate real-time changes from your code-first models to the database schema. Migrations ensure that our database structure remains in sync with your model classes without data loss as your application matures. When entity classes are modified, such as by introducing a new property, migrations allow Entity Framework to adapt the database schema accordingly, whether by adding new tables, changing columns, or changing relationships. This functionality is crucial for ensuring the continuity and evolution of your database as your application grows.

DbContext, DbSet, and Migrations work together to create a unified and efficient framework for managing relational data in .NET applications. By leveraging these components, we may take a code-first approach to database management, making it more straightforward and aligned with object-oriented programming concepts. This Entity Framework integration with your C# projects opens the way for a more streamlined, effective, and developer-friendly database administration experience.

Installing necessary tools and packages: We must install the EF Core tools on our device to integrate EF Core into our development environment. The command dotnet tool install is:

```
1. dotnet tool install --global dotnet-ef --version 8.0
```

The EF Core command line tools, specifically version 8.0, are installed throughout the entire system with this command. By installing it globally, we ensure these tools are accessible from any project or directory, allowing us to manage migrations and update database schemas straight from the command line in any .NET project.

Choose the database and use his provider/driver package to use EF Core. We need to observe what the application requires for data storage, so the choice depends on it. Here are some samples with command lines to add to your application:

```
1. // Microsoft SqlServer
2. dotnet add package Microsoft.EntityFrameworkCore.SqlServer
3.
4. // MySQL
5. dotnet add package Microsoft.EntityFrameworkCore.MySQL
6.
7. // Oracle
8. dotnet add package Oracle.EntityFrameworkCore
```

You can search the web or the manufacturer's website to use another provider. You can google **Provider for MongoDB in C# .NET**" and the result will be something like that:

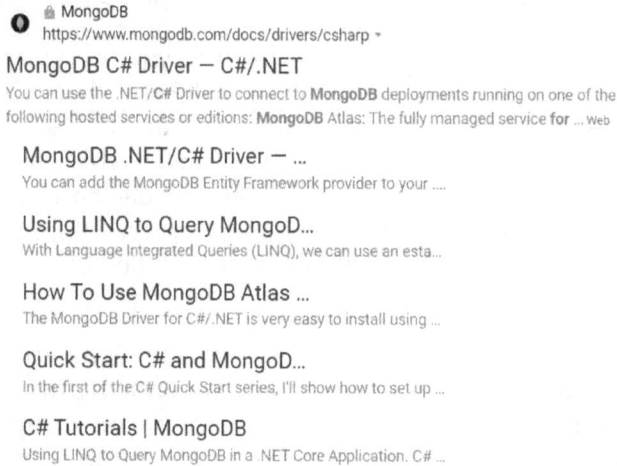

Figure 13.9: Google Search for Mongo

Then add the EF Core tools:

```
1. dotnet add package Microsoft.EntityFrameworkCore.Tools
```

The following figure depicts their appearance in the NuGet of the project:

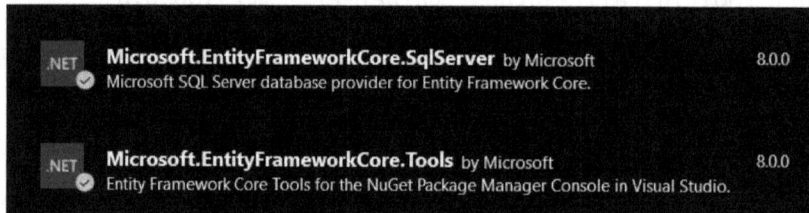

Figure 13.10: NuGet packages

Configuring Entity Framework

We must create a unique **DbContext** for each database to configure the system. Even though our application can support multiple databases and various database vendors, each database requires its own **DbContext** for proper configuration.

Create the **DbContext** class for the application. In this sample, we are creating a **HostpitalContext** that inherits from **DbContext**:

```
1. // Importing necessary namespaces
2. using Microsoft.EntityFrameworkCore;
3. using MyEfCoreApp.Models;
4.
5. namespace MyEfCoreApp.DbContexts;
```

```
6.  // Defining HospitalContext class which inherits from DbContext
7.  public class HospitalContext : DbContext
8.  {
9.      // Constructor for HospitalContext, receiving DbContextOptions
    and passing them to the base DbContext class
10.     public HospitalContext(DbContextOptions<HospitalContext>
    options) : base(options)
11.     {
12.     }
13.     // Declaring a DbSet property for Patient. This will map to a
    database table and provide access to Patient entities.
14.     public DbSet<Patient>? Patients { get; set; }
15.     // Overriding the OnModelCreating method to configure the model
    that Entity Framework uses to create the database schema
16.     protected override void OnModelCreating(ModelBuilder
    modelBuilder)
17.     {
18.         // Specifying that the Patient entity maps to a table named
    "Patient" in the database
19.         modelBuilder.Entity<Patient>().ToTable("Patients");
20.     }
21. }
```

This code snippet sets up a DbContext for an ASP.NET Core application using EF Core. The HospitalContext class, derived from DbContext, is crucial for configuring the connection to the database and mapping the Patient model to a database table. The **OnModelCreating** method provides a space to configure additional model settings, like table names and relationships. Line 19 appears in the next topic.

We now need to configure the DbContext in the **Program.cs** file by adding it to the **Services** collection as a DbContext service:

```
1.  ...
2.  builder.Services.AddDbContext<HospitalContext>(options =>
3.      options.UseSqlServer(builder.Configuration.GetConnectionString
    ("DefaultConnection")));
```

Each database from different contexts and providers requires this process.

Code-first vs. database-first approaches

When considering database design strategies in Entity Framework, two basic approaches are frequently compared: code-first and database-first. Both have distinct characteristics and cater to various developmental needs and preferences. Understanding the differences between these approaches allows us to make informed decisions about which best meets our project's needs.

Code-first methodology

We begin the code-first method by defining our domain models in C# classes. These classes reflect the information we want to keep in our database. We prioritize the business objects and their relationships over the underlying database structure. After we have designed our domain, Entity Framework generates the database schema based on these classes. This method effectively prioritizes object-oriented design while maintaining agility in our development process.

The following are some of the critical benefits of code-first:

- **Flexibility**: We can develop our application by upgrading our C# classes and updating the database schema with migrations.
- **Developer-centric**: It enables us to work in a familiar environment (C# and .NET) without requiring extensive database knowledge.

It facilitates rapid development and iterative adjustments, making it excellent for Agile approaches.

Database-first strategy

In the database-first technique, on the other hand, we begin by building our database schema directly in a database management tool. Tables, relationships, constraints, and other database objects are defined first. After we have created the database schema, we will utilize Entity Framework to produce C# classes that correspond to it. This strategy is appropriate for situations where database architecture is a primary issue or when working with an existing database.

The following are the primary benefits of database-first:

- **Control**: We have complete control over the database schema, which is critical in cases requiring specialized database optimizations.
- **Database-centric**: It is advantageous when our team has excellent database expertise and chooses to develop in a database-focused atmosphere.
- **Integration**: It is appropriate for integrating with existing databases with predefined schema.

Let us select the best approach. Some factors, including the skills of our team, project needs, and the existing development environment, influence our decision between code-first and database-first techniques. The code-first strategy is helpful if we start a new project focusing on domain-driven design and can alter our database structure. However, if we are dealing with an existing database or if our project requires a database-centric design from the start, the database-first approach is preferable.

In conclusion, each strategy has advantages and caters to different growth philosophies. When determining which technique to choose, we need to carefully analyze our project's specific needs as well as the strengths of our team.

Creating a sample database for demonstration:

Start a database using code-first, we need to create the models:

1. Let us see the entity **Patient** from *line 19* in the previous code:

```
1. public class Patient
2. {
3.     public int ID { get; set; }
4.     public string LastName { get; set; }
5.     public string FirstMidName { get; set; }
6.     public List<Doctor> Doctor { get; set; }
7. }
```

In the **Patient** model, a patient is associated with multiple doctors. Therefore, we represent **Doctor** as a List.

2. Let us take a look at the **Doctor** model:

```
1. public class Doctor
2. {
3.     public int ID { get; set; }
4.     public string LastName { get; set; }
5.     public string FirstMidName { get; set; }
6.     public string Specialty { get; set; }
7. }
```

3. Now, run the migrations command to initialize the database:

```
1. dotnet ef migrations add InitialMigration
```

4. Add **--context** to the command line if it has more than one context. Let us see the sample:

```
1. dotnet ef migrations add InitialCreate --context MyOtherDbContext
```

The following figure demonstrates our **Solution Explorer**:

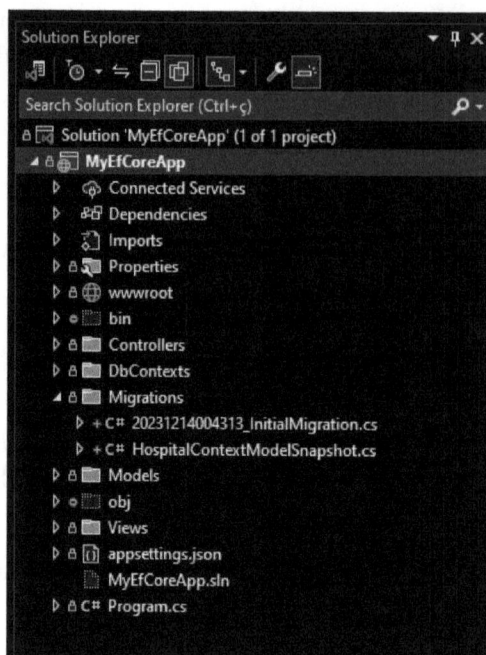

Figure 13.11: NuGet packages

5. This command will create a **Migration** folder, as shown in the image above.

6. Now, you need to execute the command to create the database: Here is the command:

    ```
    1. dotnet ef database update
    ```

7. If you change the model, run the **ef update** command to keep the database current. Let us see the command to do it. Start adding a new meaningful name for the migration.

    ```
    1. dotnet ef migrations add NameOfYourMigration
    ```

8. The **NameOfYourMigration** is a new name chosen. To update the database, run the update:

    ```
    1. dotnet ef migrations database update
    ```

Understanding LINQ queries with Entity Framework Core

LINQ is a sophisticated querying language in .NET that allows us to build expressive, legible queries against our data. LINQ becomes an even more powerful tool when combined with EF Core, allowing us to interface with our databases more straightforwardly and efficiently.

- **LINQ fundamentals with EF Core LINQ to Entities**: This is the method of querying our database with LINQ via EF Core. It converts our LINQ queries into SQL queries, which run against the database.

- **Query syntax vs. method syntax**: LINQ gives two syntax alternatives when writing queries. Query syntax is comparable to SQL syntax. However, it is typically more understandable, particularly for complex queries. Many developers prefer method syntax because it is more versatile and powerful.

- **Deferred execution**: Deferred execution is a significant feature of LINQ with EF Core. It means our query is not run on the database unless we loop over the query results or call a method like **ToList()**. It enables us to create queries dynamically and execute them at the most appropriate time.

LINQ query creation

LINQ queries are normally written by referencing a DbSet from our DbContext. This DbSet is a representation of a table in our database. We may filter, sort, group, and project our data using various LINQ operations. Here is a simple example:

```
1.  var students = context.Students
2.                        .Where(s => s.Age > 18)
3.                        .OrderBy(s => s.LastName)
4.                        .ToList();
```

In this example, we query the **Students** table, filter for students over 18, and then sort the results by last name.

LINQ advanced functions include the following:

- **Joining data**: Similar to SQL joins, we can use LINQ to join distinct tables (DbSets) based on a standard key.

- **Data grouping**: LINQ enables us to group data by a given key and execute aggregations or other operations on each group.

- We may convert our data into a different shape using the **Select** operator. Building DTOs containing only the required data is convenient.

- Eager, lazy, and explicit loading are three methods for loading relevant data. Eager loading includes related data in the first query, lazy loading includes it when the property is queried, and explicit loading includes it in a separate query.

Considerations for performance include the following best practices:

Considering performance effects while using LINQ with EF Core is critical. Complex queries, overly eager loading, or inefficient projections can all cause bottlenecks in performance. To guarantee that our queries are efficient and optimized for our individual use cases, we should continually evaluate them and use SQL profiling tools.

Understanding LINQ queries with EF Core is a powerful combination that improves data access in.NET applications. We can develop efficient, readable, and maintainable data access code by leveraging LINQ's expressive syntax and EF Core's comprehensive data modeling. We can use LINQ's full potential to construct attractive data-driven apps with practice and attention to performance.

Setting up the development environment

Begin by creating a new project to set up the development environment for an ASP.NET Core MVC project utilizing EF Core and a code-first approach.

1. To create the **MyEfCoreApp** project, choose a directory, like **C:\MyProjects**, and run the command line:

    ```
    1.  dotnet new mvc -n MyEfCoreApp
    ```

2. Then, using **cd MyEfCoreApp**, navigate to your project directory.

3. Using the **dotnet** add package, install the essential EF Core NuGet packages for your database of choice.

4. Next, define your DbContext and models that reflect your database structure.

5. Set up your DbContext in **Program.cs** and the connection string in **appsettings.json**.

6. Here is how to do it: Add to **appsettings.json** the database connection string:

    ```
    1.  "ConnectionStrings": {
    2.      "DefaultConnection": "Server=(localdb)\\
        mssqllocaldb;Database=MyEfCoreDb;Trusted_Connection=True;"
    3.  }
    ```

7. The sample above is for a local SQL Server database. Change the server, database, and other options to match your database server and preferences.

8. Add the DbContext to the **Program.cs**:

    ```
    1.  builder.Services.AddDbContext<ApplicationDbContext>(options =>
    2.      options.UseSqlServer(builder.Configuration.GetConnectionStri
        ng("DefaultConnection")));
    ```

Finally, use **dotnet ef migrations** and add **InitialCreate** to produce the initial migration based on your models, followed by dotnet ef database update to create the database schema based on this migration. This procedure lays the groundwork for developing ASP.NET Core MVC apps utilizing the code-first approach with EF Core.

Producing and consuming APIs using MVC

Producing and consuming APIs in ASP.NET Core using the MVC pattern provides a comprehensive and quick approach to constructing online apps. This method is based on a clear separation of concerns, which helps to organize and scale your application.

Making APIs in ASP.NET Core using MVC

The process of building APIs in ASP.NET Core using the MVC pattern is outlined in the following:

- **Creating our Model**: Our data model must be defined as the initial step in this journey. This model is critical since it represents the data we want to provide via our API. In ASP.NET Core, this is commonly accomplished by building a C# class with properties corresponding to the data structure. This model serves as the core of our application, laying the groundwork for the data we will be working with.

  For example, we will continue with the **Product** example used in this chapter.

- **Creating the Controller**: After our model is in place, we will create a Controller. The Controller in the MVC architecture is in charge of accepting incoming HTTP requests and returning suitable replies. In contrast to standard MVC, where Controllers return Views, our API controllers inherit from **ControllerBase**. Our primary focus is on data management rather than rendering views.

Create a folder named WebApi in the root project

Implementing actions: Within our controller, we provide several action methods that correlate to HTTP verbs, such as GET, POST, PUT, and DELETE. Each of these action methods is in charge of dealing with a specific type of request. A GET method, for example, is used to get data, a POST method to add new data, and so on. This framework enables a clear and intuitive structure, which makes our API easy to navigate and maintain.

- Add the Controller **ProductsController.cs** like this:

```
1. using Microsoft.AspNetCore.Mvc;
2. using Microsoft.EntityFrameworkCore;
3. using MyEfCoreApp.DbContexts;
4. using MyEfCoreApp.Models;
5.
6. namespace MyEfCoreApp.WebApi;
7.
8. [Route("api/[controller]")]
9. [ApiController]
10. public class ProductsController(ApplicationDbContext context) :
```

```
     ControllerBase
11.  {
12.      private bool ProductExists(int id)
13.      {
14.          return context.Products.Any(e => e.Id == id);
15.      }
16.
17.      // GET: api/products
18.      [HttpGet]
19.      public async Task<ActionResult<IEnumerable<Product>>>
     GetProducts()
20.      {
21.          return await context.Products.ToListAsync();
22.      }
23.
24.      // GET: api/products/5
25.      [HttpGet("{id}")]
26.      public async Task<ActionResult<Product>> GetProduct(int id)
27.      {
28.          var product = await context.Products.FindAsync(id);
29.
30.          if (product == null)
31.          {
32.              return NotFound();
33.          }
34.
35.          return product;
36.      }
37.
38.      // POST: api/products
39.      [HttpPost]
40.      public async Task<ActionResult<Product>> PostProduct
     (Product product)
41.      {
42.          context.Products.Add(product);
43.          await context.SaveChangesAsync();
44.
45.          return CreatedAtAction(nameof(GetProdu
     ct), new { id = product.Id }, product);
46.      }
```

```
47.
48.     [HttpPut("{id}")]
49.     public async Task<IActionResult> PutProduct(int id, Product
   product)
50.     {
51.         if (id != product.Id)
52.         {
53.             return BadRequest();
54.         }
55.
56.         context.Entry(product).State = EntityState.Modified;
57.
58.         try
59.         {
60.             await context.SaveChangesAsync();
61.         }
62.         catch (DbUpdateConcurrencyException)
63.         {
64.             if (!ProductExists(id))
65.             {
66.                 return NotFound();
67.             }
68.
69.             throw;
70.         }
71.
72.         return NoContent();
73.     }
74.
75.     // DELETE: api/products/5
76.     [HttpDelete("{id}")]
77.     public async Task<IActionResult> DeleteProduct(int id)
78.     {
79.         var product = await context.Products.FindAsync(id);
80.         if (product == null)
81.         {
82.             return NotFound();
83.         }
84.
85.         context.Products.Remove(product);
```

```
86.          await context.SaveChangesAsync();
87.
88.          return NoContent();
89.     }
90. }
```

- **Delivering data**: One of the most potent aspects of ASP.NET Core when delivering data from action methods is its ability to serialize our model objects automatically into JSON format. This simplicity ensures that the system immediately translates data returned in response to an HTTP request into a format the client can understand.

  In *line 8*, we have added the route for the API.

- Add to the **Program.cs** the necessary service to consume the API:

```
1. builder.Services.AddHttpClient();
```

- Install the **Newtonsoft.Json** using the menus in Visual Studio: **Tools | NuGet Package Manager | Package Manager Console**, and run:

```
1. Install-Package Newtonsoft.Json
```

- Alter the initializer of the **ProductsController** to add the **IHttpClientFactory**:

```
1. using Microsoft.AspNetCore.Mvc;
2. using Microsoft.EntityFrameworkCore;
3. using MyEfCoreApp.DbContexts;
4. using MyEfCoreApp.Models;
5. using Newtonsoft.Json;
6.
7. namespace MyEfCoreApp.Controllers;
8.
9. public class ProductsController(ApplicationDbContext context,
10.                                IHttpClientFactory
    clientFactory) : Controller
11. {
12.
13. ...
```

- Let us replace the **Edit** in **ProductController.cs** to use the API:

```
1. public async Task<IActionResult> Edit(int? id)
2. {
3.     if (id == null)
4.     {
5.         return NotFound();
6.     }
```

```
7.        var request = new HttpRequestMessage(HttpMethod.
   Get, $"http://localhost:5074/api/products/{id}");
8.        var client = clientFactory.CreateClient();
9.        var response = await client.SendAsync(request);
10.       if (!response.IsSuccessStatusCode) return NotFound();
11.       var jsonString = await response.Content.ReadAsStringAsync();
12.       var product = JsonConvert.DeserializeObject<Product>(jsonSt
   ring);
13.       return View(product);
14. }
```

Note the port and the path in *line 7,* observe that we are using the port from the console while running:

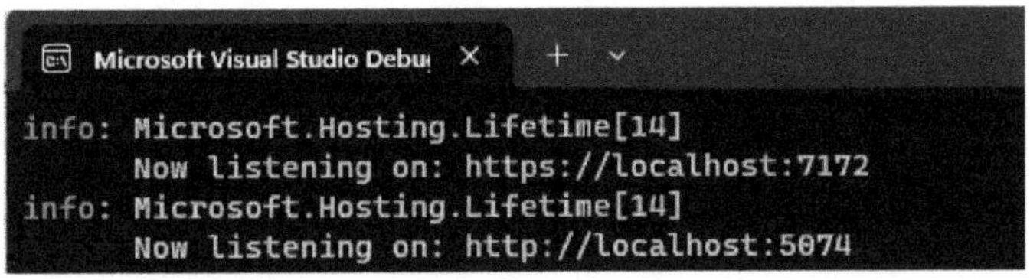

Figure 13.12: Console

Let us see what this code does. The **Edit** method is an asynchronous action designed to handle HTTP GET requests for editing. The method accepts an optional integer **id** parameter. If **id** is null, it returns a **NotFound** result, indicating the requested resource is unavailable. If **id** is provided, the method constructs an HTTP GET request to a specified API endpoint in *line 7* using **HttpRequestMessage**. It sends this request using an HTTP client obtained from **clientFactory**. If the response is successful in *line 10,* the method reads in *line 11* the response content as a string and deserializes it into a **Product** object using **JsonConvert.DeserializeObject**, and returns the View for editing this product, passing the product as a Model. If the response is not successful, it returns a **NotFound** result.

- Let us do the same for the **Edit**:

```
1. // POST: Products/Edit/5
2. [HttpPost]
3. [ValidateAntiForgeryToken]
4. public async Task<IActionResult> Edit(int id,
   [Bind("Id,Name,Price")] Product product)
5. {
6.     if (id != product.Id)
7.     {
8.         return NotFound();
9.     }
10.
```

```
11.    if (!ModelState.IsValid) return View(product);
12.
13.    try
14.    {
15.        context.Update(product);
16.        await context.SaveChangesAsync();
17.    }
18.    catch (DbUpdateConcurrencyException)
19.    {
20.        if (!ProductExists(product.Id))
21.        {
22.            return NotFound();
23.        }
24.        else
25.        {
26.            throw;
27.        }
28.    }
29.    return RedirectToAction(nameof(Index));
30. }
```

- Replace it with this code:

```
1.     [HttpPost]
2.     [ValidateAntiForgeryToken]
3.     public async Task<IActionResult> Edit(int id,
   [Bind("Id,Name,Price")] Product product)
4.     {
5.         if (id != product.Id)
6.         {
7.             return NotFound();
8.         }
9.         if (!ModelState.IsValid) return View(product);
10.        var client = clientFactory.CreateClient();
11.        var content = new StringContent(JsonConvert.
   SerializeObject(product), Encoding.UTF8, "application/json");
12.        var response = await client.PutAsync
   ($"http://localhost:5074/api/products/{id}", content);
13.        if (response.IsSuccessStatusCode)
14.        {
15.            return RedirectToAction(nameof(Index));
16.        }
```

```
17.          if (response.StatusCode == HttpStatusCode.NotFound)
18.          {
19.              return NotFound();
20.          }
21.          return View(product);
22.      }
```

- Here is the code running. The **Edit** method returned with success:

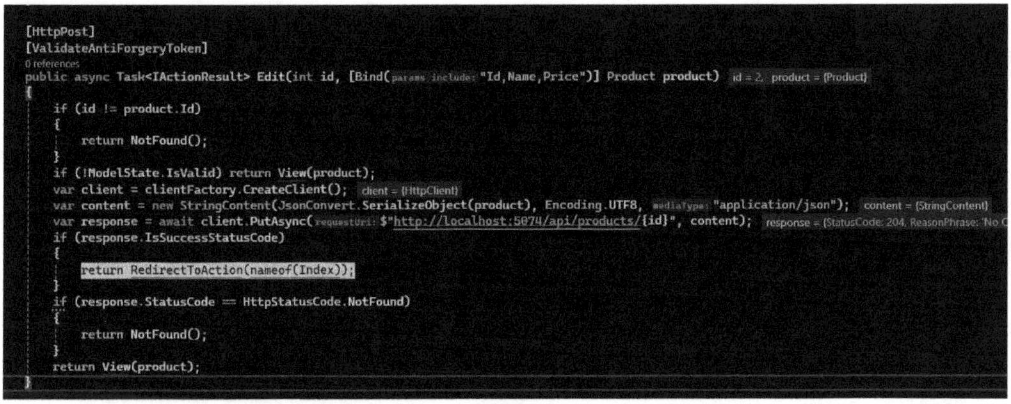

Figure 13.13: Breakpoint on execution

To summarize, developing APIs in ASP.NET Core using MVC involves designing data models, constructing controllers, implementing action methods to handle various HTTP requests, serializing data automatically for responses, and configuring URL mapping and routing. This rigorous approach results in a well-organized, efficient, scalable web application.

Testing in MVC applications

We highlight the necessity of extensive testing in MVC apps written with C# and ASP. NET Core to assure the reliability and operation of our projects. We primarily do three kinds of testing. **Unit tests** allow us to examine individual components such as Models, Controllers, and Helper methods, guaranteeing that each portion works appropriately in isolation. **Integration tests** are essential for investigating the relationships of various components, such as database access and external services. Meanwhile, **functional tests** allow us to evaluate the program from the user's standpoint, ensuring the system functions properly.

To make our testing process more accessible, we use a variety of frameworks and technologies. Depending on our needs, we frequently use xUnit, NUnit, and MSTest to write test cases. Mocking libraries such as **Moq** or **NSubstitute** are used in unit tests to replicate the behavior of real objects. Furthermore, Selenium is a helpful tool for automating web browsers for functional testing, mainly when testing views and user interactions.

Our testing strategy also includes best practices that improve the quality and maintainability of our tests. We advocate for regular and early testing throughout development to achieve complete code coverage while prioritizing key paths. Automated testing is necessary in our CI/CD pipelines, guaranteeing that new modifications do not damage current functionalities. Furthermore, we always attempt to keep our tests clear and comprehensible, reworking them as our codebase evolves and new requirements emerge. This balanced and rigorous testing methodology is critical in producing robust and dependable MVC apps in C#.

Example: Start creating a new xUnit test in the **Visual Studio | File | Start Window**, and search for xUnit:

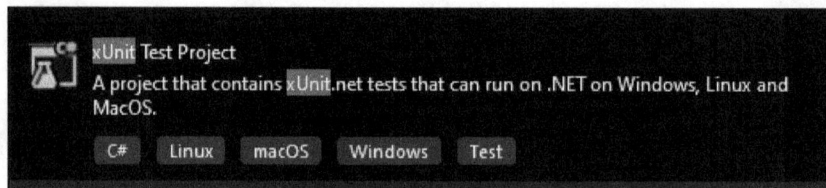

Figure 13.14: xUnit Test Project template

The project's name should start the test, plus the name of the project we would like to test.

- Create the model tests for the models like **Product**, like:

```
1.  using MyEfCoreApp.Models;
2.
3.  namespace TestMyEfCodeApp;
4.  public class ProductTests
5.  {
6.      [Fact]
7.      public void Product_SetGet_ReturnsExpectedValues()
8.      {
9.          // Arrange
10.         var product = new Product();
11.         // Act
12.         product.Id = 1;
13.         product.Name = "Test Product";
14.         product.Price = 9.99m;
15.         // Assert
16.         Assert.Equal(1, product.Id);
17.         Assert.Equal("Test Product", product.Name);
18.         Assert.Equal(9.99m, product.Price);
19.     }
20.
21.     [Fact]
```

```
22.      public void Product_Constructor_SetsExpectedValues()
23.      {
24.          // Arrange
25.          var expectedId = 1;
26.          var expectedName = "Test Product";
27.          var expectedPrice = 9.99m;
28.          // Act
29.          var product = new Product
30.          {
31.              Id = expectedId,
32.              Name = expectedName,
33.              Price = expectedPrice
34.          };
35.          // Assert
36.          Assert.Equal(expectedId, product.Id);
37.          Assert.Equal(expectedName, product.Name);
38.          Assert.Equal(expectedPrice, product.Price);
39.      }
40. }
```

- Let us test the **WebApi** and start creating the class **ProductsApiControllerTests.cs**, like this:

```
1. using Microsoft.AspNetCore.Mvc;
2. using Microsoft.EntityFrameworkCore;
3. using MyEfCoreApp.DbContexts;
4. using MyEfCoreApp.Models;
5. using MyEfCoreApp.WebApi;
6.
7. namespace TestMyEfCodeApp;
8. public class ProductsApiControllerTests
9. {
10.     private readonly ProductsApiController _controller;
11.     private readonly ApplicationDbContext _context;
12.     public ProductsApiControllerTests()
13.     {
14.         var options = new DbContextOptionsBuilder<ApplicationDb
    Context>()
15.             .UseInMemoryDatabase(databaseName: "TestDatabase")
16.             .Options;
17.         _context = new ApplicationDbContext(options);
18.         _controller = new ProductsApiController(_context);
```

```
19.      }
20.
21.      [Fact]
22.      public async Task GetProducts_ReturnsOkResult_
    WithListOfProducts()
23.      {
24.          // Arrange
25.          var products = new List<Product>
26.          {
27.              new() { Id = 1, Name = "Product 1", Price = 9.99m
    },
28.              new() { Id = 2, Name = "Product 2", Price =
    19.99m }
29.          };
30.          foreach (var product in products)
31.          {
32.              _context.Products.Add(product);
33.          }
34.          await _context.SaveChangesAsync();
35.
36.          // Act
37.          var result = await _controller.GetProducts();
38.          // Assert
39.          var okResult = Assert.IsType<OkObjectResult>
    (result.Result);
40.          var returnProducts = Assert.IsType<List<Product>>
    (okResult.Value);
41.          Assert.Equal(2, returnProducts.Count());
42.      }
43. }
```

- Create this dependency class **FakeHttpMessageHandler.cs**, like this:

```
1. namespace TestMyEfCodeApp;
2. public class FakeHttpMessageHandler : HttpMessageHandler
3. {
4.     private readonly HttpResponseMessage _response;
5.     public FakeHttpMessageHandler(HttpResponseMessage response)
6.     {
7.         _response = response;
8.     }
9.     protected override async Task<HttpResponseMessage>
```

```
      SendAsync(HttpRequestMessage request, CancellationToken
      cancellationToken)
10.     {
11.         return await Task.FromResult(_response);
12.     }
13. }
```

In our test class **ProductsApiControllerTests**, we are focusing on testing our **ProductsApiController** in the **MyEfCoreApp.WebApi** namespace. Our setup involves two main components: the API controller itself and an in-memory application context.

First, we create an instance of **ApplicationDbContext** using EF Core's in-memory database. We chose **TestDatabase** as our database name. This approach allows us to simulate database operations without an accurate database, making our tests faster and more isolated.

Then, we initialize our **ProductsApiController**, passing the in-memory context to its constructor. This setup mimics the controller's behavior in a real-world scenario, interacting with the DbContext.

In the test method **GetProducts_ReturnsOkResult_WithListOfProducts**, we are testing the GetProducts action of the controller. We start by arranging our test environment:

- Using **our _context**, we generate a list of **Product** objects and insert them into the in-memory database.

- We store these modifications asynchronously to ensure they are reflected in our in-memory database.

Next, we act on our test by invoking the **GetProducts** method on our controller. This method should retrieve the list of products we just added.

Finally, we assert several things:

- The result of calling **GetProducts** should be an **OkObjectResult**, indicating a successful operation.

- We expect the value of this result to be a list of **Product** objects.

- We verify that the count of products returned matches our expectations (in this case, 2).

This test ensures that our controller's **GetProducts** action correctly retrieves products from the DbContext and returns them in the expected format.

We could add more tests for other methods like **GetProduct**, **PostProduct**, **PutProduct**, and **DeleteProduct** to comprehensively validate the functionality of our **ProductsApiController**:

- Teste project source code for **TestMyEfCodeApp.csproj**:

```
1.  <Project Sdk="Microsoft.NET.Sdk">
2.
3.    <PropertyGroup>
4.      <TargetFramework>net8.0</TargetFramework>
5.      <ImplicitUsings>enable</ImplicitUsings>
6.      <Nullable>enable</Nullable>
7.      <IsPackable>false</IsPackable>
8.      <IsTestProject>true</IsTestProject>
9.    </PropertyGroup>
10.
11.   <ItemGroup>
12.     <PackageReference Include="Flurl.Http" Version="4.0.0" />
13.     <PackageReference Include="Microsoft.Extensions.Http"
   Version="8.0.0" />
14.     <PackageReference Include="Microsoft.NET.Test.Sdk"
   Version="17.8.0" />
15.     <PackageReference Include="Moq" Version="4.20.70" />
16.     <PackageReference Include="xunit" Version="2.4.2" />
17.     <PackageReference Include="xunit.runner.visualstudio"
   Version="2.4.5">
18.        <IncludeAssets>runtime; build; native; contentfiles;
   analyzers; buildtransitive</IncludeAssets>
19.        <PrivateAssets>all</PrivateAssets>
20.     </PackageReference>
21.     <PackageReference Include="coverlet.collector"
   Version="6.0.0">
22.        <IncludeAssets>runtime; build; native; contentfiles;
   analyzers; buildtransitive</IncludeAssets>
23.        <PrivateAssets>all</PrivateAssets>
24.     </PackageReference>
25.   </ItemGroup>
26.
27.   <ItemGroup>
28.     <ProjectReference Include="..\MyEfCoreApp\MyEfCoreApp.
   csproj" />
29.   </ItemGroup>
30.
31. </Project>
```

- It is important to add:

  1. `<PackageReference Include="Microsoft.Extensions.Http" Version="8.0.0" />`

  2. `<PackageReference Include="Moq" Version="4.20.70" />`

- Running the tests in **Visual Studio | Tests | Run All Tests**, we will have this result:

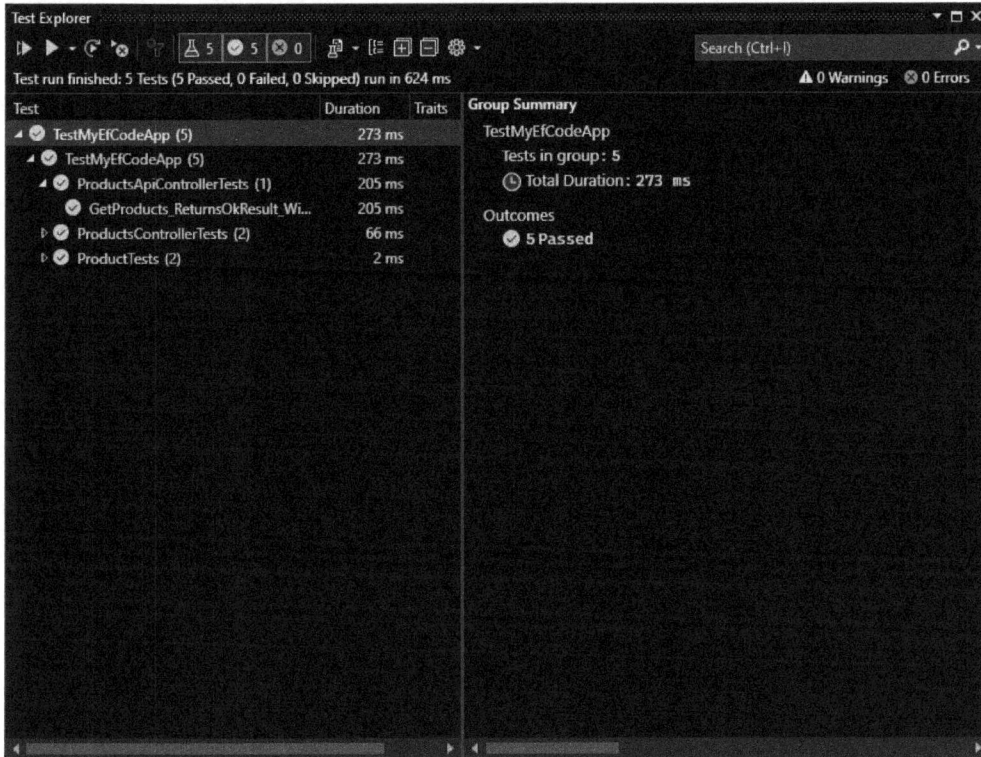

Figure 13.15: Test Explorer

Note: If we use it in CI/CD like Jenkins or GitHub Actions, we must add the `Microsoft.NET.Test.Sdk` to the project we want to test.

- Following is the NuGet package for Test SDK:

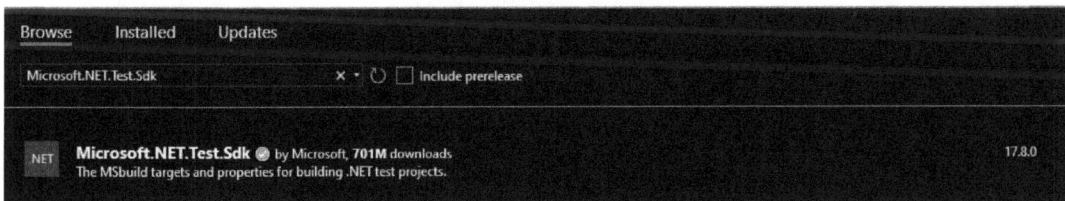

Figure 13.16: Microsoft.NET.Test.Sdk in NuGet

Finally, unit testing is critical to our development process for ASP.NET Core MVC applications, highlighting its unquestionable value. By concentrating on these tests, we verify that each component of our program, whether models, controllers, or services, performs as intended under various situations. This method not only assists us in identifying and correcting problems at an early stage, but it also considerably enhances our software's general quality and reliability. Our dedication to unit testing generates an environment of excellence and precision, allowing us to confidently make changes and updates, knowing that our foundations are solid and well-validated. We establish the groundwork for robust, efficient, and trustworthy apps through our rigorous and focused unit testing efforts.

Conclusion

We looked at the MVC pattern in ASP.NET Core and how it may help us build robust and scalable online apps. We learned how to design controllers and views, utilize EF Core to work with data, implement form validation, and use ViewModel in MVC. We also discussed the new ASP.NET Core.NET capabilities and how they improve the MVC framework. We hope this chapter provided a solid basis for constructing web apps in ASP. NET Core using MVC.

In the next chapter, we will get into the world of web development, mastering web services in the .NET platform is essential. We will explore everything from RESTful APIs to gRPC and GraphQL, with a focus on security.

Join our book's Discord space

Join the book's Discord Workspace for Latest updates, Offers, Tech happenings around the world, New Release and Sessions with the Authors:

https://discord.bpbonline.com

CHAPTER 14

Mastering Web Services

Introduction

In the ever-evolving landscape of web development, mastering web services is not just an advantage but a necessity. This chapter explores the intricate world of web services within the .NET, a realm that offers both challenges and opportunities. We embark on a journey exploring the creation and consumption of various web services, focusing on the robust .NET environment.

This chapter is designed as a comprehensive guide, from the fundamentals of RESTful APIs in ASP.NET Core to the advanced concepts of gRPC and GraphQL within the .NET. We will unravel the complexities of these technologies, offering you a clear path to harness their full potential. Whether you are a novice or an experienced developer, the insights and practical examples provided here will elevate your skills in web service mastery.

Moreover, we do not overlook the critical security aspect of web services. As we navigate these technologies, we will also focus on best practices and strategies to secure your web services, ensuring they are efficient and robust against contemporary cyber threats.

As we get into each topic, remember the versatility and power of .NET in web service development. This chapter is more than just a learning path; it is a journey toward mastering the art of web services in the .NET ecosystem.

Structure

This chapter covers the following topics:

- Introduction to web services in .NET
- Creating RESTful APIs with ASP.NET Core
- Consuming web services in .NET
- Working with gRPC in .NET
- Introduction to GraphQL and .NET
- Understanding HTTP client in .NET
- Security considerations in web services
- Understanding API versioning
- Implementing pagination in APIs
- API testing with Postman and Swagger

Objectives

This chapter's first objective is to thoroughly understand RESTful APIs within the ASP. NET Core framework. This encompasses learning the foundational concepts, design principles, and practical implementation of RESTful services, ensuring a solid grasp of building, deploying, and managing APIs effectively. The chapter aims to guide readers through the nuances of data handling and the best practices in RESTful API development, which are crucial for creating scalable and efficient web services.

The second objective expands into exploring advanced web service technologies like gRPC and GraphQL within the .NET ecosystem. This includes understanding their unique features and benefits, and how they differ from traditional RESTful services. Additionally, the chapter emphasizes the importance of web service security, teaching readers to implement robust security measures. The focus is also on practical application, using real-world examples to demonstrate how these technologies are applied in various scenarios, preparing readers for current and emerging trends in web service development.

Introduction to web services in .NET

We go into the complexities of web services within the .NET ecosystem. This introduction will guide the various subjects we will cover, giving a path for novice and experienced us in the realm of .NET web services.

Web services in .NET are software systems that enable interoperable machine-to-machine communication across a network. They are an essential component of the .NET, allowing the development, deployment, and consumption of reusable web-based applications. Here is a more in-depth breakdown:

- **Definition and usage**: A web service is a standardized method of integrating web-based applications that uses open standards such as HTTP, XML, SOAP, and WSDL. Web services in the context of .NET and C# are built on the ASP.NET and can be created in C#. They allow several apps to connect, typically spanning platforms and languages.

- **SOAP and REST protocols**: Web services are classified into two types:

  o **Simple Object Access Protocol (SOAP)**: These protocol-based services use the SOAP standard to deliver and receive data as XML. SOAP web services are popular in enterprise environments due to their high level of security.

  o **Representational State Transfer (REST)**: These services GET, PUT, POST, and DELETE data via HTTP queries. RESTful services are famous for web API development because they are more accessible and adaptable.

- **Data exchange and communication**: Web services communicate using XML-based communications. Communication with RESTful services can also include JSON, which is lighter and more efficient for web-based communication. These messages are transmitted over the web, allowing different applications built on different technologies to interact.

- **Windows Communication Foundation (WCF)**: WCF is a .NET for developing service-oriented applications. It lets us create secure, dependable, transactional applications across platforms.

- **ASP.NET Web API**: This is a system for making HTTP services that many clients, like browsers and mobile phones, can access. With this tool, you can easily make RESTful.NET apps.

- **Use cases**: In .NET, web services are used for a variety of applications, such as connecting to third-party services, allowing different applications to exchange data, building microservices architectures, and creating services that can be consumed by client apps such as web applications, mobile apps, and other services.

- **Development tools**: Visual Studio provides a complete environment for programming, testing, and deploying C# web services. Furthermore, EF and Swagger/OpenAPI technologies can be utilized for data access, API documentation, and testing.

Creating RESTful APIs with ASP.NET Core

Creating RESTful APIs with ASP.NET Core and C# is a thrilling adventure into the realm of web services and modern online application development. This section will review the fundamentals before moving on to a practical example using a hospital nursery.

RESTful APIs are the foundation of many modern web applications, providing a consistent interface for interacting with back-end services. Microsoft's ASP.NET Core, a cross-platform, high-performance framework, is a good choice for developing these APIs. It provides powerful tools and a versatile environment for designing web services in C#. ASP.NET Core, emphasizing performance, security, and scalability, enables us to design efficient, dependable, and stable APIs.

Exploring RESTful APIs

Representational State Transfer APIs (RESTful APIs) are guidelines for developing web services. They enable different computer systems to connect over the internet quickly and standardize. RESTful APIs conduct operations on resources often expressed in forms such as JSON or XML using conventional HTTP methods (such as GET, POST, PUT, DELETE).

Every RESTful architecture component, or resource, is accessible via a unique **Uniform Resource Identifier (URI)**. A server tells a client the state of the item they requested when they make a RESTful API request. This connection is stateless, meaning each client request contains the information the server requires to perform the request and return the response.

Statelessness, client-server architecture, caching, uniform interface, layered system, and code on demand (optional) are fundamental REST principles. These principles drive the design and implementation of web services that are scalable, reliable, and performant.

RESTful API history

Dr. Roy Fielding established the concept of REST in his Ph.D. dissertation at the *University of California, Irvine*, in 2000 (**https://en.wikipedia.org/wiki/REST**). It attempted to articulate the principles underlying the web's success. REST was not designed to be a new technology but rather a model for explaining existing web standards and their relationship to the web's architecture.

Due to the simplicity and ubiquity of HTTP, the early 2000s saw a shift from more complex **service-oriented architectures (SOAs)** and web services (such as SOAP) toward REST. The need for more efficient, scalable, and flexible communication between disparate systems became evident as the internet and online applications proliferated. RESTful principles, which promote stateless communication and cacheable data, answered these requirements.

With the rise of modern web development methodologies and the acceptance of **JavaScript Object Notation (JSON)** as a data transfer format, the usage of RESTful APIs has accelerated. This represented a substantial departure from the XML-dominated age. Public API companies like RESTful APIs because they are easy to use and do not take up much space.

RESTful APIs have become the backbone of web services and the standard for public APIs by the 2010s, propelling the expansion of web technologies and the evolution of the internet. They facilitated the development of a diverse range of web-based applications, from social media platforms to cloud services, and they continue to play an essential part in the architecture of current web applications.

We are creating an example of web API for a hospital nursery to demonstrate the RESTful in action.

Let us look at a real-world example: a web API for a hospital's nursery. Users can use this API to get information about the nursery, such as available facilities, personnel details, and patient information:

1. **Establishing the project**: First, we opened Visual Studio and started a new ASP. NET Core web API project. We use the ASP.NET Core web application template, the API project type, and the name HospitalNurseryAPI for our project.

2. **Model definition**: Our API requires a model to represent nursery data. In the Models folder, we build a **Nursery** class:

```
1.  using System.ComponentModel.DataAnnotations;
2.
3.  namespace MyEfCoreApp.Models;
4.
5.  public class Nursery
6.  {
7.      [Key]
8.      public int Id { get; set; }
9.
10.     [Required]
11.     [StringLength(100, ErrorMessage = "Name length can't be
    more than 100 characters.")]
12.     [Display(Name = "Nursery Name")]
13.     public string Name { get; set; }
14.
15.     [Range(1, 100, ErrorMessage = "Capacity must be between 1
    and 100.")]
16.     [Display(Name = "Maximum Capacity")]
17.     public int Capacity { get; set; }
18.
19.     [Required]
20.     [Display(Name = "Available Facilities")]
21.     public string Facilities { get; set; }
22. }
```

The use of EF Core is documented in *Chapter 13, Website Development using MVC Pattern*, of this book so that we can continue. Add the **Nursery** to **HospitalDbContext** and run the migration, adding a new one, like:

```
1.  dotnet ef migrations add Nursery --context HospitalDbContext
```

3. **Creating the database context**: For data access, we need to create a database context class. In the **Data** folder, we create a new class, **NurseryDbContext**, which inherits from **DbContext**:

```
1. using Microsoft.EntityFrameworkCore;
2. using MyEfCoreApp.Models;
3.
4. namespace MyEfCoreApp.DbContexts;
5.
6. public class HospitalDbContext : DbContext
7. {
8.
9.     public HospitalDbContext(DbContextOptions
   <HospitalDbContext> options) : base(options)
10.     {
11.     }
12.
13.     public DbSet<Patient>? Patients { get; set; }
14.     public DbSet<Doctor>? Doctors { get; set; }
15.     public DbSet<Nursery>? Nurseries { get; set; }
16.
17.     protected override void OnModelCreating(ModelBuilder
   modelBuilder)
18.     {
19.         modelBuilder.Entity<Doctor>().ToTable("Doctors");
20.         modelBuilder.Entity<Patient>().ToTable("Patients");
21.         modelBuilder.Entity<Nursery>().ToTable("Nurseries");
22.     }
23. }
```

4. **Configuring the database connection**: In **appsettings.json**, we add the connection string to the database:

```
1.  {
2.    "ConnectionStrings": {
3.      "NurseryDatabase": "Server=(localdb)\\
   mssqllocaldb;Database=NurseryDb;Trusted_Connection=True;"
4.    }
```

In **Program.cs**, we configure the context to use SQL Server with the connection string:

```
1. builder.Services.AddDbContext<HospitalDbContext>(options =>
2.     options.UseSqlServer(builder.Configuration.
   GetConnectionString("DefaultConnection")));
```

5. **Creating the repository layer**: We implement a repository layer to abstract data access. Create an **INurseryRepository** interface and a **NurseryRepository** class:

```
1.  public interface INurseryRepository
2.  {
3.      Task<IEnumerable<Nursery>> GetAllAsync();
4.      Task<Nursery> GetByIdAsync(int id);
5.      // Other necessary methods...
6.  }
7.
8.  public class NurseryRepository : INurseryRepository
9.  {
10.     private readonly NurseryDbContext _context;
11.
12.     public NurseryRepository(NurseryDbContext context)
13.     {
14.         _context = context;
15.     }
16.
17.     public async Task<IEnumerable<Nursery>> GetAllAsync()
18.     {
19.         return await _context.Nurseries.ToListAsync();
20.     }
21.
22.     public async Task<Nursery> GetByIdAsync(int id)
23.     {
24.         return await _context.Nurseries.FindAsync(id);
25.     }
26.  }
```

6. **Building the controllers**: Create a **NurseriesController** class in the **Controllers** folder. This controller will handle HTTP requests:

```
1.  [ApiController]
2.  [Route("[controller]")]
3.  public class NurseriesController : ControllerBase
4.  {
5.      private readonly INurseryRepository _repository;
6.
7.      public NurseriesController(INurseryRepository repository)
8.      {
9.          _repository = repository;
10.     }
```

```
11.
12.     [HttpGet]
13.     public async Task<ActionResult<IEnumerable<Nurse
   ry>>> GetAll()
14.     {
15.         return Ok(await _repository.GetAllAsync());
16.     }
17.
18.     [HttpGet("{id}")]
19.     public async Task<ActionResult<Nursery>> Get(int id)
20.     {
21.         var nursery = await _repository.GetByIdAsync(id);
22.         if (nursery == null)
23.         {
24.             return NotFound();
25.         }
26.
27.         return Ok(nursery);
28.     }
29. }
```

7. **Testing and deployment**: Finally, test the API using Postman or a similar tool to ensure it is working correctly. Deploy the API to a suitable hosting environment when it is ready for production.

Consuming web services in .NET

As software creation is constantly changing, being able to talk to web services is very important. Over time, the .NET has grown and improved, making connecting to different web-based tools easier and faster. Using web services is essential in creating and refining current software, whether it is web apps, mobile apps, or desktop programs.

When you use .NET to consume web services, you must send requests to remote web servers and handle the replies. Many web services exist, such as RESTful APIs, SOAP web services, and GraphQL endpoints. Each type provides a unique way to connect and share data. When coders use .NET, they have access to powerful libraries and tools that make this process easier and allow for smooth integration with web services.

The goal of this guide is to give you a complete picture of how to use web services in .NET. We will discuss different approaches and the best ways to do things, with a focus on using **HttpClient**, which is a flexible and powerful HTTP client in the .NET. This guide will teach you how to use and incorporate web services into your .NET apps, no matter how experienced you are as a developer or how new you are to the field.

Consuming web services involves making HTTP requests to a web service and then handling the responses. This can be done through various ways in .NET, but we will focus on using **HttpClient**, a modern HTTP client in the .NET:

1. **Setting up the project**: Start by making a new .NET desktop application or using a .NET project you already have. Using services directly in your controls or services is possible if you make a web app.

2. **Adding required packages**: Ensure that your project has the necessary NuGet packages. The primary package needed is **System.Net.Http** for using **HttpClient**. It is usually included by default in .NET Core projects:

   ```
   1. dotnet add package System.Net.Http
   ```

3. **Creating the HttpClient**: **HttpClient** is intended to be instantiated once and reused throughout the life of an application. We will create an instance of **HttpClient**:

   ```
   1. using System.Net.Http;
   2.
   3. HttpClient client = new HttpClient();
   ```

   For web applications, it is recommended to use **IHttpClientFactory** to handle the lifetimes of **HttpClient** instances.

4. **Making a GET request**: To retrieve data from a web service, we use a GET request. Assume we have an API endpoint that returns a list of nurseries:

   ```
   1. HttpResponseMessage response = await client.GetAsync("http://
      example.com/api/nurseries");
   2. response.EnsureSuccessStatusCode();
   3. string responseBody = await response.Content.
      ReadAsStringAsync();
   4.
   5. // Deserializing JSON to a List of Nursery objects
   6. var nurseries = JsonConvert.DeserializeObject<List<Nursery>>(re
      sponseBody);
   ```

5. **Making a POST request**: To send data to a service, use a POST request. Here is an example of creating a new nursery record:

   ```
   1. Nursery newNursery = new Nursery { Name = "Sunshine Nursery",
      Capacity = 50, Facilities = "Various" };
   2. string json = JsonConvert.SerializeObject(newNursery);
   3. StringContent content = new StringContent(json, Encoding.
      UTF8, "application/json");
   4.
   5. HttpResponseMessage response = await client.PostAsync("http://
      example.com/api/nurseries", content);
   6. response.EnsureSuccessStatusCode();
   ```

```
7.
8. // Reading the response body
9. string responseBody = await response.Content.
   ReadAsStringAsync();
```

6. **Handling responses**: Properly handle responses from the web service. This includes checking the status code and parsing the response body. You can also handle exceptions and errors gracefully.

7. **Closing HttpClient**: In a console application, ensure you properly dispose of **HttpClient** when it is no longer needed:

```
1. client.Dispose();
```

In a web application using **IHttpClientFactory**, this is handled for you.

Best practices are as follows:

- **Use IHttpClientFactory in ASP.NET Core applications**: This helps manage **HttpClient** instances efficiently.

- **Exception handling**: Implement try-catch blocks to handle potential exceptions.

- **Asynchronous programming**: Make use of async-await for non-blocking calls.

- **Content negotiation**: Be mindful of content types and character encodings when sending and receiving HTTP content.

Consuming web services in a .NET application using C# is a common requirement. Following these steps and best practices, you can effectively request RESTful services and handle their responses, allowing your application to interact with various web-based resources.

Working with gRPC in .NET

gRPC Remote Procedure Calls (gRPC) is a new, fast platform that has become very popular in the .NET community, especially for creating microservices and distributed systems. It is an open-source framework by *Google* that lets services join quickly and without worrying about language. gRPC uses HTTP/2 for transport and **Protocol Buffers (Protobuf)** as the language for describing interfaces. It also has tools like authentication, load balancing, and more. When used with .NET, gRPC provides a great mix of speed, efficiency, and cross-platform support, which makes it a top choice for us in creating high-performance, scalable apps.

In .NET, gRPC works with everything else, so it is easy for C# coders to both setup and use gRPC services. The framework supports contract-first API development, ensuring that APIs are described similarly and shared between servers and service clients. This makes the development process more cohesive. This method simplifies communication in distributed systems, making inter-service contact faster, more reliable, and more efficient than traditional REST APIs. With built-in support for ASP.NET Core, gRPC in .NET lets us make robust, up-to-date apps to talk to each other across platforms and languages. This opens up new design and layout options for software.

Google made gRPC, an open-source remote procedure call system that has become a significant player in inter-service communication, especially in the .NET environment. Because its protocol buffers are not limited to a single language, gRPC in .NET can connect services in the same context and those on different platforms and languages. This fast, light communication protocol works excellently for microservices designs that need efficiency and low latency.

Key points and benefits

gRPC is a high-performance for inter-service communication. It offers good advantages over traditional REST APIs, including the following:

- **High performance**: gRPC's transport protocol is HTTP/2, which lets requests be sent simultaneously, reducing latency and improving network connections. Due to this, it is a lot faster than regular REST APIs over HTTP/1.1.

- Protobuf can serialize structured data that can be expanded on any language or device. They are similar to XML or JSON but smaller, faster, and easier to use. gRPC uses them. Protobuf describes the structure of the service and message and makes client and server code automatically in many languages, including C#.

- **Streaming**: gRPC allows four types of RPCs: unary, server streaming, client streaming, and bidirectional streaming. This gives you more options than traditional request-response communication patterns.

gRPC is language-independent and has robust security features, such as built-in TLS-based security, making it an excellent choice for situations where data protection is vital. When developers add gRPC to .NET environments, they like how well it works with ASP. NET Core, how easy it is to define services using Protobuf, and how simple it is to set up the server and use the client. These features make cross-language communication in the .NET ecosystem quick and safe.

Using gRPC as a service

It is possible to build a service in gRPC in one language and use it in another. This makes it an excellent choice for settings with people who speak more than one language. Following are some uses of gRPC as a service:

- **Built-in security**: gRPC services support strong TLS-based security right out of the box and also allow for custom authorization and authentication methods.

- **Adding things to .NET**: Integration with ASP.NET Core: gRPC is built into ASP. NET Core to be easily used with other web tools and middleware.

- **Service definition**: Use Protobuf to define services. The .NET gRPC tools read these service descriptions and make C# code for the server and the client.

- **Server implementation**: To add a gRPC service to a .NET app, you must inherit from the base class created automatically and override its methods.

- **Client use**: .NET has a built-in gRPC client that lets you call gRPC methods as if they were local.

Useful applications

The following critical areas of excellence in gRPC should be considered to enhance the effectiveness of development projects utilizing this technology:

- **Microservices**: gRPC works incredibly well in microservices designs where many microservices need to talk to each other quickly.

- **Real-time communication**: gRPC's streaming features make it great for real-time apps like live news or chat apps.

- **Cross-language and cross-platform apps**: gRPC can make apps that work on many devices and environments because it supports many programming languages.

Here is an example of a gRPC service in .NET, including server and client implementations. The example will be split into the server and the client. We will use the same **UserService** defined by the **user.proto** file

Server implementation in C#

Let us start by setting up the server in server implementation in C#. The code given is usually part of an ASP.NET Core project. The **UserService** implementation shows you how to use C# to make a gRPC service. First, the dependencies that are needed are brought in. These include **Grpc.Core** (core library for gRPC) and the namespace are made from the .proto file (short for Protobuf file). After that, a class called **UserServiceImpl** is created. It is inherited from **UserService.UserServiceBase** and is made from the **.proto** file. The **GetUser** method is used to handle client requests inside this class. In this case, it returns a fixed **UserReply** object with sample data like name and age. **Program.cs** is where the gRPC service is set up. The **AddGrpc** method is used to add the service, and routing and endpoints are set up to map the **UserServiceImpl** class.

Setting up a client in C#: Let us make a simple client using the gRPC service next. The necessary dependencies are imported, like with the server. These include **Grpc.Net. Client** and the namespace made from the **.proto** file. The client code sets up a connection to the server at localhost:5001 and creates a **UserServiceClient** instance. It then calls **GetUserAsync** and uses a user ID to get user data. After that, the answer is shown on the console.

Running the example: To run the example, ensure the server is up and running by starting the ASP.NET Core project with the server implementation. Then, start a.NET desktop app or use a.NET project you already have for the client. To connect and send requests, ensure the client's gRPC service address matches the server's. It is essential to know that when you build the project, the `GrpcUserService` namespace and classes that go with it are automatically created from the `.proto` file. gRPC also supports other types of calls, such as server streaming, client streaming, and bidirectional streaming. The example only shows an introductory unary call.

gRPC is a modern, quick, and flexible option for making and using RPC-style services in .NET. It works well with ASP.NET Core and lets services on different platforms talk to each other quickly. This makes it a great choice for C# developers working on microservices, distributed systems, or any other apps that need to communicate between services quickly.

Let us set up the server. This code would typically reside in an ASP.NET Core project.

The following code is the **UserService** implementation:

```
1. using Grpc.Core;
2. using GrpcUserService; // Namespace generated from the .proto file
3.
4. public class UserServiceImpl : UserService.UserServiceBase
5. {
6.     // Implement the GetUser method
7.     public override Task<UserReply> GetUser(UserRequest request,
    ServerCallContext context)
8.     {
9.         var response = new UserReply
10.         {
11.             Name = "John Doe", // Example data
12.             Age = 30
13.         };
14.
15.         return Task.FromResult(response);
16.     }
17. }
```

Configuration:

In **Program.cs**, configuring the gRPC service involves setting up the necessary dependencies and routing for the gRPC server. This typically includes adding the gRPC service to the ASP.NET Core application using the **AddGrpc()** method provided by the **Grpc.Core** library. Additionally, routing and endpoints must be configured to map incoming gRPC requests to their respective service implementations. This configuration ensures that the ASP.NET Core application can adequately handle gRPC communication and effectively serve requests from gRPC clients.

```
1.  builder.Services.AddGrpc();
2.
3.  app.UseRouting();
4.
5.  app.UseEndpoints(endpoints =>
6.  {
7.      endpoints.MapGrpcService<UserServiceImpl>();
8.  });
```

Client implementation in C# client implementation involves creating a client application that consumes the gRPC service provided by the server. This includes importing necessary dependencies such as **Grpc.Net.Client** and the namespace generated from the **.proto** file. The client code establishes a connection to the server, creates a gRPC client instance, and makes asynchronous RPC calls to request data or invoke services provided by the server. This setup enables seamless communication between the client and server, allowing the client application to interact with the server's functionalities efficiently and asynchronously.

Let us set up a simple client to consume the gRPC service. The following is the source code:

```
1.  using System;
2.  using System.Threading.Tasks;
3.  using Grpc.Net.Client;
4.  using GrpcUserService; // Namespace generated from the .proto file
5.
6.  // Assuming the server is running on localhost:5001
7.  using var channel = GrpcChannel.ForAddress("https://
    localhost:5001");
8.  var client = new UserService.UserServiceClient(channel);
9.  var userRequest = new UserRequest { UserId = 1 };
10. var reply = await client.GetUserAsync(userRequest);
11. Console.WriteLine($"Name: {reply.Name}, Age: {reply.Age}");
```

Running the example: There are two steps to running the example: Get the server up and running by running the ASP.NET Core project that has the server implementation. In this way, the server is always on and ready to take client requests. Next, start up the client app. We can use an existing .NET project or start from scratch to make a new .NET desktop app. If you are making a web game, you can add the gRPC service to the controls or services of your game to let it talk to the server. Interacting with the gRPC service through the client application enables you to test how it works and ensure that the server responds correctly to client requests.

- **Run the server**: Start your ASP.NET Core project containing the server implementation.

- **Run the client**: Start from scratch and make a new .NET desktop app or use an existing .NET project. If you are making a web game, you can use services in your controls or services.

Notes:

- Ensure that the gRPC service address in the client matches the server's address.
- The server needs to be running and accessible for the client to connect and make requests.
- When you build your project, the `GrpcUserService` namespace and the related classes are auto-generated from the user protocol file.

This example demonstrates an introductory unary call. gRPC also supports other types of calls, such as server streaming, client streaming, and bidirectional streaming.

gRPC in .NET is a current, quick, and adaptable way to create and use RPC-style services. It works well with ASP.NET Core, is fast, and can run on multiple platforms. It is an excellent choice for C# writers working on distributed systems, microservices, or any other apps that need to communicate quickly between services.

Introduction to GraphQL and .NET

GraphQL, a powerful API query language, has transformed how we interact with data. It is a more efficient, robust, and adaptable alternative to *Facebook's* conventional REST API, developed in 2012 and open-sourced in 2015. GraphQL APIs obtain all the data your app requires in a single request instead of REST, which requires loading from many URLs. Users express precisely what they require, and GraphQL provides nothing more and nothing less. This leads to speedier, more efficient applications by reducing data over-fetching and under-fetching.

They are integrating GraphQL with .NET, specifically C#. Combined with it, a modern, object-oriented programming language developed by *Microsoft* results in a powerful duo capable of handling complex applications. Using GraphQL in a .NET environment allows C# to create highly optimized and scalable APIs. This integration provides a robust back-end solution that caters to complex querying requirements and ensures efficient data retrieval and manipulation.

To illustrate the integration of GraphQL with .NET, consider this example. Suppose we have a .NET Core application and want to add a GraphQL endpoint. We can use the `GraphQL` .NET library, a popular choice in the .NET community.

- First, install the necessary packages via NuGet:
    1. `Install-Package GraphQL`
    2. `Install-Package GraphQL.Server.Ui.Playground`

- Then, define a simple **GraphQL** schema. Assume we have a **Book** model in our application:

```
1.  public class Book
2.  {
3.      public string Title { get; set; }
4.      public string Author { get; set; }
5.  }
6.
7.  public class BookQuery : ObjectGraphType
8.  {
9.      public BookQuery()
10.     {
11.         Field<BookType>(
12.             "book",
13.             arguments: new QueryArguments(new QueryArgument
    <StringGraphType> { Name = "title" }),
14.             resolve: context =>
15.             {
16.                 var title = context.GetArgument<string>
    ("title");
17.                 return new Book { Title = title, Author =
    "Unknown" };
18.             }
19.         );
20.     }
21. }
22.
23. public class BookType : ObjectGraphType<Book>
24. {
25.     public BookType()
26.     {
27.         Field(x => x.Title);
28.         Field(x => x.Author);
29.     }
30. }
```

- In your startup configuration (**Program.cs**), register the **GraphQL** schema and set up the endpoint:

```
1.  app.UseGraphQL<ISchema>();
2.  app.UseGraphQLPlayground(new GraphQLPlaygroundOptions()); // to
    use Playground
```

```
3.
4.
5.  builder.Services.AddScoped<IdependencyResolver>(s => new
    FuncDependencyResolver(s.GetRequiredService));
6.  builder.Services.AddScoped<BookQuery>();
7.  builder.Services.AddScoped<Ischema, BookSchema>();
8.
9.  builder.Services.AddGraphQL(o => { o.ExposeExceptions = false;
    })
10.     .AddGraphTypes(ServiceLifetime.Scoped);
```

- Finally, create the **Schema** class:

```
1.  public class BookSchema : Schema
2.  {
3.      public BookSchema(IdependencyResolver resolver) : base(resolver)
4.      {
5.          Query = resolver.Resolve<BookQuery>();
6.      }
7.  }
```

With this setup, you have a basic GraphQL API in the .NET Core application that can respond to queries for books. This is a fundamental example of getting started with GraphQL in .NET using C#. This mix of technologies provides a strong foundation for developing intelligent, efficient, and scalable online applications.

In conclusion, integrating GraphQL with .NET using C# offers a highly efficient and flexible approach to building APIs. GraphQL's ability to fetch precisely what is needed in a single request aligns seamlessly with the robustness and scalability of the .NET. C#, with its clarity and object-oriented features, further enhances this integration, allowing for the creation of APIs that are not only powerful but also maintainable and easy to understand.

The example demonstrates the simplicity with which a GraphQL API can be implemented in a .NET Core application. This setup allows us to build more responsive, data-efficient applications catering to complex and varied client-side data requirements. GraphQL's efficient data retrieval and the .NET's performance and reliability, all harnessed through the versatility of C#, create a compelling toolkit for modern web application development.

As technology advances, the value of efficient data handling and flexible API solutions becomes increasingly important. The synergy between GraphQL and .NET, leveraged through C#, is an exemplary paradigm of this evolution, offering a pathway toward developing more advanced, efficient, and user-centric applications.

Understanding HTTP Client in .NET

In software development, particularly in web and network-based applications, understanding how to communicate over the **Hypertext Transfer Protocol** (**HTTP**) is crucial. HTTP is the foundational protocol for transferring data over the web, making it a vital component for any developer in web services, APIs, or web applications.

The **HttpClient** class in .NET provides a powerful yet flexible way to send and receive HTTP requests and responses. It is part of the **System.Net.Http** namespace and has been designed to be modern, fast, and convenient. This class allows us to interact with RESTful APIs, download files, and perform other network operations efficiently.

We will review the fundamentals of configuring and sending HTTP requests, advanced features, and recommended practices for improving performance and reliability. By the end of this guide, you will understand how to use **HttpClient** in your .NET applications, allowing you to manage web connections with simplicity and confidence. Whether creating a simple web client or a complex web service, understanding **HttpClient** is essential in your development toolbox.

To work with **HttpClient** in .NET, we need a development environment set up with:

- **.NET SDK**: Install .NET 8 SDK from the official Microsoft website.
- **IDE**: Visual Studio, Visual Studio Code, or any other IDE that supports C#.
- **NuGet Packages**: Ensure you have the **System.Net.Http** namespace available. It is usually included by default in recent .NET versions.

Basics of HttpClient

HttpClient is a class in the **System.Net.Http** namespace used for sending HTTP requests and receiving HTTP responses. A basic example of using **HttpClient** is:

```
1.  using System;
2.  using System.Net.Http;
3.  using System.Threading.Tasks;
4.
5.  using HttpClient client = new HttpClient();
6.  HttpResponseMessage response = await client.GetAsync("http://
    example.com");
7.  response.EnsureSuccessStatusCode();
8.  string responseBody = await response.Content.ReadAsStringAsync();
9.  Console.WriteLine(responseBody);
```

Making HTTP requests: When you use **HttpClient** to make HTTP requests in .NET, its methods are optimized for specific HTTP methods. The **GetAsync()** method is used for a GET request, the **PostAsync()** method is used for a POST request, the **PutAsync()** method is used for a PUT request, and the **DeleteAsync()** method is used for a DELETE request. These methods make it easier for developers to use APIs and web services in their apps by speeding up the process of sending requests to servers and getting responses.

Here is a summary:

- **GET**: `GetAsync()`
- **POST**: `PostAsync()`
- **PUT**: `PutAsync()`
- **DELETE**: `DeleteAsync()`

Example of a POST request:

```
1. using System.Net.Http;
2. using System.Text;
3. using System.Threading.Tasks;
4.
5. using HttpClient client = new HttpClient();
6. var content = new StringContent("{\"name\":\"John Doe\"}", Encoding.UTF8, "application/json");
7. HttpResponseMessage response = await client.PostAsync("http://example.com/api/users", content);
8. response.EnsureSuccessStatusCode();
9. string responseBody = await response.Content.ReadAsStringAsync();
10. Console.WriteLine(responseBody);
```

Advanced features

In HttpClient, you will find powerful tools that give you more control and flexibility over HTTP interactions. With HttpClient handlers, we can fine-tune HTTP requests and responses to meet specific needs. Headers let us add custom headers without any problems by using **DefaultRequestHeaders**. Additionally, the addition of timeout settings and cancellation mechanisms gives developers the tools to handle network timeouts effectively. They can do this by setting the **Timeout** property directly or using the **CancellationToken** to fine-tune asynchronous operations.

Here is a summary:

- **HttpClient handlers**: Customize HTTP requests and responses.
- **Headers**: Add custom headers using DefaultRequestHeaders.
- **Timeouts and cancellation**: Set the Timeout property or use CancellationToken.

Best practices

There are a few best practices that can significantly improve performance and reliability when building HTTP client functionality. To begin, it is suggested that **HttpClient** instances be reused to keep sockets from running out and efficiently utilize resources. Second, use async and await to make asynchronous methods more critical for better scalability, especially in situations with a lot of traffic. Also, make sure there are strong ways to handle errors by gracefully using try-catch blocks to handle exceptions. Also, ensure that the **HttpContent** and **HttpResponseMessage** objects are thrown away correctly to stop memory leaks and wasted resources. Lastly, the proper timeouts should be set to lower the chance of requests getting stuck and improve overall stability and responsiveness. When you combine these strategies, you get strong HTTP client implementations that work well.

Here is a summary:

- **Reuse HttpClient instance**: It is recommended to reuse **HttpClient** instances to avoid socket exhaustion.
- **Async and await**: Always use asynchronous methods for scalability.
- **Error handling**: Implement proper error handling with try-catch blocks.
- **Content disposal**: Ensure proper disposal of **HttpContent** and **HttpResponseMessage**.
- **Timeouts**: Set appropriate timeouts to avoid hanging requests.

Sample for downloading a file: In the following sample, we use **HttpClint** to download a **.zip** file from a website:

```
1. var httpClient = new HttpClient();
2. var url = "https://example.com/file.zip";
3. var localPath = "downloaded_file.zip";
4.
5. try
6. {
7.     using var response = await httpClient.
   GetAsync(url, HttpCompletionOption.ResponseHeadersRead);
8.
9.     response.EnsureSuccessStatusCode();
10.
11.    await using var streamToReadFrom = await response.Content.
   ReadAsStreamAsync();
12.
13.    await using var streamToWriteTo = File.Open(localPath, FileMode.
   Create);
14.
15.    await streamToReadFrom.CopyToAsync(streamToWriteTo);
16.
17.
18.    Console.WriteLine("File downloaded successfully.");
19. }
```

```
20. catch (Exception ex)
21. {
22.     Console.WriteLine($"An error occurred: {ex.Message}");
23. }
```

Explanation of the code:

We create an instance, specifying the file's URL to be downloaded and the local path where it should be saved. The program then sends an asynchronous GET request to the specified URL. Upon receiving a response, it reads the file data as a stream and simultaneously writes it to a file on the local machine. This process is handled asynchronously, allowing the program to perform other tasks while the file downloads. Additionally, the code includes error handling to manage any issues that might arise during the download process, ensuring a smooth and efficient file transfer.

HttpClient in .NET is a powerful tool for making HTTP requests. It is essential to understand its basics, properly use its advanced features, and follow best practices for efficient and scalable applications. With proper usage, **HttpClient** can be an invaluable asset in a developer's toolkit for interacting with web services and APIs in a .NET environment.

This explanation gives a foundational understanding of using **HttpClient** in C#. For more profound knowledge, it is advisable to refer to the official *Microsoft* documentation and explore more complex use cases and patterns.

Security considerations in web services

In the modern era of web development, the importance of security in web services cannot be overstated. As businesses and services increasingly rely on web-based applications and APIs, the potential risks and vulnerabilities associated with these services have become more pronounced. This is especially true in environments utilizing .NET and C# technologies, where these platforms' vast capabilities also bring unique security challenges. The focus on security is paramount, as the implications of breaches can range from data loss and compromised user information to severe legal and financial repercussions.

To overcome these issues, developers and IT professionals must implement a comprehensive security plan covering all web service development and deployment phases in .NET and C#. Understanding and implementing strong authentication and authorization methods, maintaining data encryption both in transit and at rest, and protecting against common vulnerabilities such as XSS and SQL injection are all part of this. Furthermore, given the ever-changing world of cyber threats, maintaining up-to-date on the latest security practices and routinely updating security measures is critical. In this context, we will look at the key security considerations in .NET and C# web services, describing best practices and presenting a practical example to show these principles in action.

In the following content, we will cover key security considerations and provide a sample implementation in .NET and C#:

- **Authentication and authorization**: Authentication ensures that only authorized users can have access to the online service. This can be performed using several approaches, such as simple authentication, token-based authentication, and OAuth.

  What an authenticated user can do is determined by authorization. RBAC is a standard method in .NET that assigns users roles and permissions depending on those roles.

- **Data encryption**: **Transport layer security (TLS)** is essential for encrypting data in transit between the client and the web service. In .NET, this is often managed through the configuration of the web server (like IIS) or libraries like **SslStream** in C#.

- **Encryption at Rest**: This is equally important. Data stored in databases or file systems should be encrypted using cryptographic libraries available in .NET, such as the **System.Security.Cryptography** namespace.

- **Input validation**: It prevents malicious data from entering the system. In .NET, you can use model validation in ASP.NET MVC or data annotations to ensure that incoming data conforms to expected formats.

- **XSS and SQL injection protection**: **XSS**: Avoid encoding user input before displaying it on web pages. ASP.NET provides built-in mechanisms to auto-encode output.

- **SQL injection**: Use parameterized queries or ORM (like EF) to prevent SQL injection attacks.

- **Error handling**: Proper error handling ensures that sensitive information (like stack traces) is not exposed to the user. In .NET, custom error pages and logging can be configured to handle this.

- **Session management**: Secure session management is critical. Use secure **HttpOnly** cookies and consider implementing session timeouts.

- **Dependency management**: Regularly update and patch third-party libraries and frameworks to mitigate known vulnerabilities.

- **Logging and monitoring**: Implement logging to track access and activities. In .NET, libraries like **NLog** or **Serilog** can be used. Monitoring can help detect and respond to suspicious activities.

- **API security**: For RESTful services, use standards like OAuth for secure API access. Implement rate limiting to prevent abuse.

Sample implementation in C#:

Here is a simple example of implementing token-based authentication in a .NET web API:

```
1. public class AuthenticationController : ApiController
```

```
2.  {
3.      public IHttpActionResult Authenticate(UserModel userModel)
4.      {
5.          if (CheckUser(userModel))
6.          {
7.              var token = GenerateToken(userModel);
8.              return Ok(token);
9.          }
10.
11.         return Unauthorized();
12.     }
13.
14.     private bool CheckUser(UserModel userModel)
15.     {
16.         // Implement user validation logic here
17.         return true; // Simplified for example purposes
18.     }
19.
20.     private string GenerateToken(UserModel userModel)
21.     {
22.         // Implement token generation logic here
23.         return "generated-token"; // Simplified for example purposes
24.     }
25. }
```

In this example, **AuthenticationController** handles user authentication. The **CheckUser** method validates the user, and **GenerateToken** creates a token upon successful authentication.

XSS, implementing input validation and encoding.

To prevent XSS, you should never trust user input. Continuously validate and encode user input before using it in your HTML output.

```
1. using System.Text.Encodings.Web;
2. using Microsoft.AspNetCore.Mvc;
3.
4. public class SafeController : ControllerBase
5. {
6.     [HttpGet("safeendpoint")]
7.     public IActionResult SafeEndpoint(string userInput)
8.     {
9.         // Validate the input
```

```
10.          if (string.IsNullOrWhiteSpace(userInput))
11.          {
12.              return BadRequest("Invalid input");
13.          }
14.
15.          // Encode the input before including it in the output
16.          var encodedInput = HtmlEncoder.Default.Encode(userInput);
17.
18.          return Ok($"Safe output: {encodedInput}");
19.      }
20. }
```

This example demonstrates an approach to handling user input safely in a web service. Remember that security is a broad topic, and staying informed about best practices and emerging threats is essential.

Further steps:

- **Content security policy (CSP)**: Implementing CSP headers can add a layer of protection.
- **Regularly update dependencies**: Keep your framework and dependencies up to date to protect against known vulnerabilities.

Creating a CSP sample: Implementing CSP effectively prevents XSS attacks. CSP is a browser security mechanism that allows you to specify the sources from which a browser should allow loading resources like scripts, styles, images, etc.

Add to the **Program.cs** the following code:

```
1. app.Use(async (context, next) =>
2. {
3.     context.Response.Headers.Add("Content-Security-
   Policy", "default-src <self'; script-src 'self'; style-
   src 'self'; img-src 'self'");
4.     await next();
5. });
```

Understanding the content security policy header

Understanding the CSP header is imperative to ensure safe browsing experiences and lower potential security risks. The CSP header controls how resources are loaded and run on a webpage. To make things safer, it limits some actions. In the given example, the CSP header is set up with specific directives: **default-src 'self'** only allows resources to load from the same origin; **script-src 'self'** only will enable JavaScript to come from the same origin; **style-src 'self'** only allows CSS to come from the same origin; and **img-src 'self'** only will enable images to load from the same origin.

Here is a summary:

- **default-src 'self'**: Allows loading resources (fonts, frames, etc.) only from the same origin.
- **script-src 'self'**: Only allows JavaScript from the same origin.
- **style-src 'self'**: Only allows CSS from the same origin.
- **img-src 'self'**: Only allows images from the same origin.

Note: CSP is a powerful tool that can break functionality if not configured correctly. Ensure that your policy allows all necessary resources for your application.

Remember that most modern browsers support CSP, but some compatibility issues may exist with older browsers.

By implementing a CSP, you add an essential layer of security that can help protect your web application from XSS attacks and other vulnerabilities.

Testing and adjusting the policy: After adding CSP, you should test your application carefully to ensure it works correctly. During this testing phase, you will ensure that your web application's intended features, such as its interactive elements and third-party integrations, work as planned and that the CSP has no unintended effects. If your app needs resources from outside domains, like scripts or styles hosted by a CDN, you must make changes to the CSP so that those resources can be safely fetched and used. Different user interactions and situations are simulated for testing to find any problems or conflicts with the CSP rules. Monitoring tools can also help keep track of policy violations and give you information about what changes need to be made. If the CSP needs to be changed after testing, it will depend on what was seen and what the application needs. This process of iterations ensures that the CSP is secure enough for your needs while letting you use it. For example, to allow scripts from a specific CDN:

```
1.  context.Response.Headers.Add("Content-Security-Policy", "default-
    src 'self'; script-src 'self' https://cdn.example.com; style-
    src 'self'; img-src 'self'");
```

Security in web services, particularly in .NET and C#, involves a multifaceted approach encompassing authentication, authorization, data encryption, input validation, and other security practices. Adhering to these principles helps ensure the security and integrity of web services. It is essential to stay updated with the latest security trends and updates in the .NET ecosystem.

Understanding API versioning

API versioning is critical to modern software development, especially with web services and applications built using .NET and C#. As APIs evolve, introducing and modifying new features becomes essential to manage different versions effectively. This ensures that clients using different API versions can still interact with your application seamlessly.

API versioning is not just about maintaining backward compatibility; it is about creating a roadmap for your API's evolution that accommodates changes without disrupting the user experience or existing functionalities.

In the .NET ecosystem, particularly with C#, implementing API versioning is a structured and straightforward process, thanks to the comprehensive tools and frameworks provided by the platform. Whether it is a mobile app back-end, a web service, or a cloud-based application, managing API versions in .NET and C# is essential for maintaining a robust and flexible interface. This approach enables us to introduce improvements, fix issues, and add new features while ensuring that all API versions operate smoothly. Understanding the strategies and best practices for API versioning in this context is critical to building and maintaining scalable and efficient software systems.

- **Importance of API versioning**:
    - ○ **Backward compatibility**: As your API evolves, older clients still need to work with the new versions of your API. Versioning allows these clients to continue using an older version of the API.
    - ○ **Phased deprecation**: Instead of abruptly removing features, versioning enables a gradual phase-out, giving clients time to adapt.
    - ○ **Variety of clients**: Different clients might have different needs. Versioning allows you to cater to these diverse requirements.

- **Strategies for API versioning**: There are several strategies for versioning APIs in .NET and C#. The most common ones are:

- **URI path versioning**: The URI path includes the version (e.g., `/api/v1/products`).

- **Query string versioning**: The query string specifies the version (e.g., `/api/products?version=1`).

- **Header versioning**: The version is specified in a custom HTTP header.

- **Media type versioning**: Also known as **content negotiation** or **accept header**, the version is supplied in the HTTP request's accept header.

- **Implementing API versioning in .NET Core**: .NET Core provides built-in support for API versioning.

    Here is a basic example of how to implement it:

1. **Install the necessary NuGet package**: You need to install **`Microsoft.AspNetCore.Mvc.Versioning`** package. This can be accomplished using the NuGet package manager or the Package Manager Console:

    1. `Install-Package Microsoft.AspNetCore.Mvc.Versioning`

2. **Configure API versioning in Startup.cs**: In the **`ConfigureServices`** method of **`Startup.cs`**, add the following code to enable API versioning:

    1. `builder.Services.AddControllers();`

```
2.
3. // Add API Versioning
4. builder.Services.AddApiVersioning(options =>
5. {
6.     options.DefaultApiVersion = new ApiVersion(1, 0); //
   Default version 1.0
7.     options.AssumeDefaultVersionWhenUnspecified = true;
8.     options.ReportApiVersions = true;
9. });
```

3. **Versioning controllers**: Decorate your controllers with the **[ApiVersion]** attribute to specify their versions. For example:

```
1. [ApiController]
2. [Route("api/v{version:apiVersion}/products")]
3. [ApiVersion("1.0")]
4. public class ProductsV1Controller : ControllerBase
5. {
6.     // Controller methods go here
7. }
8.
9. [ApiController]
10. [Route("api/v{version:apiVersion}/products")]
11. [ApiVersion("2.0")]
12. public class ProductsV2Controller : ControllerBase
13. {
14.     // New or modified methods for version 2.0
15. }
```

4. **Testing and documentation**: Once versioning is implemented, testing each version thoroughly to ensure they function as expected is crucial. Documenting each version of your API helps clients understand the changes and how to use them.

API versioning in .NET and C# is a powerful way to evolve your APIs while maintaining support for existing clients. By choosing the appropriate versioning strategy and implementing it correctly, you can ensure a seamless transition for users as your API grows and changes.

Implementing pagination in APIs

Implementing pagination in APIs is a fundamental aspect of modern web development, especially when dealing with large datasets. In the realm of .NET and C# development, efficient pagination strategies are essential for creating scalable, high-performance web applications. Pagination involves splitting an extensive data set into smaller, more manageable segments, typically called pages. This approach enhances the performance by reducing server load and optimizing data retrieval and significantly improves the user experience by presenting data concisely and organized.

In the .NET ecosystem, utilizing C# for API development offers robust tools and frameworks, such as ASP.NET Core and EF, to implement effective pagination solutions. This capability is crucial for applications dealing with extensive databases, where loading and displaying thousands or even millions of records simultaneously is impractical and resource-intensive. By implementing pagination, we can ensure that their applications remain responsive and efficient, providing users with quick access to data and a smooth navigational experience. The following guide provides a detailed overview and a practical example of implementing pagination in .NET and C# APIs, showcasing the integration of this essential feature in a real-world scenario.

Understanding pagination

Much information is broken up into smaller, easier-to-handle pieces called pages. This is called **pagination**. By cutting down on load time and bandwidth use, this method works exceptionally well in APIs to improve speed and the user experience.

Following are some reasons why we should implement pagination:

- **Performance**: Loading large datasets can be resource-intensive. Pagination reduces server load and improves response times.

- **User experience**: Provides a better, more manageable user interface, especially for large datasets.

- **Resource management**: Limits the use of server resources by fetching only a portion of the data at a time.

Pagination techniques

When managing and browsing big datasets, pagination techniques are essential for making things run faster and giving users a better experience. There are many ways to paginate, but three stand out: offset pagination, keyset pagination (cursor-based), and the seek method. Each method has its own benefits and things to consider, so it can be used in different situations and for other reasons. Let us look more closely at each method to see what it does and means for data pagination. Here is a summary:

- **Offset pagination**: The most common method, where the offset (the starting point of the dataset) and the limit (the number of records to return) are specified.

- **Keyset pagination (cursor-based)**: Uses a unique key (like an ID) to paginate through the data. This is more efficient than offset pagination, especially for large datasets.

- **Seek method**: Similar to keyset pagination but uses where clauses for pagination.

Implementing pagination

When you add pagination to your API, you must consider how to make it scalable and efficient. Pagination is essential to managing large datasets because it breaks them up into smaller, easier-to-handle pieces. This makes the server and client sides less busy. When working with databases, query optimization and indexing become essential to ensure the best performance, especially as the dataset grows. By carefully planning and implementing pagination mechanisms, you can make your API more responsive and give users a better experience. This is especially important when users interact with paginated data a lot.

Following is the environment setup we need:

- **.NET SDK**: Ensure you have the latest .NET SDK installed.
- **IDE**: Visual Studio or VS Code is recommended for C# development.

Sample scenario: Let us create a simple API that returns a paginated list of items.

1. Create a New API Project.
2. Create a new web API project using the .NET CLI or Visual Studio.
3. Define a Model. Look at the following:

```
1. public class Item
2. {
3.     public int Id { get; set; }
4.     public string Name { get; set; }
5. }
```

4. Create a Controller.
5. Add a new Controller to your project, e.g., **ItemsController**.
6. Implementing pagination.
7. Assume we have a method **GetItems** that fetches items from a database.
8. Add pagination parameters: **pageNumber** and **pageSize**.
9. Use LINQ to limit the number of items returned. Look at the following:

```
1.  [ApiController]
2.  [Route("[controller]")]
3.  public class ItemsController : ControllerBase
4.  {
5.      private readonly DataContext _context;
6.
7.      public ItemsController(DataContext context)
8.      {
9.          _context = context;
10.     }
11.
```

```
12.    [HttpGet]
13.    public async Task<ActionResult<IEnumerable<It
       em>>> GetItems(int pageNumber = 1, int pageSize = 10)
14.    {
15.        var items = await _context.Items
16.                                          .
       Skip((pageNumber - 1) * pageSize)
17.                                  .Take(pageSize)
18.                                  .ToListAsync();
19.        return Ok(items);
20.    }
21. }
```

10. **Testing the API**: Run the API and test the endpoint, e.g., **GET   /
    items?pageNumber=2&pageSize=5**.

11. **Improvements**:

    a. Implement error handling for out-of-range pages.

    b. Consider adding total count and paging metadata in the response.

Implementing pagination in APIs using .NET and C# is a straightforward process that significantly enhances the performance and usability of your application. The example demonstrates a basic implementation using EF and LINQ, which can be adapted and expanded upon for more complex scenarios.

Remember, the choice of pagination method (offset, keyset, or seek) depends on your specific use case and the nature of your data. Proper implementation of pagination can lead to more efficient and user-friendly APIs.

API testing with Postman and Swagger

Today, API testing is an integral part of the software development process, especially in .NET and C# environments. This process includes checking that **application programming interfaces (APIs)** work as expected regarding security, dependability, speed, and functionality. As web services get more complicated and development processes get shorter, it is more important than ever to test APIs quickly and correctly. This process is much easier with tools like Postman and Swagger, which give devs robust platforms for testing and documenting APIs.

When it comes to .NET and C#, which is a system known for being strong and flexible, API testing is more complex and essential. .NET works well with C#, which is a powerful language known for solid typing, object-oriented programming, and async/await for asynchronous actions. This makes it an excellent choice for creating scalable web services and APIs. We can perform thorough API tests using Postman and Swagger within this framework. Postman has an easy-to-use interface for interacting with APIs by hand, and Swagger (OpenAPI) has tools for automated documentation and a live interface for testing APIs. These tools make up a powerful arsenal for .NET workers. They make testing more manageable and ensure high-quality web services are built.

API testing is vital to software development, especially web services and microservices. Postman and Swagger are popular API testing tools in .NET and C# environments. Let us look at how these tools are utilized in the context of .NET and C#, followed by a practical situation.

Understanding APIs in .NET and C#

APIs in .NET are typically built using ASP.NET Core, a cross-platform, high-performance framework for building cloud-based, internet-connected applications. C# is the primary language for .NET, offering a range of features that make it ideal for API development, such as strong typing, object-oriented programming, and async/await for asynchronous operations.

Postman for API testing: Postman is a popular API development and testing tool. It provides an intuitive interface for sending requests to APIs and viewing responses. Postman supports HTTP methods like GET, POST, PUT, DELETE, and more, which are essential for RESTful API testing.

Features of Postman: A well-known API development tool, Postman, has features that make testing and working together easier. Postman lets developers run tests efficiently in various settings thanks to its easy-to-use GUI for sending HTTP requests and its robust environment and variable management tools. It also has features like collection organization, collaboration, and support for automated testing through JavaScript scripting. These features make it even more helpful in team workflows, making it a complete solution for API development needs. Here is a summary of his benefits:

- **Easy-to-use GUI**: Allows us to send HTTP requests without writing code.
- **Environment and variable management**: Facilitates testing in different environments.
- **Automated testing**: Enables writing test scripts in JavaScript.
- **Collection and collaboration**: Allows grouping of requests and sharing with team members.

Swagger for API documentation and testing

Swagger (OpenAPI) is an open-source framework for describing, producing, consuming, and visualizing RESTful web services. In .NET, Swagger is typically integrated using the **Swashbuckle** package.

Features of Swagger:

- **API documentation**: Automatically generates human-readable documentation for your APIs.
- **Interactive UI**: Provides a web-based UI to interact with the API endpoints.
- **Code generation**: Supports generating client SDKs in various programming languages.
- **Sample scenario**: API testing with Postman and Swagger
- **Scenario**: Testing a simple Weather Forecast API

The following steps show how Postman and Swagger can be used in tandem to test and document an API in a .NET and C# environment:

1. **Setting up the API in .NET Core**:
   a. Create a new ASP.NET Core Web API project in Visual Studio.
   b. Implement a simple API endpoint that returns a list of weather forecasts.
   ```
   1. [ApiController]
   2. [Route("[controller]")]
   3. public class WeatherForecastController : ControllerBase
   4. {
   5.     [HttpGet]
   6.     public IEnumerable<WeatherForecast> Get()
   7.     {
   8.         // implementation to return weather forecast data
   9.     }
   10.}
   ```

2. **Integrating Swagger**:
   a. Add the **Swashbuckle.AspNetCore** NuGet package.
   b. Configure Swagger in the **Program.cs** file.
   ```
   1. builder.Services.AddSwaggerGen();
   2.
   3. app.UseSwagger();
   4. app.UseSwaggerUI(c =>
   5. {
   6.     c.SwaggerEndpoint("/swagger/v1/swagger.
      json", "My API V1");
   7. });
   ```

3. **Testing with Postman**:
   a. Launch the API locally and note the base URL (e.g., **http://localhost:5000**).
   b. Open Postman and create a new request.

  c. Set the HTTP method to GET and the request URL to the API endpoint (e.g., **http://localhost:5000/WeatherForecast**).

  d. Send the request and observe the response.

4. **Using Swagger UI for testing**:

  a. Navigate to the Swagger UI URL (e.g., **http://localhost:5000/swagger**).

  b. You will see the interactive documentation of your API.

  c. Use the UI to send requests to the `WeatherForecast` endpoint and observe the responses.

This example demonstrates how Postman and Swagger can be used in tandem to test and document an API in a .NET and C# environment. Postman offers a straightforward platform for manual API testing, while Swagger provides an automated, interactive way to document and test APIs. Combining these tools can significantly enhance the API development and testing process in a .NET.

Integrating Postman and Swagger into .NET and C# environments significantly advances API testing and documentation. Postman's user-friendly interface and comprehensive testing capabilities, combined with Swagger's automated documentation and interactive testing features, provide a holistic and efficient API development and testing approach. These tools facilitate a smoother development process and ensure the creation of more reliable, scalable, and robust APIs. For us, working within the .NET and leveraging the strengths of both Postman and Swagger can markedly improve the quality and speed of their API development cycles. Ultimately, the synergy between these tools and the .NET platform with C# enriches the overall development experience, paving the way for creating high-quality web services that meet the evolving demands of the digital world.

Conclusion

We examine RESTful API development with ASP.NET Core, a powerful online service platform. This section emphasizes REST principles in API architecture and demonstrates how ASP.NET Core simplifies scalable, maintainable, and efficient web services. Our hands-on approach teaches you how to build your first API and understand ASP.NET Core RESTful services.

The client side is next examined, including .NET web service access methods and best practices. This section is crucial for app developers who use third-party services. We will cover many ways to access APIs, process different data formats, and manage network connectivity in .NET.

We continue to study gRPC, a new, high-performance inter-service communication architecture. This section introduces gRPC, compares it to RESTful services, and shows how to build gRPC services and clients in .NET. We discuss protocol buffers, service definitions, and gRPC's performance and scalability.

A major advance in data querying and manipulation is GraphQL. This section introduces GraphQL and its relationship to .NET. We compare the flexibility and efficiency of GraphQL to RESTful services and discuss how to create and deploy GraphQL APIs in .NET.

The.NET HTTP Client is essential for online applications. This section examines how it sends HTTP requests, handles responses, and handles HTTP complexity. Developers with RESTful services use this section to construct robust and efficient HTTP clients.

Web service development requires API versioning for backward compatibility and seamless API upgrades. This section explains API version management in detail and discusses API versioning methods, their pros and cons, and how to implement them in .NET.

In the next chapter, we move from core concepts and practices to a more advanced and innovative approach in the next chapter. Blazor, a cutting-edge C# UI framework for client and server-side programming, will be covered in the next chapter. Blazor's features, from designing components and forms to integrating JavaScript and executing CRUD operations using EF Core, will be covered in this chapter. Blazor lets C# developers create dynamic, responsive, highly interactive online apps by bridging the gap between server-side programming and current web development.

Exercises

Check if the following sentences are true or false:

1. .NET is exclusively used for building desktop applications.
2. RESTful APIs can be developed using ASP.NET Core.
3. SOAP is more flexible than REST for web API development.
4. gRPC is an open-source framework by Google for inter-service communication.
5. GraphQL was developed by Google and open-sourced in 2015.
6. In .NET, HttpClient sends HTTP requests and receives responses.
7. HTTP/2 is slower than HTTP/1.1 when using gRPC.
8. The primary language for .NET API development is Python.
9. Swagger is used for automated API testing and documentation.
10. Entity Framework in .NET cannot be used for data access in APIs.
11. API versioning is not necessary in .NET development.
12. Pagination in APIs enhances performance by reducing server load.
13. Postman is a tool used primarily for back-end development, not API testing.
14. GraphQL allows fetching exactly what is needed in a single request.
15. C# does not support async/await for asynchronous operations.

16. XSS can be prevented by proper input validation and encoding.
17. RESTful APIs can only use JSON, not XML, for data representation.
18. Implementing HTTPS in .NET applications is optional for security.
19. ASP.NET Core is not compatible with microservices architecture.
20. gRPC uses Protocol Buffers for language-neutral interface description.

Answers

1. False
2. True
3. False
4. True
5. False
6. True
7. False
8. False
9. True
10. False
11. False
12. True
13. False
14. True
15. False
16. True
17. False
18. False
19. False
20. True

Join our book's Discord space

Join the book's Discord Workspace for Latest updates, Offers, Tech happenings around the world, New Release and Sessions with the Authors:

https://discord.bpbonline.com

CHAPTER 15
Blazor for UI Development

Introduction

This chapter will look at Blazor, a cutting-edge UI framework that uses C# for client and server-side programming. This comprehensive exploration covers Blazor component creation, project structure understanding, form handling and validation, JavaScript interoperability, CRUD operations with Blazor and EF Core, server versus WebAssembly differences, routing, and Blazor application testing. It provides the knowledge they need to design dynamic web UIs efficiently using C# abilities across the entire stack, bridging the gap between traditional server-side programming and modern web development approaches.

Structure

This chapter covers the following topics:

- Creating Blazor components
- Understanding the Blazor project structure
- Performance and new UIs in .NET 9
- Working with forms and validation in Blazor
- Understanding JavaScript interop in Blazor
- Building a CRUD operation using Blazor

- Using Entity Framework Core with Blazor
- Understanding Blazor Server vs. Blazor WebAssembly
- Working with routing in Blazor
- Testing in Blazor applications

Creating Blazor components

Developers have historically created interactive user interfaces on the client side using JavaScript frameworks such as Angular, React, and Vue. These frameworks dominated client-side programming until recently.

To remain competitive in development, we must know both a server and client-side programming language.

Additional points to consider

Creating Blazor components has advantages like:

- **Utilizing C# for both server-side and client-side development**: It is feasible when Blazor comes into play. Blazor enables us to design interactive web UIs with C# instead of JavaScript. Blazor allows C# to be performed on the server and client browser.

- **Using existing C# skills**: Existing .NET professionals may now apply their C# abilities to client-side programming, avoiding the need to learn new JavaScript frameworks and their associated learning curves.

- **Blazor and WebAssembly**: Blazor allows you to run C# code directly in the browser using WebAssembly. This means we can run any code in the browser, including C#. WebAssembly uses the same security sandbox as JavaScript frameworks like Angular, React, and Vue.

- **WebAssembly and browser compatibility**: WebAssembly is built on open web standards, making it a native feature of all modern browsers, including mobile browsers. Unlike in the past, Blazor programs do not require installing special plugins reminiscent of Silverlight and Flash.

Using Blazor, we may optimize our workflow by using C# for server and client-side development, promoting efficiency and cohesiveness in the development process.

Understanding Blazor components

Blazor components emerge as powerful building pieces in the ever-changing web development scene, reinventing how interactive and client-side applications are created. Before constructing Blazor components, let us define what a Blazor component is.

Blazor components

Blazor components are the core building blocks of Blazor programs, containing both the user interface and its actions. Consider them modular, self-contained parts that can be smoothly integrated into your web application, providing a reusable and maintainable design solution.

Key features of Blazor components

Here we have the basic key points of componentization with Blazor:

- **Reusability**: One of the key advantages of Blazor components is their reusability. Once defined, a component can be used in other portions of your program, enabling a consistent and efficient development workflow.

- **Encapsulation**: Blazor components encapsulate the UI and the accompanying functionality, resulting in a clean and well-organized code structure. This encapsulation improves code maintenance and readability.

- **Interactivity**: Blazor components are more than simply static portions of the interface; they may react to user actions and events. This interactivity breathes life into your application, providing a dynamic and compelling user experience.

Now, that we have established a basic grasp of Blazor components, let us look at how they were created.

The following steps provide a succinct guide to creating Blazor components within your application:

1. **Setup project**: Create a new Blazor project in Visual Studio. Choose the proper project template, selecting either the Blazor WebAssembly App or the Blazor Server App based on your project requirements.

2. **Understanding razor components**: In Blazor, components are constructed using Razor syntax, which elegantly mixes HTML markup and C# code. Familiarizing yourself with Razor syntax is critical for successful component creation.

3. **Component structure**: Each Blazor component comprises two primary parts: markup (HTML-like structure) and code (C# logic). Understanding how these pieces interact and communicate is critical when designing efficient and valuable components.

4. **Parameterization**: Blazor components can accept parameters, allowing them to adapt and respond to changing input. Learn how to use parameters to increase the flexibility of your components.

Remember these fundamental notions when we begin the process of constructing Blazor components.

Before you begin Blazor development, you must prepare your machine by installing the necessary tools and prerequisites.

Follow these steps for a smooth start:

1. **Download Visual Studio 2022**: Begin by downloading and installing Visual Studio 2022, the IDE that facilitates Blazor application development.

2. **Install .NET 8 SDK**: Ensure you have the required version of .NET Core SDK installed (8). This SDK is essential for building and running Blazor applications.

3. **Verify .NET Core SDKs**: To confirm the list of installed .NET Core SDKs, run the following command from the command line:

    1. dotnet --list-sdks

4. **Check Visual Studio workloads**: Install the ASP.NET and Web Development sections if you are using Visual Studio. To check, go to Tools, then select Get Tools and Features.

5. **Server-side:** Initiating Blazor server-side and client-side projects.

Now, we discuss the steps to create a Blazor server-side and a Blazor client-side project. Follow these detailed instructions to set up your development environment for comprehensive Blazor exploration.

Creating a Blazor server-side project

After successfully installing the necessary SDKs, proceed to Visual Studio and follow these steps:

1. Click on Create New Project to initiate the project creation process.

2. Choose Blazor Server as the project template.

3. Assign a name to the project, for example, `BlazorServer`, and provide a distinctive name for the solution, such as `BlazorApplication`.

4. Click Next and select the latest targeted framework (in this case, 8.0).

5. Click Next again, and your Blazor server-side project will be generated.

6. These steps ensure the creation of a Blazor server-side project within your Visual Studio environment.

Creating a Blazor client-side project

Now, let us move on to crafting a Blazor client-side project within the same solution:

1. Navigate to the solution explorer within the server-side project.

2. Right-click on the BlazorServer solution and select Add New Project.

3. Opt for the Blazor template and name the project Blazor WebAssembly.

4. Click Next and select the latest targeted version.

5. Click Create to finalize the setup for the client-side project.

Once completed, navigate to the solution explorer to confirm that the client-side project was successfully created. These painstaking steps establish the foundation for server and client-side Blazor applications in your development environment.

In the following parts, we will look at both projects and acquire firsthand experience with Blazor's dynamic hosting models.

6. Configuring startup projects for Blazor Server and Blazor Client.

This section will walk you through selecting a startup project, including several techniques for Blazor Server and Blazor client-side applications.

Individual selection to configuring:

1. Set Blazor Server or Blazor Client as the startup project:

2. Right-click the Blazor Server solution.

3. Select Set as Startup Project from the available options.

Visual Studio will highlight Blazor Server as a starter project. Use the same method for Blazor Client, right-clicking on its solution.

Using solution properties

Another way involves using the solution properties to choose both projects:

1. Click on the solution, which is Blazor Server's parent and Blazor Client's.

2. Select Select Startup Projects.

3. A dialog window will appear, giving you two options: a single startup project or several projects.

Multiple startup projects

For choosing multiple startup projects:

1. Click on Multiple startup projects.

2. A new box under the Multiple startup projects heading will appear.

3. Both created projects will be listed, each with a dropdown option. Set both projects as Start.

4. Click Ok, then either press *Ctrl + F5* or click on Build Project.

Executing these steps initiates the build process for both projects simultaneously.

These strategies simplify the selection of startup projects, resulting in a smooth launch of your Blazor Server and Blazor Client apps.

Blazor prerequisites

Before starting Blazor development, make sure you have a working grasp of the following languages:

- C#
- HTML
- CSS

Blazor WebAssembly App template missing: Try to start a Blazor project in Visual Studio 2022. You may discover that the Blazor WebAssembly App template is missing. Here is a general command for installing Blazor templates with .NET 8.0:

```
1.  dotnet new -i Microsoft.AspNetCore. Blazor. Templates
```

This command installs the most recent version of Blazor templates. If you have problems or want to install a certain version, you can provide it in the command. For example:

```
1. dotnet new -i Microsoft.AspNetCore. Blazor. Templates:8.0.0
```

You can run this command from the Package Manager Console in Visual Studio or the command prompt.

In conclusion, Blazor is a breakthrough framework that changes how we construct dynamic web UIs. Blazor connects classic JavaScript frameworks to the robust .NET environment by letting us use C# for server-side and client-side programming. This unique integration streamlines and enhances application development by reusing talents and resources across levels. Blazor's usage of WebAssembly to run C# code directly in the browser improves compatibility without plugins and sets a new benchmark for online application performance and security.

Blazor components, a modular, encapsulated, and interactive paradigm, improve web development productivity and maintainability. Blazor's support for .NET skills helps us to shift to new technologies faster. Blazor's efficiency, user experience, and adoption of new web standards make it a crucial component in the future of web development. Its arrival gives us exciting new opportunities and signals a trend toward more coherent and efficient digital development techniques.

Understanding the Blazor project structure

Navigating a Blazor project necessitates a thorough understanding of its fundamental structure. We will peel back the Blazor project's layers, revealing each component's organization, purpose, and relevance. Look at the following figure:

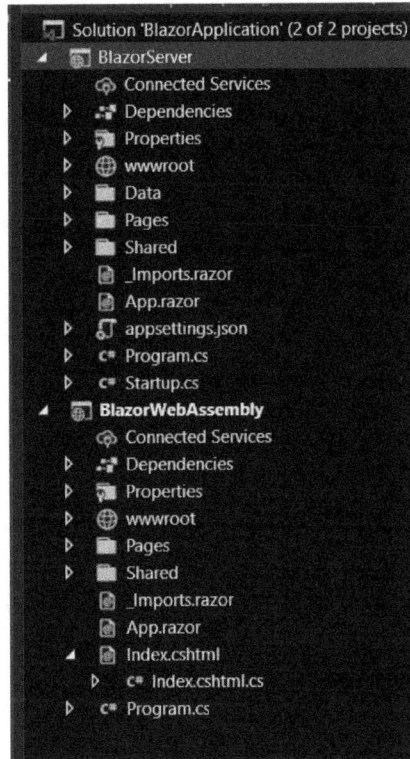

Figure 15.1: Solution Explorer

Root directory/ Program.cs

The Blazor project's root directory serves as its foundation. It contains essential configuration files such as **appsettings.json**, which holds application settings, and **Program.cs**, the application's entry point.

When exploring the heart of Blazor projects, the **Main()** method emerges as the shared entry point for Blazor WebAssembly and Blazor Server. We will have specific duties for the **Main()** method in each project type.

Main() method's dual role

In a Blazor Server project, Host Builder Choreography: The **Main()** method orchestrates by calling the **CreateHostBuilder ()** method, which sets up the Blazor Server project's ASP.NET Core host.

In a Blazor WebAssembly project: App component showcase. The **Main()** method takes center stage, specifying the application's root, the App component. This critical component is located in the root project folder within the **App.razor** file.

Blazor building blocks

A Blazor application's base is built around components.

App components serve as the root component, controlling the application's architecture.

This tantalizing glance into the orchestration of the **Main()** method, as well as the critical role of the App component, sets the foundation for a more in-depth investigation of subsequent topics. Let us take a look at the core of Blazor development:

```
1.  using Microsoft.AspNetCore.Hosting;
2.  using Microsoft.Extensions.Hosting;
3.  using System;
4.
5.  namespace MyNameSpace
6.  {
7.      public class Program
8.      {
9.          public static void Main(string[] args)
10.         {
11.             CreateHostBuilder(args).Build().Run();
12.         }
13.
14.         public static IHostBuilder CreateHostBuilder(string[]
    args) =>
15.             Host.CreateDefaultBuilder(args)
16.                 .ConfigureWebHostDefaults(webBuilder =>
17.                 {
18.                     webBuilder.UseStartup<Startup>();
19.                 });
20.     }
21. }
```

This **Main()** method starts the Blazor WebAssembly Application, establishing services and defining the root component. Specific specifications may change depending on the project's requirements and dependencies.

- **Pages/_Host.cshtml**: The **Pages** directory is critical in Blazor, holding Razor pages representing various aspects of the program. Each Razor page mixes HTML and C# code, creating a modular structure for creating interactive components.

  The **Pages/Host.cshtml** page, located at the heart of the Blazor Server program, serves as its focal point. This topic peels back the layers to expose the essence of the razor page as described by the **MapFallbackToPage("/ Host")** method. This method is used above in the **Configure** function of the **Program.cs** example.

- **The serving**: As the Blazor Server application opens, the **Pages/Host.cshtml** page takes center stage. It is the first point of contact between the application and the initial request. This page wears typical HTML clothes with recognizable **HEAD** and **BODY** tags.

- **Navigating the Razor**: **Pages/Host.cshtml**, implemented as a razor page, orchestrates the rendering of the core application component, App, encased in **App.razor**. This dynamic rendering takes place within the framework of HTML, neatly combining the worlds of markup and Razor syntax.

- **SignalR—real-time connectivity**: The **Pages/Host.cshtml** page begins an essential dance by including the **blazor.server.js** JavaScript code. This file establishes the foundation for a real-time SignalR connection, a vital link between the server and the client browser. This connection serves as a conduit for information exchange, allowing us to incorporate real-time web functionality into our application thanks to SignalR's capabilities.

In web development, SignalR demonstrates the path to real-time interactivity.

Here is an example of a razor-sharp **_Host.cshtml** page. When the program receives its first request, it returns to this page. It has the normal **HTML**, **HEAD**, and **BODY** tags. It also specifies where the root application component, App (**App.razor**), should appear. Finally, it executes the blazor.server.js JavaScript code, which creates a real-time SignalR connection between the server and the client browser. This connection is used to transmit data between the client and the server. SignalR is a good framework for incorporating real-time web functionality into programs.

```
1. @page "/"
2. @namespace BlazorServer.Pages
3. @addTagHelper *, Microsoft.AspNetCore.Mvc.TagHelpers
4. @{
5.     Layout = null;
6. }
7.
8. <!DOCTYPE html>
9. <html lang="en">
10. <head>
11.     <meta charset="utf-8" />
12.     <meta name="viewport" content="width=device-width, initial-scale=1.0" />
13.     <title>BlazorServer</title>
14.     <base href="~/" />
15.     <link rel="stylesheet" href="css/bootstrap/bootstrap.min.css" />
16.     <link href="css/site.css" rel="stylesheet" />
17.     <link href="BlazorServer.styles.css" rel="stylesheet" />
```

```
18. </head>
19. <body>
20.     <component type="typeof(App)"
    render-mode="ServerPrerendered" />
21.
22.     <div id="blazor-error-ui">
23.         <environment include= "Staging, Production">
24.             An error has occurred. This application may no
    longer respond until reloaded.
25.         </environment>
26.         <environment include="Development">
27.             An unhandled exception has occurred. See browser
    dev tools for details.
28.         </environment>
29.         <a href="" class="reload">Reload</a>
30.         <a class="dismiss">🗙</a>
31.     </div>
32.
33.     <script src="_framework/blazor.server.js"></script>
34. </body>
35. </html>
```

- **App.razor**: The **App.razor** file is the Blazor application's base component. It determines the overall layout and structure of the program and serves as the starting point for the component trees. It intercepts browse navigation.

```
1.  <Router AppAssembly="@typeof(Program).
    Assembly" PreferExactMatches="@true">
2.      <Found Context="routeData">
3.          <RouteView RouteData="@routeData" DefaultLayout="@
    typeof(MainLayout)" />
4.      </Found>
5.      <NotFound>
6.          <LayoutView Layout="@typeof(MainLayout)">
7.              <p>Sorry, there's nothing at this address.</p>
8.          </LayoutView>
9.      </NotFound>
10. </Router>
```

Navigating the Blazor router

The Blazor program relies on the **<Router>** component to navigate its complex network of routes. Let us examine the importance of the offered code snippet in the context of your current structure.

Configuring the router

Add the AppAssembly in the router:

```
1.  <Router AppAssembly="@typeof(Program).Assembly" PreferExactMatches="@
    true">
```

The **<Router>** component browses routes defined in the supplied assembly linked to the **Program** class. The **PreferExactMatches** attribute is true, indicating a preference for exact route matches.

Navigating the found routes

The following code demonstrates the route navigation:

```
1.  <Found Context="routeData">
2.          <RouteView RouteData="@routeData" DefaultLayout="@
    typeof(MainLayout)" />
3.  </Found>
```

Upon successful route discovery, the **<Found>** block activates. It encapsulates a **<RouteView>** component that dynamically renders content based on **routeData**. The **DefaultLayout** attribute is set to **MainLayout**, which designates the layout component used for rendering.

Handling unfound routes

The following code defines the 404 message:

```
1.  <NotFound>
2.          <LayoutView Layout="@typeof(MainLayout)">
3.              <p>Sorry, there's nothing at this address.</p>
4.          </LayoutView>
5.      </NotFound>
```

The **<NotFound>** block is used when a route cannot be found. The **<LayoutView>** component specifies **MainLayout** as the layout for use. A short message is displayed in the layout, apologizing for the lack of content at the supplied address.

As we explore Blazor components, the **<Router>** configuration will guide us through route handling and rendering.

Shared folder

In our Blazor application's architectural landscape, the **Shared** directory emerges as a repository for components and files that will be used on numerous pages. This purposeful structure encourages reusability and maintains a consistent look in the user interface. Let us look at the shared components contained within this directory.

Several critical components take center stage in the shared directory, each contributing to the application's overall coherence. Notable among these are:

- **MainLayout.razor**: A fundamental layout component that influences our application's overall structure and aesthetics.

- **NavMenu.razor**: This component controls the navigation ship, encapsulates the logic and presentation of our application's navigation menu.

- **SurveyPrompt.razor**: This interactive component encourages user participation by prompting surveys, resulting in a dynamic and responsive user experience.

Structuring styles .css companion

The CSS folder in the shared directory complements these Razor components. This folder is a repository for styling concerns, ensuring a clear separation of structure and presentation. The styling defined here works well with the Razor components, resulting in a visually cohesive and aesthetically pleasing user interface.

wwwroot/css folder

The **css** directory in **wwwroot** is a repository for stylesheets, with each line of code defining our application's visual presentation. These styles extend beyond individual pages, forming a cohesive image that captures the essence of our project. Essential static files stored here include the following:

- **css**: A pivotal stylesheet weaving together the overarching visual theme of our application.

  - **bootstrap**: Infusing the Bootstrap framework, this stylesheet introduces a responsive and sleek design, elevating the overall user experience.

  - **open-iconic**: A treasure trove of iconic imagery, this stylesheet contributes a library of open-source icons, enriching the visual language of our application.

- **Images**: An assembly of static images, this directory breathes life into the visual narrative, offering a reservoir of graphics that enhance the user interface.

- **JavaScript**: The dynamic counterpart, this directory hosts JavaScript files that harmonize with the stylesheets, fostering interactivity and responsiveness.

At this point we will have this structure in our solution:

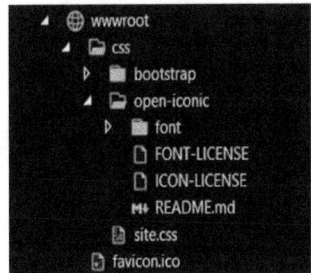

Figure 15.2: *wwwroot*

The styles within the **css** directory extend beyond the confines of individual pages, creating a stylistic symphony that resonates throughout the project.

wwwroot/index.html file

The Blazor WebAssembly Application launches from the index.html file in the **wwwroot** directory. It sets up the application and specifies the root element where the Blazor component will be rendered.

```
1.  <!DOCTYPE html>
2.  <html lang="es">
3.  <head>
4.      <meta name="viewport" content="width=device-width, initial-
        scale=1.0, maximum-scale=1.0, user-scalable=no" />
5.      <meta charset="utf-8" />
6.      <title>BlazorWebAssembly</title>
7.      <base href="/" />
8.      <link href="css/bootstrap/bootstrap.min.css" rel="stylesheet" />
9.      <link href="css/app.css" rel="stylesheet" />
10.     <link href="BlazorWebAssembly.styles.css" rel="stylesheet" />
11. </head>
12.
13. <body>
14.     <div id="app">Loading...</div>
15.
16.     <div id="blazor-error-ui">
17.         An unhandled error has occurred.
18.         <a href="" class="reload">Reload</a>
19.         <a class="dismiss">🗙</a>
20.     </div>
21.     <script src="_framework/blazor.webassembly.js"></script>
22. </body>
```

```
23.
24.</html>
```

Gateway to Blazor WebAssembly wwwroot

Nestled within the **wwwroot** directory, the **index.html** file emerges as the vanguard, acting as the first portal to our Blazor WebAssembly Application. Let us look at how it orchestrates the start of our application and defines the foundation for rendering Blazor components.

The **index.html** file serves as the beacon at the start of our Blazor WebAssembly Application. As the first point of contact, it is responsible for initializing the application and laying the groundwork for the following dynamic experience.

The foundational elements take shape within the confines of this HTML file. It articulates our application's blueprint, defining the root element through which the magic of Blazor components will unfold. This root element serves as the canvas for the entire application.

The **index.html** file starts the application and initiates the rendering of the Blazor component. This component, the heart and soul of our application, is placed within the predefined root element, ready to bring life to the user interface.

As we progress through Blazor WebAssembly, the importance of the index.html file will become more evident. It serves as the entry point, ushering us into a world where Blazor components come to life, creating a rich and dynamic narrative for our users.

wwwroot/js folder

The **js** directory within the expansive **wwwroot** repository is a home for JavaScript files. While Blazor's primary focus is on C#, there are times when seamless integration of JavaScript is required. This directory is a dedicated space for JavaScript files, bridging the C#-centric Blazor framework with JavaScript's dynamic capabilities. As we navigate the complexities of our application, the **wwwroot/js** directory is ready to facilitate the harmonious interaction of these two scripting languages.

_Imports.razor file

The **_Imports.razor** file is crucial to our Blazor project's organizational symphony. This file, strategically placed at the heart of the project structure, excels at managing namespace imports. Centralizing namespace references streamlines the referencing process throughout the project. This improves code readability while simplifying namespace management, resulting in a more cohesive and efficient development experience.

In the intricate dance of languages and organizational structure, the **wwwroot/js** directory and the **_Imports.razor** file are essential in orchestrating a harmonious and efficient development landscape.

Understanding the Blazor project structure paves the way for efficient development.

In conclusion, exploring a Blazor project's architecture from the root directory to its complex components and pages is necessary. The root is the **Program.cs** file is located to establish the application's entry point and environment, a process complicated by the Blazor Server and WebAssembly projects' **Main()** method. This core configuration is supported by Razor pages and components that render the application's UI and manage SignalR real-time communication in Blazor Server projects. Blazor's modular design relies on HTML and C# code, and the **Pages/_Host.cshtml** page and **App.razor** file initialize the application's core and enable dynamic component rendering.

Further investigation reveals the Blazor project's structured file system, including the shared directory for reusable components and the **wwwroot** directory for static resources like CSS, images, and JavaScript files, which are essential for the application's visual and functional aspects. Including **_Imports.razor** for namespace management and Router for complex route networks shows intelligent planning to maximize development efficiency and application performance.

Performance and new UIs in .NET 9

We have significant performance improvements and adaptable rendering choices in.NET 9 to maximize user interface. The new Blazor render modes—server-side, client-side, or a hybrid approach with prerendering—offer more precise control over where and how Razor components are rendered. This additional flexibility aims to enhance the user experience and the initial load time by choosing the best rendering strategy based on the app's requirements.

Blazor's Interactive Server and Interactive WebAssembly modes provide unique advantages for interactive user interfaces. For example, the Interactive Server mode uses SignalR to retain interaction while rendering components on the server. This can be a significant benefit for applications that need real-time server connectivity. On the other hand, Interactive WebAssembly is designed for situations in which we want the program to execute entirely on the client, utilizing client resources and reducing server dependencies. Furthermore, the Interactive Auto render mode offers a hybrid method where elements load server-side initially, but rendering moves to the client for later visits after assets are cached. This creates a smooth experience that strikes a compromise between user convenience and speed.

These render modes allow developers to match specific component requirements with UI performance techniques. For example, by sending HTML up front, prerendering provides a quicker initial response, enhancing **Search Engine Optimization** (**SEO**) and perceived speed. Thanks to these abilities, any company interested in web speed and adaptable app delivery will find .NET 9 a good update, enabling Blazor applications to deliver responsive user interfaces across various devices and network situations.

The new Blazor render modes in .NET 9 help us customize the user experience according to program requirements and deployment plans. By regulating where and when a component is rendered, these render modes—static **server-side rendering (SSR)**, Interactive **client-side rendering (CSR)**, and a hybrid approach with prerendering—allow applications to strike a compromise between performance and interaction.

Server-side rendering that is static

In static **server-side rendering (SSR)**, components are rendered on the server and then transmitted to the client as plain HTML. This mode works well for material that can be displayed as a static page and does not need to be interactive, such as blog entries or documentation. Since the material is already included in the initial HTML response, SSR offers quick initial load times and is SEO-friendly.

To configure a component to use static SSR, follow these steps:

1. `@page "/static-ssr-example"`
2. `@rendermode Static`
3.
4. `<h3>Static SSR Example</h3>`
5. `<p>This page is statically rendered on the server, with no interactivity.</p>`

In this example:

- The **@rendermode** static directive ensures the component renders on the server as HTML only.
- Any interactive features, such as event handling, are disabled.

The static SSR mode produces quick, SEO-friendly, non-interactive pages. For self-sustaining apps, interactive CSR transfers computation to the client. By striking a compromise, the hybrid approach with prerendering enables server-rendered content to load fully interactively on the client. Depending on the particular requirements of each component and page, developers can use these render modes to optimize for speed, responsiveness, or scalability.

CSR that is interactive

Interactive CRS makes full interaction and offline use possible. This mode downloads and launches the .NET runtime and application components straight in the browser. Applications that must function independently of the server or manage complex client-side interactions are best suited for this mode.

To activate Interactive CSR, you would utilize:

1. `@page "/client-side-example"`
2. `@rendermode InteractiveWebAssembly`
3.

```
4.  <h3>Interactive CSR Example</h3>
5.  <button @onclick="UpdateMessage">Click Me</button>
6.  <p>@message</p>
7.
8.  @code {
9.      private string message = "Initial message";
10.
11.     private void UpdateMessage()
12.     {
13.         message = "Updated on the client!";
14.     }
15. }
```

The **@renderIn** this example:

- The **InteractiveWebAssembly** directive downloads and executes the app in the browser.

- The button's **@onclick** event handler works without server calls, as everything runs on the client.

Hybrid Method using Prerendering

In the hybrid approach with prerendering, components hydrate on the client to become interactive after first rendering on the server to deliver a speedy HTML response. This method works well for complicated programs requiring rich client interaction and a quick initial load.

This hybrid behavior is made possible by Blazor's **InteractiveAuto** mode:

```
1.  @page "/hybrid-example"
2.  @rendermode InteractiveAuto
3.
4.  <h3>Hybrid Prerendering Example</h3>
5.  <button @onclick="UpdateMessage">Click Me</button>
6.  <p>@message</p>
7.
8.  @code {
9.      private string message = "Initial static content";
10.
11.     private void UpdateMessage()
12.     {
13.         message = "Now fully interactive!";
14.     }
15. }
```

In this example:

The page initially loads with static HTML from the server, allowing quick first rendering.

Once the Blazor app bundle loads on the client, the component becomes interactive, and the **@onclick** event handler works.

Configuring render modes in Program.cs

Ensure the server is configured to support these render modes. Here is how to set up services for each mode:

```
1.  builder.Services.AddRazorComponents()
2.      .
    AddInteractiveServerComponents()      // For Interactive Server SSR
3.      .AddInteractiveWebAssemblyComponents(); //
    For Interactive CSR and Auto
4.
5.  app.MapRazorComponents<App>()
6.      .
    AddInteractiveServerRenderMode()      // For server interactivity
7.      .AddInteractiveWebAssemblyRenderMode() //
    For WebAssembly interactivity
8.      .AddInteractiveAutoRenderMode();      // For hybrid prerendering
```

Mode of Interactive Server

The Interactive Server mode uses a SignalR connection and allows interactivity while rendering the component on the server. This is advantageous when you require real-time interaction and server-side processing, like with data-heavy applications.

The **@rendermode** directive can be used to set a component to interactive server mode:

```
1.  @page "/server-mode-example"
2.  @rendermode InteractiveServer
3.
4.  <h3>Interactive Server Mode Example</h3>
5.  <button @onclick="UpdateMessage">Click Me</button>
6.  <p>@message</p>
7.
8.  @code {
9.      private string message = "Initial message";
10.
11.     private void UpdateMessage()
12.     {
13.         message = "Updated on the server!";
```

```
14.    }
15. }
```

In this example:

- The button click triggers the **UpdateMessage** method on the server via SignalR.
- The message updates in real time as the connection allows the server to re-render the component and push the updated state back to the client.

Setup the project. Ensure the server has SignalR services configured.

Here is an example setup in **Program.cs**:

```
1. builder.Services.AddRazorComponents()
2.     .AddInteractiveServerComponents();
3.
4. app.MapRazorComponents<App>()
5.     .AddInteractiveServerRenderMode();
```

Interactive WebAssembly mode

While Blazor WebAssembly downloads and launches the .NET runtime and application bundle in the browser, the Interactive WebAssembly mode draws components on the client side. Applications needing client-side experience and less server reliance should use this mode.

Using Interactive WebAssembly mode, here is an example:

```
1. @page "/wasm-mode-example"
2. @rendermode InteractiveWebAssembly
3.
4. <h3>Interactive WebAssembly Mode Example</h3>
5. <button @onclick="UpdateMessage">Click Me</button>
6. <p>@message</p>
7.
8. @code {
9.     private string message = "Initial message";
10.
11.    private void UpdateMessage()
12.    {
13.        message = "Updated on the client!";
14.    }
15. }
```

In this example:

- The code executes entirely on the client side, allowing the app to respond immediately to interactions without a server round-trip.

- This setup minimizes latency and can reduce server load but requires the app's entire bundle to be downloaded to the client.

Regarding real-time server-driven interactions, Interactive Server outperforms Interactive WebAssembly, guaranteeing that the application can preserve state consistency straight from the server. However, it is not the best option for offline use because it requires constant internet access.

However, because Interactive WebAssembly eliminates server dependency and enables offline scenarios (albeit with limited dynamic data), it is better suited for isolated, self-sufficient apps. Both strategies offer the flexibility to adapt deployment and performance requirements to application requirements.

Working with forms and validation in Blazor

In this article, we will look at how Blazor implements form validation. We will look at a practical example of validating forms within the Blazor framework to demonstrate. We explain the complexities of form validation in Blazor using a hands-on example.

Employee edit form validation

The model for the employee edit form is the **Employee** class. We aim to implement form validation.

There are two simple steps:

1. **Decorate the model class with validation attributes**: These validation attributes (Required, Email Address) belong to the **System.ComponentModel.DataAnnotations** namespace.

```
1. using System;
2.
3. namespace MyNameSpace.Data;
4.
5. public class Employee
6. {
7.    public DateTime Date { get; set; }
8.    public int EmployeeId { get; set; }
9.    [Required]
10.   [MinLength(2)]
11.   public int FirstName{ get; set; }
12.   public string Email { get; set; }
13. }
```

2. **Attach validation support**:

The **DataAnnotationsValidator** component attaches validation support to our form.

The **ValidationSummary** component displays a summary of all validation messages.

The **ValidationMessage** component displays validation messages for a specific field.

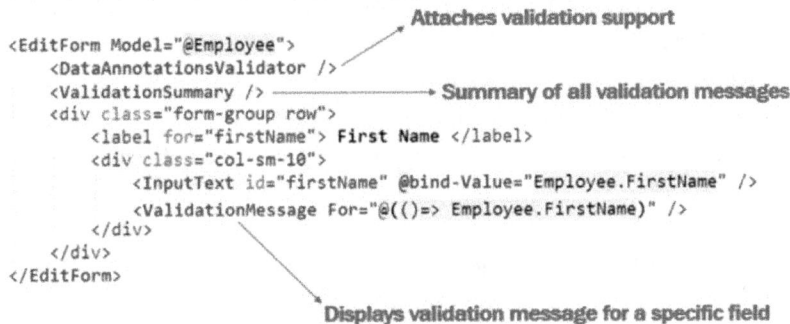

```
<EditForm Model="@Employee">
    <DataAnnotationsValidator />              Attaches validation support
    <ValidationSummary />                     Summary of all validation messages
    <div class="form-group row">
        <label for="firstName"> First Name </label>
        <div class="col-sm-10">
            <InputText id="firstName" @bind-Value="Employee.FirstName" />
            <ValidationMessage For="@(()=> Employee.FirstName)" />
        </div>
    </div>
</EditForm>
                                              Displays validation message for a specific field
```

Figure 15.3: Validation

Edit form validation—complete code:

```
1.  @page "/editemployee/{id}"
2.
3.  @inherits EditEmployeeBase
4.
5.  <EditForm Model="@Employee">
6.      <DataAnnotationsValidator />
7.      <h3>Edit Employee</h3>
8.      <hr />
9.      <ValidationSummary />
10.     <div class= "form-group row">
11.         <label for="firstName" class="col-sm-2 col-form-label">
12.             First Name
13.         </label>
14.         <div class="col-sm-10">
15.             <InputText id="firstName" class="form-
    control" placeholder="First Name"
16.                         @bind-Value= "Employee.FirstName" />
17.             <ValidationMessage For="@(() => Employee.FirstName)" />
18.         </div>
19.     </div>
```

```
20.     <div class= "form-group row">
21.         <label for="lastName" class="col-sm-2 col-form-label">
22.             Last Name
23.         </label>
24.         <div class="col-sm-10">
25.             <InputText id="lastName" class="form-
    control" placeholder="Last Name"
26.                         @bind-Value= "Employee.LastName" />
27.             <ValidationMessage For="@(() => Employee.LastName)" />
28.         </div>
29.     </div>
30.     <div class= "form-group row">
31.         <label for="email" class="col-sm-2 col-form-label">
32.             Email
33.         </label>
34.         <div class="col-sm-10">
35.             <InputText id="email" class="form-
    control" placeholder="Email"
36.                         @bind-Value= "Employee.Email" />
37.             <ValidationMessage For="@(() => Employee.Email)" />
38.         </div>
39.     </div>
40.
41. <div class= "form-group row">
42.         <label for="department" class="col-sm-2 col-form-label">
43.             Department
44.         </label>
45.         <div class="col-sm-10">
46.             <CustomInputSelect @bind-Value="Employee.
    DepartmentId" class="form-control">
47.                 @foreach (var dept in Departments)
48.                 {
49.                     <option value="@dept.DepartmentId">@dept.
    DepartmentName</option>
50.                 }
51.             </CustomInputSelect>
52.         </div>
53.     </div>
54.     <div class= "form-group row">
55.         <label for="gender" class="col-sm-2 col-form-label">
56.             Gender
```

```
57.        </label>
58.        <div class="col-sm-10">
59.            <InputSelect @bind-Value="Employee.Gender" class="form-
   control">
60.                @foreach (var gender in Enum.
   GetValues(typeof(Gender)))
61.                {
62.                    <option value="@gender">@gender</option>
63.                }
64.            </InputSelect>
65.        </div>
66.    </div>
67.    <div class= "form-group row">
68.        <label for="dateOfBirth" class="col-sm-2 col-form-label">
69.            Date Of Birth
70.        </label>
71.        <div class="col-sm-10">
72.            <InputDate @bind-Value="Employee.
   DateOfBrith" class="form-control" />
73.        </div>
74.    </div>
75. </EditForm>
```

Blazor custom form validation

In most use cases, ASP.NET Core provides a range of built-in attributes for model validation. Following are some commonly used built-in attributes:

- Required
- Range
- StringLength
- MinLength
- MaxLength
- Compare
- Regular Expression

Custom validation attribute example

If there is a validation requirement not covered by built-in attributes, we can craft a custom validation attribute. On the edit employee page, we restrict email domains to **pragimtech. com**. Any other domain triggers a validation error. While a regular expression validator could suffice, let us explore the creation of a custom validator for this specific scenario.

Create a custom validation attribute

To create a custom validation attribute:

1. Develop a class that inherits from the abstract **ValidationAttribute** class provided by ASP.NET Core and override the **IsValid()** method.

2. The **IsValid()** method returns null if there are no validation errors; otherwise, it returns a **ValidationResult** object.

3. The **ValidationResult** accepts two parameters—the validation error message and the property name to associate with this validation error message.

4. The public property (**AllowedDomain**) facilitates passing the domain name, enhancing the reusability of this **EmailDomainValidator** class compared to hard coding the domain. Look at the following code:

```
1.  using System.ComponentModel.DataAnnotations;
2.
3.  namespace MyNameSpace;
4.
5.  public class EmailDomainValidator : ValidationAttribute
6.  {
7.      public string AllowedDomain { get; set; }
8.
9.      protected override ValidationResult IsValid(object value,
10.         ValidationContext validationContext)
11.     {
12.         string[] strings = value.ToString().Split('@');
13.         if (strings[1].ToUpper() == AllowedDomain.ToUpper())
14.         {
15.             return null;
16.         }
17.
18.         return new ValidationResult($"Domain must be
    {AllowedDomain}",
19.             new[] { validationContext.MemberName });
20.     }
21. }
```

Using custom validation attribute in Blazor

Custom validation attributes are tags that direct how the properties will behave.

```
1.  public class Employee
2.  {
```

```
3.      [EmailDomainValidator(AllowedDomain = "pragimtech.com")]
4.      public string Email { get; set; }
5. }
```

Key points:

- Employ the custom validation attribute just like any other built-in one.
- The Email property is adorned with the **EmailDomainValidator** attribute.
- **AllowedDomain** property specifies the email domain against which we intend to validate.

The aforementioned are methods and techniques for implementing validation in Blazor. Additionally, we can employ compare validation and execute complex model validation.

An example of compare validation includes the following:

- Email and confirm email validation.
- Password and confirm password validation.

We can apply changes to the model class and apply validation there. In the view, use the **ValidationSummary** and **ValidationMessage** components to display the validation error message.

In conclusion, this topic covered form validation in the Blazor framework, using ASP. NET Core's built-in validation characteristics and custom validation attributes for specific needs. We covered how to validate an employee edit form to ensure data integrity and improve user experience by preventing inaccurate data submission. The procedure starts with decorating model classes with validation properties like **Required**, **EmailAddress**, and custom attributes like **EmailDomainValidator**, then adding validation support using **DataAnnotationsValidator**, **ValidationSummary**, and **ValidationMessage**. This method lets us apply several validation criteria to ensure that form data meets requirements and limitations.

Building a custom validation property to restrict email domains showed Blazor's flexibility in handling validation circumstances beyond built-in characteristics. Validation is vital in designing robust, trustworthy online apps that ensure the accuracy of user input. Blazor's comprehensive validation tools help us to build secure, efficient, and user-friendly web apps. The concepts and methods outlined enable Blazor applications to integrate complex validation logic, creating more dynamic, interactive and validated user interfaces that match business needs and increase user engagement.

Understanding JavaScript interop in Blazor

The cutting-edge framework Blazor integrates C# with web technologies to create a new web development strategy. JavaScript Interop, a bridge between C# and JavaScript in Blazor applications, is vital to this integration. This guide demystifies JavaScript interop with a complete introduction, practical examples, and full instructions on how to use it to improve Blazor apps.

JavaScript interop lets us use the best of both worlds by allowing direct communication and operation between C# and JavaScript. Interoperability lets you invoke JavaScript functions from C# or vice versa, improving user experience, integrating third-party libraries, and creating complex functionality that was previously challenging.

Unveiling JavaScript interop

JavaScript interop in Blazor bridges the robust C# functionalities and the dynamic capabilities of JavaScript. It enables the exchange of data, functions, and events, fostering a harmonious coexistence that enhances the overall flexibility and functionality of your Blazor applications.

Let us understand a practical example of the same to grasp the essence of JavaScript interop in Blazor. Consider a scenario where we want to invoke a JavaScript function from our Blazor component.

```
1.  @code {
2.      private string message = "Hello from Blazor!";
3.  }
4.
5.  <button @
    onclick="InvokeJavaScriptFunction">Invoke JavaScript Function</
    button>
6.
7.  @code {
8.      private async Task InvokeJavaScriptFunction()
9.      {
10.         await JSRuntime.InvokeVoidAsync("myJavaScriptFuncti
    on", message);
11.     }
12. }
```

In this example, we define a Blazor component with a button. Upon button click, the **InvokeJavaScriptFunction** method is triggered, which, in turn, invokes a JavaScript function named **myJavaScriptFunction** and passes the message from Blazor.

Expanding horizons

JavaScript interop in Blazor extends beyond simple function invocations. It empowers you to manipulate the **Document Object Model (DOM)**, handle events, and seamlessly integrate JavaScript libraries into your Blazor applications.

In the evolving narrative of Blazor development, JavaScript interop emerges as a pivotal tool, weaving together the strengths of C# and JavaScript to create robust and interactive web applications.

Using JavaScript in Blazor

Blazor operates seamlessly within the browser thanks to the introduction of WebAssembly in 2019, marking it as the fourth programming language alongside HTML, CSS, and JavaScript. While adopting C# instead of JavaScript is now feasible, there are scenarios where incorporating JavaScript, facilitated by JavaScript interops, remains a practical choice.

Numerous reasons may prompt the use of JavaScript despite the availability of C# for most functionalities. If you wish to incorporate a library with effects like jQuery, JS interops becomes a valuable tool.

JavaScript interops, derived from JavaScript interoperability, underscores the collaborative synergy between JavaScript and .NET. This interoperability allows the invocation of .NET methods using JavaScript and the utilization of JavaScript to invoke .NET methods.

In the case of calling a JavaScript function using .NET, we will illustrate using a Blazor Server App project. The essential files to modify are the **_Host.cshtml** file and the specific file where the JavaScript functionality is desired. For simplicity, let us consider the front page of the Blazor Server App template.

The JavaScript script tag, crucial in a Blazor Server App, must always be placed in the **_Host.cshtml** file for the script tag to function correctly. In this instance, a function named **showAlert** is added. This function accepts a parameter, the message displayed in the alert box. The function dynamically creates a new paragraph element using only JavaScript. It appends it to the div with the id of p-container.

Execute from .NET to trigger JavaScript in a Blazor Server App:

_Host.cshtml:

```
1.  @page "/"
2.  @namespace JSInterops.Pages
3.  @addTagHelper *, Microsoft.AspNetCore.Mvc.TagHelpers
4.  @{
5.  Layout = "_Layout";
6.  }
7.      <component type="typeof(App)" render-mode="ServerPrerendered" />
8.      <script>
9.          function showAlert(message) {
10.                     var element = document.getElementById("p-container");
```

```
11.                              var newElement = document.createElement("p");
12.                              newElement.innerHTML = "Appended paragraph";
13.
14.                              element.append(newElement);
15.                              return alert(message);
16.                      }
17.      </script>
```

Index.razor:

```
1.  @page "/"
2.  <PageTitle>Index</PageTitle>
3.
4.  <h1>Hello, world!</h1>
5.
6.  Welcome to your new app.
7.
8.  <SurveyPrompt Title= "How is Blazor working for you?" />
9.
10. <button @onclick="appendText">Run JS Script</button>
11.
12. <div id="p-container">
13. </div>
14.
15. @inject IJSRuntime JS
16. @code {
17.     public async void appendText()
18.     {
19.         await JS.InvokeAsync<string>("showAle
    rt", "Text will append when you close this alert!");
20.     }
21. }
```

Remember to inject IJSRuntime in the **.razor** file, and when using InvokeAsync, remember to do the function async as well.

In conclusion, this topic on JavaScript interop in Blazor shows how it bridges C# with JavaScript, opening up new options for us. Through real examples and thorough insights, we have seen how interoperability streamlines data and function interchange, improving Blazor application functionality and flexibility. The ability to invoke JavaScript functions from Blazor components and vice versa shows how well these two languages work together and makes web development more dynamic and engaging. As we studied JavaScript interop, we saw that it is a technical requirement and a strategic advantage for those who want the best of both worlds.

Blazor's JavaScript interop has great promise to help us build more robust, interactive, and beautiful web apps. Blazor's architecture is powerful and flexible enough to integrate JavaScript libraries, modify the DOM directly, and handle events without sacrificing C# features. Understanding and using JavaScript interop is crucial as we examine advanced use cases. It is essential for modern web development, allowing us to build complex, high-performance, scalable, and maintainable apps. In conclusion, Blazor's JavaScript interop improves developers' tools and the user experience, transforming web application development.

Building a CRUD operation using Blazor

Most online applications use CRUD operations, which allow users to create, read, update, and remove data. Blazor, a *Microsoft* framework, allows us to create interactive web UIs with C# instead of JavaScript. Blazor CRUD activities require server-side and client-side logic. They are frequently used with a database such as SQL Server, MySQL, or MongoDB on the backend. Here is an outline of how to implement CRUD activities in a Blazor application:

1. **Create (C)**:
   a. **Server-side**: Create a model to reflect the data structure. To interface with the database, use EF Core or any other ORM. Implement a way to add new entities to the database.
   b. **Client-side (Blazor)**: Create a form in a Blazor component (`.razor` file) to enter fresh data. Bind the form inputs to the model instance. When the form is submitted, the server-side method saves the information to the database.

2. **Read (R)**:
   a. **Server-side**: Create a method that requests the database to obtain data. It may return a list of entities or a single entity based on an ID.
   b. **Client-side (Blazor)**: To show the data, use Blazor components. To acquire the data, call the server-side API and then use data binding to show it in the UI, such as a table or list.

3. **Update (U)**:
   a. **Server-side**: Similar to create, this method updates an existing entity. It usually entails locating the entity in the database by ID and then altering its properties.
   b. **Client-side (Blazor)**: Use a form similar to create but preload it with existing data. After the user has modified the data and submitted the form, use the server-side approach to update the database.

4. **Delete (D)**: Implement a server-side method to remove an entity from the database, typically identifiable by its ID.

    a. **Client-side (Blazor)**: Include a user interface element allowing users to delete an entity, often displayed as a button in a data table row. After clicking, use the server-side technique to remove the entity from the database.

    b. **Technical implementation**: The Blazor Server paradigm allows for direct server-side CRUD operations. The UI interactions are handled via a SignalR connection. The server-side logic and database interactions are more straightforward because the code is executed on the server.

    c. **Blazor WebAssembly**: To create a client-side Blazor app, we must first configure the server's API to expose endpoints for CRUD activities. The Blazor app then sends HTTP requests to these endpoints for operations. Further configuration is required if the API is hosted separately, including **Cross-Origin Resource Sharing (CORS)**.

We will see an example of how to build up a Blazor WebAssembly project, define a model for patient records, create a service to handle data operations, and create components for each CRUD operation.

Set up the Blazor WebAssembly project

Following are the steps to set up the Blazor WebAssembly project:

1. Create a new Blazor WebAssembly App.
2. Open Visual Studio or your preferred IDE.
3. Create a project and select the Blazor WebAssembly App template.
4. Name the project OrthopedicClinic.
5. Ensure you're targeting .NET 8.
6. Add a Server Project (this is optional, for a more realistic scenario where data is stored and retrieved from a server).
7. Add a new ASP.NET Core Web API project to your solution.
8. Name it `OrthopedicClinic.Server`.

Define the Model

The following are the steps to define the Model:

1. In the `OrthopedicClinic` (client) project, define a model representing a patient record.
2. Create a `Models` folder.
3. Add a new class, `Patient.cs`.

```
1. namespace OrthopedicClinic.Models;
2. public class Patient
3. {
4.     public int Id { get; set; }
5.     public string Name { get; set; }
6.     public int Age { get; set; }
7.     public string Condition { get; set; }
8. }
```

Create a data service

This service will handle the CRUD operations. This would interact with a database in an application, but we will use a static list for simplicity, which is as follows:

1. Add a **Services** folder.

2. Add a new class **PatientService.cs**:

```
1. using OrthopedicClinic.Models;
2. using System.Collections.Generic;
3. using System.Linq;
4.
5. namespace OrthopedicClinic.Services;
6.
7. public class PatientService
8. {
9.     private static List<Patient> patients = new List<Patient>
10.         {
11.             new Patient { Id = 1, Name = "John Doe", Age = 30,
    Condition = "Knee Pain" },
12.
13.         };
14.
15.     public List<Patient> GetAllPatients() => patients;
16.
17.     public void AddPatient(Patient patient)
18.     {
19.         patient.Id = patients.Max(p => p.Id) + 1;
20.         patients.Add(patient);
21.     }
22.
23.     public void UpdatePatient(Patient patient)
```

```
24.    {
25.        var index = patients.FindIndex(p => p.Id == patient.
   Id);
26.        if (index != -1)
27.            patients[index] = patient;
28.    }
29.
30.    public void DeletePatient(int id)
31.    {
32.        var patient = patients.FirstOrDefault(p => p.Id == id);
33.        if (patient != null)
34.            patients.Remove(patient);
35.    }
36. }
```

Implement CRUD operations in the UI

Following are the steps to implement CRUD operations in the UI:

1. **CRUD**: For each CRUD operation, create a new Razor component.
2. **List patients (Patients.razor)**: Displays all patients.
3. **Add/edit patient (EditPatient.razor)**: Form to add or edit a patient.
4. **Delete patient**: Can be a button in the list with a confirmation dialog.

Example: List patients (`Patients.razor`):

```
1. @page "/patients"
2. @inject PatientService PatientService
3. @inject NavigationManager NavigationManager
4.
5. <h3>Patients</h3>
6.
7. @if (patients == null)
8. {
9.     <p><em>Loading...</em></p>
10. }
11. else
12. {
13.     <table class="table">
14.         <thead>
15.             <tr>
16.                 <th>Name</th>
17.                 <th>Age</th>
```

```
18.                    <th>Condition</th>
19.                    <th>Actions</th>
20.                </tr>
21.            </thead>
22.            <tbody>
23.                @foreach (var patient in patients)
24.                {
25.                    <tr>
26.                        <td>@patient.Name</td>
27.                        <td>@patient.Age</td>
28.                        <td>@patient.Condition</td>
29.                        <td>
30.                            <button class="btn btn-primary" @
    onclick="() => EditPatient(patient.Id)">Edit</button>
31.                            <button class="btn btn-danger" @
    onclick="() => DeletePatient(patient.Id)">Delete</button>
32.                        </td>
33.                    </tr>
34.                }
35.            </tbody>
36.        </table>
37. }
38.
39. @code {
40.     private List<Patient> patients;
41.
42.     protected override async Task OnInitializedAsync()
43.     {
44.         patients = PatientService.GetAllPatients();
45.     }
46.
47.     private void EditPatient(int id)
48.     {
49.         // Navigate to the edit page with the patient ID
50.         NavigationManager.NavigateTo($"/editpatient/{id}");
51.     }
52.
53.     private void DeletePatient(int id)
54.     {
55.         // Show a confirmation dialog before deletion
```

```
56.          var confirmed = Confirm($"Confirm
    that you want to delete the patient with ID {id}?");
57.          if (confirmed)
58.          {
59.              PatientService.DeletePatient(id);
60.              patients = PatientService.
    GetAllPatients(); // Refresh the list
61.              StateHasChanged(); // Notify the component to re-render
62.          }
63.      }
64. }
```

Example **EditPatient.razor**:

```
1.  @page "/editpatient/{Id:int}"
2.  @inject PatientService PatientService
3.  @inject NavigationManager NavigationManager
4.
5.  <h3>Edit Patient</h3>
6.
7.  @if (patient == null)
8.  {
9.      <p><em>Loading...</em></p>
10. }
11. else
12. {
13.     <EditForm Model="@patient" OnValidSubmit="HandleValidSubmit">
14.         <DataAnnotationsValidator />
15.         <ValidationSummary />
16.
17.         <div class="form-group">
18.             <label for="Name">Name:</label>
19.             <InputText id="Name" class="form-control" @bind-
    Value="patient.Name" />
20.         </div>
21.
22.         <div class="form-group">
23.             <label for="Age">Age:</label>
24.             <InputNumber id="Age" class="form-control" @bind-
    Value="patient.Age" />
25.         </div>
26.
```

```
27.          <div class="form-group">
28.              <label for="Condition">Condition:</label>
29.              <InputText id="Condition" class="form-control" @bind-
   Value="patient.Condition" />
30.          </div>
31.
32.          <button type="submit" class="btn btn-success">Update</
   button>
33.          <button class="btn btn-secondary" @onclick="Cancel">Cancel</
   button>
34.      </EditForm>
35. }
36.
37. @code {
38.      [Parameter]
39.      public int Id { get; set; }
40.
41.      private Patient patient;
42.
43.      protected override async Task OnInitializedAsync()
44.      {
45.          patient = PatientService.GetPatientById(Id);
46.      }
47.
48.      private async Task HandleValidSubmit()
49.      {
50.          PatientService.UpdatePatient(patient);
51.          NavigationManager.NavigateTo("/patients");
52.      }
53.
54.      private void Cancel()
55.      {
56.          NavigationManager.NavigateTo("/patients");
57.      }
58. }
```

Implementing **PatientService** on **Program.cs**:

```
1. using OrthopedicClinic.Services;
2.
3. var builder = WebAssemblyHostBuilder.CreateDefault(args);
4. builder.RootComponents.Add<App>("#app");
```

```
5.
6. builder.Services.AddScoped<PatientService>();
7.
8. await builder.Build().RunAsync();
```

In conclusion, building a CRUD process with Blazor is a significant step forward in developing interactive web apps with .NET technologies. Blazor's capabilities allow us to use C# on both the client and server sides, easing the development process and reducing the need to switch contexts between languages like JavaScript for client-side code. The complete procedures for building a Blazor WebAssembly project, designing a patient record model, constructing a data service, and implementing CRUD UI components demonstrate Blazor's practicality. Blazor's power and flexibility in database interactions and how we may construct rich, interactive user interfaces with less effort are shown.

Integrating CRUD activities into a Blazor application shows a thorough web application data management technique. We may create powerful applications by breaking down the process into distinct, achievable steps, from setting up the project environment and establishing data models to implementing data manipulation services and designing the user interface. This strategy creates user-friendly apps with smooth navigation and efficient data handling. The healthcare example shows Blazor's versatility across domains, giving us many opportunities to maximize modern web development with .NET technology.

Using Entity Framework Core with Blazor

Blazor is a no-cost, open-source web framework that empowers us to craft web applications using C# and HTML. It serves as a framework for constructing engaging client-side web user interfaces. NET.

Blazor, a modern web framework from Microsoft, seamlessly integrates with EF Core to facilitate efficient data management in web applications. This synergy allows us to leverage the power of EF Core for database operations within their Blazor applications.

Key features

The advantages of EF Core with Blazor are:

- Develop feature-rich interactive user interfaces using C# instead of JavaScript.
- Seamlessly share application logic between server-side and client-side, both written in .NET.
- Render the user interface as HTML and CSS, ensuring broad support across various browsers, including those on mobile devices.
- Effortlessly integrate with contemporary hosting platforms like Docker.

  Blazor allows us to build dynamic web applications using familiar C# programming, facilitating code-sharing between server and client components in the .NET ecosystem. Additionally, its capability to render UI elements as HTML and CSS ensures compatibility with a wide range of browsers, and its adaptability to modern hosting platforms enhances deployment efficiency.

Setting up Entity Framework Core in Blazor

To begin, we will initiate an ASP.NET Core-hosted Blazor App project. This project type includes all the template files necessary to set up a Blazor application. Let us launch Visual Studio 2022. If you have not installed Visual Studio yet, visit the Visual Studio downloads page to acquire it for free.

Then, on the start window, choose Create a new project, and in the Create a new project window, input or type **blazor** in the search box. Then, from the language list, opt for C#. Choose the Blazor app template and proceed by selecting Next.

In the Configure your new project window, type or enter **EFCoreInBlazorApp** in the Project name box and click the Create button.

Pick the Blazor WebAssembly App project template and check the ASP.NET Core hosted option. Click on the Create button. This will generate the app.

Visual Studio creates a new project and loads the default code files, as the Solution Explorer displays.

You will see that the following three projects are created inside this solution:

- **EFCoreInBlazorApp.Client**: It contains the client-side code and the pages displayed in the browser.
- **EFCoreInBlazorApp.Server**: It encompasses the server-side code, DB-related operations, and the web API.
- **EFCoreInBlazorApp.Shared**: It contains shared code accessible by both the client and server.

To utilize EF Core follow these steps:

1. Install the **Microsoft.EntityFrameworkCore** library in the **EFCoreInBlazorApp.Server** project.

2. In the Package Manager Console window, input the following command:

    1. Install-Package MicroSoft.EntityFrameworkCore

3. Install Microsoft for SQL Server LocalDB, which comes pre-installed with **VisualStudio.EntityFrameworkCore.SqlServer** will acquire all the necessary packages for EF Core.

    1. Install-Package Microsoft.EntityFrameworkCore.SqlServer

4. Additionally, install the following NuGet package:

```
1. Install-Package Microsoft.VisualStudio.Web.CodeGeneration.
   Design
```

Configure database connection

Follow the given steps:

1. In your **Program.cs** file, configure the database connection in the **ConfigureServices** method.

```
1. builder.Services.AddDbContext<ApplicationDbContext>(options =>
2.     options.UseSqlServer(Configuration.GetConnectionString("Defa
   ultConnection")));
```

2. **Define ApplicationDbContext**: The EF will generate an empty database. Thus, we must create a method invoked after the database is established to populate it with test data.

3. Within the DAL folder of the **EFCoreInBlazorApp**. For the server project, introduce a new class named **AuthorContextInitializer** and replace the existing code with the following.

4. Create a class that derives from DbContext to represent your application's database context. For example:

```
1. public class ApplicationDbContext : DbContext
2. {
3.     public ApplicationDbContext(DbContextOptions
   <ApplicationDbContext> options) : base(options) { }
4.
5.     public DbSet<YourEntity> YourEntities { get; set; }
6. }
```

Performing CRUD operations

Follow the given steps:

1. **Retrieve data (Read)**: In your Blazor component, inject the **ApplicationDbContext** and query the database as needed:

```
1. @inject ApplicationDbContext dbContext
2.
3. @code {
4.     var data = dbContext.YourEntities.ToList();
5. }
```

2. **Adding data (Create)**: Use EF Core to add new records to the database:

```
1. @code {
2.     YourEntity newEntity = new YourEntity { /* initialize
   properties */ };
3.     dbContext.YourEntities.Add(newEntity);
4.     dbContext.SaveChanges();
5. }
```

3. **Updating data (Update)**: Modify existing records and save changes:

```
1. @code {
2.     YourEntity entityToUpdate = dbContext.YourEntities.
   Find(id);
3.     entityToUpdate.PropertyToUpdate = newValue;
4.     dbContext.SaveChanges();
5. }
```

4. **Removing data (Delete)**: Delete records using EF Core:

```
1. @code {
2.     YourEntity entityToDelete = dbContext.YourEntities.
   Find(id);
3.     dbContext.YourEntities.Remove(entityToDelete);
4.     dbContext.SaveChanges();
5. }
```

Example: Displaying data in a Blazor component:

```
1. @page "/yourPage"
2.
3. @inject ApplicationDbContext dbContext
4.
5. <h3>Your Data:</h3>
6.
7. <table>
8.     <thead>
9.         <tr>
10.             <th>Property1</th>
11.             <th>Property2</th>
12.             <!-- Add more columns as needed -->
13.         </tr>
14.     </thead>
15.     <tbody>
16.         @foreach (var entity in dbContext.YourEntities.
   ToList())
```

```
17.      {
18.          <tr>
19.              <td>@entity.Property1</td>
20.              <td>@entity.Property2</td>
21.              <!-- Add more columns as needed -->
22.          </tr>
23.      }
24.    </tbody>
25. </table>
```

In conclusion, integrating EF Core with Blazor is a big step forward in building modern online applications. Blazor enables us to construct sophisticated, interactive user interfaces with C# and HTML, removing the need for JavaScript for client-side scripting. This connection streamlines the development process by sharing application logic between the client and server. Still, it also ensures broad browser compatibility and makes deployment easier on modern platforms such as Docker. Furthermore, the setup procedure, which includes initializing an ASP.NET Core-hosted Blazor App project and configuring EF Core, is expedited with tools such as Visual Studio, making it accessible to individuals new to the platform. This synergy enables us to handle databases efficiently.

Understanding Blazor Server vs. Blazor WebAssembly

They have some differences, Blazor Server runs on servers, sending UI updates via SignalR. Blazor WebAssembly runs entirely in browsers, downloading .NET runtime locally. Let us take a closer look at the differences.

Blazor hosting models

With Blazor, we have two hosting models, Blazor WebAssembly (client-side hosting model) and Blazor Server (server-side hosting model).

As the template names imply, use the template Blazor Server App to create a Blazor application with a server hosting model and the Blazor WebAssembly template to create a Blazor application with a client hosting model.

Blazor Server vs. Blazor WebAssembly

The project structure and layout are not that different between the two project types:

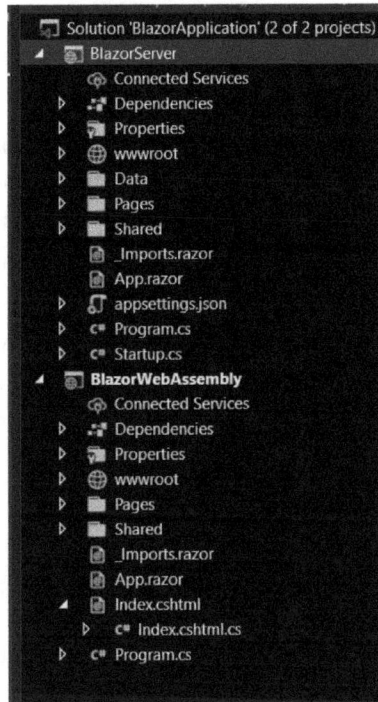

Figure 15.4: Explorer Solution.

Blazor WebAssembly hosting model

In the Blazor WebAssembly hosting model, the application operates directly within the browser through WebAssembly. All essential components, including the compiled application, its dependencies, and the .NET runtime, are fetched from the server to the client's browser. A Blazor WebAssembly App can function solely on the client, independent of a constant connection to the server. Configurations can be implemented for server interaction using web API calls or SignalR.

Benefits of Blazor WebAssembly hosting model:

- **Client-side independence**: A Blazor WebAssembly App can run autonomously on the client machine. After the initial download, no continuous connection to the server is required. This eliminates the need for the server to be operational 24/7.

- **Resource offloading**: The client's resources and capabilities bear the workload. Work is shifted from the server to the client, optimizing performance and responsiveness.

- **Minimal hosting requirements**: Unlike requiring a full-fledged ASP.NET Core web server, hosting a Blazor WebAssembly App only demands a server capable of delivering the application to the client browser. This versatility allows hosting on personal servers, on Azure as a static website, in the cloud, or even on a content delivery network.

Downsides of Blazor WebAssembly hosting:

- **Initial loading time**: The first request typically takes longer due to downloading the entire app, dependencies, and the .NET runtime to the client browser. Subsequent visits by the same client tend to be faster as the browser caches the necessary files.

- **Client-side limitations**: Since the app runs exclusively on the client browser, its capabilities are confined to those of the browser itself.

- **Hardware and software requirements**: Capable client hardware and software are prerequisites depending on the application's nature. For example, a browser with WebAssembly support is essential from a software standpoint.

Blazor Server hosting model

This hosting paradigm executes the program on the server. The client and server create a SignalR connection. The server receives information via the SignalR connection when an event occurs on the client. The server processes the event and calculates a **diff** (**difference**) for the output HTML. The complete HTML is not transmitted to the client; the diff is delivered over the SignalR connection. The browser then refreshes the **user interface** (**UI**). Since the diff is used to change the UI, the program seems quicker and more responsive to the user.

Here we have the comparison of each hosting:

- **Blazor Server hosting model benefits**:

    o The program loads quicker than Blazor WebAssembly due to its decreased download size.

    o The server-based program may leverage all server capabilities, including .NET Core APIs.

    o Clients only need a browser to utilize the app. Browsers that do not support WebAssembly can still be utilized.

    o The app is more secure since it does not serve .NET/C# code to clients.

- **Blazor Server hosting**:

    o The application requires a complete ASP.NET Core server to run. Serverless deployment possibilities, such as delivering the app via a CDN are not feasible.

    o Active connection to the server is always necessary. This necessitates the server's availability around the clock. If the server goes down, the program stops operating.

- Unlike Blazor WebAssembly hosting, there is typically more latency due to the round trip to the server required for each user interaction.

- Scalability may be problematic for programs with a large user base, as the server must manage many connections and client states. However, we may address the scalability issue by combining Azure SignalR Service with a Blazor Server app. This service enables Blazor Server apps to scale effectively by supporting many concurrent SignalR connections.

Grasping the distinctions of Blazor Server vs. Blazor WebAssembly

Blazor has two different server plans, each with its benefits. Blazor Server runs code on the server and uses SignalR to send UI changes to clients. This method lets pages load faster, download smaller files, and give you immediate access to server resources. This makes it perfect for internal apps or ones that need few client resources.

By downloading the .NET runtime along with your app, Blazor WebAssembly can run completely in the browser. This makes the experience truly client-side, with less work for the server and the ability to work offline. The runtime download makes the first load time slower, though.

Whether you choose server-side processing with few client requirements or client-side execution with offline features depends on your needs.

Core mechanism

For each type of Blazor, we have a specific mechanism:

- **Blazor Server**:
  - Operates by executing the application on the server.
  - Utilizes a SignalR connection for communication between the client and server.
  - Transmits only the calculated HTML diff to the client over the SignalR connection, optimizing performance.

- **Blazor WebAssembly**:
  - Runs the application directly in the client's browser through WebAssembly.
  - Downloads the compiled application, dependencies, and .NET runtime to the client from the server.
  - Offers client-side independence with the option to interact with the server through API calls or SignalR.

Loading dynamics

For loading they work different too:

- **Blazor Server**:
  o Swift loading due to smaller download sizes.
  o Server capabilities fully harnessed, including .NET Core compatible APIs.
  o Broad browser compatibility, supporting even those without WebAssembly support.

- **Blazor WebAssembly**:
  o Initial loading may take longer as the entire app, dependencies, and .NET runtime are downloaded.
  o Relies on client resources and capabilities for execution.
  o Requires capable client hardware and software, including WebAssembly-supported browsers.

Connection and interaction

For connections and interactions, they work differently:

- **Blazor Server**:
  o Continuous functioning requires an ongoing connection to the server.
  o A server manages multiple client connections, potentially impacting scalability.
  o Enhanced security as the app's code remains on the server.

- **Blazor WebAssembly**:
  o Independence from continuous server connections after initial download.
  o Potential latency in user interactions due to round trips to the server.
  o Security implications as the app's code is sent to clients.

Decoding Blazor Server vs. Blazor WebAssembly Dynamics

Navigating the choices between Blazor Server and Blazor WebAssembly involves unraveling the intricate tapestry of their distinctive dynamics.

Core mechanism exploration

Look at the following points:

- **Blazor Server**:
  - **Centralized execution**: The application executes its logic on the server, offering a centralized processing model.
  - **SignalR symphony**: Orchestrates communication through SignalR, facilitating real-time interaction between the client and server.
  - **Differential brilliance**: Optimizes performance by calculating and transmitting only the differential HTML to the client, ensuring efficient updates.

- **Blazor WebAssembly**:
  - **Browser ballet**: Choreographs a symphony within the client's browser, harnessing the power of WebAssembly for local execution.
  - **Downloadable symphony**: Fetches the compiled application, dependencies, and .NET runtime to the client, initiating a symphony of code within the browser.
  - **Interactivity spectrum**: Offers a spectrum of interactivity, ranging from complete client-side independence to optional server interaction via APIs or SignalR.

Loading dynamics deconstructed

Blazor provides two different hosting types that have a significant impact on user experience and application performance. It is essential to comprehend each model's loading characteristics in order to choose the best strategy for the particular needs of our project.

- **Blazor Server**:
  - **Swift beginnings**: Commences with rapid loading, boasting smaller download sizes for efficient initiation.
  - **Server's arsenal**: Exploits server capabilities fully, providing access to a repertoire of .NET Core compatible APIs.
  - **Browser harmony**: Harmonizes seamlessly with a wide range of browsers, extending compatibility to those without WebAssembly support.

- **Blazor WebAssembly**:
  - **Ponderous prelude**: Initiates with a ponderous prelude as the entire application, dependencies, and .NET runtime make their way to the client.
  - **Client-driven performance**: Entrusts execution to the client's resources and capabilities, introducing a client-centric performance paradigm.
  - **Hardware and software sonata**: Requires adept client hardware and software, demanding browsers with steadfast WebAssembly support.

Connection and interaction chronicles

Building scalable, secure, and performant applications requires an awareness of the many client-server communication philosophies found in the always changing web development framework environment. This analysis explores the key distinctions between Blazor WebAssembly and Blazor Server, shedding light on the crucial trade-offs that influence how they are implemented.

- **Blazor Server**:
  - **Tethered continuity**: Establishes a tethered relationship, requiring an active connection to the server for uninterrupted functionality.
  - **Scalability symphony**: Orchestrates scalability challenges, especially with numerous users, as the server manages multiple connections and client states.
  - **Fortified security citadel**: Bolsters security by keeping the app's .NET/C# code sheltered on the server, away from prying client eyes.

- **Blazor WebAssembly**:
  - **Liberation in independence**: Liberates from constant server connections after the initial download, granting autonomy to the client.
  - **Latency dynamics**: Introduces potential latency in user interactions, with round trips to the server impacting real-time responsiveness.
  - **Code exposure consideration**: Security considerations are raised as the app's code is dispatched to clients, necessitating vigilant safeguards.

This comprehensive decoding of Blazor Server and Blazor WebAssembly dynamics sets the stage for a nuanced understanding.

Finally, it is vital to choose one to understand Blazor Server and Blazor WebAssembly's unique features and how they meet web application needs. Blazor Server's server-side execution delivers fast load times, vast server capabilities, broad browser compatibility, and increased security, but it requires an active server connection and scaling issues. Blazor WebAssembly, on the other hand, lets apps run directly in the browser, offloads work to client resources, and requires little hosting. Its drawbacks include lengthier initial load times, client-side dependence, and code exposure that may compromise security.

Each model has advantages and disadvantages. The application's performance, scalability, client hardware, and security demands should determine the Blazor Server or Blazor WebAssembly decision. We should consider these aspects when choosing a hosting type that matches their application's aims and user expectations. This nuanced understanding of both hosting types helps make an informed choice and sets the stage for building complex, interactive web apps using Blazor.

Working with routine in Blazor

Routing in Blazor is essential for dynamic, user-friendly web apps. This technique lets us connect web addresses to application components for easy navigation and organization. Blazor's routing system supports client-side and server-side applications, making it ideal for **single-page applications (SPAs)** with minimal page reloads. Developers may utilize Blazor to construct complex web apps with efficient user flow by mastering routing essentials like route definition and navigation. This introduction will cover Blazor routing basics, including establishing routes, managing page navigation, handling static and interactive routing scenarios, and helping developers build responsive and intuitive web apps.

Basics of routing in Blazor

In Blazor, routing is primarily based on the structure of the URL. Each component corresponds to a specific route, and when a user navigates to a particular URL, Blazor renders the associated component. Routing in Blazor is case-insensitive and supports parameters, allowing for dynamic content based on user input.

Defining routes:

Routes are defined in the App. razor file. This file acts as the root component and specifies the application's layout. Each **RouteView** component defines a route and the associated component to be rendered.

```
1. <Router AppAssembly="@typeof(Program).Assembly">
2.     <Found Context="routeData">
3.         <RouteView RouteData="@routeData" DefaultLayout="@
   typeof(MainLayout)" />
4.     </Found>
5.     <NotFound>
6.         <LayoutView Layout="@typeof(MainLayout)">
7.             <p>Sorry, there's nothing at this address.</p>
8.         </LayoutView>
9.     </NotFound>
10. </Router>
```

This section pertains explicitly to Blazor WebAssembly App s. Blazor Web Apps do not utilize the **NotFound** template (**<NotFound>...</NotFound>**), although the template remains supported for backward compatibility to prevent a disruptive change in the framework. Blazor Web Apps typically handle erroneous URL requests by presenting the browser's inherent 404 UI or delivering a customized 404 page from the ASP.NET Core server through ASP.NET Core middleware. The Router component enables the app to define custom content if the content is not located for the requested route. Various items, including other interactive components, can be content within the **<NotFound>** tags.

Static routing

To identify routable components from additional assemblies for static server-side rendering (static SSR), even if the router later transitions to interactive rendering, it is imperative to expose these assemblies to the Blazor framework. Utilize the **AddAdditionalAssemblies** method, chaining the additional assemblies to **MapRazorComponents** in the server project's **Program** file.

In the provided example, the routable components in the **BlazorSample.Client** project's assembly are encompassed using the project's **_Imports.razor** file:

```
1. app.MapRazorComponents<App>()
2.        .AddAdditionalAssemblies(typeof(BlazorSample.Client._
   Imports).Assembly);
```

Navigating between pages

Blazor provides various ways to navigate between pages, whether within the application or to external links. The **NavigationManager** service is commonly used for programmatic navigation.

Interactive routing

An interactive rendering mode can be applied to the **Routes** component (**Routes.razor**), causing the Blazor router to transition to an interactive state after static SSR and static routing on the server. For instance, using **<Routes @rendermode= "InteractiveServer"/>** assigns interactive SSR to the **Routes** component. The **Router** component inherits interactive SSR from the **Routes** component, becoming interactive after static routing on the server. If the **Routes** component is located in the server project, the **AdditionalAssemblies** parameter of the **Router** component should encompass the **.Client** project assembly. This ensures that the router functions correctly when rendered interactively.

In the example, the **Routes** component is in the server project and the **_Imports.razor** file of the **BlazorSample.Client** project specifies the assembly to search for routable components:

```
1. <Router>
2.     AppAssembly="...."
3.     AdditionalAssemblies="new[] { (typeof(BlazorSample.Client._
   Imports).Assembly); " } >
4.
5. </Router>
```

Programmatic navigation: Using the **NavigationManager**, you can navigate to different pages within your Blazor application:

```
1. @code {
2.     [Inject] NavigationManager NavigationManager { get; set; }
```

```
3. }
4.
5. <button @onclick="NavigateToPage">Go to Another Page</button>
6.
7. @code {
8.     private void NavigateToPage()
9.     {
10.         NavigationManager.NavigateTo("/some/page");
11.     }
12. }
```

Links and navigation: Blazor supports standard HTML links (**<a>** tags) for navigation:

```
1. <a href="/some/page">Go to Another Page</a>
```

Routing is an essential aspect of building dynamic and interactive web applications. In Blazor, understanding how to define routes, work with parameters, and navigate between pages allows us to create seamless user experiences. The **NavigationManager** and standard HTML links provide flexibility for programmatic and declarative navigation. By mastering these concepts, you can create sophisticated single-page applications with Blazor.

Blazor routing helps structure and navigate web applications, enabling the building of dynamic, responsive SPAs for modern web development. Exploring URL formats, case-insensitivity, arguments, and route definition in the **App.razor** file shows how Blazor renders components based on URL requests. The distinction between static routing for server-side rendering and interactive routing for enhanced dynamism, along with programmatic and declarative navigation methods via the **NavigationManager** and standard HTML links, demonstrate Blazor's web development flexibility and power. With this complete understanding, we may use routing efficiently to improve Blazor app navigation and user experiences.

Testing in Blazor applications

Blazor applications, like any other software, benefit from comprehensive testing to ensure reliability and maintainability. Testing in Blazor can cover various aspects, including unit testing, integration testing, and end-to-end testing. Here are some key considerations for testing in Blazor applications:

- **Unit testing**:
  - **Blazor components**: Unit testing individual components is crucial to ensure they function as expected. Tools like xUnit, NUnit, or MSTest can be used for writing unit tests.
  - **C# code**: Test any non-component C# code separately from the UI components. This includes utility classes, services, and other business logic.

- **Integration testing**:
  - **Component integration**: Verify that components work together seamlessly. Integration tests may involve rendering components within a test environment and checking interactions.
  - **API integration**: If your Blazor app interacts with APIs, consider integration tests to validate proper communication and data handling.

- **End-to-end testing**:
  - **User scenarios**: Perform end-to-end tests to simulate real user scenarios. Tools like Selenium or Playwright can automate browser interactions, validating the entire application flow.
  - **UI testing**: Ensure the user interface behaves as expected by testing user interactions, form submissions, and navigation.

- **Testing libraries**:
  - **BUnit**: Specifically designed for Blazor, BUnit is a testing library that allows us to write unit tests for individual components.
  - **Selenium or Playwright**: For end-to-end testing, Selenium or Playwright can automate browser actions, validating the application from a user's perspective.

- **Mocking services**: When testing components that depend on services, consider using mocking frameworks like Moq to isolate components and test specific scenarios.

- **CI/CD**: Integrate testing into your CI/CD pipelines to ensure that every code change undergoes automated testing before deployment.

- **Code coverage**:
  - **Track code coverage**: Use tools like Coverlet or dotCover to monitor code coverage during testing, ensuring that tests cover a significant portion of your codebase.

- **Parameterized tests**:
  - **Test variations**: Implement parameterized tests to cover various inputs and edge cases, ensuring robustness in different scenarios.

- **Testing best practices**:
  - **Arrange, Act, Assert (AAA)**: Follow the AAA pattern in your tests—Arrange the test environment, Act on the functionality, and Assert the expected outcomes.
  - **Isolation**: Keep tests isolated to prevent dependencies between them, allowing for easier identification of issues.

Remember that a well-designed testing plan is critical to ensuring the quality and dependability of your Blazor applications. Adapt your testing strategy to your application's requirements and complications.

Blazor's introduction to C# development empowers us to extend their development across browsers without relying on traditional JavaScript frameworks like React, Vue.js, and Angular.

While setting up tests in typical JavaScript frameworks is simple, Blazor necessitates assembling specific tools and packages and then determining how and what to test in your project. Learn how to put up tests for a basic Blazor counter application and expand it to cover nearly every C# we could want to test in a Blazor app.

Setting up a test environment

Follow these steps:

1. Open Visual Studio.
2. Select App from the Web and Console menu.
3. Choose Blazor Server App.
4. Specify project details and click Create.
5. Select the desired authentication type or choose No Authentication.
6. Click Create to generate the Blazor Server App project.

The following steps will help you set up a test project for a Blazor Server App in Visual Studio:

1. **Setting up dependencies**:

    a. **Install BUnit**:

        i. In the Project Menu, click on Manage NuGet Packages.

        ii. Search and add bUnit and bUnit.core.

2. **Install xUnit**:

    a. This test project is bootstrapped as an xUnit project.

    b. By default, it comes with xUnit packages.

3. **Install Moq**:

    a. Moq is an assertion valuable library for testing if an expected result matches the returned result.

    b. Install Moq similarly to how bUnit was installed.

    c. Search for and select Moq.

    d. Click on Add Packages.

      e.   Select the test project.

      f.   Click OK.

4. **Testing with bUnit**:

      a.   xUnit is a test framework providing an interface to run Blazor applications outside the browser.

      b.   It allows interaction with the output through code.

5. **Test setup**: To test a Blazor app with bUnit, the test suite must have a test case function in a class within the test project.

The code inside the test case should look like this:

- **Configure**: Set up a TestContext (a virtual environment for rendering a Blazor component).

- **Process**: Trigger actions and make network requests to expose a component to a test context.

- **Assert**: Check if the events were triggered and the correct text was shown.

As an example, the following configuration demonstrates the steps mentioned previously:

```
1. using BlazorApp.Pages;
2. using Bunit;
3. using Xunit;
4.
5. namespace MyNameSpace;
6.
7. public class CounterTest
8. {
9.     [Fact]
10.    public void RendersSuccessfully()
11.    {
12.        using var ctx = new TestContext();
13.        var component = ctx.RenderComponent<Counter>();
14.        Assert.Equal("Click me", component.Find($".btn").TextContent);
15.    }
16. }
```

Passing parameters to components

Sometimes, parameters are required to render components correctly. bUnit provides an interface to work with. Steps to enable parameter passing:

1. Let us modify the counter component inside the application solution to look like the following:

```
1.  @page "/counter/{DefaultCount:int?}"
2.
3.  <h1>Counter</h1>
4.
5.  <p>Current count: <span id="counterVal">@currentCount</span></p>
6.
7.  <button class="btn btn-primary" @onclick="IncrementCount">Click me</button>
8.
9.  @code {
10.     private int currentCount = 0;
11.
12.
13.     [Parameter]
14.     public int DefaultCount { get; set; }
15.
16.     protected override void OnParametersSet()
17.     {
18.         if (DefaultCount != 0)
19.         {
20.             currentCount = DefaultCount;
21.         }
22.     }
23.
24.     private void IncrementCount()
25.     {
26.         currentCount++;
27.     }
28. }
```

2. Note that we have changed the default count argument and path to accept an int. The **?** tells the Blazor that this parameter is optional and unnecessary to run the component.

3. Observe the **[Parameter]** attribute on the **DefaultCount** property in the C# code. We used the **OnParametersSet** lifecycle function to alert the component when the parameter was set. This guarantees that we utilize it to update the component's **CurrentValue** field rather than beginning the count from zero.

We may render this component in a bUnit test case using the following:

```
1. using BlazorApp.Pages;
2. using Bunit;
3. using Xunit;
4.
5. namespace MyNameSpace;
6.
7. public class CounterTest
8. {
9.     public void RendersSuccessfully()
10.    {
11.
12.        using var ctx = new TestContext();
13.
14.        Action onBtnClickHandler = () => { };
15.        var component = ctx.RenderComponent<Counter>(
16.            parameters =>
17.            parameters
18.               .Add(c => c.DefaultCount, 10)
19.               .Add(c => c.OnBtnClick, onBtnClickHandler)
20.        );
21.
22.        Assert.Equal("Click me", component.Find($".btn").
    TextContent);
23.    }
24. }
```

In the test above, we render the component and then pass the callback to the component that calls (**p =>**).

4. Next, we add an **add** method on the param (**p => p.Add(c => c.DefaultCount, 10);**) to set the parameter to 10.

5. Similarly, we can pass the event callback with **p.Add(c => c.onBtnClickHandler, onBtnClickHandler)**. Thus, we implement the counter increment inside the **onBtnClickHandler** action instead of inside the counter component.

Transferring components to inputs and services

Specific components depend on external services, while others rely on external fields. In the test context, we can accomplish this using the **Services.AddSingleton** method through bUnit.

The demo Counter app has a **FetchData.razor** file that heavily relies on the **WeatherForecastService** service. Let us attempt to run this file within an xUnit project:

1. Create a new file called **FetchDataTest.cs** in the test project and add the following:

```
1.  using System;
2.  using BlazorApp.Data;
3.  using BlazorApp.Pages;
4.  using Bunit;
5.  using Microsoft.Extensions.DependencyInjection;
6.  using Xunit;
7.
8.  namespace MyNameSpace;
9.
10. public class FetchDataTest
11. {
12.     [Fact]
13.     public void RendersSuccessfully()
14.     {
15.
16.         using var ctx = new TestContext();
17.
18.         ctx.Services.AddSingleton<WeatherForecastService>(n
    ew WeatherForecastService());
19.
20.         // Render Counter component.
21.         var component = ctx.RenderComponent<FetchData>();
22.
23.         Assert.Equal("Weather forecast", component.Find($"h1").
    TextContent);
24.     }
25. }
```

2. Notice how we have utilized the **AddSingleton** interface to introduce a new service to our test runner context. When we run this test file, we should obtain a successful result.

Blazor apps undergo unit, integration, and end-to-end testing to verify reliability and performance. Unit testing isolates and tests C# code and components to ensure functionality. Integration testing checks how components and external APIs interact to ensure application ecosystem integration. Using Selenium or Playwright, end-to-end testing replicates real-user situations to evaluate the application from the user's perspective. Using BUnit for Blazor and mocking frameworks like Moq allows targeted testing. Integrating these tests into CI/CD pipelines improves development workflow by automatically testing and validating code changes. Thus, using these testing methods to Blazor apps strengthens their integrity and speeds their development and deployment, creating a robust and user-centric solution.

Conclusion

This chapter explores the Blazor framework, demonstrating its flexibility and capability for developing modern web apps in C#. You have learned how to design rich, interactive user interfaces, run CRUD operations flawlessly, and understand the differences between server and WebAssembly hosting models through hands-on examples and conversations. It demonstrates the changing world of online development and enables us to apply our C# experience in new, dynamic situations, resulting in novel web solutions. In the next chapter, we will discover the packaging and deploying .NET applications.

Join our book's Discord space

Join the book's Discord Workspace for Latest updates, Offers, Tech happenings around the world, New Release and Sessions with the Authors:

https://discord.bpbonline.com

CHAPTER 16

Packaging and Deployment

Introduction

This chapter explores the complexities of packaging and deploying .NET applications, covering key subjects such as understanding components and libraries, packaging, NuGet's critical role, and publishing code for deployment. We investigate the importance of .NET Standard and .NET Core libraries, assembly versioning, the **Global Assembly Cache (GAC)**, and the intricacies of strong-named assemblies. In addition, we walk you through using the .NET Core CLI for package management and offer best practices for packaging and distributing libraries. This thorough overview teaches developers how to efficiently manage their applications from creation to deployment, resulting in scalable, maintainable, and efficient software solutions.

Structure

This chapter covers the following topics:

- Understanding .NET components and libraries
- How to package .NET types
- Understanding NuGet and its role in .NET
- Publishing your .NET code for deployment
- Working with .NET Standard and .NET Core libraries

- Understanding assembly versioning in .NET
- Understanding the Global Assembly Cache
- Strong-named assemblies in .NET
- Using the .NET Core CLI for package management
- Native AOT improvements in .NET 9
- Best practice in packaging and distributing .NET libraries

Objectives

In this chapter, we investigate the complexity of packaging and deploying .NET programs, we will be addressing important subjects such as NuGet, versioning, publishing code, and versions of components and libraries. The purpose of this initiative is to provide developers with the knowledge necessary to effectively manage the applications throughout the development lifecycle, which will ultimately result in software solutions that are scalable and easy to maintain.

Understanding .NET components and libraries

In this section, we will explore the fundamentals of .NET components and libraries, shedding light on their significance and how they contribute to efficient and scalable software development.

Understanding .NET components

.NET components are self-contained, reusable building blocks that encapsulate specific functionalities within an application. These components adhere to the principles of modularity, making it very easy to maintain, scale, and update software systems.

Characteristics of .NET components

Some characteristics of .NET components are:

- **Reusability**: Components are designed to be reused across various parts of an application or even in different projects.

- **Encapsulation**: Components encapsulate their implementation details, exposing only the necessary interfaces to interact with the outside world.

- **Interoperability**: .NET components can seamlessly interact with components developed in other languages or technologies.

Types of .NET components

Some types of .NET components are:

- **Class libraries (.DLL)**: These are collections of reusable classes and methods that can be referenced and utilized by other projects.

- **User controls**: Custom UI elements encapsulating a set of functionalities can be embedded in different parts of a user interface. .NET Libraries

- A .NET library is a collection of pre-built classes and functions that provide standard functionalities, saving us time and effort. Libraries are integral to the .NET ecosystem, enabling us to leverage existing solutions for various tasks.

Creating a simple .NET component

Let us create a primary .NET component in C# to illustrate the concept:

```
1. using System;
2.
3. namespace ExampleNamespace {
4.     public class ExampleComponent {
5.         public void PerformAction() {
6.             Console.
   WriteLine("Action performed by the example component.");
7.         }
8.     }
9. }
```

In this example, **ExampleComponent** encapsulates a simple action that can be reused across different parts of an application.

Using .NET libraries

.NET libraries provide many functionalities, such as the widely used **System** namespace. For instance:

```
1. using System;
2.
3. class Program {
4.     static void Main() {
5.         Console.WriteLine("Hello, .NET Library!");
6.     }
7. }
```

Benefits of .NET components and libraries

Listed as follows are the benefits of .NET components and libraries:

- **Code reusability**: Components and libraries promote reusability, reducing redundant code and development time.

- **Modularity**: Modular components make maintaining and updating software systems easier.

- **Scalability**: Integrating pre-built components and libraries can scale applications more efficiently.

Having an understanding of .NET components and libraries is fundamental for building robust and efficient software applications. By embracing the principles of reusability and encapsulation, we can create scalable solutions that stand the test of time.

How to package .NET types

When working with .NET, packaging refers to bundling your code, resources, and metadata into a distributable format. It typically involves creating a NuGet package, a standardized way of sharing and distributing libraries in the .NET ecosystem.

Steps to package .NET types:

1. **Create a class library**: Start by creating a class library project using a tool like Visual Studio. This project will contain the .NET types you want to package.

2. **Define your types**: Write your .NET types within the class library. These can be classes, interfaces, enums, or other .NET constructs.

3. **Configure assembly information**: Ensure your project contains the necessary assembly information, including version numbers and metadata. This information is crucial for versioning and identifying your package.

4. **Build your project**: Build your class library project. It will generate the compiled binaries **dynamic link library** (**DLLs**) representing your .NET types.

5. **Create a NuGet package**: Use the NuGet pack command or tools within Visual Studio to create a NuGet package. This involves creating a **.nupkg** file that includes your compiled binaries, XML documentation, and other necessary files.

   Example:
   ```
   1. NuGet pack YourProject.csproj -IncludeReferencedProjects
   ```

6. **Publish your package**: If you want to share your .NET types with others, consider publishing your NuGet package to a package repository like **nuget.org**. Use the NuGet push command for this purpose.

Example:
```
1. NuGet push YourPackage.nupkg -Source https://api.nuget.org/v3/
   index.json -ApiKey YourApiKey
```

7. **Consuming the package**: Others can now consume your .NET types by referencing your NuGet package in their projects. They can use tools like the NuGet Package Manager in Visual Studio to add your package to their solutions.

   Example: Let us say you have a class library called **MyLibrary** containing a class **MyClass**. After packaging, consumers can install your package using the following command:
```
1. NuGet install MyLibrary
```

In their C# code we will have:
```
1. using MyLibrary;
2.
3. var instance = new MyClass();
```

It lets us easily include and use your .NET types in their projects.

Remember, this is a high-level overview, and the specifics may vary based on your exact scenario, tooling, and requirements. Adjust the steps accordingly.

Understanding NuGet and its role in .NET

NuGet is a package manager designed for the .NET development platform. It is crucial in simplifying discovering, installing, and managing external libraries and tools within .NET projects. Here is an in-depth look at NuGet and its role:

- NuGet is a package manager for .NET, enabling us to share and consume helpful code. It provides a centralized repository of packages, making it easy for us to include third parties or their libraries in their projects.

- A NuGet package is a distributable unit containing compiled code (DLLs) and other files like XML documentation, source code, and metadata. These standardized packages simplify sharing and reusing code across different projects and solutions.

- NuGet's role in .NET development:

  o **Package discovery**: We can explore and discover packages on the NuGet Gallery: **https://www.nuget.org/**. It is a central repository hosting a vast collection of NuGet packages.

  o **Package installation**: NuGet simplifies the process of adding dependencies to a project. We can quickly install packages using the NuGet Package Manager in Visual Studio 2022 or the dotnet add package command.

Example:

```
1. dotnet add package PackageName
```

- o **Dependency resolution**: NuGet automatically resolves dependencies, ensuring that the required versions of libraries are downloaded and included in the project.

- We can package and share their libraries using NuGet. It involves creating a **.nupkg** file containing the compiled binaries, documentation, and other necessary files.

Example:

```
1. NuGet pack YourProject.csproj -IncludeReferencedProjects
```

- We can use the Package Manager Console in Visual Studio to execute NuGet commands directly.

Example:

```
1. Install-Package PackageName
```

- The NuGet Package Manager UI provides a visual interface for managing packages, including browsing, installing, updating, and uninstalling.

- NuGet packages are managed through configuration files, such as packages. config in traditional .NET Framework projects and PackageReference in newer .NET Core and .NET 5+ projects.

- NuGet.org is the default package source for NuGet. We can also set up private package repositories if needed.

NuGet is often integrated into **continuous integration and deployment (CI/CD)** pipelines, ensuring that packages are restored and dependencies are resolved during the build process.

Publishing your .NET code for deployment

Publishing .NET code is a crucial step in the software development lifecycle, ensuring your application is ready for deployment. This process involves compiling the code, bundling dependencies, and organizing files for distribution. Here is a comprehensive guide on publishing .NET code:

1. **Dotnet publish command**: Use the **dotnet publish** command to compile and package your .NET code. This command builds the application for a specific target framework and runtime.

   Example:

   ```
   1. dotnet publish -c Release -o PublishOutput
   ```

This command compiles the code in **Release** mode and outputs the results to the **PublishOutput** directory.

2. **Output structure: Binaries and dependencies**: The **dotnet publish** command creates a directory containing the compiled binaries and necessary dependencies. The output structure includes the application's executable, DLLs, and other required files.

3. **Specify target runtime**: You can specify the target runtime using the **-r** or **--runtime** option. This ensures that the published code is compatible with the desired runtime.

   Example:

   ```
   1. dotnet publish -c Release -r linux-x64 -o PublishOutput
   ```

   This command publishes the code for the Linux x64 runtime.

4. **Specify target framework**: Use the **-f** or **--framework** option to specify the target framework. It is essential when targeting multiple frameworks.

   Example:

   ```
   1. dotnet publish -c Release -o PublishOutput
   ```

   This command publishes the code for the .NET Core 3.1 framework.

5. **Create a self-contained deployment**: For environments without the .NET runtime installed, create a self-contained deployment. This includes the runtime with the published code.

   Example:

   ```
   1. dotnet publish -c Release -r win-x64 --self-contained true
   ```

   This command creates a self-contained deployment for Windows x64.

6. **Publishing web applications**: Web applications, including ASP.NET Core projects, have additional considerations. Use the **--output** option to specify the output directory.

   Example:

   ```
   1. dotnet publish -c Release YoutProject.
      csproj --output PublishOutput
   ```

7. **Publish profiles**: For more advanced scenarios, consider using publish profiles (**.pubxml** files) to customize the deployment process, including database migrations, configuration transformations, etc.

8. **Deploying to Azure App Service**: For deploying to Azure, consider using the Azure App Service. You can publish directly from Visual Studio or use Azure DevOps pipelines for automated deployments.

9. **Publishing as a NuGet package:** If you want to share your library or package with others, consider publishing it as a NuGet package. We can use the `dotnet pack` command to create a NuGet package.

   Example:
   1. `dotnet pack -c Release`

10. **Integrate with CI/CD pipelines**: Automate the publishing process by integrating it into your CI/CD pipeline. Tools like Azure DevOps, GitHub Actions, or Jenkins can be configured to automatically build and publish your code.

11. **Customizing publish options**: Explore various options and flag the `dotnet publish` command provides to tailor the publishing process to your project's requirements.

Working with .NET Standard and .NET Core libraries

.NET Standard and .NET Core are integral components of the .NET ecosystem, providing a standardized framework for building cross-platform applications. Understanding how to work with .NET Standard and .NET Core libraries is crucial for creating modular and reusable code. Here is a comprehensive guide:

1. **Introduction to .NET Standard**: The .NET Standard is a formal specification that helps developers create interoperable libraries with multiple .NET implementations. The goal is to create a consistent base of APIs that all .NET platforms must implement. It allows developers to create libraries, components, and applications that run on different versions, like .NET Framework, .NET Core, and Xamarin, without requiring platform-specific modifications. This interoperability streamlines the development process by allowing for greater code reuse and portability of .NET programs across different contexts and platforms, allowing developers to target multiple devices and systems with a single codebase.

2. .NET Standard versions, such as 6.0 or 8.0, indicate the set of APIs available. Higher versions include more APIs, enhancing compatibility across platforms.

3. **Creating a .NET Standard library using Visual Studio**: Start creating a new project in Visual Studio 2022 and select the .NET Standard template. Choose the target framework version, such as .NET Standard 8.0.

4. **Cross-platform usage**: Reference the .NET Standard library in other projects, including .NET Core applications. Ensure compatibility across different platforms.

5. **Introduction to .NET Core libraries**: .NET Core libraries are specifically designed for the .NET Core runtime. They provide functionality tailored for building cross-platform applications.

6. **Single-file executables**: .NET Core allows the creation of single-file executables, making deployment and distribution more straightforward.

7. **DI**: .NET Core libraries seamlessly integrate with the built-in DI system, simplifying component interactions.

8. **Creating a .NET Core library using Visual Studio**: Create a new project and select the .NET Core class library template. Choose the target framework, such as .NET Core 8.

9. **Cross-platform development**: .NET Core libraries are specifically designed for cross-platform development. Write code that works seamlessly on Windows, Linux, and macOS.

10. **Combining .NET Standard and .NET Core libraries interoperability**: .NET Standard libraries can be referenced by .NET Core libraries, fostering interoperability and code reuse.

Example:

```
1. public class MyCoreLibrary
2. {
3.     private MyStandardLibrary _standardLibrary;
4.
5.     public MyCoreLibrary(MyStandardLibrary standardLibrary)
6.     {
7.         _standardLibrary = standardLibrary;
8.     }
9.
10.    public string GetCombinedMessage()
11.    {
12.        return $"{_standardLibrary.GetMessage()} {_standardLibrary.GetGreeting()}";
13.    }
14. }
```

11. **NuGet packages, distribution, and package creation**: Package your .NET Standard or .NET Core libraries as NuGet packages for easy distribution and consumption by other developers.

    Example:

    ```
    1. dotnet pack -c Release
    ```

12. **NuGet package manager**: Publish your library to NuGet.org or a private feed, allowing others to reference and use it in their projects efficiently.

13. **Choosing the right library**: Consider cross-platform requirements and target

framework compatibility when deciding between .NET Standard and .NET Core libraries.

14. **Portability analyzer**: Use tools like the .NET Portability Analyzer to ensure your codebase aligns with the targeted platforms.

Working with .NET Standard and .NET Core libraries involves creating modular, cross-platform code that meets standardized specifications. Leveraging these libraries allows us to build scalable, maintainable applications with broader compatibility across different .NET implementations.

Understanding assembly versioning in .NET

Assembly versioning is essential to managing and maintaining .NET assemblies, ensuring their deployment and compatibility across several contexts. It entails routinely assigning version numbers to assemblies to track changes over time, manage updates quickly, and ensure the stable running of applications. This procedure is crucial for identifying, managing, and distributing software components within the .NET framework. Here is a detailed look at assembly versioning within the .NET ecosystem.

Basics of assembly versioning in .NET

Assembly versioning in .NET development assigns a unique version number to each compiled assembly. This versioning mechanism is required to identify different releases of a software component, version management, and application compatibility.

Here is how the version numbers consist:

- **Version numbers**: In .NET, version numbers usually follow the format Major.Minor.Build.Revision, with each component serving a specific purpose:

  o **Major**: Denotes significant changes that are frequently backward incompatible, that means that they will not work with the last version. Incrementing the major version indicates a milestone release that may include breaking changes.

  o **Minor**: Represents the addition of new features while remaining backward compatible. Minor version updates offer capabilities while not breaking current contracts.

  o **Build**: Frequently auto-incremented for each build to reflect changes in the code that do not directly affect functionality, such as compilation or environment changes.

  o **Revisions**: Used to correct minor bugs and make enhancements. Increasing the revision number implies minor, backward-compatible modifications that improve stability or performance.

Assembly versioning for .NET projects

Working on projects using .NET allows us to set assembly versioning straight inside your project files. This method guarantees consistency across your application components and simplifies version control.

Project file configuration: .NET allows us to specify version information directly in project files (`.csproj` for C# applications), which simplifies assembly version management. An example snippet to set the file version, could look like this:

```
1. <PropertyGroup>
2.   <FileVersion>1.0.0.0</FileVersion>
3. </PropertyGroup>
```

This option allows version control at the project level, guaranteeing that all compiled assemblies include the required version information.

Best practices in assembly versioning

Refer to the following:

- **Semantic Versioning (SemVer)**: Adopting SemVer concepts can improve the clarity and predictability of version management. SemVer takes a systematic approach to versioning and clearly explains the nature of changes to developers and end users.

- **Establishing a clear versioning policy**: Development teams must create and follow a defined versioning policy. It supports consistent version control methods across the team and throughout the project's lifecycle, reducing confusion and potential compatibility concerns.

- **Tools and automation for version management, including build scripts and CI/CD integration**: Automating version increments with build scripts and CI/CD pipelines can significantly enhance version management efficiency and accuracy. This process guarantees that version numbers are consistently updated to reflect changes in the codebase.

- **Utilizing versioning tools**: Using specialized versioning tools and scripts can make managing assembly versions easier for complex or large-scale codebases. These solutions may automatically generate and increment version numbers, improving the version management process.

Assembly versioning in .NET is essential for optimal software component management and delivery. We may maintain the compatibility and reliability of .NET programs across different settings and release cycles by following recognized versioning standards and implementing strategic tooling and automation.

Understanding the Global Assembly Cache

The GAC is a machine-wide code cache that stores assemblies designed to be shared by several applications on a computer. It is a critical component of the Microsoft.NET Framework, serving as a centralized repository for .NET assemblies accessible to all .NET applications on the workstation. The primary goal of the GAC is to avoid the DLL Hell problem that plagued early Windows development by allowing several versions of the same assembly to coexist in the system while also providing a means to enforce version control and security requirements.

Key concepts

The key concepts are discussed as follows:

- **Assemblies**: In .NET, an assembly is a compiled code library that programs can use. It usually includes executable code and metadata such as types, versions, and culture information.

- **Strong naming**: Assemblies designed for the GAC must have strong names. It requires signing the assembly with a cryptographic key. Strong naming gives the assembly a distinct identity (apart from its file name), guaranteeing that references to it are accurate and secure.

- **Versioning**: The GAC allows for simultaneous execution of many versions of the same assembly. Applications can define the version of an assembly they need, assuring compatibility and dependability. This method aids in resolving version disputes while also ensuring backward compatibility.

- **Security**: Storing an assembly in the GAC enables stricter security checks. .NET employs **Code Access Security** (**CAS**) to limit what code may do depending on evidence, such as where the code is loaded. Assemblies in the GAC are often given more trust.

How it works

These are the steps:

1. **Installation**: To add an assembly to the GAC, we can use tools such as `gacutil.exe` (a command-line utility included with the.NET SDK) or programmatic access via.NET classes. The assembly must have a striking name.

2. **Resolution**: When an application starts, the.NET runtime looks for the required assemblies. Suppose an assembly is registered in the GAC. In that case, the runtime will use the version from the GAC rather than a local copy, provided the version numbers satisfy the application's requirements.

3. **Management**: The GAC is handled via the Windows shell extension or command-line tools. Administrators and developers can add and remove assemblies from the GAC and check their content.

Advantages

These are the advantages:

- **Shared libraries**: The GAC allows libraries to be shared by numerous applications, which saves disk space and ensures that applications use the correct library version.
- **Stability and compatibility**: By carefully controlling assembly versions, applications can prevent conflicts using compatible and tested versions of shared libraries.

Considerations

Working with the GAC requires considering some crucial aspects to guarantee best installation and management:

- **Deployment**: Installing apps that rely on assemblies in the GAC can be more difficult because it involves ensuring that the appropriate assemblies are present in the GAC on the target computer.
- **Security**: While the GAC improves security and versioning, administrators must carefully select which assemblies are allowed in the GAC to avoid potential security issues.
- **Performance**: Loading assemblies from the GAC incurs a minor overhead, due to the need to verify the assembly's integrity and permission. However, the benefits of shared libraries and security often outweigh this.

Hence, the GAC is a core element of the .NET framework that addresses issues such as shared libraries, versioning conflicts, and security in multi-application environments. Its proper use necessitates knowledge of .NET assembly management, robust naming, and the security model.

Strong-named assemblies in .NET

In the .NET framework, a strong-named assembly is an assembly that has a cryptographic signature, providing a unique identity through a combination of the assembly's simple name, version, culture, and public key token. This signature is produced by using a private key during the assembly's creation, allowing the runtime to verify the integrity and origin of the assembly.

Critical aspects of strong-named assemblies

Strong-named assemblies provide many main advantages that improve the dependability and security of Net-based systems. Knowing these important factors enables us to apply sensible assembly control techniques:

- **Unique identity**: The strong name uniquely identifies the assembly by incorporating information such as the assembly's name, version, culture, and a public key token.

- **Versioning**: Strong-named assemblies support versioning, allowing different versions to coexist. It is essential for managing updates and maintaining backward compatibility.

- **Security**: The cryptographic signature ensures the authenticity and integrity of the assembly. It prevents tampering and guarantees that the assembly comes from a trusted source.

- **GAC**: Strong-named assemblies are often deployed to the GAC for shared use across multiple applications.

We use tools like **Strong Name Tool** (**sn.exe**) to generate key pairs and sign the assembly during the build process to create a strong-named assembly. The firm name enhances the reliability, security, and versioning capabilities of .NET assemblies.

Using the .NET Core CLI for package management

In the .NET Core ecosystem, the CLI is a powerful tool for various development tasks, including package management. The .NET Core CLI provides commands to work with NuGet packages efficiently. Here is a brief overview of using the .NET Core CLI for package management:

1. Add a NuGet package using the following command:

   ```
   1. dotnet add package PackageName
   ```

2. Replace **PackageName** with the name of the NuGet package you want to add. This command fetches the package and adds a reference to your project.

3. If you need to **remove** a package, you can use:

   ```
   1. dotnet remove package PackageName
   ```

   This command removes the package reference from your project file.

4. The CLI automatically restores packages when you build your project, but you can explicitly restore them using:

   ```
   1. dotnet restore
   ```

This command retrieves the packages specified in your project file.

5. To see a list of installed packages in your project, you can run:

   1. ```
      dotnet list package
      ```

6. To upgrade a package to the most recent version, use:

   1. ```
      dotnet add package PackageName -version NewVersion
      ```

7. Replace **NewVersion** with the desired version.

8. The CLI allows you to manage package sources.

   For example, to add a new source:

   1. ```
      dotnet nuget add source https://api.nuget.org/v3/index.json -n MyNuGetSource
      ```

9. If you have a custom **NuGet.config** file, you can specify it during operations:

   1. ```
      dotnet restore -configFile CustomNuGet.config
      ```

These commands provide a convenient way to handle package-related tasks directly from the command line, making the .NET Core CLI an integral part of the development workflow.

Native AOT improvements in .NET 9

The **Ahead-of-Time** (**AOT**) compilation process is improved in .NET 9 by several improvements, mainly feature switching and memory efficiency. By switching feature support at build time, two attributes, **FeatureSwitchDefinitionAttribute** and **FeatureGuardAttribute**, allow conditional functionality in AOT programs. This modification minimizes the size of the application and improves runtime speed by enabling the compiler to eliminate unnecessary code during trimming. While **FeatureGuardAttribute** manages features requiring dynamic code, ensuring only the required code is left in the final build, **FeatureSwitchDefinitionAttribute** considers feature settings constants when trimming.

Additionally, more significant support for generic parameters in .NET 9 is advantageous for AOT, particularly with the **UnsafeAccessorAttribute**, which improves access to type members even when designated as inaccessible. This adaptability makes it possible to handle memory better in all AOT circumstances. Furthermore, **dynamic adaptation to application sizes** (**DATAS**), introduced, dynamically modifies the application heap size to accommodate the long-lived data requirements. This modification minimizes memory overhead by optimizing resource allocation for applications that are compiled using AOT.

Here is an example to illustrate how to construct a conditional feature switch using the **FeatureSwitchDefinitionAttribute**. This enables the inclusion or exclusion of specific functionality during trimming based on the configuration of the feature switch:

1. ```
   using System;
   ```
   ```

```
 2. using System.Diagnostics.CodeAnalysis;
 3.
 4. public class Feature
 5. {
 6.     // Define a feature switch for conditional compilation
 7.     [FeatureSwitchDefinition("Feature.IsSupported")]
 8.     internal static bool IsSupported =>
 9.         AppContext.TryGetSwitch("Feature.
   IsSupported", out bool isEnabled) ?
10.         isEnabled : false;
11.
12.     internal static void Implementation()
13.     {
14.         Console.WriteLine("Feature implementation is running.");
15.     }
16. }
17.
18. public class Program
19. {
20.     public static void Main()
21.     {
22.         if (Feature.IsSupported)
23.         {
24.             Feature.Implementation();
25.         }
26.         else
27.         {
28.             Console.WriteLine("Feature is disabled.");
29.         }
30.     }
31. }
```

To control this feature switch at compile time, add the following configuration to your project file:

```
 1. <ItemGroup>
 2.     <RuntimeHostConfigurationOption Include="Feature.
   IsSupported" Value="false" Trim="true" />
 3. </ItemGroup>
```

The **Feature.Implementation** method and any related code will not be included in the output. This configuration enhances efficiency by not loading superfluous features and helps shrink the app's size by eliminating redundant code.

Here is a real-world example that makes use of **Feature.IsSupported** switch is enabled or disabled. It can switch between various logging implementations if you wish to incorporate a more extensive logging method while the feature is activated, and a lighter one when it is disabled, this scenario might be helpful.

```
1.  using System;
2.  using System.Diagnostics.CodeAnalysis;
3.
4.  public static class Feature
5.  {
6.      [FeatureSwitchDefinition("Feature.AdvancedLogging")]
7.      public static bool IsSupported =>
8.          AppContext.TryGetSwitch("Feature.
    AdvancedLogging", out bool isEnabled) ?
9.          isEnabled : false;
10.
11.     public static void LogMessage(string message)
12.     {
13.         if (IsSupported)
14.         {
15.             DetailedLogging(message);
16.         }
17.         else
18.         {
19.             BasicLogging(message);
20.         }
21.     }
22.
23.     private static void DetailedLogging(string message)
24.     {
25.         Console.WriteLine($"[DETAILED LOG] {DateTime.
    Now}: {message}");
26.         // Add additional logging details, like stack trace, method
    info, etc.
27.     }
28.
29.     private static void BasicLogging(string message)
30.     {
31.         Console.WriteLine($"[LOG] {message}");
32.     }
33. }
34.
```

```
35. public class Program
36. {
37.     public static void Main()
38.     {
39.         Feature.LogMessage("Application started.");
40.     }
41. }
```

To control the **AdvancedLogging** feature switch at runtime, add the following to the project configuration:

```
1.  <ItemGroup>
2.    <RuntimeHostConfigurationOption Include="Feature.
    AdvancedLogging" Value="true" Trim="true" />
3.  </ItemGroup>
```

The **DetailedLogging** technique provides further logging when **AdvancedLogging** is set to **true**. If **AdvancedLogging** is set to **false**, only basic logging is carried out, which lowers output and might enhance efficiency in environments that do not need verbose logs. With this configuration, you can conditionally adjust the logging depth in various application builds.

The **FeatureSwitchDefinitionAttribute** efficiently controls code inclusion using configurable feature switches. We can use this property to create adaptive, runtime-optimized apps. When used with trimming, the **FeatureSwitchDefinitionAttribute** eliminates superfluous code, decreasing app size and improving speed. Developers may maintain robust and optimized code bases by minimizing the application's resource footprint and simplifying feature management across environments. The new feature switches allow us to construct flexible apps that meet production and development requirements.

Best practice in packaging and distributing .NET libraries

Packaging and distributing .NET libraries effectively is crucial for creating reusable and shareable components. Follow these best practices to ensure your .NET libraries are well-organized, versioned, and easily consumable:

- **Versioning**: Use SemVer to version your libraries. This helps users understand the impact of updates and compatibility. This also aids in incrementing major versions for breaking changes, minor versions for backward-compatible additions, and patch versions for backward-compatible bug fixes.

- **NuGet packages**: This distributes your libraries as NuGet packages. This also helps include necessary metadata in the NuGet package, such as author, description, license, and project URL.

- **Package structure**: Organize your library code logically within the package. Follow standard conventions for placing public APIs, implementation details, and configuration files. Clearly define namespaces to avoid naming conflicts.

- **Documentation**: Provide comprehensive documentation, including a README file, to guide users on how to use your library. Include code examples, usage scenarios, and any configuration options.

- **Dependencies**: Minimize dependencies to keep your library lightweight and reduce the disaster of conflicts with other packages. Specify version ranges for dependencies to ensure compatibility.

- **Strong naming**: Consider strong-naming your assemblies if your library needs to be deployed in the GAC or if strong-named assemblies consume it.

- **CI**: Implement a CI pipeline that automatically builds and tests your library with every change. Publish NuGet packages as part of the CI process, ensuring the latest version is always available.

- **License and copyright**: Clearly state the license under which your library is distributed. Include copyright information to protect your intellectual property.

- **Compatibility**: Regularly test your library with different versions of the .NET runtime and significant IDEs. Indicate the target framework(s) and runtime(s) your library supports in the NuGet package metadata.

- **Security**: Regularly update dependencies to address security vulnerabilities. Encourage users to report security issues responsibly.

- **Community engagement**: Establish a presence on GitHub or another version control platform to allow issue tracking and community contributions. Also, consider providing a discussion forum or chat channel for user support.

Adhering to these best practices ensures that your .NET libraries are well-structured, maintainable, and user-friendly, contributing to a positive developer experience.

Conclusion

Throughout this chapter, we have provided you with the tools and insights you need to handle the complexities of .NET application packaging and deployment. We help keep your projects current and structured for easy maintenance and scalability by concentrating on practical principles for managing components, leveraging NuGet, and comprehending the complexities of libraries. We have prepared you to face deployment issues by emphasizing the importance of version control and the GAC, ensuring that your application is robust, efficient, and ready to meet the needs of modern software environments.

Index

www.ingramcontent.com/pod-product-compliance
Lightning Source LLC
Chambersburg PA
CBHW061736210326
41599CB00034B/6698

9789365898521